PAUL AND HIS RECENT INTERPRETERS

PAUL AND HIS RECENT INTERPRETERS

SOME CONTEMPORARY DEBATES

N. T. Wright

University of St Andrews

First published in Great Britain 2015

Society for Promoting Christian Knowledge
36 Causton Street
London SW1P 4ST
www.spck.org.uk

British Library Cataloguing-in-Publication Data
A catalogue record for this book is available from the British Library

ISBN 978-0-281-06758-9
eBook ISBN 978-0-281-06759-6

Typeset by Tom Wright, St Andrews, using *Nota Bene* software
First printed in Great Britain
Subsequently digitally printed in Great Britain

eBook by Data Standards Ltd, Frome, Somerset

Produced on paper from sustainable forests

To my students, past and present

CONTENTS

PREFACE

Contemplating this book in its final form, I am reminded of a whimsical article by the journalist Bernard Levin concerning a railway enthusiast who was producing a series of articles called *Some Smaller English Signal-Boxes*. Levin imagined the life story behind this strangely humble project. Perhaps, he mused, the man had begun in his youth to research 'Signal Boxes of the World'. Then, as adult responsibilities crowded in, he decided to limit his ambitions to the English variety. Then, with the onset of middle age, realizing that further curtailment would be needed, he chose to study only the smaller signal-boxes of England. Finally, as retirement beckoned, he had to face the fact that, even there, a complete survey was out of the question, and so had introduced the tell-tale word 'some' into the title.[1]

The reader of the present volume will note that its subtitle, too, contains the word 'some'. It might have been good to write about 'Pauline Scholarship around the World', but I have had to limit my survey almost entirely to certain debates current within the Anglophone world. Thus, though my own tale is less whimsical, it still has some analogies with that of Levin's anti-hero.

When I began postgraduate studies on Paul in the early 1970s, we knew more or less where we were. The German scholars still led the way. We might disagree, but we were disagreeing with the (very different) positions of Bultmann, Bornkamm, Conzelmann, Jeremias, Käsemann and the rest. Some helpfully traced the genealogy of these views back to earlier luminaries like Wrede and Schlatter.[2] Some of us read Albert Schweitzer, and wondered why his views had not made their way into the mainstream.[3] (Perhaps it was because he was in Africa, working as a medical missionary; on his occasional return visits to Germany he was more likely to be found playing J. S. Bach on the organ than discussing F. C. Baur in a seminar.) Most of the writers we studied were wrestling with finer points of definition inside a protestant, mostly Lutheran, paradigm. Many were still writing footnotes to Bultmann. The long German counter-tradition, sometimes perhaps confusingly called 'salvation history', was usually airbrushed out of the narrative.[4]

Meanwhile, the French were introducing structuralist insights. We in Britain were still reading C. H. Dodd, and sitting at the feet of luminaries

[1] The original article appeared in *The Times* for November 24th, 1978, and is to be found in Levin 1982, 88–91. The trouble with checking a reference in a book by Bernard Levin is similar to the problem in looking up something by Albert Schweitzer: once opened, the book is hard to close.

[2] See esp. Morgan 1973.

[3] See Schweitzer 1912; 1931 [1930].

[4] See particularly Yarbrough 2004.

such as Charlie Moule in Cambridge, C. K. Barrett in Durham, and George Caird in Oxford. In America, the older work of John Knox still carried weight, though a new trend could be observed: Germans invent methods, Americans apply them, and British pragmatists sit in between, claiming that they are just trying to read the texts. Roman Catholic biblical scholarship was given official permission to spread its wings when the Second Vatican Council produced *Dei Verbum* in 1965. Since then, many Roman Catholic exegetes have produced splendid work on Paul. I think, for instance, of the creative and innovative studies of Jean-Noel Aletti in Rome.[5] There has even been a recent book entitled, somewhat ambitiously, *The Catholic Perspective on Paul*, though its author, a recent convert from my own denomination, is more concerned to demonstrate that Paul was a good Catholic than to engage with contemporary scholarship of whatever provenance.[6]

All these movements have continued. The old debates are still going on; many still pursue them energetically. But the landscape has changed completely. This book tries to describe that change; perhaps even to explain it.

An illustration may help. Someone who grew up in London in the 1950s might still be there today, living the same kind of life. But such a person now shares the city with millions of people from every corner and culture of the world. The stockbroker and the rapper walk the same streets while living totally different lives. Similarly, the scholarly discussions on Paul used to proceed in a well-known and orderly fashion. But the Pauline texts, like the London streets, now play host to a wide variety of different interpretative cultures, starting at different points, asking different questions, engaging with different conversation partners, and inevitably reaching disturbingly different conclusions. Just as the stockbroker and the rapper might stand side by side in Starbucks, and might even strike up a conversation which would reveal their worlds of difference, so the very different worlds of Pauline discussion may sometimes find themselves surprisingly adjacent, with dialogue always possible. Part of the aim of this book is to place them side by side, and to suggest that they might like to talk to one another.

Returning from metaphorical geography to literal, the main geographical focus of New Testament scholarship in general and Pauline research in particular has shifted in my lifetime from Germany to America. This has coincided with a serious glut in production. Discussions both serious and trivial appear every day on the Internet; monographs flood the markets. This makes generalization impossible. One cannot, for instance, point to any single movement in Germany and say, 'This is where German New Testament scholarship is going', let alone German Pauline scholarship.[7] The

[5] e.g. Aletti 2010 [1992].

[6] Marshall 2010. Marshall pays tribute to my own work, and in an appendix (219–27) invites me to consider ten questions . . . which I am still pondering.

[7] There are, however, two very helpful recent volumes: Frey and Schliesser 2013 (discussing, in particular, the work of Wolter 2011); Horn 2013. Perhaps we may hope that a project many of us found helpful at the time, Rengstorf 1969 (a collection of seminal articles), might be emulated at least in time for its fiftieth anniversary. Meanwhile, the article by Simon Gathercole in the Frey and Schliesser volume (Gathercole 2013) is helpful in bringing relevant issues into focus.

same is true, if anything more so, in Britain and in America. And, just as older German scholars tended not to refer to, let alone discuss, non-Germans,[8] the Anglophone world has all too often repaid the compliment. I regret that this book continues the trend, for reasons (in my case) of time and space.

A different sort of shift has taken place which creates the social and cultural conditions for some of the key elements in the story this book tries to tell. In the 1960s, most people who wrote about Paul (there were important exceptions) stood within some kind of Christian confession. Now a good deal of biblical research, particularly in the United States, happens in faculties of 'religion'. People in that environment sometimes hint that this setting makes their work 'objective', by comparison with the 'subjective' or faith-driven work of seminaries, 'divinity schools', or even the church itself. In Europe, including Britain, there used to be a regular commerce between church and scholarship, though this has worn thin of late. But in America the split between church and state has been defended as much by Christians who forswear the messy business of public life as by secularists who want nothing to do with dangerous outworn superstitions. This new either/or maps all too easily on to other social, cultural and political issues within the culture.[9]

This shift to America, and to 'religious studies', has had many spin-offs when it comes to understanding the big picture of Paul and his thought. Two of the early flagships of the movement are still important; the present book highlights one in Part I and the other in Part III (we shall come to Part II presently).

The first is E. P. Sanders's *Paul and Palestinian Judaism*, whose subtitle makes it clear that this is not a work of theology but rather 'a comparison of patterns of religion'. The second is Wayne Meeks's *The First Urban Christians.*[10] For my money, Meeks's analysis of Paul's communities is far more shrewd, and historically grounded, than Sanders's. It is ironic that Sanders has become the founding father of one particular so-called 'perspective' on Paul, when actually his really important work was his protest about misrepresentations of the Jewish world. Meeks's work on Paul's communities got closer, in my view, to the heart of what those communities actually believed. Both works, however, are symptomatic of the double shift I am talking about: from Germany to America, and from a (usually Lutheran) theological framework to the secular study of 'religion'. Some at least of the sharp and puzzled reactions to the so-called 'new perspective' are as much to do with context as with content (see chapter 5 below).

[8] Schweitzer touchingly explains that he did not treat English and American works, partly because they were not all available to him, and partly because of the barrier caused by 'insufficient acquaintance with the language' (1912, xi). It is reassuring that the great medical missionary, who could write books on Jesus, Paul, Goethe and J. S. Bach in his spare time, had at least some intellectual limitations.

[9] I have written about all this in various places: see, for instance, Wright 2014c, esp. chs. 7–12. Sometimes the pressures are not so subtle: see e.g. Boer 2010.

[10] See Sanders 1977; Meeks 1983.

The immediate antecedent of Sanders's protest was, however, neither American nor secular. Krister Stendahl had challenged the ruling consensus on Paul in a famous article. But Stendahl, who went on to serve as a bishop in his native Sweden, was himself a practitioner, not merely a theoretician, of 'religion'. Käsemann, in his response to Stendahl, expressed surprise that a Lutheran could say such things; one correspondent wrote to me (perhaps expressing a typically British viewpoint!) to enquire why the rest of us should worry about a dispute between a Swedish Lutheran and a German one.[11] Anyway, this was the kind of debate that caught the eye in the early 1970s.

Discussions like that, and others that have followed on from them, have not stopped. But since the 1970s and 1980s there have emerged several new schools of Pauline thought in America in particular. Part of the problem faced by students and teachers alike is that these have often been conducted in isolation, both from one another and (often enough) from the earlier framing debates. We need a map, and this book aims to provide one.

Maps, of course, can be totally accurate and totally inaccurate at the same time. Another metropolitan illustration suggests itself: the London Underground map. I used to be puzzled, on my rare youthful visits to London, that the actual underground lines had far more twists and turns than I could see on the card in my hand. It gradually dawned on me that the Underground map tells you exactly what you need to know but not much else. It would be useless, for instance, to a construction crew digging foundations for a new building and needing to avoid the existing tunnels.

All history is, in a sense, map-work, and is subject to the same challenges. Like a map, history excludes many things in order to highlight a few others. In ancient history, the sources (or the lack of them) often do the excluding for us. In modern history – and this book presents some slices of the modern history of Pauline interpretation – we are bound to produce something much more like the London Underground map and much less like a detailed aerial photograph. Such a map exists mainly to help people see where the main lines go, and also to avoid making wrong connections. Not every train stopping at King's Cross is travelling on the same track or heading for the same destination. A station may have many platforms, sometimes joined by confusing passages and escalators. The same is true of a commentary on Romans, or a book on Paul's Christology.

The three main Parts of the present book exemplify the point. In Part I, after the opening chapters setting the scene, we meet the so-called 'new perspective', commonly held to be launched in 1977 by the work of E. P. Sanders. In the second Part, we examine the revival of so-called 'apocalyptic' interpretations of Paul, associated with J. C. Beker's work of 1980 and J. L.

[11] My correspondent was the Very Revd. David L. Edwards, in a private letter in 1981. For Käsemann's surprise see Käsemann 1971 [1969], 61; for the original article, see Stendahl 1976, 78–96, embodying an *HTR* article of 1963 which itself was based on an earlier Swedish text. Behind both Stendahl and Sanders stands the massive work of G. F. Moore: see Moore 1921, and his *magnum opus*, Moore 1927–30. Moore, an ordained Presbyterian, embodied an earlier American scholarship which combined 'history of religion' with Christian ministry.

Martyn's 1997 commentary on Galatians. In the third Part, we examine a wider range of discussions centring upon Paul's social and cultural context, a movement whose main flagship remains the 1983 work of Wayne A. Meeks. These three movements have run in parallel for a generation. Each has pursued its own agenda without much reference to the others.

This creates confusions, to put it mildly. A recent commentary on Galatians links the 'active' meaning of *pistis Christou* ('the faithfulness of Christ') with a 'salvation-historical' account of Paul. That link is indeed sometimes made. But the author, by way of illustration, cites the commentary of J. L. Martyn, which certainly does defend the 'active' meaning of *pistis Christou* but does so within a sustained polemic *against* anything that could be called 'salvation history'.[12] We are all in danger of arriving at the right station but then getting on the wrong train. That is why we need map-work such as this, regularly updated.

The three main areas I have mentioned, which are the focal points of the three Parts of this book, subdivide further. Even more confusion can result. I list here ten such subdivisions; there are undoubtedly many others, but this is enough to be going on with. In the present book, Part I addresses the first four; Part II, the fifth; Part III, the last five. I list them here partly to indicate where the present book will focus, and partly to note where a relevant discussion can be found instead in *Paul and the Faithfulness of God*.[13]

1. The so-called 'new perspective on Paul' is regularly associated with the work of Sanders (from within the American 'religious studies' movement), but also with that of J. D. G. Dunn and myself, working from more traditional settings. The family resemblance should not be allowed to mask some fundamental disagreements. Sanders's work points to a particular subcategory, namely the study of Paul's own 'religion'.

2. The 'new perspective' has prompted a sharp response. This has now gained its own momentum, often calling itself the 'old perspective', and often operating with minimal reference to any of the other categories. It has continued earlier debates about the nature and centre of Pauline theology.

3. Within a broadly 'new perspective' reading of Paul, there have been major developments in areas such as Paul's use of Israel's scriptures. This work should relate to all the other categories, but is often ignored there.

4. Sanders's work has rightly been seen as giving new impetus to the study of Paul as a Jew. How did he relate to the Jewish world in which he had grown up? What difference did his Messiah-belief make?

5. One of the most vigorous recent movements, at least in America, has been the attempt to see Paul as an 'apocalyptist'. This movement, focused on J. L. Martyn's commentary on Galatians, has become popular among theologians as well as exegetes. Since my work in many ways (not all) cuts across the line taken by Martyn and his followers I will need to engage in

[12] Moo 2013, 160. Moo is referring to Martyn's contrast between the 'old era' of Torah and the 'new age' of Christ; but Martyn sharply distinguishes this from 'salvation history'.

[13] Hereafter *PFG* (London and Minneapolis: SPCK and Fortress Press, 2013). For the relation of the present work to this 'parent' volume see below.

head-on debate with this whole school in a more direct way, in Part II, than I do with the writers surveyed in Parts I and III.

6. The study of Paul's social world, with Meeks's 1983 book *The First Urban Christians* as a flagship, has continued unabated. How can we appropriately describe Paul's communities, and what conclusions can we draw from that about their beliefs and self-identity?

7. This vigorous movement has itself subdivided, into what may be called the 'social history' branch, represented by Meeks himself, and the 'social-anthropological' branch exemplified by the work of the self-styled 'Context Group'. The latter bring their anthropological analysis of the 'Mediterranean world' to Paul, whereas Meeks and his followers prefer to work from the ground up. I discuss categories 6 and 7 in chapters 10 and 11 below.

8. When we put 'apocalyptic' and 'social context' together, we ought to expect 'political' readings of Paul, and that is what we find in another whole wave of studies, though these are not usually joined up with the worlds of Martyn or Meeks. Here again there is a subdivision. Horsley and others, writing from within the North American context, have explored the possible relation between Paul and 'empire'…

9. … while, in Europe, radical philosophers have explored Paul's potential relevance for their ongoing contemporary political dilemmas. This exploration mostly ignores, and is ignored by, the other categories with which it would seem to share much in common. I also note here that neither in category 8 nor in category 9 has there been much attempt to engage with Paul's economic world. An important start has been made, but this is hardly, yet, a separate category of current research.[14]

10. Others have explored Paul's links with the philosophical movements of his own day (I say 'links' to leave it open whether Paul was deriving ideas from his non-Jewish contemporaries or confronting them adversarially, or perhaps both). This research would ideally link arms with all the other categories above; in practice this has not usually happened.[15]

These ten movements are all alive and well at the time of writing, but with a few exceptions they are not really talking to one another. The present book is, in part, a plea that they ought to do so, difficult though that may be. These are the movements with which I have been concerned in my own work, some more than others, inevitably, but all of them from time to time. I see them in the three broad categories which form the three Parts of this book: Part I, Paul and his Jewish world (categories 1–4); Part II, Paul and 'apocalyptic' (category 5); Part III, Paul and his 'social world' (categories 6–10). Thus, though I still regret that I cannot here discuss the many other contemporary movements not only in European scholarship but further

[14] See esp. Longenecker 2010, and the work (broadly within the 'social history' category) of Meggitt 1998. The work of Steven Friesen is also important here: see e.g. Friesen 2010.

[15] Many of these categories are discussed in the present book. Among those that are not, or not so much: on Paul's religion, see *PFG* ch. 13; on Paul's use of scripture and his relations with his Jewish world, see also *PFG* ch. 15; on Paul and empire see *PFG* ch. 12; on Paul and the philosophers see e.g. Martin 1995, Rowe 2015, and the work of Engberg-Pedersen, for which see the discussion in *PFG* ch. 14.

afield, this will perhaps do for a start. I hope that by distinguishing these various strands of thought, and placing them within at least a sketchy social history of scholarship, I will give to the reader coming to Pauline studies at least a sense of the territory, and hints as to possible connections and overlaps which the detailed focus of so much scholarship sometimes ignores. Perhaps the stockbroker and the rapper may have more to say to one another than we might have thought. Perhaps they might even share their experiences of finding their way around the London Underground ...

As they do so, they will find themselves engaging in four tasks which overlap and interlock. All categories of Pauline study engage in these, at least by implication, though often giving them different weight. These tasks are well known. They are history, theology, exegesis and contemporary relevance. But since these form the real start of the book, I will save any further remarks about them for the first chapter itself.

A brief word about how and why this book came to be. I have listed ten different areas of Pauline research, but the first book I ever read on the 'back story' of Pauline studies categorized its material in terms of two questions, which do not map directly on to any of these ten. First, can we best explain Paul in terms of his Jewish or his non-Jewish background? Second, and related to this, what is the 'centre' of Paul's thought? Is it 'justification', or is it 'being in Christ'?

Albert Schweitzer, offering this sketch of research, used an image from the lunar landscape. For him, 'being in Christ' was the 'main crater' which the impact of the Pauline meteorite had left on the surface of the history of humankind. The theme of 'justification' was a *Nebenkrater*, a smaller crater formed within that larger one. Perhaps misleadingly, he called the larger one 'Mysticism'.[16]

That verdict, and that metaphor, have resonated down through the last hundred years of Pauline studies, even though Schweitzer's own arguments have often been quietly sidelined. The two main terms have been explored, modified, sometimes played off against one another and sometimes brought into fresh conjunction. Such discussion, however, has taken place *within* an assumed pair of questions which the present wave of studies has exploded into fragments: how to place Paul historically, and how to understand him theologically. My own work, particularly in the parent volume from which the present book is an offshoot, tries to approach these questions from further angles again. My own proposal for a synthesis has some analogies with that of Schweitzer, but with every element examined on the basis of wider evidence, and brought into dialogue with many other issues of which Schweitzer himself, busy as he was with medicine and music, did not take account.

The lunar image haunts this book as well, for another reason. Like the moon which orbits our own planet, this book started out life as part of a larger whole. It was originally part of the Introduction to *PFG*, my own

[16] Schweitzer 1931, 225.

detailed exposition of Paul's thought. The purpose of such a section, or (now) such a volume, has not been to map a large and complex area of scholarly terrain for its own sake, but to explain why certain topics have loomed so large in my own work, why some issues have become particularly important, and why certain problems now demand a fresh angle of vision. This map-work quickly became more complex than I had imagined, to the point where it could no longer be contained within the larger book. Critics have noticed that *PFG* is itself quite long. One obvious way of stopping it growing still larger was to let the present material escape and do its own thing.

Like our moon, this book is thus intended to circle its parent volume, shedding a varied and I hope pleasant light on it, now from this angle, now from that. There are times when it will be like a full moon, shining brightly on particular issues and writers. At other times it will appear only as a thin, tantalizing arc, enough for us to glimpse some objects but not shedding much light on them. Sometimes this particular moon will shed no light at all: the present book makes no claim to exhaustive coverage.

A work like this, after all, has to make difficult choices. I am familiar in other contexts with the problem that once you mention one person in a speech of thanks you have to mention everyone. That is clearly impossible here; it would result in little more than a lightly annotated bibliography. The alternative is that it might become the literary equivalent of those one-day tours of 'England' which, having 'done' Oxford in the morning and Stratford-upon-Avon in the afternoon, dash back to London to see Big Ben and Buckingham Palace before flying on to Paris the next day. I have taken the risk of making this book less like the former and more like (though not, I hope, too like) the latter. Anyone who knows the present state of play in New Testament studies, the flood of monographs and articles, the multiple questions which sometimes interact with one another and sometimes do not, will understand the problem. For similar reasons, I have made no attempt to note reviews of the books I here discuss, or other works by the same authors. I regret the many omissions, not least because they will inevitably appear arbitrary.[17]

Unlike the parent volume, this one has aimed at being as lean as was compatible with a helpful sketch of the chosen terrain. Thus some topics are missing entirely. I do not here discuss Paul's so-called 'conversion';[18] nor the standard questions about Pauline chronology, the relationship between the letters and Acts, or the authorship of disputed letters.[19] Nor have I engaged with the other surveys which have appeared from time to time, all of which struggle, as does the present volume, with the confusing plethora

[17] I said this already (Neill and Wright 1988, v), and it is even more true today.

[18] On which see *PFG* 1417–26.

[19] On the latter topics, see now the stimulating if controversial proposals of Campbell 2014.

of new lines of investigation and angles of vision.[20] This itself is of course as nothing compared with the daunting task of mapping New Testament scholarship as a whole.[21]

All this points to a particular apology: that I have not been able to introduce, let alone to do justice to, the work of many valued continental colleagues. The fact that there used to be a German tradition of ignoring Anglophone work is no excuse. There is a larger gap, too, relating to the scholarship of the so-called 'second world' of Eastern Europe, and the so-called 'third world' which comprises most of the human race, including many of the most energetic (and sometimes the most persecuted) churches. We in the western academy have much to learn from other such readers, while they, for their part, might well wonder why they should need to learn from us. Those who read Paul in Africa, Asia and Latin America might glance at the discussions here in the way that I look at my neighbour's bee-hives: there's a lot of buzzing going on, I trust he gets some good honey, but I am busy enough with the chickens and the sheep, thank you very much. Worse: those churches may well come to regard our western preoccupations as simply another sign of our self-centred, self-serving arrogance. It would be nice to think that 'post-colonial' studies might lead to fresh openness to, and integration with, writings from outside the charmed western circle.

Some overlap is inevitable between the present work and the final chapter of the book originally written by Bishop Stephen Neill, which I updated at his request after his death.[22] Those who would profit from fuller discussions of Schweitzer, Bultmann and Davies might wish to refer to that earlier work; the discussions of Käsemann and Sanders in the present volume will supplement the previous ones rather than starting again from scratch. In addition, in 2012 I wrote a survey article on 'Paul in Current Anglophone Scholarship'.[23] Some of that material is likewise inevitably repeated here, though in most cases developed and expanded. Finally, I gave a paper on the 'shifting paradigms' of Pauline scholarship, particularly in relation to Paul's theology, at the Cambridge seminar of Professor Judith Lieu in January 2014. Some of that material, too, has found its way into the present book. I am

[20] e.g. Zetterholm 2009 is interesting, though not entirely on target; Seesengood 2010 is embarrassingly unreliable (see my review in *JTS* n.s. 63.1, April 2012, 263–5). The collection of essays in Given 2010 raises several of the contemporary issues mentioned above from particular angles; the debates in Bird 2012 show the startling disconnect between four competing visions of Paul. The substantial work of Westerholm 2004 is in a different league; his subtitle, 'The "Lutheran" Paul and his Critics', indicates both the sharp focus and the limitation of his study. See the discussion in ch. 5 below. The discipline badly needs someone brave enough to do the full sketch. Sanders already said this a generation ago, but it hasn't happened, and the task is now much greater and more complex: see Sanders 1977, 435, in the course of a brief but characteristically sharp summary (434–42) of Schweitzer, and of the way in which mainstream scholarship never really assimilated his insights.

[21] On this larger project, see, in addition to Neill and Wright 1988 [1964], Kümmel 1972/3 [1970]; Riches 1993; and the remarkable three-volume survey of Baird 1992, 2003, 2013. Among older works which themselves indicate the perspectives of a very different generation from our own, compare Hunter 1951; Ellis 1961; Fuller 1963 [1962].

[22] Neill and Wright 1988 [1964], 403–30.

[23] In the *Expository Times* (123, no. 8 [2012], 367–81), now reprinted in my *Pauline Perspectives* chapter 29 (474–88).

grateful to Professor Lieu and her colleagues for the stimulating discussion we had on that occasion.

As we get down to business, I thank especially my colleagues at St Mary's College in St Andrews, and in the various discussion groups at the Society for New Testament Studies and the Society of Biblical Literature, for stimulating conversations over many years. Special thanks are due to the Center of Theological Inquiry in Princeton, my hosts for the sabbatical in 2009 in which this book, as well as *Paul and the Faithfulness of God*, was planned and partly researched; and to my assistant during those months, Chad Marshall. My present assistant, Dr Jamie Davies, has been developing his own interest in many of the topics covered here, particularly the question of 'apocalyptic'. After many conversations on that topic, I no longer know which ideas were original to me and which to him – or which ones emerged from our ongoing discussions. He is not, of course, responsible for what I have done with them (though his help has been invaluable at every stage). The same applies to those other colleagues with whom these ideas have been discussed, and who would disagree with at least some of them: Scott Hafemann, Grant Macaskill, Alan Torrance and Richard Hays. I note with special gratitude the careful comments I received, at a late stage, from David Moffitt, David Horrell, Todd Still and Carey Newman; they, too, are likewise exonerated from any responsibility, as is my son Julian, who has once again helped me to think through some of the relevant issues in modern political philosophy. My thanks go as always to my friends at SPCK and Fortress Press, who have waited longer than they, or I, thought they would have to; especially to Simon Kingston for his wisdom and encouragement over many years and now in relation to this project; to Sam Richardson and Will Bergkamp, at the helm of SPCK and Fortress respectively; to Philip Law, Alan Mordue, Joe Riley and Amy Sleper for their cheerful support; and to the enthusiastic teams, both in London and in Minneapolis, who produce and distribute my work.

Since I envisage that this volume may be of particular interest to those coming fresh to the study of Paul, I dedicate it to my own students here at St Mary's College. Their lively discussions and eagerness for exegesis have been refreshing. Their enthusiastic discovery of mistakes in an early draft of the present book has been delightful. Old men ought still, of course, to be explorers. But part of their gift to the young may be the sketch-map of their previous wanderings, so that those who come after may at least understand why they got excited by the things they did, and also why they made the mistakes they did.

N. T. Wright
St Mary's College
St Andrews, Scotland

Easter, 2015

ABBREVIATIONS

1. Stylistic Shorthands

ad loc.	at the [relevant] place
cf.	confer
ch(s).	chapter(s)
C*n*.	*nth* century
cp.	compare
ed(s).	edited by
edn(s).	edition(s)
e.g.	for example
esp.	especially
et al.	and others
etc.	et cetera
f.	and the following (verse, page or line)
idem.	the same person
i.e.	that is
introd.	introduction/introduced by
loc. cit.	in the place cited
MS(S)	manuscript(s)
n.	(foot/end)note
n.s.	new series
orig.	originally
passim	throughout
pub.	published
ref(s).	reference(s)
rev.	revision/revised by
sc.	presumably
sic	thus (acknowledging an error in original)
tr.	translation/translated by
v(v)	verse(s)
vol(s).	volume(s)

2. Primary Sources

1QS	Rule of the Community
2 Bar.	*2 Baruch*
4 Ez.	*4 Ezra*

4QMMT	Halakhic Letter
bB.M.	Babylonian Talmud, Baba Metzia
bYom.	Babylonian Talmud, Yoma
Eumen.	Aeschylus, *Eumenides*
Jos.	Josephus (*Ant.=Jewish Antiquities*; *War=The Jewish War*)
LXX	Septuagint version of the Old Testament
mAb.	Mishnah, Abodah Zarah
mBer.	Mishnah, Berakhot
mB.M.	Mishnah, Baba Metzia
mKid.	Mishnah, Kiddushin
MMT	Halakhic Letter
mPe'ah	Mishnah, Pe'ah
mSanh.	Mishnah, Sanhedrin
NT	New Testament
OT	Old Testament

3. Secondary Sources, etc.

CD	Karl Barth, *Church Dogmatics*. Edinburgh: T & T Clark, 1936–69.
Exp. T.	*Expository Times*
FS	Festschrift
HTR	*Harvard Theological Review*
JBL	*Journal of Biblical Literature*
JSNT	*Journal for the Study of the New Testament*
JT	Justification Theory
JTS	*Journal of Theological Studies*
LSJ	H. G. Liddell and R. Scott, *Greek–English Lexicon*, 9th edn. by H. S. Jones and R. McKenzie, with suppl. by P. G. W. Glare and A. A. Thompson. Oxford: Oxford University Press, 1996 [1843].
NP	'new perspective' (on Paul)
NRSV	New Revised Standard Version
PPJ	E. P. Sanders, *Paul and Palestinian Judaism: A Comparison of Patterns of Religion*. Philadelphia/London: Fortress/SCM Press, 1977.
RSV	Revised Standard Version
TFUC	W. A. Meeks, *The First Urban Christians: The Social World of the Apostle Paul*. New Haven: Yale University Press, 1983.

4. Previous Works by N. T. Wright: Short Titles and Acronyms (full details in Bibliography)

Climax	*The Climax of the Covenant: Christ and the Law in Pauline Theology*, 1991.
JVG	*Jesus and the Victory of God* (vol. 2 of Christian Origins and the Question of God), 1996.

NTPG	*The New Testament and the People of God* (vol. 1 of Christian Origins and the Question of God), 1992.
Perspectives	*Pauline Perspectives: Essays on Paul 1978–2013*, 2013.
PFG	*Paul and the Faithfulness of God* (vol. 4 of Christian Origins and the Question of God), 2013.
Romans	'Romans' in *New Interpreter's Bible*, vol. 10, 2002, pp. 393–770.
RSG	*The Resurrection of the Son of God* (vol. 3 of Christian Origins and the Question of God), 2003.

Part I

PAUL AMONG JEWS AND GENTILES?

Chapter One

SETTING THE STAGE

1. Introduction

If Paul had never been heard of, and his letters had suddenly come to light in a hoard of papyri long buried in the sands of Egypt, there are certain questions we would want to ask about them. Who was the author? Did the same person write all these letters, or only some? In what culture did the author(s) live, and how might that culture help us understand what was being said? When were they written? Were they real letters, or was the literary form simply adopted as a teaching tool? Supposing them to be real letters, who were they addressed to? How would they have been understood? Can we get a sense, from the letters, of the larger world in which the author and the readers lived? What human motivations can we discern both in the letters themselves and in their circumstances, so far as we can reconstruct them? Historians ask questions like these all the time. Any academic study of Paul, a letter-writer from two thousand years ago, must be grounded in the attempt to answer such questions with all the tools available to us. The aim, all along, is 'exegesis': to get *out* of the text what is there, rather than, as with 'eisegesis', to put into it ideas from somewhere else.

We engage in this historical task neither out of mere antiquarian curiosity nor out of nostalgia for a long-forgotten past. We do it because we crave genuine understanding, a real meeting of minds and even of worlds. As soon as we think about it, we know we should do our best, in reading any texts from other contexts, to avoid two dangers: anachronism, imagining that people in a former *time* saw the world the way we do, and what Coleridge called 'ana*top*ism', imagining that people in a different *place* saw things the way we do.[1] Of course, we are at liberty to read the texts how we like – just as, notoriously, the guardians of ancient scrolls and manuscripts have sometimes been known to use them for shoe-leather, or for lighting the fire. But we know instinctively, I think, the difference between use and abuse. History is about what happened, and why it happened. We do not advance that quest by projecting our own personalities, or cultural assumptions, on to material from other times and places.

Of course, we see things through our own eyes, and imagine them within our own worlds of understanding. But history is about learning to let the

[1] Coleridge 1836, 1.317: librarians who arrange books by geographical subject-matter 'must commit an anachronism in order to avoid an anatopism'.

evidence guide us into seeing with other people's eyes, and into imagining the world in other people's visions. The task is to understand, so far as we can, what it was like to live, to think, to imagine and to believe within worlds other than our own. The otherness is important, and remains so. We can never attain complete knowledge, a 'God's-eye view'. But nor does the act of knowing collapse into the projection of our own prejudices. We are not positivists; but nor are we solipsists.[2]

Part of the historical task, when one is faced with a new document from an older world and a different place, is to try to understand the train of thought expressed in the writing, and, behind that again, the mind of the writer. We usually assume that there *is* a train of thought that made some sense to the writer. People do sometimes deliberately write 'nonsense', but even this is usually for a purpose. In other words, within the general historical questions about who, when, where and how, there are the more focused questions of *what* and *why*: what is being said here, and why is it being said? Often, with ancient papyri, this is quite easy: a short letter home from a soldier, a shopping list, an IOU. But with many documents, be they poetry or philosophy, plays or biographies, it may take time to get inside the flow of thought, to see how the various ideas expressed relate to one another. The aim, however, is the same: to move towards an *historical* description of the *themes and ideas* in the document. When, as is the case with Paul, the subject-matter is regularly and emphatically concerned with a being referred to as *ho theos*, 'the god', and with what this divinity has done and is intending to do, and with how both writer and readers are supposed to be relating to this being, then we naturally give a particular label to the themes and ideas we are finding. We call them 'theology'.

And now the danger of anachronism or anatopism comes back with a vengeance. We in the western world know a bit about 'theology', at least if we belong to some tradition that teaches it or perhaps sings about it. (The same problem would occur, of course, if the subject-matter appeared to be medical, and we knew a bit about medicine; or philosophical, and we had studied philosophy.) We will easily assume that technical terms mean what similar terms mean in our world; that ideas we are accustomed to think of as compatible, or indeed incompatible, will be seen in that way in the text; that arguments we find convincing now would be found convincing then. But the point for the moment is that in order to listen to the text, to let it be itself, to engage in dialogue with it, and to advance towards understanding it, we must allow the basic questions (who wrote it, to whom, at what time, and by what means) to lead us to the historical questions: what is being said, what it meant at the time to the writer and indeed to the readers, and not least why this writer wanted to say these things to these people at that moment. (Actually, in practice things do not move in a straight line. Often the way to find out who wrote the letter and why is first to be sure we have picked up the train of thought.) Historical study of our hypothetical new-

[2] See my discussion in *The New Testament and the People of God* (*NTPG*) ch. 4, itself predicated on the discussion of knowledge in ch. 2; also *PFG* 48–56.

found texts thus necessarily includes historical study of *meaning* and *motivation*. When the subject-matter has to do with *ho theos*, the meaning and motivation have to do with theology.

This task always *involves* the interpreter. We never have a mere fly-on-the-wall role, let alone, as we said, a God's-eye view. This involvement, the dialogue between text and interpreter, can easily get muddled up with the question of 'what might this mean for us today', but wise interpretation will always recognize the difference between 'granted I am looking through my own eyes, what seems to be going on in this text?' and 'granted this text says X, how does X apply in my world today?' The task of interpretation thus involves going to and fro, as in a real-life conversation. Our culture supplies us with other models, for instance the dialogue of the deaf one sometimes hears when a politician is interviewed on the radio. Real dialogue is the path to understanding; it is the task of 'interpretation', of 'hermeneutics'. (There are cultural differences here in our own world. Montreal has – at least, it had when I lived there – two radio stations offering classical music. The English-language one told us who was 'playing' the music; the French-language one told us who was 'interpreting' it.)

This task is often focused not simply on the question as to whether *we* have understood *this* text. As I have just suggested, it frequently looks in the other direction: what has this text to say to us in our own world here and now? That question might well emerge, not simply from 'religious' or specifically Christian texts, but from any discovery. An ancient philosophical text might be hailed as offering good advice about happiness, or relationships, or money. An ancient poem might shed light on dark corners of human experience. An entire genre of fantasy novels, of which Dan Brown's *The Da Vinci Code* is the best known example, works on the assumption that a new discovery from the ancient world might radically transform not only how people today understand the first century but also how they understand themselves, and the church they belong to (or perhaps don't belong to), today. This is one of the reasons people do history and indeed archaeology: in the hope of a moment of rich connection, of water from an ancient spring slaking our modern thirst.

But now at last we must give up the pretence that we have just discovered these Pauline letters, making us the first people to read them. We are simply the latest in a long line of readers. And the question, What might this mean for us today? is one we share with that long line. Serious readers have pondered these questions before us. We do not want to be enslaved by their ideas, but nor should we suppose that we have nothing to learn from them. We do not want to end up reinventing the wheel.

I approach the matter like this because it might be easy to imagine that the question of 'What does this mean today?' confronts us in the Bible in a way that is not true with other writings. Though I believe that there is indeed a sense in which this might be so, that sense is found *within*, not detached from, the wider truth that the letters of Paul meet us as documents from the past, and that our engagement with them has a lot in common with our engagement with all other documents from the past. Biblical hermeneutics is a sub-branch of hermeneutics more generally. Careful thinking about the nature of our engagement with texts from the past ought not to diminish any sense that the early Christian documents are *sui generis*. It ought to enable us to be much clearer as to where exactly that supposed uniqueness might lie.

We should not make the mistake of thinking that addressing the question of contemporary relevance is only done by those who read Paul within a faith-community committed to regarding his letters as authoritative. Many today want to learn from Paul, but to be selective about which parts of his writings they will embrace and which they will decline. Many want to apply a hermeneutic of suspicion, exposing his supposed prejudices and shortcomings both personal, intellectual and perhaps cultural. This, too, is a form of 'interpretation for today': it is a way of saying, 'Yes, these texts have been important', but also 'That has been a disaster.' My point here is not to adjudicate between such approaches; simply to point out that all readers of any text worth reading, whatever its content, are engaged in this fourfold task: history, content (in Paul's case, 'theology'), exegesis and application. These four strands intertwine like the four parts in a string quartet. You can study them individually, you can write out the separate parts; but you only get the music if all four are playing simultaneously.

The people who have read Paul's letters before us include scholars, both ancient and modern; and all such scholars have their own contexts, their own cultures, their own reasons for wanting to study Paul, their own hopes and fears about what he might be saying. The movements of scholarship which have been most influential in the last two hundred years have again and again been attempts at *historical* analysis, often in the belief that such work, by proposing different analyses of *content*, will challenge certain elements, perhaps foundational elements, within the Christian church. Some have, for that reason, done their best to ignore what has been called 'historical criticism', or even to vilify it: those scholars, they suppose, are always undermining the gospel! But the protest is in fact very similar, in form though not in content, to the protests of Luther and Calvin against the mediaeval church. Read the Bible afresh, they said, and you will see that things have gone wrong. Such a protest cannot be ruled out a priori. Even if it is ultimately wrong, it may have important points to make.

All this leads to the underlying thesis of this book. First, many of the roots of contemporary discussions of Paul go back to one such movement in the nineteenth century, which was offering a new would-be historical reading of Paul through which he would appear differently from how people had seen him before. Second, the main movements of Pauline scholarship in our own day have launched a similar, supposedly historically based protest, against that dominant nineteenth-century construct. The middle term in all this is Bultmann: it is only a slight oversimplification to say that he sums up in the middle of the twentieth century the movement that began in the nineteenth, thereby raising questions for the twenty-first. Certainly the three main movements I shall chronicle (those focused on Sanders, Martyn and Meeks) are all reacting to him, albeit in strikingly different ways. Since these more recent movements form the main subject of this book we need to understand why the nineteenth century said what it did, and why its legacy in the first half of the twentieth century was found to be historically inadequate in the second half.

Here is an irony, one of many within this story. More 'conservative' readers of Paul have often ranged themselves against Bultmann, but they have often been closer to him than they might have cared to acknowledge. Some at least of the reaction against Sanders (the 'old perspective') has come from such quarters. These great movements of thought have not taken place in a rarefied atmosphere, detached from or irrelevant to the 'popular' use of Paul's letters in preaching, teaching, counselling and evangelism. Such activities have regularly been far more bound up with the larger currents of modern thought than is usually supposed. The 'popular Paul' has all too often been addressing sixteenth-century questions in a nineteenth-century tone of voice, whether philosophical or pietistic. This book is about the struggle to hear his first-century voice as part of our own task of addressing twenty-first-century questions.

But is even this task appropriate? There was a short period, in the 1960s and 1970s in particular, when some scholars challenged the viability of any such reading of the New Testament. Since (they said) the writings came from a culture so different from our own, and especially since they were rooted in the ancient world (sometimes people added, 'in the ancient *Jewish* world', or 'in the ancient *apocalyptic* worldview'), whereas we are rooted in the modern world, the best we can do is to demythologize them, that is, to discern what they might be saying about some timeless or abstract truth and then to try to re-express that in ways appropriate for our own day. That was of course central to Bultmann's agenda, and was picked up by some in the English-speaking world to raise the question like this: granted that the early Christians saw the truth through their spectacles, how can we, whose spectacles are so different, say in our own way the core of what they were saying?[3] Hence the quest for the 'centre' or 'core' of Paul, which continues to this day. But most readers of Paul, whether friendly or hostile to his central claims, have made more direct connections. There has always been a strong sense that his writings do in fact pose questions which retain a sharp relevance and challenge across time and across cultures. So exegesis, as a branch of history, has regularly been accompanied by what we might call 'application', both inside the Christian church and outside it. Almost all exegetes look over their shoulder at this question, whether or not they address it specifically. It is better, in my judgment, to bring it out into the open.

All history, after all, at least glances at the question, not just 'How can we best describe what we are seeing?', but 'How might this be relevant to us?'

[3] One of the most enthusiastic advocates of this extreme relativism was D. E. Nineham: see e.g. Nineham 1976.

Historians and biographers both ancient and modern have hinted at, or even highlighted, parallels between societies, empires, leaders, popular movements, cultural forces and pressures, in the world they are describing and in their own. Plutarch was one of the first, but hardly the last, to sketch 'parallel lives'. One of the greatest ancient historians of the twentieth century, Ronald Syme, offered a dramatic and disturbing parallel between Augustus and Hitler.[4] Sometimes the question is not so much about parallels as about appropriate continuity: American and French theorists look back to the late eighteenth century, and to what their founding fathers did and said at that time, in order to discern what should be done today. Even those weary souls who declare that the only thing history teaches us is that we never learn from history are paying lip service to the possibility that the study of the past might have relevance for the present. Thus a specifically Jewish, Christian or Muslim invocation of a sacred text is a special case of a much broader phenomenon, however many other dimensions it may also possess. One of the ironic features of the movement mentioned earlier (the new interest in Paul on the part of atheistic philosophers) is that it has skipped right over the agonized wrestlings of some liberal Christians ('we can't let the past dictate to the present') and is doing with Paul what many today do with Epictetus or Marcus Aurelius, studying them not because they will tell us everything we need to know but because they resonate, they carry weight, they stimulate thought and sometimes give it a new sense of direction.

Thus the four tasks facing all serious readers of Paul are history, theology, exegesis and 'application'. These four intertwine and impinge on one another, however hard we might try to stop them. But there is a problem with how this has been done. Understanding this problem, and its lasting effects, will occupy us for the rest of the present chapter.

2. History and 'History of Religion'

(i) Introduction

The problem to which I refer has to do with the fact that when people have tried to locate Paul in 'history' they have often done so in terms of a larger implicit project about the history of 'religion', or indeed 'religions'. This, though understandable at one level, has been thoroughly misleading at some others. For a start, the word 'religion' means something quite different, in the modern western world, from anything that would have been recognized in the first century.[5] Anachronism here is therefore both easy and fatal for any fully historical study of Paul. Talking of Paul and 'religion' while ignoring the huge differences between his day and ours first narrows

[4] Syme 1939.

[5] See *PFG* chs. 4, 13.

the historical focus, screening out everything else that might be relevant, and then gives that focus a modern meaning.

Take the first point, the narrowing of focus. Why limit historical study of Paul to 'religion'? There are much wider historical questions to ask: Who was this man? What can we know about him? What sort of family was he from, where did he grow up, was he rich or poor or not really either, what outline sketch can we give of his life and work, who did he engage with both positively and negatively, and what impact did he have on subsequent history? Any interesting figure who emerges from the shadows of history generates questions like these. There is nothing here specific to Paul's being a 'religious' figure. 'Religion' in the ancient world touched all aspects of life. Even the rather few genuine atheists usually kept up 'religious' appearances; and religious appearances were all over the place, woven in to every aspect of life. There was no separate sphere in the ancient world called 'religion'. Or, for that matter, 'politics'; or indeed 'economics'. Life may not have been completely seamless, but it was, more or less, a complex whole. Historical enquiry, at least in the modern western world which has regarded its habitual separation of these 'spheres' as a virtue, needs constantly to be reminded of this. By all means let us study the 'religious' element in any given society, any particular biography. But if we try to isolate that from everything else, particularly in studying the ancient world, we will radically distort the whole picture, and fail to understand even the 'religious' bit we were trying to look at.

Of course, once we discover that a particular historical figure had an impact in a particular area of life, we might, as historians, home in on that area and ask more questions. But which area should that be? Some might want to say that Paul resembles most closely the founder or teacher of a philosophical school. Like the philosophers, Paul had plenty to say about cosmology, epistemology and ethics, none of which featured prominently in ancient 'religion'.[6] Or perhaps we might see him as a 'political' person, either as a thinker (with his views about God's kingdom administered through Jesus) or as a doer (setting up communities that sat at an awkward angle across the political landscape), or both.[7] In each of these areas, philosophy and politics, it would be appropriate to ask how Paul came by his ideas, whether he had a moment of sudden enlightenment, whether what he said placed him within one of the well-known schools of ancient thought and practice, whether his ideas and beliefs changed and developed, whether we can give a clear and consistent account of them, and indeed whether they were, from his own point of view, consistent within themselves. In particular, as historians we would undoubtedly want to situate him within a larger context: what strands of thought or life was he particularly indebted to, which did he resist, where was he prepared to compromise, and so on? Was

[6] See *PFG* chs. 3, 14; and below, ch. 10 in relation to the proposals of Edwin Judge.

[7] See *PFG* chs. 5, 12; and below, ch. 12.

he, like many philosophers, political thinkers and activists in antiquity, part of a 'school' from which he then developed in his own new way?

I have tried to address these questions in the main volume, but I raise them here for a different reason: to show that, though we have been accustomed to thinking of Paul as a 'religious' figure, that is a function of the way our culture has seen things in the last two hundred years, not a necessarily 'correct' way to approach him. Separating out anything to do with 'God' and calling it 'religion', assuming that it has nothing much to do with the rest of real life, is a distinctly modern western phenomenon, part of the movement we loosely call 'secularization'. The roots, causes and deep problems of that movement are beyond our scope here, but it is important to note that this was the wider context for what, by the early twentieth century, came to be seen as the natural way to approach someone like Paul.[8] Thus if you want to study Paul in a modern university you would probably find your way to the Faculty of Religious Studies, or of Theology, or even (as in my own institution) 'Divinity'. You would not so naturally go looking in Ancient History, Middle Eastern Culture, Philosophy or Politics. All of these, however, might have a good claim to Paul, and such claims have recently been made.[9]

A telling sign of what has been taken for granted is that if you wanted to make a television programme about Paul you would probably be directed to the 'religious' department of the broadcasting company. A strong case could be made, however, for making a film or series of programmes about Paul in terms of his social, cultural, political and economic impact. Large elements of the western media are still controlled by the simplistic divisions of modernist thought. I was shocked when I learned that the British Broadcasting Corporation, for all its highly sophisticated technology (funded by the licence-payers, which means almost all British households), retains a clunky modernist division of material into 'Factual' and 'Non-Factual'. No prizes for guessing which side of the line St Paul would come; he is bound to be seen as part of 'religion', and therefore 'Non-Factual'. If, however, you were planning a documentary on Cicero or Seneca, showing how their public life and philosophical thought had to be seen together as part of a complex whole which had an equally complex impact on their entire social environment, the decision would go the other way. They, at least, would be 'factual'. To protest against the division might be difficult. It has often been reinforced by the churches and theologians themselves.[10]

But Paul was a *public* figure. He was not inviting people into a private 'religious' world. That was the gnostic fantasy, cherished by some from the second century onwards, and embraced too eagerly, as an explanatory hypothesis, by some Pauline expositors in the early twentieth century, notably the great Rudolf Bultmann himself. But it has nothing to do with the

[8] On secularism the obvious and challenging texts are Milbank 1990; Taylor 2007.

[9] See ch. 12 below.

[10] I think of the basic position of e.g. Barth 1963, 109, insisting on clear water between 'theological knowledge, thought, and speech' and 'general truths' or 'general knowledge'. Barth's well-known and long-lasting hostility to 'natural theology' gave hostages to fortune, to put it mildly.

relentlessly Jewish message of the Apostle, which was about the real creation of the one and only God, and the real new creation which was already transforming it. Perhaps, after all, this is why some earlier writers were eager to distance the historical Paul from, say, the Areopagus Speech in Acts 17. Their 'Paul' would not have accepted the invitation to speak in such a forum; not that Paul seems to have had much choice, since he was not there as a 'visiting lecturer', but was, at least implicitly, on trial for serious social and cultural (and hence also 'religious') offences! The 'Paul' of this essentially modern 'religious' imagination would certainly not have wanted to explain his message in the philosophical and cultural terms of his day.[11] But the real Paul seems to have done exactly that. Here both 'history' and 'application' urge us into areas, and in directions, which many classic studies of a 'religious' Paul, not least in Germany, have not wished to go.

My point in all this is that we meet Paul primarily as a figure in ancient history. Ancient history includes everything from dates and events (such as the fall of Jerusalem in AD 70) to the social, cultural and political climate of the times, and on to the reconstruction of the ideas and beliefs of particular actors (whether Paul, Nero, Seneca or anybody else) within the multiple dramas of the day. This is the sort of thing that 'history' does, and the broader we make the basis of that historical study the better. What seems to have happened, however, is the double movement in which, first, the most influential Pauline studies of the late nineteenth and early twentieth century created certain problems from which, second, more recent scholarship has been trying to escape, in different ways and with different results. The first part itself is what we must now examine, and it too divides into two parts: the 'secularization' that has forced the 'historical Paul' to appear simply as a 'religious' figure, and the Hegelian Idealism which analysed 'religion' itself into two broad hypothetical streams: 'Judaism' and 'Hellenism'.

(ii) Paul between 'Judaism' and 'Hellenism'?

Once historical study has narrowed its focus to the 'religious' question, this generates the more specific puzzle: What kind of 'religion' did Paul teach and practise, with what 'religious' ideas as its core? What was the origin of these 'religious' ideas? Can we give a clear and coherent account of them? Was there a moment when they appeared to him in a new way? How did his 'religious' thought develop? In particular, where can we place him within the 'religious' world of late antiquity, and especially within the developing early Christian movement? Was he – here comes the all-important but highly misleading either/or! – essentially a *Jewish* religious thinker or a *hellenistic* one? These questions have generated debates over the last two centuries. Such questions distort, but these are the distortions we have lived with for a long time, and which have shaped today's debates. Even when we

[11] See e.g. Vielhauer 1966. Vielhauer is now well answered by many, esp. e.g. Rowe 2011.

try to get out of their grip, it is this prison, rather than some other, from which we are trying to escape.

Paul has thus been studied, for better and for worse, within the 'history-of-religions' movement of European scholarship, which flourished a century or so ago but whose influence is still strongly felt.[12] As we have noted, 'religion' as seen by the eighteenth-century Enlightenment is, by definition, that which is *not* about 'public life', not about 'politics', not about anything much in human life except those moments when the individual (or, sometimes, a group of individuals meeting for worship) believe themselves to be in touch with, worshipping, invoking or celebrating some divinity or other. The history-of-religions paradigm posed questions to do with the historical origins and setting of the 'religion' of a figure like Paul. Was his 'religion' basically Jewish or basically hellenist? Where did it belong on the map? And, granted that at least by the middle of the second century the Christian movement seemed to show a strange blend of both Jewish and non-Jewish elements, how was this to be explained? Furthermore – since the other questions cannot be ignored – how does any answer to this historical question impinge on theology, on exegesis, and on 'application'?

(iii) F. C. Baur

A particular set of answers to all these questions emerges from the stream of scholarship going back to the remarkable work of Ferdinand Christian Baur (1792–1860).[13] Baur taught in Tübingen from 1826 to his death in 1860, working tirelessly on the history of the early church as well as preaching regularly in the university church. He was the centre of the 'Tübingen School' which is perhaps the best-known of all nineteenth-century German theological and exegetical movements.[14] Baur stood firmly in the tradition of Hegelian Idealism, and his entire reconstruction of early Christianity was shaped according to these principles. As Baur himself put it on the first pages of his monumental work on Paul, reflecting on the independent mood of thought in his own day:

> This independence of thought, attained after such great effort ... naturally turns its gaze back into the Past, the spirit reposing in the self-certainty of its consciousness, is now first placed on a standpoint from which it can review the paths along which it has passed, driven by the force of circumstances, and it reviews them in order to illumine the unconscious Past with the consciousness of the inward necessities of the Present.... Christianity is on one hand the great spiritual power which determines all the belief and thought of the

[12] See Neill and Wright 1988 [1964], 367–78. Schweitzer's account of the main elements in the history-of-religions approach to Paul in the late C19 and early C20 remains clear and helpful (Schweitzer 1931 [1930], 26–40). See too Kümmel 1972/3 [1970], Part V.

[13] See particularly Baur 2011 [1873].

[14] On this, see Harris 1990 [1975]. On Baur see, among many other treatments, Schweitzer 1912, 12–16; Kümmel 1972/3 [1970], 127–43; Neill and Wright 1988 [1964], 20–30; Baird 1992, 258–69, and the important collection of essays in Bauspiess, Landmesser and Lincicum 2014.

> present age, the ultimate principle by which the self-consciousness of the spirit is produced and maintained . . .[15]

This meant, more or less, a collapsing of history and theology into one another. History was not simply the sphere in which one might occasionally encounter the divine, but 'the self-expression of God as Absolute Spirit in the unfolding process of history', so that 'God lives in history, and history is the life of God.'[16] We note that the word 'history' here basically means 'what has happened', rather than the historian's task of reconstructing it or the work in which that reconstruction is written down, though of course Baur did a great deal of reconstruction and writing as well. He believed his work to be constructive, aiding an apologetic for the truth of the essential Christian mystery.

A vital part of this task, one which would prove fateful a century after Baur's day in social and political life (ironically!) as well as in theology and exegesis, was his insistence that it was essential to break Christianity off from its Jewish roots. The crucifixion put an end to the particularity of Jewish hopes, including messianic hopes, so that the resurrection, which Baur took to be an event in the experience of Jesus' followers, was the moment when Jesus' spirit was made available to all humanity. Thus

> . . . there next follows the historical and critical enquiry into the question how Christianity, so closely interwoven with Judaism, broke loose from it and entered on its sphere of world-wide historical importance . . . becoming of itself a living power, the idea found in the bounds of the national Judaism, the chief obstacle to its universal historical realization . . . [H]ow Christianity, instead of remaining a mere form of Judaism . . . broke loose from it, and took its stand as a new enfranchised form of religious thought and life, essentially differing from all the national peculiarities of Judaism is the ultimate, most important point of the primitive history of Christianity.[17]

The echoes of this basic principle continued to resonate through much German scholarship throughout the twentieth century.

Baur recognized only four of Paul's letters as original: Romans, Galatians and the two Corinthian epistles. From these he sketched a basic conflict 'between Pauline and Jewish Christianity', which was the point at issue in the apostolic debate in Jerusalem and also in the row at Antioch.[18] It was also what was at stake in the party squabbles in Corinth. In a famous article, Baur saw the four 'parties' which Paul mentions in 1 Corinthians 1.12 (the Peter party, the Paul party, the Apollos party, and the 'Christ party') as basically two: Paul was the representative spokesman for something called 'gentile Christianity', with Apollos taking his side, while Peter, who articulated the position of the 'early Jewish Christians', was joined by the 'Christ party', stressing contact with Jesus himself and his first apostles. This enabled Baur to make another Hegelian move. The 'spirit' at work within the dialectical

[15] Baur 2011 [1873], 1.1f.

[16] Baird 1992, 259.

[17] Baur 2011 [1873], 1.3.

[18] cf. Baur 2011 [1873], 1.125–36.

historical process made its way by 'thesis', followed by 'antithesis', and then 'synthesis': thus, for Baur, the 'thesis' of Petrine (i.e. Jewish) Christianity and the 'antithesis' of Pauline (i.e. gentile) Christianity were destined eventually to reach a 'synthesis' in the 'early Catholicism' of the second century. This, Baur thought, could already be seen in Acts and the Pastoral Epistles.

This essentially Idealist scheme provided Baur with his supposedly 'historical' analysis of early Christianity in general and Paul in particular. It also provided him with a *theological* focus: the new experience of the spirit which Paul referred to as 'justification'.[19] Baur held together Paul's language about 'justification' with the idea of 'union with Christ' and indeed with God, all being accomplished by the spirit (remembering that for Baur the word 'spirit' was heard in Hegelian terms):

> Thus the spirit, the principle of the Christian consciousness, which is the highest stage of justification, is also the principle in which the adequate relation in which justification places man towards God, is practically realized. The spirit presupposes faith as the subjective form in which man takes up the spirit into himself. Through the spirit, that which he is as a justified person in his relation to God, in his consciousness of sonship of God, is practically operative.[20]

Thus, as Baird comments (following Schweitzer), Baur makes it sound as though Paul had been reading Hegel (and, we might add, thereby reinforcing a cultural version of Lutheranism's 'freedom from the law'):

> The principle which takes possession of his consciousness is now the immanent principle of his own self-consciousness; he knows himself free from everything by which he was formerly constrained; he is conscious of his own independence and autonomy. The position which the apostle took up as the logical and necessary consequence of his conversion, involved of course that all those shackles of religious authority which he had recognised up to that time at once fell away.[21]

Thus the breaking away from 'Judaism', and the authenticity and autonomy of Paul's experience, were both bound up with 'justification'. This, in a sense, is all we need to know about Baur: the lines from here to Bultmann and beyond are clear, as is the hostile reaction of Nietzsche to such an Idealist Paul. Baur stands, in fact, at the fountain-head of that Idealist strain of western Protestantism against which the historical protests of the last generation, in their multiple ways, have been launched.

This might seem ironic, in that Baur was supposedly himself an historian. But his 'history' was, relentlessly, the projection onto the ancient world of the Idealist scheme we have just described. Documents were dated early or late, ascribed to this author or denied to that one, on the basis of this grand scheme.

[19] See Baur 2011 [1875], 2.135–68.

[20] Baur 2011 [1875], 2.168.

[21] Baur 2011 [1875], 2.271f.; cf. Schweitzer 1912, 15; Baird 1992, 263, 265: 'In this justification, the believer is united with the Divine Spirit so as to become a new creation: justification is union with God.'

One particular long-term result of Baur's picture must be noted here. Baur used his vision of history progressing as the incarnation of the divine spirit in the service of a radical Protestantism which broke decisively with Judaism. But in the nineteenth and early twentieth centuries there was another movement which likewise saw God at work in history, only this time including the Jewish history as a 'salvation history' which would eventually culminate in Jesus. This movement is not so well known as that from Baur to Bultmann, and was routinely marginalized no doubt because it presented a kind of shadow side to all that Baur and his successors stood for.[22] But in our own day, when the protest of Käsemann against Bultmann matched the protest of Walter Benjamin against all theories of 'historical progress', any and all such ideas of an immanent historical process have been cast aside in the name of an 'apocalyptic' which, as with Barth's protest against a post-Baur liberalism, denies any sense of an immanent or divine progress within 'history'. The distinction which has to be made today, as I shall argue in Part II of the present book, is that between any Baur-like suggestion of an immanent 'process', on the one hand, and a genuinely Pauline view of the providentially guided, though often dark and twisted, Israel-narrative to which the Messiah really does provide the *telos*. In rejecting Baur, in other words, one is not rejecting everything that might usefully be named by the shorthand 'salvation history'.

Baur's agenda, to separate off Paul from 'Jewish Christianity' on the one hand and 'early Catholicism' on the other, had a philosophical and theological outworking. It went, rather obviously, with a particular sort of liberal Protestantism which wanted to retain something approximating to Paul's doctrine of 'justification', not least his rejection of 'works of the (Jewish) law', and which saw the history-of-religions proposal about Paul's battle on two fronts as being a way of gaining that point. Just as Martin Luther opposed the Roman Catholicism of his day, aligning it more or less with the 'works-righteousness' of Judaism against which Galatians in particular had protested, so Paul, opposing Peter and 'those who came from James' in Antioch (Galatians 2.11–14), was standing out against much the same sort of thing in the first century. Paul thus stood in the middle, between the 'early Jewish' Christianity and the (later) 'early catholic' variety, opposing them both and for broadly the same reasons. And just as Martin Luther also opposed the radical 'enthusiasts' of the Reformation period,[23] so Paul firmly resisted those, especially in Corinth, who supposed themselves to have already attained a higher spirituality. This was the picture that dominated German scholarship in the late nineteenth and early twentieth centuries: (a) a focus on 'religion' as the primary category; (b) a sharp distinction between 'Judaism' and 'Hellenism', with Paul as the pioneer of 'gentile Christianity'; (c) the centrality to Paul of 'justification', in Baur's sense of a new spiritual

[22] See the detailed description and discussion in Yarbrough 2004.

[23] The word 'enthusiasts' is used in the sense of the German *Enthusiasmus*, and the eighteenth-century English 'enthusiasm' as described and criticized by Knox 1950, and as exemplified in Wesley and others; the point being the claim to special divine inspiration or illumination.

experience. Sanders, Martyn and Meeks do not often refer to Baur, but his picture is the one they are ultimately rejecting.

(iv) Life after Baur

The picture drawn by Baur has now been discredited on historical grounds, though like a not-quite-exorcised ghost it still haunts the libraries and lecture-halls of New Testament scholarship. The ancient evidence, both Jewish, Christian and pagan, is stacked against it. Baur's categories do not in fact correspond to, or well describe, any actual phenomena in the first century or the centuries on either side. Study of the nineteenth century itself, however, indicates that the construct emerged quite naturally from within certain cultural and philosophical contexts which were, indeed, those which shaped Baur himself.[24] A recent major study of this point has argued that Baur shared with Hegel and others certain fundamental ideas we now see as 'Orientalist',

> which are inherently racist, presupposing that in order to attain 'freedom' the Jews or Jewish-Christians must be influenced by Greek thinking. Being a main architect of such Orientalist thinking in New Testament exegesis, Baur had created a dialectics where Jews would continue being the antithesis of everything Christian theology deemed valuable ... Thus ... historiography like Baur's resulted in a a systematic marginalisation of Jews and Judaism within Enlightenment theology.[25]

The writer concludes that by putting Baur in his own historical and cultural context, tracing the strands that made him think as he did and the further strands by which he influenced others, we see the urgent need for 'a reconstruction of profound structures in New Testament historiography'.[26]

The need for this is everywhere apparent in the scholarship of the twentieth century. Baur's model did not disappear when the social and cultural landscape shifted. From the middle of the nineteenth century until at least the great Romans commentary of Ernst Käsemann his picture of Paul continued to be massively influential. The apostle has continued to be seen as a sign of contradiction to an earlier 'Jewish Christianity' which was clinging to legal and covenantal ideas that Paul believed had to be either abandoned or radically redefined around the cross of Jesus, and at the same time he was warding off both the triumphalist 'enthusiasts' and any who would lead the way back to the kind of 'religion' which would become, despite his best efforts, the early catholic church. In my experience, a great many students in the Anglophone world have no idea that when they are reading scholars in the tradition from Baur to Käsemann these are the supposedly historical parameters within which they are working. The fact that such categories fail

[24] See esp. e.g. Meeks 2001; Martin 2001.

[25] Gerdmar 2014, 125f. The whole article is important for understanding this seminal moment in scholarship.

[26] Gerdmar 2014, 127.

on all fronts *as history* (long before we begin to ask theological questions) ought to make us wary of any supposed 'results' that emerge from such analysis. That in no way implies, however – and we must emphasize this – that the scholars who addressed the questions did not, at the same time, produce a great deal that remains both useful and important. To that we shall return.

We must now, however, investigate the way in which this history-of-religions task dominated the landscape in the generations following Baur. The underlying question was, What sort of a thing is genuine Christianity? How can it be preached today, and how can its key texts best be understood? But the way to those questions was perceived to be through the prior challenge: was earliest, somehow 'normative', Christianity basically Jewish or non-Jewish? There was always an assumption, appealing tacitly to the protestant return to scripture against tradition and, behind that again, to the Renaissance return *ad fontes*, that one should go in search of some kind of 'original' form and make that the norm. Since the putative 'Jewish Christianity' had not yet fully thrown off the shackles of 'Judaism', one would then look to Paul's developed view as the true 'original' of the worldwide movement. However misleading we now see that way of looking at things to be, that is how the question of Christian origins, and particularly of Paul's writings, has been approached.

(v) A Gentile Origin?

The scholarly endeavour to uncover the 'religious' roots of Christian origins included many very different emphases which we cannot track here. At the risk of oversimplification (unavoidable in a task like our present one), we can see the work proceeding in two great waves. First, there was the relentless quest for the supposed hellenistic, non-Jewish, sources of Paul's religion. If Paul had opposed 'Judaism', he must have got his basic ideas from somewhere else. The mystery religions of Egypt and other parts of the ancient Near East were combed for signs of what we find in Paul's 'being-in-Christ' language and similar phenomena. (Perhaps, people thought, Paul's idea of 'baptism into Christ' was borrowed from the mystery religions.) The gnostic movements, known principally at that time through the writings of the early Fathers, were projected back into the pre-Christian period and probed for signs of a pre-Pauline religion which focused on a redeemer coming down from heaven and returning there with his work complete. This, famously, was the line taken by Bultmann, particularly in his commentary on John, but also in the expectation, continued by Bultmann's followers, that the roots of Pauline Christology might be found in the same material. (The search for gnostic origins received an unexpected boost with the discovery of the Nag Hammadi texts in 1945.)

Other non-Jewish elements were brought into the picture, not least the burgeoning cult of Rome and the emperor. Perhaps, it was thought, these provided Paul with some of his raw material. Perhaps it was the familiar title used for Caesar that gave Paul the idea of Jesus as 'son of God'. But the main point was to demonstrate historically that Paul was not primarily a *Jewish* religious figure. Explain him in terms of Hellenism and you have explained the break with Judaism – and thereby, perhaps, justified it: Judaism was still seen, after all, in more or less the way Baur had seen it, as the religion of 'works' rather than faith, of a material culture rather than a spiritual one, a messianic religion looking for a this-worldly kingdom rather than a religion of the heart looking for the kingdom of heaven or a religion of the spirit looking for union with the divine ('the unity of the subjective spirit with the objective spirit', as Schweitzer summed up Baur's Hegelian doctrine[27]). Hindsight quickly perceives the dark side of all this in the European culture of the nineteenth and early twentieth centuries. So, in ways which still emerge (for instance, in the resolute refusal to let *Christos* mean 'Messiah' in Paul!), the quest was on not so much for a 'neutral' historical analysis which would place Paul firmly outside 'Judaism', but for such an analysis as a way of saying, 'There, that's what Christianity was supposed to be; that's how the narrow particularistic religion of Israel was gloriously transformed into the worldwide faith of the church.' There are echoes of this even in Schweitzer's more nuanced study, whose conclusion is that though Paul's own view of Jesus remained firmly rooted in Jewish thought, the way he expressed 'Christ-mysticism' meant that the new faith could the more easily spread into the non-Jewish world. Thus Schweitzer took the antithesis of Deissmann ('The dogmatic Messiah of the Jews is fettered to his native country. The spiritual Christ could move from place to place'[28]) and explained both halves in terms of the contemporary Jewish world, even while showing that the second part could prove more accessible outside it.

This kind of history-of-religions research was then developed two significant notches further. First, it was suggested that within Paul's own writings we could detect signs of an earlier 'Jewish-Christian' theology, which Paul sometimes quoted in order to relativize or refute it. Thus the apparent echoes in Paul of, say, 'covenantal' ideas are to be explained as the residue of a pre-Pauline Jewish Christianity. Second, it was suggested that, although Paul was the centre of one kind of 'hellenistic Christianity', there was another variety, which he opposed, which held an over-realized eschatology and a kind of super-spirituality which, as we saw a moment ago, could be labelled 'enthusiasm'. These constructs, for which the only evidence is the angled mirror the scholar applies to Paul's own writings, were then used to 'position' Paul in opposition to both of these hypothetical groups – a difficult and exegetically dangerous task, since most of the 'evidence' consists of things that he actually wrote, from which we have to 'deduce' things he only

[27] Schweitzer 1912, 15.

[28] Deissmann 1926 [1912], 133. For Schweitzer's criticism: Schweitzer 1931, 33–6.

mentioned in order to undermine them. All this is well known as part of the 'back story' of modern scholarship.[29]

(vi) A Jewish Origin?

Such agenda-driven historiography has invited an equal and opposite response. Faced with the post-Baur proposals just outlined, it was not difficult for others, particularly from within the world of modern Jewish scholarship, to respond that if Paul really did find an early Jewish religion and transform it into an essentially pagan one we shouldn't be surprised at the muddles and confusions that Christianity then got into. Such critics have developed the point: Paul, they assert, seems not to have known much about pure and genuine Judaism, the real Palestinian article; he was, after all, from southern Turkey, where no doubt there was a form of Judaism but not a very fine example of the genre; so what else could you expect? Thus the whirligig of historical study brings in its own revenges.[30] It is only in the light of these much longer debates that we can appreciate the significance of Sanders's protest in 1977. Those who have rushed to attack Sanders without noticing the longer scholarly narratives and debates to which he was contributing have inevitably missed at least some of the point.

But revenge comes in different forms. Several factors combined to move the historical study of Paul's religious setting from a relentlessly hellenistic project to a relentlessly Jewish one. W. D. Davies's ground-breaking book *Paul and Rabbinic Judaism* was more than a straw in the wind. It was part of the wind itself, blowing freshly through the academic corridors and reminding everybody that Paul was a Jew, spoke like a Jew, thought like a Jew, and reasoned like a Jew – and that when he became a Christian he did not put away any of these things, but continued in the same way, only now with the belief that the Messiah had come at last.[31] Some rabbis had spoken of a new Torah for the messianic age; this, Davies suggested, was at the heart of Paul's vision, explaining both his rejection of the Mosaic law as it stood (in other words, this was no Marcionite or antinomian move) and his embracing of the *nomos Christou*, the 'law of the Messiah'.[32] Here at last was a very Jewish Paul, for an age that had suddenly woken up, too late, to recognize the earlier dark prejudices for what they were.

Davies at least broke the log-jam of hellenistic interpretations of Paul: perhaps, after all, Schweitzer was right, and a Jewish context would explain

[29] An obvious example is the work of Käsemann, for instance his surgical operation to separate an earlier Jewish-Christian formula in Rom. 3.24–6 from what Paul then makes of it (Käsemann 1980 [1973], 95–101), and his insistence that a passage like Rom. 8.31–4 ('if God is for us, who is against us?', etc.) is a quotation by Paul of an 'enthusiastic' slogan which the apostle counters: 'though the enthusiasts raise their cry of victory, . . . believers are regarded as sheep to be slaughtered' (Käsemann 1971 [1969], 68).

[30] See again Moore (as above); also e.g. Montefiore 1914; Schoeps 1961 [1959]; Maccoby 1986, 1991.

[31] Davies 1980 [1948]. See Neill and Wright 1988 [1964], 412–15.

[32] As, for instance, in 1 Cor. 9.21 or Gal. 6.2.

things that had previously been thought to need a gentile one. But what sort of Jew might Paul prove to be? If not an apocalyptist, then a rabbi? If not one of those, then what? There were, and are, plenty more options to choose from. But a start – or at least a return in outline to Schweitzer's start – had been made.[33] There remain all kinds of questions, about (for instance) the dating of rabbinic material. But Davies was a pioneer, going boldly where few mainstream western scholars had ventured before. (Quoting Strack-Billerbeck's monumental collection of 'parallels' hardly counts, and was, in any case, put very firmly in its place by a now famous article decrying what has become known as 'parallelomania'.[34])

Davies's project, to explain Paul in terms of rabbinic Judaism in particular, coincided with an explosion of interest in second-Temple Judaism brought on by the discovery of the Dead Sea Scrolls. This was important because it soon became clear, even to the non-expert, that one could not simply pick up rabbinic texts which might well have been written several centuries later and assume that they reflected the views and practices of Paul's day. The twin disasters of AD 70 and 135 changed the Jewish world for ever; the rabbinic texts reflect the later world in which they were produced, rather than the time of Jesus and Paul. One could not simply appeal to the rabbis' own strong sense of tradition as evidence that sayings in the Mishnah (roughly 200) or the Talmud (roughly 400) did in fact reflect first-century reality, any more than one could appeal to the strong sense of tradition in Irenaeus or subsequent Christian writers as evidence that their second- and third-century views were accurate reflections of what the first apostles had said in the middle of the first century. Once, however, you raise the question that maybe Paul was a much more deeply Jewish thinker than had been supposed, newly-discovered texts such as the Scrolls, and new editions of other second-Temple works such as the Pseudepigrapha, could provide some solid help where the rabbinic material might be less reliable.

The question of continuity and discontinuity between Jewish thought and practice in the first century and in the later rabbinic period has itself become further confused by the problem of labelling. We have learned to shudder at the word *Spätjudentum*, 'Late Judaism', because of its associations with the older view in which post-exilic Judaism became corrupt and degenerate, declining away from the supposedly pure early religion of the prophets, and then contributing to all those features of the hypothetical 'first-century Judaism' against which Jesus and Paul were thought to have reacted. It is not clear, however, at least not to me, that the currently favoured alternative, 'Early Judaism', is any better at achieving appropriate historical clarity. It tends to lump together everything from immediately after the Babylonian exile to the early mediaeval period, and to assume (for instance) that the Pharisees in the days of Herod the Great were pretty much the same as the later rabbis themselves, who of course liked to cast

[33] Davies was a pupil of C. H. Dodd, whom we have not discussed but who perhaps deserves more notice, particularly in his reading of eschatology: see Matlock 1996, 76–100.

[34] Sandmel 1962.

themselves as their successors. Some have proposed 'Middle Judaism' as a compromise, though this has not caught on.[35]

I have in the past tended to prefer the phrase 'Second-Temple Judaism' because it labels the period in terms of its own central institution rather than through an implied relationship, whether positive or negative, with an earlier or later stage of Jewish life. It does, of course, have the very considerable drawback that the second Temple itself ceased to exist once the Romans had destroyed it in AD 70, whereas arguably many features of the pre-70 period – not least a strong revolutionary element, allied to a strict Torah-piety, and for that matter a tradition of 'apocalyptic' writing as evidenced by *4 Ezra* and *2 Baruch* – continued until the doomed bar-Kochba revolt.[36] It also has the drawback of the very word 'Judaism' itself, which, despite its regular use by Jewish scholars themselves, can be shown to carry overtones (especially because of the give-away implication of the 'ism') of much later categorizations.[37] But all this only goes to show that, however much one might applaud Davies's attempt to align Paul with 'rabbinic Judaism', if one really wanted to earth the apostle in his own first-century Jewish environment things would have to be made more complex before they could once more be clarified. When studying Jesus, we have learned that it isn't enough to speak of 'the Jewish Jesus'; one must enquire as to *what sort of* 'Jewish Jesus' one might be talking about. So it is with Paul: we may agree with Schweitzer and Davies that the apostle is best explained from within the first-century Jewish world, but we cannot assume that either Schweitzer's blend of apocalyptic and mysticism or Davies's hypothetical rabbinic thought will by themselves provide the right historical, cultural and theological setting.

That is why, soon enough, others came forward to declare that Paul wasn't simply, or even primarily, a rabbi, but rather a Jewish sectarian not too unlike an Essene, though again with a particular belief in the Messiah.[38] Similarly, other Jewish 'backgrounds' have been tried out: Josephus, Philo, the apocryphal literature, and so on. One of the greatest agents of transformation in New Testament studies has been the ready availability, in good new editions and translations, of texts such as the Pseudepigrapha, hitherto much harder to obtain and use.[39] One might also cite the massive impact made by the work of Martin Hengel in Tübingen, particularly his studies of the Zealot movement and his monumental survey of *Judaism and Hellenism* – arguing, in great detail, that all Jewish life and thought of the period had to be seen as part of the wider hellenistic world, rather than as a separate and detachable entity.[40] But the main point was this: Paul was a Jew, he still saw himself as a Jew while working as the Apostle to the Gentiles, and he

[35] See e.g. Boccaccini 1991.

[36] On all this see esp. *NTPG* Part II; and now *PFG* ch. 2.

[37] See esp. Mason 2007; and again Meeks 2001, Martin 2001.

[38] See e.g. Murphy-O'Connor 1995. For a nuanced Paul-as-rabbi see e.g. Chilton 2004.

[39] See esp. Charlesworth 1983, 1985; and now Bauckham, Davila and Panayotov 2013.

[40] See Hengel 1974a; 1989 [1961].

had to be seen as such if one was to understand what he was talking about. The impact of these studies was immeasurably heightened by the slow but horrified awakening of Europe and America to the facts of the Nazi Holocaust, and the gradual realization that the ideology which had been able with comparative ease to dehumanize the Jewish people and so to justify killing millions of them was no mere contemporary aberration, but had at least some of its roots deep within western culture, not least western Christian culture in both its catholic and its protestant forms.

The world was thus ready for a hasty inversion of the earlier prejudice: Paul the Hellenizer is bad, Paul the Jewish thinker is good! To praise Paul, you now had to go by the second route; to blame him, the first. Albert Schweitzer had long ago said much the same, but it was only after the Second World War that popular opinion came into line.

(vii) Beyond 'History-of-Religions'?

There are many comments one might make on this whole way of studying early Christianity in general and Paul in particular. But we must confine ourselves to a few pertinent observations. One might comment already on the danger of allowing agendas of the kind just mentioned to influence not only the subject-matter of historical study but also, in a measure, its results. We should not of course be naive. Agendas are what get people, even historians, out of bed in the mornings, though one might hope that, once at the desk, they allow the data to challenge the hypotheses they have dreamed up overnight. These agendas have produced, among other things, the set of history-of-religion categories which we mentioned earlier when discussing F. C. Baur ('Jewish Christian', 'gentile Christian', 'enthusiast' and 'early catholic'), which are still regularly employed and invoked.[41] In particular, there is the obvious but devastating mistake of imagining that once you have discovered where an idea has come from you have found out where it's going to.[42] Just as, in lexicography, the etymology of a word does not necessarily provide a reliable guide to current usage, so it is with beliefs and ideas. In particular, just because something (an idea, a symbol, a story) is demonstrably 'Jewish', that does not mean it has no critique of Judaism. In fact, one of the main characteristics of Judaism from at least the time of the eighth-century prophets onwards was *critique from within*, something a normal 'history-of-religions' analysis has always found hard, if not impossible, to allow for. Thus, just as Baur, Bultmann, Bousset and others eagerly produced 'hellenistic' contexts for Paul's ideas because they knew he was opposed to 'works of the (Jewish) law', W. D. Davies produced a would-be

[41] These formed the backbone, for instance, of Dunn 1977.

[42] See the parallel comment of Geertz 2000 [1973], 23 about 'social actions': 'where an interpretation comes from does not determine where it can be impelled to go'.

'Jewish' Paul from whom more or less all critique of Judaism had been removed.[43] Misleading categories produce misleading analyses.

But there are two more subtle dangers here as well. First, there is the obvious problem that history and 'application' will be linked up without even a proper glance at theology. One might simply assume that to be basically Jewish (or basically non-Jewish) is bad, or, as it may be, good; and Paul might then be fitted into whichever box is preferred, with evidence duly marshalled, but without real reflection on what those boxes might mean, how Paul's thought-patterns fit together when seen from that angle, why we are assuming a certain moral judgment on particular cultures, or the extent to which Paul, like so many other Jewish thinkers ancient and modern, resists our attempts to flatten him out in such a way.[44]

In particular, such a move assumes that the way to find the appropriate 'application' of Paul's letters to today's world is first to discover the 'right' sort of 'religion' and then to attempt to reproduce it. This assumption cuts both ways. Some have assumed that the main thing about Paul is that he discovered and propagated a new sort of 'religion'; others, indeed, that he gave up something called 'religion' and had something new, perhaps a 'revelation', instead (an antithesis favoured by some early twentieth century theologians, and now retrieved by some 'apocalyptic' interpreters). Others have seized upon some elements of the twentieth-century 'Jewish Paul' (Schweitzer, Davies, Stendahl, Sanders) as a sign that scholarship was now moving inexorably and irreversibly towards the view that Paul had no critique of 'Judaism', so that any attempt to see him as a nascent 'Christian theologian' would represent a regressive move against the tide of scholarship, and perhaps society – though one would have thought that such polemics would recognize the analogy with Hegelian developmental schemes and prefer to keep clear. Anyway, the attempt to jump straight to an 'application' of Paul's work on the basis simply of a would-be 'history-of-religions' analysis must be resisted, especially when the analysis in question, like Baur's, was rather obviously a back-projection of views reached on other grounds. History sets the context for exegesis, and must always remain in close dialogue with it; history and exegesis together must always remain in dialogue with theology itself. And theology, as I have argued in *Paul and the Faithfulness of God*, shows that the reasons for Paul's stance had to do, not with a 'religious' critique ('you have an inferior kind of religion, but I've discovered a superior one'), but with the *eschatological* belief that the crucified Jesus had been raised, and was Israel's Messiah. Only in the light of that belief, and its theological outworking, can appropriate 'application' begin.

The second more subtle danger has to do with the point we made earlier: the limiting of 'history' to 'history of religion'. This as we saw belongs with

[43] Davies 1980 [1948]: there is no discussion, for instance, of Rom. 2.17–29 or Phil. 3.2–8, and no mention at all of anything in Rom. 9.6—10.4 except for one cursory ref. to 10.3. This continues to be a problem in today's Jewish 'retrievals' of Paul: see *PFG* ch. 15.

[44] See, rightly, Agamben 2005 [2000], 3–5.

the post-Enlightenment ideology, according to which 'religion' becomes detached from all other aspects of life, and especially from politics. This bears no relation to Paul's world. Any attempt to impose a modern meaning of 'religion' on Paul or anyone else in his day is bound to fail. Any attempt to build an 'application' out of such an analysis will fail with it.

Perhaps partly because of this latter danger, more recent study has seen various attempts to locate Paul historically in relation to the philosophies of his day, particularly Stoicism. I have written about this elsewhere.[45] The danger here is that we fall back into the false either/or in which Paul must *either* be a 'Jewish' thinker *or* a 'hellenistic' one – or into an equally damaging antithesis in which Paul must be *either* a 'political' thinker *or* a 'religious' one. I have argued that he is both. Paul himself, however, given half a chance, will remake all our modern categories around his gospel.[46]

What is needed is history, genuine history, multi-faceted history, 'thick description' history that takes seriously the full range of human life and culture. We need to ask, not simply 'who did what', 'who ruled when' and 'who won which battles' – or, in the case of the New Testament, 'who wrote what', 'what were their main ideas', and 'where did they clash?' but, more particularly, why did people think and behave as they did? What motivated them, and why? What were they aiming to do? For this, I have employed the 'worldview' model, which I use heuristically, not to import any particular philosophical framework but to make sure, as with the social map-work of writers like Clifford Geertz and Charles Taylor, that we pay attention to cultural elements like narrative and symbol.[47]

3. From History to Theology?

If the historian is to make headway with exegesis, it is vital to understand the nature of the subject-matter. In the case of Paul, that will include all sorts of things about the ancient world, including tent-making and travel as well as politics and philosophy. But it will also include, centrally, what we broadly call *theology*. I have made this case in *PFG*. But how can we put the history and the theology together? They have been uncomfortable bedfellows for a long time, and particularly since the Enlightenment in which they were consciously split apart. We cannot pursue that long and complex story here, but we must note it as the wider context of historical scholarship on the New Testament. The results of the separation of history and theology, of faith and public life, are inscribed across western culture, biblical scholarship included. When this post-Enlightenment division is combined with a Lutheran 'two kingdoms' theology, the conclusion is even more inevitable.

[45] See *PFG* ch. 14; and see now esp. Rowe 2015.

[46] See *PFG* chs. 5, 12.

[47] See Geertz 2000 [1973]; Taylor 2007. See too Barclay's exposition of the notion of 'habitus' as found in Bourdieu (Barclay 2011, 26f.); this is an attempt to achieve the same kind of wider cultural grid of interpretation. See further ch. 10 below.

And when, as in Bultmann and some of his followers, history itself has been under suspicion lest, in offering an apparent foundation for faith, it might turn that faith into a 'work', it appears that much of the mainstream scholarly enterprise has been proceeding with unchallenged and unquestioned assumptions that have made it impossible to understand some of the key texts. The so-called 'new perspective' on Paul, to which we shall presently turn, ought not to be seen simply as a rejection of some older perspectives about justification, faith, the law and so on. It ought to be seen as part of a much larger turn, away from the Idealist world where 'history' in the sense of 'the immanent progress of the divine spirit' called the tunes and 'history' in the sense of 'what we can say about what actually happened' had to dance to them.

The present state of Pauline studies, then, emerged from many agendas and many aspirations, mixed with a great deal of historical research. The complex world we have sketched can neither be placed on a pedestal as the 'objective' results of 'neutral' scholarship nor dismissed as the mere 'subjective' projections of various cultural, ecclesial and theological movements. We must not absolutize our predecessors; nor must we ignore them.

They appealed, ultimately, to history. If we disagree with their findings it must be because, grateful for the stimulus of their labours, we ourselves are engaging in that same historical task, and attempting to do it more thoroughly. And that thorough task, applied to Paul, will quickly reach one particular *historical* question: what was Paul's '*theology*', and what sense did it make to him and his hearers?

Chapter Two

THE THEOLOGICAL QUESTIONS

1. Introduction: The Fireworks and the Framework

Mention 'Pauline theology' in a church, a seminary or even a university department of religion, and people will assume that you are talking about one or more of several different sets of questions. Trying to describe what was going on in Pauline theology used to be like trying to board a moving train. It is now more like trying to describe a box of fireworks seven seconds after someone has thrown a match into it.

But we have to try. The present chaotic display, fizzing and crackling all round the contemporary academy, provides the shape of one of the main problems to which my larger book, *Paul and the Faithfulness of God*, is offering an answer. The ultimate 'main problem' is, of course, 'how to understand Paul'. But we come to this problem, not with a *tabula rasa*, but as part of a conversation with at least some of the other voices that are trying to answer it too. One of the chief difficulties here is that many people, reading a book on Paul, assume that it is fundamentally addressing *their* questions, while there may in fact be other questions on the table, other debates taking place at the same time.

These discussions all relate closely, though this is not always made explicit, to several other issues as well. They relate, rather obviously, to the historical questions we looked at in the previous chapter: the history-of-religions standoff between 'Judaism and Hellenism'; the wider issues that accompanied it. They relate in particular to the exegetical problems raised by particular letters, passages and key terms. They also relate, crucially, to the question of 'application' or 'relevance'. Keeping these connections in mind is important throughout.

The resultant picture is bound to be multi-dimensional, and hence potentially confusing, especially for newcomers. The task before us, changing similes, is like the task confronting any attempt to analyse the later paintings of Claude Monet. When painting his celebrated 'Water Lilies' series he worked longer and longer, adding layer upon layer of paint, allowing the different layers to blend, to contrast in both colour and texture, to peep through or past one another, and so on; so that any attempt to describe one of his paintings, after the manner of some commentators on Paul, by saying 'this part of the painting is blue' or 'this part is green' simply misses the point. Every square inch is partly blue, every square inch is partly green, and a thousand things besides. To change from one art to another, to suppose that we can mount a serious discussion of Paul's theology without keeping these different dimensions constantly in mind would be like trying to accompany a song with only two or three strings on the guitar. In fact, study of Paul has often proceeded as though it were a one-string instrument, though different corners of the Pauline-studies world have been using different strings. It is time to have Paul's full harmonies heard again, even if it means that scholars and others will have to learn how to play on all six strings. Only so will the full harmonies be revealed. And sometimes, perhaps – Ephesians? – Paul decides, for reasons of his own, to switch to a twelve-string guitar instead. Why not?

One good metaphor, as Paul might have observed, deserves another. Coming to Paul's theology might be likened to someone going to watch a football match. (Note to American readers: I am thinking of soccer. But you can make the necessary transpositions. And your turn will come.) Imagine the consternation as the game gets under way and you realize that, instead of eleven players on either side, each with a literal and obvious goal in view, there are all sorts of other people on the same field, trying to play different sports: rugby, tennis, hockey – and perhaps American football, too, where, disconcertingly to British viewers, people appear to tackle one another with the ball nowhere in sight. That, too, has its scholarly counterparts. There are even some, in one corner of the field, who are trying to get friends together to play Australian Rules football. This could get dangerous. And many of these wildly different sports are trying to use the same ball . . .

For many, the football match they thought they were going to watch is quite straightforward. Paul, they have been taught, has written about one thing above all else: how to be saved, how to be 'justified by faith', how to be assured that one has been rescued from the consequences of one's own sin. This, it is still widely assumed, is the 'centre' of Paul (the quest for a 'centre' has been a running feature of Pauline studies for many years now, though I regard it as a bit of a side-track). Because the post-Enlightenment study of Paul grew out of an essentially protestant environment, the main lines of interpretation of Paul were already sketched out, and some have seen the Pauline football match as a re-run of the great games of old, the rival interpretations of Luther and Calvin in the sixteenth century. Many, indeed, read (and report on) the multiple cross-currents of scholarship solely in terms of the sport they thought they had come to watch.[1]

Let us then take a moment to review the rules of this older game, which continues to provide, for better and for worse, the framework within which most people come to Paul. I hasten to add that I am here concerned not so much with what Martin Luther or John Calvin themselves actually said – they deserve a much fuller treatment – but with certain key elements associated with them which have shaped Pauline studies in the western church and academy.

For Luther, the Mosaic law had indeed been necessary because of human sin (which had to be named, shamed and dealt with); but it was not God's ultimate word, and could often be spoken of, no doubt with pardonable hyperbole, as not really God's word at all. Famously, Luther read Paul's polemic against his Galatian opponents as the direct equivalent of his own struggle against the legalism of late-mediaeval Catholicism.[2] Thus he saw 'the righteousness of God' as the 'righteousness' which God gives, or accounts, or reckons, to those who believe; the 'works of the law' as the human attempt to make oneself good enough for God, even by apparently 'religious' performance; and 'faith' as the glad acceptance of what God had done, in Jesus Christ and his cross, to enable sins to be forgiven. Luther wrote so much that one can prove almost anything from his works; but it is fair to say that in the broadly Lutheran and evangelical traditions which have continued in lively forms to this day this emphasis on justification as central, and on the rejection of the law as the means to that justification, has remained constant.[3] One need only glance at commentaries on key passages like Romans 10.4 ('Christ is the end of the law'? or 'Christ is the goal of the law'? Or something else?) to see the vehement emphasis placed by the Lutheran tradition on the law as having been abolished through the gospel. Or one could look at Galatians 3.19, where Paul comments that the law was given by angels. Many have declared that he must be referring to *evil* angels, or at least to angels who gave the Torah to Israel as it were behind God's back.[4]

The response of Calvin, one of the most thorough and careful exegetes of his century or perhaps almost any century, was to challenge this Lutheran reading of the Mosaic law. What sort of a God is it, after all, who gives his people a law at one moment, and then, discovering them to be incapable of keeping it, changes his mind and decides to save them by a different method

[1] See, again, the shrewd remarks of Sanders 1977, 434, summarizing Schweitzer: if one relegates eschatology to the last place in a discussion, following the traditional *loci* of systematic theology, one will never understand Paul; and, likewise, if one assumes 'righteousness by faith' as the centre, one will never understand Paul's view of 'incorporation'.

[2] This was already pointed out by Barth long before Sanders said the same thing: see below, 89.

[3] For details, one might consult Westerholm 2004, ch. 2; for justification in Luther and his immediate followers, see McGrath 1986, 2.1–32.

[4] See e.g. Martyn 1997a, 364–70, in the form of a question: 'one could ask whether in writing Galatians Paul anticipates Marcion by suggesting that the Law did not come from the Father of Jesus Christ' (365).

altogether? For Calvin and his followers, perhaps already mindful of the potential antinomian tendencies which might follow from a simple 'rejection of the law', the law was to be seen also as a gift of grace. God redeemed his people when he led them out of Egypt; the law, given subsequently on Sinai, was *the way of life for a people already redeemed*. It was not a bad thing, given to condemn people and then swept aside by the gospel. It was a good thing that led up to the coming of the Christ. Compare, once more, that crucial verse Romans 10.4: Christ is the 'end' of the law. In the Lutheran tradition, 'end' regularly means 'termination'; for the Calvinist tradition, it comes out as 'fulfilment'.

Calvin made another crucial move which subtly but emphatically adjusted the focus of the post-Luther understanding of justification and salvation. We are justified, he said, *in Christ*. It is not just that the death and resurrection of Jesus are effective as the ground of our justification. Christ himself is the locus, the place where we find ourselves, and when God sees us there he declares that we are, as Christ is, 'righteous'.[5]

We thus have already, within the Reformation traditions, a negative and a positive view of the law. For both the great Reformers, justification was based on an event concerning Jesus Christ which happens, as it were, away from and outside us, as against a supposed Roman theory that justification consists in a divine work inside and within us. But for Calvin, here following Paul closely,[6] the divine verdict of 'righteous' is spoken *because we are in Christ*. This then points forward to the Westminster Confession, which has recently come back to prominence in some circles: we are justified because of the double achievement of Christ, his saving death *and* his perfect 'obedience'. Whether this construal of 'obedience' corresponds to Paul's use of that term in Romans 5.15–21 is another matter. But this was at least a natural extension of a Calvinist reading, in which the law was not a dangerous or bad thing now abolished by Christ, but a good, God-given thing now fulfilled in Christ. These two positions then go with a reading of the whole history of Israel in which, again, the Lutheran position tends towards the negative, seeing Israel as part of the problem, and the Calvinist towards the positive, seeing Israel as the start of the solution. That is why Calvinist theology has tended to issue in 'covenantal' schemes, with the scriptural covenant(s) not destroyed but fulfilled in Christ.

The football match many have come to watch is thus played between two teams, two variations within the essentially Reformational heritage – though the composition of the teams and the style of play has changed over the years, as was only to be expected. But it will be obvious that they are playing the same sport, on the same field and, mostly at least, by the same rules. *They are answering in biblical terms the questions posed by the western world and church in the fourteenth and fifteenth centuries.* They are doing their

[5] More details on Calvin in McGrath 2.32–9; and, not least, Westerholm ch. 3 (though Westerholm gives the impression of being more at home with Luther than with Calvin).

[6] e.g. Rom. 3.24f.; Gal. 2.17; Phil. 3.8f.

best to give biblical answers to mediaeval questions.[7] But what if those were not the questions Paul himself was addressing?

To be sure, in many passages – not, perhaps, as many as some might suppose – Paul is indeed talking about salvation. The letter to the Romans, in particular, announces that as a main theme, though even careful readers sometimes seem not to notice that the subject is never mentioned in Galatians. But was Paul meaning by 'salvation' what the western mediaeval church meant? Was he addressing the question in their terms? Was it, more especially, as central to his thinking as it was for theirs? Most works on 'Paul's theology' have proceeded as if salvation were after all the key topic, a process which reached its climax with Bultmann's concentration on 'man under sin' and 'man under grace' (see below). Some, noting this, have gone in a different direction, and have used the traditional topics of patristic theology as the framework (Trinity, creation, fall, and so on).[8] It might be the case that, with hindsight, we might conclude that Paul had supplied some of the materials for those later formulations. But this is not how he himself argues.

We thus find the mainstream western discussion about Paul caught uncomfortably in a post-mediaeval moment – a moment which, to be sure, has now gone on for nearly five hundred years. Paul himself, a millennium and a half earlier, was, as I have suggested elsewhere, asking subtly different questions. In any case, the multifarious scholarship of today's confusing world is asking radically different ones again. Most Pauline scholarship today is not writing footnotes to either Luther or Calvin. To revert to my previous sporting metaphor, the playing-field where the different teams are battling it out in terms of Paul's soteriology (this, too, is now not merely a game of two teams; they have subdivided) is crowded out by other teams, bent on playing other games. The sociologists have come on the field to play their game, which has to do with locating Paul within the social world of late antiquity, and his leading ideas within the moral discourse of the time. Jewish writers have taken more interest in Paul, but there is no agreement as to whether Paul really was a very bad Jew indeed, a very good Jew indeed, or something in between. And the sudden rise of interest in Paul as a political thinker cuts right across all these scholarly games, like someone setting up a tennis net sideways across the football pitch and proceeding to mark out the lines and get ready to serve. The scholarly journals, and the annual meetings of the Society of Biblical Literature (and, to a lesser extent, the Society of New Testament Studies) are increasingly full not only of straightforward debates between people who are at least trying to play the same sport, but also of sidelong engagements between the soccer players trying to get round the tennis net, the rugby players ('apocalyptic') tripping over outstretched hockey sticks ('covenant theology'), and the heavy-duty American football

[7] On the mediaeval questions involved, see esp. McGrath 1.155–87.

[8] e.g. Whiteley 1964. Sanders 1977, 435 says, rightly, that this may 'distract from seeing Paul's thought on its own terms'; but Sanders himself, as we shall see, cannot seem to help returning to soteriology as a central topic.

players, replete with helmets and padded shoulders, annoyed because other people keep catching their ball when they were about to score. And let's not even think what the Australians are up to, especially when they line up with one of the original soccer teams. Those who have ears may hear; those who do not can dismiss this as mere foolishness – though without forgetting that Paul, too, was not above such rhetorical tactics. And Paul might well, I think, have approved of such a way of marking the frustration of trying to track so many themes and discussions which have emerged from his writings. Let us take a step back from this playing-field, and describe the scene in a slightly more conventional manner.

Once we have grasped the original protestant conversation about Paul, it would be easy for those with an appetite for such debates to be carried along by the flow, without ever stopping to ask the question, which surely needs to be asked: why *these* topics? Why should one read Paul primarily to discover a system of salvation, a doctrine of justification, a means of dealing with sin? Why not read him for all the other things he rather obviously spends a lot of time talking about – Jesus Christ himself as the one through whom the world was made, the spirit as the one who brings the life of God himself to dwell within believers both corporately and individually? Why not focus on his frequently-stated eschatology, on the new creation, the resurrection, the final 'appearing' of Jesus? Why not look in more detail at his concrete and definite teaching about human character and conduct, all focused on faith, hope and love? Why not – a truly radical thought! – look at what Paul says about God himself?

Why not indeed? But the answer is: Luther, Calvin and their sixteenth-century colleagues, understandably granted the age in which they lived, were dominated in their approach to soteriology by the questions bequeathed to all Europe by the later mediaeval period, with its often short and brutal human life. *What will happen to me after I die*? In particular, (a) Can I know, and if so how, that I will be 'saved', rescued from eternal torment to enjoy a blissful heaven? (b) Even so, will I have to spend a long time being purified of my still-present sins in a 'purgatory'? And, not least, (c) What can I do in the present to be sure that the answer to (a) is 'Yes', and the answer to (b) is 'Not for very long, preferably not at all'? The mental hold that these questions had on ordinary people across a whole continent by the end of the fifteenth century – and the spiritual and even financial hold over those ordinary people that the existence of these questions gave to the clergy – was, by today's standards, quite remarkable.[9] And because all human beings ask themselves questions of that sort from time to time, even when freed from clerical threats and a late-mediaeval mood, Luther's and Calvin's focus on the matter of justification – on the question of whether, and how, one might know in the present that one was saved for all eternity, with no anxious striving in the present and no purgatory in the future – has retained its power to this day. Its Pauline power, we might say. (Of course,

[9] On the role and power of 'purgatory' etc. see e.g. Greenblatt 2001.

Luther and Calvin were interested in many other things as well, not least in how to make a living Christian faith real in the concrete circumstances of actual communities and cities. But much retrieval of them has concentrated on soteriology.)

Had Paul faced the questions asked so urgently by the early sixteenth century, we can safely say that he would have given moderately similar answers, albeit nuanced and narrated differently. If Paul had had to choose between Martin Luther and Johann Tetzel (the Dominican preacher who went around Germany selling 'indulgences' to enable people to get out of purgatory), he would undoubtedly have chosen Luther. But just because I would rather eat part of a dead cow than part of a dead rat, that doesn't mean that I don't care whether my steak is properly cooked; and Paul might have queried whether Luther's skill in the kitchen was equal to his choice of menu. So, too, more subtly and also controversially: if Paul had had to choose between Luther's strident rejection of the law and Calvin's strong affirmation of it, he would have chosen Calvin. But once again, just because I prefer Guinness to lemonade that doesn't mean I am not particular about the temperature at which the Guinness is served; and I believe Paul would have told Calvin to take his dark Irish beer out of the fridge, to let it come up to room temperature and taste its full flavour. In other words, I believe that Paul himself compels us to say both Yes and No to both Luther and Calvin – and, in consequence, to the traditions that have been shaped by both of them, especially the later dogmatic and philosophical traditions that have in turn shaped so much reading of Paul, right through to the worlds of contemporary historical scholarship.

Even a casual reading of Paul's letters, in other words, will indicate that when Paul did come near to the Reformers' questions (not that he ever dreamed of Purgatory!) he framed them, and fashioned his answers to them, in quite a different way. Their questions, and the answers to those questions which they culled from Paul, were not nearly so important for Paul as they were for the sixteenth and seventeenth centuries. Paul can write whole, long letters, dealing with several different vital topics, without going near justification and salvation. He can write a little gem of a letter, the one to Philemon, concentrating all the resources of the gospel into a small, sharp and perfectly formed pastoral appeal, but without stopping to remind Philemon about his future salvation or to warn him that, even though he now has something concrete he must 'do', his justification remains by grace through faith. But gradually, bit by bit, starting with Schweitzer and coming forward with the speed but also the relentlessness of a glacier, scholarship has been working towards the problem: what questions *was* Paul asking? What were the burning issues in his world, in his day? How was 'salvation' itself conceived within that world?

Here we meet once more the question of Paul's cultural (not just 'religious'!) context: are we looking for ancient Jewish questions, or ancient non-Jewish questions, or both? Even granted that Paul gave fresh, gospel-driven answers, what were those answers *to*? Did such answers force a reframing of the questions? Until we catch up with the complexities of such an enquiry – until, in other words, we allow a properly historical vision of Paul to take priority over later images – we will not advance towards fuller understanding.

This process has been delayed by a scholarly move which is, in fact, remarkably *un*scholarly. So strong have been the traditions of Pauline interpretation in the western academy that many have assumed they knew, sometimes better than Paul did himself, what questions he was 'really' asking (despite what he seems to have been saying) and what answers he was 'really' trying to give (despite what he actually said).[10] Unfortunately, the apostle did not have the benefit of a relaxed sabbatical in an accommodating German university so he could sort these things out at leisure ... so the twentieth-century scholar will have to do it for him. This generates a process (it seems too kind to call it a 'method') known as *Sachkritik*, 'material criticism', 'the interpreter's criticism of the formulation of the text in the light of what (he thinks) the subject-matter (*Sache*) to be'.[11] In other words, we know better than Paul what he 'really' wanted to say, and we now have ways of making sure he will say exactly that.[12]

The mainstream exponents of Pauline theology, then, have focused on the questions raised over the last five hundred years within the protestant tradition: justification, the law, grace, faith and salvation, all in relation to an assumed ultimate goal of reaching heaven and an assumed intermediate goal of being assured in the present of that future destination. Other things then come close behind, not least Christology – by which is usually meant, 'What did Paul say in relation to Jesus' "divinity" on the one hand, and the meaning of his death on the other?' The meaning of Jesus' death is itself then integrated into whatever view of Paul's soteriology is being advanced. But what about the spirit? What about the question of God? The topic of God has been conspicuous by its absence in much Pauline theology; notoriously, for Bultmann it came in on the side as part of the analysis of human

[10] I add these qualifying parentheses because, of course, I once wrote a book with the hostage-to-fortune title *What St Paul Really Said* (= Wright 1997). In my case, the 'really' was implying a contrast, not with some of the ideas which happen to occur in Paul's letters, but with some of the interpretations given by both scholarly and popular writers.

[11] Morgan 1973, 42. The whole discussion (42–52) is important.

[12] e.g. Bultmann 1951–5, 198: what Paul wanted to say in 1 Cor. 15 was that human existence both before and beyond death would be 'somatic' in Bultmann's sense; but Paul, whose 'capacity for abstract thinking is not a developed one', muddles this up with bodily resurrection. On *Sachkritik* see also e.g. Matlock 1996, 124 (noting that it seemed as though 'Paul deserved a hand up from the modern interpreter at those points where he found it beyond his power to maintain against the currents of his time his critical insights'); 126 n. 135, quoting Conzelmann 1968, 175 in summary of Bultmann's programme to present Paul's theology 'as anthropology in order to do justice to its own intention'. In other words, we know better than Paul himself what he was 'really' saying, and like a wise sub-editor must help the author make his meaning clearer by slicing through all those awkward bits which didn't quite fit. My other favourite example of this genre is Dodd 1959 [1932], 71, striking through Rom. 3.1–8 like a tutor responding to an essay from a dull pupil: 'The argument of the epistle would go much better if this whole section were omitted.' In other words, 'I am determined that Paul should talk about what I think he was talking about, whatever ideas he may have to the contrary.' Whatever else this may be, it is not responsible historical exegesis.

sin, a sign of failure in a 'theological' architecture if ever there was one.[13] From this angle, the question of Paul's theology can be quite simply posed: how do these various concepts line up and integrate with one another? How do these concepts appear, singly and combined, within Paul's various letters? Was he consistent, or at least coherent both from letter to letter and within the individual letters themselves, in what he meant by them? How can we sort them out in our own minds in a way which does justice, rather than violence, to their varied expressions in Paul's writings? This is the framework within which the vast majority of Pauline study has taken place over the last few hundred years. It still shapes the way in which many approach the subject, even though now, with fireworks exploding all around us, everything is far more confused than once it was.

2. From Schweitzer to Sanders: A Necessarily Impressionistic Sketch

We return to Albert Schweitzer, who gave a decisive new twist to the shaping of Pauline debates in his review of the literature over a hundred years ago.[14] Like all Paul's greatest modern interpreters, he recognized a fundamental *historical* question and offered a fundamental *theological* analysis as the key to the answer. The historical question is, simply: where does Paul belong in the development of earliest Christianity? How does he relate to Jesus himself, to the earliest ('Jewish-Christian') followers of Jesus, and then to the next generation, the world of Ignatius of Antioch and the wider second-century church?

Here Schweitzer did battle with those who saw Paul as the Hellenizer of the early Jesus-tradition: with those who, instead of seeing Paul as the bridge *between* 'early Jewish Christianity' and 'later hellenistic Christianity', had him already standing on the further bank. No, insisted Schweitzer: Paul remained firmly Jewish, but his Judaism was that of the radical eschatology called 'apocalyptic'. Paul was dominated by 'the exclusively eschatological conception of the Gospel'.[15] Even where non-Jewish ideas had made their way into his mindset, such material 'has been poured into Jewish moulds and received a Jewish impress.'[16] In the very place where his contemporaries thought they could see the influence of the mystery-religions, namely in Paul's sacramental theology, Schweitzer insists that here 'the eschatological interest breaks through'. The sacraments will then 'effect, not re-birth, but

[13] Bultmann 1951–5, 228 (God's creatorship is not 'a cosmological theory', but 'a proposition that concerns man's existence'), following from his opening statement that since all statements about 'God' are statements about 'man', and all statements about Jesus Christ are about soteriology, we should frame the discussion in terms of 'man', his sin and his salvation (191). On Bultmann see further below. A noble exception to the rule about not discussing God: Das and Matera 2002, with the revealing title, *The Forgotten God*. An earlier straw in the wind was a famous article of Nils Dahl: Dahl 1977, ch. 10.

[14] Schweitzer 1912. Fuller summary and discussion in Neill and Wright 1988 [1964], 403–8; and see esp. Matlock 1996, ch. 1; Gathercole 2000.

[15] Schweitzer 1912, x–xi.

[16] ibid., 177.

resurrection. That which in the near future is to become visible reality, the sacraments make in the present invisibly real by anticipation.'[17]

The point for our purposes, as we summarize all too briefly one of the greatest minds of the twentieth century addressing one of the greatest minds of all time, is this. Schweitzer's answer to his own question was that Paul remained a thoroughly eschatologically-grounded and essentially Jewish thinker. What Schweitzer called Paul's 'Christ-mysticism', rooted in his Jewish thought, was nevertheless able to form the bridge across which early Christian thought moved into the second and third generation, the period in which the dogmatists of Schweitzer's day (he is in dialogue particularly with von Harnack) saw the origins of Christian theology (and also the origins of what they saw as its more degenerate formulations). When Schweitzer's long-promised systematic treatment of Paul came out, nearly twenty years after his review of the background literature, its title, *The Mysticism of Paul the Apostle*, was perhaps misleading.[18] It was not a book about Paul's prayer life or techniques of spirituality. It was a sustained exegetical and theological exposition of what Schweitzer called Paul's 'eschatological mysticism of the Being-in-Christ'.

This was, for Schweitzer, the centre of Paul's thought and life. The experience of 'being in Christ' was a matter of being caught up in the present time in the state which anticipated the soon-to-be-expected eschaton. Subsequent generations, he said, could not follow Paul in this eschatological rooting of the 'being-in-Christ'. They kept his central formulation, but they gave it a different framework, that of 'current hellenistic concepts'.[19] Paul was not therefore himself the Hellenizer of Christianity. But in this central doctrinal concept 'he gave [Christianity] a form in which it could be Hellenized.'[20]

Schweitzer, tantalizingly, suggests towards the end of his book that the letter to Philemon 'exhibits the lofty charm of Paul's personality in a unique degree'. If this was the only letter of Paul's that we had, he suggests, 'we should still know a good deal about him.'[21] Tantalizing: because, as I argued in the first chapter of *PFG*, the heart of that little letter is indeed the eschatological being-in-Christ which Paul insists is shared by the three actors in the drama, namely Philemon, Onesimus and Paul himself. Schweitzer does not, however, draw attention to this.[22] More important in the history of the discipline, and for our present brief survey, Schweitzer declared, following the insight of William Wrede, that the entire system of thought we might label 'forensic', the 'law-court' language of justification and the law, was not after all the centre of everything for Paul. Following

[17] ibid., 216.

[18] Schweitzer 1931: see below.

[19] Schweitzer 1931, ix.

[20] ibid.

[21] 1931, 331f.

[22] He notes the relevant passages, as part of a long list, at 124, but does not discuss them or comment on the way they form the driving heart of the letter.

the line by which he had divided up Paul's interpreters in his earlier survey of German research, and setting a course which is still the major division in the subject to this day, Schweitzer insisted that

> in Paul's writings there are two independent conceptions of the forgiveness of sins. According to the one, God forgives in consequence of the atoning death of Jesus; according to the other, He forgives, because through the dying and rising again with Christ He has caused the flesh and sin to be abolished together, so that those who have died and risen with Christ are, in the eyes of God, sinless beings.

How did these two viewpoints come to be combined in Paul? Here Schweitzer sounds a bit like J. L. Martyn, seventy years later:

> The former of these doctrines [forgiveness because of Jesus' atoning death] is traditional, the latter [the abolition of flesh and sin because of the Christ-event] is peculiar to Paul, and is a consequence of the mystical being-in-Christ. Though he can express himself in both ways, his thinking follows by preference the lines of the latter, because in this the fact of forgiveness of sins falls into its due relation to the complex of facts involved in redemption. For it results, like them, from the fundamental event of the dying and rising again with Christ.[23]

These two ways are not ultimately at loggerheads, because Paul's preferred way can subsume the other within it. Hence the famous metaphor (Schweitzer could match Paul stride for stride in vivid imagery):

> The doctrine of righteousness by faith is therefore a subsidiary crater, which has formed within the rim of the main crater – the mystical doctrine of redemption through the being-in-Christ.[24]

This combination is not, however, natural to either topic, but rather an 'unnatural construction of thought', resulting in 'the idea of a faith which rejects not only the works of the law, but works in general', and which thus 'closes the pathway to a theory of ethics'. These large themes, 'incorporative Christology', 'righteousness by faith', and 'ethics' (or whatever else we choose to call them), have remained to this day three of the major elements which any fresh reading of Paul must correlate. And, as Schweitzer himself would insist, such a reading must not only correlate them so as to give a coherent account of Paul himself. It must also show how, in such a correlation, they form a demonstrable bridge between Jesus himself and his earliest followers on the one hand and, on the other hand, the post-Pauline developments that point towards Ignatius and the second century.

We note in particular the strong exegetical implication of all this. Once you divide 'forgiveness through the atoning death of Jesus' from 'being in Christ and so sharing his once-for-all dying and rising', you will be tempted to draw a thick line between Romans 1—4 and Romans 5—8, or at least 6—8, and to demand that we choose between the two. That is what people have been doing ever since – though, as we shall see, they are regularly disturbed

[23] Schweitzer 1931, 223.

[24] ibid., 225.

in this false either/or not only by those who point out that Romans 9—11 and 12—16 are part of the same tight-knit structure, but also by those who remind them that the third and fourth chapters of Galatians contain all the basic themes of both sections, and that they seem there to be mutually compatible and integrated. The sharpness of Schweitzer's vision, coupled with his unrivalled skill as a lively writer about complex abstract issues, thus crystallized a way of looking at the subject which, in the cold light of a postmodern morning, appears to have more clarity than historical accuracy.

There is no indication in either of Schweitzer's books on Paul that he realized how close he was, structurally, to the thought of John Calvin. Paul is a Jewish thinker following through a Jewish line of thought, and 'justification' happens basically because one is 'in Christ'. That is more or less exactly what the Reformer of Geneva had proposed, though one would not have realized that either from reading Schweitzer or from reading many today who claim Calvin's heritage but would be shocked to find 'justification' as a 'secondary crater'. And it is this proposal of Schweitzer's, variously modified over the course of the following generations, that re-emerged in the late 1970s in the work of E. P. Sanders, for whom 'participation' was the centre and 'justification' a secondary matter to do with the admission of gentiles into the church, as Wrede had already insisted two generations earlier.[25] There are some analogies, too, with the 'apocalyptic' theory of J. L. Martyn, which highlights God's cosmic rescue operation and downgrades the notion of Jesus' atoning death and consequent 'forensic' categories of justification; and, even more, with the recent work of Douglas Campbell, for whom 'participation', in a slightly different sense, remains central, and for whom 'justification' has been pushed off the table altogether.[26] The terms in which Schweitzer posed the question have thus been hugely influential, whether or not acknowledged.[27] There is a sense in which all these have the character of 'reformed' or 'Calvinist' responses to a perceived 'Lutheran' construal of Paul, however much they now diverge both from Calvin and from one another. 'Participation' and 'justification' are regularly spoken of as two major and quite different categories of thought in Paul's mind. The relationship between them, historically, theologically and (not least) exegetically remains one of the major questions in the discipline.[28] Since I have argued elsewhere that this dichotomy is fundamentally ill-conceived, and that the two are outworkings of a larger theme which the discipline has not normally recognized or worked with, it is at least important that we recognize how powerfully present within the whole discourse of Pauline studies this distinction has been, and acknowledge the role of Schweitzer in stating so

[25] Wrede 1907; see Schweitzer 1912, 166–73. As Schweitzer pointed out (173), Wrede's view was ignored at the time because the dogmaticians of the day could make nothing of it.

[26] See Part II.

[27] Sanders is more conscious than many of his debt to Schweitzer. Käsemann, who took 'apocalyptic' as his guide, appears to have been more reluctant to tip his hat to his distinguished predecessor. For Käsemann, as we shall see, 'apocalyptic' functions within his hypothetical history-of-religions scheme in the place formerly occupied by the discredited 'Gnosticism'; see the discussion of Käsemann below.

[28] See now esp. Macaskill 2013 (on Schweitzer: 21–4).

clearly the historical, theological and (in a measure) exegetical problems as they appeared a hundred years ago.

Schweitzer's massive reinterpretation of Paul also did its best to reframe the questions that had to be asked, away from the narrow focus of 'how can I find a gracious God', or even 'how can I go to heaven', and on to the questions of what exactly 'being in Christ' might mean, and its consequences, and the question of how the early Christian 'apocalyptic' perspective can be retrieved, granted that even Paul's successors found that task impossible. But this does not seem to have had much immediate effect, even among the German theologians who were Schweitzer's natural conversation partners. There were two rather obvious reasons for this (apart from the fact that Schweitzer had left the academic life to pursue other vocational goals, so it was easier to ignore him; he was not attending conferences, or writing for the theological *Zeitschriften*). First, the apparent relativization of justification in favour of 'participation' was not congenial to most of his German contemporaries. Second, the word 'mysticism', despite the fact that Schweitzer meant it in a specialized sense, sent shivers down the spine of most Protestants of his generation. It spoke of a vague, dreamy, sacramental, possibly even pantheist piety which they associated with the popular Catholicism against which, in Germany at least, Lutherans defined themselves.[29] So it is not surprising that, in terms of further scholarship, Schweitzer's view of Paul had little apparent impact. For the next generation, the landscape was dominated by the man whose influence is still felt in many quarters: Rudolf Bultmann.

Reading the section on Paul in Bultmann's famous *New Testament Theology*, one would hardly know that Schweitzer even existed. His two books are listed in the Bibliography, but there is no sign of engagement, of wrestling with issues freshly stated, except possibly for one or two side-swipes at 'mysticism', which we should probably take as a way of saying, 'Don't bother me with that strange stuff.' The 'in Christ' theme is ecclesial and eschatological but not 'mystical'.[30]

This is not the place for a detailed study of Bultmann, whose influence on mid-twentieth-century readings of the New Testament must be deemed quite extraordinary given just how counter-intuitive most of his proposals now appear.[31] Ironically, his work was taken by many, not least in the English-speaking world, as 'objective scholarship', so that several of his more outlandish proposals, which we now see were driven by a priori theological agendas, are still faithfully recorded and discussed by would-be

[29] On the misinterpretations of Schweitzer's use of 'Mystik', see e.g. Sanders 1977, 434f.

[30] Bultmann 1951, 311, 335. Bultmann had engaged with Schweitzer elsewhere, and twice promised a fuller discussion which never came. On this, and on Bultmann's reading of Paul in general, see Matlock 1996, 100–29.

[31] On Bultmann see now the full assessment, with updated bibliographies, by Robert Morgan in Bultmann 2007 [1951–5], xi–lxiii. Morgan's account is not uncritical, but it remains more positive than many today would allow. From a quite different angle: Thiselton 1980, chs. 8, 9 and 10.

wissenschaftlich scholarship.[32] Ironically, Bultmann himself had declared that one cannot do exegesis without presuppositions. It now seems obvious to us that his proposals belonged within the turbulent and often dark world of Europe from the 1920s to the 1950s, where they were proclaimed as a matter of pastoral urgency. To study Bultmann while taking this context fully into account is, in fact, to be awed and humbled by the integrity with which he wrestled with the questions of what Christian faith might mean in those appalling times. To read the conclusion of his study of Paul, knowing what he had lived through, and indeed preached his way through, is to find oneself grateful for a giant of courageous faith:

> In God, freedom, righteousness, and life have their cause, and it is in them that the glory of God as ultimate meaning and ultimate goal comes to its own. To the glory of God, Christ is confessed as Lord. To the glory of God, prayers of praise and thanksgiving are to sound forth in the congregation. Our eating and drinking and our every undertaking is to be done to His glory as well as the work of the apostle. To His glory, Christ accomplished his work and to Him he will resign his reign 'in order that God may be all in all'.[33]

That is a noble statement. One can sense from it, as well as from his published sermons, what it would have been like to listen to Bultmann on a Sunday morning, with Europe in tatters but with God's word issuing a fresh summons to hope, and even to joy, as well as (of course) to faith. People have asked again and again whether this Bultmann is compatible with the dry, devastatingly negative Bultmann of the *History of the Synoptic Tradition*. That is not a question for us at present, but we may reflect that his analysis of Paul, for the most part, stands about half way between those two extremes.[34]

Bultmann was a classicist, a student of the wider world of greco-roman antiquity. He shows a strong inclination throughout his work to 'explain' Paul in terms of non-Christian and especially non-Jewish influences. Indeed, the major difference between Bultmann and Schweitzer might be said to lie just here: Schweitzer insisted on interpreting Paul within the Jewish world of his day, particularly that of 'apocalyptic eschatology' (as Schweitzer understood it), and Bultmann showed almost no interest either in that world or indeed in the Old Testament, but rather supplied a hypothetical 'gnostic' framework as the explanatory grid for one theme after

[32] e.g. his theories about pre-Pauline formulae (e.g. Rom. 1.3f.; 3.24–6) which were driven by a desire to protect Paul from supposedly primitive Jewish Christianity, i.e. to fit him in to his proper place within a post-Baur developmental scheme. These were then taken up with equal enthusiasm by Käsemann and developed by his students, all still working within the same frame of reference. This was basically an intellectual confidence-trick, predicated on the assumption that German scholarship was massively and objectively historical – an assumption that a positivistically-inclined English-speaking liberalism was eager to seize upon in support of its own very different agendas.

[33] Bultmann 1951, 352 (the closing paragraph of the section on Paul): biblical refs. omitted (Phil. 2.11; Rom. 15.6; 2 Cor. 1.29; 9.12–15; 1 Cor. 10.31; 2 Cor. 4.15; Rom. 15.7; 1 Cor. 15.28). In the fourth sentence, the text reads 'it' for 'is'; in other ways, too, one senses that the translator (Kendrick Grobel) may understandably have been a bit tired by this point.

[34] Some of Bultmann's sermons can be found in Bultmann 1960a; another collection is at Bultmann 1960b.

another.[35] Paul's 'body of Christ' language is 'gnostic terminology'; the angels through whom the law was given in Galatians 3.19 are part of a 'gnostic myth'; and so on. Even 1 Corinthians 15, which echoes the first chapters of Genesis all the way through, is derived according to Bultmann not from Genesis but from gnostic ideas.[36] If not gnostic, then Stoic: the formula of praise to God at the end of Romans 11 is derived from 'Stoic Pantheism'.[37] Bultmann's Paul is not, like Schweitzer's, forming the bridge which others will cross from the Jewish world into the hellenistic. He has himself crossed the bridge, leaving Judaism behind well, truly and for ever. Christ is, after all, the *end* of the law (Romans 10.4); and by 'end' Bultmann understands 'termination'.[38]

This set of assumptions about 'where Paul got it from' plays out in terms of the theological analysis of the material. The grid of interpretation which Bultmann chooses is essentially that of protestant soteriology, seen in the light of his classical researches on the one hand and his neo-Kantian Idealism and Heideggerian existentialism on the other: the two main divisions are 'Man prior to Faith' and 'Man under Faith'. The letters are treated as though they are collections of theological *topoi*; almost no attention is given to the actual flow of thought in which those short discussions are embedded.[39] As a result, Israel – its hope, its life, its national eschatology, its messianic expectations; its history, its exile and restoration; even its anthropology – is more or less ignored. Romans 9—11 is not discussed as a section. What matters is that the law has merely made the plight of humans even more serious, because the law has lured 'man' into trying to keep it, and so becoming guilty of a kind of meta-sin.

This, I confess, was the hardest thing for me to grasp when I first read Bultmann nearly forty years ago, and I suspect it remains a puzzle to many today. Bultmann, and Kümmel alongside him in his famous analysis of Romans 7, insisted that the problem was not that the 'I' was struggling to keep the law and failing, trying to do what the law required but not coming up to the standard.[40] The problem was that the law itself was enticing 'man' to try to keep it, and thus, in the apparent success of that effort, to commit the sin of pride. I now believe that Kümmel and Bultmann were trying to say something that needs to be said about Romans 7, but that the tools available to them to say that needful thing were about as helpful as giving a sledgehammer to someone trying to install a new hard drive on a computer. Having held at bay both Israel's scriptures and the post-biblical Jewish literature, and the whole worldview they instantiate, there was no way

[35] See the revealing remarks in Stuhlmacher 1986 [1981], ix: 'In the school of Rudolf Bultmann (in which I myself, through my teacher Ernst Käsemann, was trained), the New Testament was interpreted to a large extent without reference to the Old Testament.'

[36] e.g. Bultmann 1951, 310; 268; 228.

[37] 1951, 229.

[38] 1951, 163f., 280.

[39] The main exception is an interesting passage on the sequence of thought in the first half of Romans (1951, 278f.).

[40] Kümmel's famous treatment of Rom. 7: Kümmel 1974 [1929].

Bultmann would understand what Paul was on about in this passage. He was too good an exegete not to see that there was a problem. But he had long since forsworn the tools he needed to solve it.[41]

The exception to this point is in Bultmann's treatment of justification. This is almost the only place where he allowed small parts both of Israel's scriptures and of the post-biblical literature (in this case, the Psalms of Solomon) to play a role. They enabled him to say, with clarity and conviction, two things about Paul's language about justification: it was both 'forensic' and 'eschatological'.[42]

On 'forensic', he is clear that 'righteousness' means 'the "favourable standing" that a person has' when the court has found in his or her favour.[43] Quoting Psalms 37.6 and 17.2, 15, he insists that the word refers not merely to 'innocence' but to the fact that someone 'is *acknowledged* innocent'.[44] He does, however, combine – unhelpfully to my mind – the idea of 'the verdict of the law-court' with the slippery idea of 'relationship'. If we import the idea of 'relationship' into the courtroom setting itself, it makes nonsense, or worse than nonsense. In a law-court, the 'relationship' of the judge and the defendant is neither here nor there. The better they know one another, the more the suspicion will arise that the case is not being tried fairly. Paul does of course correlate 'justification' with 'reconciliation'. But correlation, as for instance in Romans 5.1–11, is not the same as identification.

Bultmann is correct, however, to see that 'relationship' comes into the overall picture, and that in both Judaism and Paul 'the forensic term "righteousness" became an eschatological term', referring to 'God's rightwising verdict' that would come 'from His eschatological judgment'.[45] Bultmann is clear that Paul speaks, in line with his Jewish context, of a *future* 'judgment', and that Paul also declares that, through the 'apocalypse' of the gospel, this future judgment has been brought forward into the present. Thus

> The contrast between Paul and Judaism, then, is not that each has a different conception of righteousness as a forensic-eschatologican [*sic*: presumably 'eschatological'] entity. Rather, the immediate contrast is that what for the Jews is a *matter of hope* is for Paul a *present reality* – or, better, is also a present reality.[46]

[41] On his failure to grasp Paul's Jewish context, cf. e.g. 1951, 222f., where he discusses 2 Cor. 3 in terms of Paul producing a formulation 'determined by reminiscences of the Old Testament', as though there were no thought-through or thematic coherence, but rather a few bits and pieces of ancient Hebrew fragments about which Paul just happened to 'reminisce'.

[42] 1951, 270–4.

[43] 1951, 272. I have anglicized the American translation ('favorable').

[44] 272, italics original. He recognizes the 'ethical' sense of the word (271) but insists that when Paul uses it in soteriological contexts it is strictly forensic, that is, to do with 'the verdict of the "forum"', i.e. the law-court (272).

[45] Bultmann 1951, 273. The translator's use of the old English 'to rightwise', as a way of retaining the same root for verb and noun rather than switching between 'justify' and 'righteous', was one of several experiments in that area which have not caught on, though Sanders tried it as well.

[46] 1951, 278f. (italics original).

It would be hard, I think, to improve on this. Again, however, Bultmann introduces extraneous notions, bringing 'adoption' into the picture but without seeing how it works, for Paul, in relation to the law-court language and the eschatological context.

A better solution was at hand. The move Bultmann could have made at this point would have been exactly parallel to the move he made to join eschatology with the forensic use of 'righteousness'. The 'Jewish piety' which he cites as evidence for the 'eschatological' meaning (273) was also deeply and foundationally *covenantal*. And, just as he sees that Paul has retained the Jewish eschatology but revised it around the events concerning Jesus, so that it is now a present reality as well as a matter of hope, so he could have concluded that Paul had retained the Jewish covenantal theology – the 'relationship' between Israel's God and his people – and had revised that, too, around the events concerning Jesus. This would have provided a perfect context for understanding how 'adoption' related to this whole train of thought. And it would have clarified numerous other points on the way.

The other extraneous notion Bultmann introduced here has to do with one of the most famous of the mid-century Pauline debates. He insisted that the 'righteousness' which someone comes to possess, within this forensic and eschatological scenario, *is* 'the righteousness of God'. That is demonstrably a mistake, despite its venerable ancestry, but it was the sort of mistake likely to occur to one whose grid of interpretation owed much to Luther on the one hand and to the classical world on the other, and who had more or less bracketed out the world of ancient Israel (Isaiah and the Psalms were quite clear on the point) and also the world of second-Temple Judaism. This point will be central in our later discussion of Käsemann. Bultmann's analysis of justification, though, while needing to be recontextualized within that larger Jewish world, is otherwise on target. There is more to be said than simply that justification is both forensic and eschatological. But that provides two large steps in the right direction.

Bultmann says remarkably little, in his analysis of Paul within the *New Testament Theology*, about the place and role of Jesus Christ and the spirit. The death of Jesus 'for us' is, he concludes, a pre-Pauline formulation which Paul picks up and develops. The resurrection is confusing in Paul's hands, because he sometimes writes as if it actually happened, and as if one could prove it by citing witnesses. The spirit is given as a response to faith, not as the cause of it.[47] Bultmann's treatment of 'faith', though, is striking, because, again as a good exegete, he does not shrink from bringing Paul's meaning of 'faith' into close relation with 'obedience'.[48] The gospel, Bultmann rightly sees, is for Paul a *summons* to be obeyed, and that obedience consists in

[47] 296; 305; 330. On Bultmann's analysis of the resurrection see *RSG* 625–7 and elsewhere via the index.

[48] Rom. 1.5; noting too the parallel of 1.8; 16.19, and of 1 Thess. 1.8 with Rom. 15.18; and comparing Rom. 10.3 (referring tacitly to 9.32), with 10.16 (not all believed; not all obeyed). Similarly 'disobedience' is correlated with 'lack of faith': Rom. 11.30–2; Rom. 15.31; Gal. 5.7. Bultmann also compares 2 Cor. 9.13; 10.5f.; 10.15 (all this at Bultmann 1951, 1.314f.).

'faith'.[49] This faith is not, however, a 'work' (a regular charge made by Calvinist exegetes against Lutherans), because of its very nature. Bultmann's way of making this point is to distinguish such 'obedience', which is a *renunciation* of one's own will, from 'accomplishment', which would be an *assertion* of that selfish will. This arbitrary distinction, corresponding to nothing in Paul's Greek or indeed in his thought or argument, nevertheless gives Bultmann a telling summary not only of Paul as Bultmann reads him but also of his own existentialist analysis of 'authentic' existence:

> As true obedience, 'faith' is freed from the suspicion of being an accomplishment, a 'work'. As an accomplishment it would not be obedience, since in an accomplishment the will does not surrender but asserts itself; in it, a merely formal renunciation takes place in that the will lets the content of its accomplishment be dictated by an authority lying outside of itself, but precisely in so doing thinks it has a right to be proud of its accomplishment. 'Faith' – the radical renunciation of accomplishment, the obedient submission to the God-determined way of salvation, the taking over of the cross of Christ – is the free deed of obedience in which the new self constitutes itself in place of the old. As this sort of decision, it is a deed in the true sense: In a true deed the doer himself is inseparable from it, while in a 'work' he stands side by side with what he does.[50]

We may properly question whether this subtle distinction will actually work, both historically and exegetically in terms of Paul and, perhaps equally important, in the pastoral and homiletic application of this challenge. Is it really possible for someone to be sure that their 'obedience of faith' is not always threatening to turn into an 'accomplishment'? Is not that question itself, a natural one indeed granted Bultmann's scheme, a sign that one is seeking, precisely by asking it, the kind of security which Bultmann thinks we should not seek? To follow this up here would take us too far afield. Suffice it to say that, as many have pointed out, Bultmann's Paul is an ancient version of a Lutheran existentialist, with little relation to Israel's scriptures or to the world of contemporary Judaism, drawing instead on gnostic categories to construct a challenge, a daily summons, to live by faith in a world of apparent chaos. We may thank God for the pastoral challenge Bultmann thereby offered his contemporaries, both in the Nazi period and after the Second World War. We may still, however, regret that he allowed these contexts to flatten out his exegesis so that he seemed either unwilling or unable to hear all the other things which Paul was saying, through which alone a fully integrated picture and a richer pastoral message might have emerged.

I have deliberately spent a bit of time with Schweitzer and Bultmann because, even at this distance, perhaps especially at this distance, we can see clearly that they set the terms in which subsequent study has been conducted, whether by modification or disagreement. We must move on; but

[49] Bultmann 1951, 314f.

[50] 1951, 315f. The use of existentialist categories in this extract is particularly noteworthy, for instance the careful analysis of a 'true deed' in terms of its authenticity (the doer being inseparable from the deed) as against the kind of inauthenticity in which one remains detached from what one does. This, once more, owes nothing to Paul and everything to Heidegger.

unless we recognize that these were the issues which shaped the later debates, and that this was how they were approached, we will not understand those debates themselves.

In particular, it is important to see that the so-called 'new perspective', itself diverse from the start, constituted a retrieval of Schweitzer and a departure from Bultmann – and, with that, a re-opening of the question about 'Jewish' or 'non-Jewish' contexts. Many of its critics, failing to realize all this, have criticized the movement as though it were something else. Likewise, the new so-called 'apocalyptic' readings pay homage to Käsemann; but Käsemann himself was also retrieving Schweitzer, at least by invoking 'apocalyptic', and also rejecting some of Bultmann's key moves, especially his anthropocentric rather than cosmological soteriology (signalled by the debate over 'the righteousness of God'). Thus, once more, we need to locate today's debates on the Schweitzer/Bultmann playing-field to understand where they have come from and why they have taken the shape they have.

One might, of course, want to object, whether on historical or dogmatic grounds, that the whole playing-field was sloping so dangerously, or perhaps that it was so uneven and muddy, that no sensible games could be played on it at all. One might then propose rescheduling our Pauline matches for a different venue altogether. One might, in other words, take the view that since subsequent research has shown up so many weaknesses in the arguments of both Schweitzer and Bultmann it would be foolish to go on trying to make sense of the bits and pieces they left behind. There would be a certain refreshing air to such a proposal: clear away the rubble and start again! But it would be hopelessly naive. And here we return to the fact that the core task of studying Paul is *exegesis*. We are still faced with *these* texts. They still contain the same Greek words and sentences, and even if we decide to reinvent all the earlier wheels by doing our own lexical studies and concordance-checking – which is also a refreshing and salutary exercise – we will soon bump our noses against the same large questions. It would be going too far to say of Schweitzer and Bultmann what W. S. Gilbert said, with tongue firmly in cheek, about 'conservatives' and 'liberals' in British political life ('that every boy and every girl, that's born into the world alive, is either a little liberal, or else a little conservative'); but one can still see the marks of the Schweitzer/Bultmann division etched into today's debates, and it is better to take account of them than to pretend we are doing something completely different. One of the reasons why Käsemann has remained such a towering figure forty years after the publication of his major commentary on Romans is that he offered a new resolution of this dichotomy, in at least implicit dialogue with his two great predecessors. Even if we reject his solutions, we should acknowledge that this was what he was trying to do, and that the rest of us are still trying to do it as well. One of the reasons why the opposition to the 'new perspective' has sometimes been a bit too noisy may be that, in rejecting a new variation on Schweitzer, it finds itself drawn back into the orbit of Bultmann, whether it recognizes it or not.

The other reason why we cannot ignore these earlier debates has to do with the larger fusion of horizons. Schweitzer and Bultmann, and the lesser lights who followed them, were embedded in their own culture and history. They believed that their work on the New Testament would contribute to the task of addressing that culture and history with fresh, life-giving words from God. The early twenty-first century, to be sure, faces significantly different challenges from those of Schweitzer before the First World War or Bultmann before the Second. But Europe and America still bear the scars of those terrible years, as much in our cultural perceptions and moral judgments as in our family memories, though these may be important as well. We cannot stand aside and pretend we are not part of the history which included Paschendaele and the Somme, Hiroshima and the Holocaust. The multiple crises of today's democracies, the inept short-term pragmatism of international politics, the collapse of trust in many areas of public life, the rampant inequalities of rich and poor both between and within nations – all these and more are the muddled legacies of the culture within which the earlier debates about Paul took place and by which they were shaped. Again, we might wish it otherwise, but if the study of Paul has any sense of hermeneutical responsibility it should recognize that if we are the heirs to the questions and proposals of Schweitzer and Bultmann we are also the heirs to the cultures they were addressing. However much we start the exegetical task afresh in every generation – as young men and women are gripped by the challenge of figuring out for themselves how the argument of this or that letter actually works! – we do so with the older issues still on the desk, even if we try to cover them up. Hermeneutics is complicated, but inevitable. And if someone were to say that we need not worry about all that, because the message of Paul had to do with being saved out of this world for a better one – or even, that because we believe in 'apocalyptic' we can forget the past and rely on an entirely new word from God in our own day! – then we may remind them that that way of seeing the matter, too, has its own long history, and that the gnostic impulse it follows has itself contributed to some of the problems of which we are now aware.

We must now proceed more briskly through seven scholars of the post-Bultmann period whose work has remained influential and important for the further study that has taken place. Of Bultmann's successors, the most straightforward is Gunther Bornkamm. His book on Paul, backed up by various articles, remained in the Bultmann line: a Lutheran gospel message, located within a history-of-religions account drawn mainly from the non-Jewish context, taking as axiomatic that every statement about God, Christ, the spirit and so forth 'is at the same time one about man in his world'.[51] Bornkamm's work is more user-friendly than Bultmann's, and has done a lot to continue disseminating the view that Paul was more or less as Luther had described him. Christ is the end, i.e. the termination, of the law.[52] A

[51] Bornkamm 1971, 118 (subsequent refs. are to this work). His index has even fewer references to Jewish literature: 12 OT refs. (4 from Isa.); one each to 4 Ezra, Qumran, Philo and Josephus.

[52] 134.

new world of Christian 'experience' opens up which has left behind the world of Judaism with all its 'legalism' – and also its promises: Paul uses Abraham to 'illustrate what it means to have faith', but his statements about Abraham 'are, of course, fundamentally different in content from traditional Jewish ideas'.[53] Romans 1.16–17 'does not fit any apocalyptic pattern' (despite, we note, its use of the Greek word *apokalyptō*!), but 'expounds and develops the Christian gospel *as the gospel of justification by faith alone.*' Paul's thought is in fact 'totally opposed to apocalyptic'.[54] All this, it seems, is a way of saying 'no' to Schweitzer (and, explicitly, to Käsemann as well) and 'yes' to Bultmann. And, therewith and quite explicitly, 'no' to any idea of a cosmic reach to the gospel, and 'yes' to an individualism which goes beyond even that of Bultmann: 'justification' is 'not properly forensic, but "existential".'[55] Bornkamm does, however, insist that the language of justification and that of incorporation into Christ belong closely together, not least in Romans 8, though there too he is careful to hold Schweitzer at arm's length. Whatever this 'incorporation' is, it is not 'mysticism'.[56]

Bornkamm thus offers a brief, elegant exposition of the way Paul was being read in many parts of Germany in the 1960s. The opening of his main exposition of Paul, though, is very revealing in the light of 'the Sanders revolution'. Whatever we may think of the 'new perspective' and its critics, I doubt if anyone will ever again introduce Paul with a first chapter entitled 'Lost: Man and the World', with the first section of that chapter being 'The Law'.[57]

More important, but quite puzzling, is Oscar Cullmann. Cullmann reacted strongly to both Bultmann and Barth, and was very much aware of Schweitzer. He insisted in two famous books that 'salvation' in the New Testament, and in Paul in particular, was not to be dissociated from time or history. The appearing of Christ had been at the 'mid-point of world history' and was to be interpreted thus, not in the sense (as in the early Barth at least) of a 'vertical invasion' by God into the world without visible or organic connection to what came before or followed after.[58] Cullmann explains that he has been rebuked by followers of Barth and others,

> for my stress upon the *horizontal line of salvation*. These critics say that the crucial thing in the New Testament is the *vertical saving act of* God in Christ – '*senkrecht von oben*' (vertically from above).

[53] 143. The slightly nervous 'of course' gives the game away: yes, all right, he seems to be saying, I know these are in a sense Jewish ideas, but let's not get carried away! So too 148: of course, Paul appears to be dealing with 'theodicy' when he speaks of God's righteousness, but 'the two modes of thought' (Paul and 4 Ezra) are 'totally different'.

[54] 125, italics original; 147.

[55] 151.

[56] 155.

[57] 120.

[58] Cullmann 1962 [1951]; 1967 [1965]. On Cullmann see esp. Matlock 1996, 129–85; and, from a different and important point of view, Yarbrough 2004, 213–60. A less provocative, less influential, but in some ways more attractive writer than Cullmann on similar themes is J. Munck: see Munck 1959 [1954], 1967 [1956].

He is eager to rebut the charge, and to show how this emphasis is taken care of within his larger scheme:

> In what follows I shall try to show that I do not dispute the verticality of the saving event, but that this verticality becomes significant and understandable only on the basis of the horizontal nature of the line of salvation, and that the vertical line, as in a co-ordinate system, derives its meaning from, and is defined by, the basic, horizontal line.[59]

All Christian theology, he says, is '*in its innermost essence*' biblical history. God reveals himself 'on a straight line of an ordinary process in time', and from that line God 'controls not only the whole of history, but also that which happens in nature!'[60] This is exactly what Barth was so worried about, both when he reacted sharply against the easy-going *Kulturprotestantismus* of the German liberalism of the early twentieth century and particularly when he opposed the quasi-Darwinian theology of the *Deutsche Christen*, who claimed that God had, through the immanent and evolving process of history, raised up the German nation to be the new great world power, and that Christian obedience demanded that one should discern what God was doing in history and get on board. That was the context for Barth's famous 'Nein!' against Emil Brunner, and also for the Barmen Declaration.[61]

One can readily understand, in that social, cultural and above all political context, why Cullmann's line of thought was simply not wanted. If 'salvation history' meant that God was at work throughout the natural processes of the created order and of human history to bring about 'salvation' by an immanent process, an evolution, a steady development which could contain or muzzle the radical inbreaking of something quite new, then this was to be seen as a political as well as an exegetical and theological *faux pas*. The idea of history as an immanent development, as we saw, is a Hegelian concept, which drove, among other things, the Tübingen scheme of F. C. Baur on the one hand and the dreams of both the Marxists and the Nazis on the other. Cullmann seems not to have realized the seriousness of the charge, or the dangers he was in simply as an exegete in appearing to license a 'steady development' or 'evolutionary' approach in which 'salvation', and perhaps even Christ himself, merely 'emerged' from their background, like a new mutation within a Darwinian scheme of genetic selection. I do not think that Cullmann, or indeed his contemporary apologist Robert Yarbrough, have taken fully into account the deep-seated reasons why so many Germans reacted strongly to this renewed version of salvation history. It was not simply because they were wedded to Bultmannian existentialism, or, behind that, the proposals of F. C. Baur. Some like Käsemann were themselves also reacting against that. It was rather that Cullmann, and the earlier

[59] Cullmann 1967 [1965], 16 (italics original).

[60] Cullmann 1962 [1951], 23: italics and exclamation original.

[61] On Barmen see Scholder 2012 [1987], esp. 122–71.

writers in the 'alternative tradition' in German scholarship, seemed oblivious to the philosophical and ideological company they were keeping.[62]

In particular – this came as a shock to me as I reread *Salvation in History* after thirty years – Cullmann, for all his insistence on the Jewishness of his proposed historical reading, never engages with the question of what it might have meant to a first-century Jew to live within the biblical and post-biblical narrative, or indeed what that implicit narrative actually was, which texts had formed it, and how second-Temple Jews struggled variously with hope deferred and promises both realized and not. For a book of the size, theme and stated scope of *Salvation in History*, it is breathtaking to find that the Index lists a mere twenty-two passages from the Old Testament: nine from Isaiah, none from Deuteronomy, and none from the narratives of either creation or exodus.[63] If one is going to reconstruct a Jewish 'salvation-historical' perspective within which to read the New Testament, one might have thought it important to investigate the narratives (in their multiple forms) embedded within the scriptures themselves, and also the ways in which they were retrieved and reworked within the second-Temple world.[64] Simply ignoring all this was asking for trouble. Cullmann got it.

He was, however, unrepentant. He was very conscious that in his 'salvation history' he was doing his best (inadequately, as I have suggested) to locate early Christianity within its specifically Jewish context, and that those who were denying it that context, both in their history-of-religions assumptions and in their theological analyses, were themselves colluding with the deep anti-Judaism which had so horribly infected the culture of the day. Judaism and Christianity, he wrote, had been *dehistoricized* by Bultmann's move to explain things via Gnosticism: he, Cullmann, was standing with Irenaeus against Gnostics ancient and modern.[65] What kept the faith alive in the second century, and ought to keep it alive now, was precisely 'the idea of salvation in history'. Hardly daring to name the horror that had taken place under the Nazis, Cullmann nevertheless levels a serious charge against those who had accused 'salvation history' itself of complicity in wickedness:

> I dare to ask, however, whether that decisive debate in Church history with Marcion and Gnosticism does not contain a lesson for our time.[66]

[62] Yarbrough offers a sharp polarization: on the one hand, critical orthodoxy from Baur through Wrede to Bultmann; on the other, salvation historical approaches from J. C. K. von Hofmann through Schlatter and Cullmann to Goppelt. It is true that the latter tradition – if that is what it is – has often been ignored rather than refuted. But things are more complicated than this polarization implies. Yarbrough virtually ignores Käsemann, whose would-be followers today reject 'salvation history' in the name, not of Bultmann, but of 'apocalyptic' (see, however, Yarbrough 2004, 149f., 238; and also 150f., noting, with Watson 1997, 165, that Bultmann, like Käsemann, made a tacit identification between the Nazi ideology and a biblical *Heilsgeschichte*).

[63] The two refs. to Ex. are incidental side-notes, not part of an argument.

[64] I have tried to do just this in *PFG* 108–79.

[65] 1967 [1965], 26.

[66] 27.

– in other words, whether the utter rejection of Jewish categories, including of course the idea of salvation being somehow connected with history, might not be linked to the rejection of the Jewish people themselves within European society.[67]

These internecine polemics, so urgent and so necessary as Europe and particularly Germany shook itself and shuddered in horror at the events of the 1930s and 1940s, must be seriously re-evaluated today. Each side is accusing the other of holding an analysis of early Christianity which somehow colluded with Hitler and all his ways. You can't believe in salvation history, because that's what got us into the mess! You must believe in *Heilsgeschichte*, because if you reject it you're saying that Judaism itself is a category mistake! From the safe, comfortable distance of one born after the war and the Holocaust, and for whom, despite family involvement, that war remains like a strange tale from a far-off land, I say with due respect to those who lived through that period that neither of these positions strikes me as particularly helpful for doing historical exegesis, or for the attempt to reconstruct the worldview and theology of the apostle Paul. Granted, as I said before, we are all the children or grandchildren of the ideological debates and horrible wars of the previous generations. But we cannot simply project the ideological confusions of one part of Europe in the early twentieth century on to the much larger screen of world history, and insist that, now that *we* have been through *this period*, we understand at last the categories of thought within which all previous writing must be understood, the scales in which they must be weighed. Such a suggestion would be a new form of cultural imperialism: you *must* see the ancient world like this, because of *our* modern history! Indeed, a key feature of our rootless western world is that, having given up the theological and moral foundation of an earlier assumed Christian civilization (honoured of course more in the breach than in the observance, but still a reality), the post-Enlightenment world has tried to invent a new 'morality' by reaction, in a sort of trial-and-error fashion: (a) something horrible happens, (b) we ask ourselves how we got into that mess, (c) we react angrily against anything that looks as though it was part of that cause, then (d) we elevate our new 'insight' into an absolute standard by which everything and everybody else is to be judged, whether ancient or modern, European or 'Oriental', North or South.

It might be good, instead, to turn Barth's 'Nein!' into a position simply of humility. It would be good to put the exegetical hand on the theological mouth: to declare that we do not know. It would be good to return to the tasks of history without assuming that our own experience has given us a yardstick by which to judge which ancient writers were preaching the genuine gospel and which were not – and which may need our 'help' to make

[67] See too Stendahl's less restrained response to Käsemann (1976, 131): 'I could list how pogroms and the Holocaust found fuel and comfort in an understanding of Judaism as the eternally condemned and evil way to serve God', etc.; further, the 'profound warning' in Rom. 11.11–35 'against that kind of theological imperialism which triumphs in its doctrine of the justification of the ungodly by making Judaism a code word for all wrong attitudes towards God' (132). On Stendahl and Käsemann see below.

sure that what they 'really' intended to say can be set free from the shackles of some of the unfortunate paragraphs they actually wrote. Rereading some of these writers, one is tempted to say that if anyone needed help to struggle against some of the unfortunate things they committed to paper, it was not Paul, but some of his twentieth-century interpreters.

Cullmann has sparked these more general reflections, not least because it was in reaction to Cullmann that the third of my post-Bultmannians wrote some of his sharpest material. Ernst Käsemann, declaring that 'controversy is the breath of life to a German theologian', sprang to the attack when Krister Stendahl wrote his famous article on Paul and the 'introspective conscience of the West'.[68] The real target of the polemic, however, was not Stendahl himself but Cullmann, and deeper and darker forces behind him.[69] Reflecting on the 'conception of salvation history which broke in on us in secularized and political form with the Third Reich and its ideology,' Käsemann described himself and his contemporaries as youngsters who had learned an unpleasant lesson. 'As burnt children,' Käsemann insisted,

> we are unwilling to add fuel to the fire which at the present day, for the third time in a century, is awakening such general enthusiasm. Our experience has made a theology of history suspect for us from the very outset, whatever the reasons may be which are urged in its support. It determined the liberalism whose faith in progress was finally shattered by the First World War. However erroneously and improperly, it was capable of serving as a shield for Nazi eschatology. We do not want to be called back to the place where our fathers and grandfathers stood a hundred years ago and where they came to grief fifty years later.[70]

Being tarred with those brushes, we might think, was enough to kill off any project. But there is more. Salvation history, declares Käsemann, encourages one into an easy-going Catholicism in which one is 'always on the safe side'; a triumphalism in which the church itself will 'ultimately triumph over its Lord, by organizing him instead of listening and obeying'; and, at the heart of the ideological, as opposed to the political, critique,

> an immanent evolutionary process whose meaning can be grasped on earth, or which we can control and calculate.[71]

Now all this is fine so far as it goes. We can see where, in today's slang, Käsemann is coming from – though it ill becomes him, with all these contemporary warning signs, to claim that he, unlike his opponents, is standing for a ruthless historical-critical reading of scripture *against* 'a theology which is guided by the needs of the church or its traditions'. He deprecates

[68] Käsemann 1971 [1969], 60.

[69] See Hays 2002 [1983], 58 n. 96, referring also to Stendahl 1976, 129–33.

[70] Käsemann 1971 [1969], 64.

[71] ibid., 62f. See too Käsemann 1980 [1973], 264: 'salvation history is obviously not an immanent process of development into which justification can be fitted at the proper place'. Käsemann says that this is directed against Stendahl; but neither at the passage cited nor anywhere else does Stendahl, to my knowledge, say anything like what he is here accused of. Käsemann is here tilting at windmills, as again in 1969 [1965], 250, speaking of 'the superstitious belief in history and salvation history as sources of revelation'.

an exposition of scripture which has been 'regulated and confined by considerations of edification', but it is hard to see how his fierce situational and contextual polemic could be read except as another example of that very thing.[72] That, however, is what makes Käsemann, particularly in his great commentary on Romans, such an exciting exegete to read. All the questions are on the table all the time, bumping into one another and bouncing off in different directions.[73]

The debate between Käsemann and Stendahl, which I addressed in my own first major statement on Paul, points the way to the heart of Käsemann's theology.[74] For him, 'apocalyptic' is both 'the mother of Christian theology' and the shaping, driving force within Paul in particular.[75] This represents of course a return to Schweitzer. Some reviewers, pointing this out, wondered if Käsemann should rather more obviously have expressed a kind of collective post-Bultmannian apology for the way in which the previous generation had missed the point. Whatever we may think about that, the stress on 'apocalyptic' is massively important for the contemporary debates about Paul in America in particular. Martyn's famous commentary on Galatians, dedicated to Käsemann, has followed ostensibly the same line, albeit as we shall see with significant modifications. We must be sure therefore that we understand Käsemann, at least in outline, well enough to be aware of an entire stream of thought which still strongly influences the way Paul is read.[76]

When Käsemann put 'apocalyptic' at the centre of early Christianity and of Paul in particular, he was quite clear what he meant. 'Apocalyptic', he wrote to me in a letter, 'for me always means "imminent expectation", *Naherwartung*.'[77] Early Christian and Pauline thought, in other words, was decisively shaped by the hope that the 'end' was about to happen. The question of 'apocalyptic', what it is and where it belongs within the history of religions, has been itself a matter of enormous discussion in the last two generations. For Käsemann, it performed a similar, though not I think identical, task to what it had done for Schweitzer. Certainly when we stand the two of them over against Bultmann, we see that 'apocalyptic' provided for both of them an apparent religio-historical framework for understanding Paul, though Käsemann was, to put it mildly, less concerned than Schweitzer had been to join up the edges of his Pauline picture with Jesus on the one hand and Ignatius of Antioch on the other. The hypothetical 'apocalyptic' framework avoided the (Bultmannian) problem of invoking

[72] Käsemann 1971 [1969], 62. One caution, though: it may be that by 'edification' Käsemann meant, scornfully, what passes for 'edification' in ordinary, humdrum, bourgeois Christian circles.

[73] I have engaged further with Käsemann's great commentary at appropriate points in *PFG*, and confine the present remarks mostly to his trenchant and fascinating collections of essays.

[74] Wright 1978, now in *Perspectives* ch. 1. My fuller discussion of Käsemann is in the same vol., ch. 4.

[75] See esp. Käsemann 1969 [1965], ch. 5.

[76] For a much fuller treatment, see *Perspectives* ch. 4; and Neill and Wright 1988, 416–21. I was grateful for a personal letter from Käsemann himself, expressing his approval of my analysis of his thought. See too Way 1991; Zahl 1996. On Martyn see below Part II.

[77] See too 1969 [1965], 109 n. 1.

some form of early Gnosticism, which Schweitzer had not wanted and which Käsemann already knew was unhistorical.[78] But Käsemann's framework, too, can be disputed historically – a point which will recur, *mutatis mutandis*, when we come to contemporary would-be 'apocalyptic' readings. As Klaus Koch showed in his famous monograph, there was in fact little appetite in the post-Bultmannian world (Käsemann's world, in other words) for serious engagement with the 'apocalyptic' texts either of Israel's scriptures, or of post-biblical Judaism, or indeed of early Christianity (Revelation, Hermas, and so on).[79] Even Mark 13 and its parallels were treated as a kind of extraneous addition. And, as I have said before, 2 Thessalonians tended to be shunted off into deutero-Pauline obscurity, lest it contaminate its pure Pauline neighbour with strange, dark, 'apocalyptic' thought-forms.

But for Käsemann the point of 'apocalyptic' was not primarily to link Paul to a particular strand of second-Temple Judaism. In fact, in the way he used it, it was a way of *not* linking him so directly, except to (Käsemann's version of) a strand of thought in Qumran and one or two other texts. There, so he claimed, 'God's righteousness' had become a technical term, removed from its 'covenantal' framework so that it no longer referred to the divine faithfulness to the covenant with Israel, and meant instead 'God's salvation-creating power', with a cosmic *rather than a covenantal* reach and goal.[80] 'Apocalyptic' was thus about the whole cosmos, not primarily, if at all, about Israel, 'salvation history', or 'covenant'.[81] Käsemann, in fact, may have been subtly demythologizing 'apocalyptic' itself, making it do the job that the now discredited 'Gnosticism' had done as an explanatory hypothesis, but within an apparent Jewish framework, though the history-of-religions evidence for this particular proposal always was thin. Käsemann had ways, however, of making sure that this theory would stick: passages which appeared to be 'covenantal', such as Romans 3.24–6, actually contained embedded quotations from pre-Pauline 'Jewish-Christian' formulae, which could be carefully extracted, like a doctor removing a foreign body from the patient's flesh, leaving Paul himself innocent of such covenantal ideas. The problem with this is not the suggestion that Paul could and did quote bits and pieces of earlier material which he knew as traditional. Paul himself says as much.[82] But always, when he does this, he is quoting in order to agree with the tradition, to build on something which he and his hearers knew was common ground. We have no actual evidence, apart from a few Corinthian 'slogans', that he quoted material in order to subvert it. Yet this

[78] See Käsemann 1980 [1973], 144.

[79] Koch 1972 [1970].

[80] See esp. Käsemann 1969 [1965], ch. 7. This antithesis of 'cosmic' and 'covenantal' persists to this day, despite having no warrant in ancient literature.

[81] It seems to me that towards the end of his life Käsemann was more prepared than he had previously been to allow that Paul did indeed include the sense of 'covenant faithfulness' into the meaning of *dikaiosynē theou*. I have explored this in Wright 2014b.

[82] e.g. 1 Cor. 15.3–8, though the last line of this is presumably a Pauline addition.

was what Käsemann insisted on. The same method has been employed by some of his own successors.[83]

This was part of the larger, more complex history-of-religions proposal, going back as we saw to F. C. Baur. The idea was that one might reconstruct both the early *Jewish*-Christian community, which was assumed to be at least linked with the people who came 'from James' in Galatians 2, and which focused on issues of nation, law and covenant; and then again an early *hellenistic* Christian community, which had eagerly, perhaps too eagerly, embraced a 'realized eschatology' and so had turned into an 'enthusiasm' which no longer needed 'apocalyptic' (i.e. 'imminent expectation') because everything that had been hoped for had already happened.[84] In between these two one might then discover the supposedly pure 'Pauline' gentile Christian message, a 'law-free' gospel which generated a suffering, struggling, but radically hopeful community.

One does not have to be particularly cynical to notice what has happened here, however subtly and cleverly these hypothetical communities and messages may be distinguished. The effect is that Paul can be situated against 'Jewish Christians', with their insistence on law and covenant, on the one hand, and against 'enthusiasts' on the other hand. And the weapon Käsemann's Paul employs against both is 'apocalyptic' itself: the radical inbreaking of God which declares that there can be no 'steady state' or 'evolutionary development' in 'salvation history', and which declares that, since the hope remains in the future, one cannot become an 'enthusiast' and imagine that one already possesses all God's promises.[85] In other words, 'apocalyptic' as reconstructed by Käsemann (or at least reimagined; there is not much sign that he was actually studying 'apocalyptic' texts and coming up with a careful historical construct) is what the apostle needs in order to be located exactly at the point where Martin Luther himself had stood, facing the legalistic Roman Catholics on the one hand and the dangerously radical 'enthusiasts' on the other. For Käsemann, these opponents could easily be transformed into the comfortable bourgeois churchgoers on the one hand and the charismatics or fundamentalists (as he would see them) on the other.

Here is the irony of Käsemann's position. For all his relentless polemic against 'safety', being comfortable within the church, and so on, he has used every ounce of his religio-historical skill to construct a double-sided 'early Christianity' in such a way as to make his hero, Paul, fit exactly into the

[83] For the Corinthian 'slogans' see e.g. 1 Cor. 6.12f.; 8.1. For the use of this method see e.g. Jewett 2007, 283 (we must 'distinguish between the original significance and provenance of this material [Rom. 3.25f.] and its meaning in the context of Paul's letter'); Martyn 1997a, 89–91 (90: 'Paul quotes the Jewish-Christian formula [Gal. 1.4a] in order affirmatively to correct it by means of an additional clause').

[84] Käsemann 1969 [1965], 131.

[85] Käsemann 1969 [1965], 124–37.

mould which his own Lutheran tradition would suggest.[86] He is fighting battles on two fronts and remaining solid in the middle. Anyone, of course, can reinvent themselves as 'centrists', simply by describing what they see to left and right of them, no matter where they are on a larger spectrum. But with Käsemann the irony is more acute than with most. It is after all not only Anglicans who try to follow a *via media*.[87]

Käsemann's Lutheran tradition was centred, of course, on the doctrine of justification. For Käsemann, 'God's righteousness' did not refer, as with Bultmann and Luther before him, to the 'righteousness' which the believer has *coram Deo*. It was God's own righteousness, seen as that characteristic because of which God would act to put the whole world right at last. This had clear political implications. Käsemann had learned the hard way, being imprisoned by the Nazis, that a 'confessing' stand for the gospel might well mean opposing the powers that be. But it was not only Nazis who earned the great man's wrath. Käsemann had a horror of bourgeois, comfortable pietism (though, as one leading German theologian once remarked to me, 'Käsemann ist auch Pietist': he too was a pietist, as we can observe in his posthumously collected addresses[88]). His watchword remained Paul's great doctrine of 'the justification of the ungodly', as in Romans 4.5. The mere suggestion that a person or community might become 'godly' would instantly trigger his reflex: that way danger lies, that way you are playing safe; you are settling down, insulating yourself against a fresh word from God which might disturb you and call you to radical obedience.[89] One sometimes gets the sense that Käsemann, like Luther perhaps, would prefer a good old-fashioned sinner, openly and straightforwardly doing bad things, than someone engaged in 'pious works'.[90] This is no doubt an overstatement, but it is one to which he frequently lays himself open. He would no

[86] See too the wonderful knockabout polemic in Käsemann 1969 [1965], ch. 12. Here, as in the concluding paragraph (250), the twin targets are 'orthodoxy' and 'enthusiasm'. Paul remains, even for the church, 'the apostle of the heathen; the pious still hardly know what to make of him.' Speaking as a bishop, I know exactly what Käsemann is getting at, and I share his frustration. Speaking as an exegete, I do not regard these challenges as necessarily the best tools for getting at Paul's historical situation or his historical message. See Stuhlmacher 1986 [1981], ix–x: 'Bultmann and his students . . . proceeded from the view that in the New Testament a sharp distinction had to be drawn between Palestinian and Hellenistic churches, and also that Hellenistic Christianity, before and parallel to Paul, the Apostle himself, as well as the Gospel of John and its traditions were already exposed to the influences of pre-Christian and Christian Gnosticism. We have now learned to judge matters differently . . .' The key thing to note, especially for British and American readers who may have thought that Bultmann and Käsemann were doing 'neutral' or 'objective' 'history-of-religions' research into early Christianity, is that this entire strategy was a way of making sure that elements within the NT – including within Paul himself – would be allowed house room only if they fitted an already-given view of 'the gospel'.

[87] It is only fair to say that when I sent Käsemann my 1978 article, warning among other things against a retrojection of Lutheranism into the New Testament, he commented wryly, 'Doch gibt es auch eine Retrojektion des Anglikanismus in den NT, und ihr Aufsatz könnte das demonstrieren': 'actually, there is also a retrojection of Anglicanism into the New Testament, and your essay could demonstrate that'! The reader must judge; but I fear that the only one of Paul's churches in which I can recognize the present Anglican Communion is the congregation in Corinth.

[88] See Käsemann 2010 [2005].

[89] e.g. Käsemann 1971 [1969], 92.

[90] See e.g. 1980 [1973], 250, 302.

doubt have retorted, with some justification, that similar things were said about Paul himself.

Käsemann's great emphases thus remain firmly within the Lutheran tradition, even though he disagreed so clearly with his own teacher, Bultmann, on some key issues. (This can be seen not least in his insistence on the importance of historical-Jesus research. Having seen the Nazi invention of an Aryan 'Jesus', he realized that, whatever the problems, the real Jesus must be anchored in real history.)[91] But, as Stendahl pointed out, Käsemann was too quick, rejecting what he saw as 'salvation history', in joining the long tradition of labelling 'the Jew' and 'Judaism' as essentially part of the problem. Saying that Paul 'here strikes at the hidden Jew in all of us' sends a chill into the heart of any post-Holocaust thinker, Jewish, Christian, whoever.[92]

This fits with the way in which Käsemann follows Bultmann in his reading of Romans 7. Here, he says, is 'the heart of Paul's teaching', a big claim even for someone like Käsemann to make:

> It is not just that the creature repeatedly comes up against its limits after the fall, but precisely the religious person crashes and the pathway under man fails. The path which leads by the Mosaic Torah blinds him like Adam and delivers him up to sin. He agrees with the will of God, which is oriented to the salvation of the creature. He delights in it, so long as he desires salvation and strives to attain it by obeying the commandments. In the process, however, he becomes entangled in his own desire for life which tries to snatch what can only be given and thus falls subject to the powers of the world. This pious person typifies as no one else can the nature of self-willed, rebellious, perverted, and lost creation.[93]

Käsemann himself was too good an exegete not to see, in a way that many previous Lutheran exegetes had not, that there is indeed something in Paul that could properly be called 'salvation history'. One of his big disagreements with Bultmann was against the latter's over-individualizing of the gospel; he insisted that the larger history should always be in view.[94] Salvation history does indeed 'form the horizon of Pauline theology', but it is the significance of that horizon that is in dispute.[95] Käsemann insists (it is

[91] See 1964 [1960], ch. 1; 1969 [1965], ch. 2.

[92] 1969 [1965], 186. The whole passage is important: 'Paul is obliged to destroy those claims of Israel which are grounded in its own history in exactly the same way as those of the individual religious man. The express fashion in which he does this shows that Israel has exemplary significance for him; in and with Israel he strikes at the hidden Jew in all of us, at the man who validates rights and demands over against God on the basis of God's past dealings with him and to this extent is serving not God but an illusion.' See too e.g. 1980 [1973], 302f.: Israel as 'example' of the general truth that it is 'not sins, but pious works' which get in the way of salvation.

[93] 1980 [1973], 209 (towards the end of the exegesis of Rom. 7).

[94] 1971 [1969], 63, 65, 74 (agreeing with Stendahl at this point); 1980 [1973], 236, pointing out the neo-Marcionite tendencies of 'an existentialism which individualizes salvation and thereby truncates Paul's message by describing freedom formally as openness to the future' (against Schlier). Such a theological reduction (this is the sort of sentence which lures us back to Käsemann again and again) 'derives from a world view which no longer knows what to do with Pauline apocalyptic, allows anthropological historicity to conceal the world's history, obscures the antithesis of the aeons of 1:20ff. by natural theology and here through the assertion of mythology, and for this reason can no longer speak adequately of the dominion of Christ in its worldwide dimension.' In other words: if you follow Bultmann all down the road, the scope of the church's mission will be radically shrunken.

[95] 1971 [1969], 66.

not clear against whom: are we once again fighting shadows here?) that in Romans 5 'the apostle does not understand history as a continuous evolutionary process but as the contrast of the two realms of Adam and Christ'.[96] Thus 'salvation history' is always paradoxical, always a journey 'in the face of Sarah's justifiable laughter'.[97] The gospel is about freedom, one of Käsemann's great watchwords. He does not seem to have commented on Philemon (no references appear in the Indexes to his collected essays), but the underlying theme of freedom we find in that letter would surely have been grist to his mill.

Käsemann remains justifiably influential, not least but not only through the work of J. L. Martyn, to which we shall return. His major history-of-religions reconstruction of groups and parties in the pre-Pauline church is a kind of scholarly fiction, a modern 'myth' in the sense of 'a story told to legitimate a worldview'. But to hold aloof from those reconstructions is not to deny that as an exegete, an historian, and a preacher of uncomfortable truths to a would-be comfortable church, Käsemann is formidable. Some of what I regard as the most important insights in current Pauline studies were things he pioneered a generation or more ago in the teeth of powerful criticism. In particular, his affirmation of the cosmic scope of 'God's righteousness', and his vision for how it was expressed and embodied in the letter to the Romans, is foundational for a good deal which I believe we today must say in our turn. I do not think his analysis of 'apocalyptic' (or for that matter of 'early Jewish Christianity' or 'early hellenistic enthusiastic Christianity') will stand up to historical scrutiny, but then in a sense it doesn't need to. It was, ultimately, a heuristic device to enable him to draw attention to certain emphases of Paul's thought which, having been ignored for a long time, needed to come back into centre stage. It was a way of affirming Paul as in all sorts of ways a *Jewish* thinker, despite the Lutheran currents which pushed Käsemann also to regard 'the Jew' as the type of *Homo religiosus*, the official representative of the wrong sort of theology and piety. But if that helped to create the context in which the 'new perspective' was necessary, Käsemann's other emphases laid down markers which that movement would ignore at its peril.

Time would fail to list, let alone to expound, the many other great German scholars of the last generation. I think particularly of Ulrich Wilckens, whose earlier seminal articles pointed forward to a great commentary on Romans and then a career-crowning 'New Testament Theology'. These works urgently require translation into English; when that happens, I believe their impact will be considerable. Wilckens has long championed a more positive relationship between Paul and the scriptures of Israel. In his view, Christ is both the 'goal' and the 'termination' of the law, and this nuanced view must be worked out in detail.[98] He is critical of Bultmann and

[96] ibid., 67.

[97] ibid., 70. Käsemann notes that Cullmann 'sees the problem clearly' but does not bring out the paradox as fully as Käsemann thinks he should.

[98] See e.g. Wilckens 1974, 101; 1978–82, 2.221–3.

many others for the view that the real problem, for Paul, is not 'sin' as such but 'nomism'; this puts him, as we have just seen, against Käsemann as well.[99] He has done important work on the resurrection.[100] For Wilckens, the fact that the Jews did not attain the goal of the law, because they transgressed it, does not mean that the law is done away with. Believers are commanded to fulfil it through the work of the spirit, which enables them to love one another (and, since that is the centre of the law's demands, it means that cultic and ritual requirements are no longer necessary). In some ways this is a fairly traditional presentation of a post-Reformation reading of Paul, though many in that tradition would not follow Wilckens in his bold affirmation that when Paul speaks in Romans 2 of a future judgment according to works he means what he says. But, in standing over against some key elements of a post-Bultmannian reading, without being pulled in the direction of Käsemann either, Wilckens represents a more moderate Lutheran position, which has moreover been worked out in great exegetical detail, not merely asserted.[101]

A very different position is represented by Hans Hübner, whose famous monograph on Paul and the law addressed the problem of an apparently negative view of the law in Galatians and a positive view in Romans, and argued that Paul's thought had significantly developed in between the two letters. This view, though in some ways attractive, has not found its way into much subsequent scholarship, though the problem remains of how to give an account of 'Paul and the law' which allows for the very different things that are said in different letters.[102]

Before we get to the 'new perspective' as such, a word about two very different Pauline exegetes who, though standing just as much in the Reformation tradition as Käsemann, were consciously in the Calvinist stream rather than the Lutheran.

First, Charles Cranfield. Many of us owe a great debt to Cranfield for the high-quality education provided by working carefully through his great commentary on Romans, even though we may have concluded in retrospect that many of his central judgments were wrong.[103] He follows Bultmann, not Käsemann, on the meaning of 'the righteousness of God'. He insists that the 'wretched man' of Romans 7 is the genuine, no-nonsense Christian, despite the clash between being 'sold under sin' in 7.14 and Paul's insistence in Romans 6 that the baptized person is no longer in that condition. And

[99] e.g. 1974, 82–4.

[100] e.g. Wilckens 1977.

[101] See the discussion in Westerholm 2004, 154–9.

[102] See Hübner 1984. Hübner was a powerful presence in the 1994 Durham conference on Paul and the Law (whose papers were published in Dunn 1996b). One seminal moment came when he spoke passionately about the negative portrayal of the law in Galatians, quoting all the passages where Paul says that people were *hypo nomon*, 'under the law'. He repeated, '*hypo, hypo, hypo*'. Martin Hengel responded, 'Aber es ist doch eine *heilige hypo*'; 'But it is after all a *holy "hypo"*.' That is precisely the point. It is for moments like this that one attends conferences.

[103] More details in my review article, now in *Perspectives* ch. 3; see too Neill and Wright 1988, 421–4. Cranfield died in his hundredth year in March 2015, as the present volume was nearing completion.

his interpretation of chapters 9—11 leans too heavily in the direction of Barth for some of us to follow him all the way. But all this, in my view, is forgiven for the stunning vision, essentially Calvinist rather than Lutheran, which Cranfield offers of the single plan of God, and the positive view of the Jewish law that goes with it. It may be hard for students today to realize just how firmly the world of German and English-speaking scholarship was in thrall to a basically Lutheran view of the law when Cranfield published his article 'Paul and the Law' in the *Scottish Journal of Theology* in 1964.[104] Up to that point, it was normal for commentaries to assert, with minimum argument, that Paul saw the law as a bad thing, perhaps not even given by the true God in the first place but rather by angels or even demons; that the law simply condemned people, and that in order to save them God had to declare that the law itself needed to be swept out of the way; that when the Messiah bore 'the curse of the law' in Galatians 3.13 this meant that in Jesus' resurrection the law was shown up as having, so to speak, got it all wrong, and that this was the primary meaning of Paul's vision on the Damascus Road (the law cursed Christ; God has reversed that verdict; therefore the law is a bad thing and must itself be condemned and removed); and so on, resulting in the famous 'law-free' gospel of a hypothetical Lutheran Paul. Often this was based on Galatians, but the same view spilled over into exegesis of Romans and, more importantly, into an overall view of Paul and Judaism, and even of God. Assuming, with Paul, that the God of Israel had actually given the law, one common construal of this was that God had given the law as a way of saving people, but that when this plan had failed to work after one and a half millennia, God decided to scrap it and switch to a 'plan B' called 'faith' – faith being, after all, so much easier. God was lowering the bar so that sinners could get in with less difficulty. One of the most respected commentaries of a former generation said more or less exactly that.[105]

This negative, often scornful, view of the law emerged from the Lutheran critique, going back in its essence to some of the more arm-waving declarations of Brother Martin himself. But it was deeply entrenched in the protestant theology and exegesis of the 1950s and 1960s for a quite different reason. As those of us who grew up in that period remember well, it was a time for throwing off restraint of all sorts. The word 'duty' had become a dirty word; respect for authority dwindled rapidly; a sense of common moral standards withered on the vine; the emotivist ethic of Logical Positivism became the fashion of the day (when I say 'honesty is good', all I mean is 'I like honesty'; and when I say 'theft is bad', all I mean is 'I don't like theft'). Plenty of churchmen – they were mostly men – went along for the ride, resenting the hidebound and often hypocritical moralism of much traditional church life, longing to throw the doors open to welcome people of whatever background, and making the interesting mistake of supposing

[104] See Cranfield 1975–9, 845–62, a revision of that article (details at ibid., 845).

[105] Sanday and Headlam 1902, 278, 283, 287f.

that when Jesus and Paul welcomed people in that way they cut a swathe through traditional moral standards in order to do so. 'The law' was taken to mean 'the practice of self-righteous judgmentalism'.[106] The watchword for all this was Romans 10.4, read (as in many translations) as 'Christ is the end of the law'. In such a context, that meant: no more moral codes; 'situation ethics' will do instead; and actually 'all you need is love'. Beatles-style 'morality', masquerading as Paul's 'law-free gospel'.

Many of us who were troubled by this mood, and the exegetical weight that seemed to lie behind it, were enormously grateful to read Cranfield: 'the law has Christ for its goal and meaning', a sentence repeated with variations over three dense pages of a positive exposition of Romans 10.4. What was 'wrong' was not the law itself, but 'legalism', the failure to recognize that Christ was its goal and the attempt to use it to establish a claim upon God. But that was never its intention. Neither in Romans, nor in 2 Corinthians 3, nor yet in Galatians 3 or the two relevant passages in Colossians and Ephesians, is the law abrogated; Paul meant what he said in Romans 3.31 ('Do we then abolish the law through faith? Certainly not. Rather, we establish the law').[107] Rather, the gift of the spirit is the establishment of the law. Thus Cranfield launched a detailed and scathing attack on 'that modern version of Marcionism which regards the law as a disastrous misconception on the part of religious men from which Jesus desired to set us free.' Further, in the article's peroration, Paul's authority cannot be claimed for

> the view that the law was an unsuccessful first attempt on God's part at dealing with man's unhappy state, which had to be followed later by a second (more successful) attempt (a view which is theologically grotesque, for the God of the unsuccessful first attempt is hardly a God to be taken seriously); nor yet the view that in law and gospel two different modes of God's action are manifested, the ultimate unity of which, while it may indeed be supposed to exist in God, has not yet been revealed to us men.[108]

These were, obviously, demons against which Cranfield had battled long and hard, and his commentary on Romans was designed, if not to put them to flight once and for all, at least to inflict on them a severe tactical defeat. Instead, on the positive side, we are, he says, true to Paul's teaching

> when we say that *God's word in Scripture is one*; that there is but one way of God with men, and that an altogether gracious way; that gospel and law are essentially one, and their unity, so far from being a mystery still hidden from us, has been once and for all revealed to us in that one gracious Word of God, whose name is Jesus Christ, in whom at the same time God gives Himself wholly to man, and claims man wholly for Himself.[109]

[106] A remarkable example of this may be found in Eduard Schweizer's commentary on Colossians: Schweizer 1982, 22.

[107] Robinson 1979, 51, records that when the New English Bible translation committee got to that point, C. H. Dodd exclaimed 'What rubbish!'

[108] 1979, 861f.

[109] ibid., 862.

Thus, in a fascinating further essay on Paul's use of the scriptures, Cranfield let fly with a splendid but tantalizing sentence in which one glimpses, though behind the veil of anonymity, his lifetime theological opponents:

> Because he kept his eyes so steadily fixed on Jesus, the author of Romans was able to hear and to comprehend the message proclaimed by the OT; and, because in his total commitment to Jesus as Saviour and Lord he never ceased to be seriously engaged with the OT scriptures, he perceived with amazing clarity of vision vast and splendid reaches of the truth of Christ which lie beyond the ken of all Marcionites and semi-, crypto-, and unwitting, Marcionites.[110]

All this needs to be said, even if we lack a detailed typology, or list of suspects, to decode those four final categories of false readings. And we should note, in particular, that for Cranfield this 'Marcionism', of whatever type, was solidly associated with an essentially *Lutheran* theology. His was a Reformed protest against the broad mainstream of New Testament scholarship of the day.[111]

And yet. Cranfield's Achilles heel, it seems to me, is Galatians. He cannot fully explain Paul's critique of 'the law' in that letter. He recognizes this, and falls back on the suggestion that we should interpret the puzzling, sharply polemical statements there in the light of Paul's clearer, fuller statement in Romans.[112] That, of course, begs the question raised by Hübner: did Paul's position change? Is there actually a different critique of the law in Galatians, so that Paul was a Lutheran when writing to Galatia but a Calvinist when writing to Rome? Or what? I fully take Cranfield's point that the view of the law, and indeed God, in what had been the 'normal' reading was inadequate on several grounds, and that a unified vision, such as we associate with good Reformed theology, was greatly to be preferred. But how could such a thing make headway? That, for this reader, was the problem to which one version at least of the 'new perspective' provided the answer.

Our seventh and final post-Bultmann writer, like Cranfield a representative of Reformed rather than Lutheran theology, comes from Holland.[113] His massive work is characterized throughout by care and caution, but there is no question where his own exegetical results lead and where his theological sympathies lie. As with W. D. Davies, Herman Ridderbos explains the

[110] Cranfield 1975–9, 867.

[111] Which makes it all the odder that Westerholm 2004, 201–8, makes him his first representative of 'Lutheran' responses to the 'new perspective'. Granted that Cranfield had indeed distanced himself from Dunn in particular, there is far more in common between Cranfield's essentially Reformed view of the law, and of Israel, and much of the 'new perspective', than there is between either of them and the continuing 'Lutheran' line. Westerholm knows perfectly well that Cranfield stands in the Calvinist and Reformed tradition (e.g. Westerholm 202, 208). But to label him a 'Lutheran' is like saying that a Welshman or Scotsman is 'English'; or, indeed, that a Canadian is an 'American'. It would not be going too far to say that the inner strength of the new perspective is that which it shares with the Reformed tradition in its view of Israel and the Law – not least as expounded by Cranfield himself, no doubt with significant differences here and there.

[112] Cranfield 1975–9, 858.

[113] Ridderbos 1975 [1966]. Dutch readers of my work have frequently commented that many of the ideas I expound were already familiar to them, at least in outline, from Ridderbos. How much I learned from him forty years ago, and how much I was thinking independently, it is now impossible to say.

many features of Paul's thought which had formerly been supposed to derive from 'Hellenism' in terms of a Jewish context. Here, however, instead of 'apocalyptic' as with Schweitzer or 'rabbinic thought' as with Davies, Ridderbos is closer in many respects to Cullmann: Paul is to be understood as a 'redemptive-historical' theologian. Ridderbos's Index is revealing by contrast with Cullmann's (not to mention Bultmann's!): there is a solid rank of references to Genesis, Exodus, Deuteronomy, the Psalms, Isaiah and the other prophets. Ridderbos's range of secondary reference, too, is much wider than most other writers I have mentioned.[114] He constantly engages with Bultmann and Cullmann, but also refers extensively to scholars such as Berkouwer, Bornkamm, Dibelius, Käsemann, Kümmel, Lietzmann, Schlatter and a host of others. It is a major work which, in my view, has been taken with insufficient seriousness in the guild of biblical studies.

Much of Ridderbos's outline corresponds to the standard soteriological categories of regular protestant exposition: sin, God's righteousness, reconciliation, the new life, the church, sacraments, and eschatology. But the shape and pattern of everything is thrown into a new light by his opening of the main exposition with a chapter entitled 'Fundamental Structures'.[115] The whole book is framed by this chapter's opening section on inaugurated eschatology: the 'fullness of time' has come, the mystery is revealed, and it turns out to be 'the mystery of Christ'. Eschatology and Christology go inalienably together: Jesus is the 'last Adam', the 'firstborn from the dead', and with this the whole world has changed. Everything that now opens out before us comes from this eschatological act of God in Christ. Ridderbos does not regularly employ the terminology of 'apocalyptic', and indeed his strong opening statement that in Christ the fullness of time had come indicates that he saw strong continuity between the whole preparatory history of Israel and the event of Christ himself. What he says about that event, however, corresponds closely with what several have seen as the true meaning of 'apocalyptic' (if one may speak about 'true meanings' in that connection): the sudden sharp and surprising unveiling of what turns out to be something long promised but never anticipated in this form.

Ridderbos's exposition of Christology, in the sense of who exactly Jesus Christ is for Paul, goes on and on, page after page, as though here, right at the start of the book, he can hardly wait to talk about Jesus Christ, to say the many things he wants to say about him and his significance. This Christ-centred vision is also emphatically a God-centred picture, and, as becomes clear, is also a worldwide vision: Christ is the Lord of the whole world, and the aim of this new time, this new revelation, is to rescue the whole creation from corruption and death.[116]

[114] Something interesting is going on here. Ridderbos, as a Dutch scholar, was no doubt conscious of the need to engage in wider circles. No such awareness seems to have bothered some others we have studied.

[115] Ridderbos, 44–90.

[116] e.g. Ridderbos, 90.

Starting the book in this way enables Ridderbos to locate his key discussions *within* Christology, rather than, as with Bultmann and many others, merely bringing in Jesus Christ to deal with the problem of sin. Here, as a good Calvinist (he footnotes Calvin explicitly at this point), he declares that 'the foundation for the doctrine of justification ... lies in the corporate unity of Christ and his own.'[117] Ridderbos sees that for Paul the concepts of 'being in Christ' and 'Christ for us' do not need to be played off against one another, but that the redemptive and forensic ideas, and the corporate ones, are in fact mutually explanatory. He insists that Paul did not switch, somewhere around Romans 5, from one 'conception' of salvation to the other, 'as though for him the first represented merely the traditional and the second the real, the adequate, idea' (a theory which has recently re-emerged in the work of Douglas Campbell). Rather,

> both belong to the unbreakable subsistence of Paul's preaching, and for him they have become an indissoluble unity. It is also in this unity of the 'Christ-for-us' and the 'we-in-him' that the theme of the revelation of the righteousness of God by faith exhibits in a clear fashion the basic eschatological-christological structure of Paul's preaching. For Christ's death was the demonstration of the judging and justifying judgment of God in the eschatological sense of the word because the old aeon and the old man were judged in him, and justification unto life and the new creation came to light in him as the second Adam. And the justifying power of his death and resurrection could for this reason benefit his own, because he as the second Adam was their Representative and they were in him.[118]

I happen to think that there is a major step missing in the argument, here and elsewhere in Ridderbos's thorough and close reading of Paul. I refer to the Israel-dimension of the Apostle's thought; it is surprising, in a Reformed theologian, to see this given such comparatively little space. How this would have helped (for instance) in the passage I have just quoted will be apparent to any reader of *Paul and the Faithfulness of God*. But the significance of this passage, and the surrounding and supporting arguments, ought to be clear. There are some ways of reading Paul – serious, carefully thought-out ways, not casual let's-hope-it-works ways – in which the antithesis maintained by Schweitzer, Bultmann, Käsemann and, as we shall see, Sanders, Campbell and others has been called into question: the antithesis, that is, between 'being in Christ' on the one hand, expressed either in 'incorporative' or in 'participationist' categories, and 'justification by faith' on the other, expressed in 'juristic', 'forensic' or 'relational' categories.[119] Ridderbos, like Cranfield, is innocent of the 'new perspective', but his Reformed theology anticipates some elements of it – the positive view of the law, Judaism, and 'redemptive history', for a start. It remains to be worked out how the integration he glimpsed, which he tried to attain by one route, can be more thoroughly and effectively arrived at by another.

[117] Ridderbos, 169.

[118] ibid.

[119] Another example, to which we shall return: Hays 2002 [1983], 212f.

The writers we have surveyed so far constituted, more or less, 'the state of play' for a great deal of New Testament scholarship in the mid-1970s. As we have seen, there were significant variations, both within the Bultmann school itself and between that school and other quite different options. In particular, a strong reaction had begun to set in against the earlier belief that one was bound to interpret Paul's ideas and beliefs in the context of Hellenism rather than Judaism – a distinction which in any case the massive work of Martin Hengel had already called into question.[120] The relationship between Paul (and his churches) and 'Judaism' – whatever one means by that term – had emerged, in a way that was not true fifty years earlier, as a major and divisive topic. The questions of the integration of Paul's different leading ideas, their possible development over the course of his writing career, and the different impact that they might have on the western church and world as it struggled to reorganize itself after the horrors of the 1940s, were all on the table. This was the moment when a new voice, echoing things that had been said before but for which the time had apparently not been right, spoke a word which rearranged the furniture throughout the house. If Karl Barth's *Römerbrief* fell like a bomb on the playground of the theologians, Ed Sanders's *Paul and Palestinian Judaism* exploded like a volcano over the fields where the exegetes had been busy at their usual sports. The lava is still flowing as we speak. And since this brings us into what might be seen as the modern period of Pauline studies, we had better address it with a new chapter.

[120] Hengel 1974a.

Chapter Three

THE NEW PERSPECTIVE AND BEYOND

1. The Launch of a Protest

In the late 1980s my younger son attended New College School in Oxford. I often thought, seeing the sign outside, that one should never call anything 'new'. New College, together with its Choir School, was founded in 1379. It is not quite as 'new' as it was. At the time I used to reflect that the so-called 'new quest for the historical Jesus', started by Ernst Käsemann in 1953, was not so 'new' either. By the late 1970s, never mind the 1980s, the novelty had worn off.[1] Thirty years can be a long time in scholarship.

That same passage of thirty years has now overtaken the 'new perspective on Paul'. By common consent, the normal starting-point for this movement, if that is what it is, has been reckoned from the 1977 publication of Ed P. Sanders's blockbuster, *Paul and Palestinian Judaism*. Life after Sanders has been rumbling on for some time. Perhaps we are now entering a new period: Life after 'Life after Sanders'.

The 'new perspective' has been described so many times that it seems otiose to do so again.[2] For the same reason, I am shortly going to drop the inverted commas, and also the qualifying phrase 'so-called'. But I hope the reader will realize, not least because of what I am going to say in the present chapter, that there never was one single entity called the 'new perspective'. It was always a loose movement containing sharply divergent presuppositions, aims, methods and results. Its main players never met as a group, thought as a group, or planned their next work together. The very different things that different new-perspectivists have said do not come as a package deal, even within the work of any single scholar, but are separate proposals, even if some of us think that some of these proposals are mutually supportive. That

[1] Details in Wright 1996b (*JVG*), 23.

[2] See, for a start, Neill and Wright 1988 [1964], 424–30.

is why I have so often thought of it as 'the so-called "new perspective"'; but I shall know it thus no longer.

The movement does, however, remain formative, for good and ill, in much contemporary writing on Paul. Since I have been closely associated with it in the minds of many throughout its history, I can hardly avoid it.[3] I therefore cheerfully make a virtue of necessity: I shall take this opportunity to say what I think is important about this many-sided movement, and where I think we need to move forward into new areas.[4] Several writers have spoken of going 'beyond the new perspective', and certainly that needs to happen, if only to squash once and for all any idea that the new perspective was a single 'thing', a dramatic point where two roads diverged.[5]

Various things need to be said right from the start. To begin with, when Ed Sanders published *Paul and Palestinian Judaism* (hereafter *PPJ*), his main point was not really new. It had simply not caught people's attention.[6] This is often the frustration of scholarship. The purist assumes that because an article or book has been published it will 'make its way' into the minds and hearts of the guild as a whole, but this is manifestly not the case. The race is not always to the swift, nor the battle to the strong. The reason why ideas do not percolate into the larger consciousness often has little to do with the merits of the argument, the careful handling of sources, or even the clarity of presentation. Sadly, what counts all too often is the play of other non-academic and non-intellectual factors, such as the profile of the author, the publicity given to the book by the publisher, the receptivity of the target audience, and, not least, the fashionability of the ideas. This is a world where Chaos sits as umpire, with Chance as his co-regent. Were this not so, to glance at a different field, Ben Meyer's remarkable book *The Aims of Jesus* would by now be in its thirtieth reprint, and one or two commentaries best

[3] For a recent summary, see Zetterholm 2009, ch. 4.

[4] I discover to my surprise, in Dunn 2008 [2005], 7 n. 24, that I am credited with the first recorded use of the phrase 'new perspective on Paul' (Wright 1978, 64; in *Perspectives*, 6). Jimmy Dunn was sitting in the front row when I gave the original lecture in Tyndale House, Cambridge in July 1978, but as he then made the phrase 'new perspective' his own with his 1982 lecture (= Dunn 2008 ch. 2) I had forgotten I had even said it. But, as Dunn points out (ibid.), Krister Stendahl had suggested long before, in his famous 'introspective conscience' essay (1963; originally given as a lecture in 1961, based on a shorter article published in Swedish the previous year), that 'the framework of "Sacred History" which we have found to be that of Pauline theology . . . opens up a new perspective for systematic theology and practical theology' (Stendahl 1976, 95 = Stendahl 1963, 214). In his famous essay of 1983, Dunn credits me simply with the phrase 'national righteousness' (2008 [2005], 114 n. 36); but cf. Watson 2007 [1986], 4 n. 3, which tells a larger story.

[5] 'Beyond the New Perspective' is the subtitle of Watson 2007, and was the title of a conference based on Douglas Campbell's work at Kings College London, and also at Duke University Divinity School, in late 2012 (the papers are now published, with Campbell's responses, in Tilling 2014). A group referring to itself by the phrase 'beyond the new perspective' (abbreviated BNP, unfortunately for British participants for whom that acronym denotes the far-right British National Party) was the subject of discussion in a paper by J. B. Tucker at the Evangelical Theological Society in New Orleans in November 2009: he named William S. Campbell, Katharine Ehrensperger, Peter Tomson and Mark Nanos as constituting the core of this group. I have discussed the position in question in *PFG* 1426–49. Unfortunately, Tucker's paper repeats the mistaken idea that Sanders, Dunn and I share the same views.

[6] Some, clearly, would have preferred it to stay that way. Sanders told me once that SCM Press decided to publish the book against the strong advice of one outside reader, a senior British scholar.

left unnamed but still in print would have long been a rare curiosity in the second-hand shops.

Nor is it the case that Sanders's book made the impact it did because of its size and scope. That, no doubt, had something to do with it, but many heavy books, even from established scholars, fall into the pond with neither splash nor ripple. Nor is the reason for Sanders's impact the fact that he has one of the most enviably clear prose styles of any contemporary biblical scholar. Even when the issues are at their most complex, you never have to read a sentence twice. No: the reason for the impact – and this needs to be taken very seriously by those who want to reject the new perspective and all its works – was that, as we say in the trade, it was an idea whose time had come. There are five convergent reasons for this, which together explain both its power and its problems.[7]

First, Sanders's book was the culmination of a long, growing chorus of protest at the way Judaism had been regularly characterized in 'Christian' scholarship. G. F. Moore had registered a similar protest many years before, but it had gone unheard. The scholars who ought to have paid attention to it 'knew' that 'Judaism' was what Schürer and Bousset and others had said it was, and they were not going to be disturbed by evidence to the contrary.[8] Hans-Joachim Schoeps had voiced a similar challenge in the form of a protest against Paul's self-description as a Pharisee: Schoeps took it for granted that the normal picture of 'Paul's protest against Judaism' was an accurate description of what Paul had said, and pointed out that if that was the case then clearly Paul didn't know much about real Judaism.[9] Krister Stendahl, as we have already seen, had challenged the ruling consensus, in terms more of Paul than of Judaism, but he was certainly pushing in the same direction. Other voices had come in from other angles, protesting that 'Christian' mischaracterizations of Judaism had been partly responsible for the climate of opinion in which the Holocaust had become thinkable.[10] People were at last asking questions that had taken a generation to work through. Now someone at the heart of the guild of biblical scholarship had put up a hand and said that enough was enough.

Second, Sanders brought to a head a long though broken line of scholarship which had insisted that Paul was basically a Jewish thinker rather than a hellenistic one. As we have seen, Sanders's pedigree in this respect goes back to Schweitzer and Davies, particularly the latter (Sanders's teacher) with his special interest in the rabbinic writings. Though Sanders was not concerned to argue a case about the *derivation* of Paul's ideas, the fact that he so massively lined up the Jewish sources and read Paul in that context

[7] See Stuhlmacher 2001, 40 (despite his severe disagreements with Sanders).

[8] Hence the answer to the surprise expressed by Hagner 2001, 76f., quoting Silva also: these things had been said (Moore, Montefiore, Schechter, Travers Herford, and Marmorstein), but nobody was listening. See e.g. Moore 1921, 1927–30.

[9] Schoeps 1961 [1959].

[10] See e.g. Klein 1978; Ruether 1974. Watson agrees (2007, 1f.): in the post-Holocaust world, people were at last ready to reconsider things previously taken for granted.

carried its own weight.[11] Unlike Davies, however, Sanders recognized both that Paul held a critique of his contemporary Judaism and that it was difficult to articulate this critique. Perhaps the fact that he held back from a history-of-religions theory about the origins of Paul's thought made it easier to recognize at least that there *was* a 'critique'. History-of-religions research, notoriously, has been better at inventing hypotheses about where an idea came from than imagining what it might have been critical of, and it more or less rules out a priori anything like a *Jewish* 'critique of Judaism' – even though Jewish traditions both ancient and modern are full of exactly that. Sanders seems to have concluded, in fact, that it was the death and resurrection of Jesus which generated Paul's belief:

> Paul appears as one who bases the explanations of his gospel, his theology, on the meaning of the death and resurrection of Jesus, not as one who has fitted the death and resurrection into a pre-existing scheme, where they take the place of other motifs with similar functions.[12]

In other words, though the Jewish world formed the context for what Paul believed and did, those beliefs and actions were not a natural outgrowth from within that world. Here, not for the only time, Sanders sounds a bit like J. L. Martyn, though in other ways their projects are quite different.

The third reason why Sanders's protest gained such a hearing (though this was not something Sanders highlighted, or perhaps even noticed) was its resonance with the Reformed tradition of theology. His stress on Judaism as a religion of grace, and on the Torah as a good thing to be obeyed out of gratitude rather than a bad thing to be obeyed out of a toxic mixture of fear and pride, resonated powerfully with a long tradition of Calvinist protest against Lutheranism's perceived semi-, crypto-, or unwitting Marcionism. (I say 'Lutheranism', but many other strands of Protestantism, and indeed many strands of Catholicism, not to mention Anglicanism, have been guilty of the same basic faults.) As we saw with Cranfield and Ridderbos, the usual anti-law rhetoric simply could not capture certain major elements in Paul's thought, and it was time to pause and look at key topics through the other end of the telescope. The main stream of scholarship had not been listening to the Reformed tradition, any more than it had been listening to Jewish objections about caricatured stereotypes.

This point is valid in relation to Sanders's positive proposal as well. As with Calvin himself, and many subsequent Reformed theologians, Sanders saw that Paul's doctrine of justification meant what it meant *within* the idea of 'participation', of 'being in Christ'. Hence, of course, the irony: some Jewish scholars have now reacted against Sanders and his successors in one direction, and many Reformed thinkers have reacted against him in another

[11] Sanders does say, at the end, that 'it may be just as difficult to peg [Paul] as a Hellenistic Jew who thought that Christ presented the true mystery or true *gnosis* as it is to characterize him as a Rabbinic Jew who thought that Jesus was the Messiah' (1977, 555). Sanders 2009, 75 is clear (see too Sanders 2008a, 24): he has never tried to write about the *source* of Paul's ideas, only to *compare* him with Jewish texts.

[12] Sanders 1997, 555f. This is the final sentence of the book.

direction. That is perhaps inevitable with any far-reaching set of proposals. But part of the purpose of scholarship, after all, is not to solve all the problems but to raise new questions which get people looking at familiar texts from new angles. Sanders has certainly done that.

The fourth reason for Sanders's impact is that he was resonating with a strand of exegetical scholarship which had not been sufficiently noticed and had not made its way into the wider discourse. I think particularly of the work of George Howard, whose monograph on Galatians appeared after Sanders's book but whose preliminary articles had raised questions about the standard reading of several key Pauline passages without, to my mind at least, offering a larger synthesis within which new ways of reading might be seen to make sense.[13] These questions – such as the apparently close relation of Romans 3.29–30 with 3.21–6, raising doubts as to whether 3.27–8 were after all about 'boasting' in the normal protestant sense – refused to go away, and Sanders offered a fresh angle of vision from which they could be addressed. This is linked in my own mind, perhaps simply because I was reading these works in the early and middle 1970s, with Charles Cranfield's resolutely 'Reformed' understanding of Paul, the law and the Jewish people, and with my sense that however hard he tried he could not quite make Galatians fit.

There was, in other words, an *exegetical* imperative at work. Sanders has never really been, in the strict sense, an exegete. He has written no verse-by-verse commentaries, and has only seldom addressed head on the question of what an entire chapter, let alone an entire book, is actually all about.[14] But exegesis needs a wider historical vision. He provided one, and we verse-by-verse people found that, up to a point at least, it made a lot of sense of passages that had otherwise been puzzling.

The fifth and final reason for Sanders's impact had to do with his social and cultural location. He clearly belonged (as a giant, admittedly) within the ranks of the new American 'religious studies' world. He was neither ordained within a denomination nor teaching in a seminary. In an autobiographical aside in his major book on Jesus he described himself as coming from a Christian tradition with a low Christology and a high social concern.[15] He has also spoken of theological topics as things he was once interested in but is no longer. Whatever his personal position, however, he was clearly not engaging in the implicit attempt to find the true Pauline gospel so he could preach it and teach it, but in the explicit attempt to *compare two patterns of religion*.[16] With the increasing turn to, and high profile of, the 'comparative religion' model of study, particularly in America but also in Britain and Europe, Sanders embodied and represented a new kind of

[13] See Howard 1967; 1969; 1970; 1979. Hays mentions Howard in a similar vein as one who had anticipated some of his own lines of thought (see the Index to Hays 2002 [1983]).

[14] The main exception is Sanders 1983, which is, as Sanders says (2008a, 37 n. 40), 'basically a long footnote to the Paul section' of *PPJ*.

[15] Sanders 1985, 333f.

[16] See again Sanders 2008a, 24.

Pauline investigation, closer perhaps to Wrede than to anyone else since. This brought with it a dimension also seen in Stendahl, and now extended more widely: a *relativist* agenda, at least to the extent that, as in much 'comparative religion', one holds back from any evaluative comment on the different religions being compared, sometimes to the extent that one implies, or actually argues, that two or more religions are equally salvific, or more or less so. This, I suspect, is another reason why Sanders has been eagerly taken up in some quarters and just as eagerly rejected in others. It ought not to be necessary to make the adjacent point, that other new perspective writers such as Dunn and myself shared neither Sanders's aim of comparing patterns of religion nor the theological conclusions which some thought they found in his work. And Sanders himself was careful, at least in *PPJ* itself, not to draw any conclusions about the contemporary relationship, or evaluation, of 'Christianity' and 'Judaism', even though some heard that implication and may not have been totally wrong.[17]

All this means that the study of 'life after Sanders' ought to look more widely than simply to the question of whether Sanders was right or wrong in his central argument. The new wave of Pauline studies as part of 'comparative religion' has taken many forms, but it was Sanders who opened the floodgates and let them all through.

It is not surprising, then, that the book was quickly recognized as drawing a line in the sand, as declaring a new day. People were ready for it, for a variety of different reasons not always appreciated either by the enthusiasts or by the anxious traditionalists. At least, people were ready for *something* down these lines. The serious questions which have been raised about both the outline and the detail of Sanders's construction should not quench our enormous appreciation for his achievement.

2. Sanders on Judaism

So what did Sanders achieve?[18] He tells us, with his usual clarity, the six things he was aiming to accomplish:

- to consider methodologically how to compare two (or more) related but different religions;
- to destroy the view of Rabbinic Judaism which is still prevalent in much, perhaps most, New Testament scholarship;
- to establish a different view of Rabbinic Judaism;
- to argue a case concerning Palestinian Judaism (that is, Judaism as reflected in material of Palestinian provenance) as a whole;

[17] For Sanders's own position see e.g. Sanders 1978, 185: Paul thought that Jews who did not believe in Jesus would not be saved, but Sanders thinks they ought to be. This also indicates his hermeneutical stance, being prepared to state his own disagreements with Paul. This stance appears to free the historian from the danger of distorting evidence to fit the desired conclusion. But there are different kinds of desired conclusions, and different ways in which historical exegesis may lend them subtle weight.

[18] I am here dealing with Sanders 1977. He followed this with two further books on Paul (1983, 1991) as well as a major book on Judaism (1992).

– to argue for a certain understanding of Paul;
– to carry out a comparison of Paul and Palestinian Judaism.[19]

The fourth and sixth are, he says, the 'general aim' of the book: to argue a case about Palestinian Judaism, and to compare Paul with the Judaism thus described. The others he aimed to accomplish on the way. We note that he is *not* saying that he will analyse Paul's *theology*. 'A certain understanding of Paul' is a vague phrase which tacitly admits in advance that the following exposition of the Apostle will not be particularly well worked out in an organic or systematic fashion. That is indeed part of the difficulty. But since the theologians, or quasi-theologians (perhaps semi-, crypto-, or unwitting theologians) had had things all to themselves for a long time, they could hardly grumble if for once someone approached things from a different angle. (I say 'for once'; but of course what Sanders represents in all this is a return to the days of Deissmann or, up to a point, Wrede.[20]) I suspect, though, that part at least of the anti-Sanders backlash has come from those who are engaged, in their institutions, in the kind of 'theology versus religious studies' sniping which is part of the long-term fallout from the Enlightenment's split worldview.

Sanders's great success – I say this in the teeth of the regular protests to the contrary – was to remind the non-Jewish academic world that first-century Jews, and the early rabbis in particular, were not early forerunners of mediaeval Catholics, or indeed Pelagians.[21] I still lurch between amusement and embarrassment to think of Christian scholars writing about Judaism in terms borrowed from the fifteenth century ('works of supererogation' and the like). It is of course possible to produce apparent 'parallels' to almost anything. There is after all only a limited range of things that one can say in any 'religion', and some statements, taken cold and out of context, will look a bit like other statements whose own setting would actually indicate significant differences. We shall come to some of those. But the great strength of Sanders's proposal, greater indeed I think than he even realized, was to see that the entire structure of rabbinic *halakah*, the classified 'law',

[19] 1977, xii. In his autobiographical essay (2008a, 24f.) Sanders gives an even fuller summary, with eleven points.

[20] Sanders 2008a, 32, explains that as a young man he had been 'very attracted to the Religionsgechichtliche Schule and, in fact, to pre-World War I German New Testament scholarship in general – before the turn toward Luther, which has narrowed that scholarship, to its detriment.' This will cause further gnashings of teeth in some circles. But Sanders continues (32f.) with a sentence that should serve as a challenge to all of us, whatever our theological interests: 'I still think that many of the people now engaged in New Testament research know far too little about ancient history and far too little about ancient sources other than the Bible.'

[21] It will not do to object pedantically that the Reformers could not have been opposing Pelagians because 'the Roman Catholic Church had officially renounced such teaching long before' (Allen 2013, 109). (a) The normal post-Reformation polemic, against both Catholicism and Judaism (and other 'isms' too for that matter) charges people simply with trying to save themselves by their own efforts. (b) One of the best known shorthands for this is 'Pelagianism', not in the technical sense either of what Pelagius himself taught or of what the church had officially renounced, but as a useful signpost to a basic position. (c) Anyone who supposes that, because a church has officially renounced some doctrine, nobody thereafter will hold to it, has little experience of real church life.

took place within a larger context still: the context (Sanders did not explore this, but it is important) of a *story*, the story of a *people*. It was the story of God's redemption of Israel, based on God's election and ultimately on God's love and grace. God loves; God chooses; God redeems; God gives Torah. Only then does Israel obey, within that context and for that reason. There was always a danger in reducing this story, as Sanders understandably did, to a formula, namely 'covenantal nomism'; though, as formulae go, that one seems to be sharp and clear, pointing back beyond itself to the narrative which is its own bottom-line reality. I would greatly prefer something like 'covenantal narrative', and to this, too, we shall return.

This is how Sanders himself spells out the 'pattern' (which is, after all, what he has undertaken to expound and compare):

> The pattern is this: God has chosen Israel and Israel has accepted the election. In his role as King, God gave Israel commandments which they are to obey as best they can. Obedience is rewarded and disobedience punished. In the case of failure to obey, however, man has recourse to divinely ordained means of atonement, in all of which repentance is required. As long as he maintains his desire to stay in the covenant, he has a share in God's covenantal promises, including life in the world to come. The intention and effort to be obedient constitute the *condition for remaining in the covenant*, but they do not *earn* it . . .
>
> [The rabbis'] legalism falls within a larger context of gracious election and assured salvation . . . they did not think that they earned their place in the covenant by the number of *misvot* [commandments] fulfilled. Nor did they think that the transgression of more commandments than were fulfilled would damn them . . . The failure to understand the relationship between the *framework* of covenantal election and assured atonement on the one hand, and the *intra-covenantal* reliability of God to reward and punish on the other, has led to the complete misunderstanding of the essentials of Rabbinic religion.[22]

Sanders was aware of the obvious challenge to his 'covenantal' reading of first-century Judaism: the word 'covenant', *berith*, hardly occurs in the rabbis themselves. He offers it as a construct, an explanatory tool for indicating the larger worldview within which they always, implicitly, see themselves:

> Word studies are not always deceptive, but they can be, and this one is . . . I would venture to say that it is the *fundamental nature of the covenant conception which largely accounts for the relative scarcity of appearances of the term 'covenant' in Rabbinic literature*. The covenant was presupposed, and the Rabbinical discussions were largely directed toward the question of *how* to fulfil the covenantal obligations . . . The covenant is directly mentioned in the Dead Sea Scrolls relatively frequently because the very existence of the sect was based on the sectarians' conviction that they had the true covenant (or the true interpretation of it) and because of the need to define special requirements for being admitted to and staying in the covenant. Generally, however, the word does not much appear in the literature of the period, even though covenantal ideas are absolutely common.[23]

The result, central to Sanders's case, is that the role of law-keeping in rabbinic and other relevant branches of Judaism was not about 'getting in' but

[22] 1977, 180f.; cp. too e.g. 422: 'election and ultimately salvation are considered to be by God's mercy rather than human achievement.'

[23] Sanders 1977, 420f. (italics original). Sanders refers further to this in his article of 1976.

about 'staying in'. One kept the Torah, not to become a member of God's people but to demonstrate that one already was a member. Call this 'legalism' if you like, as Sanders does. Note, with Caird, that even if it is to be read within a covenantal framework, the Mishnah itself, and still more the Talmud, simply is what many people think of as 'legalism', the endless casuistical probing ever deeper into what counts as proper obedience.[24] But for Sanders the framework is everything; and in principle I think he is right. Certainly his point is proved *over against the old caricatures* in which it could be assumed that 'the Jews', lock, stock and barrel, were automatically and inalienably investing in a degenerate, dehumanizing and ineffective form of 'religion', doing their best to lift themselves out of the mud by their own hair and lurching from pride (when they thought they were being successful) to despair (when they realized they were just as stuck as they had been before). One can read many, many pages in the Apocrypha and Pseudepigrapha, in the Scrolls, in Philo and in Josephus – not to mention the rabbis – without coming upon anything remotely like this.

If people object, as they will, that nevertheless most Jews believed in a final judgment that would be based on 'works', the obvious answer – which Sanders gives as well – is that Paul did so too.[25] Here the problem, which is at the heart of some of the anti-new perspective rhetoric, is that just as the Reformers in general never quite sorted out their eschatology, so their successors often had difficulty with the relationship between the three tenses of justification.[26] For Paul, there will be a *future* verdict which will take into account the totality of the life that has been led. He says this again and again. But this verdict is anticipated in the *present* by the 'justification' which consists of the divine declaration when someone believes the gospel. And this, in turn, is based on the *past* act whereby the one God vindicated Jesus by raising him from the dead.

Many are understandably confused here, and some of that confusion has spilled over into the post-Sanders discussions. If one fails to see Paul's emphasis on a *future* judgment related to 'works', one will continue to insist that Judaism, which clearly teaches such a thing, is radically opposed by Paul on this point. But what Paul has done is to allow the fact of the crucifixion and resurrection of the Messiah its full effect. The verdict of the last day has been anticipated already: God has condemned Sin in the flesh of the Messiah (Romans 8.3), and God has issued, through the resurrection, the verdict that Jesus really was and is 'God's son' (Romans 1.4). The resurrection, the defeat of death, clearly implies that sin has been defeated as well (1 Corinthians 15.17). This same verdict – that sin has been dealt with, and

[24] Caird 1978, 539, points out that the Mishnah can easily give the impression that 'the Rabbis were deeply preoccupied with legal minutiae, almost to the exclusion of other concerns'.

[25] See Sanders 1977, 515–18, though he does not always pick up the particular nuances. The obvious passages, which have naturally proved a thorn in the side of some post-Reformation dogmatists, include Rom. 2.1–16, esp. vv. 6–10, 13; 14.10–12; 2 Cor. 5.10, on which see e.g. *PFG* 1087–90. On all this see Wright 2014a.

[26] cf. Barth *CD* 4.1.332: 'Like the other Reformers, [Calvin] was not always at his best when dealing with eschatology.'

that new life has been granted – is then announced *in the present time* by God on the basis of the sign that declares that this person is 'in the Messiah': in other words, by *pistis*, faith. Justification thus does indeed remain a crucial point of distinction between Paul and his pre-Christian Jewish belief. But this is not because Jews believed in a final judgment according to works and Paul did not. It is because he believed that, in the Messiah, that verdict had already been announced in advance.

But this – crucially for the ongoing debates – is in no sense a matter of *two different types of religion*, as though one were to declare that, having compared them, one now finds (by what criteria?) that Christianity is somehow 'superior'. Paul would have snorted not just at that suggestion but at the misunderstanding it betrays of the gospel itself. The point is that *in the Messiah Jesus the one God has acted decisively to do what he had always promised and to rescue the world from the grip of death*, together with all that contributed to that death and followed from it. By setting up his argument in terms of a 'comparison of patterns of religion', Sanders laid himself open to the misunderstanding that he was suggesting that Paul himself compared 'Judaism' and 'Christianity' and decided in favour of the latter. By failing to see how the eschatological dimensions of justification work, his critics have often fallen into an equal and opposite trap. There is a sense in which Ed Sanders was trying to explain, to a scholarly guild whose value-laden assumptions were conditioned by western Christian beliefs in the importance of grace, and of not 'working' to earn God's favour, that Jews believed in those things as well. This already imported into the discussion, of course, the 'Christian' prejudice in favour of 'grace' and so on, but that is not my point for the moment. My point is that Sanders's argument had the opposite effect. In appearing to bring Judaism more into line with Pauline Christianity, he was instead seen to be bringing Pauline Christianity into line with Judaism. Hence the call to arms from the defenders of the faith.

This is all the more ironic, in that, as I have hinted, Sanders's view of the Jewish law corresponds structurally more or less exactly (a point Sanders did not make) to the normal Reformed view of the giving of the law and its 'third use'. God gave the law to Israel, not as a ladder of good works up which one might climb to a self-generated salvation, but as a way of life for a people already redeemed through the exodus.[27] This does not correspond to the normal non-Reformed protestant viewpoint, in which 'good works' are simply ways in which people (including people who are already Christians) try to make themselves good enough for God in the first place, or indeed to consolidate that status in the period between initial justification and final justification. Battle is thus joined, albeit confusingly, with the Reformation tradition: confusingly, that is, not least because the Reformation tradition itself is not united on these issues. There is still a lively debate on what role

[27] The idea of a 'third use of the law' goes back at least to Calvin's *Institutes* 2.7.12 (the first 'use' is to drive sinners to seek salvation; the second is to put a bridle on impenitent wickedness). Ridderbos 1975, 278–88 uses this as the heading of his relevant section.

(if any) the Christian's moral obedience should play in the period leading up to final judgment.[28]

What Sanders did not do, which would I think have helped his case considerably, is to offer a *worldview* analysis, a social-historical study, which would do the very thing he was wanting to do: to probe down under the surface message of a text for the symbolic structure and, not least, the implicit narrative. Worldview analyses are particularly good at reaching the parts which other analyses – including those of 'religion' and even 'theology' – cannot reach, and indeed in showing how all these things ultimately join up. There are three possible reasons why Sanders did not do this, and it may help to explore them, since unlike most of Sanders's critics on Judaism and the law I disagree with him not because I want to go back to something called the 'old perspective' but because I believe he did not ground his thesis deep enough, and seemed not to notice some of its weaknesses at that level.

First, Sanders may simply not have known, or may not have bothered much about, the work of Geertz, or Berger and Luckmann, or others who have so helpfully explored a number of cultures with the tools which we and others have summarized under the word 'worldview'.[29] Second, he was not particularly interested in 'narrative' as a category, either for studying Judaism or for getting to the heart of Paul. Third, and tellingly, Sanders's primary expertise, at least when he wrote *Paul and Palestinian Judaism*, was the rabbis themselves. He had spent ten years studying them in Jerusalem and Oxford. But the rabbis themselves *lived in a world in which narrative had ceased to mean what once it had meant*. This marks a vital difference between the world of the rabbis and the world of Paul himself.

Rabbinic literature, though it includes plenty of material from before AD 135, tends to see everything in the light, not of a continuing story about God and Israel within the ongoing flow of world history, but of the much thinner, often dehistoricized world of Torah-piety. As I argued in the second chapter of *PFG*, the key point about second-Temple Judaism, certainly the Judaism that Saul of Tarsus knew intimately, is that it was not an abstract system of either religion or salvation, but *an acted narrative*, a millennia-old drama in which each generation took up its role, with some understanding at least of the plot and how it was supposed to work out, hoping to see the God-given denouement of the story in its own day. One of the frustrations of reading through the myriad books and articles about the new perspective, this way and that – not that anyone, except possibly Jimmy Dunn and Michael Bird, has actually read all the material; certainly I have not – is that writers on both sides simply screen this element out of consideration, thus reducing the debate to the swapping of alternative systems for attaining an essentially ahistorical salvation. My problem, then, with Sanders's analysis of Judaism is that it actually reinforces this ahistorical scene-setting, which does indeed then lay him open to critique from the traditionalists. (This is

[28] It is impossible even to begin a chronicle of these ongoing debates. For the sixteenth-century material, see McGrath 1986; for recent discussions, see e.g. McCormack 2006; Beilby and Eddy 2011.

[29] For the background, see *NTPG* ch. 5; for the developed account, *PFG* 22–68.

all the more ironic in view of Sanders's own protest about New Testament scholars needing to do more history.) But my solution to this problem is to go deeper into the narrative substructure, not to abandon ship at the first sign of gunfire from Deerfield, Illinois. What matters is the world of the great story; and the great story is what the rabbis, by and large, seldom if ever explicitly tell us.

When I have made this point in seminars, someone has usually said 'But what about the *Haggadah*, all those wonderful rabbinic stories about Moses and Abraham and Rabbi This and Rabbi That?' Yes, of course. Judaism has never lost its character as a story-telling religion. The average rabbi to this day possesses, in my experience, a fund of shrewd, quirky, funny stories, poignant and pointed by turn, that even the best Christian clergy cannot match. But that is not what I mean. Those are *small-scale* stories designed to *illustrate* or embody a larger truth about Torah, about piety, or about the sadness and hope, the gloom and the glory, of the human condition in general and the Jewish predicament in particular. They do not, normally, evoke the *large-scale* story that many (not all) second-Temple Jews believed themselves to be living in, the historical narrative I explored in *PFG* chapter 2. That story received its death-blow in AD 70, and it finally died altogether in 135. True, the Rabbis still certainly believed in the eventual 'Age to Come'; but the retreat into Torah-piety was precisely a retreat from the larger story which had led to the cataclysm, the story of God, Israel and the world – the story we find in coded but powerful form in Daniel 7, in *4 Ezra*, and in literally dozens of other second-Temple works. And though the great story has today been revived in a new form with the events of the late 1940s and all that has followed from them, many devout Jews continue to insist that that is a category mistake, that the talk of a Messiah and a return to the Land should be seen simply as an evocative allegory, challenging them to obedience and hope. This is obviously a larger theme than we can pursue here.

All the story that seems to be left in the worldview of the rabbis, then, is the one Sanders tells in the long quote on page 71 above. The other stories we examined in *PFG* chapter 2, the stories to which second-Temple Judaism clung for dear life, remain a closed book to them. The fact that Sanders can discuss Judaism and Paul in terms of the 'covenant', while offering no discussion of Deuteronomy 27—30 and how it was retrieved in the second-Temple period, speaks for itself.

Sanders's great strength is that he really *knows* the rabbis. His great weakness is that he really knows *the rabbis*, and reads their largely dehistoricized, de-storied world back into the other Judaisms of the first century. He makes the case that has to be made, that they lived within an implicit covenantal framework. But he sees neither the essentially narrative quality of that framework *nor the fact that Paul himself shared it*. What is more, I suspect that part of the gut-level reaction to Sanders on the part of the so-called 'old perspective' is a worldview-level reaction to the very idea of a narrative world, any narrative world at all *except that of the narrative of the individual sinner needing to find personal salvation*. This is the narrative that many assume, without reflection, as the framework for their entire reading of Paul. Such readings go unchallenged because they seem 'natural'. Historically speaking, they are anything but.[30]

There are many more questions to be raised about Sanders's basic case on first-century Judaism. They will come up frequently hereafter. As I say, I regard the case as broadly made. Jews did not see their 'works of Torah' (a phrase they mostly did not use; see below) as good fifth-century Pelagians might have seen theirs, or even as hard-working moralistic fifteenth-century Roman Catholics might have seen theirs.[31] No doubt there is more to be said on that front as well. Nobody much speaks up for fifteenth-century Roman Catholics these days, at least among the guild of biblical scholars.[32] But I suspect that, if somebody cared to do so, a case could be made that they too saw their piety and virtue in terms of a larger narrative that was both initiated and sustained by grace. That might of course spin back again into the normal denunciations we hear from the Reformation lobby, but it is a conversation that might usefully be had. This is where one would need to revisit some of the complexities of the debates both between the early Reformers and the pre-Tridentine Roman Catholics, and between different protestant writers themselves.[33]

Another conversation that might have grown out of Sanders's project, but seems hardly to have begun, concerns the way in which the mainstream protestant view of *Spätjudentum* ('Late Judaism', the older and derogatory term) massively affected Old Testament scholarship. The theories that have dominated that world (including the Documentary Hypothesis of Pentateuchal origins) were just as much rooted in 'the wrong view of Judaism' as the older views of Paul. They too depended on the idea of a late, 'degenerate' form of Israelite religion, corresponding to late-mediaeval Catholicism, with its priests, its sacrifices, and its works of supererogation. That was what drove scholars to see the 'J' source as specially early and the 'P' source as particularly late. I remember the shock when I first heard a scholar speaking positively about the source 'P', the so-called 'priestly' material; then I discovered he was a Roman Catholic, who did not share the normal liberal protestant prejudice against that kind of supposedly degenerate, hierarchical and sacrificial religion. Are there signs that the 'Sanders revolution' is undermining Graf, Wellhausen and Noth in the same way that it undermined Bultmann and Bousset?[34]

[30] cf. *PFG* 140–2.

[31] Interestingly, most of the essayists in the collection designed to refute Sanders (Carson, O'Brien and Seifrid 2001–4) actually provide a good deal of back-up evidence for his view of Judaism, despite Carson's concluding piece which tries to reassert the old view none the less. Like Balaam, the writers who were hired to curse Sanders found the task harder than they might have imagined. Perhaps that old donkey called 'history' had had a quiet word with them.

[32] Though cf. e.g. Duffy 2005 [1992].

[33] See the nuanced discussion of Lane 2006.

[34] One answer might be found in the renewed interest in Temple-cosmology. Levenson 1984 does not challenge the Documentary Hypothesis, but he, in parallel as it were with Sanders, exposes the prejudices that have distorted perceptions of both Temple and cult. See also *PFG* 95–108 and other refs. there.

3. Plight, Solution and Critique

Having presented his argument for seeing first-century Judaism in terms of 'covenantal nomism', Sanders's second main point concerns Paul. Here there is an irony: Sanders has placed the question of 'plight and solution' at the start of his exposition, precisely in order to argue from the beginning that Paul proceeded not from plight to solution but from solution to plight.[35] It is almost as though the question, 'What's wrong?' has for so long begun expositions of Paul's thought that, even when Sanders wants to say that this is the wrong place to begin, he still begins with it. Anyway, on this topic Sanders insists that here, too, the post-Reformation tradition has simply got it wrong. Paul did not start off, like Luther, with a troubled conscience (this was the point of Stendahl's famous earlier article) and then find that the fact of Jesus Christ, or the message about him, resolved his personal anguish. Nor did he have a 'problem with the law', either a struggle to fulfil it, a fear that he had not done enough to earn such merit as it could award, or a pride that in fact he had fulfilled it perfectly and had thus earned favour with God. (Sanders is not so concerned to refute this last suggestion, but it is important as part of the picture.) Sanders, like others, picks up what Paul says about himself in Galatians 1 and Philippians 3. 'Official status under the law? Blameless.' That is Philippians 3.6, and this is what it means: Paul had been a good Jew, already in the covenant and successful in keeping Torah not to earn that status but to express it, aware that for any failure there was the well-known and regularly-used system of repentance, atonement, forgiveness and restoration. The anguished cry of Romans 7 was not uttered by Saul of Tarsus in his pre-Christian state. Sanders does not read Romans 7 as profound or important, in which I think he is profoundly and importantly mistaken, but I agree with him at least in this: it is not a transcript of 'how Saul felt before his conversion.'[36]

So what was 'the problem' with the law and with Judaism as a whole, and how did Paul arrive at that analysis? Sanders's answer is that there wasn't a problem – except that Paul discovered 'salvation' to be 'in Christ', and concluded that since he had been given this gift by this means it could not therefore be 'in Judaism'. Hence the famous statement, for which Sanders has been criticized but which was always intended as a kind of gnomic summary: 'this is what Paul finds wrong in Judaism: it is not Christianity.'[37]

In the build-up to this final summary Sanders says many other important things which were not grasped by all who read this quotation out of context in reviews and elsewhere. In a letter to me dated 3 November 1982, expressing frustration with oversimplifications of his argument, Sanders declared, 'Perhaps I should have had the entirety of p. 551 printed in bold type.' Well,

[35] Sanders, 442–7, explaining (442) that he is excluding one of the traditional ways of setting up the discussion, namely, by describing the pre-existing 'plight' to which Paul found Christ as the 'solution'.

[36] See Wright 2002 (*Romans*), 549–90; and, in *PFG*, 892–902.

[37] Sanders 1977, 552.

perhaps; but that would have demanded more work from reviewers and summarizers. On that page, and the one before it, he stresses that

> It is the change of 'entire systems' which makes it unnecessary for [Paul] to speak about repentance or the grace of God shown in the giving of the covenant. These fade into the background because of the surpassing glory of the new dispensation . . .

First, then, a change of dispensation, not because of anything wrong with the old one (though Sanders admits that Paul does sometimes say stronger things 'in the heat of the moment'), but because the new one has come, and offers the real thing. Paul's point, in other words, is not actually a comparison between two 'religions', but a claim about eschatology. In this respect at least I believe Sanders is profoundly correct, though this conclusion, again ironically, calls into question the ultimate importance of the 'comparison of patterns of religion' he sets out to perform.

Second, though, Paul knows perfectly well what the Jewish covenant and the doctrine of election are all about, and how they 'work'. But he denies that they are effective for salvation. Sanders goes on to say, in italics, that Paul thus consciously denies 'the basis of Judaism'. But immediately afterwards he quotes what Paul says in Romans 4 and Galatians 3, which he summarizes thus, again in italics: 'the covenantal promises to Abraham do not apply to his descendants, but to Christians'. I think this means that, for Paul, the covenant with Abraham – which one might well consider 'the basis of Judaism' – has not been denied after all. There seems to be a confusion here that needs further teasing out. Anyway, unlike W. D. Davies, Sanders is clear that Paul *did* have a critique of 'Judaism' and the law, but in his view this critique did not have to do with what traditional protestant theology of whatever type had assumed, i.e. the wrongness, badness, legalistic crypto-Pelagianism or whatever of 'Judaism' per se. It was rather that Paul had been overwhelmed by the discovery of salvation in Christ, and everything else was a reflex of that. Unlike H.-J. Schoeps, Sanders thinks that Paul really did know what genuine Judaism was all about, and that he really did turn his back on exactly that 'because knowing King Jesus as my Lord is worth far more than everything else put together' (Philippians 3.8).

Elsewhere Sanders articulates a sharper reason why Paul rejected Torah. I am not clear why it did not feature more strongly in his closing summary:

> It is the Gentile question and the exclusivism of Paul's soteriology which dethrone the law, not a misunderstanding of it or a view predetermined by his background.[38]

This, I think, is closer to the truth, though as I have shown elsewhere there is more to be said. In any case, Sanders clearly believes that Paul's mind moved not from 'plight' to 'solution', from a perceived personal problem to the solving of that problem in some way by Jesus Christ, but in the other direction. Having found salvation in Jesus Christ, he deduced that it was not to be found in the law. That explains, for Sanders, the otherwise puzzling

[38] 497.

scattershot nature of Paul's varied statements about, and against, the law: they were not the real reason for the rejection, but rather the unsystematic attempts to 'explain' something which was in fact an a priori deduction.[39] This question of 'plight and solution' has been one of the major ongoing puzzles in attempts to understand Paul in the post-Sanders world.

I have argued in *PFG* for a rather different view: that when we look at the first-century Jewish world, we see plenty of 'problems', or different views of a 'plight'.[40] It seems clear, from Qumran, Josephus, *1 Enoch*, *4 Ezra* and plenty of other sources, that, however zealous and holy a first-century Jew might be, there was still a 'problem'. Not, to be sure, Martin Luther's personal problem, but the national problem of Jews under Roman rule, with scripture unfulfilled, Israel unredeemed, and, not least, Israel's God still not returning in glory as had been promised.[41] If, as it appears, Paul's own mature analysis of what was wrong, both with humans in general and with Israel in particular – and, we might note from Romans 8, the whole creation itself – grew out of what he believed God had revealed through the events concerning Jesus, this is to be seen as a *radicalization* of the 'problem' of which he had previously been aware, not as a new point from nothing. This is important not only for discussing Sanders but in relation to the various theories about 'apocalyptic', which we shall discuss in Part II.

4. Paul's Own Thought

When it comes to Paul's own thought, Sanders's organization of the material is unusual. In a sense, it is a reverse of Bultmann: after the opening section on 'plight and solution', we first meet 'Pauline Soteriology', and then 'The Law and the Human Plight'. 'Justification' is treated in the latter section rather than the former; so too is 'Righteousness and participation'. We then find three short concluding sections: 'Covenantal nomism in Paul', 'Justification by works and salvation by grace' and 'Coherence, relevance and sources'. I applaud any attempt to rethink categories, but I do not think Sanders allowed that process to run its full course. It looks more as though he has simply provided brief essays on certain topics.

Perhaps this is because his controlling question and category, namely 'religion', proved inadequate for the task. Like Deissmann, one of Sanders's early heroes,[42] he tried to subsume 'theology' under 'religion', and it doesn't work. Indeed, one significant problem with Sanders's project was his ready embrace of the category 'religion' as bequeathed to modern scholarship by

[39] Another important voice in this debate, supporting Sanders and often going beyond him, is the Finnish scholar Heikki Räisänen: see Räisänen 1986, 2008. On the question of 'consistency', and of the difference between how someone arrives at a position and how they then present it to others, see Wright 1991 (*Climax*), esp. ch. 1.

[40] See *PFG* 737–64.

[41] See *PFG* 737–72.

[42] Sanders 2008a, 32.

the Enlightenment. This, as I argued in detail in *PFG* chapters 4 and 13, has at best only a tangential relationship to anything that would have been recognizable as 'religion' – or as anything at all! – in Paul's own world. Sanders managed to defamiliarize us all in relation to the species 'Judaism', but not to the genus 'religion'. Until that is done, even the most helpful remarks about the species will still be heard within the wrong echo-chamber.[43]

In particular, the categories with which Sanders conducts his 'religious' analysis seem more inappropriate the more one looks at them. 'Getting in' and 'staying in', Sanders's major categories, are not topics suggested by the Jewish material. Apart from the occasional discussion of proselytes, and the question of initiation within the Qumran community, the sources are not interested in how someone 'gets in'. Again, apart from occasional questions of discipline within that kind of community, the matter of 'staying in' is not a focus either. Nor would ancient greco-roman religion have been comfortable with a discourse framed in that way. Apart from what happened in relation to the mystery religions, 'getting in' and 'staying in' are simply not what ancient religions were about. Such categories might conceivably apply to a philosophy, but apart from the official 'schools' themselves there were no structures to police who was 'in' and who was 'out'. No: these phrases look like the retrojection of modern categories of 'religion', where 'religion' is something that you choose, that you enter, and from which you might perhaps be ejected. There may be a loose analogy, of course, with what happened when a pagan converted to following Jesus and then, in a Pauline church, was threatened with expulsion (as, for instance, in 1 Corinthians 5). But one can hardly elevate that unusual question into a founding principle. I do not find these categories helpful either for Judaism or for Paul.

That said, the main points of Sanders's proposal about Paul are fairly clear, even though they may not work well within the model of 'getting in and staying in', and hence are not well served by the 'patterns of religion' framework. He sees very clearly that Paul's first 'readily identifiable and primary conviction' has to do with Jesus himself:

> that Jesus Christ is Lord, that in him God has provided for the salvation of all who believe (in the general sense of 'be converted'), and that he will soon return to bring all things to an end.[44]

– in other words, a global message about God and what he has done in Jesus, set in an eschatological framework. (Sanders naturally and rightly identifies Paul's second conviction as his call to be the Apostle to the Gentiles.) The question is, how does this conviction about God, Jesus and eschatology work out? And how does the 'salvation' take effect? At this point, Sanders has effectively abandoned comparative religion and lapsed into theology. The main theme of Paul's gospel, he asserts, 'was the saving

[43] See *PFG* ch. 4; also my critique of Sanders at 1321–4 (including some overlap with the present treatment).

[44] Sanders 1977, 441f.

action of God in Jesus Christ and how his hearers could participate in that action'.[45] It isn't quite clear how that summary lines up with the one quoted above, but in either case 'we now have to consider ... how Paul understood and formulated human participation in God's saving action.'

The main impression I still receive, rereading Sanders nearly forty years on, is that in his discussion of Pauline soteriology most of the key elements are present but not yet joined up.[46] Believers are to wait for the return of Jesus, and their present possession of the spirit is a guarantee of their coming salvation.[47] This 'participation' in both the spirit and the death of Christ leads to a strong account of believers forming 'one body, one spirit' 'in Christ', serving the Lord under the spirit's direction.[48] It is within this larger category that Sanders then locates 'transfer terminology', discussed under 'participation in Christ's death', 'freedom', 'transformation, new creation', 'reconciliation', and last of all, as one untimely born, 'justification and righteousness'.[49] This leads to a final short section on 'salvation of mankind and the world', in which Sanders proposes that, though for Paul salvation does have a cosmic reach, it is normally only about humans; and that, though he does sometimes seem to be proposing a universalism, in many other passages it is clear that he thinks only believers will be saved.[50]

This ordering of topics – 'participation' first, 'transfer terminology' second – is Sanders's overall main point. As with Schweitzer, and as with strong elements of the Reformed tradition (is the Schweitzer/Bultmann debate after all simply a fresh vision of the Calvin/Luther polarization?), whatever Paul means by 'justification', it must be located within his larger christocentric participatory ecclesiology. There might be plenty of details to quibble over, but this claim is central. Unlike Schweitzer and some of his followers, Sanders does not think that this relativizes justification. This section, however, does little more than list the topics, discuss them briefly, and propose this ordering. As we shall see, what Sanders then means by 'justification' is rather different from some traditional understandings.

But if participatory soteriology is what Paul's teaching is centrally about, what are humans saved *from*, and what role does the law play in it all? This brings us to the second main section of Sanders's exposition, 'the law, the human plight, and the relationship of the solutions to it.'[51] Here Sanders's main thesis is that Paul's apparent polemic against the law is not the result of an analysis of human sin in which the law entices people to try to save themselves by keeping it (as in Bultmann). Rather,

> in Christ God has acted to save the world; therefore the world is in need of salvation; but God also gave the law; if Christ is given for salvation, it must follow that the law could not

[45] Sanders 1977, 447. Subsequent refs. are to this work unless otherwise indicated.

[46] Sanders himself admits as much: e.g. 452f.

[47] Sanders, 447–53.

[48] Sanders, 453–63.

[49] Sanders, 463–72.

[50] Sanders, 472–4.

[51] Sanders, 474–511.

> have been; is the law then against the purpose of God which has been revealed in Christ? No, it has the function of consigning everyone to sin *so that* everyone could be saved by God's grace in Christ.[52]

I agree with Sanders that this is a more plausible account than Bultmann's. But I do not find it persuasive. It is still tortuous and peculiar, and is in any case exegetically, theologically and historically unnecessary, as I have tried to show elsewhere.[53] It is a pity that the discussion of 'righteousness' within this section has been cut off from the discussion of 'justification' in the earlier passage. This contributes to a certain disjointedness in the whole treatment, and to the sense that Sanders, for all his great learning, has not got to the heart of what 'justification' is actually all about. At the same time, the passage on 'righteousness and participation' seems to me correct in locating the 'righteousness' language within the 'participatory' categories, as at the end of Galatians 3 and the key passage in Philippians 3.2–11 (he might have added Galatians 2.15–21 for good measure), though I do not think Paul here changes what he means by the (admittedly complex) term 'righteousness'.[54] I agree in principle that Paul did not in fact distinguish the things which appear to us as two categories; that, at least in general terms, 'righteousness by faith and participation in Christ ultimately amount to the same thing'; that 'we cannot … think that Paul was conscious of any bifurcation in his own thinking,' and that 'the two conceptions of man's plight [transgression and bondage] go together … and thus the two main sets of soteriological terms also go together.'[55] He is right to resist a common but shallow reading of Romans in terms of 'righteousness as the preliminary juristic status which leads to life in Christ'.[56] However, he concludes, in another moment of *Sachkritik*, that 'once we make the distinction between juristic and participationist categories,' 'there is no doubt that the latter tell us more about the way Paul "really" thought.'[57] Käsemann had gone the other way: the justification of the ungodly, and righteousness by faith, are central, but they are to be seen as a cosmic and corporate act.[58] Both want to retain both ideas. Neither sees how to do it in full Pauline balance.

Granted where the main lines of debate had been up to his day (not least with Schweitzer and Bultmann), Sanders's argument represents, I believe, a real advance. It takes a lot of effort to wrestle with these issues and bring

[52] Sanders, 475 (italics original).

[53] See, among many passages in *PFG*, the summary on Torah at 1032–7.

[54] Sanders, 502–8. One of the ways by which Sanders brings the categories together is to deny that 'righteousness' in Paul has the 'forensic-eschatological' meaning which Bultmann saw in it (506). Here I believe Bultmann was exactly right and Sanders exactly wrong – though that does not, in my view, prevent an appropriate fusion of 'juridical' and 'participationist' categories and terminology. It is as though, to adapt Schweitzer's metaphor, Sanders has shrunk the crater called 'justification' to the point where it will now fit within the crater called 'participation'. Something vital is lost with that shrinkage.

[55] Sanders, 502, 506, 507, 508. Here we note that Sanders thus holds together what appear to some as completely different modes of thought (see Part II below).

[56] Sanders, 506f.

[57] Sanders, 507.

[58] 508, quoting Käsemann 1971 [1969], 165, which Sanders discusses at 438 n. 41.

them so near to a full resolution. Many exegetical traditions are the poorer to this day for not making this effort. Yet a final ironic sense persists. Sanders has seen that what have appeared to some as two separate things are in fact two different angles of vision on the same thing. But he cannot reach out and grasp the category through which they might be finally and satisfyingly reconciled: that is, the covenant. He considers the possibility that Paul is articulating a new form of 'covenantal nomism', and rightly rejects it; but in doing so he also rejects, on what seem to me insufficient grounds, the possibility that there might be other ways of articulating covenantal categories which would be adequate for understanding the apostle.[59] Since I have advanced the alternative hypothesis at length in *PFG*, especially chapter 10, I need not develop the point further here.

But one thing must be said loud and clear before we leave Sanders. There are various succinct passages in which he sums up 'participation in Christ' with no apparent need of justification language:

> The main theme of Paul's gospel was the saving action of God in Jesus Christ and how his hearers could participate in that action ... The principal word for that participation is 'faith' or 'believing', a term which Paul doubtless took over from the earlier Christian missionaries.[60]

> God has appointed Christ as Lord and saviour of the world. All who believe in him have the Spirit as the guarantee of future full salvation and are at present considered to participate in Christ's body, to be one Spirit with him. As such, they are to act in accordance with the Spirit, which is also to serve Christ as the Lord to whom they belong.[61]

> What he really thought was just what he said: that Christ was appointed Lord by God for the salvation of all who believe, that those who believe belong to the Lord and become one with him, and that in virtue of their incorporation in the Lord they will be saved on the Day of the Lord.[62]

It is puzzling, reading these strong, clear sentences, to suppose that Sanders could ever have meant what some of his critics have taken him to mean: that Paul was only interested in saving gentiles from the hassle of being circumcised, and that he had no particular interest in humans being rescued from their sin and enjoying an eternal salvation. Sanders says exactly these latter things – that Paul is centrally concerned with final salvation – again and again. As with his own analysis of 'plight and solution', it appears that his critics have assumed a priori that he must be wrong, and have then cast about in an arm-waving fashion for reductionist things to say about him.[63]

Granted, Sanders's Paul is not nearly as interested in 'justification by faith' as the traditional Paul used to be. Perhaps this is why Sanders's discussion of 'final judgment according to works' sits by itself without much

[59] Sanders, 511–15.

[60] 447.

[61] 463.

[62] 523.

[63] I think in particular of Westerholm, whose work I shall discuss later.

relation to the flow of the argument.[64] Sanders is clearly right to say that Paul, just like Judaism, expects a final judgment according to works; but he has not integrated this into the rest of the structure, or attempted to engage with the puzzles this Pauline language has generated. This is itself an indication that he is not dealing with the normal discussions of 'justification', perhaps because he considers them to be more relevant to post-Reformation theological traditions than to Paul himself.

My own view of all this is that both Käsemann and Sanders are correct (against, for instance, Campbell on the one hand and some of the recent Germans on the other) to hold the two 'categories' together, but that neither of them has discovered the properly Pauline way in which to do that.[65] Sanders points out that the 'participationist' language is hard for many to grasp today, at least in the modern individualized western world. He rejects the demythologized account given by Bultmann and his followers, who were trying in their own way to overcome the same communication gap. But we lack, says Sanders, a category of 'reality' which will enable us to do justice to the full depth of what Paul was saying. Not for the first time, Sanders is impressive when he comes upon something for which we do not have good language and is not afraid to say so.

Here, in the final page of exposition, Sanders raises a massive question which *Paul and the Faithfulness of God* has attempted to answer. Rejecting on the one hand the idea that Paul was referring to some kind of 'magic transfer' of people into a new state of existence, and on the other that all Paul was talking about was their existential self-understanding (more or less, Schweitzer to the right and Bultmann to the left), he concludes:

> I must confess that I do not have a new category of perception to propose here. This does not mean, however, that Paul did not have one ... Although it is difficult today to formulate a perceptual category which is not magic and is not self-understanding, we can at least assert that the realism of Paul's view indicates that he had one.[66]

The irony is that Sanders frequently comes close to a much larger view which would enable him to discover Paul's key category, and always turns away from it.[67] When he discusses Paul and 'covenantal nomism', he lines up Davies's insistence on Paul's belief in Jesus as Messiah against the view that Paul saw Jesus as Lord of the world. (Here Sanders is close to Käsemann, but he does not seem to realize it.) This is extraordinary in terms of the historic biblical view that Israel's true king, when he arrives, will be the Lord of the world; but that was something which Sanders, like most others, never noted. Likewise, in comparing Paul's 'pattern of religion'

[64] Sanders, 515–18.

[65] Hübner 1980, 468f. criticizes Sanders for separating justification and participation, but I think Sanders has done his best, other things being equal, to hold them together. I do not find Hübner's alternative proposals any more impressive.

[66] Sanders, 522f.

[67] This question is addressed by two essays in the Sanders *Festschrift*: see Hays 2008; Stowers 2008.

with that of Judaism, he holds out the hypothetical possibility that the key category might be that of God's people, but then rejects it:

> The body of Christ is not analogous to Israel, and being in Christ is not formally the same as being in the covenant between God and Israel.[68]

> One may hazard the guess that the experience of being 'in Christ' was not the same as the experience of being 'in Israel'. This is a matter which is much more opaque to research than is thought, and we must be content with analysing how religion appears in Jewish and Pauline thought.[69]

It is just here, I suggest, that Sanders is pressing his nose against the window through which one might view the correct solution, but the bright light of his overall agenda (a patterns-of-religion comparison), shining from behind him, means that he cannot see through the glass. There before him is the very solution he is looking for, the clue that might enable us to grasp, as first-century historians, not only how Paul's 'participation' language actually worked, but also how it rested snugly beside the 'juristic' language, without either of them being subsumed, swallowed up, or swept off the table by the other. The category in question is the people of God: Israel. Sanders cannot see how that might help, so he pushes it aside. It was to explain this solution – the scholarly 'solution' to the 'plight' stated poignantly and honestly by Sanders at the end of a massive investigation full of sharp observation and shrewd insight – that I wrote the central section of *Paul and the Faithfulness of God*.[70] Caird expressed disappointment that Sanders had not drawn what he (Caird) thought the obvious conclusion: that Paul was critiquing the genuine Judaism as expounded by Moore and others, including himself.[71] To this we may add the disappointment that, having sketched something he called 'covenantal nomism', Sanders did not see the possibility of sketching a Pauline 'new-covenantal fideism'. Such shorthands can, of course, deceive. But this one might just point to the larger solution which, by Sanders's own admission, was still needed.

My last critical comment concerns eschatology. Sanders is of course right to stress the importance, for Paul, of the future return of Jesus. But I do not think he even recognizes, much less factors into his analysis, the extent to which Paul regularly saw the death and resurrection of Jesus in terms of an eschatology already inaugurated. All the weight, for him (as for Käsemann), lies on the future event, and on the way in which people are being prepared for it. But when we look at many of Paul's key passages – we might think, for instance, of the great set piece on the resurrection in 1 Corinthians 15 – we find that what has *already* happened is just as important as what is *still to* happen. It is not just that, as Sanders sees, Jesus is already installed as the Lord of the world. It is that, with his resurrection, the new world has already

[68] Sanders, 547.

[69] Sanders, 549.

[70] See too the recent work, independent of mine, by my colleague Grant Macaskill (Macaskill 2013).

[71] Caird 1978.

begun. The Pauline gospel issues a summons to discover that new world as a reality. This helps to explain why Sanders's discussion of justification is so unsatisfactory. In rejecting Bultmann's 'forensic-eschatological' meaning, he loses the eschatological tension and balance as well as the forensic shaping.

I have devoted an entire chapter to Sanders for the obvious reason that his work has remained, throughout the last generation, one of the most significant reference points for subsequent research. It is, to be sure, a sign of contradiction in many circles; but it is a sign none the less. I have given an account of why I think *Paul and Palestinian Judaism* had the impact it did in the aftermath of its publication. I have suggested that in some respects Sanders has made his case, and that in other respects, despite some important points, there are things to disagree with and things that need different nuance. I have suggested in particular that his stated aim, a comparison of 'patterns of religion', was ultimately at odds with his exposition of Paul's theology. But none of this detracts from the fact that this book is one of the great milestones of twentieth-century New Testament scholarship. Sanders had the courage to see a big picture, to realize that others were not seeing it, and to bring it to their attention. The discipline would be better served if there were more who would devote the best years of their life to studying the primary sources and the best energies of their maturity to communicating what they had seen.

A tail-piece. One of the things that has horrified many of Sanders's readers (and many of mine, for that matter) is his suggestion that the great Reformers, Luther, Calvin and the rest, misread Paul by projecting their own problems back on to his day. Often, when this question comes up, people like to quote a famous saying of Karl Barth:

> how energetically Calvin, having first established what stands in the text, sets himself to re-think the whole material and to wrestle with it, till the walls which separate the sixteenth century from the first become transparent! Paul speaks, and the man of the sixteenth century hears. The conversation between the original record and the reader moves round the subject-matter, until a distinction between yesterday and to-day becomes impossible.[72]

This is cited, often enough, as though to put paid to any cheeky suggestion from later, perhaps 'secular', biblical scholars that perhaps the great Reformers read Paul wrong. But, as Paul himself might say: Tell me, you who quote Barth, will you not hear Barth? Here is the same man, writing thirty years later:

> The Reformers dared to see the situation in their own time in the light of the situation of Galatians, and therefore indirectly (and often very directly) to equate the Law of Israel with the cultic and general order of the late mediaeval Roman Church, the doing of its works with the achievements of the ostensible or actual piety of their contemporaries in correspondence with that order, the Galatian errorists with the exponents of the ecclesiastical doctrine of justification current in their day, and finally the apostle as the preacher of

[72] Barth 1968 [1933], 7 (from the preface to the second edition of the famous *Romans* commentary, dated 1921).

> the faith which alone justifies – with themselves. We have only to read Luther's exposition of the Romans in 1516, and especially his commentary on Galatians in the definitive form of 1535, to see to what extent exposition and application – this exposition – intermingle with one another almost from the very first verses of the New Testament text to the very last. And fundamentally the same is true of the commentaries of Calvin, who was a much more careful exegete, and who occasionally at least did bring out the difference between the two ages. The risk involved in this kind of *explicatio* and *applicatio* was a very big one. The strength of Reformation theology is the directness with which it tried to place itself under Scripture and listen to it and allow it to speak . . . But this very strength was perhaps its weakness – a too hasty identification of the biblical situation with its own, and therefore as a result of its own impetuous understanding of the present a failure to see many of the nuances and differentiations in its judgment of the present. Only those who have tried to understand and expound the Bible, and especially Paul as a man of his own day, only those who have happily escaped the dangers which threaten us on these two sides (exposition and application), are entitled to cast the first stone. Certainly in Galatians (not to speak of other parts of Paul's writings and of Scripture generally) there were and are many more things to be discovered than what Luther discovered then.[73]

Wise words from a seasoned theologian, more than twenty years before *Paul and Palestinian Judaism*. But then, Barth belonged fundamentally to the Reformed tradition. As I have suggested, Sanders's protest may well have gained accidental traction through its retrieval of that tradition, if only by the non-traditional method of highlighting the larger Jewish context of Paul's thought. Whatever John Calvin would have thought of the result, I think he would have approved of that way of approaching the question.

[73] Barth *CD* 4.1.622f. Barth goes on to say, and I agree, that the Reformers were doing their best to reverse what had happened in the quite early church, namely, a move 'too far away from the world of the Old Testament' (623).

Chapter Four

LIFE AFTER SANDERS

1. Introduction

Nothing will ever be the same again. The new perspective on Paul – not that there is any single thing which can now be called by that name, despite the ambitious title of Jimmy Dunn's collection of related articles[1] – has burst in, like the delightful Goldilocks, to disrupt the peaceful scene where the Three Reformation Bears were planning to have an undisturbed breakfast. She has sat on the chair of traditional justification-theology, and it now seems to be broken (though they have called in the carpenters from Louisville, Sydney and elsewhere to try to fix it). She has eaten the exegetical breakfast, scooping up favourite texts and swallowing them whole. Now she is asleep in the theological and religio-historical bed, claiming the private room of Pauline studies as her own. And the Three Bears, quite understandably, are cross about it.

In some versions of the story, Goldilocks is chased away from the house, never to be seen again, and peace can return.[2] Part of the point of the present book, though, is to place this nursery story (which, to be sure, carries its own overtones in sociology and psychology, topics for which the somewhat conservative Bears never had much time) within a much larger set of stories in which the Bears themselves will come under scrutiny for the terms of their tenancy. The arrival of Goldilocks, though obviously an intruding nuisance, might then be seen as an accident that had been waiting to happen, perhaps even the necessary disturbance of a too-cosy household.

It is important not to imagine that the post-Sanders debate is either straightforward or the only game in town. It is complex, and there are many other things going on to which these debates are tangential if they are present at all. As I have stressed before, not least with my opening illustration of

[1] Dunn 2008 [2005].

[2] See esp. Carson, O'Brien and Seifrid 2001–4; Kim 2002; Westerholm 2004; and a host of lesser lights. Some of this work I shall discuss below.

the London Underground map, many of the lively conversations about Paul now taking place may happen to share one or two intermediate stations, but they are on different journeys with different starting-points and different goals. Just as there is no such thing as a straightforward new perspective reading, so there is no such thing as a straightforward old perspective reading either. Even if such things did exist, neither would correspond, in outline or in detail, to the major new 'apocalyptic' readings to which we shall come, let alone the sociological, philosophical and political readings which have become such a feature of the present landscape. The 'apocalyptic' readings are in some ways parallel to Sanders (stressing eschatology and, in some cases, 'participation', and downplaying the traditional meanings of 'righteousness'), but in other ways they are quite different, owing more to Käsemann's negative view of the law and of Israel than to Sanders's much more positive retrieval.

Similar things could be said about what I have called the 'fresh perspective', that is, the newer 'political' readings of Paul. This was something to which neither Sanders nor his main critics gave any attention one way or the other, though in one case (Seyoon Kim) an attempt has been made to see off the 'fresh' perspective along with the 'new'.[3] Nor has the neo-'apocalyptic' school attempted to incorporate it, though one might find this strange in view both of its homage to Käsemann on the one hand and its invocation of the obviously and thoroughly 'political' world of ancient Jewish apocalyptic on the other. We could make parallel comments about the newer 'philosophical' readings. To all this we shall return. My point is that the present debates about 'old' and 'new' are important, but they are not the whole map. One cannot treat the rest of that map as if it were offering merely a few other options for undertaking the same journey.

With that reminder, then, my task in this and the following chapters is to look at the different waves of post-Sanders development. I begin with the two most prominent scholars to have developed fresh ways of reading Paul within his Jewish context; then I look at those who have pushed back hard against the new perspective and all its works; then I examine those who are, in various ways, claiming to go 'beyond' the new perspective, particularly in relation to Paul's view of Judaism itself.

2. New Tasks within New Perspectives

The year 1983 saw the publication of five works each of which has had a lasting impact on the field. One of these, by Wayne Meeks, we shall examine in Part III.[4] Another of them, the work in which Sanders supplied more exegetical back-up to his original volume, we will pass over;[5] we shall also

[3] Kim 2008; see *PFG* 1313f.

[4] Meeks 1983.

[5] Sanders 1983.

take as read the solid work of Martin Hengel, which underlies quite a bit of the newer investigations but which focuses primarily on the interval between Jesus and Paul rather than on Paul himself.[6] Two of them we must deal with here: the first is a seminal article, and the second is one of the most important Ph. D. theses of modern New Testament scholarship.[7]

James Dunn picked up the thread of Sanders's argument early in the 1980s and has been sewing new patterns with it ever since. He is almost single-handedly responsible for thinking through and working out a basic post-Sanders position, in verse-by-verse exegesis of the key Pauline letters, in a way which Sanders himself had not done. What is more, he has been responsible, through his tireless organization of cross-channel conferences, for bringing together scholars, not least from Germany, who might not otherwise have had the relevant conversations face to face, and who might have been tempted to ignore one another or even to write one another off. For all this and much besides, the world of scholarship is grateful to him. This is not the time either for a full exposition of Dunn's reading of Paul (though he himself has provided his own account in several recent places, so the need is less obvious), or for the many anecdotal reminiscences which might shed light on the complex and mostly friendly relationship, scholarly and personal, which he and I have enjoyed.[8] I want here simply to highlight three major features of his work which have left their mark on the discipline in a way that has been characteristic of the post-Sanders world.

First, Dunn accepts a good deal of Sanders's case about Judaism, but insists that Sanders has still not read Paul in the right way. This reminds us once more of the most important thing that needs saying about the new perspective: right from the start, it has been a plurality of perspectives, an ongoing conversation, containing within itself at least as much disagreement as agreement. Those who think that having read a summary of Sanders they have understood what other scholars with a similar label are saying should think again. In Dunn's 1983 article, now reprinted in his larger collection, he criticizes Sanders sharply for failing to understand Paul, saying that he finds Sanders's Paul not much more convincing, or much more attractive, than that of Luther.[9] Sanders's Paul, argues Dunn, is

> an idiosyncratic Paul who in arbitrary and irrational manner turns his face against the glory and greatness of Judaism's covenant theology and abandons Judaism simply

[6] Hengel 1983.

[7] There are of course many other scholars who have carried forward elements of Sanders's proposals, not least into exegetical studies. I think particularly of the fine, careful work of John Ziesler, especially his commentary on Romans (Ziesler 1989).

[8] See esp. Dunn 2008 [2005], which he kindly dedicated to me (a compliment I returned in Wright 2009 [*Justification*]); and also his numerous commentaries, notably Romans (Dunn 1988), Galatians (Dunn 1993), Colossians and Philemon (Dunn 1996a) and also such major books as his *Theology of Paul the Apostle* (Dunn 1998) and now his massive *Christianity in the Making*, whose second volume focuses on Paul (Dunn 2009, 322–77 and 497–954). As his near-namesake put it nearly four hundred years ago: 'when thou hast done, thou hast not done, for I have more' (John Donne, 'A Hymn to God the Father' [1623], in C. Ricks, ed., *The Oxford Book of English Verse* [Oxford: OUP, 1999], 117f.).

[9] 2008 [2005], 103–5.

> because it is not Christianity ... [H]e still has Paul making an arbitrary jump from one system to another and posing an antithesis between faith in Christ and his Jewish heritage in such sharp, black- and white-terms [*sic*], that Paul's occasional defence of Jewish prerogative (as in Rom. 9.4–6) seems equally arbitrary and bewildering, his treatment of the law and of its place in God's purpose becomes inconsistent and illogical, and we are left with an abrupt discontinuity between the new movement centred in Jesus and the religion of Israel which makes little sense in particular of Paul's olive tree allegory in Rom. 11.[10]

Dunn therefore sets about taking all he sees as good in Sanders's proposal ('I believe that the new perspective on Paul does make better sense of Paul than either Sanders or his critics have so far realized'[11]), and elaborating it so as to address or even eliminate these peculiarities and weaknesses.

How well he has succeeded is a matter of judgment for those who have worked carefully through the several large volumes that Dunn has written on Paul between that early article and the present day (far more pages on Paul than Sanders or indeed the present writer have ever published, perhaps by a factor of four or five). My own view is that he has made a great many good points, but that his synthesis still lacks some of the dimensions necessary for a full account. But, to repeat, the first thing to note about the new perspective and 'life after Sanders' is that Sanders raised questions in a new way to which, from the very beginning, there was a variety of incompatible answers. Let nobody suppose that the new perspective is monochrome. Its main proponents are at least as sharply critical of one another as they are of other points of view, other 'perspectives'.

The second point about Dunn's remarkable contribution is his solution to one of the puzzles left by Sanders, and not addressed in my own work prior to Dunn's article.[12] Why does Paul say what he says about the *works* of the law? Might this not imply that he is, after all, attacking either something like what Luther was worried about (people trying to save themselves by good moral behaviour) or what Bultmann was worried about (people trying to grasp control of their own destiny)? These two are after all variations on the same theme, namely human pride (for Luther, pride in moral achievement; for Bultmann, pride in gaining control of one's destiny). Does this not mean that Paul was attacking the human tendency, and within that the Jewish tendency, to suppose that we can *do* something because of which God will be pleased with us, will justify us, will save us? I remember Bishop Stephen Neill making this point to me when we discussed my not-quite-complete dissertation some time around 1979: he was very interested in where I was going in my own post-Sanders reconstruction, but he pointed out that Paul's rejection of 'the works of the law' seemed to count strongly

[10] 2008 [2005], 103, 105.

[11] 2008 [2005], 105.

[12] My doctoral dissertation (Wright 1980) was examined by Dunn in the autumn of 1980; Dunn had also attended my Tyndale Lecture (= *Perspectives*, ch. 1) in 1978 (see above, 65 n. 4). I gave a paper to his seminar in Nottingham in February 1981, where we really began our still-continuing conversation; I do not think that Dunn at that stage had arrived at his now-famous hypothesis about 'works of the law'.

in favour of the traditional protestant interpretation. At that stage neither he nor I could see what was lying so close at hand.

Dunn's solution was staring us in the face in the ancient Jewish evidence. The 'works' of Torah to which Paul refers in Galatians and elsewhere, and which he rejects as the key to justification, are not the 'good moral works' performed by the would-be self-help moralist whom we and many others have thought of, with whatever historical inaccuracy, as 'Pelagian'. They are not the things someone might do in order to impress God. They are, quite specifically, the things *the Jew* does, not in order to *earn* God's favour but to *demonstrate* it: specifically, to demonstrate that he or she really is a member of God's people.[13] In the first century more or less everyone, whether Jew or gentile, knew what those 'works' were: circumcision of male children, various food taboos, and sabbath observance. These were particularly important for Diaspora Jews, living outside from the holy land itself, for whom such 'works' marked them out from their pagan neighbours. Those who lived in Judaea or Galilee had the land itself, and especially the Temple, as their great symbols, their badges of allegiance and cultural identity. For them the 'works' which Torah commanded, not least the sacrificial code, related to the Temple in particular. The wide variation in the style and intensity of observance of these 'works' does not reduce the overall point one whit.[14] What Paul was concerned about, particularly in Galatians and then in the more broad-based exposition in Romans, was that what Israel's God had accomplished in and through the Messiah Jesus was done for all people, Jew and gentile alike. This is the point which I myself had drawn out further than Sanders had done. Therefore, the things which marked out the Jewish people from the surrounding gentiles – *in other words, the 'works of the Jewish law'* – were now irrelevant, and worse than irrelevant. If they were highlighted, they were separating that which God had joined together once and for all and for ever. That, rather than a concern about proto-Pelagianism or crypto-Catholicism, is what Paul 'finds wrong with the works of the law'.

Dunn expounded this view in his original 'new perspective' article of 1983, and has returned to the point again and again ever since.[15] One might almost say that the badges of identity worn by Dunn himself include one which says, 'I know what "works of the law" is all about.' And I think, for the most part, and despite the continuing chorus of the unconvinced, that he is right.[16] I have myself tried to nuance things this way and that in my own exegesis and synthesis, but I believe that this was a major step forward.

[13] In the one text from second-Temple Judaism that certainly refers to 'works of Torah', i.e. 4QMMT, the 'works' in question demonstrate that the person doing them is a member of a particular subset of Judaism, which the writer takes to be the true covenant people. Dunn and I have taken rather different positions on this text: see his 2008 [2005], ch. 14, and my *Perspectives*, ch. 21.

[14] On the variations, see *PFG* ch. 2.

[15] Dunn 2008 [2005], chs. 2, 3, 8, 14, 17, 19, and some of the more general chapters as well.

[16] Among those still unconvinced: Gathercole 2002; 2006.

It was also, by the way, anticipated by Karl Barth, but this is not normally noticed.[17]

It is vital to realize that neither Dunn nor I have proposed a disjunction at this point. We have not said that Paul is now unconcerned about the larger range of 'works of the law' which would include the avoidance of murder, theft, adultery and so on. It will not do to shrink Dunn's proposal to the small scale of 'table manners', or of a politically correct 'social inclusion', and then to sneer at him for ignoring the weightier matters of the law, or indeed the gospel. The point is that *in the key texts*, that is, Romans 3, and Galatians 2 and 3, the phrase belongs closely with the question of Jewish identity. 'The works of the law' in this sense are the things which, by definition, the gentile cannot do. Of course, Paul knows perfectly well that 'the work of the law' (note the singular) is something which, by the miracle of heart-renewal, the Christian gentile can and will do.[18] And of course Dunn knows, as Paul knows, that those who are marked out by these badges from the surrounding culture are also under obligation to avoid murder, theft, adultery and so on.[19] Those injunctions, however, correspond broadly to the general moral principles articulated by many in the wider non-Jewish world as well – though Paul would have been quick to remind us that when it came to the worship of idols on the one hand and sexual behaviour on the other (the two being closely linked) he was reinforcing, certainly not relativizing, the broadly Jewish position over against the accepted norms of the non-Jewish world.

Anyway, the problem in this debate has been a false disjunction in the modern mind. For a long time readers of Paul have simply forgotten that the God-given purpose of Torah was to mark out Israel not simply as being different from the gentiles but as being different in this thing specifically, that Israel would demonstrate to the world the genuine way of being human. Ethnic identity and ethical behaviour went together. When Paul speaks about 'the works of the law' in Romans 3.20, and declares that nobody can be justified that way, he explains that 'what you get through the law is the knowledge of sin' – a point he then explains at length in Romans 7. But then in Romans 3.28 he declares that 'a person is declared to be in the right on the basis of faith, apart from works of the law', and then immediately continues, by way of explanation, 'Or does God only belong to Jews?' The 'or', missing in many translations, is the tell-tale sign that 'works of the

[17] See Barth *CD* 4.1, 621: 'Paul obviously meant by *erga* the works which the Old Testament demanded of the members of God's chosen people Israel to mark their distinction from other peoples or positively to attest the fact that they belonged to the covenant which he had made with them.'

[18] Rom. 2.15, followed up by 'the righteous deeds of the law', *ta dikaiōmata tou nomou*, in 2.26.

[19] I do not think this is the point being made in Gal. 5.3. There, Paul is saying, in effect, that if non-Jewish believers get circumcised they will also have to keep the other commandments which separate Jew from gentile, and thus (5.4) they will separate themselves from *Christos*, the single family (as in 3.15–29) which is marked out, by faith, from Jew and gentile alike. This passage is thus a reminder (cf. *palin* in 5.3) of the point made in 2.15–21. Paul here distinguishes the 'work' of moral character ('faith, working through love', 5.6, then expanded in 5.13—6.10) from the performing of 'the whole law' (5.3).

law' here are precisely the *Jew-specific* performances which mark out the Jewish communities from their pagan neighbours.

But how do these things go together? The answer cannot be that Paul 'really' means one of them and not the other. The answer must lie in the implied narrative: the Jewish person of whom Paul speaks is counting on the possession of the Torah, and the maintenance of the boundary-markers which it sets up, as the guarantee of ultimate security. No, says Paul: if you appeal to Torah to do that job for you, you must hear what Torah itself says to you, namely, that *you too are a sinner* just like the gentiles from whom you are claiming to be separate. Let us be clear, against the chorus of opposition and misrepresentation: *the new perspective is not saying that sin does not matter or that the gospel is not about being rescued from sin and its consequences.* Just as, in Galatians 3.21–2, Paul points out that without the problem of sin the Torah would indeed have been the way of life, so he might well point out that without sin the Torah really would have been the effective fence around the Jewish people. This is the key, also, to Galatians 2.15–21, though there is no space here to develop the point; and also to Philippians 3.2–11. The problem about using the law as a boundary-marker was not primarily, for Paul, that boundary-markers were a bad thing in themselves, or that there was something particularly wrong or unpleasant about 'exclusivism' (that central boundary-marker in the strange new post-modern moral landscape!). It was just that the fence which the God-given law built around the ancient people of God was covered on the inside with mirrors, and what the mirrors revealed, to those with the courage to look into them, was that (to quote a saying which I first heard from Rabbi Lionel Blue) Jews are just like everybody else, only more so.[20]

All this highlights a very important point which has emerged through the new perspective though in various different ways. *When Paul speaks of 'the law', he is talking of the Jewish law, the Torah.*[21] We cannot, without ruining his arguments, make *nomos* into something universal.[22] It is not a generalized 'law', a moral code, a quasi-Kantian 'categorical imperative', hanging in the sky over the whole human race, demanding moral obedience and making people feel vaguely guilty. Nor can *nomos* in Paul be flattened out into a generalized principle, as in some translations and many commentaries.[23] It is the law which God gave through Moses to Israel. Part of the point of that law, the prized possession and covenant instrument of Israel in particular, was to keep Israel separate from the gentiles.

[20] This saying seems to have passed into modern Jewish folklore (see e.g. Fredriksen 2005), being variously attributed to Heinrich Heine, Chaim Weizmann, or even Sigmund Freud.

[21] Das 2009, 110–13, suggests that there is a steady move of scholars towards this conclusion. See already Wright 1991 [*Climax*], *passim*, esp. chs. 7–12.

[22] In Rom. 3.19f., often cited against this, Paul is making the point that (a) he has already laid the charge against the gentiles, in 1.18—2.16; (b) he has now added to that charge, with the catena of quotations from 'the law' (in the wide sense of 'Israel's scriptures as a whole') (3.10–18), the specific charges also against 'those who are "in the law"'. Thus (a) plus (b) equals (c): now, 'the whole world may be brought to the bar of God's judgment'.

[23] See the discussions in e.g. Wright 2002 [*Romans*], 480; *PFG* 1034 n. 736.

This point has sparked another kind of controversy, as some Jewish scholars have felt done down by what they hear as an accusation of xenophobia or 'exclusivism'. I shall discuss this later, but we may note here that the function of Torah to keep Israel separate from the nations is not only evidenced by, but is regularly celebrated within, both the second-Temple literature and the scriptures themselves. Pointing this out might accidentally overlap with some patterns of would-be contemporary moral discourse, but this is not the point.[24]

More significantly for the present discussion, I suspect that the negative reaction to Dunn's proposal has to do with a deep-seated western protestant reading of the whole question. From the sixteenth century onwards, many have taken it as axiomatic that God made a 'covenant of works' with the first humans: they should obey, and then they would have life.[25] They disobeyed, of course, but God then gave the Torah, which was like the first covenant of works only (so to speak) more so. The human plight, and the divine solution to it, then appears like this: the law, as a general moral code, condemns us all, but Jesus has obeyed it in our place. Thus, to say that 'the law' is not after all this general moral code has repercussions on the larger picture of salvation. That is why the issue has generated such heat. Make 'the law' in Paul Israel-specific, and you shake a foundation of some branches at least of Reformed theology. As Barth realized, however (in the passage quoted at the end of the previous chapter), once you do business with the actual historical context of the New Testament, there may well be elements of traditional exegesis and theology which have to be reconsidered. The good news is that when this reconsideration takes place, nothing of value need in fact be lost.

A further important side-point to emerge from this discussion is that with Dunn, more clearly than with Sanders but drawing out the full implication of his work, we have returned to the point made a century ago by Wrede and Schweitzer: the questions about the law, works and justification occur in the context of Paul's discussion of the admission of gentiles into full membership of the 'Christ'-community. It is important to note that for Dunn this never meant (as it tended to in Wrede and Schweitzer, and also with Sanders, and now, far more, with Campbell and also in a quite different way with Gorman) a downgrading of 'justification', whether by subsuming it under a larger category, shrinking it so that it loses some of its sharp edges, pushing it to one side, or eliding it into other categories. Dunn

[24] See *PFG* 92–5. Zetterholm 2009, 117f. accuses Dunn of perpetuating the old 'Christian–Jewish' divide in a new guise: instead of Judaism as works-righteousness, Judaism as particularism instead of universalism/inclusivism. This would be a charge against me, too. What counts is historical exegesis: in *PFG* chs. 6, 10 and 15 I demonstrated that Paul did more or less what Zetterholm is worried that Dunn ascribes to him, namely making 'Jewish identity markers' no longer relevant for membership in God's people (not quite the same as 'valid', Zetterholm's word). It might be possible to state this in such a way as to claim a postmodern superiority rather than a protestant one (substituting 'we are inclusive, not exclusive!' for 'we believe in grace not law!'). As far as I know, neither Dunn nor I have tried that line.

[25] This received classic expression in the Westminster Confession, ch. 7 (2). A more recent articulation of the same point is in Gresham Machen 1982, 187f. (cited in Keller 2014, 69, 298f.).

remains a good, strong Protestant at heart: 'justification by faith' is still central to his reading of Paul. But he has seen very clearly that its location within Paul is bound up, not with the question of 'how do I get converted' or 'how do I find a gracious God', but with the question, which Dunn as also an ecumenical enthusiast sees as very important: how do gentiles come to be full members of God's people?

Dunn has thus drawn out from Sanders's position one of the most important aspects of new perspective work. The retrieval of Schweitzer is not simply a matter of an implied Jewish, rather than hellenistic, history-of-religions account. As we saw, Sanders was not attempting to offer such an analysis, though his whole project was leaning in the Schweitzer/Davies direction. Nor is it simply a matter of declaring that 'participation' (Sanders's equivalent of Schweitzer's 'Christ-mysticism') is Paul's central soteriological category rather than 'justification'. What Dunn has argued goes beyond this: 'justification' is part of Paul's treatment of how God's people in Christ are united across the Jew–gentile barrier, the barrier marked out by 'works of Torah'. This in turn indicates that, though 'justification' does indeed have to do, in a broad sense, with 'soteriology', it also has to do with Paul's vision of the renewed people of God. That I regard as massively important, initially for the reasons of good exegesis (e.g. of Romans 3.21–31, especially the relationship between 3.21–6 and 3.27–31; and also of Galatians 2.11–21), and then, as a corollary of that point, within the attempted reconstruction of the larger frameworks of Paul's theology.

The third point which is associated with Dunn in the course of the post-Sanders debate is his running debate with Richard Hays on the question of the phrase *pistis Christou*, particularly in Galatians 2 and 3, Philippians 3 and Romans 3. Traditionally this has been translated as 'faith *in* Jesus Christ', and that is how Dunn takes it in his commentaries on the relevant letters and in various articles. But Hays, along with some other modern American writers (and claiming older ancestry too), has insisted that it should be translated 'the faith[fulness] *of* Jesus Christ', so that, though Paul still clearly speaks of the faith of the individual believer, the weight of these particular passages falls, not on that individual faith, but on the accomplishment of Jesus Christ, or rather of God through Jesus Christ, and the 'faithfulness' of Jesus Christ to the purpose and will of God.[26]

One or two clarifications are in order. Among earlier explorers in this area, some have suggested that Paul, referring to Jesus' own 'faith', meant that Jesus himself (like a good Protestant!) refused to live by 'works' and lived by faith instead.[27] That is an anachronistic suggestion, designed (so it seems) to strengthen a kind of liberal antinomian use of an apparently protestant principle. Others have focused on Jesus' 'faith' in terms of his

[26] Hays's doctoral dissertation, published in 1983, was entitled *The Faith of Jesus Christ*. Unusually for a doctoral dissertation, it was republished almost twenty years later (with new material added): 2002 [1983]. It remains influential: see below.

[27] e.g. Hanson 1974, 39–51. Hanson glimpsed many then unfashionable points which have since become mainstream; but this particular suggestion seems to me a blind alley.

own deep and rich religious experience.[28] However important this is, I do not think (and, for our present discussion, Hays does not think) that this is what Paul is referring to with the phrase *pistis Christou*. Others, even earlier, have tried to link a subjective genitive reading both with linguistic phenomena on the one hand and larger theological constructs on the other. Here again caution is required.[29]

The polarization between the objective genitive ('faith *in* Christ') and the subjective genitive ('the faith[fulness] *of* Christ') might seem like a small exegetical either/or. But a good deal hangs on it, which is no doubt why the debate has run on in public, private and print.[30] At these key points in the letters, is Paul speaking about God's achievement or about human response? Both are of course included in the overall account of what has happened. But for Hays, following a more Reformed perspective at this point, the weight rests on God's action in Christ, whereas for Dunn the weight rests on the individual believer. Whether we can correlate this with the other significant features of Dunn's exposition of Paul – Dunn's insistence, with Cranfield, that Romans 7 describes the Christian's normal struggle with sin, or his deep anti-sacramentalism – are questions that would take us too far afield at the moment. But this debate is linked with, and is indeed symptomatic of, a deeper one still.[31] Here we arrive at one of the main new things to emerge in 'Life after Sanders'. Though as we have seen Sanders did not work out his position in terms of underlying narratives, the picture he drew of Judaism included such a narrative: the election and covenant, creating a religious space in which Israel would obey the law out of gratitude. Sanders could have extended this, but did not, into the larger biblically-based narrative of Israel, perhaps because, as we suggested in the previous chapter, his picture was drawn from the rabbis and then developed backwards to the regular second-Temple Jewish texts. This larger biblical and post-biblical narrative constantly reaches forwards with the key question: not, How can I find a gracious God, but, When will the gracious God fulfil his promises to Israel? What Hays saw in his dissertation (1983), and

[28] e.g. Wallis 1995, ch. 3: another important discussion, making several good points, but in my judgment Wallis confuses Jesus' faithfulness with his personal faith, and tries to make the resulting construct perform too many functions in Paul's argument. Hays discusses Wallis's work sympathetically – giving particular attention to his point about the patristic interpretation of the phrase – in Hays 2002 [1983], xlviii–li.

[29] See the famous short article of Torrance 1957, discussed in various places in Hays 2002 [1983]. Hays concludes (161 n. 145) that 'while Torrance's methods are subject to criticism, his interpretive intuition was fundamentally correct.'

[30] Dunn's main piece is printed as an appendix in Hays 2002 (249–71), followed by Hays's response (272–97). These reflect a public debate at the Annual Meeting of the Society of Biblical Literature in November 1991. I cannot resist recalling that, after some hours of exciting discussion, someone in the large crowd called for a vote on the issue. 'Nope,' said Professor Lee Keck, from the chair. 'This ain't the Jesus Seminar.'

[31] I thus disagree with Westerholm 2004, 305 n. 18, who suggests that the importance of this debate is 'easily exaggerated'. Dunn suggests (1998, 384f.) that the 'faith of Jesus Christ' reading results from atomistic study of the texts in isolation from 'the flow of Paul's argument'. I think this is exactly wrong: it is the flow of Romans 3 in particular which has convinced me of the subjective genitive reading. See *Perspectives* ch. 30; *PFG* 836–51.

has elaborated ever since, is that this question, posed thus in narratival terms, found its Pauline answer also in a narrative: the story of Jesus the Messiah. And the point of raising all this in a discussion of Dunn's work lies just here: this narrative framework, I believe, is what is lacking throughout Dunn's work, causing him to reject Hays's proposal about *pistis Christou*. The way Dunn reads this phrase is not just an exegetical decision to do with the key passages in question. It is the encapsulation of a whole way of reading Paul.[32]

Hays's own way of reading the apostle has been set out much more fully in his second book, which like his dissertation has been not only influential but paradigm-changing. In *Echoes of Scripture in the Letters of Paul* he argues, through close readings of several key texts, that when Paul quotes Israel's scriptures, or even alludes to them, he is demonstrably thinking not just of that one verse or even one word but of the larger context within which it comes, and that when we put that larger scriptural context alongside the argument Paul is making we find, again and again, that a flood of light is shed on the Pauline passage in question.[33]

This proposal, which has been taken up by many scholars and elaborated in many directions, has not been without its critics. Some have said that Paul couldn't have written that way, because his first audience would never have picked up the allusions and echoes.[34] Others have come up with counter-proposals, insisting that Paul only intended what we find on the page, that he used scriptural allusions as a rhetorical power-tool to stun his audiences into submission with his superior knowledge, and that anything else is a figment of our imagination rather than his.[35] But my own view, corroborated in many fresh readings on top of those Hays already offered, is that the thesis is confirmed in practice again and again.

It is important, as with Dunn, to point out that the route taken by Hays was a route Ed Sanders himself did not go, and indeed that when faced with such a proposal he has tended to resist it stoutly. For him, the reason why Paul quoted Genesis 15.6 in Galatians 3 and Romans 4 – and hence the reason why he referred to Abraham in the first place – was because he wanted to join together 'faith' and 'righteousness'. Paul, according to Sanders, had himself discovered a new way of 'righteousness' which was marked by 'faith', and he wanted to find some 'scriptural proof' for this startling new insight. So Paul, on Sanders's view, with the Septuagint in his lifelong memory, ran through his mental concordance and came up with the only two passages where this combination occurs: Genesis 15.6 and Habakkuk 2.4. In

[32] This is also cognate with Dunn's steady refusal to take the point about the 'extended exile', which I have now argued at length in *PFG* 108–79.

[33] See further Hays, Alkier and Huizenga 2009; for detailed application of Hays's method to Romans and Galatians, Keesmaat 1999; to Paul's use of Isaiah, Wagner 2002.

[34] cf. e.g. Tuckett 2000. For a classic and frustrating example, see Westerholm 2004, 359 n. 26: Paul's Galatian and Roman audiences might have understood a claim about the promises made to Abraham, but 'the Thessalonians (and, I suspect, the Corinthians . . .), bless their hearts, would have been clueless.' Maybe; but Paul was determined to give them not only clues but a whole new worldview.

[35] e.g. Stanley 1992; 2004. On this and related matters see *PFG* 1449–56.

Galatians he quotes the two nearly side by side; in Romans they come three chapters apart; but that was what was going on. No reference to context was intended. Paul would not otherwise have brought them into the argument. Abraham remains a convenient early example of someone who was 'justified by faith'.

Yet, on Sanders's own view of Paul's memory, this should be questioned. He has recently insisted that even moderately educated Jews of Paul's day, let alone one such as Paul himself who by any standards was extremely bright, not to say intellectually brilliant, would know much if not all of the scriptures by heart. That was, after all, much easier than carrying around cumbersome scrolls and having to look things up, a complex task in itself. Memorizing itself, as many educationalists have forgotten, is not difficult if begun sufficiently early.[36] And Sanders himself can speak, as we saw, of Paul arguing in terms of the promises to Abraham, not as isolated sayings but as promises which imply a narrative. Hays's proposal should thus properly be seen as part of 'life after Sanders', even though Sanders himself did not go that route and did not embrace it when offered. It may well be that Hays would have developed the same line of thought even if Sanders had never written a word. But it is fair to say that the world of scholarship which has taken up Hays's ideas so eagerly is the same post-Sanders world in which every effort is now being made to read Paul in terms not of a sharp polemic against 'Jewish legalism' (or something with the same function) but in terms of an essentially Jewish apostle discovering, perhaps to his surprise, that the fresh revelation he believed had come from Israel's God through Jesus the Messiah was the very thing to which Israel's scriptures had in fact been pointing all along.

The manner of that pointing, though, has not been straightforward. I have detected a shift, over the last twenty years, between Early Hays and Later Hays on this point. In *Echoes*, the fundamental thrust is to see Paul thinking through Israel's scriptures in what might be called a typological manner. In the scriptures, Paul hears voices which echo and resonate with things that need to be said in and to his churches. There is no linear continuity; God's word through Deuteronomy to Israel becomes, by a strange alchemy, God's word to those who are 'in Christ'. Indeed, one of the great emphases of *Echoes* is that the echoing word addresses and forms the church, the community of the 'in Christ' people, the people 'upon whom the

[36] See Sanders 2008b, 347: 'He carried the Bible safely tucked away in his head, where it belongs.' Contrast the suggestion of Schnelle 2005 [2003], 110: 'as a rule, the apostle could only refer to particular quotations when he had sufficient time and could support his argument with written texts.' Compare Schnelle's view (111) that Paul would only introduce scriptural material 'when the necessity arose ... for the clarification of controversial theological problems.' The picture of Paul, when writing Galatians and Romans, 'reaching for his Bible to find texts that can serve to resolve the severe conflicts and arguments in which he is engaged' is counter-intuitive ('reaching for his Bible' would be a complex activity) and indicates a completely different view of how Paul's mind worked: all the signs are that he was not *first* figuring out what he wanted to say theologically and *then* looking for back-up material in the scriptures, but that his whole project involved thinking through a fresh reading of the whole scriptural narrative in the light of the Messiah. (That this in no way implies a smooth, immanent process should be clear: see Part II below.) On the question of how much scripture Paul's churches already knew see Hays 2005, 24.

ends of the ages have now come'.[37] 'The Word leaps the gap':[38] the echoes of Wisdom 18.15 do not explain which 'gap' this is (between heaven and earth, as in Wisdom? between past and present, as in 'two horizons' hermeneutical theory? Or what?). Certainly Paul frequently implies that the *ekklēsia* stands in parallel, rather than in continuity, with the ancient people of God.

But from the time of Hays's commentary on 1 Corinthians, and particularly with his article on 'The Conversion of the Imagination', now published as the title-piece of a collection of essays, the note of continuity has emerged.[39] Here again we find something which Sanders never envisaged, but which brings together Hays's earlier emphasis on *story* with his later emphasis on *echo*. The 'echoes' are now to remind the *ekklēsia* of *the earlier parts of their own story*. A good example is 10.1–2: 'our fathers', Paul says to the ex-pagan Corinthians, 'were all baptized into Moses in the cloud and in the sea'. The fact that Paul then sets the two stories in parallel (what happened to *them* might happen to *you* if you don't watch out) is held *within* the larger narrative *continuity*: this is the same people who, though clearly transformed by the gospel, are the descendants of the exodus generation, and so can learn from them not because they are merely related typologically but because they are part of the single historical family:

> Israel's story is not somebody else's history; rather, Paul addresses the Gentile Corinthians as though they have become part of Israel. They are invited to understand themselves now as descendants of the characters who appear in the pages of Scripture ... It should be noted that Paul is not trying to convince his Gentile readers to accept this identity description as a novel claim; rather, he assumes their identification with Israel as a given and tries to reshape their behavior in light of this identification.[40]

So too in 1 Corinthians 5: 'Paul thinks of his Gentile Corinthian readers as having been taken up into Israel in such a way that they now share Israel's covenant privileges and obligations.'[41] Paul's challenge to the ex-pagan Messiah-believers is not simply that they learn behaviour by looking at scriptural examples. It is that they learn to think of themselves as characters in the story of God and his people, whose earlier chapters set out characteristic lessons to be mastered by those who find themselves in the later chapters. But the overall point is this: they are in *the same* story, not a different story which happens to be parallel to another earlier one. Something drastic has happened to that story, something which has burst in on it, turned it inside out, set the house on fire and rebuilt it, however you like to say it:

> Paul was not promulgating a linear *Heilsgeschichte* in which Gentiles were simply absorbed into a Torah-observant Jewish Christianity. Rather, the 'Israel' into which Paul's

[37] 1 Cor. 10.11, in a passage explaining the relevance for the Corinthians of the exodus-events.

[38] This is the title of the Hays *Festschrift*, ed. Wagner, Rowe and Grieb (2008): cf. *PFG* 73 n. 158.

[39] See Hays 1997; 2005.

[40] Hays 2005, 9. Hays points out that Bultmann said more or less the opposite.

[41] ibid., 23.

Corinthian converts were embraced was an Israel whose story had been hermeneutically reconfigured by the cross and resurrection.[42]

But it is nevertheless the same story. 'You are Abraham's children, heirs according to promise.' Not, *like* Abraham's children. Not, following their example but in a different family. 'Paul is urging the Galatians to understand themselves as heirs of God's promise to Abraham, by virtue of their union with Christ.'[43] The single narrative is the most powerful element in Paul's reconceived worldview. And Hays's elegant literary phrase, 'hermeneutically reconfigured', is scholarly language for 'put to death and brought through to new life.' Hays has thus been central to the newer focus on Paul's narrative world, though as with all his work this has opened up new questions rather than shutting them down.[44]

These brief and no doubt inadequate thumbnail sketches of two of the most obvious post-Sanders expositors of Paul, both of whom go in significantly different directions from that taken by Sanders himself yet both of whom breathe the air of the different world he ushered in, may be drawn together in a particularly interesting point. Dunn and Hays alike stress that for Paul the categories of 'justification' and 'participation in Christ' are both important, and actually belong closely together. Dunn, in a fine and wide-ranging passage, insists that at this point we must look to Calvin rather than Luther, and that when we study some of Paul's most central passages, such as Philippians 3.8–14, we find that all the key themes run together: being found in Christ, having the righteousness which is from God upon faith, knowing Christ and the power of his resurrection (which, as Dunn points out, is for Paul another way of talking about the work of the spirit), sharing Christ's sufferings, being conformed to his death in the hope of the resurrection, and so straining forward to make his own that which has been promised.[45] Hays, more briefly but no less tellingly, put it like this in his dissertation over thirty years ago, referring to Galatians 2.17:

Here justification and participation in Christ are merged, and it is clear that Paul intends this phrase to be synonymous with his words in the previous verse, *hina dikaiōthōmen ek pisteōs Christou*. To be justified *ek pisteōs Christou* is the same thing as being justified *en Christō*. Thus, 'justification' and 'participation in Christ' do not belong to divergent theological spheres; for Paul, they belong together because he understands salvation to mean our participation in *Christ's* justification.[46]

[42] Hays 2005, 5, referring also to Donaldson 1997, 236. Hays is here carefully distancing himself from what Käsemann and others – and, in our own day, Martyn! – have rejected as a kind of evolutionary, steady-state development in which the new creation, and Christ himself, merely emerge from an immanent process. See above, 46–50, on Cullmann; and below, Part II, on 'apocalyptic'.

[43] Hays 2000, 274.

[44] For further discussion of Paul's narrative world see *PFG* ch. 7, and among other monographs those of Witherington 1994, Longenecker 2002.

[45] Dunn 2008 [2005], 92–5, here at 94.

[46] Hays 2002 [1983], 212f.

Whether either Dunn or Hays has thereby given a full account of how these two elements may be reconciled – two elements still widely regarded as entirely different types of thought – I am not sure. Hays has suggested that the place to look for further help might well be the Greek Fathers, and that suggestion has recently been followed up in an important monograph.[47] But Hays and Dunn, in their different ways, are determined to hold them together, in a tight exegetical and theological unity which goes beyond what Sanders had suggested. These parts of the post-Sanders world have been creative and positive, and there is much more to come.[48]

One of the key writers to follow Sanders, in a different manner from Dunn and Hays, was Francis Watson. I say 'was', because Watson's early work *Paul, Judaism and the Gentiles* (1986), a brilliant essay in its own way, does not exactly represent where its author now stands. The new edition of the book retains the same title and shape, and a fair amount of the original wording, but with a significantly different angle of vision.[49] Watson has reflected on this change not only hermeneutically but also autobiographically. Here there is scope for a redaction-critical analysis. But the first edition remains important, not because it got Paul right – indeed, I reviewed it critically when it came out, and I shall not repeat that analysis and critique here – but because it may well have been part of the post-Sanders development that generated part of the anti-Sanders backlash.[50] This is the more ironic in that, in line with what I have already said, Watson is clear that there is no such thing as '*the* new perspective'. The book was essentially, he says, 'an *alternative* response to Sanders's challenge to rethink Paul', an alternative (that is) to the responses offered by Dunn or myself, 'taking a far more positive view of [Sanders's] perspective on Paul himself.'[51]

Watson's initial argument pushed further than Sanders towards a relentless, almost reductionist, sociological analysis. Paul was seeking to generate and sustain communities of a certain sort, and what the tradition has taken to be 'theology' and 'soteriology' was actually carefully crafted rhetoric to create and hold in place sectarian communities of a particular type. The Preface set out the stall: the book was to argue that

> the view of Paul's controversy with Judaism and Jewish Christianity which derives from the Reformation is seriously misleading, and that the Pauline texts become much more readily comprehensible when one abandons this overtly theological approach . . . Sociological analysis . . . shows up serious shortcomings in the more traditionally theologically-oriented approach.[52]

[47] See Hays 2002 [1983], xxxii; and Hays 2008; and see now Macaskill 2013, esp. ch. 2.

[48] See the striking proposals of Vanhoozer 2011; Macaskill 2013.

[49] Watson 2007 [1986] has a new subtitle: 'Beyond the New Perspective' has replaced 'A Sociological Approach'.

[50] For my original review see Wright 1989.

[51] 2007, 9 (italics original).

[52] 1986, ix, x. Watson now explains (2007, 347–9) that it was never his intention, even then, to abandon or supplant theology, but it is clear that he laid himself open to that (mis)interpretation.

Not only Reformation theology is to be abandoned, it seems, but theology as a whole. Whether or not that was Watson's ultimate intention, that is how most people read him. Several other passages in his original book appear to confirm this line.[53]

Watson's book was part of a larger movement of thought which we shall study in Part III of the present book, and which has in my view redressed a necessary balance.[54] Paul was indeed centrally concerned to establish and maintain united communities of Messiah-people. Those communities were of great symbolic and practical importance. Where Watson spoke of 'sociology', however, he did not actually root that work in actual sociological method as practised by sociologists.[55] As he says himself, what he was really doing was a form of secularized ecclesiology. But the apparent either/or of Watson's analysis, *either* 'theology' *or* 'sociology', *either* 'salvation' *or* 'sectarian formation', may have been one of the factors that caused critics of the new perspective to react in horror, and, as we shall see, to overreact.[56]

Watson's subsequent work has taken a different line. I have discussed it in some detail in the parent volume.[57] But I note his original contribution here as a key marker in the early story of the new perspective, a signal which was picked up perhaps too enthusiastically by those eager to say 'the old is better'. To that reaction we shall shortly turn.

Before we do so, a quick note on how things stand within 'life after Sanders'. For a start, there has been a considerable emphasis on continuing to read Paul within his larger Jewish context. This is not easy. The more we know of the widely diverse Jewish world of the first century, the more we scratch our heads as to where Paul belonged within it, and in how contested a manner. He himself, after all, had persecuted the first followers of Jesus on what he had taken to be good Jewish grounds; and he speaks with a certain bitterness of the similar hostility he has received from his own kinsfolk.[58] Persecution itself implies, of course, that one is in some sense or other still part of the basic group: one does not persecute someone who is living in a

[53] Thus e.g. Rom. 2 was Paul's attempt 'to persuade the Roman Jewish Christians to abandon the remaining ties that bind them as a (failed) reform-movement to the Jewish community, and to join with his own followers in sectarian separation' (122).

[54] My own investigation in *PFG*, esp. Part II, has continued the same approach, though like Meeks 1983 I have tried to integrate this with Paul's theology rather than set them in opposition.

[55] In 2007, 10 Watson speaks of his earlier monograph being revised (from his original dissertation) in the light of the deep impression made on him by Berger and Luckmann (1984 [1966]; Watson refers to the 1967 first UK edn.). They do not, however, appear in the book, even in the bibliography; and the opening section on 'sociology' (19–22), though referring briefly to Esler, Theissen, Elliott and Meeks, does not attempt to set out a full sociological method.

[56] This was perhaps inevitable, granted statements such as this (1986, 179): 'It is therefore completely wrong to regard the phrase *sola gratia* as the key to Paul's theology; Paul does not believe that salvation is by grace alone ... the faith–works contrast is primarily sociological rather than theological in meaning. The faith–works contrast is only absolute as a contrast between the incompatible ways of life practised by two different religious communities.' In Watson 2007, 306 this has been dramatically softened: 'The Reformational assumption that Pauline theology is summed up in the phrase *sola gratia* should be treated with considerable caution'.

[57] See *PFG* 1456–71.

[58] 1 Thess. 2.14–16, on which see *PFG* 1151–6.

different world entirely. So, for all that Sanders's Paul finds that Judaism is 'not Christianity', he still shows up to the synagogue, and still gets beaten there.[59] So Paul belongs within, and is to be understood historically within, that larger Jewish world, however problematic that may have been both for his contemporaries and for today's historians. At the same time, Sanders's initial apparent sharp distinction ('not Christianity') might itself have pointed the way, however ironically, to the newer attempts to place Paul not so much within his Jewish world as within the wider world of hellenistic philosophy.[60] It also opened the possibility of an analysis in which Paul was the apostle of a movement essentially for gentiles, leaving Jews to continue with their own way of life.[61] This proposal, however superficially attractive in the late-modern western world, has not commended itself either exegetically or theologically.

The theological legacy in 'life after Sanders', then, has continued to focus on a more Jewish Paul, and in particular – in a way returning to Schweitzer, in a way going beyond him – has highlighted 'participation' as the controlling category, while still finding it a challenge to know what Paul himself understood by the language for which that word serves as a summary. I have myself underlined the covenantal nature of Paul's whole thought, and I find it ironic that, despite his whole emphasis on a covenantal understanding of the Jewish world, Sanders himself did not go in this direction. To be sure, the category is itself in need of more exploration and explanation. It might well be, as we mentioned a moment ago, that we need to bring into the picture some of Paul's early expositors, such as the Greek Fathers. I am not at the moment entirely convinced by this. My fear is that the categories developed in the third and fourth centuries may have tended to ignore or radically to downplay the biblical and Jewish roots of Paul's incorporative language. If we want, as some do, to embrace the notion of incorporation into the divine life itself, we must always equally embrace the notion of incorporation into the family of Abraham.[62] Of course, since much of the modern scholarly tradition has wanted nothing to do either with mysticism or with belonging to the family of Abraham, it is perhaps not surprising that neither element of this combination has received the attention it may deserve.

To say that both of these – incorporation into the divine life, incorporation into Abraham's family – find their *telos* in Jesus is of course to restate, more adequately perhaps, a soteriology rooted in the old combination of Jesus' 'divinity' and his 'humanity'. In particular, all this seems to me to have a lot to do with Jesus' Messiahship, which again is normally ignored in both halves of this combination. Putting that back into the mix might make

[59] cf. *PFG* 1498f., and the ref. there to Sanders 1983, 192.

[60] See the various discussions in Engberg-Pedersen 2001.

[61] So, famously, Gager 1983; Gaston 1987.

[62] The idea that Paul's 'incorporative' language had to do with Jesus' 'divinity' was one of the leading ideas in the important work of Moule 1977. Though this particular line has not found favour, the book itself remains a masterpiece of patient and insightful scholarship.

quite a difference, too. Paul at least seems to be aware that 'Son of God' is simultaneously a 'messianic' title and a way of speaking about Jesus as the one in whom Israel's God comes, in person, to fulfil Israel's strange destiny. At certain key points, like Galatians 2.19–20 and Romans 8.3–4, he seems to be drawing all this together in deliberately rich and dense formulations. Exploring these themes further will undoubtedly go a long way beyond anything Sanders said. But this sort of exegetical task, constantly aware *both* that Paul is to be seen within a Jewish context *and* that he was himself conscious of bursting the normal boundaries of that context, is what one might expect 'life after Sanders' to look like.[63]

[63] For Paul as an 'anomalous Jew' see e.g. Barclay 1996, ch. 13. See again *PFG* ch. 15.

Chapter Five

'THE OLD IS BETTER'?

1. Introduction

In a characteristically cryptic saying, Jesus declares that people who taste the old wine first and then the new wine afterwards will declare that 'the old is better'.[1] Robert Gundry has used that phrase as the title of a collection of essays, putting together a lifetime of scholarly protest against new fashions, including perhaps predictably the new perspective on Paul.[2] If it is difficult to describe such a pluriform phenomenon as the new perspective, it is even harder to describe, in short compass, the multiple negative reactions to it. But something must be said at the present point. I here choose a small sample out of the enormous flood of related literature.[3]

For some, it seems, saying that a writer on Paul belongs to the new perspective is one of the harshest criticisms available. Even without consulting websites and, even worse, blogsites (Paul would have had sharp words for those who cloak themselves with anonymity and fire off intemperate messages into the void of cyberspace from the privacy of their own computers), rumour has reached me that entire denominations have passed solemn resolutions banning new perspective readings of Paul, and refusing to ordain candidates unless they forswear them.[4] That is only the tip of the iceberg,

[1] Lk. 5.39. Some mss. have simply 'good', but the intention is still to compare the two.

[2] See Gundry 2005; the essay on the new perspective (originally published in 1985) is ch. 11.

[3] A good recent bibliography is provided by Bird 2007, 196–211, with references to websites where information is regularly updated. This includes recent works defending the new perspective against its critics. To footnote more than a tiny sample of all this would be unthinkable. Further interaction with writers of all sorts is of course found in *PFG*.

[4] Indeed, I once received a solemn letter from the Synodical Secretary of a small denomination based in California informing me that my work was heretical and that I should repent and publish a retractation to prevent the faithful from being led astray. Did they, I wonder, send similar letters to Ed Sanders, Jimmy Dunn, Richard Hays, Francis Watson, Terry Donaldson, Bruce Longenecker and at least half a dozen others? If not, why not? Cf. Bird 2007, 183–93, a serious engagement with my work and a warning against making rejection of it a touchstone of 'Reformed' orthodoxy.

though, and there are all kinds of less intemperate, often simply puzzled, views being expressed in both scholarly and popular literature. I have responded elsewhere, in a somewhat different genre, to certain attacks on my views in particular. But some account, however brief, cannot be omitted here.[5]

2. The Reaction

There was a temporary lull after Sanders's original work. Perhaps it was the sort of pause that corresponds to the moment between stubbing your toe really badly and the onset of the pain that you know will come within a few moments. Then, in the middle 1980s, reaction began to set in.

Robert Gundry's measured article, mentioned above, concentrated on 'synergism', a doctrine in which God 'does' some bits of the saving process, and humans 'do' other bits, resulting in a 'doing-together' or 'working-together', which is what the Greek '*syn-erg*' means. Judaism taught this, Gundry declared, but Paul rejected it; that was the real difference.[6] Another early reaction to Sanders came from Frank Thielman, who lodged a careful and shrewd protest against Sanders's idea about 'plight and solution', following this up with a more systematic appraisal of the question of 'Paul and the law'.[7] These were the early signs of serious dissent against Sanders's proposals.

Then, in the early 1990s, there was rather more frantic activity at both scholarly and popular levels. The battlefield might have appeared lost (certainly many new perspective advocates assumed they had swept the board), but evidence now began to emerge of a powerful, indeed often angry, reaction, of a courage never to submit or yield. Some, indeed, were content to write the whole new perspective phenomenon off as another example of 'liberal' theology, assuming that anyone who questioned the classic (essentially Lutheran) understanding of justification probably did not believe in the atoning death of Jesus, or several other doctrines regularly associated with justification. Such high words had semblance of worth, not substance, though they served no doubt to raise fainting courage and dispel fear among the faithful. Whole churches and movements have, as I indicated, made rejection of the new perspective a touchstone of orthodoxy, thereby creating a private sphere where they could reign secure, untouched by the ravages of historical or even exegetical research or debate. But others went into battle, producing since the early 1990s a veritable deluge of monographs, articles,

[5] Fuller accounts in e.g. Westerholm 2004; Bird 2007; Zetterholm 2009. For my earlier rebuttal of some charges see Wright 2009 [*Justification*].

[6] Gundry, as above. The debate between 'synergism' and 'monergism' was important in the sixteenth and seventeenth centuries; it seems strange to me to try to use that either/or as a tool for understanding first-century texts. See further Hagner 2001, 86f.

[7] Thielman 1989; 1994. See too his more recent *Theology of the New Testament* (Thielman 2005), esp. 438–79.

commentaries and collections of essays, coming at the issues from this angle and that, squabbling over small details of exegesis and huge questions of providence, foreknowledge, will and fate, righteousness and judgment, glory and shame.[8]

Part of this new floodtide has come from the school of D. A. Carson and his pupils and associates, with varying degrees of energy and accuracy.[9] Learned works from scholars such as Simon Gathercole and Andrew Das have mounted detailed exegetical arguments to push back at elements within the new perspective, Das even offering a 'newer' perspective which he claims solves outstanding problems.[10] Seyoon Kim has returned to the question of the way in which Paul's 'conversion' shaped his whole theology, and has defended his view, with its basically traditional justification-theology, against Dunn in particular.[11] The great, and much missed, Martin Hengel produced several monographs on Paul, though perhaps not the one that would have drawn his massive learning together in the way we had hoped; regularly, towards the end of his many volumes, he offered trenchant restatements of a solid Lutheran faith, warding off the new perspective rather than engaging with it.[12] Other German writers have begun in greater numbers to take on board the fact that something strange has been happening in America, and have begun to engage with it rather than simply reaffirming their traditional position.[13] Meanwhile, others have responded to this increasing flood, restating and clarifying a variety of positions within the new perspective.[14] The discussion often seems to get lost in wandering mazes of footnotes and multiple interlocking references, with writers who agree with one another referring eagerly to each other's work as though that strengthened their argument, when often – in many quarters of the battlefield, not only one! – the effect is more like Austin Farrer's simile about a line of tipsy revellers linking arms on the way home from the pub. Each is supported by those on either side, but the whole line can drift this way and that without encountering any solid object.[15]

The solid objects do exist, however, and it may be as well to name them. They consist, obviously, of two large and unwieldy entities: first-century Judaism and the letters of Paul. Where then does the issue lie? Rather than

[8] A very small selection, almost at random: Piper 2002; 2007 (to which I responded in Wright 2009 [*Justification*]); Waters 2004; Vickers 2006. There is a sub-debate continuing between those for whom the 'imputation of Christ's righteousness' is the centre of the biblical view of justification (as in the Westminster Confession) and those who hold to some variety of a Lutheran position in which 'imputed righteousness' is not seen as a necessary element: see e.g. Seifrid 2004.

[9] See esp. Carson, O'Brien and Seifrid 2001–4; Seifrid 1992; 2000a; 2000c.

[10] See Gathercole 2002; 2006; Das 2001; 2003.

[11] Kim 2002.

[12] See esp. Hengel 1983; 1991; Hengel and Schwemer 1997.

[13] The need for a survey of these reactions is now met, for the moment at least, by Gathercole 2013. Earlier German reaction was coloured by the fact that Sanders, especially in his work on Jesus, had severely attacked Joachim Jeremias, whom many Germans held in high esteem and affection.

[14] e.g. Garlington 2004; above all, of course Dunn (see the previous chapter).

[15] Farrer's original simile was describing the way in which scholars dated the New Testament documents: see Farrer 1964, 37.

getting into detailed discussion at this stage, thereby repeating things that have been said elsewhere, I propose to name the key areas of debate and point out some features of them which are not always noted. I will then look more specifically at two representatives of the best kind of scholarly responses, one from Germany and one from America. That will at least put down some markers as the conversations continue.

First, there is the description and evaluation of first-century Judaism. From one point of view, the renewed stress on God's grace in election and covenant has been widely welcomed and was no doubt long overdue.[16] There is no doubt, at this distance, that Sanders greatly oversimplified and indeed oversystematized the massive and complicated Jewish evidence. One of the first serious challenges to his work came at this level, from the learned, careful, and late lamented Friedrich Avemarie. He insisted that in the early rabbis we find two quite different principles articulated, without any attempt at harmonization. Sometimes we are told that everything depends on God and his electing grace towards Israel; at other times we are told that it depends on human effort and obedience. The rabbis do not seem bothered by what appears to the modern western mind as a contradiction, or at least a paradox.[17] Then there appeared the substantial volume of essays from the American/Australian counterattack: but it has often been observed that many of the contributors ended up giving qualified support to Sanders, despite what the editor tried to say in his summing up.[18] But that volume highlighted the issue which has become one of the main topics of post-new-perspective conversation about Judaism, namely the relationship between divine sovereignty and human responsibility.[19] How do 'grace' and 'works' relate to one another, from text to text and passage to passage? It has not been difficult for people to argue that many Jews of the period really did believe that solid 'obedience', perhaps even to the 'whole law', was required.

But 'required' – for what? Insofar as the rabbis answer this question, the answer they give is 'the age to come'. Can we take this as meaning 'salvation' in a sense which would correspond to the meanings of that word in western Christianity over the last few hundred years (that is, a meaning to do with 'going to heaven')? Many voices have warned against this kind of equation, but much of the debate has simply assumed it.[20] Sanders himself, indeed, seems more or less to have assumed it as well. But the western meanings of 'salvation' are in some respects quite different from the aspirations and hopes of first-century Jews. As I have argued elsewhere, there is all the difference in the world between the hope to 'go to heaven when you die' and the hope for resurrection within new heavens and new earth, a resurrection

[16] Though Hagner 2001, 84 goes too far in saying that 'few will want to deny that what is found in the Old Testament ... is a religion of grace rather than works-righteousness'. Sadly, quite a lot of people do indeed want to deny that.

[17] See Avemarie 1996.

[18] Carson 2001.

[19] See the volume of essays edited by Barclay and Gathercole (2006).

[20] e.g. Loewe 1981.

and renewal which would retain significant continuity with the present world and its struggles.[21] And it was the latter scenario, rather than the former, that characterized at least the kind of Judaism to which Saul of Tarsus gave his passionate allegiance.

This in turn points to another feature which is usually ignored. The question of final hope, whether we call it 'the age to come' or 'salvation' or whatever, was intimately and essentially connected with the whole *story of Israel*: when would this great story of the creator and the covenant, Israel's God as the world's creator, responsible for bringing it to judgment and for rescuing the righteous – when and how would *this* story come to its conclusion? If one had said to a Pharisee in the early first century (I think this would apply to many other types of first-century Jew as well, but let's stay with the Pharisees), 'When you die, God will provide a heavenly dwelling for you in his nearer presence, and you can forget all these troubles Israel is presently suffering', he might well have responded, 'Thank you; that sounds very nice for me; but are you implying that God will abandon Israel to whatever fate may come? Are you saying that Israel's destiny doesn't matter? Isn't God the creator, and hasn't he promised that there will come a day when the fields and the rivers will sing for joy because he is coming to set everything right, and to vindicate us as his people? How can I be happy going off to a distant spiritual bliss if God hasn't saved his people? How do I know which "God" we are talking about any longer, if he doesn't do this?' Gnosticism had not been invented in the early first century. But, if it had been, such a Pharisee might well have accused such an interlocutor of teaching it.

This relates directly to the question of 'grace and works', and the associated questions about providence, foreknowledge, will and fate and all the other issues around which people then and now have wandered, getting lost in philosophical mazes. When Josephus described the different 'parties' within Judaism, he *translated their particular beliefs into terms of 'fate and free will'*, because that was language that his Roman audience might be expected to understand. But it has not been difficult to translate what he said back into the real life of first-century Palestine. The Sadducees believed in 'free will': well, of course, they were the ruling party, they could make decisions and put them into effect. The Essenes, says Josephus, believed that everything was determined: well, naturally, they were without power, they could only sit in the desert and wait for God to do whatever God was going to do (though some of them may have had contingency plans to change that policy, and with it the 'philosophy', should God delay too long). The Pharisees believed in a mixture of fate and free will: well, they would, wouldn't they, since they believed *both* that God had made promises and would keep them *and* that part of the way God would keep those promises would be through Israel (and particularly the Pharisees themselves) being obedient, indeed super-obedient. The 'zealous' revolutionaries, in their various submovements, lived on the 'free will' edge of strict Pharisaism: it was not

[21] See Wright 2008 [*Surprised by Hope*].

enough to wait for God to act, since the way he would act might be precisely through the violent acts of the faithful as they tried to emulate Phinehas or Elijah.[22] Once we think in terms of the actual social and political situation, and the actual hope for God to do a new thing *within the great story of covenant and creation*, the philosophical abstractions come to life.[23] And the abstract post-new-perspective discussions about 'grace and works', and indeed about 'salvation' itself, look very, very different.

All this means, I think, that Sanders actually gave several hostages to fortune in describing Judaism in the way he did, hostages of which fortune has been making use from time to time. I think, in fact, that instead of *covenantal nomism* he might have done better to think in terms of *covenantal narrative*. Or, to be clear (since I am not replacing 'nomism' with 'narrative', but bringing out the full flavour of the narratival element which was already there), what we are dealing with is *covenantal/nomistic narrative*. Here is the point: it is actually the *narrative* to which the anti-new-perspective camp are most deeply objecting. I do not mean that (in their view) they are being offered the wrong narrative, and want to get back to the right one. They are being offered *a narrative*, an historical story whose hope of 'salvation' lies not in a flight *from* history but in a great convulsive change *within* history, a transformation in which there will be continuity with the present as well as discontinuity. That is what they do not want at any price. Until we recognize, name, and flesh out the *narrative* of the covenant, as it was inhabited by many first-century Jews and in particular the Pharisees, all the debate about grace and works, about the exact balance between what God does and what humans do, about how all this contributes to 'salvation', will simply go round and round in circles, ending up with a lot more footnotes and a lot less illumination.[24]

Consider the case of *4 Ezra*, which Sanders, with his usual disarming candour, admitted did not fit into his scheme.[25] Why did it not fit? Because the writer, seeing chaos and destruction all around in the wake of the awful events of AD 70, could no longer envisage that God would do something for 'all Israel', with only the real renegades being left out. The historical cataclysm produced a new perspective of its own: Israel's God would now have to start from scratch. The only thing that would make any sense in this appalling new world, the only thing that could bring back together anything that might be called 'Israel' at all, would seem to be a sharp and complete observance of Torah. The author was not asking an abstract question about how people 'got saved' in some modern western sense. He was asking how on earth, granted the recent disasters, Israel's God would – could! – be faithful to the covenant, what it would look like when he acted (as surely he would), and, granted all that had now been learned about the depth of evil

[22] On 'zeal' see e.g. *NTPG* 176–81, 191f.

[23] See Jos. *War* 2.162–5; *Ant.* 18.13–18.

[24] See esp. *PFG* ch. 7.

[25] Sanders 1977, 409–18.

within Israel itself, who among Israel might share in the blessings of the covenant when that great day finally arrived.[26]

But already I have gone way beyond what Sanders said – and certainly way beyond what his critics have said, about this and about other texts. It isn't a matter of merely coming to yet another text in the abstract and saying, Well, what does this writer say about grace and works, about 'getting in' and 'staying in'? – assuming that, despite all the signals to the contrary, *we know ahead of time that all these second-Temple texts were 'really' talking about 'how to go to heaven when you die'*, and were addressing this question in terms of a grace/works antithesis, or indeed of a 'forensic' or 'apocalyptic' antithesis (see Part II below). That pays no attention to what the texts are actually talking about.

Or consider that other now famous text, 4QMMT. The main chapter on Qumran in the volume edited by Donald Carson chose to focus on the material from the Community Rule (1QS). This was understandable, since that scroll contains some remarkable material which, in the dark with the light behind it, might deceive a casual observer into supposing it was part of a lost letter of Paul, full of sorrow because of the weakness of the flesh but full of gratitude for a justification which comes by the righteousness of God and which lasts for ever.[27] But MMT, despite numerous scholars who have brought their own questions to it and taken away commensurate answers, is not talking about how people can 'be saved' in anything remotely like the western sense that has obtained in catholic and protestant thought for the last half-millennium. It is talking about what will happen 'at the end of days', as in the prophecy of Deuteronomy 30, and how the performance of various specialized Torah-interpretations in the present time will enable one to know, even now, who the 'righteous' are, ahead of that final moment.[28]

The point, in other words, is that simply saying 'grace or works?' merely reinscribes the old pattern of analysis from which Sanders was trying to free the discipline. As I have said, I do not think he was completely successful, because he substituted an alternative 'pattern', a 'pattern of religion', as his model, rather than looking beyond it to the essential underlying Jewish *narrative*. And when we look at the narrative, which is of its very nature historical, even when it points to the final apocalyptic denouement ('the end of days', which is actually an allusion to Deuteronomy[29]), we find the questions reframed in such a different way that much of the recent post-Sanders discussion of Judaism appears simply beside the point.

[26] See e.g. Longenecker 1991.

[27] i.e. 1QS 11. In this article (Bockmuehl 2001), Bockmuehl says that Sanders is basically right, but that now, with much greater textual material available, we can see that the Qumran community shows evidence of unresolved tensions and various developments over a considerable period of time. It was left to Roland Deines, in the same vol., to look more closely at 4QMMT (Deines 2001, 461–74).

[28] This undermines the comments of e.g. Das 2009, 105f. On MMT see Wright 2013b (*Perspectives*), ch. 21.

[29] 31.29 cf. 32.20; see the full discussion in *PFG* ch. 2.

What we have seen, in fact, is people projecting onto the post-Sanders debate issues *which were already puzzles within Protestantism itself*, never mind within western Christianity itself. The question of how exactly we should relate 'grace' and 'works' has been a bone of contention between Calvinists and Arminians, between Lutherans and Reformed, between Wesleyans and Presbyterians, and so on in ever-diminishing groups, defining themselves this way and that, and insisting that only their way is true to scripture and pastorally or evangelistically effective. We all know (so we say) that the gospel is about the free grace of God. No-one is going to deny that. We all know (so we say) that this doesn't mean that God doesn't care how you behave between the time you first believe and the time you die. No-one is going to deny that, not even the most laissez-faire liberal; they have ways of reinventing quite sharp ethics. Where we have difficulty is describing how those two, God's grace and human behaviour, relate together. Well, of course we do: because in today's western tradition the philosophical framework we assume is basically that of Kant, who split the 'indicative' so sharply from the 'imperative' that we struggle to see any way across the great divide, a gulf as deep, and dug by some of the same workmen, as Lessing's 'ugly ditch'. But who says it has to be like that? Who says people saw things like that in the first century? Are we not in danger of massive philosophical or theological anachronisms, which amount to a post-Enlightenment (to say nothing of post-Reformation) cultural imperialism?

In particular, the now regular 'proof' that first-century Jews were after all 'legalistic' simply misses the point (Look! All those detailed regulations! And you really did have to keep them!). It misses *Sanders's* point. Sanders never denied that rabbinic Judaism offers a kind of casuistry. His point was that it was always contained, by an implication so deep as not to need stating, within the framework of covenant, of election. That was what was at stake. But here we run up against two further key points: first, a problem with the analysis, then, an anachronism in response.

First, a problem with the analysis. Sanders demonstrated massively that, within that covenantal framework, the rabbis and other second-Temple Jews believed firmly in some sort of 'nomism': keep the law, and you'll 'stay in' the covenant. When the 'final judgment' occurs, these 'works' will matter. No disagreement there.[30] Sanders also pointed out, in a very brief section, that to all intents and appearances Paul fully agreed. When he talks about the final judgment, he always envisages that 'works' will matter. But what Sanders never did was to track the narrative which said, 'At some point God is going to *renew* that covenant, and then there will be a *different kind of* nomism.' That is how many second-Temple Jews read Deuteronomy 30. And when Sanders set Paul's supposed 'pattern of religion' alongside that of Judaism, he never factored in the possibility that Paul might have

[30] Das's insistence (part of his 'newer perspective') that most forms of Judaism demanded *complete* obedience misses the point. Of course nobody was going to say 'all right, just keep one-third of the commandments, if that's all you can manage'. But Jewish thinkers developed, out of scripture itself, regular means for dealing with failure.

been saying 'Yes: and that covenant renewal is exactly what has happened in the Messiah; so now we are living within the new mode, with a renewal more radical than anyone ever thought.' That, actually, is what MMT was saying as well, *mutatis mutandis*.

In other words, the problem of analysing 'patterns of religion', in which 'eschatology' was simply one belief among many, has come home to roost. Better to do it the other way round. First, varieties of 'Judaism' in which the hope for the covenant God to act creates the context for covenantal and narratival 'nomism'. Second, a Pauline framework in which that hope has been realized in Messiah and spirit, and has generated a new, second-order version of the same hope, in which a radically different 'pattern' will fit.[31]

This problem of analysis leads to a major problem of anachronism, which happens when people get worried about 'judgment according to works', and think that, when they have proved that many first-century Jews seem to have believed that they 'had to do works' of some sort, this constitutes evidence of 'synergism', which we know by definition (because Paul was a good Protestant) that the apostle did not accept. We leave aside the fact that the one relevant occurrence of the word *synergeō* in Paul is entirely positive. Immediately after the famous sentence about God making the Messiah sin for us, and our 'becoming the righteousness of God' in him, he declares, 'So, as we *work together [synergountes] with God*, we appeal to you in particular: when you accept God's grace, don't let it go to waste!'[32] That might just be a trick of the concordance. There is no reason to suppose that the relatively modern term 'synergism' should correspond to the Greek word as Paul occasionally used it. The point is wider: the problem of 'how our behaviour corresponds to the final judgment' is already an *intra-protestant* dispute, which has been seized on by the guardians of the protestant traditions and projected back, via the post-Sanders debate, onto the first century.

In other words: there is already a long tradition of theological argument, in western theology before and since the Reformation, about how the 'good works' enjoined upon believers actually relate to the 'final judgment'. There are, no doubt, a thousand ways of saying what has to be said on this topic, and most people who have addressed it have done their best (not always to one another's satisfaction, of course) to say *both* that we are under obligation to live in a particular way *and* that our final salvation remains a gift of God's grace.[33] But to suppose that if we discover the rabbis (or anybody

[31] This is the case I have argued, from various angles, in *PFG*.

[32] 2 Cor. 6.1 (see *PFG* 955f.). The other uses of the verb are Rom. 8.28 (where the subject is either 'God' or 'the spirit' or 'all things': see Wright 2002 [*Romans*], 600f.); and 1 Cor. 16.16 (where it refers to people 'working together' with one another).

[33] See Moule 1967: 'it is not that grace abolishes law, but that dependence on grace, instead of the attitude of legalism, is the only way to fulfil God's law. There is obligation, but it is to grace, not law' (394); one is not 'released from obligation by ceasing to be under law' (396). By itself, 'justification' might mean the removal of 'all logical grounds from obligation'; but since justification is *by faith*, which is intimately entwined with being 'in Christ', this provides a fresh, solid ground for 'obligation' without the slightest hint of 'legalism' (400f.). Thus Paul retains the belief in judgment according to works (403), but those works are of an utterly different character. For neither the first nor the last time, one could wish that more attention had been paid to Moule.

else) talking about proper moral behaviour as a key factor in the coming judgment we have thereby unmasked Sanders's proposal about the rabbis' 'nomism' being 'covenantal', i.e. taking place within a framework of grace, is to make a massive double category mistake. (a) Just because people had to exercise moral effort to keep Torah, that didn't mean there was therefore no longer any overarching 'covenantal' framework. (b) You cannot assume that our relatively modern western categories for getting at the theological point about framework and obligation can be straightforwardly projected back, putting Judaism in the 'synergism' camp and Paul in the 'non-synergism' camp. Unless we learn to think within first-century categories rather than mediaeval ones, we will never understand either the ancient Jewish world or Paul.

What is missing from all these discussions is Paul's strong, clear teaching at exactly this point *both* on the new status of the believer as having died and risen with Jesus Christ *and* on the new gift of God to the believer, the gift which Paul calls the holy spirit. It is astonishing to see how much of the debate has been conducted without the help of these two categories, as though the 'doctrine of justification' had to proceed with minimalist theological tools in order to be pure. You might as well try to play Wagner on a tin whistle.

When it comes to the analysis of Paul himself, attention has focused, in the anti-new-perspective camp, on the meaning and place of justification. It is important to note that this was by no means the only or the most appropriate reaction to Sanders. Why not discuss his view of 'being-in-Christ', which he argued was so much more central? Why not look at the way he analysed various other aspects of Paul's thought, such as the occasional mention of repentance, or his treatment of atonement? Why not discuss Sanders's intriguing mentions of 'truth'? The answer, of course, is that the word 'justification' at once conveys, within many parts (not all) of today's protestant world, an entire worldview, a way of being Christian, a way indeed of being human, a deep-rooted, wide-ranging and enormously powerful construct with not only theological but also ecclesiological meanings (*our* churches believe in the *proper* doctrine of justification, and that's why we're so faithful/fruitful/happy in our faith) and even, dare we say, sociological and political meanings (to be 'conservative' on 'justification', it is sometimes observed, has sometimes accompanied a 'conservative' position in today's American 'culture wars', and their ecclesiological spin-offs). That is why some (not all) of the anti-new-perspective brigade will stop at nothing to vilify, malign, slander and misrepresent anyone who has anything to do with the post-Sanders way of reading Paul. Any mud will do: you can suggest that some of us do not believe in Jesus' atoning death; you can insinuate that we have no gospel to preach, nothing to say to a dying 'enquirer'; you can declare that we are false shepherds leading the flock astray; you can accuse us of crypto-Catholicism or quasi-Platonic moral Idealism; anything rather than pay attention to the actual arguments, the reframing of debates, and above all to the texts themselves.[34]

What, after all, is the problem with a post-Sanders view of justification? The problem is that for a large swathe of would-be post-Reformation Christianity, particularly in North America, the word 'justification', or at least the term 'justification by grace through faith', has come to denote everything one really wants to say about the point of being a Christian, from initial conversion to final salvation. That is why both the question of Paul's own conversion (*was* it a 'conversion', or simply a 'call', or what? and how did whatever-it-was affect and shape Paul's theology?) and the question of final judgment (what role, if any, will 'works' play?) have both loomed so large. Despite the theological niceties of separating out an *ordo salutis* which might include some or all of predestination, election, foreknowledge, conversion, regeneration, justification, sanctification, glorification and salvation,[35] for a great many Christians in the western protestant tradition the word 'justification', and the phrase 'justification by faith' and/or 'by grace' has expanded so as to become a shorthand which can include 'conversion' on the one hand (since the initial 'coming to faith' is clearly, within the scheme, the moment when one is thereby 'justified') and 'salvation' on the other (partly because Paul can use the word 'save' in the *past* tense (e.g. Romans 8.24) as well as the future).[36] So strong has this slippage become that one often hears in popular discourse, and one sometimes even reads in supposedly scholarly work, the phrase 'salvation by faith'. The closest thing to that in the Pauline corpus is Ephesians 2.8, 'you have been saved by grace, through faith', which is not quite the same. Moreover, because of a particular reading of Romans 1.16–17, and of various passages in Galatians, it has been assumed that 'justification' simply *is* 'the Pauline gospel': that 'the good news' is, in effect, 'you don't have to do good works; all you have to do is to believe'.

Here is the point. Because of the way in which 'justification' has carried this large set of implications around with it, including a theology and/or experience of conversion; because of the way in which debates about 'justification' have regularly been covert debates about the Westminster Confession's notion of a 'covenant of works' in which 'righteousness' basically means 'goodness' or even 'merit', with the only question being how the human lack of this 'righteousness' can be made good; because of the sense that all this relates directly and immediately to the offer of salvation, and that it actually overlaps to the point of identification with Paul's 'gospel' – *it has been assumed that when Sanders, Dunn and others speak of 'justification' as playing a subordinate role in Paul's thought they mean that conversion, salvation and 'the gospel' are of less relevance than was once supposed*, that

[34] All of these things have been said about the present author. Some critics have insinuated even worse ideological devilries.

[35] cp. Paul's list in Rom. 8.28–30. On the whole notion of *ordo salutis* see *PFG* 959f.

[36] e.g. Rom. 8.24: 'we were saved (*esōthēmen*) in hope.' The 'in hope' qualifies, but does not nullify, the 'were saved'.

sin and forgiveness are not particularly important, and that new-perspective scholars can therefore be assumed to believe that Paul was interested merely in a sociological or ecclesiological struggle, to enable non-Jews to become full members of the *ekklēsia* without having to be circumcised, and not in the life-and-death issues of human salvation and the personal conversion and spirituality which is assumed to accompany it. Hence the mud-slinging. In the remarkable words of Stephen Westerholm, to which we shall return:

> The issue that divides the 'Lutheran' Paul from his contemporary critics is whether 'Justification by faith, not by works of the law' means 'sinners find God's approval by grace, through faith, not by anything they do,' or whether its thrust is that 'Gentiles are included in the people of God by faith without the bother of becoming Jews.' In the one case justification is directly connected to the Pauline gospel summed up in the words 'Christ died for our sins' (1 Cor. 15:3) and 'Be reconciled to God' (2 Cor. 5:20). It promises deliverance from sin. In the other case the good news of justification is found in the best-of-both-worlds scenario that it paints for Gentiles: 'You people want to become Jews, but you are afraid of the knife. Have I got an offer for you!' It promises deliverance from a good deal of hassle ... The former is the position of the 'Lutheran' Paul and the latter isn't.[37]

Observe what has happened here. Westerholm, speaking at this point I believe for more or less the whole anti-new-perspective group, first sums up accurately what the new perspective has been saying (following Wrede, Schweitzer and many others): that the Pauline language of 'justification' relates directly to the question of the inclusion of gentiles without circumcision. But then the leap is made: for the 'Lutheran' Paul,[38] 'justification' is 'directly connected to the gospel', the message of forgiveness and reconciliation to God. And the corollary follows directly, hard as nails behind the jokey caricature: the new perspective *doesn't care about forgiveness of sins, reconciliation to God, and salvation*, whereas of course the 'Lutheran' view does. The new perspective has sold its soul, its gospel, its salvation, for a mess of opportunistic sociology.[39]

The rhetoric, like a badly aimed blunderbuss, is fired into thin air. Where does Sanders say that Paul is not interested in salvation, that it does not remain hugely important for him? Where does Dunn say that it is no longer important for sinners to be reconciled to God? Where do I, or Richard Hays, or any of the other new perspective representatives who might be wheeled out at this point, suggest that 'deliverance from sin' has ceased to

[37] Westerholm 2004, 257f.

[38] By which Westerholm, for all his teasing of Seifrid on this point (221), does indeed mean 'Lutheran' rather than 'Reformed'.

[39] Somewhere along the line, too, this has led to the strange view that the new perspective teaches that only gentiles, not Jews, need to be justified by faith (e.g. Hagner 2001, 77). There may be some who have suggested that (perhaps in connection with the kind of two-covenant theory which some have developed out of NP materials?), but I have not met that view in NP writers, only in their muddled critics. Paul is quite clear (Rom. 3.29f.). Similarly, Hagner 80 suggests that for the NP Paul was concerned with the Jew–gentile question *rather than* 'any universal human problem'. This is simply a misunderstanding. All main NP authors are quite clear that Paul was very concerned about the 'universal human problem'. They just do not think Paul's way of addressing that problem had 'justification' as its primary focus.

be of major importance, and 'deliverance from hassle' has taken its place? (Not that 'hassle' has gone: as any reader of Paul knows, he emphasizes to gentile Christians as much as to anyone else that plenty of 'hassle' awaited them. And, whatever other reasons he gives for not requiring circumcision of gentile converts, deliverance from hassle is never mentioned, either by Paul or by, so far as I know, his new perspective interpreters.)

What the new perspective interpretation *does* say, however, but which so many of its critics have failed to hear, is this: salvation remains enormously important; conversion remains enormously important; 'the gospel' remains central, powerful, vital; *but the language of 'justification' is not the key term used by Paul to convey all this.* It isn't that the new perspective has downgraded conversion, salvation, and the gospel, or indeed 'justification' itself. It has simply explored, in one exegetical context after another, the job which 'justification' language in fact performs in Paul's writings.[40]

What the new perspective has said, though you might never know this from reading many books on the subject, is that the triple reality of conversion, salvation and 'the gospel' is conveyed by Paul not primarily through the language of justification, though that is indeed closely aligned with this reality, but through the language about Jesus Christ; more exactly, about Jesus as the crucified and risen Messiah, and about what is true of humans who come to be 'in him'. If only Romans had been read as it stands, i.e. with 1.3–4 constituting Paul's initial statement of his 'gospel', and 1.16–17 constituting the thematic statement of what the gospel then means in practice, this would already have been clear. Instead of this, 1.3–4 has been treated as a largely irrelevant pre-Pauline formula (because 'we all know' that Paul wasn't interested in Jesus' Davidic Messiahship); and 1.16–17, despite Paul's explicit wording, has been made to stand as a statement of 'the gospel'. No: the gospel message, for Paul, is the message about Jesus the Messiah. All that follows in terms of the revelation of God's righteousness means what it means in that context.

Sanders, as we saw, is clear about the centrality of Jesus Christ for Paul. Here he is exactly in line with Schweitzer, though without the use of 'mysticism' as a category. Conversion means coming to be 'in Christ'. Salvation is what people are given, and then guaranteed, 'in Christ'. The gospel is the message about Jesus Christ and him crucified, and the summons to that believing obedience which characterizes those who are 'in him'. Remarkably, one writer after another opposing the new perspective has managed to write as though the real issue were the fine-tuning of the grace/works balance in the life, the moral effort, the psychology almost, of Jewish covenantal nomism on the one hand and of Paul and his churches on the other. No. The real issue is whether the terminology of 'justification' is Paul's way of summing up conversion/salvation/gospel, or whether in fact his preferred and primary way of talking about conversion/salvation/gospel is the whole universe of discourse drawn together by 'being in Christ'.

[40] This is a major theme in *PFG*; see e.g. 912–1032.

The irony is that at this point Sanders and others, including the present writer, are standing firmly in line (via Albert Schweitzer) with Calvin himself, though it is from would-be Calvinists that some of the sharpest criticism has come. This point should be well known. Michael Bird quotes two of the most venerable Reformed thinkers putting it well:

> Richard Gaffin remarks: 'Not justification by faith but union with the resurrected Christ by faith (of which union, to be sure, the justifying aspect stands out most prominently) is the central motif of Paul's applied soteriology.' John Murray is similar: 'Union with Christ is really the central truth of the whole doctrine of salvation not only in its application but also in its once-for-all accomplishment in the finished work of Christ.'[41]

In my larger work I have tried to show that, precisely from within the new perspective, and despite those who have continued to subsume one aspect under the other in such a way as to reinterpret the 'lesser' one almost out of existence, it is not only possible but essential to integrate the two. This integration can in fact be much tighter than either the Reformed tradition, or Sanders, or even Dunn and Hays, quoted above, have imagined.

Notice what happens once this point is grasped. The five other major bones of contention all look very different.

First, there is no question as to whether the death of Jesus was, for Paul, the basis upon which everything else rested. Of course it was. There remains, to be sure, plenty of room for debate about how Paul sees that death functioning theologically, but that can be worked through.[42]

Second, the conversion of Paul is obviously important (not only in Acts, but also e.g. in Galatians 1, and perhaps elsewhere), but it is not all-important either for Paul himself or in recent debates.[43] Certainly it is not the case that almost everyone who writes about Paul foregrounds it, as has recently been claimed.[44] The question of the precise relationship between (a) what Paul saw on the road to Damascus and how his belief and thinking changed as a result of that, on the one hand, and (b) what he came to articulate as his mature theology, on the other hand, remains an interesting topic, but it does not relate directly to the new perspective. The matter of how we describe it ('call'? 'conversion'? or both, or something more?) naturally relates to some outworkings of the new perspective, particularly for those who have followed Krister Stendahl. But for many of us, such as Sanders and myself, it has not been a major issue. What mattered to Paul, for himself and for anybody else whether Jew or gentile, was coming to be 'in Christ'.[45] How that happened, whether in a blinding flash of light or a slow turning

[41] Bird 2007, 86f., n. 127, referring to Gaffin 1978, 132, Murray 1955, 201.

[42] Highlighting 'participation', as we shall see, does not at all entail discarding 'vicarious' meanings for Jesus' death: 'representation' and 'substitution', despite popular opinion to the contrary, are not mutually exclusive, but rather mutually determinative. On this see now Williams 2015.

[43] On Paul's Damascus Road experience see *PFG* 1417–26.

[44] Eisenbaum 2009.

[45] Again: Hagner 77 suggests that according to the NP a Jew does not need fresh justification, since there wasn't anything wrong with Judaism. So far as I know no NP author has ever said this. Such a view might perhaps be associated with Gager 1983, or Gaston 1987.

towards the source of light itself, did not matter; if part of the reaction to the new perspective has been a fear lest 'conversion' be downgraded, all I would appeal for is that it be understood in its myriad different forms. Coming to be 'in Christ' mattered because, in the words of Donald Hagner, who though a critic of the new perspective is here expressing a view I think most new perspective writers would agree with:

> Christianity, for Paul, is nothing other than the faith of his ancestors come to an eschatological phase of fulfillment before the final consummation ... Paul did not think of a second religion for the Gentiles. He was calling them to his fulfilled Judaism, nothing other than the faith of Israel beginning with Abraham.[46]

The objection might then come up, of course, as to what this says about the continuing 'Israel according to the flesh'. Well, yes; it came up for Paul, and it comes up for any interpreter who wants to do justice to his thought. I have written about this in chapter 11 of *Paul and the Faithfulness of God*. But in text after text Paul says just what Hagner has said here; and this is substantially what Sanders, Dunn and I have said in our various ways.[47]

Third, the question of 'solution and plight' can be addressed in a fresh way. I am largely with Thielman on this: a strict line of thought from 'solution to plight' is not necessarily implied within the basic new perspective. Actually there was, as I have stressed, plenty of 'plight' in first-century Judaism, though not necessarily the sort of personal *angst* which, via Luther and Augustine, has often been projected back onto Paul.[48] But the revelation of Jesus Christ on the road to Damascus presented Paul with an 'answer' or a 'solution', not just to the 'plight' of which he was aware, but to depths and dimensions of 'plight' never hitherto glimpsed. This is a very important turn in his thought, and in the argument of Romans in particular, and I have addressed it elsewhere with good hope of a 'solution' to this particular academic 'plight'.[49]

Fourth, there should no longer be any problem about 'imputation'. The idea of 'imputed *righteousness*', whether of God himself or, as in some constructs, of Christ himself, is not the only way of addressing the question. The idea of 'imputed righteousness' was in any case a latecomer to Reformation theology. Plenty of the anti-new-perspective writers themselves make nothing of it. Some who do discuss it declare that it is not a Pauline idea at all.[50] But its place is taken by something even better, and far more explicitly Pauline: the imputed *death and resurrection of the Messiah*, as in

[46] Hagner 93f.

[47] Hagner 99f., however, then seems to take back with the other hand what he has just said: 'Paul's Christianity includes a break with Judaism', he declares, and concludes that this 'amounts to a denial of the new perspective at its very center'. The NP at its centre never said there was no 'break with Judaism'; what is at stake is an analysis of what that break consisted of; and why and how, and indeed when and perhaps where, it took place.

[48] Despite Gundry 2005, ch. 13, on Paul's moral frustration before his conversion.

[49] See *PFG* 737–73.

[50] Westerholm, so far as I can see, says nothing about it, a remarkable enough thing in a long survey of current debate. Gundry 2005, ch. 12 argues against 'imputed righteousness'.

Romans 6 and Philippians 3. That does all the theological work that the Reformed doctrine of 'imputation' was trying to do, and more besides. It has the merit of being firmly present, and loadbearing, in Paul's own text.

Fifth, the question of final judgment, and of the relationship between the Christian's 'works' in the present and that final judgment to come, can be handled completely differently. Instead of agonizing over 'who does what' (is it God doing it, or me, or both, or what?) we have Paul's own clear statement: there is no condemnation for those *in the Messiah, Jesus*, ... because, through the incarnation and death of the Messiah, and 'in [his] flesh', God 'condemned sin', thereby dealing with 'the law of sin and death' in order that 'the right and proper verdict of the law could be fulfilled in us, as we live not according to the flesh but according to the spirit' (Romans 8.1–4). Because you are in the Messiah, the Messiah's spirit dwells within you. And the moral effort now required (if Romans 8.12–16 is not about moral effort, then words have no meaning) is not subject to a zero-sum calculation, just as God's action in the world is not subject to a decision (as in some Deist or Epicurean theology) about whether God was responsible for an event or whether it was the result of 'natural processes'. *Of course* we do it; but *of course* it is 'by the spirit'.[51] Some have even suggested that this eliminates 'free will'.[52] But that is to force Paul onto a philosophical Procrustean bed. For Paul, the spirit is precisely the one who sets the believer free. To understand this we need a much fuller discussion of pneumatology, and indeed of the whole business of how the God in whom Paul believed works in and through individuals and communities. I have tried to provide that elsewhere. Here we simply note that the principle articulated from within Reformed theology itself, the principle that Paul's primary soteriological category was that of 'being in Christ', will do the jobs about which the critics of the new perspective are anxious, and indeed will do them much better.[53]

The new perspective does not diminish Paul's concern for 'salvation'. It does not undermine his theology of conversion (for which, by the way, he uses the word *kaleō*, 'call'). It does not devalue the continuing work of grace in the life of the believer. It certainly does not devalue or undermine his 'gospel'. It sets all these on a firmer footing. And in doing so it liberates the word 'justification' itself, and its cognates, to do the job which in Paul it so manifestly does, linked to all the above but saying something which the western church has been in grave danger of forgetting: that this gospel is for all alike, Jew and Greek, slave and free, male and female. And it shows how that new definition and identification of the community of those who are 'in

[51] See Westerholm 351: for Lutherans, 'humans contribute *nothing* to their salvation' (italics original). That raises obvious questions: for instance, What difference does the spirit make?

[52] Smith 2007.

[53] See again e.g. Vanhoozer 2011. Hagner takes issue with Yinger 1999 for saying that for Paul there was no theological tension between judgment according to works and justification by faith. Why then, asks Hagner, did Paul argue against 'works-righteousness'? This misses the point. 'Judgment according to works' is about the *future* judgment; justification by faith (rather than by 'works of Torah') belongs to the *present*. One of the merits of the NP is that it helps avoid the confusion of 'works-righteousness' with 'judgment according to works'. To repeat that confusion is simply to stop the conversation in its tracks.

Christ' functions vitally within Paul's worldview and theology. It cannot be, of course, that western Protestants, so eager to be 'biblical', have ignored Paul's repeated injunctions about ecclesial unity . . . Or can it?

What then about those who have written so strikingly against the new perspective? Some concluding remarks about two very different books, chosen out of a hundred possible ones.

Peter Stuhlmacher has been one of the leading German Pauline scholars for the last several decades. His work is widely respected. As a pupil of Käsemann and hence a scholarly grandchild of Rudolf Bultmann he represents a long and noble tradition.[54] His brief but wide-ranging work challenging the new perspective therefore deserves to be taken very seriously.[55]

As was to be expected granted his previous work, Stuhlmacher insists, with me and several other new perspective writers, that Paul's phrase 'the righteousness of God' refers to God's own righteousness, rather than to the ('righteous') status of God's people.[56] For him, this 'righteousness', in Israel's scriptures, is an active power

> which creates welfare and salvation in the creation, in the history of Israel, and in the situation of the (end-time) judgment.[57]

He thus reiterates points he has made before about 'God's righteousness' invoking an entire apocalyptic drama in which God will act on behalf of the whole world, through which God's kingdom will be established (28, 52, 73). He shows clearly the way in which Luther went beyond Paul into a 'soteriological intensification and theological evaluation', though he insists that this was an entirely correct development (36). He suggests that Stendahl and Dunn, at least, 'evade the question about justification in the final judgment' (42), a comment easier to make with Stendahl, whose works remain slim if powerful, than with Dunn, who has explored every nook and cranny of Paul's writings at least twice, if not more. But then, insisting that he wants to hold together 'juristic' and 'participationist' categories, Stuhlmacher rejects the distinction between them (perhaps because of the continuing German protestant dislike of 'mysticism'?) and says that the distinction between the two categories comes about because of 'a deficient understanding of the atonement' (44). This is strange, and perhaps needed to be spelled out more, as did his attempted counter to Dunn on 'works of the law'.[58] In fact, Stuhlmacher's own attempts at holding together 'juristic' and 'participatory' schemes look fairly similar to those of Sanders, Dunn

[54] He follows both these mentors, for instance, in seeing a Pauline meaning of 'sin' not only as the transgression of commandments but the pious zeal for them (25).

[55] Stuhlmacher 2001. Stuhlmacher has written many other works, including a commentary on Romans; I am working on the principle, however, that when senior scholars set out ideas in a short compass, they summarize the heart of what they really want to say. I assume that this is true of the little book now to be discussed.

[56] See Stuhlmacher 1966.

[57] Stuhlmacher 2001, 19; refs. that follow are to this work.

[58] 43f. It is particularly strange to read about the use of the Greek terms *erga* and *erga nomou* at Qumran.

and Hays, though no doubt nuanced differently. His lively view of Paul's 'baptismal justification' strikes me as closer to Schweitzer than to a good many of the anti-new-perspective group, not least in North America (62–3).

What mainly distinguishes Stuhlmacher from the new perspective, I conclude, is his downplaying of the 'Israel' category. For him, as for his teacher Käsemann, the 'covenantal' hints in Paul turn out to be vestiges of an earlier Jewish-Christian formulation which Paul has not endorsed, but which he has instead translated into talk of God's faithfulness to *creation*. As I have suggested elsewhere, this is a false either/or. Stuhlmacher is surely right to stress the *final* judgment as the hermeneutical context within which 'justification' means what it means, but he does not to my mind show how what Paul says about justification in the present (in baptism! – where not all will follow him) is directly linked to that final judgment. And, though Stuhlmacher has of course written commentaries, it is frustrating that, despite his repeated insistence that the solution is to follow Paul's own train of thought, he does not in fact do that, but instead imposes his own train of thought, selecting key texts and omitting the ones that do not fit so well.[59] However, studying his little book has made me reflect that, if this is really what German scholarship has to say to the new perspective, the two sides, at least in their more scholarly representatives, are not actually that far apart, and that the remaining questions are things which could be quite easily taken up in further study.

What then shall we say about the large, carefully laid out and highly engaging work of Stephen Westerholm, called now to stand as a representative of the revived 'old perspective', and certainly among the finest scholars to do so? I have already highlighted his remarkable caricature of the new perspective, which, to be fair, he flags up as such.[60] This way of coming at things is a shame, since the first half of his book is so fair, so clear, so remarkably open- and even-handed, that to turn to the second half is a serious disappointment. Basically, Westerholm has done the opposite of what normally happens, being clear and fair in describing other people's views but doing less than justice to his own. Let me explain.

First, we should note Westerholm's other remarkable and puzzling caricatures. At one point he seems to affirm the recent turn:

> That the issue of boundary markers compelled Paul to formulate the thesis that one is declared righteous by faith in Jesus Christ, not by the works of the law, is the entirely appropriate emphasis of recent scholarship.

A sigh of relief for the new perspective, then? Not a bit of it:

[59] e.g. 42f., where he considers Rom. 3.28 in isolation from 3.29f.; at 55 he says that we must follow 'Paul's own train of thought' rather than 'subordinating it immediately to the typical questions of Western justification theology'. I naturally applaud this programme but do not see that in what follows Stuhlmacher has carried it out.

[60] Westerholm 2004, 249: 'caricature will of course be indispensable'. Subsequent refs. to Westerholm are to this book unless otherwise noted.

> That the point of this was *merely* that Gentiles did not need to be circumcised, and *not* that all human beings, sinners that they are, can only be declared righteous extraordinarily through the death of Christ Jesus, represents the shortsightedness of which some recent scholarship is guilty.[61]

Perhaps it is telling that Westerholm does not footnote that last statement. I do not think any of the main new perspective exponents has ever denied that Paul thought all human beings were sinners and in need of rescue by the death of Jesus Christ. Perhaps Westerholm's copy of Sanders has some blank pages in which the ultimate truth might have been revealed.

The false either/or is repeated. At one point Westerholm solidly refutes a view that nobody in the new perspective, to my knowledge, had dreamed of affirming:

> 1 Thessalonians gives no hint that Paul thought loyalty to the Jewish covenant provided a viable alternative to salvation offered in Christ, or even that he considered it an option sufficiently enticing to his readers to warrant refutation.[62]

Well, no: and the new perspective gives no hint that any of us imagined that Paul thought that kind of thing, or even that we considered it an option warranting refutation. Where did it come from? Westerholm's footnote does not enlighten us, but goes on straight away to deny, as though it was an even stranger point of view, the idea, which is foundational for Paul but totally unlike the point Westerholm has just 'refuted', that God's solution to the problem of the world's sin began with the promise to Abraham – a position common to Judaism and to Paul alike.[63]

And so on, through long pages of complex exegesis. All this culminates in the chapter-heading of Westerholm's final summary: 'Grace Abounding to Sinners or Erasing Ethnic Boundaries?'[64] At this point I want to reply, 'Both, of course – and in their proper Pauline correlation'. To my astonishment, after all that has gone before, Westerholm then backtracks, and suddenly admits that the new perspective has actually made an important point which needs to be factored in properly to any overall solution. Is this a volte-face? Was it a new 'revelation' vouchsafed as his chapter 20 began to take shape? Or does it mean that the previous caricatures were only a game, a feint? Whatever: we take comfort from these expressions of synthesis:

> Recent scholarship has rightly underlined that it was in the context of *this* dispute [i.e. the admission of Gentiles], *not* a debate whether one is saved by human effort or divine grace, that Paul formulated the doctrine of justification 'by faith apart from the works of the law'.[65]

[61] 389.

[62] 358f.

[63] 359 n. 26. Westerholm notes later (376) the way in which Abraham's blessing 'has now, in Christ Jesus, become a reality'; why could he not make the connection?

[64] ch. 20.

[65] 441. Note, though, the imprecision of 'saved by human effort' etc. (see above).

> It is thus both true and important to say that the Pauline gospel will not allow that the distinctively Jewish practices of the law be imposed on Gentiles; and it is true and important to note that it was in response to such an insistence that Paul formulated his doctrine of 'justification by faith apart from works of the law.'[66]

> The most important and salutary emphasis of the new perspective on Paul is the insistence that Judaism was not 'legalistic': Jews did not think they 'earned' their salvation; they acknowledged God's goodness in granting Israel his covenant and strove to respond to that goodness by fulfilling its requirements ... [There follow various qualifications; but] none of these qualifications should obscure the fundamental truth that Judaism, described in its own terms, knew and depended on God's grace and did not promote a self-righteous pursuit of salvation by works.[67]

And, finally, concluding the book:

> The critics have rightly defined the occasion that elicited the formulation of Paul's doctrine and have reminded us of its first-century social and strategic significance; the 'Lutherans', for their part, rightly captured Paul's rationale and basic point. For those (like Augustine, Luther, Calvin, and Wesley) bent on applying Paul's words to contemporary situations, it is the point rather than the historical occasion of the formulation that is crucial. Students of early Christianity must attempt to do justice to both.

Well, it seems that if we are not exactly agreed – I would not concede that 'the point' actually trumps 'the historical occasion' in that way – certainly we have a reasonably clear 'both/and' position. This is remarkable, granted the strong either/or which Westerholm had earlier formulated, and granted the way in which, time and again in the second half of the book, he attempts to undermine new perspective readings and to insist, like Robert Gundry, that 'the old is better'.

So how has Westerholm reached his conclusions? Several things emerge, which I note here more as points for further debate, signposts to later discussions, rather than things we can take up here in detail.[68]

First, it is quite remarkable that there is no recognition, throughout Westerholm's long and careful book, that the real underlying problem is that of the integration, or lack thereof, between 'juristic' and 'participationist' categories. Indeed, there is simply no discussion, so far as I can see, of the whole theme of 'being in Christ', far less of the way(s) in which it might be integrated with 'justification' and its cognates. In terms of the history of the debate this is extraordinary. In terms of a survey of exegesis, it is (to be frank) unpardonable.

Second, there is no real discussion of 'the righteousness of God', which has played such a large part in the debate down the years. We are offered an extremely short (and to my mind muddled) discussion of the phrase, followed by some indications that Westerholm is going with a basically

[66] 442. Westerholm continues with an 'on the other hand', which takes away some of the force of this, but the statement stands, and any new perspective writer will approve it.

[67] 443f.

[68] cf. Zetterholm 2009, 192: 'Thus at the end of the day, this is what Westerholm finds wrong with Judaism – it is not Lutheranism, and a Lutheran reading of Paul appears fully possible also in the post-Sanders era.' I agree that that is what Westerholm has argued, but the following questions remain.

Bultmannian view over against Käsemann and the increasing number who have seen the phrase as referring in some sense to God's own righteousness. But this issue, fundamental to the interpretation of all the key passages in Romans, is not even parked. It is simply dodged.[69]

Third, there is no sign of recognition that the real argument of Romans 4 and Galatians 3 concerns the question, who are the true children of Abraham? Nor is there any indication that the context of Galatians 2.15–21, one of the most crucial statements, is the question which was raised so sharply at Antioch: who is allowed to share table-fellowship with whom?[70]

Fourth, fascinatingly considering how the debate has played out in some quarters, Westerholm never even notices that there is a question on the table about 'imputed righteousness'. Even when discussing 2 Corinthians 5.21, it does not seem to occur to him that there is something there to worry about. Is this the result of his insistent 'Lutheranism', and his continuing marginalization of the Reformed perspective?[71]

Fifth, and more particularly, there is no serious consideration whatever of the role of (what we might call) 'covenant' theology. Westerholm waves this aside, caricaturing it, quoting Seifrid on 'covenant romanticism' (an interesting concept in itself)[72] and suggesting revealingly that just because Israel's scriptures do indeed include God's faithfulness to his covenants (note the plural) within the notion of his righteousness, 'it does not follow that God's righteousness can be *reduced* to covenant faithfulness.'[73] *Reduced*? Where did that idea come from? The answer in the footnotes seems to be, 'Mark Seifrid'; but why would anyone familiar with Israel's scriptures and their long retellings in the second-Temple period think that God's covenant faithfulness to Israel was a small, insignificant thing? As I have argued at length, it is the hinge upon which the divine plan for the world was supposed to turn. Westerholm, in company with most of the anti-new-perspective scholars, never sees the key connection for Paul between the language of *dikaiosynē* and the covenant, despite the obvious passages where that makes best sense of the evidence.[74] The point is clear in 2 Corinthians 3. In Romans 9.6–29, the reason Paul retells the story of

[69] 284–6; and cf. e.g. 322, 'God's "righteousness" is available . . .'

[70] On 367 Westerholm admits that he cannot see the point of Paul's response to Peter; then, on 370f., he offers no account of the context of 2.15–21 where his argument urgently needs it. He denies (390) that Abraham has anything much to do with the argument of Rom. 3.21 onwards, citing him as an 'example' (392), and he skirts round the telling passage 3.27–31 (390).

[71] 365. Westerholm notes (202) that the earlier edn. of his book was criticized for its failure to take account of Reformed views; but his inclusion of Cranfield has not noticeably increased his engagement with the actual specifics of Reformed theology on justification.

[72] 287 n. 61: see Seifrid 2000b, 124.

[73] 285 (italics original). Actually, for 'righteousness' Westerholm, here and elsewhere, uses the regrettable coinage 'dikaoisness', which I have deemed it unwise to inflict on the main text here. See too 359, suggesting that Paul's readers would simply not have understood the idea that the solution to the problem of the sin of the world lay in a promise God once made to Abraham. According to Romans 4 and Galatians 3, that was exactly what Paul believed. He was, after all, simply following Genesis 12, as I and others have frequently pointed out. Paul's energies were regularly bent to getting ex-pagan converts to *think Jewishly*, however hard it may have been for them (and for some contemporary scholars).

[74] See my recent restatements in e.g. Wright 2014a, 2014b.

Abraham's covenant family is to ask, 'is God unrighteous?', *mē adikia para tō theō*; and to give the answer, 'No, God is not unrighteous,' which leads him to the fresh exposition of God's 'righteousness' in and through Deuteronomy 30, the long-cherished promise of covenant renewal. We might note, in addition, Romans 4.11, when Paul, quoting Genesis, changes the key term: Abraham received circumcision as a sign and seal of . . . what? Genesis 17.11 says 'the covenant'; Paul says 'the righteousness of faith'. That can hardly mean that Paul is saying, 'Don't bother about covenant; think instead about righteousness'. The point of the passage (which is an exposition of Genesis 15, the chapter where God establishes his covenant with Abram in the first place) is that *this is what the covenant really meant and means.*[75] Note too, finally, the parallels between Romans and *4 Ezra*, where the question, urgent to screaming point, is, How is God then to be faithful to the covenant, to be *tsaddik*, to be 'righteous'? That does not 'reduce' the massive, cosmic question which 'Ezra' is facing to a small, 'romantic' idea. It gives it its full, resonating, earth-shattering scope. The creator God is the covenant God, and the covenant is his means of addressing the woes of all creation. If the covenant is irreducibly broken, chaos is come again. That is the point.[76]

So, too, Westerholm routinely allows himself, despite his closing summary, to fall into the trap we outlined earlier. He sets off on a long exposition of 'Justification by Faith in Paul's Thought' – a chapter of over fifty pages – without saying what it is that we are looking for. It gradually becomes clear that he has begged the whole question by assuming that the answer is 'a doctrine about how sinners get saved'. Thus he grossly caricatures the new perspective when he says that Paul is 'no longer allowed to ask' the question about how humans face God's wrath and must respond to the gospel (355). In his reading of 1 Thessalonians, he naturally sees that 'justification' does not occur, but says that since 'justification entails a divine initiative by which sinners meriting condemnation are reprieved and granted a place in God's kingdom', then the doctrine itself, though not the expression, is found there (360). But that is the very thing at issue: not whether Paul believed all that about the saving of sinners, but *whether he used the language of 'justification' to state that point.* So too with the first letter to Corinth: Paul's 'message of salvation' had not altered (361). No indeed, but the point at stake is whether Paul was talking directly about *that* question when he used the language of 'justification'. The Paul who wrote 1 Corinthians 1.18–29 'could *not* have conceived of salvation as a cooperative enterprise for which human beings could claim any credit' (364, italics original). No indeed; whoever would have thought otherwise? Westerholm has simply missed the point. To say that 'justification was a polemical doctrine designed to make it clear that believing gentiles have equal rights with Jews, and that both are full members of Abraham's family, the Messiah's family,

[75] Gen. 17.10f.; Rom. 4.11.

[76] See in particular Longenecker 1991.

through faith alone' is *not* saying 'therefore Luther and his friends were wrong, and salvation is a cooperative enterprise'. He is tilting at windmills. So far as I know, neither Sanders nor Dunn nor any other main new perspective interpreters have said that Paul, going to Corinth, was going 'to invite the local gentiles to share in a salvation already enjoyed by their Jewish neighbours under the Jewish covenant'.[77] That might be the view of some scholars whose work we shall mention later, but it does not feature in new perspective writing. Nor will it do, finally, to cite Ephesians 2.8–10, as many 'anti-new-perspective' writers have done, as though to prove that, whether or not Paul himself wrote Ephesians, either he or a close imitator was fully on board with the 'Lutheran' view (406). Westerholm, like many others, does not point out that Ephesians 2.8–10 is followed at once by the emphatic, indeed climactic, 2.11–22, in which the coming together of Jews and gentiles in Christ is the central theme, contributing its own weight to the main argument of the letter. One might suggest that Ephesians 2.1–10 represents the old perspective, and 2.11–22 the new; in other words, that the two belong firmly together at least in the mind of the author of that particular letter.

It gives me no great pleasure to take issue with Stephen Westerholm over all these issues. Indeed, one might have chosen a different target. But it is precisely that fair-minded, well-reasoned first half which makes the book (as the distinguished blurb-writers say) just the sort of thing to give to first-time Paul-readers; and they would be led into a trap. If the book 'will surely help us escape the impasse in our current debates', as John Barclay writes, it will be because the puzzles and gaps in Westerholm's own exegetical work might just drive others to do better. Simon Gathercole may be right, in his blurb, to say that Westerholm is 'head and shoulders above almost everyone else', but not 'as an interpreter of Paul'. As an interpreter of some debates about Paul (though not others), we might perhaps agree. But if stature as a Pauline interpreter is measured by the themes one manages to integrate and the passages of which one gives a convincing exegesis, then we must beg to differ. Perhaps Stephen Westerholm, himself master of a quiet irony I would not dream of imitating, will not mind my saying that anyone trying to be a Pauline exegete while still in thrall to Luther should consider a career as a taxidermist. Heroes are to be engaged with, not stuffed and mounted and allowed to dominate the room.

3. Life after 'Life after Sanders'

Meanwhile, in another part of the forest, all sorts of other plots have been hatched, all kinds of different agendas explored and advanced. As recent surveys indicate, the last two or three decades have seen, particularly in

[77] 366; cf. 374: 'Nowhere has Paul suggested that the Christian gospel was needed if Gentiles were to enjoy blessings already experienced by Jews under their law (or covenant).' Who says Paul did suggest such a thing? Nobody in the new perspective.

North America, that sudden explosion of new questions, of 'perspectives' of many radically different kinds, that caused us earlier in this survey to speak of watching the sudden explosion of a box of fireworks.[78] One might have thought that the debates between old and new perspectives would resolve into a reasonably straightforward and clarified debate about the relative weight and proper integration of 'juristic' and 'participationist' categories in Paul. That debate, indeed, remains important and central. But the decline of the Bultmann school in Germany, with Pauline exponents now following a variety of approaches, and the rise of 'religious studies' in parts of Europe and North America, opening up supposedly non-theological discussions and lines of enquiry, have given a new and confused appearance to the field. Some of these developments, which go not just 'beyond the new perspective' but in quite different directions altogether, remain important conversation partners for the present book. Indeed, in seeking to take my own earlier new perspective work into different dimensions, I am hoping to provide a larger viewpoint which will include the apparent strengths of at least some of these recent explorations. This is an exciting time in terms of history, theology, exegesis and (in the old, restricted sense) hermeneutics. We should be grateful that so many people have been reading Paul from so many different points of view, even if sometimes the whooshing of unexpected rockets and the displays of unnervingly close Catherine wheels can prove challenging.

What has caused this sudden explosion? Two things, I think. First, as we mentioned in the Preface, Paul is now studied and taught in the context, not just of seminaries and divinity schools, but of university departments of 'religion'. We may regret the implied shrinking of Paul into that post-Enlightenment category, but often the effects have been just the opposite, expanding Pauline horizons to include politics, ethics, philosophy and even economics. Second, the partial collapse of the Enlightenment worldview on many fronts – the turn in thought and culture now loosely known as 'postmodernity' – has meant that the watertight divisions between academic subjects has increasingly disappeared. The big narratives and truth-systems within which Paul, like many other writers ancient and modern, had been carefully labelled and put on a particular shelf, have been replaced by the swirling multiple engagements and cross-disciplinary studies which, not worrying about old ideas of 'objectivity' (honoured so often in the breach rather than the observance), have allowed the new questions of today's world, both western and non-western, to impinge on classic texts, whether this means post-structuralist readings of Jane Austen or post-colonial readings of Aristotle.

Why not? The older 'objectivity', and the older imprisonment of Paul within 'theological' questions, now looks threadbare. It is a shame, of course, that some of the new interpreters now play the 'either/or' game in the other direction, and declare (for instance) that because we are now discovering Paul to be a seminal *political* thinker this means that 'theology' is

[78] See esp. Zetterholm 2009, chs. 5, 7; Given 2010. Note the subtitle of Given's collection: 'Other Perspectives on the Apostle.'

irrelevant. But this too will pass, and I hope the present book, and the larger project of which it is a part, will speed its passing. Paul is a multiple, complex, but basically *integrated* thinker. What he says about God, Jesus and the spirit, which is obviously of more than minor importance for him, must be thought through in close relation to what he says about Caesar, money, women, ethnicity, philosophy and rhetoric – to name but a few.

It will not do, as we engage in this kind of work, to object that so many of these investigations have been launched from a particular 'ideological' point of view.[79] Of course they have been. That is what makes it all so very exciting. Let us not pretend that Schweitzer and Bultmann, Käsemann and Sanders didn't have axes to grind.[80]

What then counts is whether those who offer new proposals are willing to engage in *historical* debate with others who come not only with different assumptions and starting-points but with actual evidence that doesn't fit the new theory. It is fine to bounce one's own ideas and aspirations off texts of all sorts. It ill becomes those who for long years have been accustomed to read their own theology back into Paul and then claim his authority (and, while they're about it, to tell him off for not expressing himself clearly enough and introducing irrelevant and extraneous material) to look down their noses at those who come to Paul with definite moral, social and cultural questions and, reading him, find themselves sometimes in agreement (Look! Paul agrees with me! That helps my case!) and sometimes in radical disagreement (Look! Paul was wrong at this point!). No doubt we have all done that to a lesser or greater extent, without always realizing that using Paul or anyone else as an echo chamber to magnify our own voices is ultimately a kind of confidence trick. No: let us come with our questions, tell it like we see it, *and then submit to critical questioning on the basis of the evidence, not simply on the basis of alternative prejudices*. This is what critical realism is all about. It does not mean pretending that we have a God's-eye view. It means recognizing that truth can indeed be approached through shared investigation.

And – to say it before someone else does – I do not of course pretend that I am a mere disinterested spectator myself. For twenty years of my middle life I was daily and hourly involved in the challenge of what it might mean, in a confused late-modern or postmodern ecclesial and political context, to retrieve 'what St Paul really said'. Those challenges have given me a particular angle of vision, but I do not think that they have distorted my view any more than the newer challenges addressed in some quite different contemporary writing. We need one another in this enterprise, and I remain of the opinion that to come to Paul as a would-be practitioner (prayer, preaching, pastoral ministry, political involvement) is no more distorting than to write about Bob Dylan while continuing to practise the guitar. Someone who was tone deaf, or for whom English was a fifth language,

[79] See Friesen's response (2010, 32) to Barclay.

[80] See above; and the brief summary in e.g. Wright 2005 [*Fresh Perspectives*] ch. 1.

might indeed see things in Dylan that are opaque to me; but I am inclined to think that trying to sing some of his songs since the 1960s means that there may be some aspects of his work on which I have at least the chance of an inside track.

So how many roads must Paul walk down, before we can call him an apostle? Plenty, it seems. I listed ten in the Preface, and no doubt there are others. None of them owes all that much to the new perspective or indeed the old, except that some tip their hat to Krister Stendahl as they go their separate ways. The question of Paul the 'apocalyptist' has become a powerful element in the post-post-Sanders world, at least in the country where most biblical scholarship now takes place. This has been so important that the entire second Part of the book will be devoted to it, necessitating a change of voice. Up to now, even in discussing cheerfully polemical writers like Westerholm, we have been looking back at well-worn debates, but at the time of writing the question of 'apocalyptic' is one of the hottest topics, and we must engage more directly with its key exponents.

After that, however, there come all kinds of attempts to locate Paul in his world – and in ours. This is where newer political, philosophical and related questions come in. Occasionally this exhibits similar weaknesses to the older theological approaches: a theological *Sachkritik* is sometimes replaced by this or that cultural or philosophical one ('Paul clearly believed in X; sometimes he seems to say Y, its opposite, but we must let his X override this particular Y'). In Part III of this book we will sketch, at least in outline, some of the key developments that have taken place in the task of placing Paul in his world and in ours. In all this, it will be sufficient for our purposes to gain a sense of the various lines of thought that are now fanning out, in fresh historical and hermeneutical work, into questions and discussions which, though comparatively new to modern Pauline studies, are perhaps not so new to the apostle himself.

We have thus traced the rise of modern Pauline studies as far as the Sanders-led new perspective, and the reactions to that movement. These still set the agenda for a great deal of research. But, while Sanders was working away comparing Paul with the rabbis, a very different American scholar was doing his best to locate Paul within a world which the rabbis mostly shunned: that of 'apocalyptic'. To this new movement we therefore turn in the second Part of this book.

Part II

RE-ENTER 'APOCALYPTIC'

Chapter Six

THE STRANGE CAREER OF 'APOCALYPTIC'

1. Introduction

Not long after Ed Sanders published *Paul and Palestinian Judaism*, and not long before Wayne Meeks brought out *The First Urban Christians*, a very different American scholar – to be accurate, American by residence, though Dutch by birth – produced a very different sort of work. In his remarkable *Paul the Apostle: The Triumph of God in Life and Thought*, J. Christiaan Beker, who taught at Princeton for many years, re-introduced into the discourse of English-speaking Pauline studies a term which, however slippery and polymorphous, has become the watchword for a whole new family of interpretations: 'apocalyptic'.

Beker's book is rambling, repetitive, and rambunctious – but also compelling. Beker had suffered terrible things, as a young man, at the hands of the Nazis. His reflections on the horrors of that period led him, like Ernst Käsemann, to react against the individualistic existentialism of Bultmann and to think in terms of a much larger, more apparently powerful, message.[1] The human plight was much worse than Bultmann had imagined; the Pauline solution was much grander than Bultmann had proposed. It was equal to the task. What's more, Beker argued, when you read Paul like this, you find that, behind some apparently disparate emphases, he makes sense. Beker proposed that

> The imminent triumph of God is defined by the death and resurrection of Christ and constitutes the basic coherence of the Pauline gospel in the midst of the contingent particularity of the needs of his churches.[2]

There are Beker's two main themes in a nutshell. First, Paul's central and coherent theme was 'the triumph of God', that is, the divine victory over the powers of evil. This victory, won on the cross, resulted in the new creation

[1] For Beker's early life see Ollenburger 1994.

[2] Beker 1980, 367.

which, launched in the resurrection, is to be completed in the final triumph, which is yet to come. Second, Beker proposed that in Paul we find a rich mixture of this coherent overall theme and of the varied expressions called forth by the 'contingent' situations to which his letters were addressed. The latter was an important point in itself, arguing that Paul was not merely a situational thinker, trimming his sails to every wind. But the former is the theme which has now come into prominence not only in several fresh readings of Paul but also in various appropriations of his thought among theologians and philosophers. The 'apocalyptic triumph' in which God wins the victory over the forces of evil, highlighting the 'cosmic' dimensions of Paul's gospel rather than focusing on the 'individual' meaning, has become, in many circles, the new orthodoxy.

I shall return to Beker presently. But I begin with him because, in terms of the English-speaking world with which the present book is, perforce, mainly concerned, he seems to have been the first to grasp the significance of the revolution which Käsemann had effected in German scholarship, and to attempt a systematic presentation of this 'apocalyptic' perspective on Paul. Käsemann had stated his case in the form of short articles and a long commentary on a single book. Somebody needed to stand back and say, Very well, if that's what Paul was saying, how did it all work out? Beker was that man.

This revolution was all the more surprising in that for a century or more the very notion of 'apocalyptic' was avoided by exegetes and theologians alike. Beker is so eager to stress the earlier negative portrayal of 'apocalyptic' against which he is reacting that he cites three times, in very similar terms, the view held by the great Julius Wellhausen at the end of the nineteenth century:

> In the first place, apocalyptic suggests armchair speculation, sectarian rigidity, egocentric particularity, ethical passivity, and an adherence to an obsolete world view and to misleading language that cannot and should not be resuscitated.[3]

The same negative portrayal, offered by a good many exegetes in the first half of the twentieth century, was laid bare by Klaus Koch in his rightly famous and eye-opening book *The Rediscovery of Apocalyptic*, whose original German title, *Ratlos vor der Apokalyptik*, had put the point more sharply: 'Clueless in the face of Apocalyptic'.[4] In the great nineteenth-century constructions of ancient Jewish thought, coming as they did with a heavy and Hegelian evaluative agenda, 'apocalyptic' was seen as one of the

[3] Beker 1980, 18; see too 139 ('armchair sophistry, degeneration of prophecy, utopian speculation, ethical passivity, and so on'; the whole of 135–43 expands this discussion) and 361 ('armchair speculations and spiritually inferior reflections'). The 'second place' that goes with this statement is the theological objection according to which it would be wrong to require acceptance of 'the apocalyptic world view' as a prior commitment before one could believe the gospel – a view which is still alive and well in some circles today. In addition to Wellhausen, Beker cites B. Duhm and, more recently, R. Schnackenburg as representing the view he is opposing.

[4] Koch 1972 [1970]. This short book should be compulsory reading, preferably on a regular basis, for all who find the word 'apocalyptic' rising unbidden to their lips.

degenerate features of what was called 'Late Judaism'. It represented a declining away from the (supposed) pure, early prophetic message of God's action in the world, from the ethical demands of monotheism, and from all that the exegetes of that period and that tradition wanted to highlight and retain from pre-Christian Judaism. It reminded them far too much of the sectarian movements, from the sixteenth-century Anabaptists to their own day, which had specialized in secret revelations, speculative readings of texts like Daniel, and, not least, the dangerous and regularly deluded belief that the end of the world was close at hand. Albert Schweitzer stood out boldly against this fashionable dismissal of 'apocalyptic', arguing that both Jesus and Paul did indeed belong in the world of ancient Jewish thought for which that word might be an appropriate marker. But that only seemed to make things worse, because many who read Schweitzer found his pictures of the Messiah and his apostle so unwelcome that it merely reinforced the old stereotypes. If that was 'apocalyptic', so much the worse for it. Much safer to assume, as Koch puts it, that one could leap over five hundred years of Israelite religion and place Jesus immediately after Deutero-Isaiah.[5]

While scholars writing about the Hebrew Bible and ancient Judaism thus laboured to identify a 'pure', non-apocalyptic stream of thought, students of the New Testament engaged in what Koch called 'the agonized attempt to save Jesus from apocalyptic'. Bultmann demythologized it; C. H. Dodd, not so far from Bultmann as one might think, went for a 'realized eschatology' in which the 'kingdom' had already come. Bultmann's scheme resulted in an existentialist 'faith'; Dodd's, in the neo-moralism of the 'new law'. Though some of today's exponents of a would-be 'apocalyptic' look back behind Käsemann to the early Barth as their prototype, in many ways the neo-orthodoxy for which Barth became well known had itself offered alternative construals, characterized by Beker as the insistence on a kind of Christomonism over against the theocentric emphasis of the ('apocalyptic') divine victory over evil.[6] Whether this is fair to Barth and his followers is beside the point at the moment. What matters is that we should understand just how powerful had been the anti-apocalyptic mood of mainstream western scholarship through much of the twentieth century, and hence how shocking it was when Käsemann launched his protest, insisting that 'apocalyptic' was after all 'the mother of Christian theology'.[7]

2. What Is 'Apocalyptic'?

I shall come back to Käsemann presently. But before we go there it is important to note some of the other things that prepared the way for the

[5] Koch, 115.

[6] Beker 1980, 142f., and elsewhere.

[7] The relevant essays by Käsemann are 'Sentences of Holy Law in the New Testament', 'The Beginnings of Christian Theology', 'On the Subject of Primitive Christian Apocalyptic', and 'Paul and Early Catholicism', in Käsemann 1969 [1965], chs. 3, 4, 5 and 12.

present confused state of the discussion. Whatever else the word 'apocalyptic' does in western scholarship, it always appeals implicitly to an *historical context* within the so-called 'history of religions' of the time. That is, it implies that there is a larger worldview and/or religious movement and/or theological perspective for which the label 'apocalyptic' is appropriate; and it claims, again at least by implication, that the material under consideration can best be understood as belonging within *that* worldview, movement or perspective, rather than within some other. When pressed, most would say, uncontroversially, that 'apocalyptic' means, more or less, the worldview (or movement, or perspective) which we see in biblical books like Daniel and (parts at least of) Zechariah, with apparent roots in Ezekiel and (parts at least of) Isaiah; in post-biblical books like *1 Enoch* and *4 Ezra*; and, obviously, in the New Testament book known as the Revelation of St John the Divine. If the word 'apocalyptic', as a label for a mode or type of thought, is intended to carry any implication in terms of the religio-historical context to which appeal is being made, it must be to these books, and the many others like them, that the writer is appealing. Otherwise the word has been cut loose from any recognizable historical moorings. Like an advertiser's barrage balloon, originally tethered above a shopping mall or car showroom, it can then float free, giving the onlookers the false impression that the designated product is to be had at the new location. That, I think, has happened on a massive scale in recent discussions.[8]

In fact, we know far more about actual 'apocalyptic' literature, and in a measure about the people who wrote it and treasured it and the movements they represented, than we did a hundred years ago. The Qumran Scrolls have helped enormously. They have spotlighted not only certain lines of thought but a community in which such thought found its home. And Qumran, though containing much writing that on anyone's analysis deserves the label 'apocalyptic', also contains much else: 'wisdom' texts, prayers and liturgies, scriptural exegesis, community rules, and so on. 'Apocalyptic' does not 'come away clean' as though it represents a single, and single-minded, worldview, movement or perspective. Likewise, although (so far as most of us think) the Qumran Scrolls were produced by and for a group that we can call a 'sect', it is a moot point whether this 'sect' was actually as 'sectarian', as separated from the rest of the parent body (i.e. Judaism – itself a slippery term at this period), as we might have supposed. One person's 'sect' is another person's 'renewal movement'. In a world which cherished prophecies of a glorious future, it was not necessarily outlandish, dualistic, world-denying, sectarian or any such thing to suggest, and to come to believe, that these prophecies might at last be finding a new sort of fulfilment. (Of course, in a world which believed in a steady-state Hegelian or even Darwinian 'progress', and which still had bad memories of revolutions, such denigration of renewal-movements might all the more easily spring to mind.)

[8] I have set out my own views of 'apocalyptic' in *NTPG* ch. 10. Standard discussions now include Rowland 1982; Collins 1987; and see below.

We know, in fact, a good deal more than we did a century ago not just about 'apocalyptic' texts but also about the multiple varieties of second-Temple Jewish life, and the multiple varieties of its literary remains. We have newly discovered texts, and newly produced editions of the ones we knew already. We have new historical surveys and specialist studies which provide three-dimensional cultural, social and political models within which we can aspire to fresh understandings of these texts. In particular, books like Daniel and *1 Enoch* have emerged as literature of *political protest*, of subversive symbolic narratives to strengthen resistance to alien imperial rule and to encourage those suffering under it.[9] Such a reading challenges at its core the old idea, so popular in the time of Wellhausen, that 'apocalyptic' was necessarily dualist, or quietist, or ethically passive. Its language about the 'present age' and the 'age to come' did not mean that its authors or readers were anticipating the imminent collapse of the world order of space, time and matter. Like their predecessors in the better known (and formerly better liked) prophetic literature, the writers of Jewish apocalypses believed in a God whose definitive self-revelation was found in the events surrounding the exodus from Egypt, a powerful act of liberation which was, in a sense, the end of one 'world' and the start of another – with, to be sure, an awkward gap in between, during which the Israelites were both free from slavery and not yet at home in their promised inheritance. That idea of two conditions, two states of being, with an in-between time to be negotiated with difficulty, remained as an important echo in many early Christian retrievals of the same traditions. And one vital part of the exodus narrative was the making of the Tabernacle, in which the glorious divine presence (referred to by later rabbis as the *Shekinah*) came to dwell. If ancient Jews spoke or wrote of their God 'rending the heavens and coming down' in a new way – the phrase comes from Isaiah, but it might be seen as characterizing much 'apocalyptic' thought – this was not because they held a static and dualistic worldview in which 'heaven' might one day 'invade' the present world, but because, in the eyes of many, Israel's God had abandoned his people at the time of the Babylonian exile, and had promised to return in glory at last. Though the rebuilt Temple in Jerusalem held, of course, powerful memories, no second-Temple Jews claimed that the glorious divine presence had returned. Indeed, later rabbis agreed that it had not.[10]

The older analyses, in short, are highly misleading. 'Apocalyptic' is not 'dualistic' in and of itself. That is, it might or might not be; but the fact that a piece of writing exhibits the signs of the genre we may call 'apocalyptic' does not itself indicate dualism. Granted, it all depends what you mean by 'dualism'. I earlier catalogued no fewer than ten senses which that word has been given in modern writing about ancient Judaism, and if we do not insist on clarity at this point our discourse threatens to collapse.[11] Indeed, the

[9] See e.g. Portier-Young 2011.

[10] For all this, see *PFG* 104–7, 653–6 and elsewhere. The Isa. ref. is 64.1; the rabbinic reference is bYom. 21b; see *PFG* 106.

[11] See *NTPG* 252–6, 297–9.

hope of resurrection and new creation, strongly apparent in some apocalyptic writing, indicates a concern that the present world should be renewed, not abandoned.[12] What is more, when we engage in a three-dimensional historical study of the writings normally considered 'apocalyptic', we soon discover many continuities, as well as some discontinuities, with other expressions of Jewish life and thought, both then and in subsequent centuries. Books such as *Jubilees*, the *Psalms of Solomon* and many of the Qumran Scrolls share features with the obviously 'apocalyptic' literature. Even the Wisdom of Solomon, often too easily categorized as 'wisdom' literature and hence, in some eyes, the very opposite of 'apocalyptic', opens with a five-chapter account of divine judgment which is suddenly revealed upon an unready and wicked world. In particular, the feature of 'apocalyptic' often cited as most central and characteristic – the belief in the 'two ages', the 'present age' and the 'age to come' – is not at all unique to 'apocalyptic' thought, but is present as a regular feature in the later rabbinic writings, which, almost by definition, and certainly by political intent, are very far from being 'apocalyptic'.[13] I thus find myself in company with several other scholars who have suggested that the word 'apocalyptic' has become so slippery, capable of so many twists and turns of meaning, that it would be safest to confine it simply to a literary genre: that of 'revelations', which is after all what the word basically means, in which reports are given of visions vouchsafed to a 'seer', and then (sometimes) interpreted, by an angel or other intermediary, in relation to socio-political events, and to the divine disclosure which might accompany them.[14]

This plea, however, has been regularly made and equally regularly ignored by the many for whom the word 'apocalyptic' has become too useful to be dropped. What has happened, I think, is this. A hundred years ago, certain key ancient Jewish texts were known to scholars, who understood them within the ideologies of their own day. The word 'apocalyptic' was used to denote not only certain texts but the ideology (or worldview, or perspective, or movement) which these texts were supposed to enshrine. This easy-going categorization was helpful in enabling people to distinguish the bits of ancient Jewish tradition of which they approved (and which they supposed to have carried forward into the teaching of Jesus and his early followers) from the bits of which they disapproved. But from that unpromising start two quite different movements have developed. The first, the

[12] So, rightly, Beker 1980, 223.

[13] On the 'two ages' (*ha-olam ha-zeh* and *ha-olam ha-ba*) see below 158 n. 12. This calls seriously into question the assertion of Vielhauer in a well-known article (Vielhauer 1964, 588) that 'The essential feature of Apocalyptic is its dualism ... above all, in the doctrine of the Two Ages ... the entire course of the world is comprehended.' Vielhauer notes that earlier Jewish thought also looked for a coming Age, but suggests that, in contrast to the supernatural and irruptive notions found in 'apocalyptic', the earlier hopes were for a glorious earthly messianic kingdom in continuity with the present world. This seems to me a classic case of mistaking form for substance, the 'form' here being the characteristic apocalyptic metaphor-system, designed to give dramatic emphasis and theological depth to historical substance.

[14] The literature here is of course vast. For recent clear summaries see the articles by Collins (on 'Apocalypse') and Rowland (on 'Apocalypticism') in the *Eerdmans Dictionary of Early Judaism* (Collins 2010 and Rowland 2010), both with recent bibliographies.

scholarly study of the texts themselves and their location within the wider history of the ancient Jews, has demonstrated that the earlier ideological constructs were historically unwarranted. The second, the theological use of the word 'apocalyptic' (and even 'apocalypticism': the nineteenth-century love of inventing 'isms' lives on!) to denote a particular kind of ideology has continued to assume something like the earlier construction, not noticing, so it seems, that the theory had lost its historical anchorage. The word has then, as in my earlier simile, been able to float free, gaining or losing different meanings at different times and in relation to different texts.[15]

We should note in particular two *historical* features which explain a good deal of the mood of so much ancient Jewish 'apocalyptic' writing, and which ought to call in question the abstract generalizations often made about it.[16] First, this literature emerges from the period after Alexander the Great, when for the first time the Jewish people had to understand their own calling within the larger history of the world. Second, most of the literature was written at a time of persecution or national danger. Thus

> It is hardly surprising ... that these documents are full of cryptic but easily decodable references to current affairs; or that they evince a pessimistic helplessness on the part of the Jews in the face of world powers over which they have no control.[17]

As a result, we should not be surprised that these writings do not sound like Amos or Micah. But a small breeze of historical contextualization can dispel a thick fog of theological muddle:

> This is no symptom of spiritual or intellectual decline. One does not expect a programme of social reform from the liberation front.[18]

What we face in consequence is an exciting and confused mess. Historical scholars discuss the significance of the literary genre; theologians and philosophers use the same word to denote mutually incompatible points of view. Exegetes, as often, are caught in between. Often the word 'apocalyptic' is reduced to a loose, generalized, arm-waving adjective, introduced into sentences to suggest a vague atmosphere of 'cosmic' significance rather than merely private or personal relevance. Phrases like 'apocalyptic powers' – meaning, it seems, the kind of 'powers' that 'apocalyptic' writers refer to, taken to be supramundane or suprahuman forces – function as shorthands which those in the know can decode. This then becomes self-referential, with such writers doing what 'apocalyptic' characteristically does, using a private language which initiates can understand, a code for transmitting subversive ideas. Koch's suspicion that scholars are projecting their own times back into the early period may have the ring of truth.[19] Scholars afraid

15 See Caird 1980, 260–71. Caird, as often, managed to say a great deal in a short space.

16 For these points, see Caird 1980, 261f.

17 Caird 1980, 261.

18 Caird 1980, 261f.

19 See Koch 1972 [1970], 15.

of revolutionary disturbances in their own world were anxious to escape into the world of faith and theory, and thus came to read ancient texts which really were expressing revolutionary aspirations as if they were expressing cosmic dualism. And so on.

An example of the confusion can be seen in the two major movements within American biblical scholarship in which 'apocalyptic' has played a key role. The much-heralded 'Jesus Seminar', which met under the chairmanship of the late Robert Funk, made the rejection of 'apocalyptic' one of its basic criteria for distinguishing genuine Jesus-sayings from spurious ones. Jesus himself, they decreed, was not an 'apocalyptist', because that would have made him bombastic and judgmental, announcing the end of the world and threatening sinners with hellfire – in other words, doing all those things which American fundamentalists were supposed to do and which the 'Seminar' rejected. Jesus, by contrast, belonged in the cooler, more savvy atmosphere of 'wisdom', conveying by stories and clever sayings an alternative way of life.[20] Some members of the Seminar, to be sure, argued that Jesus did use 'apocalyptic' language, but that this was to be taken metaphorically.[21] Others occasionally pointed out, with obvious examples like the Wisdom of Solomon, the Qumran Community Rule, and Matthew's gospel, that the antithesis between 'wisdom' and 'apocalyptic' did not seem to be found in the actual texts.[22] But these views went unheeded. 'Apocalyptic' meant fundamentalism (the Seminar was born not long after the Jonestown massacre), and Jesus was to be separated from it by a wide margin. This was part of the outworking of Koch's 'agonized attempt', noted above. Over against the Seminar, more recent scholars have argued that Jesus was indeed an 'apocalyptic prophet' – not always noticing, perhaps, that the word 'apocalyptic' is so ambiguous that to affirm that identity of Jesus is merely to arrive at a point from which several roads fan out in different directions.[23] Thus, for the 'Jesus Seminar', 'apocalyptic' represented all the things about popular American Christianity which those particular scholars most disliked.

The move for an 'apocalyptic Paul', however, seems to work in the opposite direction. As we shall see, partly with Beker but more particularly with Martyn and his followers, 'apocalyptic' interpretations aim to highlight the 'cosmic', global and supraglobal dimensions of Paul's thought, over against individualistic and even privatized readings. Here is the irony: in Martyn at least, as we shall see presently, one sometimes has the impression that the main thing to be avoided is the kind of fussy, who's-in-who's-out sort of Christianity one finds in – popular American religion! Thus, at the risk of

[20] On the 'Jesus Seminar' and its presuppositions and practices see *JVG* ch. 2 and other literature cited there. One of today's enthusiastic promoters of a Pauline 'apocalyptic', Beverly Gaventa, notes the dangerous associations with contemporary fundamentalism: Gaventa 2007, 82f.

[21] e.g. Borg 1986, 1987 and elsewhere, dependent on the larger arguments in e.g. Borg 1984; see the discussion in *JVG* 75–8.

[22] See e.g. Wright 1996a.

[23] See e.g. Allison 1998 and elsewhere.

oversimplification, it might appear that the 'Jesus Seminar' disliked fundamentalism, and so avoided 'apocalyptic', whereas Martyn and others also dislike fundamentalism, and so have embraced 'apocalyptic'.[24] This oversimplification actually makes the necessary point: a word that can, within the same larger world (American biblical scholarship), connote both X and not-X, fundamentalism on the one hand and its avoidance on the other, is singularly useless as an historical or a theological marker for accurately describing anything in the modern world, still less in the ancient one.

In any case, I see no reason here, any more than in the 'Jesus Seminar' discussions, to be drawn into such either/or polarizations, which are rather obviously modern distinctions read back into first-century material where they are out of place. Once more we may refer to Koch:

> We still have to enquire whether it is really historical apocalyptic which is looming up so suddenly at the centre of theological thinking. There is a widespread suspicion that, basically, certain contemporary ideas are being projected back and fathered upon the apocalyptic writers; whether the reason be to make modern ideas more cogent and plausible, or whether it be to represent certain contemporary theological ideas as being from the outset unbiblical and uncanonical. The apocalyptic writings could be particularly suited to such conscious or unconscious manipulation, because little work has been done on them by scholars and they have always for that reason appeared to observers as equivocal and open to many interpretations.[25]

In particular, there is the constant danger that Martyn, in his reconstruction of the Galatian situation, may be ascribing to the 'Teachers' (Paul's opponents) some things which Paul himself strongly affirmed. Martyn might respond that Galatians, of all the letters, cries out for mirror-reading, and he would be right. He might also respond, as he says more than once in his commentary, that some scholars, including the present writer, ascribe to Paul certain beliefs which were instead held by the 'Teachers'![26] But all such work must be subject to continual check and critique. Otherwise, the impression is that Martyn's 'Teachers' are simply a construct of the bits and pieces of Paul's writings that he, Martyn, does not want to see in his own would-be 'Pauline' theology.

We must remind ourselves again that using the word 'apocalyptic' in New Testament studies is itself a rhetorical device whose power lies in its implicit appeal to an explanatory history-of-religions map. Such appeals invoke a larger body of literature, and/or a more widely evidenced worldview, which serves as a matrix for understanding themes, elements or indeed whole books and movements within the New Testament and early Christianity. By designating something 'apocalyptic', one is saying, 'You can see what sort of thing we are dealing with here because it belongs in the larger world reflected in Daniel, *1 Enoch*, *4 Ezra*, Revelation and so on.' As

[24] Martyn's own agenda – the particular contemporary movements he approves or disapproves – does not emerge clearly in his writings. Some of his followers, however, are less reticent: see e.g. Rutledge 2007 and particularly Campbell 2009.

[25] Koch 1972 [1970], 15.

[26] See Martyn 1997a, 347; and esp. de Boer 2011, 154. On these writers see ch. 8 below.

with all historical analysis of this kind, such a judgment may have to do with the *origins* of a theme or idea ('this came from an "apocalyptic" context'), or with its *destination* ('this idea, borrowed from elsewhere, came to serve an "apocalyptic" purpose'). But the point, to say it again, is that when people use the word as a label for a text, a theme, an idea or an entire book, they are saying, in effect, 'There: we have located this within an already-known matrix; now we can move forward from that to draw further conclusions about its meaning.' It is therefore vital to be sure that the matrix itself is carefully described.[27]

One further important wrinkle needs to be mentioned. Part of the earlier rejection of 'apocalyptic' by Wellhausen and others, in a line forwards at least to Vielhauer, had to do with the fact that this category was inalienably *Jewish*, in a scholarly environment where it was assumed that genuine Christianity had broken free from 'Judaism' and its dark world of 'works-righteousness'. Thus Schweitzer's reaction was itself a plea, not only for 'apocalyptic' as the matrix for Jesus and Paul, but for an essentially Jewish context for both. This itself has proved, of course, far too simple. There were plenty of non-Jewish 'apocalyptic' movements (to use that language for the moment) in the ancient world, as indeed in the modern; and there were many Jewish movements which, so far as we know, did not characteristically use the literary genre 'apocalyptic' or appear to think like some who did. But we need to remind ourselves that this debate, like most others in the last century, carries in itself overtones with particular resonance in the world of scholarship which still looks back to F. C. Baur and his highly misleading Hegelian categories ('Jewish Christianity', 'gentile Christianity' and 'Early Catholicism', in particular). From this quagmire of agenda-driven analyses only history can save us. Fortunately, history has been doing so. Unfortunately, not everyone has noticed.

[27] For an early example of careful description in relation to some of Paul's key 'apocalyptic' terms, see Court 1982, who however argues his case in relation to Cullmann and not at all to Käsemann.

Chapter Seven

FROM KÄSEMANN TO BEKER

1. The Käsemann Revolution

If any twentieth-century movement in Pauline studies deserved the title 'new perspective', a strong case could be made for the revolution launched by Ernst Käsemann after the Second World War. Käsemann, whose pre-war political stance had got him into trouble and indeed into prison under the Nazis, was horrified by all that had happened. But he was if anything even more shocked by the fact that the churches had neither understood the depth of the structural evil which had wreaked such havoc nor articulated a biblical message that would address the problem in its fullest dimensions. Bultmann's existentialism, and its individualistic application, could not be enough. The Bible itself, and Paul himself, had things to say which the previous generation had screened out. A fresh reading was called for, in which the biblical message about the divine victory over suprahuman evil would stand out, providing an altogether larger context for understanding the message of redemption.

Käsemann's writings, not least his personal reminiscences and final lectures, make it clear that he was urgently concerned throughout his life with social and political issues, and that he was addressing them, not as an 'extra', a mere late-blooming 'implication' of a 'gospel' which was about something else, but as the deep dimension of one and the same 'gospel' which Paul proclaimed. Since I have various questions to raise about the way in which the Tübingen master developed this insight, and about the ways in which it has been taken forward subsequently, I should make it clear that, in these general terms at least, I am in substantial agreement. To put it bluntly, if we have to choose between Bultmann and Käsemann, we must choose Käsemann.

But that does not mean that we have to follow him all the way. Since the Käsemann revolution has been the platform upon which the highly influential work of Beker and Martyn has been built, it is important to understand what he said, what he did not say, and what the strengths and weaknesses of his proposal might be.[1]

As a New Testament scholar within the German tradition, Käsemann's proposal naturally focused on an essentially history-of-religions analysis. When he proposed that 'apocalyptic' was 'the mother of Christian theology', he was explicitly replacing an earlier candidate, the Gnosticism made famous in the work of his teacher Rudolf Bultmann. It is not clear, at least not to me, whether Käsemann rejected the 'gnostic' hypothesis because he found it unconvincing at an historical level (the relevant sources are much too late; the Pauline exegesis simply doesn't work), or because he found it grossly inadequate in enabling the church to be the church at a time of crisis (why oppose the Nazis if what matters is the secret authenticity of your own personal faith?). Perhaps it was both. Some German scholars continued for a while to try to place Paul's thought within a 'gnostic' environment.[2] But Käsemann had seen that this was not enough. He therefore struck out on a new line, as the mood of the times seemed to demand, replacing Gnosticism with 'apocalyptic'.

Two important corollaries followed from this. First, 'apocalyptic' as envisaged by Käsemann was still *doing the same job* that 'Gnosticism' had done, that is, providing a hypothetical religio-historical matrix within which Paul's thought developed and could be appropriately interpreted. Perhaps that is why, in the hands of Käsemann and at least some of his would-be followers, 'apocalyptic' still retains a radical dualism at its heart, rejecting the present world and its structures and insisting on the utter superiority of the world to come. There are strong echoes here of some elements of Barthian thought: Käsemann was as good as Barth at saying 'No!' to the present world of nature, of 'religion', of the bourgeois way of life which had so easily been duped into demonic idolatry. Though, as we now know, ancient Jewish 'apocalyptic' was not designed to combat any of those things, that was the job Käsemann needed his sort of 'apocalyptic' to do.

For that reason, second, this would-be history-of-religions analysis had an uncomfortable position to maintain. The move from 'Gnosticism' to 'apocalyptic' involved a move, massive in its implications within German scholarship, from an essentially hellenistic analysis to an essentially Jewish one. (Käsemann's anti-Bultmannian protest was thus, at this level, a kind of 'apocalyptic' equivalent to the radical 'rabbinic' proposals of W. D. Davies which were put forward around the same time.[3]) But for Käsemann, despite his radical rejection of the anti-semitism that had cast its dark shadow over Europe, 'the Jew' was still the classic type of *Homo religiosus*. 'Religion' was something humans did to impress God, and the Jewish 'religion' was the

[1] There have of course been many analyses of Käsemann's thought. See e.g. Morgan 1973, 52–62; Koch 1972 [1970], 75–8; and the monographs of e.g. Way 1991; Zahl 1996. For my own earlier assessment, see *Perspectives* ch. 4. I noted above (51 n. 76) the letter in which Käsemann thanked me for that article and congratulated me on having understood him.

[2] Notably e.g. Schmithals 1971 [1956].

[3] See above, 19–22.

archetypal form of that phenomenon – thus collapsing the analysis back into yet another version of the 'old perspective', with Judaism as the 'wrong' sort of religion and Christianity as the 'right' sort. For Käsemann, the gospel was of course about 'faith', which was completely different from 'religion', accepting the sheer gift of the gospel through which God justified not the 'religious' but precisely the ungodly. So Paul's argument in Romans 2.17–29, and above all in Romans 9—11, is aimed at *Homo religiosus* in general, under the label of 'the Jew'. But this made it very difficult for Käsemann to argue at the same time for the essentially *Jewish* historical matrix which his 'apocalyptic' proposal needed. He needed Paul to be arguing from an essentially Jewish vision of the divine victory over the whole wicked world. But he needed this Jewish vision to be shorn of several of its most characteristically Jewish elements, not least any strong sense either of the divine covenant faithfulness or of salvation history. Käsemann's vision was of a Paul who embraced a whole-world gospel, a vision of all of reality, not a particularistic Paul who endorsed local or national aspirations.

The trouble was, and is, that the texts where one might find the 'apocalyptic' vision which the theory required, texts like *1 Enoch*, Qumran, *4 Ezra* and so on, were soaked in exactly that particular local and national vision and hope. They were rooted in covenantal theology, and again and again highlighted fresh retellings of the long story of the world in general and Israel in particular. This problem does not seem to have impinged on Käsemann as much as it might have done, perhaps because he, like most other western scholars of the period (as Koch remarked), does not seem to have made a close study of those texts in their own right. There is no sign that, when he invoked 'apocalyptic' in the way he did, he had in mind what the relevant writers were actually saying and hoping for, or how they were retrieving and re-applying the ancient biblical promises. It was enough for Käsemann that they represented a worldview called 'apocalyptic', well known in German history-of-religions analysis, though to this point seen as a dark and unwelcome intruder. Thus, like the early Gnostics themselves, Käsemann was driven through the disillusionments of history to embrace what had formerly been considered the dark side of theology. What Bultmann had regarded as the husk, Käsemann saw as the kernel; what Bultmann had hastily demythologized, Käsemann celebrated as the heart.

The most obvious exegetical result was Käsemann's view of *dikaiosynē theou.*[4] This meant a break with the entire Reformation tradition, but Käsemann was undeterred. 'The righteousness of God' was not, he declared, the human status given by (or approved by) God. It was God's own 'righteousness'. This was not, however, the *iustitia distributiva* against which Luther had reacted, a blindfolded divine 'justice' which distributed rewards to the good and punishments to the wicked. It was rather the 'salvation-creating power' through which God, the creator, overturned the powers of the world in order to establish his own sovereign rule of justice, freedom

[4] See, famously, the article in Käsemann 1969 [1965], ch. 7; and of course the exposition of the relevant passages in Käsemann 1980 [1973].

and peace, for the benefit of the whole creation – not just for individuals who happened to believe the gospel. For this meaning, Käsemann drew on the work of associates, claiming the background of a supposed 'technical term' in a few texts from apocalyptic Judaism.[5]

The advantage of this 'technical term' was that it might seem to have bypassed the otherwise awkward national and covenantal meaning of 'God's righteousness', to which the older biblical usage would naturally have pointed.[6] The disadvantage was that the evidence for the use of the phrase as a non-covenantal and 'cosmic' technical term is lacking. All the signs are that the national and covenantal meanings were there, not only in the Jewish texts to which appeal had been made, but also in Paul himself, notably at the very heart of Romans 3. That, too, could be dealt with by the proposal that in 3.24–6 Paul was quoting, but modifying, an earlier Jewish-Christian confession which had originally emphasized the divine covenant faithfulness but which Paul was now altering in a global or 'cosmic' direction. That rather desperate suggestion (the victory of theory over exegesis) is itself unnecessary, as I and others have argued elsewhere.[7] Similar moves, however, have continued to be made by Käsemann's followers, as we shall see. Koch could speak of the agonized attempts to save Jesus from 'apocalyptic'; we still have agonized attempts to save Paul from covenantal Judaism, or at least some supposed features of it. The fact that this latter task invokes 'apocalyptic' to achieve that goal ought to be seen as ironic.

Käsemann's main theme, however – the divine victory over the powers, rescuing the whole world from their grip – really was and is there in Paul. Romans 8.18–25 does indeed promise the redemption and renewal of the whole created order. Taken together with 1 Corinthians 15.20–8, this means that the creator God will overcome all opposing powers, up to and including sin and death itself. Since Romans 8 forms the climax of the argument about the divine righteousness, it is important that all this be given full weight. But what Käsemann never saw was that this itself was part of *the christologically redefined covenant with Israel.* The hint was there in Romans 4.13, where God's promise to Abraham was that he would inherit 'the world'. It was there in the messianic redefinition of the promises, through passages like Psalm 2.8, in which the inheritance of the royal 'son of God' would include the nations and 'the ends of the earth'. In Paul's reading, the creator's purposes for the creation would be accomplished *through* the covenant with Israel, not bypassing it, and likewise *through*, not despite, the Messiah's accomplishment of the worldwide covenant purposes. To put it the other way, the covenant with Abraham and his family was there in order to undo the sin of Adam and its results. (In exegetical terms, this represents the reading of Genesis implied in Romans 4, 5 and 8: now that the covenant

[5] In the relevant article, Käsemann gestures towards the Qumran *Hodayoth*, but without specific passages. The details were filled in by e.g. Stuhlmacher 1966; Müller 1964.

[6] Perhaps the most obvious passage is Dan. 9 (see esp. 9.4, 7, 13, 16, etc.), but the point could be made from dozens of passages in Isa. and Pss.: see *PFG* 795–804.

[7] See e.g. Wright 2002, 464–8.

with Abraham has been explained (Romans 4) we can see how the Adam-problem has been solved (Romans 5), so that the world can be put right at last (Romans 8).[8]) The covenant was not intended, as far as Paul was concerned, to create a different, 'religious' group who were somehow untouched by the fate of the wider world.

For Käsemann, the great unveiling, the 'apocalypse', lay in the future. He took the word 'apocalyptic' itself to mean, simply and unambiguously, 'imminent expectation' (German *Naherwartung*). In this interpretation, what was revealed in the gospel was the ultimate divine intention – and, of course, the 'power' through which it would be accomplished. The death and resurrection of the Messiah was the sign that God would overcome all the forces of evil and bring about new creation. But here there were problems.

Käsemann shared the widespread view that the early Christians expected the world to come to an end and that they were disappointed. I have argued elsewhere that the end-of-the-world idea is a modern scholarly myth, caused partly – ironically! – by a failure to understand 'apocalyptic' language itself, with its rich symbolism and imagery from its early biblical beginnings through at least as far as the second century AD, and partly by a back-projection from the crises of mid-twentieth-century Europe.

To take the first point: the authors of *1 Enoch* or *4 Ezra* – or, for that matter, Ezekiel and Daniel – were not expecting the world to come to an end. They were expecting, and struggling to find appropriate imagery to explain, a massive turn-around within the ongoing world of space, time, matter and history, for which nothing short of the language of new creation would do. But the older reading of 'apocalyptic' as essentially dualistic (and hence looking for the destruction of the world) persisted.

To take the second: an extra spur to seeing things this way came with the deep sense of cultural disappointment that Europe had suffered in the 1930s and 1940s. After all those years of expecting Utopia just around the corner, what happened instead was the multiple horror of the Nazi regime and war. It was natural to see the same thing in the first century: the early church, expecting the world to end (whatever that would mean), was disappointed. This, I am convinced, is a radical misreading of first-century history.[9] It is significant that neither J. Christiaan Beker nor J. Louis Martyn follows Käsemann at this point. For Beker, the apocalypse was 'now and not yet': the events of Jesus' death and resurrection were the inauguration of the new world, and the final triumph would be the ultimate consummation of something already begun. For Martyn, as we shall see, the real apocalypse, the real divine triumph, was the death of Jesus itself.

There is one more important point to make about Käsemann. It would be easy to imagine, granted his regular emphases, and granted the use of his work by Martyn in particular, that he had nothing positive to say about the

[8] On the Adam–Abraham link see now *PFG* 784–95 and elsewhere. See also the suggestive essays in Anderson and Kaminsky 2013.

[9] cf. *NTPG* 459–64; *PFG* 1082–5, 1098, 1482f. For the point about language and imagery: Caird 1980, ch. 14, esp. 260–71.

divine covenant with Israel. This would be a mistake. For all his political and cultural passion, Käsemann remained an exegete to his fingertips. In his final lectures and essays he returned continually to a theme to which he had previously given little attention.[10] For him, 'apocalyptic' was not antithetical to all forms of 'salvation history', even though the latter had of course been drastically reshaped by the cross. He did not believe that 'apocalyptic' ruled out some kind of covenant fulfilment. Ironically, however, when Käsemann mentioned the latter theme he always saw it in terms of a renewal of the Sinai covenant rather than a fulfilment of the Abrahamic covenant. But my point is quite simple. In our present climate, forty years after the first publication of Käsemann's great commentary on Romans, it is regularly assumed, by theologians and philosophers as much as by some exegetes, that to invoke the word 'apocalyptic' is to stand over against all forms of 'salvation history' and all forms of 'covenant' theology. That was not Käsemann's position, however much he resisted Stendahl on 'salvation-history' (actually, as we saw, he was resisting movements of immanent progress, which was not what Stendahl was proposing) and however much he tried to ward off the covenantal sense of 'God's righteousness' in Romans 3.

It is of course possible that Käsemann was wrong, that he did not draw the radical conclusions he should have done. It is possible to say he was inconsistent – in other words, to apply to him the same kind of *Sachkritik* that the Bultmann tradition applied to Paul, correcting the apostle on the basis of what he really ought to have said. But it is not possible to invoke Käsemann himself in favour of an 'apocalyptic' from which all trace of salvation history, all trace of the covenant with Israel, has been removed. This will be important in the later stages of the present Part of the book. But first, we return to the man who introduced the post-Käsemann world of Pauline 'apocalyptic' to America: J. Christiaan Beker.

2. Triumph Now and Not Yet: J. C. Beker

Beker's ground-breaking book was published in 1980, the year in which there appeared the English translation of Käsemann's commentary on Romans. Like Käsemann, Beker was principally concerned to oppose the Bultmannian reading of Paul which had held sway in mainstream scholarship for so long.[11] Like Käsemann, he highlighted 'apocalyptic', no longer as a dark or negative strain in Jewish or early Christian literature, but as the glorious news of 'the dawning triumph of God'.[12] For Beker, the death and resurrection of Jesus mean that the new creation really has begun: there is

[10] I have explored this further in Wright 2014b, drawing on the posthumous collection Käsemann 2010 [2005].

[11] Bultmann has 56 index-entries in Beker's book; the nearest competitors are Käsemann with 29 and Schweitzer with 25. Key discussions may be found at e.g. 18, 213, 275.

[12] e.g. Beker 1980 (subsequent refs. are to this work), ix, xi, 8, 16, etc. See the summaries at e.g. 207, 278, 354f., 366f. Beker later published a shorter, popular version of his thesis (Beker 1982).

an 'already' to the divine triumph, not merely a 'not yet'.[13] He borrows from Cullmann – not the favourite scholar in the Bultmannian world, no favourite either of Käsemann – the Second World War imagery of 'D-Day' and 'V-Day'. The decisive invasion has taken place, and final victory is assured.[14] Jesus is already exalted as Messiah, but his kingdom has not yet appeared.[15]

This 'apocalyptic' vision is, for Beker, the very centre of Paul's 'coherent' gospel. Even when local circumstances might have suggested a dose of 'contingency' to soften the blow for the congregation in question, Paul insists on his 'apocalyptic' perspective, as for instance in 1 Corinthians 15, where despite the natural cultural and philosophical position of the Corinthians Paul nevertheless gives them the full apocalyptic measure.[16] Beker's signature theme of 'coherence and contingency' is then deployed, in the main, to address the vexed question of the relation between Galatians and Romans, where some had postulated a decisive development.[17] Galatians he deems to be less directly 'apocalyptic', since there is only one mention of the future event (at 5.5), and virtually no mention of Jesus' resurrection, with which the new creation was launched.

There is little direct engagement in this book with 1 Thessalonians or Philippians. Furthermore, despite Beker's invoking of 'apocalyptic' as the key category, 2 Thessalonians is deemed to be post-Pauline, along with the more predictable Ephesians and Colossians.[18] Nor does Beker actually engage with the key Jewish texts that stand behind his account of 'apocalyptic'. Some are cited, none expounded. Perhaps for this reason, we hear nothing of the themes which dominate the Jewish literature in question: exile and restoration, the hope for a restored Temple and a returned glorious divine presence, the defeat of political enemies. Indeed, one would hardly know that apocalyptic literature as a whole had inalienable political overtones and intentions. The word 'apocalyptic' functions, for Beker, as a shorthand for an essentially *theological* position: that the gospel which Paul proclaimed was not about how individuals get saved, but about the divine triumph over the powers of evil and death that have usurped control over God's good creation.

What I notice particularly about Beker, rereading his book a generation on, is that unlike Käsemann before him and Martyn after him he has no hesitation in combining the main theological themes which generations of

[13] Beker 149, 155.

[14] Beker 159f.; he modifies Cullmann's position, though, at 355, since he takes Cullmann to be placing too much emphasis on the 'now' as against the 'not yet'. There are of course problems with the imagery, implying as it does a more or less smoothly progressing 'mopping-up operation', leading to a kind of postmillennial ecclesial triumphalism. Here is another irony, which Richard Hays pointed out to me: Martyn, too, regularly uses the Second World War language of 'invasion' to push for a picture very different from Cullmann's.

[15] Beker 346; this despite passages like 1 Cor. 15.20–8, where Paul really does seem to think (like Matt. 28.18) that Jesus is already reigning.

[16] Beker 144f., 171.

[17] e.g. Hübner 1984. On 'coherence and contingency' see Beker's summary statements at e.g. 351.

[18] e.g. 161–3.

scholars have forced apart. 'Justification' and 'participation' are not to be separated.[19] Nor (against Schweitzer) are 'juridical' and 'mystical' types of thought to be split apart.[20] In particular, Beker has no problem – any more than do the relevant second-Temple texts! – in combining 'apocalyptic' with something one might call 'salvation history'.[21] Apocalypticism, after all,

> often comprises a universal history that concerns the rise and fall of world empires and expects a cosmic redemption that will be inaugurated by a preexistent redeemer figure.[22]

The death and resurrection of Jesus are the centre point of history, indeed the point at which the world is judged and reborn:

> According to Paul, the cosmic dimensions of the death and resurrection of Christ signify that the cross is God's judgment of the world and that the resurrection is the beginning of the ontological renewal of creation that will come to completion in God's new age.[23]

Paul thus takes Judaism and its traditions seriously, and sees them as fulfilled, however unexpectedly, in the crucified and risen Christ. Beker does sometimes appear to think that Paul was capable of leaning in the direction of Marcion.[24] But this, he says, is not in fact Paul's position. Rather,

> He believes that Christ is the surprising answer to Judaism's religious search, and thus he never considered himself a 'founder' of a new religion. For Paul, *the Hebrew scriptures climax in Christ as their eschatological confirmation* ... The 'New Testament' is ... the authoritative interpretation of the Scriptures in the light of the crucified Messiah, that is, 'the gospel concerning his Son' that God 'promised beforehand through his prophets in the holy scriptures' (Rom. 1:2, 3).[25]

Having myself tried to articulate just such a vision – an 'apocalyptic' reading of Paul, in line with the traditions of second-Temple Judaism, and drawing them to their 'climax' while yet transforming them with the shocking news of the cross and resurrection – I naturally warm to this formulation.

As a result of all this, Beker has no use for the kind of anti-historical understanding of 'apocalyptic' which has recently become such a regular feature, to the extent that for some people this simply *is* what the word means. He refers back to 'classical' theories of the atonement, but he could equally have been referring forward to their present-day successors:

[19] Beker 151, 275, 286, etc. The question of whether Beker really understands 'justification' is a separate issue which we cannot pursue here.

[20] Beker 256, 259f.

[21] Beker 49, 56, 99, 181. Cf. too e.g. 116: 'Like Second Isaiah, Paul interprets Israel's traditions in the light of new divine eschatological acts in history.' I do not think J. L. Martyn could or would have written that sentence.

[22] Beker 138. I am not so sure about the pre-existent figure, but the rest of that sentence is a good summary, in the teeth of what is now often called 'apocalyptic', of what was common coin in the second-Temple period.

[23] Beker 211.

[24] e.g. 30f, 58, 107f., 186f.

[25] Beker 314, italics added.

> ... the 'classical' view threatens to view sin and redemption in terms of a dualistic power struggle in which God in Christ simply conquers enemy territory *by an invasion from heaven*. In this scheme, sin is less a responsible guilt that must be forgiven than a power that must be eradicated, so that Anselm's dictum is relevant here: 'Nondum considerasti quanti ponderis peccatum sit' (You have not yet considered the weight of sin). The death of Christ is here so conflated with his victorious resurrection that the depth, burden, and costliness of God's love in Christ are not accentuated. This results in an interpretation of 'the righteousness of God' as simply God's redemptive act and ignores its Hebrew moral meaning of God's 'just order'. A Christology 'from above' overshadows a Christology 'from below,' and our new creation in Christ threatens to become discontinuous with our former moral responsibility under the power of sin. This view ignores the fact that sin needs to be not only eradicated but also forgiven.[26]

This remarkable argument, to be sure, contains some problems. I do not think Anselm was responding to the 'classical' view when he warned against underestimating the weight of sin. It is more likely that he had in mind the Abelardian view in which what the sinner needed was simply the loving example of the cross. Nor is it necessarily helpful to categorize these different visions of the problem of sin and its solution in terms of Christologies 'from above' or 'from below'. But when Beker, against the grain (one might think) of his larger argument, insists that what was achieved in the death and resurrection of Christ was not simply an 'invasion' by which the powers of evil were defeated but also a dealing-with-sin that would address the problem of guilt and forgiveness, all the signs are that he has Paul on his side. The fact that some modern versions of Christianity may have overemphasized guilt and forgiveness does not justify the interpreter in excising all such material from the apostle, or re-expressing it in terms of 'invasion' and 'victory'. Beker is right, exegetically and theologically, to offer a more nuanced and multi-layered view. Yes, he sees 'grace' as an *event*, something that happens in history as God triumphs over evil.[27] Yes, he sees 'faith' itself within an 'apocalyptic' framework (though he is innocent of the recent interpretation in which *pistis Christou* refers to the Messiah's own faithfulness).[28] Even the spirit, in Paul, is to be understood 'apocalyptically'.[29] But none of this adds up to a pan-'apocalyptic' reading from which other elements, normally found in Paul, are pushed to the margins. Beker does not indulge in *Sachkritik*. Nor does he suggest that Paul sometimes writes things he does not mean in order then to offer an alternative perspective.

Perhaps the strangest thing in Beker's book (there are many strange details; Beker was by all accounts not a straightforward character, and his writing reflects a craggy, angular approach) is that, despite his insistence on an 'apocalyptic' approach to Paul, despite his obvious similarity to Käsemann, and despite his inevitable foregrounding of Romans, there is very little here about the *dikaiosynē theou*. Beker discusses it, of course, but he never makes it a central focus. Yet this is where some of Paul's most

[26] Beker 209, italics added.

[27] Beker 265f.

[28] Beker 268f.

[29] Beker 281f.

obviously 'apocalyptic' language is focused. In the gospel, Paul declares, God's righteousness is unveiled, *apokalyptetai*.[30] We should of course beware of imagining (though as we shall see some have not heeded this danger) that the occurrence of the Greek word *apokalyptō* can be held up as evidence that the writer espouses or expounds a worldview which some scholars two thousand years later have come to call 'apocalyptic'. Yet one might have thought that Beker would be eager to point out that Paul, in the thematic statement of Romans 1.16–17, was insisting on the sudden gospel-driven disclosure of the divine faithfulness both to covenant and to creation.

So many strands in his book point in this direction. The 'imminent triumph of God' is the triumph of the divine *faithfulness*, the divine commitment to put the whole creation right at last, expressed in the present through the putting-right of those who believe, achieved through the divine accomplishment of the ancient covenant promises. This way of expressing it is, of course, my own, but I do not think it is very different from what Beker was saying. Let us, by all means, put the 'apocalyptic' triumph of God in the middle of the picture. Let us insist that this triumph is 'defined by the death and resurrection of Christ', and that it 'constitutes the basic coherence of the Pauline gospel', expressed contingently in relation to the varying needs of the churches. But let us, like Beker, insist that this 'apocalyptic' theology contains within itself, and does not displace, contradict, or render redundant those other features of Pauline thought (history, including salvation history, 'justification' and 'participation', and indeed sin, guilt, forgiveness and atonement) which must be integrated in any full exegetical and theological account of his letters.[31] What Beker saw as coherent ought not lightly to be dismissed as incoherent.

[30] Rom. 1.17; cf. 3.21, where the verb is *pephanerōtai*, but with similar effect and an obvious echo of the earlier passage.

[31] One scholar who has followed Beker in holding together what others have pulled apart is B. W. Longenecker: see e.g. Longenecker 1998.

Chapter Eight

THE 'UNION SCHOOL'? DE BOER AND MARTYN

1. M. C. de Boer

Käsemann's leading follower in America in the last generation has been, without a doubt, J. Louis Martyn. In a distinguished and influential career, Martyn taught at Union Theological Seminary in New York from the 1960s until the 1980s, before retiring to continue his writing. His name is the one now most readily associated with the newer 'apocalyptic' interpretations of Paul, and is invoked as such by many outside the ranks of biblical scholarship who have sought to anchor their own philosophical, theological, homiletical or indeed political ideas in this way of reading the apostle. Because of Martyn's tenure at Union, and because two of his pupils who have most obviously carried forward his work studied there under him, one or two have referred to the vessels that sail alongside the flagship of Martyn's massive commentary on Galatians as 'The "Union" School'.[1]

Martyn studied with Käsemann in Tübingen, and he writes warmly about the influence and example of his teacher.[2] Yet his work diverges significantly from Käsemann's, both in emphasis and in exegesis. If we are to understand what 'apocalyptic' has come to mean in the post-Martyn scholarly world, it is important to be clear about these differences, and about many other tensions and puzzles within his position at large.

Martyn and his followers have produced a substantial body of literature in the last two decades, and it is out of the question to discuss it all in the present context. I will focus on two works in particular: the now famous commentary on Galatians, and the proposals of Martinus de Boer upon which Martyn relies heavily. For this movement, which now fans out to include many others, 'apocalyptic' is the watchword, and Käsemann the guru: the gospel of Jesus breaks in upon the present world, bringing about a

[1] See the complicated little discussion in Ziegler 2011, 420. The world of scholarship was saddened to hear of Martyn's death, in his 90th year, in June 2015.

[2] Martyn 2012.

new creation, overthrowing in the process not just one 'religion' but the whole concept of 'religion' itself, ancient and modern. One could write a whole book simply expounding and engaging with J. L. Martyn, whose influence has ensured that this reading of Paul is taken very seriously in many parts of America at least, giving rise to some fascinating further studies by, not least, Beverly Gaventa, one of the Union students mentioned above.[3] But puzzles remain, which will have to be worked out in the course of our investigation.

I begin with the seminal proposals of Martinus de Boer. (We cannot tell whether de Boer, the student, initiated these ideas, or whether Martyn, the teacher, suggested them first; in the hurly-burly of graduate work, ideas emerge.) De Boer has now produced his own substantial commentary on Galatians where, to borrow the Martynesque phrase which was used as the title for one of his *Festschriften*, 'the conversation continues'.[4] Both Martyn and de Boer make regular and frequent reference back to de Boer's doctoral dissertation, published in 1988, as the historical and textual foundation for the wide-ranging theories which then determine their exegesis and the theology which claims it in support.[5] We note as an aside, but an important one for anyone trying to understand the landscape of English-speaking Pauline studies in recent decades, that the Union School has not really engaged with the new perspective in any of its variations. The two have run on parallel tracks. Insofar as Martyn and others have read Paul and particularly Galatians in terms of a radical opposition between 'grace' and 'religion', the former being all about divine action and the latter being all about human attempts to please God, there are overtones of the so-called 'old perspective' – which is hardly surprising considering the essentially Lutheran background of Käsemann's thought. Insofar as Martyn and de Boer have tried to understand Paul within a Jewish context, and more particularly insofar as they have read Paul's phrase *pistis Christou* as referring to Christ's 'faithfulness', climaxing in his death, there are some analogies with some elements of the new perspective. All this serves as a warning against mixing up different conversations.

Martinus de Boer is to be congratulated for having undertaken a task which, surprisingly perhaps, neither Käsemann nor Beker seems to have regarded as necessary: an investigation of the Jewish 'apocalyptic' literature deemed relevant to the quest for an 'apocalyptic' understanding of Paul.[6] (As with Käsemann, this represents the implicit shift from a hellenistic to a Jewish history-of-religions context, but the Union School has not normally drawn attention to this.) De Boer is clear that this historical study of the key

[3] See esp. Gaventa 2007; and e.g. Gaventa 2011 (a revised form was subsequently published as Gaventa 2012), 2013b, 2013c.

[4] See Fortna and Gaventa 1990.

[5] See too de Boer's article in the other Martyn *Festschrift* (de Boer 1989), which repeats and expands some of the key arguments.

[6] cf. Koch 1972 [1970], 123: 'It is hard to detect any study of the primary texts, at least in continental theology.'

texts must form the basis of his interpretation of the relevant motifs and passages in Paul. Our modern phrase 'apocalyptic eschatology', he writes,

> is used by students of Paul because they discern certain conceptual affinities between Paul's eschatology and Jewish eschatological expectations that are also labelled 'apocalyptic'.[7]

The point may be obvious, but it is worth making because the word 'apocalyptic', as we have already seen, has had such a varied career that de Boer's determination to anchor his use of it in actual ancient texts can only be applauded: 'Apocalyptic eschatology', he writes, 'is that type of eschatology usually associated with a genre of works known as apocalypses', though elsewhere he broadens this to include 'texts that bear witness to Jewish apocalyptic eschatology, i.e. "revealed" eschatology, whatever the precise literary genres of such works'.[8] Following Käsemann and Beker, the study of Pauline 'apocalyptic eschatology' must proceed

> in light of their conceptions [i.e. Käsemann's and Beker's conceptions] of Jewish apocalyptic eschatology which is the assumed *religionsgeschichtlich* backdrop to the apostle's own views.[9]

De Boer is, in other words, appealing directly, in the regular mode of New Testament scholarship, to an aspect of the wider cultural matrix as the explanatory grid on which to plot the exegesis of early Christian texts. So far, so good.

The problems begin almost at once, however, with the motif which, for de Boer (and for Martyn following him, and for Vielhauer, regularly cited in this connection), is the surest sign of the presence of something that can be called 'apocalyptic'. This motif is the distinction (sometimes misleadingly called 'dualistic') between the 'two ages', that is, between 'the present age' and 'the age to come'. It is of course true that this distinction characterizes several writings normally known as 'apocalyptic', from the book of Daniel onwards.[10] But it is equally characteristic, if not more so, of more or less all Jewish thought in the rabbinic period; and this should lead us to suppose that it is highly likely to have been even more widespread in the early period. The rabbis, after all, turned their backs on 'apocalyptic' after the disasters of 70 and 135, and instead concentrated on the study and practice of Torah.[11] But they retained the strong sense that 'the present age' (*ha-olam ha-zeh*) was a time of sorrow and wickedness, and that the one God would at last usher in 'the age to come' (*ha-olam ha-ba'*). Of course, those who

[7] de Boer 1988, 7. References in what follows are to this work unless otherwise indicated.

[8] de Boer 19, 40.

[9] de Boer, 19.

[10] e.g. *4 Ez.* 6.9; 7.12f., 113; 8.1, 52; *2 Bar.* 44.15; 48.50; 73.5. The relevant phrases themselves are not found in Daniel, but the idea of a present time of oppression and wickedness, to be followed eventually by 'the time of the end' when God will establish his kingdom, runs throughout much of the book: e.g. 2.36–45; 7.9–14, 21f., 23–7; 8.13f., 17, 19; 9.24–7; 12.1–4.

[11] See *NTPG* 197–9; and the recent brief but helpful survey of Schiffman 2010.

wrote 'apocalypses' in the sense of the literary genre did indeed speak in these terms, sometimes undertaking to reveal matters concerning the character and timing of the 'age to come'. Sometimes they advanced specific chronological proposals about when this would happen, usually dependent on Daniel 9. But the existence of a 'two-age' scheme of thought – we can hardly emphasize this enough in the present context – *has no automatic connection to anything that can meaningfully be called 'apocalyptic'*. A two-age scheme is neither a necessary nor a sufficient condition for giving a text, or the ideas expressed in it, that label. The two-age scheme is simply a widespread feature of Jewish thought throughout the second-Temple period and on into the high rabbinic period. We may assume that Saul of Tarsus, as a zealous Pharisee, took it for granted, and we may take it as read that this of itself is not sufficient to affix the label 'apocalyptic' around his neck. One might just as well say 'rabbinic'. I agree broadly with Käsemann and the rest that Paul had a great deal in common with the Jewish 'apocalyptic' writings, but this is not the best way to access that material. To be sure, the ancient Jewish world contained many varieties of speculation about how precisely the 'age to come' would arrive, not least the way in which that might, or might not, involve the arrival and activity of a Messiah. There are different points of view on the question of whether anything God's people might undertake in the present would hasten the coming day. But to speak of 'the present age' and 'the age to come' in this period is a sign, not of 'apocalyptic' specifically, but of the Jewish world in general.[12]

The same could be said of the other supposed signs of 'apocalyptic' to which de Boer appeals, namely the mention of angels, including wicked ones, and a sense of cosmic drama.[13] Of course, not all Jewish sources mention everything all the time. Nobody can say, in one short writing, everything they believe. Paul himself leaves big gaps in every letter – at least, if what one was expecting was some kind of complete 'systematic theology'. Thus, for instance, Galatians itself says almost nothing about sin, salvation or resurrection – which we know from other letters to have been extremely important for Paul.[14] But the 'two ages' scheme, a belief in angels (including evil ones), a sense of cosmic drama as well as the local and personal challenges faced by individuals and groups – all this is to be found as far back as early biblical texts, and as far forward as the mediaeval and modern Jewish writings. And once we have said this we have insisted that the entire history-of-religions discussion of Paul must be moved from the narrow screen of something labelled 'apocalyptic' on to the much larger screen

[12] It is of course quite possible that some Jews – perhaps the Sadducees are the most likely contenders – would have regarded two-age speculations as dangerous or unnecessary. For the phenomenon, see e.g. mBer. 1.5; mPe'ah 1.1; mKid. 4.14; mB.M. 2.11; mSanh. 10.1–4; mAb. 2.7; 4.1, 16f.; 5.19; and the classic discussions in e.g. Moore 1927–30, 377–95; Schürer 1973–87, 2.537f. See too e.g. Davies 1980 [1948], 287f., with more refs. including the collection of passages in Strack and Billerbeck, 1926–61, 4.816f. The rabbis discussed subtle possible distinctions between 'the age to come' and 'the messianic age' (a distinction which may find an advance echo in 1 Cor. 15.24–8), but this is beside our present point.

[13] de Boer 30 notes that Käsemann expands his definition of 'apocalyptic' to include these elements.

[14] See *Perspectives* 520f.

which has the multiform, complex, swirling history, culture, thought and writing of ancient Israel as its backdrop and the equally multiform life of early Judaism as its foreground. That is where Paul belongs. To notice that he, like many other early Christians, thought in terms of the 'present age' and the 'age to come', and to deduce from this that he is therefore to be seen within a rather narrow subset of 'Judaism' called 'apocalyptic' (and within that, as we shall see, a narrower one again) is entirely unwarranted.

Once we make this point all sorts of other things come into play. To appeal to the larger world of Jewish life and thought is to remind ourselves that even the texts commonly regarded as 'apocalyptic' *are not simply about the issue of how people get 'saved'*. De Boer, and Martyn following him, often speak as if the only thing that really mattered in the texts under consideration was, so to speak, the analysis of 'plight and solution', in some kind of universal soteriology, playing out in terms of whether one speaks of 'sins' or of 'Sin', and in terms of how one envisages 'agency' in the complex analysis of human action, divine initiative, and evil powers. Thus the question upon which de Boer fastens, in making his critical distinction of 'two types of apocalyptic' (see below) is the question of *responsibility for evil* on the one hand and of *rescue from evil* on the other. And though 'responsibility' and 'rescue' are indeed themes in the books under discussion, we may rightly protest that these abstractions are not, in fact, the primary things the books in question are talking about.

How has this happened? The answer is quite simple: through the posing of the central question in terms of an essentially modern dichotomy. Martinus de Boer opens his key dissertation with a discussion of two twentieth-century scholars, our old friends Käsemann and Bultmann; he then postulates that there were two types or 'tracks' of second-Temple 'apocalyptic', which correspond broadly to the distinction between those two great men; he then argues that Paul just happens to fit into the type of 'apocalyptic' which resembles Käsemann's thought rather than the type which corresponds to Bultmann's. This inevitably arouses the suspicion of anachronism, even when de Boer (and Martyn, following him) arrive at a view of 'apocalyptic' which, as they note, is significantly different from that of Käsemann himself, for whom the 'apocalypse' is all still in the future while for them it has happened in the death of Jesus. It would indeed be strange if one very specific and highly contingent mid-twentieth-century debate just happened to correspond to a hypothetical distinction, not recognized by most scholars of the relevant texts, between two strands of ancient Jewish thought.

But my point, in any case, is that we cannot isolate themes like 'two ages' and angelic activity and declare that writings which contain them are 'apocalyptic'. Nor can we, by focusing solely on the question of responsibility for evil on the one hand and redemption from it on the other hand, separate these themes off from the larger topics which, demonstrably, preoccupy more or less all the books and writers under consideration. Such larger topics include the divine purpose for Israel and the world; the end of exile and the return of the glorious divine presence; the building or cleansing of the Temple; the coming of an anointed leader, whether royal or priestly; and so on.[15] In particular, more or less every book that might be called 'apocalyptic', and a great deal of Jewish writing that might not merit that label, has to do with the *covenant*, whether by implication or directly, as de Boer admits but does not develop.[16] For the Jewish apocalyptists, the one God has made unbreakable promises to Israel, so that the question to be addressed is not the generalized one of 'how can humans be saved' (with the answers varying according to whether evil is the fault of humans or of evil angels – see below), but 'how will the divine plan to rescue Israel be fulfilled?' And the answer, again and again from writings of many different types, comes in terms of an *historical sequence*: not, to be sure, a smooth, evolutionary narrative of immanent 'progress', against which Martyn, following Käsemann, quite naturally sets his face, but the kind of thing we find in Daniel 2, Daniel 7 or, particularly, Daniel 9. One might actually suggest that a far more accurate indicator of 'apocalyptic' than the 'two ages' (which as we have seen are prominent in a much wider sphere) would be the way in which 'apocalypses' regularly concern themselves with *telling the story of Israel and the world* in a way that leads the eye up to the eventual moment of divine rescue.[17] Since there are now some writers who assume (a) that Martyn has offered a compelling 'apocalyptic' reading of Paul and (b) that this compelling reading involves denying any such narrative-reaching-a-climax, it is important to get this straight. Once we expand the question of Paul's history-of-religions context beyond the narrow confines of the Bultmann–Käsemann debate, it is impossible either to isolate 'apocalyptic' in general or to play this notion off against either 'covenant' or 'salvation history' (as long as the latter is carefully defined). It is likewise impossible, within this expanded horizon, to separate out the two strands of 'apocalyptic' which de Boer claims to find in some Jewish texts, and which Martyn, following him, turns into the backbone of his analysis of the Galatian situation. Finally, it is impossible then to call one of these strands 'apocalyptic' and to play it off against everything else, as some of Martyn's followers have tried to do.[18]

What, then, are these two 'strands' or 'tracks', and how does de Boer discern and describe them? The first hints come in his early comments about the Syrian 'Apocalypse of Baruch'. This book, he notes, has little or nothing to say about 'cosmological powers', by which he means principally the evil non-human beings of Genesis 6 (who play such an important role in, for instance, parts of *1 Enoch*). Further, *2 Baruch* operates with a linear

[15] de Boer 85 more or less admits that he is omitting much relevant material.

[16] de Boer 1989, 173.

[17] See Koch 29, 33, 40f. 43, 51f., 84. I have argued the point from the actual texts in *PFG* 121–8. Koch's point is well taken (51f.): on the one hand, the apocalyptists stress 'the divine direction of the whole of history' (Koch puts the whole phrase into italics); on the other hand, the glorious future which will come at the end of this history 'does not issue from human energy [nor, we might add, from an immanent process] but from God's conferring grace.' If this balance had been maintained a lot of trouble might have been avoided.

[18] e. g. Harink and Campbell: see below.

sequence of the two 'ages', rather than with two 'spheres' which might better be conceived of 'vertically'. Finally, *2 Baruch* envisages an 'ontological' change between the two ages rather than a 'cosmological' one.[19] Once we put this writing back into its historical context, however (probably in the late first or early second century), these are simply not the issues with which the writer seems to have been concerned. For him, the problem was that Jerusalem had been destroyed, and with it the urgent hopes of the day. Of this, however, de Boer tells us almost nothing.

Instead, he claims that *2 Baruch* and its close cousin *4 Ezra* exhibit something he calls 'forensic apocalyptic eschatology', to be distinguished from the 'cosmological apocalyptic eschatology' he finds in books such as *1 Enoch*, or, to be more precise, in its first thirty-six chapters, commonly called 'The Book of the Watchers'.[20] This scheme works less well for the 'Similitudes' of Enoch (*1 Enoch* 37–71), since there, while human life has been subject to evil angelic forces, it is human sinning itself which enables death to destroy human beings.[21] And in the 'Epistle of Enoch' (*1 Enoch* 91–105), we find that, while the fallen angels are indeed to be judged, 'human beings are themselves responsible for sin'.[22] Here de Boer in my view overplays his hand, claiming that the author of this section 'has rejected cosmological subjection as an explanation for sin and for death', highlighting instead personal responsibility and accountability. This problem comes into focus at the end of the discussion, where de Boer claims that 'You cannot ascribe to an alien force what is your own fault and responsibility!'[23] This essentially modern ethical perspective is challenged by a great many Jewish texts ancient, mediaeval and modern. Where a modern might see contradiction (between, say, 'determinism' and 'free will'), Jewish tradition would see a mystery which was ultimately both incomprehensible and indissoluble.[24]

One other feature which assists de Boer in making his all-important distinction between the 'two tracks' he discerns within ancient Jewish apocalyptic is the presence of Adam as the origin of human sin. Though Adam plays a minor role in some other texts, it is in *4 Ezra* and *2 Baruch* that this theme comes to the fore. This assists de Boer in constructing his division. These books, he says, offer a system of salvation in which humans are responsible for evil (a responsibility going all the way back to the beginning); humans are therefore responsible for choosing to follow God and his law, and so finding life after all. The law, in fact, gives them a 'second chance', encouraging a 'legal piety'.[25]

[19] de Boer 35–7. In his commentary, however, de Boer (2011, 31) allows that at least in *2 Bar.* 56 the wicked angels put in an appearance.

[20] de Boer 52f.

[21] de Boer 56.

[22] de Boer 57.

[23] de Boer 58: exclamation original.

[24] See Moore 1927–30, 1.453–6, etc. De Boer's own textual analyses indicate the ease with which these antinomies could be held together: see, e.g., his account of the *Testaments of the 12 Patriarchs* (67–9).

[25] de Boer 86–8. The student of twentieth-century Pauline scholarship will recognize 'legal piety' as a code for 'works-righteousness', though de Boer leaves this hanging in the air.

There are many problems with all this. I here mention only three.

1. The labels that de Boer uses are imprecise and, more to the point, misleading. The words 'cosmic' and 'cosmological' are almost as slippery as 'apocalyptic' itself. They gain such precision as they possess within the Bultmann/Käsemann debate, where they demarcate Käsemann's emphasis on the supramundane and suprahuman dimensions both of the human plight and the divine solution over against Bultmann's individualistic, human-centred account ('anthropology'). But in relation to ancient Judaism they are less helpful. 'Cosmic' and similar terms easily collapse into arm-waving gestures with little exact content.[26] In part this is a problem of the contemporary western world, which, soaked in an implicit Epicureanism, has little practice and less skill in discussing non-human and non-spatio-temporal realities. This leaves de Boer's first category very vague. And, once more, it is hard to think of any Jewish literature, of that period or any other, in which some kind of 'cosmic' perspective is entirely lacking. Just because *4 Ezra* and *2 Baruch* do not ascribe responsibility for evil to fallen angels, that does not mean they are not thinking 'cosmically'.

The same is true, if not more so, for de Boer's next category, 'forensic'. Properly speaking this means 'relating to the law-court', but de Boer uses it (so it seems) to mean 'having to do with sin, guilt, atonement and forgiveness' – as opposed to 'having to do with enslavement to evil angels and rescue by divine invasion'. The label 'forensic', like the label 'anthropology', has the function (within the debates to which de Boer is contributing) of signalling a view that might be associated with Bultmann rather than with Käsemann. (Behind this one might detect older echoes, for instance of Gustav Aulén's grossly overdrawn antithesis between a supposed 'classic' view of the atonement and a supposed 'Latin' view.[27]) But this, too, is highly misleading. Both Bultmann and Käsemann, in their reading of Paul, emphasize his 'forensic' theology of justification. I think Käsemann would have been astonished to be associated with a 'non-forensic' account of justification; exegete that he was, he knew perfectly well that the crucial passage in Romans 3.10–20 set up precisely a 'law-court' scenario, i.e. a 'forensic' model, to which the admittedly complex passage 3.21–6 supplied the resolution. Shorthands are inevitable. But these ones, employed in this way, seem to me to distort the material just when precision is required.

2. The most important point, however, is my next one. It has to do with the real content of all the texts under consideration. As I suggested earlier, the books which might properly be called 'apocalyptic' – whether we confine this, as I think we should, to a genre of that name, or whether we launch out into the stormy waters and apply the label to a type of theology or worldview – are never simply about (a) the human plight and (b) the divine solution. They are, again and again, about *Israel's* plight – a subset of the

[26] See Meeks 1983, 240 n. 20, quoting (without a page reference) Beker's description of Christian eschatology as 'realistically chronological (but without any real *measure* of time)' and 'cosmological'. Meeks comments 'I confess that I do not know what this means.'

[27] See Aulén 1969.

human plight, to be sure, but specific, historical, and urgent – and the divine *covenantal* solution.[28] The question is, What is Israel's God up to, in the world and with his people? These writers were always striving for what might be called a theopolitical vision: their question was not 'how do people get saved' so much as *What is going to happen to Israel*? These books, as a result, are again and again preoccupied with the strange dark story of Israel from earliest days to the present time.

This has nothing to do with a smooth evolutionary progress, the straw man much beloved of some 'apocalyptic' theorists, against which they can shoot their fiery darts, speaking of a 'vertical invasion' over against a 'horizontal process', sometimes reclaiming an implicit high theological ground of a Reformational emphasis on 'grace' over against 'human religion'. The dark story in question is there in Daniel 2, 7 and 9; it is there throughout *1 Enoch*, *4 Ezra*, *2 Baruch*, *Jubilees*, *Pseudo-Philo* and many books besides. It comes in various shapes and sizes which do not admit of an easy analysis into 'cosmological' or 'forensic' patterns. To imagine that such stories are really about an immanent process *within* history, rather than having to do with the divine sovereignty *over* history, is to impose a nineteenth-century scheme on first-century material.

The strange thing is that all this is well known. The major writers on Jewish apocalyptic in the last generation – one thinks at once of John Collins at Yale, or Christopher Rowland at Oxford, but of many others from different backgrounds – have explored and expounded 'apocalyptic' from many points of view, setting it in its historical, cultural and theological contexts. None of them has come up with anything remotely like the 'forensic' and 'cosmological' models proposed by de Boer. It simply will not do to say, as de Boer and his fellow 'Union School' members sometimes do, that there are different meanings of 'apocalyptic', and that they are choosing these ones rather than the ones offered by Collins, Rowland and others. The word only carries force within the historical study of the New Testament because of its implicit appeal to an actual historical context, as de Boer specifically and rightly insisted. History, and the historical exegesis of relevant texts, is what matters, not the projection of modern antitheses onto ancient writers.

In particular, there is a rather obvious reason why *4 Ezra* and *2 Baruch* ascribed responsibility for evil principally to Adam. This was not because they held a different abstract theory. It was not because they were thinking like Bultmann rather than like Käsemann. It was not because they had a 'forensic' scheme rather than a 'cosmic' one. It was because *Jerusalem had been destroyed by the Romans*. The 'apocalypse' had come, and it had been a day of darkness, not of light. Earlier writers could ascribe blame to evil angels, whose malevolent power was driving the pagan nations to oppress Israel, but these two books glimpsed a harsher truth. The only explanation for such a disaster, they reckoned, must have been that the problem which had infected humans in general had infected the Jewish people as well. In

[28] As Sanders pointed out with reference to the rabbis, the reason 'covenant' is rarely mentioned is that it is everywhere presupposed.

Pauline language, Israel, too, was 'in Adam'. The horrific disaster of AD 70 demanded a deeper analysis: don't blame the angels, blame the human from whom all, Israel included, are descended! There is no evidence that Jewish writers of this period thought in the patterns de Boer has described, distinguishing a 'forensic' idea associated with Adam's sin from a 'cosmic' one associated with wicked 'powers'.[29] There is good evidence that something actually happened in AD 70 as a result of which the whole world seemed to be a different place, demanding a different analysis. Here is irony indeed: an 'apocalyptic' event really did occur, with visible results; and those who have studied 'apocalyptic' have translated it out into abstract systems of thought. My second point, then, is this: that a more detailed historical study of 'apocalyptic', such as has been carried out in recent decades, does not support either the overall analysis which de Boer offers or his specific 'two tracks' proposal, upon which Martyn, as we shall see, has built so much.[30]

3. The last point is almost equally important. As de Boer himself candidly recognizes, the hypothetical 'two tracks' do not 'come away clean' from one another. Even when there are significant differences of emphasis as between 'cosmological' and 'forensic', these do not play out in the way de Boer, followed by Martyn, require if their interpretations of Paul are to work.

De Boer himself frequently points out that his 'two-track' theory is a generalized, heuristic model which glosses over a lot of the detail. His aim was, after all, to understand specifically the role played by 'death' in the different texts, and he does not pretend

> to account for all that is of importance in Jewish apocalyptic literature (e.g. messianism, national destruction and restoration, the Temple, repentance, atonement).[31]

Once those major themes are eliminated from consideration, one might express doubts about the likelihood of a balanced account upon which entire worldviews can be reconstructed. But this is not the greatest weakness in the theory. De Boer himself admits that hardly any of his texts exhibit the 'tracks' in the way they have then been used. He does not wish, he says,

> to suggest that the various documents we have discussed can be assigned simply to one of the two tracks. Rather, I present the two tracks as *heuristic models* that may be used as interpretive tools to understand the dynamics of the various texts.[32]

The two tracks occur, he says, 'in *relatively* pure form' (italics original), in *1 Enoch* 1—36 and *2 Baruch* respectively. Elsewhere, however,

[29] Which Martyn 1997a, 97 described as 'extraordinarily perceptive'.

[30] Martyn 1997a, 97 n. 51 declares that the 'two track' proposal is 'essential to the reading of Galatians'. De Boer's work is also held up by Gaventa 2007, 83 as having done the necessary work on the relevant Jewish texts. A further example of recent 'apocalyptic' study going in quite a different direction is the remarkable work of Portier-Young 2011, which offers a detailed historical and not least political analysis of the relevant texts.

[31] de Boer 85.

[32] de Boer 85 (italics original).

> Other works to one degree or another exhibit significant elements of both tracks, most notably the Dead Sea Scrolls.

Thus

> The metaphor of the two 'tracks' ... is used to denote two internally consistent or coherent configurations of motifs that, like railway tracks, may lie parallel, crisscross, or overlap, even within a single work.[33]

This is indeed the case, and de Boer is to be congratulated not only on the careful modesty of his proposal but on describing, in relation to several of the works under discussion, points at which that crisscrossing and overlap occurs. The question, of course, is what counts as 'consistency', and according to whose standards. As de Boer says disarmingly, in relation to notions of resurrection but then more widely,

> We must, however, acknowledge that the correlation ... with the two 'tracks' of Jewish apocalyptic eschatology does not always hold. (Jewish apocalyptic literature is not noted for its systematic consistency and I remind the reader that the two 'tracks' I have outlined are heuristic models.)[34]

As a result,

> in some works both 'tracks' of Jewish apocalyptic eschatology appear equally prominent. The Dead Sea Scrolls provide the most notable instance of this combining of the two 'tracks' ... Much the same may perhaps be said for *Jubilees* and the *Testaments of the Twelve Patriarchs*, works that have much in common with the Scrolls though the balance they keep between the two forms of Jewish apocalyptic eschatology may not be the same as that found in the Scrolls.[35]

When the architect provides the client with so many warnings about the foundations, we may well be excused for wondering whether any structure built here will remain standing for long.

The fact is that the classic 'apocalyptic' texts are suffused with elements of both supposed 'tracks'. The book of Daniel, the fountainhead of so much writing in this genre, regularly makes it clear that the history of global empires, and of Israel caught in between them, has always been under the sovereignty of God, and also the battleground of supramundane powers. But at the same time God's people are summoned to a costly and law-observant covenant loyalty. Israel's present distress is the direct result of its covenant disobedience, for which penitence is offered, and for which atonement will be made.[36] Meanwhile, the centrepiece of the book, in chapter 7, is a massive law-court scene, with God as the judge, the 'beasts' (representing successive empires) being judged and condemned, and 'one like a son of man' being vindicated, 'coming on the clouds' to be seated beside 'the

[33] de Boer 85. He makes more or less the same point in de Boer 1989, 176f.

[34] de Boer 87f.

[35] de Boer 89. Cf. too 205 n. 94, where de Boer admits that both *4 Ezra* and *2 Baruch* 'consist of various and often conflicting material'.

[36] Dan. 9.3–19, 24–7.

Ancient of Days' and given kingly authority. It is hard to imagine a scene more worthy of that slippery word 'cosmic' than this one; and yet it is obviously also 'forensic'.

It is also, of course, 'salvation-historical'. When read as a whole, with special emphasis on chapters 2, 7 and 9, Daniel presents a typically apocalyptic overview of human history in terms of imperial epochs, which have nothing to do with a steady development or progress and everything to do with the divine overruling of history. This history is 'going somewhere', but the destination in (God's) mind is not to be arrived at by slow and steady steps gradually approaching the target. We are not talking about 'progressive revelation'. The destination, the final divine verdict on human wickedness and the final divine vindication, comes suddenly, intruding into the last great blasphemous speech of the final 'beast'. But it is none the less the end which God had had in mind all along – the end, indeed, which in chapter 9 can be given a chronology, the famous 'seventy weeks of years'.[37]

Faced with all this, in the book which by common consent launches second-Temple 'apocalyptic', we should not be surprised that the categories which de Boer brings to the other texts simply do not fit there either.[38] Even *4 Ezra*, which ought to be one of his best 'forensic' examples, 'seems to represent a mediating position', including elements which the theory would suggest do not belong together.[39] Meanwhile *1 Enoch* 1—36, supposedly 'cosmological' and hence not concerned with human responsibility for sin, makes the wicked angels responsible instead; but de Boer qualifies this with 'at least ultimately', implying once again that the dichotomy is not so sharp (or perhaps so important to the writer) as the theory demands.[40] The 'Similitudes' of Enoch combine both themes; the Wisdom of Solomon offers a rich blend of types; the *Psalms of Solomon* stress human responsibility, but nevertheless treat 'death' as a personified power. (Once again we may wonder whether these considerations were uppermost in the mind of the writer, who, under the pressure of Pompey's invasion of Jerusalem, may have momentarily forgotten that he was supposed to be choosing to follow either Bultmann or Käsemann – that is, to decide between 'forensic' and 'cosmic' apocalyptic eschatology.) *Jubilees* certainly offers 'a decidedly cosmological cast of contending angelic forces', but equally holds out long and peaceful life 'to those who devote themselves to the study of the Law and life in "the way of righteousness"'.[41] A similar balance between the supposedly alternative theories is offered by the *Testaments of the Twelve Patriarchs*, and as already noted the Scrolls cannot be parcelled out neatly into either of the supposed alternative paradigms.[42] That leaves *4 Ezra*, which de Boer admits

[37] On which see now *PFG* 142f. and frequently.

[38] One could also cite the book of Revelation, the other great biblical example of 'apocalyptic' writing, where the motifs prised apart by de Boer live happily alongside one another. On this, see Davies 2016.

[39] de Boer 77.

[40] de Boer 53.

[41] de Boer 54f., 59–62, 64f.

[42] de Boer 67–73.

to be ambiguous on the point; Pseudo-Philo, which is likewise ambiguous; and *2 Baruch*, the supposed parade example of 'forensic apocalyptic eschatology'. In short, the texts barely support the theory; and since the theory is self-confessedly a projection into the first century of a twentieth-century (and highly culturally conditioned) German discussion, we may conclude that it is in fact an anachronism. Despite de Boer's pioneering attempt to inject some actual study of actual texts into a debate that had largely ignored them up to that point (and has continued to do so apart from referring back to his work), the result cannot claim to be historical. These issues, in the way that de Boer has presented them, are simply not what the texts were trying to talk about. The third point, then, is that despite de Boer's best efforts to construct a two-track hypothesis, most of the relevant texts simply do not fit. Even if we were to allow that there were two different theological emphases at work here, most of the literature seems happy to accommodate them both.

I have chosen to spend time analysing and critiquing de Boer's work because of its foundational importance for Martyn's commentary on Galatians, one of the most influential books on Paul to be written in America since Sanders, Beker, and Meeks. De Boer, as I say, is to be credited both for adding some textual discussion to a discourse which had previously struggled along without it, and for the cautious, indeed modest, way in which he himself has drawn attention to the flaws in his own theory. This caution seems less evident in some of those who have put his theory to use.

2. J. Louis Martyn

J. Louis Martyn is among the giants of modern American biblical scholarship. His early work on John was justly regarded as establishing a new framework for understanding that gospel.[43] But it is his major commentary on Galatians in the Anchor Bible series that has earned him his place in the scholarly pantheon. Martyn prepared the way for this substantial work with numerous articles and studies, and has followed it up with further reflections.[44] But the weight of discussion must lie on the commentary itself. (Since de Boer has himself now published a substantial commentary on Galatians, I shall include some mention of that here as well; one could, of course, attempt to track the ways in which he now diverges from his teacher, as indeed Martyn does from his, but that exercise must be left for another occasion.) Though Martyn is more of a theologian than he really admits, he would himself agree, indeed insist, that the case he is making must be established on solidly exegetical grounds.

The case in question is one whose time had fully come. Despite the efforts of Beker, 'apocalyptic' had been held at bay in American biblical scholarship

[43] See Martyn 1979 [1968].

[44] See the collection of articles published at the same time as the commentary (Martyn 1997b).

for quite some while. Martyn gives few clues as to the particular theological or cultural pressures to which he was responding – like many exegetes, he might simply say that he was trying to read the text – but there are plenty of similarities to the explicit protests of Käsemann against comfortable bourgeois religion on the one hand and 'enthusiasm' on the other. For Martyn, as for his teacher, Paul believed that in Jesus Christ God had invaded the world, overthrowing the dark hidden powers that had held it captive. Paul's gospel was not simply offering a way of being pious or 'religious' while the world carried on as before. It was about an *event*. Something had *happened* as a result of which the entire world – the whole creation – was different. The imperative of the gospel was all about coming into line with this new reality. This, substantially, is what Martyn means by 'apocalyptic', at least in connection with Paul. At this level it is hard to fault his emphasis, either exegetically or in what seems to be its implicit relevance to church life in the late twentieth or early twenty-first century. I have myself frequently tried to make similar points, in relation both to Jesus, to Paul, and (in their different ways) to the gospels.[45]

I begin there because I have some serious questions to place beside Martyn's commentary on Galatians, but I would not wish those questions to distract attention from the deep-level agreement between us. As often happens, however, we agree on what should be affirmed, but not on what must be denied in order to make room for that affirmation. Nothing that I now say is intended to undermine Martyn's emphasis – Paul's emphasis! – on the gospel as, in that sense, *apocalyptic event*: that is, something that took place as a free and fresh gift of grace, something through which God's new creation has burst upon a surprised and unready world, winning the victory over the forces of darkness and death. Paul says as much in 1 Corinthians 15.20–8, a passage I have long considered central to Paul, not peripheral as some see it. Martyn has emphasized this, and in that I rejoice.

The problems begin when Martyn attempts to root his thesis – a thesis about the nature of Paul's gospel, seen through the lens of the letter to the Galatians – in the work of Martinus de Boer which we have just been examining. Where de Boer is cautious, Martyn is adamant. There are two types of 'apocalyptic'; Paul belongs to the first, his opponents in Galatia (whom Martyn calls 'The Teachers') belong to the second.[46] Martyn himself does not offer any fresh account of the 'apocalyptic' texts and themes of second-Temple Judaism. He relies on de Boer's analysis, shorn of the caveats and qualifying remarks de Boer himself inserted. Behind de Boer, Martyn is of course relying on the proposals of his teacher Käsemann, to whom the commentary is dedicated.

This, as we have seen, causes problems. De Boer was clear, in his earlier work at least, that the distinction between the two supposed 'tracks' or types of apocalyptic was somewhat arbitrary and anachronistic, and that in actual

[45] See, for instance, Wright 2011 [*How God Became King*].

[46] Martyn 1997a, 97f., 587 and *passim*. Subsequent references to Martyn are to this book unless otherwise noted.

second-Temple Jewish literature, such as the Scrolls, the two crisscrossed and interpenetrated one another. Why then should he, or Martyn, be so sure that Paul was highlighting the one and relativizing or marginalizing the other? How can we be sure that the Galatian 'Teachers' whom Paul was opposing had embraced 'forensic apocalyptic' and that Paul, in response, was occasionally using their language but subverting and transforming it with the 'cosmic apocalyptic' he preferred? Granted that Paul did not use either the literary genre 'apocalypse' or, as the main points in his argument, any of the themes to which de Boer draws attention, might the entire discussion not be getting off on the wrong foot? Might the whole thing not be a way of pursuing our own contemporary concerns (recalling that de Boer opens his discussion with the debate between Bultmann and Käsemann) by way of distinctions that meant nothing in the first century, as Koch suggested in relation to the earlier discussions of similar topics? Why, in particular – since de Boer was clear that Jewish apocalyptic eschatology focused on the covenant, and since de Boer never said anything about either 'track' of 'apocalyptic eschatology' entailing a rejection of history – did Martyn leap so quickly into supposing that the 'Teachers' were offering a covenantal and historical construal and that Paul was opposing them at just these points?[47] These vital elements in Martyn's analysis – his opposition to 'covenantal' theology, and to some kind of 'salvation history' – have nothing to do with historical analysis of actual 'apocalyptic' texts (including de Boer's analysis on which Martyn says he is relying), and far more to do with similar themes in Käsemann (though he, too, was more nuanced, as we have seen) which Martyn was retrieving for his own polemical purposes.[48]

Does it matter how we use the word 'apocalyptic'? Is there a problem with giving such a term different meanings? Not necessarily. We can, as Lewis Carroll suggested, make words mean what we like and pay them extra on Fridays. But, as we saw, de Boer's explicit intention, in the work on which he and Martyn (and hence Martyn's many followers) have built so much, was to locate Paul's supposed 'apocalyptic' within its actual historical context, that is, within the 'apocalyptic' of second-Temple texts. The problem is that, with the discussion set up in terms of Käsemann's debate with Bultmann – remembering that neither of those great Germans seems to have spent much time studying the Jewish texts in question – what started off as an historical quest has quickly turned into a study in twentieth-century themes, projected back fuzzily onto a would-be 'historical' screen.

[47] On the importance of history in 'apocalyptic' writing see once again Koch 19, 33, 40f., 43, 51f., 84. At 101–3 Koch discusses Pannenberg's retrieval of this theme, but we should avoid tying down what is manifestly there in the texts to the work of any one modern theorist.

[48] See e.g. Martyn 347–9, suggesting that the present writer and others offer 'a fascinating synthesis of a *biblical theology*, in some regards reminiscent of the nineteenth-century works of J. C. K. von Hoffmann and J. Tobias Beck' (347, italics original). Martyn seems to suppose that any kind of 'redemptive continuity' would have the law playing a positive role (see too 346 n. 179), which of course I deny. The parallels with von Hoffmann and Beck are, I think, superficial only; one might as well reply that Martyn is himself in some regards reminiscent of the nineteenth-century work of F. C. Baur and his followers, pitting Paul's liberating gospel against a hypothetical 'Jewish Christianity'.

Käsemann's serious attempt at a fresh 'apocalyptic' reading of Paul was notionally at least standing on the shoulders of studies such as those of Vielhauer, which would bear little weight today. It relied heavily on the supposed 'apocalyptic', 'technical' meaning of *dikaiosynē theou* in such settings, in which that term was 'cosmic' *and not covenantal.* The major recent studies of 'apocalyptic', however, from Rowland and Collins through to Stuckenbruck and others, simply do not recognize the kind of thing de Boer and Martyn are talking about as being within the world they are describing.[49] (The same goes, far more, for Vielhauer and Käsemann, and even for Schweitzer himself, who confessed that his own knowledge of second-Temple Jewish apocalyptic was second-hand and based on a limited selection of texts, and who offered a 'literal' reading of some of their metaphors, an amusing irony.)

It will not do to sweep these objections away by saying, in effect, 'This is what Vielhauer and Käsemann meant by "apocalyptic", so that's good enough.'[50] Nor can one simply say, 'Well, "apocalyptic" has different meanings.' The only point in invoking the category was that it appeared to offer historical anchorage. If that is denied or ignored, it would be better to find a different term. The use of the word carries at least an implicit claim to be *placing Paul within a particular religio-historical context*, as de Boer claimed in his dissertation. When those most expert on that context say, 'We don't recognize this', we should conclude that something has gone wrong.

Nor will it do to say 'Look how many times Paul uses the word *apokalypsis* and its cognates at key moments in his argument.'[51] That sort of proposal involves a triple begging of the question. (1) It cannot be assumed that Paul's use of a particular Greek term corresponds to the use within twentieth-century scholarship of a cognate word as a label for a particular genre of writing. (2) It remains to be demonstrated that a particular literary genre, which hardly appears as such in Paul, carried with it an entire worldview that could be thus read across into the rest of his work.[52] (3) It

[49] See e.g. Rowland 1982; 2010; Rowland and Morray-Jones 2009; Collins 1987, 2000, 2010; Stuckenbruck 2014. To be clear: de Boer has always, I think, allowed that Jewish apocalyptic eschatology, of whatever type, finds 'its focus in God's covenantal relationship to Israel' (e.g. de Boer 1989, 173; and see de Boer 2011, 219f., 267, 296). De Boer does not link this to Gen. 15 (surprisingly in view of Paul's use of that chapter in Romans and Galatians), and does not allow the covenant to become a major theme in his exposition.

[50] This would be a caricature of the careful statements in de Boer 2002, 22–4, but at times his argument seems to lean in that direction; see too e.g. Gaventa 2007, 82, 111, explaining that she had earlier held out against using the word because of its ambiguities and because – an important point – 'it does not do justice to the continuity reflected in [Galatians]', a continuity she explains, exactly against Martyn, 'with Israel's history and Israel's Scripture' (111). Actual second-Temple Jewish 'apocalyptic', including both the 'tracks' hypothesized by de Boer, would be thoroughly at home with these continuities.

[51] de Boer 2002, 25–33, frequently. Even Gaventa (2007, 81), in her interesting discussions of the term (80–4, 111), allows herself to use this argument.

[52] de Boer 2002, 23 n. 8 suggests that the book of Revelation has always been 'the touchstone for any understanding of apocalyptic, whether Jewish or Christian'. That does seem to make it difficult to see Paul as a representative of the same type of thought; and it certainly makes it difficult to distinguish two 'tracks' of the sort de Boer has proposed. It is ironic that discussions of Pauline 'apocalyptic' have made virtually no use of Revelation (though see again Davies 2016).

remains to be demonstrated that, even if such an 'apocalyptic' worldview existed, it was what Käsemann, Beker, Martyn, de Boer and others have assumed it was. The proof of the pudding is in the exegesis, and Martyn has nobly undertaken the hardest task, which Beker said couldn't be done: to demonstrate this worldview in Galatians, which had until then seemed the least promising place to start.

The reason it seemed least promising is that 'apocalyptic' used to be concerned more or less entirely, for Käsemann in particular, with the *future* event, the *parousia* or second coming. 'Imminent expectation' was the key thing. That gets only one small mention in Galatians.[53] But for Martyn this has changed, albeit it seems without much comment: 'apocalyptic' now designates a worldview in which the decisive 'inbreaking' or 'invasion' (a term Martyn and his followers use a great deal) *has already happened* in the death of Jesus. This represents, I think, not simply a modification, but a serious deconstruction of Käsemann's future-oriented worldview, and its replacement with a decisively inaugurated eschatology. For Käsemann, everything had to be shifted to the future, because otherwise one would open the door to that unwelcome phenomenon *Enthusiasmus*.[54] For Martyn, however, 'apocalyptic' means 'a cosmic drama in which there are three actors', God, humans and evil powers, and in which God in Christ *has already* defeated the evil powers and liberated humans.[55] I am not sure how happy Käsemann would have been with this. More importantly, I do not think that the many 'apocalyptic' writers of the second-Temple period would recognize a statement of their major concern that did not include, as central elements, the question of Israel itself, the ongoing and ultimate divine purposes for Israel and the world, and the ways in which the long story of Israel was to be understood as falling under the divine sovereignty, with the promise of eventual dramatic rescue and reversal of fortune.

The problem of labelling, of giving names to types and strands of thought, emerges particularly when Martyn himself, and then particularly his later followers, end up using the word 'apocalyptic' simply for the first 'track' in de Boer's analysis – which, we remind ourselves again, de Boer himself warned was heuristic and not clear in most of the texts. By the time this way of thinking reaches, say, Douglas Campbell (see the next chapter), we are faced with an 'apocalyptic' reading of Paul standing over against something else, perhaps a 'forensic' one – at which point we are more or less back with Albert Schweitzer, if anything more so. De Boer's more careful distinction of two types of 'apocalyptic' theology has been left behind. Only one of the 'tracks' is now to be allowed to use the word.

But then comes the really critical move. In Martyn's hands, the polemic between Paul and 'the Teachers', seen through the lens of de Boer's 'two types of apocalyptic eschatology', has turned into the familiar neo-orthodox

[53] 5.5: 'waiting for the hope of *dikaiosynē*'.

[54] It is noticeable, in Käsemann's seminal articles as listed above, just how much this (essentially Lutheran) concern preoccupies him.

[55] Martyn 2008, 177f.

polemic of 'revelation' against 'religion'. This can be, and now often is, cast in terms of the 'vertical' against the 'horizontal': the divine initiative breaking into the world, over against any human project, system or effort.[56] But this goes a very long way beyond anything one could deduce even on a generous reading of de Boer's 'two tracks'. Granted that the two tracks overlap and crisscross this way and that in almost all the relevant Jewish texts, how can we possibly say that the first ('cosmic') track is about a genuine divine 'revelation' and the second is about 'religion'? If, in addition, the second track ('forensic apocalyptic eschatology') is capable of being combined, in many of those key texts, with the 'cosmic' variety, why should not Paul, precisely because of what he believed about God's action in Jesus, have seen that there is a new *kind* of 'forensic apocalyptic eschatology', one which does not put its trust in the keeping of Torah but only in the victory of the cross? Why should not both 'tracks' have been rethought, reworked, around the events concerning Jesus? At this point Martyn seems to me to have stepped back from the history-of-religions analysis on which his work was supposedly based, and to have taken his stand instead on the familiar but dangerous territory in which Judaism was a 'religion' while (Pauline) Christianity was a 'revelation'. This is exactly what Koch said the older German 'theology of the Word' had done, only for the apparently opposite reason:

> The onlooker cannot avoid associating the widespread aloofness from apocalyptic literature with the theology of the Word which was in vogue in those decades [between 1920 and 1960] . . . [A]ll were at one in their ultimate conclusion: that the Christian kerygma has nothing in common with history and that church and world, faith and knowledge, lie on two completely different planes.[57]

Ironically, of course, those older writers assumed that 'apocalyptic' would be the dead weight that would anchor faith to history, because of the regular feature of symbolic history-telling which is clearly found in so many actual apocalypses. What happened with Käsemann to some extent, and then with Martyn completely, was that, despite the warnings of Beker and others, the theological *desideratum* – separating the Christian *kerygma* from history – was now to be achieved, not by resisting 'apocalyptic', but by invoking it, and giving it the now regularly assumed but historically spurious meaning of 'vertical invasion'.

This in turn means, as some commentators from different traditions have already noted, that the heart of Martyn's proposal is not, after all, so very different from the so-called 'old perspective'. Perhaps this is why, despite twenty years of the 'Sanders revolution', we hear nothing about that, or the relevant post-Sanders debates, in the Galatians commentaries of either

[56] Thus e.g. Martyn 87, 151, 155, 164 ('Judaism was now revealed to be a *religion* [italics original], as distinguished from God's apocalyptic and new-creative act in Christ'; 'the whole of the letter shows . . . that the advent of Christ is the end of religion'); 382f., 474, 478 (the Teachers are 'nothing more than men who place their trust in religion rather than in the God of the crucified Christ'). At 417 n. 82 Martyn suggests that 'the promissory voice' of the law had an 'original, nonreligious, Abrahamic form'.

[57] Koch 1972 [1970], 63; cp. too 98f.

Martyn or de Boer. Instead, we have a highly sophisticated version of an older Lutheran reading. Käsemann's apple has not, after all, fallen so far from the tree.[58]

This is problematic for many reasons. It is not simply that the new perspective arguments have not been heard. It is more that Martyn has slid back into the worrying position of suggesting, like Käsemann, that 'the Jew' is the archetype of *Homo religiosus*, and as such must be opposed in the name of the Pauline gospel. This is clear beyond cavil in Martyn's work.[59] It is also clear in de Boer's own commentary.[60] It might of course be the case that they were correct, that Paul really did think in terms of the ending of a 'religion' called 'Judaism'. But, as I and others have argued, there are other, and I think better, ways of approaching this difficult and sensitive issue.[61]

All this leads us to the question of exegesis, which is after all where a commentary stands or falls. Naturally, we cannot here work through Martyn's commentary (or for that matter de Boer's) in any detail. But there are certain key moments that stand out.

One natural place to begin is with Martyn's analysis of Galatians 1.4, remembering that Paul's opening greetings often contain microcosmic statements of points he intends to develop later. Here is 1.4, in the context of 1.3–5, with the two key elements labelled (a) and (b):

> Grace to you and peace from God our father and Jesus the Messiah, our Lord, (a) who gave himself for our sins, (b) to rescue us from the present evil age, according to the will of God our father, to whom be glory to the ages of ages. Amen.

Martyn here discerns the 'two tracks', side by side. He proposes that (a) would have been what the 'Teachers' wanted to hear (Jesus 'giving himself for our sins'), and that (b) was what Paul wanted to say in response (the rescue from the present evil age). Thus he claims that

> The formula [in 1.4a] is to a significant degree foreign to Paul's own theology; for it identifies discrete sins as humanity's (in the first instance Israel's) fundamental liability; and it sees forgiveness of sins as the remedy provided by God . . . As we have noted, Paul, when he is formulating his own view, consistently speaks not of sins, but rather of Sin, identifying it as a power that holds human beings in a state of slavery. And he sees liberation rather than forgiveness as the fundamental remedy enacted by God.

[58] So, rightly, Westerholm 2004, 240.

[59] For details, see *PFG* 807f. I should make it clear that when, in 808 n. 109, I accuse Martyn of 'prevarication', I am using that word in the British sense, which means 'evasion', rather than in the apparently American sense of 'lying'. I am grateful to Beverly Gaventa for pointing out this (to me) linguistic novelty, and I apologize for any apparent offence. For Käsemann's position, see e.g. Käsemann 1969 [1965], ch. 8.

[60] de Boer 2011, 324 (the cross 'has brought about the end of a religion'), 398 (the cross 'signifies the end of what [Paul] has called "Judaism"'); similarly, 401f. De Boer's attempt to get off this hook (406) is comparable to Martyn's (204–8).

[61] My own attempts – which, to put it mildly, have themselves not met with universal favour! – are now in *PFG*, esp. chs. 10, 11 and 15.

Why would Paul, or any writer, highlight at the start of an important letter a point significantly different from the one he wishes to make? Martyn raises this question, and is ready with his answer:

> We therefore have to ask why Paul, intent on turning his customary epistolary greeting into a prayer, should do so by quoting a confessional formula, the origin and theological dimensions of which are partially alien to him. The next clause suggests an answer. Paul quotes the Jewish-Christian formula in order affirmatively to correct it by means of an additional clause.[62]

This kind of would-be exegetical move inevitably reminds us of what Käsemann and others did with Romans 3.24–6. Martyn refers to that explicitly in the same context. Theories like this depend on the view that it was pre-Pauline 'Jewish Christians', rather than Paul himself, who were concerned, not only with the covenant and perhaps also with the Torah, but now also with sin, atonement and forgiveness. Martyn is here repeating this post-F. C. Baur tradition, and applying it in a new context. But why should we regard these two things as incompatible (forgiveness of sins on the one hand, rescue from the present evil age on the other), granted that they sit side by side in so many 'apocalyptic' works from Daniel to Revelation and beyond, as de Boer himself has admitted? The only possible answer is that the supposed incompatibility is in the eye of the beholder, specifically, the modern western theologian who stands in a particular tradition and projects this false either/or back onto the first century.[63] We see the same move made, often enough, in commentaries on Romans 1.3–4. Despite the fact that this constitutes Paul's clear and formal opening statement, balanced by a similar scriptural and Davidic statement at the very end of the theological exposition (Romans 15.12), most writers in the Bultmann school and beyond regard the passage simply as a *captatio benevolentiae*, saying something the Roman Christians will want to hear but something which Paul himself will then leave behind as he expounds 'justification by faith'.[64]

Over against this whole line of thought certain things need to be said. First, as a principle of good exegesis, when Paul offers what looks like an opening summary, which turns out to cohere rather well with themes that are then developed later in the letter, we should assume that he actually intends to say what he has in fact said, rather than trying to divide up his carefully balanced statements. Second, the attempt to chisel off this kind of 'early Jewish-Christian' formula from Paul's key statements is doomed to failure. It represents a demonstrably Procrustean technique: here is an idea we cannot fit with our thesis, therefore Paul cannot really have meant it.

[62] Martyn 90.

[63] As I write this I discover that a theologian (Spence 2004, cited in Ziegler 2012, 200f.) has actually accused me of the same fault, of highlighting a *Christus Victor* motif and so ignoring sin, atonement and so on. A glance at my commentary on Romans – or almost any of my other books – should lay this strange suggestion to rest.

[64] See e.g. Jewett 2007, 103–8.

Third, when Paul quotes a parallel tradition in 1 Corinthians 15.3, there is no question that he means every word of it. 'The Messiah died for our sins in accordance with the Bible': whether this formula was quoted by Paul or by anyone else, it was as basic to his gospel as to anyone's. The Corinthians must have known that, and he must have known that they knew it. There is not the slightest sense that this was an emphasis he needed to modify, or a point from which he wished to step back a pace or two. But this turns out to be the foundation of that most obviously 'apocalyptic' of all his chapters, 1 Corinthians 15, which could be seen from this point as a large-scale expansion of just what Galatians 1.4 – in both of its parts! – actually means. The death of Messiah Jesus was 'for our sins', and that is proved by the resurrection: if the Messiah has not been raised, 'you are still in your sins' (15.17). There is no indication in that latter passage that Paul does not mean this in much the same sense as in 15.3, or indeed Galatians 1.4a. Nor can 15.17 be set aside, as Martyn seems to do, as simply the repetition of a tradition.[65] It is a vital part of Paul's larger argument. Of course the 'death for our sins' is not to be separated from the resurrection, or the combination of the two from the cosmic victory they herald (15.20–8). Indeed, it is the resurrection that demonstrates the effectiveness of the cross. Without the resurrection, nobody would have supposed that Jesus was Messiah in the first place, much less the sin-bearer. But now, with sins dealt with on the cross, *this is how Jesus is liberating us from the present evil age*: by the means described in 15.20–8. 1 Corinthians 15.3 thus corresponds to Galatians 1.4a, and 15.20–8 to Galatians 1.4b. Paul not only affirms both of them; he shows how they must go together, how each only makes the sense it makes when conjoined with the other.

The strongest arguments for Paul meaning both halves of Galatians 1.4 come in the parallel, but fuller, statements of similar points within Galatians itself. The combination of ideas in 1.4 seems nicely to anticipate 3.13–14. First, Christ became a curse 'for us'; second, the result is the larger, perhaps 'cosmic', arrival of 'the blessing of Abraham' upon the gentiles.[66] There is of course far more to say about that highly contested passage, but Paul seems happy to affirm *both* the redemptive curse-bearing of the Messiah *and* the larger effect of that death, linking them as achievement and purpose (i.e. the Messiah bore the curse *in order that* the Abrahamic blessing might flow to the gentiles), just as in 1.4 the Messiah 'gave himself for our sins' *in order to* liberate us from the present evil age. We might suggest – though working this out in detail would be too complex here – that a similar sequence is visible in the crucial passage 4.4–7, and on into 4.7–11. The redemptive act of God in the Messiah, redeeming those 'under the law', was accomplished *in order that* those so redeemed might receive adoption, might receive the spirit, might be made 'heirs', and might thus be liberated from the 'elements', whatever they are, that had formerly enslaved them (4.8–11). If Paul

[65] Martyn 89.

[66] cf. Rom. 4.13: the promise was that Abraham's seed would inherit the *kosmos*.

had wanted to put down an advance marker for these two crucial passages (3.13–14 and 4.4–11) within his opening statement and prayer he could hardly have done better than to write what he did in 1.4. There is no need to see either part of that seminal verse as other than fully intentional, fully in line with the letter's complex but coherent argument.

In particular, 1.4a anticipates exactly the emphatic and rhetorically charged 2.20c. There can be no question but that 2.15–21 constitutes a dramatic and powerful statement of some of the main themes not only of Galatians but of all of Paul's thought. And this statement reaches its climax in 2.20, deliberately placed and emotionally powerful:

> ... the life I do still live in the flesh, I live within the faithfulness of the son of God, who loved me and gave himself for me.[67]

The closing phrase echoes 1.4a: *kai paradontos heauton hyper emou*, 'and gave himself for me', repeating, personalizing but only slightly expanding the *tou dontos heauton hyper tōn hamartiōn hēmōn* of 1.4a. If Paul meant 2.20 as strongly as he seems to have done, there is no reason why he should not have meant 1.4a with equal emphasis. Martyn in his commentary moves quickly past the point, saying that the two parts of 2.20c ('the son of God who loved me' and 'who gave himself up for me') are 'drawn from christological formulas', citing 1.4a and Ephesians 5.2, and then adding 'but the major point is that Paul uses them here to answer two questions: Who is this Son of God, and what is his faith?'[68] I agree that Paul is addressing those two questions, among other things. But to take such a careful, powerful and rhetorically placed statement, unparalleled in its singular reference (except perhaps for Romans 8.1–2, which may be significant), and to minimize it by making it simply the repetition of a couple of formulae, has the same feel as someone firing a tranquillizer dart into an energetic pony to stop it prancing round the tidy garden and ruining the carefully arranged flowers. This text, if taken seriously, would spoil the neat either/or pattern upon which Martyn's whole reading of the letter depends.[69]

What I think we have in Paul, which classic protestant readings have screened out in one direction, and Martyn in another, is a double problem with a double solution, the one problem nesting within the other. This is clearest in Romans, but it is clear enough, I believe, in Galatians too. I have argued elsewhere that it was a fundamental assumption of many Jews that the creator God had chosen Israel to play a central role in his purpose for the wider world. That project, and that means to that end, remained unaltered. But the failure of Israel, as set out in the scriptural prophets, meant that God had had to deal with Israel's problem *precisely in order thereby to*

[67] My point would be the same if one were to adopt the alternative translation, 'by faith in the son of God'.

[68] Martyn 259.

[69] Martyn also refers to 'the latter part of the next Note', but the Note in question (on 2.21) does not seem to me to add particular strength to his case.

deal with the cosmic problem. 'Delivering from sins' is exactly the way by which God 'rescues us from the evil age'. The two belong tightly together. 'Dealing with Israel's problem' is *not*, then, a straightforward affirmation of 'the law' in the way Martyn is so concerned about; though, we remind ourselves, the revelation of God's righteousness is still witnessed by 'the law and the prophets', as in Romans 3.21b. What Martyn has done, I think, is to invent a theology for 'the Teachers' which includes a significant element in Paul's own theology, forcing him to take a razor-blade to passages which are actually tightly integrated. This, to my mind, is a sure sign that something has gone structurally wrong, exactly as with the equivalent passages in Käsemann.[70]

This is linked to a further serious problem in Martyn's exposition of Galatians, namely, his insistence on translating the abstract noun *dikaiosynē* ('righteousness' or 'justice') as though it were the active noun *dikaiōsis* ('rectification' or 'justification'). (This in turn is linked to the deeper question of what precisely Martyn and de Boer intend to highlight, or indeed to avoid, in regularly speaking of 'rectification' rather than 'justification': see below.) In the translations familiar from older work, 'righteousness' or 'justice' is not the same as 'justification'. We cannot, it seems to me, assume that an abstract noun can be replaced with an active one without explicit warrant. When Paul intends the active noun, he uses it; when he intends to refer to 'righteousness', or 'justice', or (in Martyn's preferred terminology) 'rectitude', he uses it. This comes to the fore in Martyn's treatment of 2.21, which he translates as

> For if it were true that rectification comes through the Law, then Christ would have died for no purpose at all.

Martyn does not explain, or comment on, the change he has effected here.[71] Throughout the passage Paul has not been talking about the *event* of someone being 'justified', but rather the *status* (of *dikaiosynē*) that people have as a result.[72] To use Martyn's chosen word-group, Galatians 2.21 does not speak of 'rectification', but of 'rectitude', the *status* of 'being in the right'. In 2.15–21 Paul is concerned with the actual present status of those who have been justified, not with the event by which they arrived at that status. And with that we are not far from recognizing that this is in fact the status of *being in the covenant*, the thing which Martyn, like many 'old perspective'

[70] Not to mention Bultmann's famous article 'Glossen im Römerbrief' (Bultmann 1967, 278–84) which is basically *Sachkritik* on steroids. *Sachkritik* says 'Paul shouldn't really have said this, but he did; never mind, we'll help him out of a jam.' Postulating 'glosses' says, in effect, 'Paul shouldn't have said this, *and actually he didn't*.' That way lies chaos (and O'Neill 1975). See also ch. 9 below, on Campbell.

[71] Martyn 260; similarly 297, on 3.6.

[72] On 'justification' see the full discussion in *PFG* 912–1038; and my earlier statement in Wright 2009 [*Justification*].

writers, appears anxious to avoid, but which Paul will almost at once explain by retelling the story of God's promises to Abraham.[73]

It is a measure of how fascinating Martyn's commentary is that one is tempted to discuss a good many other points, themes and passages. But one more must suffice. Throughout the work Martyn insists – though actually nothing in de Boer's earlier analysis had suggested this – that the 'cosmological apocalyptic eschatology' he finds in Paul can have nothing to do with the ongoing flow of history. It seems that, despite Käsemann's nuanced acceptance of certain types of 'salvation history' in Paul, and, more to the point, despite the fact that many if not most actual 'apocalypses' do in fact deal with the history of the world and of Israel, Martyn takes as axiomatic the either/or stated sharply in Käsemann's rejection of Stendahl.[74] And, since Käsemann is seen as the true prophet of a 'cosmological' apocalyptic reading of Paul, Martyn assumes that Paul, too, must reject *Heilsgeschichte* as a matter of principle. But what shall one then do with Galatians 4.3–5?

> When we were children, we were kept in 'slavery' under the 'elements of the world'. But when the time of fulfilment arrived, God sent out his son, born of a woman, born under the law, so that he might redeem those under the law, so that we might receive adoption as sons.

'But when the time of fulfilment arrived' is my slightly loose translation for Paul's *hote de ēlthen to plērōma tou chronou*, 'but when the fullness of the time came'. Does this not suggest exactly what Martyn has ruled out, a chronological sequence at the end of which the redemption occurred?

Yes, it does, and we should not be surprised. Nor is this *in any way* to remove Paul from his putative or actual 'apocalyptic' context. Nothing in the real history-of-religions context of second-Temple Jewish apocalyptic rules out such a statement. Everything, in fact, speaks in its favour. This is precisely how the apocalyptists thought, taught and wrote. Did not the most famous apocalypse of them all reach its central climax in a similar way?

> As I looked, this horn made war with the holy ones and was prevailing over them, until the Ancient One came; then judgment was given for the holy ones of the Most High, and *the time arrived* when the holy ones gained possession of the kingdom . . .
>
> They shall be given into his power for *a time, two times, and half a time. Then* the court shall sit in judgment, and his dominion shall be taken away . . . [and] the kingship and dominion . . . shall be given to the people of the holy ones of the Most High.[75]

[73] As for the other occurrences of *dikaiosynē* in Gal.: at 359f. Martyn neither quotes nor expounds the final clause of 3.21, which at 352 he had translated as 'things would have been made right by the Law', so that we cannot tell there, either, why he has transformed the abstract noun (denoting status) into the active one (denoting divine action). The single other occurrence of *dikaiosynē* in Gal. (at 5.5) Martyn again translates as 'rectification' (472). Here at last he sees the theological (though not the verbal) problem, and attempts to solve it in an excursus (478f.).

[74] Which itself looks back, as we have suggested, to the older German debates: see 46–56 above.

[75] Dan. 7.21f., 25–7.

Fascinatingly, in both ancient Greek versions of Daniel the word for 'time' in these passages is *kairos*, the normal designation of a particular or special time, an opportune moment. That is what we might have expected in Galatians 4.4. But Paul has written *to plērōma tou chronou*, the fullness of *time*, chronological time, one day succeeding another. What can he mean?

Two answers suggest themselves, both telling heavily in favour of Galatians as a classic piece of first-century Jewish apocalyptic thought (if such a thing exists!) rather than a projection of twentieth-century would-be 'apocalyptic'. A detailed study of one 'apocalyptic' text after another reveals that in the second-Temple period the books that took their inspiration from Daniel, and that were themselves set in the troubled period of the Hasmoneans, the Herods and the fateful first century, were looking for a sudden divine act of redemption that would occur at (what we would call) the social and political level. It would of course be 'spiritual' and 'theological' as well, because all these things went together. This act of redemption, of rescue from pagan enemies (the 'beasts' of Daniel's vision), would be like *a new exodus*. Hence the 'apocalyptic' imagery of slavery under the powers, and the divine, yes even 'invasive', act of rescue. That was what Israel's God had done for his people by overthrowing Pharaoh. But, according to Genesis, this divine action took place *at the right time*, the time which God had promised to Abraham four generations earlier. Where was that promise made? Genesis 15 (verse 16). Which biblical passage does Paul expound as the backbone of Galatians 3? Genesis 15. What is the end of Galatians 3? That 'if you belong to the Messiah, you are Abraham's family; you stand to inherit the promise' (3.29). How does Galatians 4 begin? With a statement about slaves being freed so that they could be 'sons of God' (another exodus-motif) and heirs according to the promise, no longer under the rule of the 'powers'. When, at the heart of that argument, soaked in allusions to, and echoes of, the exodus-promise to Abraham, and of the exodus narrative itself, we find the arrival of the 'redemption' (yet another exodus-word) occurring 'when the time had fully come', we should be in no doubt. This is an echo of Genesis 15 and Exodus 3, where the promise is reaffirmed and the rescuing action begun, and it invokes the idea of a chronological sequence (hidden no doubt in the inscrutable divine purpose, and not open to human calculation) which has now arrived at its goal. No first-century reader of apocalypses, whether 'cosmic', 'forensic', or any other kind, would have had any difficulty in recognizing what Paul was talking about. This was the long-awaited new exodus, and it happened, quite properly, 'when the time had fully come' or 'when the fullness of time arrived'.

Of course, there is no suggestion here, any more than there was in the exodus narratives, that this referred to a steady process of maturation, a slow and gradual build-up, a long crescendo finally reaching its triumphant fortissimo of freedom (the sort of thing imagined by some nineteenth-century philosophical traditions, offering a kind of theopolitical social Darwinism). Anything but. The slavery got worse. The night became darker. The burdens became heavier – and *then*, suddenly, all at once (and yet at the very time promised long before), the day came. Exegesis has for too long been in thrall to the false either/or of (1) a Hegelian idea of development and 'progress' and (2) its angry, disappointed rejection.[76] When Paul speaks of the time having fully come, he has no thought whatever of progress, of development, of some kind of immanent force that would stand over against the inbreaking divine rescue-operation. He is thinking like a prophet, not a Marxist; like an apocalyptist, not a liberal.

If the exodus-event, as the fulfilment of the promise to Abraham, thus forms one rather obvious background to Galatians 4.1–11, the other obvious background is once more in classic 'apocalyptic' thought. This is perhaps the heart of my objection to the either/or which Martyn has applied to the material (far more than de Boer, more even than Käsemann, and not at all like Beker). In one text after another within the broadly 'apocalyptic' world to which Martyn appeals as his history-of-religion matrix there is hardly anything more common than *retellings of the story of Israel*. In fact, one of the central and regular characteristics of actual second-Temple Jewish 'apocalyptic' literature is *a long narrative in search of a resolution, a conclusion*.[77] Often, as with Jubilees and similar writings, this narrative runs from creation to Abraham to Moses, pointing on through the exile to the writer's own day, looking for resolution or conclusion in the immediate future. It is precisely not looking for what some have supposed, that is, a moment at which one will declare that everything that has gone before is dust and ashes, a misleading waste of time.[78] Why, if that were so, would one bother to tell the long story? Yet that is how Martyn and his followers now seem to use the label 'apocalyptic'. If, however, I read Galatians as 'apocalyptic', *using that word to place the document within an historical matrix*, I will *expect* the kind of narrative, running from Abraham to the present, which Paul really does seem to be offering – offering, that is, as his own proposal, not as something the 'Teachers' have invented which he feels constrained to oppose and so is compelled to discuss.

Martyn, however, constantly resists this conclusion, until at last he agrees that there *is* an 'Abraham-story' after all ... but he classifies it as a kind of 'law' narrative, which is of course just what Paul says it isn't.[79] As far as I

[76] See Koch 1972 [1970], 67f.: 'nearly all discerning Christians had finally lost faith in a divinely willed progress in history after the outbreak of the Second World War ...'. See too *PFG* 1477–83, in relation to Walter Benjamin.

[77] See *PFG* ch. 2, esp. 108–79. Koch 1972 [1970], 29 lists as one of the 'generally accepted' characteristics of 'apocalyptic' that 'The end-time is closely connected with the previous history of mankind and of the cosmos. The *time of this world* is divided into fixed segments ...' (italics original). He goes on to claim that apocalyptic literature 'gives an impressive insight into the coherent progress of world history according to God's plan, from creation to the end of the world, a history which includes the whole of mankind' (41). He later quotes Goppelt: 'Apocalyptic interprets history as a sequence of events tending towards the End' (84, quoting Goppelt 1964, 328).

[78] That is the despairing position of the disappointed Walter Benjamin, and it is telling that Harink 2012, 84 cites these ideas as having 'penetrated deeply into my understanding of the gospel, precisely because they resonate so profoundly with the apocalyptic character of the gospel that I have learned from Martyn.' On Benjamin's similarities to and radical differences from Paul, see *PFG* 1473–84.

[79] Martyn 505: 'the voice of the Abrahamic Law that speaks in God's behalf', which is now fulfilled and becomes 'pertinent to the daily life of the church'.

can see, that recognition of an Abraham-narrative stands in tension with the emphasis, throughout Martyn's exposition of Galatians 3 and 4, that there is only minimal continuity between Abraham and Jesus Christ, let alone between Abraham and the church. Indeed, 'continuity' seems to be what Martyn is most concerned to avoid. Hence the 'invasion' motif, with its echoes of the early Barth, raising for me the question of some kind of over-transcendent dualism – as well as the question of whether the later Barth would have been so happy with that non-narratival 'invasion' language.[80]

Thus – to return to this crucial text – Martyn effectively neutralizes Galatians 4.4. His Paul has rejected the idea of 'redemptive history' as held by the 'Teachers', so how could he now embrace a version of it? Instead, he insists that the 'time' in question has nothing to do with a slow or steady maturing process. If the 'Teachers' had held a view like that, they would have been very peculiar first-century Jews; Martyn is here once more fighting nineteenth-century shadows. The 'time' in question has to do rather, he says, with a 'punctiliar liberation' taking place 'at the time chosen by [God] alone'.[81] Well, yes, but what then does *to plērōma tou chronou* mean? For Martyn, it seems to mean 'at a time selected by [God]'.[82] I understand what he is fighting against (the idea of 'a gradual maturation'[83]), but here as elsewhere he throws out the banana with the peel.

Nor does de Boer, in his own commentary, deal successfully with the relevant phrase. He rightly rules out the idea that 'God's action is somehow dependent on time, on the course of human history'.[84] But he is wrong, I think, to say that the idea of the periodization of history (which he admits is found in some Jewish and Christian apocalypses; he cites Daniel 9, which as I have shown elsewhere was influential throughout this period) is an optional extra in 'apocalyptic' writing, while the 'two-age' contrast is 'the essence of apocalyptic eschatology'. As I pointed out earlier, the 'two-age' contrast is central to most Jewish thought from at least Daniel to the Mishnah and far beyond; and it is precisely the periodization of history that is more characteristic of 'apocalyptic' writing.[85] Failing to see this, de Boer makes Galatians 4.4 say more or less the opposite of what *to plērōma tou chronou* actually means:

[80] On 'dualism' see esp. *NTPG* 252–6, which remains foundational. On Barth see *CD* 4.1: at 640–2 he sounds like Martyn, warning against any form of 'progress' or 'religion'; but the long and powerful discussion at 166–77 shows that Barth realized the importance both of the continuity of the gospel with Israel's story and of the fact that this continuity was always under the sign of suffering, of the cross. See too Beker's warning against the bare idea of 'invasion' (above, 153).

[81] Martyn 389. See too 99, where Martyn describes 'the fulness of time' as 'a clear apocalyptic motif', meaning by that a reference to the 'two-age' scheme. That is quite true; but the 'apocalyptic' context, not least its implicit invoking of the exodus-theme, means that a mysterious sense of time-to-be-fulfilled, as in Genesis 15 or Daniel 9 (not, once more, as in a nineteenth-century immanent process!), is rendered more likely, not less.

[82] Martyn 388, within a paraphrase.

[83] Martyn 389.

[84] de Boer 2011, 261.

[85] See again *PFG* ch. 2, and Koch as n. 77 above.

> For Paul, God's action in Christ in and of itself demonstrates that the fullness (and thus in a sense the 'end') of time had – and has – been reached ... The 'fullness of time' thus signifies *a clean break with the past* and may be regarded as an apocalyptic assertion on Paul's part: it announces the end of 'the present evil age' (1:4) and the beginning of the 'new creation' (6:15).[86]

Yes, of course, the redemptive action has rescued people from 'the present evil age'; yes, indeed, it has launched the 'new creation'. But, however hard this phrase might try, *to plērōma to chronou* cannot mean 'a clean break with the past'. It cannot mean it either linguistically or theologically. Of course the divine action is not 'dependent on' human history. God's action is always dependent on God's promise and grace. But God's promise – in the very chapter quoted by Paul in Galatians 3 – always envisaged a particular time, even though that time always remained under God's own sovereign command. Of course when you reach 'the fullness of time' you reach, in a sense, the end of the journey; but it is 'end' as *goal*, not 'end' as 'thankful termination'. One is reminded of the debates about *telos* in Romans 10.4.

These exegetical points, at crucial moments in the letter, indicate to my mind that the way Martyn and, to a lesser extent, de Boer apply their notion of 'apocalyptic' to Paul fails the most basic test. It cannot make sense of what he actually wrote in the letter to which they appeal. It correctly identifies his basic belief, that in the gospel events the one God had acted decisively to deal with the slavery of the 'present evil age'. But it fails to see that the way this needed to be done was through the fulfilment of the covenantal promises to Abraham, a fulfilment which took place when 'the son of God loved me and gave himself for me', bringing about the 'new exodus' at the moment when 'the fullness of time had come'. All this, ironically, would I think be understood in principle by the truly 'apocalyptic' writers of the period, from *1 Enoch* to *2 Baruch*. If it remains incompatible with this newly reconstructed scheme which sets 'cosmological apocalyptic eschatology' (or, in the simplified versions invoked by some of Martyn's followers, merely 'apocalyptic' itself) over against the other elements of Pauline theology, so much the worse for the scheme.

Three much shorter reflections bring us towards the fullness of time as it concerns the present chapter.

First, the more Paul is deemed to be 'apocalyptic', the more I want to press a cheeky question: why then shouldn't he have written Second Thessalonians, the most obviously 'apocalyptic' book in the Pauline canon? (And, also, the most overtly political, once we learn to 'read' apocalyptic texts in their first-century context.) And, even more, why not Colossians, with its defeat of the powers in 2.14–15 and the larger Christ-and-powers scenario in 1.15–20? Even if that passage may well be quoted from somewhere else, it is nevertheless quoted *by this author*, and used as a source and reference point throughout the letter. And if Colossians, then why not

[86] de Boer 2011, 262 (italics added). This is de Boer's way, not unlike Martyn's, of trying to escape from the direct challenge to their view presented by Gal. 4.4. The implausibility of these readings of *to plērōma tou chronou* demonstrates the weakness of the theory.

Ephesians as well, which sees the victory of Christ over the powers as central (1.19–23), and which finishes by reminding the readers that they are part of that same cosmic battle (6.10–20)? And if the answer is, 'Because Colossians and Ephesians have too high an ecclesiology', doesn't that simply beg the question? If *they at least* seem to combine those high-octane Christ-and-powers 'apocalyptic' motifs with that ecclesiology (which to my mind grows out of the very similar Jewish 'ecclesiology' found in some second-Temple apocalyptic literature), how do we know, a priori, twenty centuries later, that the authentic Paul would rule out such a combination? And if, perhaps more to the point, the answer is 'Because Colossians and Ephesians have too realized an eschatology', referring to the idea of believers being *already* 'seated in heavenly places in the Messiah', *already* 'raised', and so on,[87] then I reply that it is Martyn who has radically modified Käsemann's essentially futurist apocalyptic eschatology, so that instead of the 'imminent expectation' upon which everything depends we have an apocalypse that has already taken place. Why then is Martyn's seriously inaugurated eschatology so different from that of Ephesians and Colossians? And if the answer is that Martyn emphasizes the event of the cross rather than the resurrection (in line, after all, with Galatians, where the resurrection is mentioned only once, and that in the opening greeting[88]), is this not a sign that we should be more wary about trying to produce a complete construction of Paul's thought from one letter only, and that a highly polemical one?

Second, and following from this, we face the now well-known question about the political meaning both of 'apocalyptic' and of Galatians. Martyn mentions the Caesar-cult in ancient Turkey, but makes nothing of it. But if Galatians is 'apocalyptic', we might well expect it to be in some way 'political' because so much genuine 'apocalyptic' literature undoubtedly is, and Paul might well be using features of the genre as a way of making political points, after the manner of Daniel.[89] If we were to follow through on that line of thought, might it not make a radical difference to the exegesis, not simply as 'another dimension' bolted on to the outside, but actually as part of the theology and exegesis? In particular, if it is true that in ancient Near Eastern thinking the duties of the king would oscillate between the cosmic and the political, the two fusing together much more than would be assumed today, then it might even be thought that the 'cosmic' ought to *entail* the 'political', rather than the two being mutually exclusive.[90]

[87] e.g. Eph. 2.6; Col. 3.1–4.

[88] Gal. 1.1; but cf. too the awkward but important *zō de* of 2.20, coming right after *Christō synestaurōmai*, with this pair itself (crucifixion and then new life) coming right after 'through the law I died to the law, so that I might live to God' in 2.19.

[89] See again Portier-Young 2011; and e.g. Moore 2006. In a recent Martyn-dominated collection of essays, Neil Elliott makes the point, drawing on Portier-Young xxiii, 27, 37, that the apocalyptist seeks to assert 'the transience and finitude of temporal powers, [to affirm] God's governance of time and the outworking of God's plan in history' (Elliott 2013, 150). Thus, so far from 'apocalyptic' standing over against the idea of a historical plan and its political implications, it ought actually to insist on it.

[90] On the political significance of Paul's beliefs see *PFG* ch. 12 (where I debate with John Barclay, who has argued against me that Paul's concern is 'cosmic', even 'apocalyptic', and therefore *not* 'political'); Heilig 2015; and see below, ch. 12.

The third comment is inevitable but it has to be made all the same. It does seem a serious weakness, in a commentary on Galatians, that one cannot easily understand how the Paul of this 'Galatians' could transmute into the Paul of Romans. Of course, all kinds of developmental schemes have been offered. Beker, as we saw, envisaged a mixture of 'coherence and contingency'. Hübner and others have postulated significant development, not least perhaps from a negative view of the Jewish law to a positive one. But, starting where Martyn starts, the only way of holding the two letters in any kind of relationship to one another would be either to shrink Romans beyond the bounds of credibility, until it became simply a fuller version of (this) 'Galatians', or to postulate some massive rethinking in between the two, such that one would then be forced to choose between two radically different visions of God, Israel, the gospel and the world. Romans, after all, has a strong and thematic *narrative* core, and the narrative in question is the classic Israelite and Jewish story of Adam, Abraham, and Abraham's family. In particular, the clearly positive view of the law in Romans, insisted upon even when the law is doing devastating things,[91] stands in sharp contrast to Martyn's reading of Galatians. And Paul's positive view of Israel does the same. Martyn's Paul, faced with the question of Romans 3.1 ('what advantage has the Jew'), ought to have responded 'none at all'. With that, we would be back with the shallow reductionism of C. H. Dodd.[92]

Some final reflections on Martyn's project are in order. I reiterate what I said at the start: I believe Paul's message is thoroughly 'apocalyptic', in the sense that he believed that the events concerning Jesus constituted the long-promised and long-awaited moment when the divine saving purpose for Israel and the world was at last revealed. I fully agree with Martyn and the others that this event is *cosmic* in the sense that the unseen suprahuman powers that have tyrannized the world have been overcome, even though we today find it difficult to say (a) what precisely we think we are referring to when we speak of those powers and, not least, (b) what we are actually affirming in claiming their defeat, granted the ongoing existence in the world of evil, including massive structural evil, and death itself. Actually, I think Beker said it more clearly than Martyn, because he emphasized the resurrection as the launching of the new creation; but then, he was not restricting himself to Galatians. So, if I am faced with the choice between an 'apocalyptic' and a 'non-apocalyptic' Paul, I unhesitatingly and enthusiastically choose the former. Once again, Käsemann rather than Bultmann.

But why should that be the only choice – and why should it rule out all the things which Martyn wants it to rule out? Answer: it shouldn't. Jewish apocalyptic was more rich and many-sided than he has supposed. So was Paul's fresh reworking of it around Messiah and spirit.

It would be good to know what really energized Martyn in this enterprise, with all the problematic exegesis that it produced. What agenda was driving

[91] Rom. 3.19f.; 4.15; 5.20; 7.5, 7–25.

[92] Cf. Dodd 1959 [1932], 68.

the project? For his hero Käsemann, it was obvious. Käsemann was reacting against at least five positions: first, against Bultmann's neo-Kantian and Heideggerian collapse of Paul into individualistic anthropology; second, against the tame *Deutsche Christen* who went along with Hitler under the mistaken idea of a kind of secular *Heilsgeschichte*;[93] third, against anything that smelt of Catholicism (Käsemann was after all still deeply Lutheran, as his fierce reaction to anything like an *imitatio Christi* or a *devotio moderna* indicates); fourth, against what he saw as the smug bourgeois piety of south Germany after the war; and fifth, against the 'enthusiasm' which in Britain would probably be called 'charismatic' Christianity and in American might be somewhere between 'evangelical' and 'fundamentalist' (German *evangelisch*, of course, means 'Lutheran'). In other words, as we saw earlier, Käsemann was taking his stance as a new Luther, fighting off traditional demons to right and left, and newer political ones as well. Fair enough, in all sorts of ways, and very exciting stuff it is. But what is going on when all those battles are transposed from mid-century Germany to fin-de-siècle America, where comparatively little of Käsemann's enemies (except fundamentalism, of course) are to be found? What was Martyn anxious to ward off? He did not say. The fact that his commentary was dedicated to Käsemann implies that there might be parallels. One might hazard a guess – mirror-reading Martyn as he mirror-reads Galatians! – that it could have something to do with his implicit opposition to (a) a casual, cheap-and-cheerful evangelicalism or fundamentalism which is constantly fussing about sin and salvation, defining its own group tightly and ignoring larger, cosmic issues, and (b) the easy-going socially conformist liberalism of the mainstream churches. But even if we agree that those are battles worth fighting (and even supposing, granted that this is only mirror-reading, that these really are the implicit targets of Martyn's polemic), it is hard to see that this is a good starting-point from which to read Galatians. Isn't that the mistake Luther made, to understand Paul's enemies as though they were an earlier version of his own? Martyn remained, at this point, emphatically outside the new perspective, however much in other respects he was a post-Sanders writer. Indeed, as we saw earlier, some might think that the way he flattened out de Boer's 'two tracks' of 'apocalyptic' into an 'anti-religious' position called 'apocalyptic', on the one hand, and a 'religious' view, on the other, including covenant, salvation history, and the forgiveness of 'sins', constituted a subtle return to the older, pre-Sanders way of reading Paul.

The positive side of the same question relates to the assumed proposal that Martyn was putting forward. How did he imagine that a Pauline 'apocalyptic' might play out in terms of the life of the church or the Christian? This is of course a question for me as well. I am conscious here of the insistence of Troels Engberg-Pedersen in *Paul and the Stoics* that 'we' are 'unable to adopt Paul's theology and cosmology', that it isn't an 'option' for us – presumably because we are post-Enlightenment thinkers who 'cannot' view

[93] See above, 50f., on Käsemann's reaction to Stendahl, and behind him to Cullmann.

the world that way.[94] Did Martyn think that his reconstruction of 'apocalyptic' was in fact an 'option' for people in today's world? If so, what did it mean? How (to use the vernacular) would it 'preach'? I am used to people telling me that I seem to be inviting them to embrace an outdated and impossible ancient worldview in order then to become Christians; how does Martyn respond when people say that to him? What happens if, equipped with Martyn's 'apocalyptic' worldview, one approaches the major theological, political and ethical questions of today? How, in other words, would Martyn have addressed the question which perplexed German scholarship a hundred years ago ('how can we, in the modern world, believe in ancient apocalyptic?') and which led, through twists and turns, to Bultmann's solution, namely, demythologization? How, in addition, might Martyn have addressed the apparent difference between his own views and those of his teacher, Käsemann, that for Käsemann what mattered was the 'imminent expectation' of the *parousia*, ruling out any over-realized eschatology and hence a triumphal 'enthusiasm', whereas for Martyn the crucial event had already taken place? How might one declare, in the face of the principalities and powers all too evident in the twentieth and now in the twenty-first century, that the decisive victory has already been won? I am not suggesting that it is a weakness in a commentary on Galatians that these questions are not addressed. I do think, though, that it calls into question the parallel some have drawn between Martyn on Galatians and Barth's early commentary on Romans. At least with Barth everybody knew what he was getting at.

The 'apocalyptic' reading of Paul offered by Martyn in particular must therefore be questioned as a complete or adequate account. As with Käsemann himself, when we contrast this reading with many others on offer, it scores highly. But when we match it up against Paul's letters themselves, it raises problems. I have argued in detail elsewhere that Paul really was an 'apocalyptic' theologian, who believed that God had done a radical new thing, a fresh gift of grace, in the sending, and the dying and rising, of Jesus the Messiah, and that he had indeed thereby liberated Israel from its plight and the world from the powers of evil. But this, Paul argues again and again, was the original purpose of the divine covenant with Israel. This was where the strange, dark, non-immanent salvation history had been going all along. As exegetes we are bound to challenge modern distortions by arguing for genuine historical readings. I therefore regard de Boer's historical proposals as unproven and, given the difficulties to which de Boer himself drew attention, unlikely, and certainly incapable of bearing the weight which Martyn then rested on them. Martyn's followers have made notable contributions in many areas, but it is hard to see how the superstructure of a building can be any more secure than its foundation.

[94] See Engberg-Pedersen 2000; see, on this point, *PFG* 1388 and related passages.

Chapter Nine

AN APOCALYPTIC REREADING OF ROMANS? DOUGLAS CAMPBELL

1. Introduction

There is one main problem with Douglas Campbell's already famous book, *The Deliverance of God: An Apocalyptic Rereading of Justification in Paul* (2009). It is much too short.

This may not, I grant, be the first problem that comes to mind when the reader is faced with over 900 pages of text and nearly 250 further pages of small-print end-notes. (That size alone, by the way, justifies a substantial discussion at this point in the present book, just as the cheerfully polemical tone of Campbell's work, and the way in which he throws down the gauntlet to those who would disagree, may serve to justify the slightly different tone of voice in my response.) Let me explain.

The main argument of Campbell's book is (a) that the normal way of reading Romans 1—4 is wrong, (b) that Romans 5—8 offers an altogether superior way of understanding Paul in general and Romans in particular, and therefore (c) that we need to find a radically different way of reading Romans 1—4, and indeed of understanding Paul. For Campbell to make his case, one might suppose, he would not only have to demonstrate the wrongness of the normal reading of the first four chapters. He would also have to explain the theological superiority of the next four. This book makes no attempt to do this. It offers the barest summary, early on, and then some scattered notes (under the heading 'Loose Ends in Romans') towards the end.[1] We look in vain for the exposition of the master-theory, the grand vision, the full 'apocalyptic' glory of Romans 5—8, that will supposedly upstage the wrong reading of Romans 1—4 and compel us to accept an alternative reading. But, as in a Pinter play, the main character (in this case, the 'apocalyptic' vision of Romans 5—8) remains off stage throughout.

[1] Campbell 2009, 62–73, 821–7.

When I realized this, I thought, 'He must have set out his view of Romans 5—8 somewhere else.' But no. It is not to be found in Campbell's earlier book, *The Quest for Paul's Gospel: A Suggested Strategy*.[2] There are several passages dealing with various aspects of the relevant chapters of Romans, but no sign of the full-dress exposition needed for the larger theory to work. The closest we get, so far as I can see, is a thirty-page article in a recent paperback where four scholars were invited to summarize their views of Paul and then to respond to one another.[3] But the article in question, as the other contributors to that short volume were not slow to point out, was a strange piece. It gestured towards various traditions in systematic theology, and only briefly, and in the most general terms, outlined a reading of Romans 5—8.[4] And, surprisingly, though Campbell insists that this is an 'apocalyptic' reading, he neither draws attention to, nor expounds, what might be thought the most obviously 'apocalyptic' passage – the climax, indeed, of the argument! – in Paul's vision of cosmic renewal in Romans 8.18–25. Thus, despite Campbell's right and proper insistence on seeing texts as wholes, I do not think he has yet offered us a 'whole' vision of Romans 1—8 – to say nothing of Romans 1—16 in its entirety.[5] I can think of some books that might be described as short, but still too long. Campbell's is long, but still too short.

This leads directly to another basic problem with the book. It has the wrong title.

The main title, 'The Deliverance of God', is the translation Campbell offers in the book for Paul's central phrase *dikaiosynē theou*, as in Romans 1.17 and 3.21. Fair enough: this is, broadly speaking, in line with Käsemann's proposed meaning for the phrase. But Campbell never shows – never *attempts* to show – how, exegetically or theologically, this phrase functions in relation to the soteriology he finds in Romans 5—8. And, though he has returned to Romans 3.21–6 from many angles over the years, and does so again in this book, I am not yet convinced by his reading of that vital passage, or by his account of its relation to the larger unit in which it comes.[6] And, since 'the deliverance of God' is what Campbell thinks Paul expounds in Romans 5—8, the book, as I said a moment ago, promises something it does not in fact deliver.

But it is the subtitle of the book that begs the question (a fault Campbell is quick to spot in others). This book claims to be, but is not, 'An Apocalyptic Rereading of Justification in Paul'.

[2] Campbell 2005.

[3] Campbell 2012.

[4] See the responses from T. R. Schreiner, L. T. Johnson, and M. D. Nanos in Bird 2012, 144–58.

[5] For the insistence: Campbell 2009, xxix. Campbell does attempt various proposals about the overall purpose of Romans, but these fall a long way short of the kind of demonstration required to explain how his would-be 'apocalyptic' reading of chapters 5—8 is superior to the normal reading of chapters 1—4.

[6] See esp. Campbell 1992; 2005; and *Deliverance* chs. 15 and 16. Campbell declares (*Deliverance*, 935f.) that he will not accept it if people say, without argument, that they remain unconvinced. My arguments will follow presently.

For a start, it is not a 'rereading' of justification. It is a demolition, a hatchet job, a bomb on the playground of the justification-theorists. Schweitzer had allowed 'juridical' thought a secondary place as a *Nebenkrater*, a subsidiary crater, within the larger, apocalyptically conceived, crater he called 'mysticism'. Campbell places it on another planet altogether. By the time he is finished, 'justification' has not been 'reread'. It has been despatched to outer darkness.

For another thing, by this stage in the post-Käsemann world the blessed word 'apocalyptic' has become so exhausted that it seems to be wandering around in a daze, unsure of its own identity, lending accidental support to this or that theory, forgetting the way back to its own front door, indeed appearing to forget that it ever *had* a real front door, or a home, in the first place. As Tom Schreiner points out crisply in his response to Campbell's essay in the 2012 volume, what 'apocalyptic' seems to mean here is 'über-Reformed, or even hyper-Calvinist'.[7] Campbell is quite explicit, in many places, about the theology which is driving his work. This is refreshing, of course. Many exegetes pretend to be neutral observers, just reading the texts and trying to understand them, when their own agendas are in fact poking through at point after point. But what Campbell seems to mean by 'apocalyptic' (and his regular use of the word, and his invoking of Martyn as the leading exponent of 'apocalyptic' readings of Paul, indicate that we are right to discuss him within the present Part of the book rather than elsewhere) is basically that he believes in the sovereignty of God and therefore in a covenantal rather than a contractual soteriology;[8] that he believes that Paul thought everything through 'backwards' on the basis of the revelation of God in Jesus Christ, rather than coming with an already worked-out system and then fitting Jesus into it; and that he believes in a gospel of the surpassing love of God as opposed to a message about the dangerous anger of God. With all this, 'apocalyptic' has changed its meaning yet again. It now has to do with a *theological method*: *Nachdenken*, thinking *backward from* Jesus rather than *forward to* Jesus from some other 'foundationalist' starting-point.[9] As his frequent annotation indicates, all this places Campbell somewhere in an orbit defined by Calvin and Barth in particular. I do not think this is necessarily a bad place to be. But it does not have very much to do with 'apocalyptic' either in a recognizable first-century sense or, for that matter, in a sense we might recognize from the relevant twentieth-century scholarship up to and including Käsemann.

Let me stay on this point for a moment, since the issues in question are of much wider current importance than simply the question of what Campbell is arguing and whether it makes sense. Campbell claims to be standing in the tradition of Käsemann and Martyn (and Martyn, we recall, based his

[7] Schreiner, in Bird ed. 2012, 144.

[8] See e.g. the summary at the top of Campbell 2009, 903: an 'apocalyptic' approach to Paul 'emphasizes the revelatory and hence unconditional nature of his soteriology. In contrast to Justification, it consequently works backward, not forward.'

[9] See e.g. Campbell 2012, 129.

reading firmly on de Boer's analysis). But Campbell makes little attempt to line up closely with any of them. He warmly endorses Käsemann's emphasis on the divine sovereignty over against the 'insipid optimism' of the voluntarist and individualist liberalism which was powerless to resist tyranny.[10] But there is no sign, in Campbell, of Käsemann's meaning of 'apocalyptic', that is, the 'imminent expectation' which the great German saw as 'the mother of Christian theology'. Nor is there any reference to Käsemann's particular reading of Romans 3.24–6 (as containing a pre-Pauline 'Jewish-Christian' formula about the divine covenant faithfulness, then amended by Paul's addition of his non-covenantal reading of *dikaiosynē theou*), though one may detect some of the same post-Baur thinking underneath Campbell's own new proposals. Campbell passes lightly over the fact that for Käsemann the result of reading Paul in relation to 'apocalyptic' was precisely a fresh emphasis on justification by faith as expressed in Romans 1—4, the very thing against which Campbell protests.[11]

Nor is there the slightest sign in Campbell of de Boer's hypothetical and heuristic 'two tracks' of 'Jewish apocalyptic eschatology'. (Already, as we have seen, de Boer's careful and cautious proposal has been flattened out by Martyn and his followers, so that the first track simply becomes 'apocalyptic' and the second one something else that the writer wants to bracket out.) Nor is there any sign of the 'two ages' which in de Boer's proposal is the central feature of 'apocalyptic'. Campbell could respond that this is indeed what Romans 5—8 is all about, but he does not seem actually to have made that case. Nor is there any sign of J. C. Beker's nuanced and contextualized 'apocalyptic', which was able to sit down comfortably alongside 'justification', 'salvation history' and various other things, without needing to bundle them all out of the room as Martyn, and now particularly Campbell, think it ought to do. Nor, even, is there much sign of Martyn's own great emphasis on the divine *victory* over the 'cosmic powers'.

What we have instead, as I suggested before, is an explicitly stated form of Calvinism. Of course, that label has been enthusiastically adopted by many today, especially in parts of North America where the seventeenth-century Westminster Confession has made a significant comeback. Campbell would not, however, wish to be associated with that branch of a diverse family. In his frequent statements about his own personal theological starting-points he leans considerable weight on the difference, in varieties of Calvinism, between two things. First, there is a basically *contractual* divine–human relationship, which leads to the 'federal' views which have been widespread in parts of the 'Reformed' world, and have shaped not only churches but also those societies which have either embraced such principles or reacted, and perhaps over-reacted, against them. Second, there is a genuinely *covenantal* divine–human relationship, in which the sovereign love of God

[10] See Campbell's excellent summary of Käsemann's motivations: 2009, 189.

[11] See Campbell 2009, 191. Käsemann was after all a Lutheran, not a Calvinist.

remains paramount.[12] Campbell, unsurprisingly, insists on emphasizing this latter position; though, as we shall see, he regularly superimposes on this debate a running battle with a more popular, low-grade form of Arminian evangelical preaching.

Just when we might think he is going to be more precise about his key term, Campbell is instead unhelpfully vague. The signifier 'apocalyptic', he says,

> is a useful label at an introductory level of discussion when broad loyalties and orientations are being sketched in relation to different basic approaches to Paul; it denotes fairly that an approach to Paul is being pursued that ultimately aligns with the concerns and readings of – in this context in particular – Lou Martyn, and that therefore is in sympathy with the alternative texts and soteriological paradigm that he endorses, and sensitive to the tensions that he detects between that paradigm and Justification concerns.[13]

Campbell seems well aware (partly because of the proper warnings issued at various points by Barry Matlock[14]) that one cannot legitimately argue forwards from this a priori affirmation into exegetical or interpretative conclusions. But, as I shall presently suggest, many readers of his book might come away with the impression that this is what he has in fact done. Likewise, though he rightly says that the use of the *apokalypt-* word-group does not automatically mean that we are faced with a large theological category we might call 'apocalyptic', he allows himself to fall into that very trap from time to time.[15] Like Schweitzer, he draws together 'apocalyptic' and 'participatory' categories, and 'mystical' ones too. There is room for them all, just so long as they all agree to gang up and exclude that unpleasant outsider, 'Justification'.[16]

This position seems to me fraught with danger. First, Campbell explicitly leans all his weight on Martyn; but Martyn himself (a) leans heavily on de Boer's model, which we have seen good reason to question, and then (b) adds to it other crucial elements which do not appear in de Boer's original work, but which fit a recognizable twentieth-century pattern (e.g. 'religion' against 'revelation'). This is not a recipe for good historical analysis. Second, Campbell does not in fact line up all that closely with Martyn after all, except in the general sense of privileging divine over human initiative; and if that is 'apocalyptic', then all the great theologians, from Augustine to

[12] See Campbell's frequent references, scattered throughout his writings, to James B. Torrance and his son, Alan J. Torrance.

[13] Campbell 2009, 191. When Campbell uses the capital J for 'Justification' he is referring to what he normally, more fully, calls 'Justification Theory' or JT, a popular reading of Romans 1—4 which his book aims to demolish.

[14] See esp. Matlock 1996; and Campbell's discussion at 2009, 190f.

[15] For the point, 2009, 191; for the falling into the trap: 2012, 123 n. 25; cf. 171 n. 51.

[16] Campbell 2009, 192. Lest it be thought that I am over-egging Campbell's pudding, compare e.g. Campbell 2005, 4, where he announces his own model ('pneumatologically participatory martyrological eschatology', or PPME), and declares, in relation to Justification by Faith (JF) and Salvation History (SH), that 'the JF and SH models ought to be subordinated to the PPME model, or failing this, to be exegetically eliminated.' The 2009 book is devoted to this task in relation to 'JF'; I sense that Campbell may now see a way of subordinating 'SH' to 'PPME', though this is not really clear in *Deliverance*.

Luther and Calvin and many besides, turn out to be 'apocalyptists', which I suspect would surprise most of them (as we might imagine that the genuine 'apocalyptists' such as the authors of Daniel, *1 Enoch* or *4 Ezra* would be surprised to learn that they were saying the same sort of thing as those three wise men).[17] Third, and most important, we must re-emphasize that the point of using a word like 'apocalyptic', in describing a first-century text, is to make a strong implicit claim, namely that the text in question belongs to a supposedly well-known first-century worldview or a universe of discourse and that it will be illuminated if understood within that larger context. 'Here', we are saying, 'is a way of looking at the world which is visible in the wider culture; now we shall claim that Paul belongs here too.' If the word 'apocalyptic' is not intending to make a claim like that, it would be clearer, more honest even, to find a different term. Why not 'Calvinist'? Why not 'Barthian'? And if the objection is that those terms have many meanings, and that other people use them to denote different theological positions, well, the same applies to 'apocalyptic', only much more so.[18] But if the meaning of 'apocalyptic' is reduced to 'what Lou Martyn is talking about' (as, explicitly, in the passage from Campbell just quoted), then we must once more recall that Martyn himself has claimed to base his work on de Boer's analysis of actual Jewish apocalyptic texts ... and then the fat will be in the fire, because the texts themselves, as de Boer candidly admits, are not so clear-cut. To put it mildly. Indeed, as many have pointed out, the 'apocalypses' of the second-Temple period *are simply not discussing the issues which occupy Martyn, Campbell and others.* People were not writing urgent tracts in the first century in order to address the questions that would later separate Bultmann and Käsemann. Nor were they debating the same things as the seventeenth-century federal Calvinists and their sovereign-grace opponents. Books like *1 Enoch* and *4 Ezra* were not debating the question of *Vordenken* and *Nachdenken* as theological methods.

Even if the second-Temple apocalypses had been discussing these essentially modern and culture-conditioned questions, we should remind ourselves again that the analysis upon which all this construct stands, that of de Boer himself, was not a distinction between 'apocalyptic' and something else.[19] It was between (1) 'cosmic apocalyptic eschatology' and (2) 'forensic apocalyptic eschatology'. This of course entails that the latter category, the one Martyn so dislikes, is already seen as *both* 'forensic' *and* 'apocalyptic'. If Campbell is standing on Martyn's shoulders, and Martyn on de Boer's, there is no easy way for any of them to claim that they have in their hands a category called 'apocalyptic' which must at once be set over against 'forensic', that is, juridical or justification-related ideas.

[17] Campbell claims at one point that Ephesians is 'thoroughly and consistently apocalyptic' (2009, 930), a claim which I think has a good deal going for it, but which Martyn repeatedly denies.

[18] As Gaventa suggests (2007, 111).

[19] Gaventa 2007, 83 suggests that de Boer's work answers the charge of Matlock that the meaning of 'apocalyptic' offered by Martyn and others is not well grounded in second-Temple texts. Matlock himself, of course, wrote about the modern interpreters rather than the ancient sources.

What then is the argument of Campbell's remarkable book? Simply this: that Romans 1—4 as it stands exhibits something called 'Justification Theory' (JT);[20] that this is theologically problematic, socio-culturally dangerous, exegetically unwarranted, and incompatible with the heart of Paul's teaching; that attempts to solve this problem have all failed; and that a radical new reading of the passage is therefore called for. This argument is worked out with great ingenuity, massive attention to detail not only in exegetical discussions but in relation to other meta-fields too numerous to mention here, and with a great many 'excursuses' on related topics and on the work of specific scholars. Some of the end-notes are small articles in themselves.[21] It is important, however, to see that the main thesis of the book is essentially quite simple. (1) Normal readings of Romans 1—4 are demonstrably wrong (a) historically, in that they misrepresent what was actually going on in Paul's writing of these chapters, and (b) theologically and socio-politically, since this misreading has generated all kinds of bad effects. (2) This new reading, supposedly based on Romans 5—8, will sort the matter out.

The new reading turns out to be a variation on Martyn's analysis of Galatians. There, Paul is clearly opposing a group whom he calls *hoi tarassontes hymas*, 'those who are disturbing you', whom Martyn labels 'the Teachers'.[22] At this point Campbell injects a new proposal into the old debates about Paul's reasons for writing Romans. Someone of the same sort as Martyn's 'Teachers' – Campbell calls him 'the Teacher' – is on his way to Rome; perhaps he has already arrived there. Paul writes Romans 1—4 in order to set out the debate he needs to have with this person. Thus, whereas Martyn sometimes has Paul alluding to the position of 'the Teachers', only then to 'correct' it with an added clause of his own (this, as we saw, was Martyn's view of Galatians 1.4a and 4b), Campbell has Paul setting out the viewpoint of 'the Teacher', much more extensively, and then engaging with it and, by proposing an alternative view, refuting it. 'The Teacher', according to Campbell, is on his way to offer the Roman church a faulty theology, which is foundationalist, contractual, rationalistic and ultimately concerned with a different God altogether. Paul, by contrast, is offering the true, 'apocalyptic' theology, with the true (and Trinitarian) God revealing himself in the gospel. Thus the entire western tradition of reading Romans 1—4 (I suspect the eastern one as well, though Campbell does not say that) has been duped into supposing that these chapters are a single argument in which Paul himself is expounding the 'Justification Theory' which he is in fact opposing. And from that problem have arisen ills of every kind – up to fifty of them, variously classified.[23]

Three things may be noted: the placing of Campbell's proposal within the larger history of scholarship; the underlying theological reasons he invokes

[20] Sometimes confusingly called simply 'Justification': e.g. 81f., 309.

[21] It is a problem, though, that there is no bibliography, so that short-title references are not always easily identifiable, and that there is no index of key topics.

[22] Gal. 1.7; cf. 5.10, where it is in the singular.

[23] Campbell offers a remarkable catalogue of problems at 168f., 171f., and then 396–406.

to address the perceived problem; and the specific proposals of the theory itself.

First, the placing within scholarship. Campbell sets up his treatment in terms of Schweitzer, Sanders and the recent debates on 'the reasons for Romans'. I take each in turn. (1) Like Schweitzer, he notes that Romans 1—4 and 5—8 seem to offer different theological schemes; unlike Schweitzer, he neither attempts to 'nest' the former within the latter, nor reckons with the continuing presence of 'justification' language in chapters 5—8,[24] nor points out that Paul's language of 'justification' is employed when arguing for the inclusion of gentiles within the church. Indeed, the latter point, so important for Paul (and highlighted of course in the various 'new perspectives'), seems to drop from view. (2) Like Sanders, Campbell notes that traditional readings of Paul, especially Romans 1—4, have tended to misdescribe first-century Judaism. But Campbell's 'Teacher', who by definition is not just Jewish but is a Jewish follower of Jesus, has so many theological failings that Campbell accuses him, as Marcion accused the Jews, of believing in a very different God. (3) As for the situation in Rome, Campbell's proposal (the presence, or at least the imminent arrival, of a Jewish-Christian 'Teacher') is novel, though of course it has the more generalized antecedents (within the broad perspective of Baur, Bultmann and the rest) of supposing that Paul represents a certain type of Christianity over against something called 'Jewish Christianity', and that this is as visible in Romans as elsewhere. The difference is that for Baur and Bultmann Romans 1—4 was one of the places where Paul's 'gentile Christianity' struck out at 'Jewish Christianity'. For Campbell, Romans 1—4 consists of a dialogue between these two theological positions . . . except that he does not call Paul's position 'gentile Christianity', but rather 'apocalyptic'.

When it comes to the theological roots of Campbell's argument, we need be in no doubt, because in many places he – unlike many other New Testament scholars! – has disarmingly laid his hand on the table. Though he pays lip service to the normal historian's imperative to let exegesis lead the way,[25] his autobiographical account of how he arrived at his present view includes a heavy dose of a particular form of Reformed, particularly Barthian, theology.[26] As we indicated earlier, he comes at everything with a very definite theological contrast in mind, that between a genuine covenant theology and a kind of contractual arrangement, a low-grade pseudo-covenant, popular in many churches and societies, in which humans figure things out from first principles and then play the system to their own advantage. Campbell offers several examples.[27]

In particular, Campbell sees in western readings of Romans 1—4 a *rationalist* and also *foundationalist* account of how people 'get saved'. People have to be convinced, on the grounds of general observation and reason, first,

[24] On this point see now Wright 2014a.

[25] cf. e.g. 2009, xxvi.

[26] Campbell 2009, xxiv–xxvii.

[27] cf. 2009, 15–23, 24–8.

that they are *sinners*; then, that they are *helpless* sinners; then, that Jesus died *for their sins*; then, that if they *believe* this message they will be saved. They have to work themselves up, as it were, from the problem to the solution, and moreover to do so by a series of rational steps which lead to a rational conclusion. Thus Romans is to be read as providing an apparently watertight argument that all are helpless sinners (1.18—3.20), followed by the gospel announcement that Jesus has taken the punishment in their place, so that, by believing this good news, sinners can be saved (3.21—4.25). This is a *forward-moving* argument, from apparent first principles (all are sinners) to the eventual conclusion (the remedy provided). Campbell traces this type of thinking to two of the greatest names in western theology, Anselm and Melanchthon.[28] He also links it to 'popular' preachers, such as Billy Graham, and to the 'Four spiritual Laws' and associated ideas and methods used by organizations like Campus Crusade.[29] One feature of Campbell's book which becomes more marked as his exposition goes on is his repeated use, as a shorthand for what Paul is opposing, of the slogan 'Turn or burn' – a phrase one might associate with a particular kind of would-be 'evangelism'.[30] I do not know if Anselm or Melanchthon ever said such a thing. I do not know, for that matter, if even Billy Graham regularly employed such a phrase; but it summarizes Campbell's view of what this foundationalist, rationalist apologetic is all about. Either you allow yourself to be convinced by this rational argument from first principles, or you will go to hell. One sometimes has the impression that Anselm and Melanchthon (and, for that matter, the author of Romans 1—4) are picking up the bill for the excesses of a certain type of modern low-grade preaching and teaching, but we must let that pass for the moment.

Over against all such movements, Campbell places the tradition of Athanasius, Calvin and Barth: not only a Christology 'from above' rather than 'from below', but also a soteriology *and an epistemology* 'from above'. Salvation is not a matter of humans starting at a fixed observational point and thinking rationally about their disastrous moral failings, and their need for rescue, and then about the fact that this rescue has in fact been provided. It is a matter of the sovereign grace of God reaching unconditionally into the human situation – and thus *revealing*, in the light of the remedy offered, that there had been a problem in the first place.

At this point those who follow debates in New Testament scholarship will recognize a familiar feature. E. P. Sanders argued in *Paul and Palestinian Judaism* that Paul's 'critique', of Israel in particular, was retrospective: that is, until Paul found salvation in Christ, he had not been aware of a problem,

[28] On Anselm, see 2009, 50–5, 75f., and sundry other refs.; for Melanchthon, 258–61, 482f., etc. Campbell's positioning of himself over against (a standard picture of) Anselm is another indication that the modern would-be 'apocalyptic' reading of Paul is trying to make the same basic point as Gustav Aulén's *Christus Victor*: see 162 above.

[29] 2009, 284, 290f., 337 ('Campus Crusade' is now known as 'CRU'). At one point, memorably, he likens Billy Graham's theology to that of Rudolf Bultmann (290); again, we may suppose that both would be surprised at the comparison, though in this case I think there may be something to be said for it.

[30] See Campbell 2009, 205, 617 n. 42 [=1097], 697, 707f., 891.

but after discovering Christ he reflected in retrospect that there must have been a problem, since he had, to his own surprise, been given a 'solution'.[31] Sanders's argument has, as it were, some accidental analogies with the position of Barth. For Sanders, it was a matter of historical analysis, constituting his answer to a different sort of problem: (a) Paul's polemic against the Torah seems to be muddled and inconsistent; (b) this is because it wasn't where he began; (c) it was in fact the reflex of his finding salvation in Christ; (d) this explains its random, scatty nature. Though Sanders's analysis, as we showed earlier, does have some important similarities to the Reformed tradition, his view of Paul's thought moving 'from solution to plight' was argued on these historical and critical grounds (the need to explain Pauline inconsistencies about Torah), rather than from any theological a priori. For Barth, however, his similar position was part of a much larger theological agenda, including the rejection of 'natural theology': humans *could not* learn anything important, including their own sinfulness, through unaided and natural study of their world and their own condition, but only in the light of the revelation in Christ. Only when rescued and placed on dry ground could people formerly in danger of drowning see how bad their plight had been. As we might expect, granted his frequent references to Barthian theology, Campbell's view is here a variation on Barth, rather than on Sanders.[32]

With these explicit theological foundations, Campbell proceeds to his bold hypothesis: that significant parts of Romans, especially of its first four chapters, do not represent what Paul himself wanted to say, *but what he imagined 'the Teacher' wanting to say*. In *The Deliverance of God* Campbell advances, to explain this, a phenomenon fairly well known in ancient literature, that of 'speech in character' (the technical term is *prosōpopoeia*), as found in the rhetoric of old law-court masters such as Demosthenes in Athens or Cicero in Rome. As a well-known ploy, such speakers might put into their opponents' mouths entire sentences and paragraphs which they would then undermine or refute. A similar (though smaller-scale) phenomenon can be found in the rhetorical style known as the 'diatribe', widely recognized as being a feature of Paul's writing, especially in some parts of Romans and Galatians. ('You will say to me then . . .' followed by a sentence or line of thought, and then a refutation.[33]) Arguably, Paul does something similar, too, in 1 Corinthians 6 and 8, though exactly which words he is putting into the mouths of hypothetical opponents is disputed.[34] The most extensive Pauline passage normally seen as having been put in the mouth of

[31] Sanders 1977, 442–7 and elsewhere; see above, 77–9.

[32] I have set out my own account of how Paul arrived at his view of the 'plight' in *PFG* 747–72; and of his view of Torah in *PFG* 1032–7, summing up earlier discussions. Martyn 1997a, 95 n. 43 and 266 n. 163, notes the partial parallel between Barth and Sanders at this point, and suggests that Barth reached his position because he was 'an exegete as well as a systematic theologian'. Granted Barth was indeed an exegete – too good an exegete, in fact, to ignore the biblical themes of covenant and salvation history! – this particular point is rather obviously driven by his characteristic emphasis on *Nachdenken*.

[33] Obvious examples include Rom. 9.19: 'You will say to me, then, "So why does he still blame people? Who can stand against his purpose?".' For the 'diatribe' in Paul, see *PFG* 222–4, 453, 458, 1366f.

[34] See 1 Cor. 6.12f.; 8.1–5, with the standard commentaries.

someone other than Paul himself is Romans 7.7–25, where many exegetes, myself included, take the view that Paul is expressing with hindsight (*Nachdenken* again!) the actual theological position of the devout Jew living under Torah.[35]

Nobody up to now has suggested that Paul employed an analogous technique on a larger scale to set out views which he did not hold, and perhaps had never held, but which he was 'quoting' in order to refute.[36] But that is what Campbell now does. He offers a breathtaking analysis of Romans 1.16—3.20, setting out the words of the 'Teacher' in italics, and Paul's responses in normal type.[37] Campbell proposes that the 'Teacher' is to be imagined as saying all of 1.18–32, 2.2–13 (with small inputs from 'Paul' in verse 3), 2.16a, 2.17b–20, and certain phrases in 2.25–9. The opening of chapter 3 lends itself more obviously to this treatment, since here Paul's use of the 'diatribe' lies on the face of the text in the rapid-fire sequence of questions and answers – though, against normal expectations, it now seems to be Paul who is asking the questions and the 'Teacher' who is answering them. The 'Teacher' is then assigned 3.19b, while 'Paul' has 3.19a and 3.20.

Campbell then does similar things with Romans 3.21—4.25 (and indeed, later on, within chapters 9—11), though here the 'Teacher' has much shorter interjections. One gets the impression that Campbell is less wedded to these analyses than he is to his understanding of the crucial passage 1.18—3.20.

What are we to say to these things? We may, for a start, gently lay to rest the full-blown theory of *prosōpopoeia* – for many reasons, including the good one that Campbell himself has already done so. Overwhelming objections from classicists have persuaded him to reconsider.[38] In particular, the great classical examples of the phenomenon stand against him, because there it is always obvious *in the texts themselves* that a new 'speaker', or at least a new 'voice', is being introduced and then answered. I understand from personal conversation that Campbell has now abandoned, too, his earlier suggestion that the reader of the letter (Phoebe?) would signal the change of speaker by gesture and tone of voice. One cannot of course rule out the possibility that a letter-reader might have done such a thing. But such a proposal, about a text without obvious clues to this effect, is hardly the sort of guess on which one would bet five pounds in real life. Campbell now speaks, instead, of irony, parody or even sarcasm. Paul, he suggests, intended the tone of the relevant passages to come across as sarcastic, though how this would work in practice is not clear, at least not to me.

[35] See Wright 2002, ad loc.; and Campbell 2012, 133–6. We disagree about details, but not about the fact that Paul here articulates a theological position which is not his own present one.

[36] Campbell does not, I think, make it clear whether the views of 'the Teacher' are views that Paul himself might once have held or taught.

[37] For the analysis: 2009, 522–87; the display, 587–90.

[38] See particularly Griffith-Jones 2014. Campbell's response (in the same volume: 175–81) indicates that he will now call the relevant material not *prosōpopoeia* but 'parody' (176).

Paul's letters are, of course, full of changes of tone, pace and style. That is how good writers often write. We see it at several points in Romans itself; in passages like Galatians 4.12–20; in 1 Corinthians, switching from chapter 12 to chapter 13 and back to chapter 14; and, perhaps particularly, in 2 Corinthians. I know Paul was not usually writing poetry as such, but one's mind goes to the famous passage in *East Coker* where T. S. Eliot, after a perfectly good seventeen-line stanza ('What is the late November doing/ With the disturbance of the spring ...'), responds to himself with five lines in which he describes the stanza as 'not very satisfactory' and as 'a periphrastic study in a worn-out poetical fashion'. This, he comments, still leaves one with 'the intolerable wrestle with words and meanings.' Quite so.[39] There are all sorts of tricks people can play with words and meanings, and this by no means necessarily signals that they are expounding a particular case at one moment and undermining it at the next. Nobody doubts that there are significant changes of mood, pace, style and flavour at various points in Romans, of which the most obvious is between the end of chapter 8 and the start of chapter 9. This does not of itself tell us anything about whether the author intended to affirm, or to undermine, the statements he appeared to be making.

The major apparent exception does not, in fact, help even the more moderate case that Campbell now wants to press.[40] Romans 7.7–25 is not an *objection* to something Paul is saying; nor is it an argument which someone might want to make and which he is going to refute or undermine. It is a highly charged way of saying, 'This is where *autos egō*, "I myself", would be, under Torah.' He means every word, not as a statement of his present life, but as a true statement of the plight of Israel under Torah (in other words, of his own former self under Torah), recapitulating, as in 5.20 the sin of Adam. Even if the passage is thus, in some sense, to be read as an example of *prosōpopoeia*,[41] it is a very different sort of thing from what, say, Romans 1.18–32 would be if Campbell's original case were to hold.

What is more, it is a serious objection to the case even for a 'sarcastic' reading that not a single one of the Greek Fathers appeared to get the point. It was not just 'western readers' who failed to see what was going on.[42] It was eastern readers as well, who shared Paul's language and, in a measure, his culture. Granted, one does not lightly appeal to the Greek Fathers as a way of establishing what Paul was saying. There are often cases where something deep in the Jewish culture of early Christianity was covered over within a century or two, so that exegetes and theologians had to make heavy

[39] Eliot 1944, 23.

[40] There are other, shorter examples, e.g. Rom. 11.19, where the short 'speech in character' ('Branches were broken off so that I could be grafted in') is introduced with an explicit *ereis oun*, literally 'You will then say ...'.

[41] As is argued by, for instance, Stowers 1994, 264–72. Stowers is one of the few pre-Campbell scholars to have investigated the phenomenon in Paul.

[42] As Campbell suggests (2009, 529). Stowers, loc. cit., points out that Origen understood Rom. 7.7–25 to be 'speech-in-character', but no early exegetes seem to have recognized the phenomenon earlier in the letter in the way Campbell proposes.

dogmatic bricks with the thin straw of alternative philosophies. But here the point is important. If Phoebe had 'performed' Romans in the way Campbell needs her to have done for his theory to hold (there are no clues in the words themselves to tell a reader who had not been schooled by the author where the invisible inverted commas were to be placed), one might have hoped that *some* such tradition might have been preserved. It has not.

In any case, though there is such a thing as *prosōpopoeia*, and though there are such things as sarcasm or irony, it is abundantly clear from Campbell's own explanation of his theological agenda that he has not arrived even at his now moderated proposal for reasons of history or exegesis. The whole thing is a priori. He has come to see the 'straight' reading of Romans 1—4 as a dangerous, almost hateful, thing, speaking of a different God, and of, as we have seen, a rationalist and foundationalist 'gospel'. Rather than suggest that 'Paul changed his mind', or even 'Paul got it wrong, and so started again in chapter 5 and got it right this time' (much as C. H. Dodd declared in relation to Romans 3.9) Campbell is determined to find a way of saying that Paul did not mean what the 'normal' reading of chapters 1—4 thinks he meant.

The result is, once again, a new and fiercer form of *Sachkritik*. That notion, we recall, says in effect, 'Paul said X, but we can see from the rest of his thought that he really meant Y, so we will help him out of the muddle into which he has got himself.' Bultmann and others, as we saw, proposed that certain verses were 'glosses', added by a later redactor; this was a way of saying, 'The present text says X, but this is so out of character that we must assume the line to have been added by a foolish scribe at a later stage.'[43] But Campbell's hypothesis, even in this moderated version, is that Paul did indeed write the passages in question, but that he intended them to be 'heard' as the voice of someone - perhaps someone already known to the first audience, or someone to whom they would shortly be listening - whom Paul was quoting, or at least sketching, in order to refute. Though this does not involve actually excising portions of text, as the 'gloss' theory would do, it comes under the same critique, as in words from a seasoned scholar and teacher:

> Excising a piece of text on the grounds that it does not fit a broader theory of a letter's provenance is clearly methodologically muddled. The data of the text should underlie the broader explanation, and not vice versa.

The scholar in question is Douglas Campbell himself, wisely pushing back against any theories which would excise Romans 16.17–20.[44] Of course: that

[43] See above, 177 n. 70. In one of his famous *Essays in Satire* Ronald Knox caricatures this procedure by imagining a learned commentator discovering that the narrator of the Sherlock Holmes stories is called 'John H. Watson' but that in one story his wife addresses him as 'James'. 'Nihil aliud hic latet', writes Knox's fictitious commentator, 'nisi redactor ignorantissimus' ['what lies hidden here is nothing other than a very ignorant redactor']. This error, says another fictitious pundit, is what 'gave the original impulse to [the] theory of the Deutero-Watson'. See Knox 1928, 148.

[44] Campbell 2009, 513.

text, a sudden sharp warning against dangerous false teaching, is one of the pegs on which his own theory can be hung (though, since it is a peg capable of supporting many different hypotheses, it does not actually advance his own case much further). Granted, he has not tried to excise the relevant portions of text. But he has done his best to neutralize them, to prevent them being taken seriously as things that Paul himself wishes to say as part of his developing line of thought.

Some scholars, it is true, have imagined that *Sachkritik* is necessary, to some degree, to prove that one is not after all a naive fundamentalist; but this is a category mistake. If a Plato scholar assumes that Plato meant what he wrote, and that the text has its own logic even if we cannot at first understand it, we do not accuse her of naive or uncritical reading. If an orchestral conductor takes the tempo markings in a Beethoven symphony seriously, despite the normal traditions of performance, he is more likely to discover otherwise hidden meanings in the music. Letting the text be the text, whatever the discipline, is the sign of humble, patient scholarship, not of naivety.

Let us suppose, however, for the sake of argument, that Paul was, by some means or other, trying to warn his Roman hearers about a particular false teaching to which they might soon be exposed. What sort of teaching is it, and where does it come from? Campbell is quite clear: 'the Teacher' is a Jewish Christian. (Paul himself, of course, was a Jewish Christian; this is the problem with all post-Baur theories of this type; but we press on to see where the argument goes.) Campbell is close at this point to the now largely discredited theories according to which Paul represented a middle stage in early Christianity, a genuine gospel moment between 'Jewish Christianity' (which must be left behind) and 'Early Catholicism' (which represents a declining away from the truth). What does this 'Jewish Christianity' teach?[45] Answer: the 'Teacher' teaches all the things that Campbell so strongly disapproves of. He is a foundationalist; he thinks you can prove by observation that all humans are sinful; he thinks that sinners will be condemned by God unless they turn and obey the Torah. It is not really clear, I think, just what the 'Christian' bit in the phrase 'Jewish Christian' would then mean: how did the 'Teacher' integrate Jesus, not least his death, into his system? But what matters here is that the 'Teacher' is going to begin his theological statement with a 'fiery rhetorical entrance, which is lit – like that of so many preachers – by the flickering backdrop of hell'.[46] The 'Teacher', in other words, is the one whom Campbell will increasingly invoke with the phrase 'turn or burn'. And it is the Teacher's position that has become, according to Campbell, the foundation (within an overtly 'foundationalist' way of thinking) for what has become 'Justification Theory'.

Let us put this point gently. There is no actual evidence for any 'Jewish Christians' preaching this kind of message, in Paul's day or at any other

[45] In theory there ought to be a distinction between a 'normal' reading of Rom. 1—4 and the particular theology of the 'Teacher', since even when divided up at least half the text is by Paul. But in practice Campbell fails to take this into account.

[46] Campbell 2009, 529.

time. Yes, there are analogies between some aspects of Romans 1 (and Romans 9) and the Wisdom of Solomon. But the author of Wisdom does not sound like either a foundationalist or a fundamentalist. Yes, of course many Jews believed in a coming judgment in which – to take one obvious passage – the 'beasts' of Daniel 7 would be destroyed when the creator God finally took his seat and performed the justice for which the whole creation had been longing. Actually, when it suits him, Campbell can mount a careful apologia for divine 'wrath', explaining it as the proper reaction of a good God to the wickedness that defaces his good creation: 'a loving God's anger directed against any situation that is evil'.[47] He describes this as 'an apocalyptic account of God's wrath'; and he goes on to explain how this will differ from what he has heard in 'Justification Theory' and in the speeches of the 'Teacher' which, expressing something like this theory, have earned the scorn and the refutation of Campbell's 'Paul':

> Anger can be the reflex of benevolence or love just as much as it can spring from concerns with desert. And, as such, it can be a response to a prior initiative and its repudiation, and hence function in a secondary position just as much as it can be the first action undertaken, functioning in a primary location.

This, then, is how texts like 1 Thessalonians 1.10 are to be understood: not in the way the 'Teacher' has explained it in Romans 1 and 2, but in terms of

> God's reaction against a sinful situation and hence conceivably understandable as part of an account of divine benevolence.

Such passages, Campbell claims, do not 'attribute this activity to God in a fundamental fashion.'

In other words, there is good wrath and bad wrath. Good wrath is simply an outworking of divine benevolence, and is never 'foundationalist'; bad wrath is the core characteristic of a different God, and appears as the foundation of the argument, not a secondary or reactive mode.

The first problem with this proposal is that we lack any clear evidence of second-Temple Jews, let alone first-century Jewish Christians, thinking in the 'bad wrath' way. There is no sign of them making this the foundation for a 'turn or burn' style of preaching.

The second problem is that *Romans 1.18 itself proclaims itself to be precisely the 'secondary' turning of the good and loving creator to administer 'good wrath' against all that spoils and defaces his creation.* The very passage which is the heartland of Campbell's case points in the opposite direction. And if Campbell and others can quote the word *apokalyptetai* as an indication of 'apocalyptic' thought – I have already indicated that this begs several questions, but let the point stand for the moment – then we are bound to notice that Romans 1.18 offers precisely what, in the passage just quoted, Campbell refers to as 'an apocalyptic account of God's wrath.' *Apokalyptetai gar orgē theou*; 'for the wrath of God is *revealed*'. If we are to transliterate

[47] For this and the following quotations, cf. Campbell 2009, 929f.

rather than translate, we will say that the wrath is 'apocalypsed'. Where? Not, to be sure, in a 'neutral' observation of the moral decay of society. This is the problem with dividing up the passage too tightly. The argument runs forward, through its rhetorical stages, until it comes to rest at 2.16: God will judge all human secrets through the Messiah, Jesus, according to the gospel Paul proclaims – in other words, this entire section is dependent upon the gospel events and their meaning, not on some foundationalist platform. Starting there, and working back, Paul can see at last that the divine wrath is 'revealed'. In the light of the gospel of Jesus, and only as we look backwards in that light, we now know how the game will end.

Granted, exegetes have struggled to make sense of this. Granted, people have found the *gar* at the start of 1.18 very difficult: what is the logical connection with what has gone before?[48] But, on the face of it, Romans 1.18 makes it very difficult to produce the kind of foundationalist 'turn or burn' message Campbell wants to find there and to have Paul rebut. The fact that some preachers may have used Romans 1—4 in the way Campbell dislikes is not a proof that Paul himself meant it in that way.

It is nearly time to turn to exegesis itself, since as Campbell rightly says any case must stand or fall on how it actually handles the text. But before we get there we must make a central and vital point. It comes in three stages.

First, when I initially read Campbell's book (in a pre-publication copy), I was genuinely puzzled about his 'Justification Theory'. I have been in and out of churches of various kinds all my life. I have attended, and heard sermons in, avowedly 'evangelical' churches in various traditions and on various continents (as well as a great many 'liberal', 'catholic' and other kinds of churches). But I simply did not recognize the rationalist and foundationalist message which Campbell refers to as JT, 'Justification Theory'. Yes, I had heard preachers starting with sin and moving to the cross; but it was always in terms of the love of God reaching out to embrace sinners where they – we – actually were. There was always a strong element of *appeal*, not simply to the emotions, but not simply to a blind, calculating 'reason' either. (All this is really rather hard on preachers. I remember a fuss in Cambridge in advance of the 1979 Billy Graham mission because people were afraid that Graham was going to use techniques of 'mass indoctrination'. The mission came and went, and the protesters were puzzled: he had simply talked about Jesus, told stories, and urged people to welcome the transforming love of God into their lives. No 'mass indoctrination' anywhere to be seen. So now we find the opposite objection: he wasn't emotional – so perhaps he was rationalist, or foundationalist, instead.) Yes: I have known evangelists who would talk about 'the Romans road', leading potential converts through the first four chapters of the letter in a way that might be open to Campbell's objections. But I have known many others who, when people were seriously

[48] Campbell 2009, 340f. is unconvincing in his attempts to avoid the normal meaning of *gar*. His 'looser' or 'weaker' senses, however, include English phrases like 'you see', which, like the 'because' which he rejects, is also introducing an explanation. I have discussed this problem in Wright 2002 [*Romans*], 432, and more fully in *PFG* 764–71.

enquiring about the Christian faith, would give them instead a copy of John's gospel, and tell them to read it and open themselves to the one they would meet there. So, on my first reading of Campbell, I racked my brains but couldn't think of any sermons I had heard that fitted the hard, rationalist, foundationalist model Campbell was describing.

Since then I have learned otherwise. Many people have told me that this is indeed the way things have been presented in their churches. And I am aware that in the work of James B. Torrance in particular we find detailed and widespread studies of a 'federal Calvinism' which works more or less as Campbell has said, with, in some documented cases, worrying links to the social and cultural problems he mentions. So I hold my hand up: 'Justification Theory' does indeed exist. It does cause problems. And it has undoubtedly claimed authority from a particular reading of Romans 1—4.

But – and this is the second point – this is essentially a *modern* phenomenon, not an ancient one.[49] When Campbell suggests 'a set of strong affinities between Justification theory and the modern liberal *political* project',[50] and goes on to make similar connections with modern capitalism, he does not seem to realize that this link has implications in both directions. To put it bluntly: *it is far more likely that the post-Renaissance world has shaped the way western Christians have read Romans than that earlier 'Justification-Theory' readings of Romans have shaped the post-Renaissance world.* It is simply not the case that Romans 1—4, read 'straight', caused Constantinianism, imperial wickednesses, capitalism and so forth. It is overwhelmingly more likely that the western church, seduced by a slow and steady cultural process (helped by, but certainly not caused by, some aspects of the Reformation), came to read Romans 1—4 in an individualistic, foundationalist and (sometimes) rationalistic fashion because the people who were doing that reading were sixteenth- and seventeenth-century individualists, foundationalists and (sometimes) rationalists. To blame Romans 1—4 for the evils and problems listed by Campbell is like blaming the company that made your walking boots for the fact that you got lost in the mist.

In other words: Yes, there is a problem about 'Justification Theory'. A 'contractual' and foundationalist approach to the gospel does no justice to Paul or to the gospel itself, and it has done considerable damage by seeping out into the wider culture in the form of systems of government, punishment and so on. I was particularly interested in Campbell's point that JT does not know what to do with the *life* of Jesus (for JT to work, all that is

[49] As Campbell concedes (2009, 3, 935). The final paragraph of the book stresses that the reading he is opposing is 'an essentially modern reading of Paul' which belongs to 'European conceits'.

[50] Campbell 2009, 284f. (italics original); see too 305 ('Justification theory fits liberal politics like a glove'); and especially 935: 'the ostensibly evangelical construct I am criticizing throughout this book is in reality a contractual and liberal construction (although "liberal" of course in the political sense) and so is a characteristically *modern* gospel' (italics original). Campbell then goes further: 'Paul is often currently being read under its impress in a way that is in effect uncritically North American. Certain modern readers ... are constructing Paul in their own image.' That might indeed be the case; by the same token, perhaps certain other modern readers are constructing Paul's *opponents* in the image of their own opponents. Stranger things have happened in exegesis.

needed is for Jesus to be born of a virgin and to die on a cross), and hence with the whole theme of the kingdom of God.[51] Yes, all this matters. But the first four chapters of Romans are not to blame for subsequent misunderstandings. They do not teach what they have sometimes been supposed to teach.

Thus (1) I agree that there may well be a serious distortion of the gospel of the sort that Campbell is attacking, though I do not think it is nearly as widespread as he imagines; (2) this is essentially a *modern* phenomenon rather than an ancient one; and (3) if 'Justification Theory' gets Paul wrong, this is not because it has failed to hear the different 'voices' in his text, but because various parts of the post-Renaissance western world have misread Romans in the light of their own cultures, pressures and questions. All this tells us nothing about the first four chapters of Romans except that, like all writings, scriptural or otherwise, they are open to serious misinterpretation.

2. Campbell's Rereading of Romans

But is 'Justification Theory' a misinterpretation of Romans 1—4? Campbell claims to have examined the various proposals which would mitigate the charge, and that he has found them wanting.[52] This is not the place to speak up for any of those options. Nor is it possible here, of course, to argue in any detail for a fresh exegetical proposal that would make Campbell's entire complex structure unnecessary. Some of that I have done elsewhere. But some brief points must be made, if only to gesture towards the fuller account that could easily be given.[53]

First, we must acknowledge that Romans 1.18—3.20 has been badly served – and this is the heart of Campbell's point – by being treated simply as a 'demonstration that all are sinful', with 'the Jews' as a special case, supposing themselves exempt from the general condemnation only to discover that they are included after all. True, that is part of the overall effect. That is where Paul lands up in 3.19–20. But, crucially, that account simply ignores the point which is vital if we are to understand the central notion of 'God's righteousness' itself. In Romans 2.17–20 Paul lists, not the ways in which 'the Jew' might suppose Jews to be exempt from the general charges (that was already undermined in subtle ways throughout 1.18—2.16), but rather the ways in which 'the Jew' might rightly plead that Israel's own scriptures gave the people of God the vocation of being the light of the world, the solution to the global problem. Paul *agrees with* this account of Israel's vocation – only to show, from the same scriptures, that it fails because of Israel's sins

[51] Campbell 2009, 212; for my own work in this area, see Wright 2011 [*How God Became King*].

[52] Campbell 2009, 412–60.

[53] I am here drawing in particular (and summarizing somewhat drastically) the accounts of Rom. 2.17—3.9 and Rom. 4 in *Pauline Perspectives* chs. 30 and 33 (see also Wright 2014a). Readers of my 2002 Commentary may like to know that my reading of these passages has developed in various ways over the last twelve years.

(2.24). The point is not (to answer the boringly regular objection to 2.21–2) that 'all Jews' committed adultery or robbed temples or whatever. That would indeed be a 'crude attack', and ineffective at that, since it could easily be avoided by pointing to Jews who were obviously not guilty of these sins (people like Paul himself in Philippians 3.4–6).[54] There may well be a hint at recent scandals in Rome, but this is not the main point.[55] Nor is 'the Jew' here to be seen as 'the bigot', the archetypal *Homo religiosus*, as in Jewett's commentary.[56] The point is that 'the Jew', here apostrophized in the singular but referring to Israel as a whole, really had received the divine call to be the *solution* to the problem sketched in 1.18—2.16. For this remarkable plan to work, however, Israel would have needed to be perfect, and this was clearly not the case. But then the last paragraph of the chapter (2.25–9) holds out a tantalizing 'What if . . .?' What if there was a rejuvenated 'Israel', circumcised in heart by the spirit? What then?

This is a tease, a hint, a remote but haunting possibility at this stage of Paul's argument. He will later amplify it and explain what he was driving at. But even in this cryptic form 2.17–29 is enough to raise the question of 3.1–2 in a way not normally noticed. God has said that he will save the world through Israel; that is the point of 2.17–20, and Paul has not denied it. Israel has been 'entrusted with God's oracles' (3.2), charged to be the bearer of divine revelation for the wider world. But if Israel has been 'unfaithful' *to this commission*, what then? God will still be 'faithful' to his promise – the promise not principally *to* Israel but *through* Israel for the world. And that 'faithfulness', expressed in specifically legal or forensic terms in 3.5, is what constitutes the *dikaiosynē theou* in this passage, and hence by implication in 3.21 – and hence, by implication, in 1.17. That then sets off the train of thought in 3.5–9; and it is this question, of the divine faithfulness to the promise not only *to* Israel but *through* Israel, that dominates the rest of chapters 1—4. Yes: for the moment, universal sin is to be acknowledged. Israel joins the pagans in the dock, guilty as charged – not, we note again, because of some foundationalist assertion of sinfulness, but in the light of the Messiah and his gospel (2.16). In the Messiah, the one and only faithful Israelite, Israel's God has after all been faithful to his covenant promises and purposes (the promises and purposes to rescue the world through faithful Israel). This is why, through his death and its effects, a worldwide community has come into existence marked out simply by *pistis*, the faith or faithfulness which was the Messiah's own badge, which was indeed the character of God himself (3.3). Romans 4 then takes its place, not as a mere ad hominem response to a 'Teacher' who had asked 'Well, what about Abraham?',[57] not as a showcase for a handy prooftext in which 'righteousness'

[54] For the idea of the 'crude attack': Campbell 2009, 371f.

[55] See Campbell 561f., discussing Jos. *Ant.* 18.81–84.

[56] Jewett 2007, e.g. 223.

[57] Campbell 625.

and 'faith' happened to be conjoined,[58] and certainly not because Abraham is a 'heroic' example, an individual whose faith and its reward become the archetype for Christian believing (though there is a grain of truth there too, as 4.18–25 indicates).[59] Rather, Abraham belongs here, or rather, Genesis 15 belongs here, because this is where, as Paul reads the story, God made the covenant which promised Abraham a family and a land. But the family in question was a vast, uncountable family from every nation, and the land in question was the whole *kosmos*, the world, not just one small country (4.13). By the end of Romans 4, Paul has laid the foundations for the real thrust of the letter as a whole, which has to do not simply with the message of 'how to get saved', but with the carefully balanced and skilfully displayed message that the one God has, in the Messiah, created a single people out of Jew and gentile alike, thereby unveiling his own powerful, rescuing covenant faithfulness. Campbell is quite right to say that the first four chapters of Romans do not present a foundationalist, rationalist argument designed to bludgeon people into an intellectual 'faith'. He may well be right, even if he has overstated the point, that reading this section in that way has done considerable damage to the modern western church and society. He is wrong, however, to think that the chapters can only be rescued from this misreading by reconstructing them as a dialogue between a Jewish-Christian 'Teacher' and Paul himself. He has missed the golden stream of thought that flows through these chapters and right on through the three later sections of the letter, chapters 5—8, 9—11 and 12—16. Romans is all about the mission and unity of the people of God in the Messiah (and, yes, by the spirit). Chapters 1—4 lay the perfect foundation for that exposition. Campbell never notices the strong ecclesial argument that permeates Romans 3.21—4.25. This is why he, like so many, gets into tangles at 4.16–17.[60]

Romans 1.18—4.25 is thus a much more complex and intricate passage than has normally been supposed. Campbell is absolutely right that it has been badly misread, as part of the effort (which I suspect predates the Reformation but was certainly given a major boost at that time) to find a key text on 'how to be saved'. Romans will indeed tell you 'how to be saved', but it will do that as part of its larger project: to unveil the divine covenant faithfulness, and as part of that to explain what one is saved *for*. It will tell you, in particular, that 'the wrath of God is *revealed* from heaven' (1.18), and if anything is 'apocalyptic', that certainly is. As I said before, when we read 1.18—2.16 as a single section (albeit of course containing different twists and turns), we find that it is neither 'foundationalist' nor 'rationalist'. Of course it has been read like that, but that only goes to show that people have not taken seriously either its opening or its closing. What is 'revealed', as in Acts

[58] Campbell 396; this is the regularly-stated view of E. P. Sanders, a sharper version of the normal 'proof from scripture' point, which is also arguably inadequate.

[59] For the 'heroic' idea: Campbell 2009, 405, 603, 625.

[60] Campbell 735. Campbell says (724; cf. 1122 n. 19) he is broadly following Hays's rereading of 4.1, but had he done so – especially with my modification (Wright 2002 [*Romans*] 489f.; *PFG* 849), which has Hays's approval – he would have seen the point and saved himself some trouble.

17.31, is that the long-awaited promise (that Israel's God would put the whole world right at last, that is, that he would 'judge' it) is now to be performed through the human being Jesus, the Messiah. Only in the light of that 'revelation' can the dark miscellany of human degradation be seen for what it is. Romans 1.18—2.16 is not 'foundationalist'. It is 'apocalyptic', and the 'revelation' in question has come about through the events of the gospel.[61]

All this brings us to the second point. If it is possible to offer an alternative reading of 1.18—4.25 which is significantly different from the normal majority reading, and not open to the problems which Campbell has identified, how then does the argument about 'justification' actually work?

The answer is fascinating, and undermines not only Campbell but also all those who, in the line from Schweitzer, have been misled by Paul's clever stylistic change between the opening two movements of this 'symphony' (Romans 1—4 and 5—8) into imagining that these two blocks of teaching contain two different kinds of theology. (That should already have been difficult to maintain in view of the fact that in Galatians 3.1—4.11 we find all the different 'strands', which in Romans are apparently separated out, woven together into a single argument. We could also compare Philippians 3.2–11.) The first two main sections of Romans are often discussed as though they were set awkwardly next to one another like a camel and an elephant side by side at the zoo. Either will give you a ride; either will serve as a pack animal; but they are not part of the same family, and some will say (as some say about Justification Theory) that in the end the camel is not to be trusted. That is how chapters 1—4 and chapters 5—8 of Romans have often been seen. *But that is not how Paul saw them*, and though once again there is no space to demonstrate this in any detail we can at least point to the signs which show that, for Paul, chapters 1—8 as a whole formed a single great argument, summed up in 8.29–30: 'those he justified, he also glorified'.

Here we meet the odd feature I noted at the start of this discussion: that Campbell, though claiming to rely on a reading of chapters 5—8, has not actually given an account of these chapters in any detail. He falls back on the usual proposal that this is where Paul speaks about 'ethics' (in response, supposedly, to a Jewish interlocutor who was frightened that Paul's gospel might lead to moral slackness), and about 'assurance' of final salvation.[62] That is fine, up to a point; there is certainly plenty of ethical exhortation here, and there is also, arguably, the most ringing argument for 'assurance' anywhere in the New Testament. But the odd thing about this is that these are the categories normally proposed by those who have offered some variety of 'justification theory' for chapters 1—4. It seems as though Campbell, despite claiming 5—8 as his 'apocalyptic' heartland, has not in fact worked out that idea in detail. As we saw, he never draws attention to the most obviously 'apocalyptic' passage, 8.18–25.

[61] See *PFG* 764–71.

[62] e.g. Campbell 607f., 708; in the 2012 article Campbell emphasizes 'ethics'.

In particular, he manages to distract attention from the fact that *the argument about justification has not finished at the end of chapter 4*. Paul has set up the terms of the argument in 2.1–16, and he returns to these in chapter 8.[63] The question here is about *final* justification (hence the need for 'assurance'), and it is in chapter 8 that he revisits the scenario posed in chapter 2 in terms of 'condemnation' and 'justification', now that at last – particularly with the strong teaching about baptism and the spirit! – it can be answered. Romans 3.21—4.25 is about *present* justification; but what Paul had set up in 2.1–16 was the question of *future* justification. That is the point to which he returns at the end. The sign of this is that Paul has not stopped talking about *dikaiosynē* and its cognates. We obviously cannot explore the passages here, but we note them in order to make the point, which ought to be grist to Campbell's mill, that the normal western reading in which chapters 1—4 are 'about' justification and that chapters 5—8 are 'about' something else (sanctification, ethics, 'mysticism', 'participation' or whatever) is the malign result of projecting later theological schemes onto Paul's text.

Thus, after the opening statement in 5.1, crucial references to 'justification' or 'righteousness', or other terms from the *dik-* root, occur in chapter 5 at 5.9 (being justified by [the Messiah's] blood); 5.16 (the *dikaiōma* which contrasts with the *katakrima*, as in 2.12–13 and looking on to 8.1–4 and 8.33–4); 5.17 (those who receive the gift of 'being in the right' will reign in life, looking on to 8.30); 5.18 (the contrast between *katakrima* and *dikaiōma* again); 5.19 (the future 'justification', again corresponding to 2.12–13); and 5.21 (grace reigns 'through *dikaiosynē*'). I think this is why some scholars, noting all this, have placed chapter 5 together with chapters 1—4 rather than as the start of the new section, and though I prefer the traditional arrangement one can see the point. Nor will it do to say that chapter 5 refers so much to justification, righteousness and so on because it is summing up what has been said so far. That is certainly true as well, but in several different interlocking ways the two halves of chapter 5 (verses 1–11 and 12–21) are also laying foundations for what is to come. And what is to come continues to be about *dikaiosynē*, right up to the celebration at the close of chapter 8.

Thus the incidental references to *dikaiosynē* in chapter 6 (6.7, 13, 16, 18, 20) indicate well enough that Paul is not finished with the topic. It will not do to suggest that he has switched to a different meaning (an 'ethical' one, say, as opposed to a 'forensic' one). Chapter 6 draws in several ways on chapter 5, and chapter 5 as we have seen is continuing the theme from the earlier chapters. Then, after the dark interval of chapter 7, we find at the start of chapter 8 the same contrast (*katakrima* and *dikaiōma*) that we had in chapter 5, where Paul was summing up and moving forward, not leaving 'justification' behind but developing and filling it in towards the future eschatological conclusion which, as chapter 2 indicated, was always required. This is where the spirit comes in; one of Campbell's great

[63] See again Wright 2014a.

strengths has always been his insistence that you cannot do Pauline soteriology without including (and perhaps also invoking) the spirit. That is what 'Justification Theory', isolating Romans 1—4, has long tried to do. But, in 8.10, we find that 'the spirit is life because of *dikaiosynē*'. This points forward through the great 'apocalyptic' section of the chapter to the dramatic conclusion (8.30): 'those he justified, he also glorified'. Again, we note that this effectively repeats 5.17, once one realizes that 'glorification' is not about 'going to heaven' but about sharing the Messiah's glory, which is his sovereign rule, as in Psalm 8.

Then, in the closing 'coda' to this symphonic movement, we find 'justification' and 'condemnation' side by side once more, just as in chapters 2 and 5. 'It is God who declares them in the right. Who is going to condemn?' (8.33–4). In other words, *the whole of Romans 1—8 is about justification*, with the argument developing, snowballing, picking up more themes as it goes along, resonating now with Genesis, now with Exodus, now with Leviticus and Numbers, now gloriously with Deuteronomy (the promised 'inheritance'). *But the whole of Romans 1—8 is also about more than justification.* It is about God bringing into existence, in fulfilment of his covenant promises, a single worldwide faith-family who will 'inherit the world'.[64] *And since all of this is about the long-awaited fulfilment of age-old prophecy, resulting in the defeat of sin and death and all the other powers (8.1–3, 37–9), the renewal of the whole creation and the resurrection of the dead, one of the genuinely appropriate words to describe what Paul has done is 'apocalyptic'. Here he is on much the same ground as the second-Temple literature which is regularly given that label.* 'Apocalyptic' is not something other than 'justification', and vice versa. For Paul, one is the mode, the other is the result. And all is accomplished through the Messiah, through the spirit, through incorporation by the latter into the people of the former. Justification; participation; salvation history; spirit-driven fulfilment; and, not least, 'apocalyptic'. We can join Campbell in dismissing the essentially modern and rationalistic 'Justification Theory', like Abraham letting Lot go off to the Cities of the Plain. But we are then told to lift up our eyes and look to north, south, east and west: to the whole sweep of Romans, and to the creation of the new single family that must struggle for unity and holiness because it is a sign and foretaste of the coming great cosmic renewal. And at the centre of that vision of an entire renewed creation there remains Paul's apocalyptic vision of justification: justification in the future; justification also, by faith alone, in the present.

Justification, moreover, achieved through the death of the Messiah. In his earlier works Campbell highlighted the background of Paul's language about Jesus within the Jewish martyr-literature. That proposal clearly has some mileage.[65] But it is a considerable embarrassment for his theory that

[64] In 4.13, anticipating 8.18–25, Paul is deliberately following Jewish traditions, going back at least to Psalm 2, of expanding the land-promise to Abraham by means of the world-promise to the Messiah.

[65] Hence his scheme PPME (pneumatologically participatory martyrological eschatology), as in Campbell 2005, 4.

one of the great climaxes of Romans 5—8 comes at 8.3–4, in which the substitutionary and penal death of Jesus is clearly stated. This motif belongs (it is normally thought) to 'Justification Theory'; in Campbell's own construct, 'apocalyptic' should have no room for it.[66] In almost any of the definitions of 'apocalyptic' that have been flying around throughout this whole Part of the book, the idea that Sin ('Sin-as-a-*power*') has been 'condemned' is precisely an 'apocalyptic' theme. Paul has built up to this very carefully through chapter 7, so that by the time we reach 8.1–4 we know that 'Sin' is virtually the equivalent of 'Satan'. And 'Sin' is *condemned.* Significantly, once this sentence has been declared we hear no more of Sin. We hear plenty about the 'flesh', and the urgent necessity of not living in accordance with it. But Sin itself, now that its condemnation has been pronounced, disappears from view. This is 'apocalyptic', if anything is.

And it is also forensic:

> There is no condemnation for those in the Messiah, Jesus ... For God has done what the law ... was incapable of doing. God sent his own son in the likeness of sinful flesh, and as a sin-offering; and, right there in the flesh, he condemned sin. This was in order that the right and proper verdict of the law could be fulfilled in us, as we live not according to the flesh but according to the spirit.[67]

This is without a doubt *substitutionary.* 'There is no condemnation for those in the Messiah' ... because God 'condemned sin' in the Messiah's flesh. 'Condemnation' is undoubtedly *penal.* But this 'penal substitution' is not fitted in to the kind of 'justification theory' to which Campbell is understandably so allergic. It is in support of the larger, apocalyptic, cosmic vision which Paul is unfolding in Romans 8: the divine victory over all 'powers', death included, so that the whole creation will be set free from its slavery to corruption. Paul's expression of what can properly be called 'penal substitution' has nothing to do with the western mediaeval idea of an angry God being pacified by a merciful Jesus, as in many a frightening painting, many a frightening sermon. It has everything to do with the ancient Jewish theme of the *dikaiosynē theou* as an *apocalyptic* theme about the divine covenant faithfulness through which the divine purposes for the creation are at last brought about through the condemnation and overthrow of the powers of evil.

This is where we need to invoke the category Campbell admitted elsewhere, that of 'good wrath' as opposed to 'bad wrath'. For God to condemn 'Sin' can hardly be an act of hatred towards the human race. It was the ultimate act of self-giving love (5.8; 8.31–9). I do not think it will do to separate out, as Campbell tries to do, a 'forensic-retributive' or 'judiciary' theology

[66] We look in vain, in Campbell's works of 2005, 2009 or 2012, for any recognition of what Paul is saying about 'no condemnation ... because God condemned sin in the flesh ...'. The closest he comes is when he says (2012, 126) that God 'dealt decisively and powerfully with the evil that surrounds [humanity].' A few pages later he says that 'a trinitarian dynamic has liberated humanity' (2012, 136).

[67] 8.1–4. The translation of *dikaiōma* in 8.4 remains difficult, but the contrast in the context with *katakrima*, picking up the similar balance in 2.12f. and 5.16, and anticipating 8.33f., shows that we are dealing with the same law-court theme.

(which 'the Teacher' apparently holds) and a 'forensic-nonretributive' or 'executive' theology (which Paul apparently holds).[68] Underneath the complex language, this is simply a re-run of Luther's polarization, coming by a circuitous route into Käsemann's work, between the old *iustitia distributiva*, in which God punished sinners and rewarded the righteous, and the newly-discovered *iustitia salutifera* of the gospel. But this is just as unconvincing as de Boer's 'two-track' theory of 'apocalyptic'. If the word 'retributive' means anything, it must include 'condemnation'. At the crucial moment in this passage – this 'apocalyptic', 'participatory' and 'mystical' passage we know as Romans 5—8! – Paul roundly declares that God *condemned Sin in the flesh*. Near the centre of the newer so-called 'apocalyptic' readings of Paul is the fundamental rejection of the kind of low-grade 'forensic' readings into which some popular theology has collapsed the apostolic message.[69] But the genuinely 'apocalyptic' Paul includes a 'forensic' account both of the death of Jesus and of the inclusion of believers within its effects. If we, with our complicated theological, philosophical, historical and socio-political baggage, find it difficult to express that larger whole in our own language, that is our problem, not Paul's.

But if all this is so – if, at the heart of his launching of the great argument of Romans 8, Paul states so clearly that God condemned Sin in the Messiah's flesh so that those 'in the Messiah' would now have 'no condemnation' – then there is no reason in principle to deny that a similar theological position may lie underneath the dense and vexed passage 3.24–6. We do not need to develop or demonstrate the point; merely to note that if the whole of the first eight chapters of Romans are about 'justification', accumulating other dimensions as they go, then we would expect that the meaning of Jesus' death, though invoked differently at different stages of the developing argument, would exhibit a deep coherence.

To see Romans 1—8 as a single coherent argument, moving through its different stages but with one basic developing line, alerts us to another important exegetical point. There are many ways in which the elements of 1.18—4.25 which Campbell assigns to 'the Teacher' are in fact woven tightly with other passages, both in chapters 1—8 and in the letter as a whole, so that to pull away the bits that Campbell gives to 'the Teacher' robs the letter of some of its tight argumentative links. Again, there is no space here to explore this in detail; but a few obvious points may be noted.

First, the great commands at the start of chapter 12 appear as a direct reversal of the indictment in 1.18–32 – the primary passage Campbell gives

[68] Campbell 2009, 662 and elsewhere.

[69] At 1120 n. 87 Campbell quotes Martyn on Gal. 1.4, attempting to marginalize Pauline references to 'sins', plural. Campbell himself speaks of 'two irreconcilable conceptions of God and the Christ-event' (705–7), which turns out to be a new version of the old polarization between the 'angry God' and the 'loving God' which, in sundry times and diverse manners, has led theologians to the brink of Marcionism. See too Campbell's suggestion, in the book's final paragraph (936), that his reading will produce 'a kinder, gentler Paul'. The nasty 'Paul' proclaimed a nasty god; now, Campbell's gentler Paul will proclaim a nice one! Underneath the breathtaking sophistication of the argument, in other words, we find a familiar cliché.

to 'the Teacher'. We may note in particular the role of the 'mind': 12.2 reverses 1.28, while the overall command of 12.1 reverses more or less the whole sweep of 1.24–32. Even within chapters 1—4 we see a similar process of reversal taking place, as the faith of Abraham in 4.18–22 seems to be a carefully phrased reversal of the corruption of humankind in 1.19–25.[70] In the same vein, the positive view of creation in 1.20 is finally answered by the redemption of creation in 8.19–21.There are other tightly interlinked passages as well, far too many to mention. The questions of 3.1–9 go very closely with the questions of chapters 9—11, which hints strongly that the passage which gave rise to those early questions, namely 2.25–9, might be seen as an anticipation of the passage which gives rise to chapters 9—11, namely Romans 8 (or perhaps we should say Romans 7 and 8). You cannot start picking away at one section and parcelling it out in bits and pieces to different 'voices' without beginning to unravel the tightly woven fabric of the whole. Whether Romans was written to a particular sharp-edged local situation, or (as I think) to a broader though still specific set of needs in the Roman church, all the signs are that it contains a very carefully arranged sequence of arguments which dovetail and interlock at point after point. I agree that insofar as a foundationalist, rationalist, individualist, conditional and contractual 'justification theory' still exists, it is necessary to expose its follies and failings and offer an alternative. But you don't throw out the bathtub just because you sometimes find a spider in it. And in the case of Paul's letters there is no need to create new shadowy actors and then persuade Paul to part with sections of his own script so that they may have something to say as well.

A final point might be made, perhaps by a bolder scholar than I. It could be argued, no doubt by someone 'speaking as a fool' after the manner of Paul in 2 Corinthians 11 (another 'speech in character'?), that the greatest irony in Campbell's massive book is that *his own argument works exactly like the one he is criticizing*. 'Someone might say' something like this:

First, Campbell tries to convince us, in a 'foundationalist' manner, of the dozens of problems that are linked with or even caused by 'Justification Theory'. In his own words, he decided to enter the argumentative circle

> with a set of preliminary characterizations that were largely incontestable and could serve to establish and initiate the principal issues.[71]

That is more or less the definition of 'foundationalism'. Then, having laid his preliminary charge (much like the 'Paul' of 'Justification Theory', with the long list of sins in Romans 1), he faces the possibility (much like Paul on any normal reading of 2.17–24) that there might be exceptions, and he rules them out (in his chapter 12). All standard readings of Romans 1—4, he concludes, have erred, and fall short of the glory of 'apocalyptic'. Thus the long list of problems (helpfully categorized into 'Intrinsic Difficulties', 'Systematic

[70] See Wright 2002 (*Romans*), 499–501.

[71] 2009, xxvii.

Difficulties' and 'Empirical Difficulties', followed in turn by Textual 'Underdeterminations' and 'Overdeterminations'[72]) 'will provide much of the leverage for the hermeneutical and exegetical discussions that follow'.[73] The model possesses, Campbell says, 'an impressive rational integration'.[74] A good deal of the argumentation proceeds in this explicitly 'rational' way, deducing what 'must' be the case from foundational principles.[75]

Then, since there is no escape from the charge, our Teacher provides us with a Solution – to the problems he has 'convinced' us exist. An atoning mechanism is needed through which this wrong-headed thinking can be put right. The coherence of Romans 1—4 as it stands must be sacrificed, with 'the Teacher' as the scapegoat, bearing the guilt of 'Justification Theory' into the wilderness, in order that Paul's real 'apocalyptic' intention may emerge, rescued from its captivity to false readings. In case anyone should appeal to the great theologians of the past (as the hypothetical 'Teacher' might have appealed to Abraham), Campbell will invoke the great theologians – Athanasius, Augustine, Calvin and of course Barth – on his side, even though (as with Abraham and circumcision?) a certain amount of fancy exegesis may be needed before those august personages will 'support' the required position. (All of them, of course, to be serious for a moment, believed in justification, and found it in Romans 1—4; none of them ever imagined reading Romans the way Campbell does.)

The payoff – the equivalent, in Campbell, of the rationalist and foundationalist appeal of 'the Teacher' – is clear. For 'the Teacher', it was 'turn or burn'. Not that any first-century Jews we know of actually said that; if Sanders accused Luther of projecting a supposed picture of late-mediaeval Roman Catholics onto Paul's opponents, one can imagine Campbell being accused of a similarly modernizing misreading. For Campbell, it is equally blunt and uncompromising: submit, or face extinction! I have already quoted his remarkable threat, from an earlier book, that 'Justification' and 'salvation-historical' models must either be subordinated to his model or be 'exegetically eliminated'. Now he expands this:

> The conventional reading ... needs now to justify itself positively and not merely assume its superiority. And it needs to deal with its numerous problems, of which over fifty have been enumerated. It also needs to refute my rereading positively in the same ways, undermining its positive supports and/or finding problems in its account of the text or implications ... In the absence of these, any simple retort to my rereading of 'I am unconvinced' must immediately itself be judged unconvincing. Things have moved well past the stage of mere dismissal. The conventional construal of Paul's Justification texts has been only the least worst alternative, and with a new, superior alternative now present, it has much work to do beyond the hermeneutics (and politics) of assertion. Justification must adapt to a brave new world – or quietly expire.[76]

[72] Campbell 2009, 168f., 171f., 396–408.

[73] 2009, 8.

[74] 2009, 35.

[75] e.g. 2009, 32, 41 and frequently.

[76] 2009, 935f.

In other words: Turn or burn. A foundationalist argument leading, at this meta-level, to a fundamentalist conclusion. A bolder critic than I might well want to make such a point.

But this is not the only irony. Campbell frequently invokes the well-worn image of the blind people studying the elephant: students of Paul grab on to the tail, the leg, the trunk or the tusk and declare that the 'elephant' of Paul's theology 'really' consists of 'justification', or 'participation', or 'salvation history', or whatever. But the real elephant in the room, throughout Campbell's work, is rather obviously the *covenant* between God and Israel, the covenant to which in the gospel events Israel's God has been faithful, the covenant made with Abraham which involved the promise of a worldwide family and a cosmos-wide inheritance. This theme is capable, as I have tried to demonstrate elsewhere, of holding together the otherwise disparate emphases in Paul's writings.[77] It has, of course, been scorned precisely by the proponents of various 'Justification Theories' because it seems to threaten (among other things) the individualism of the modernist 'gospel'. One might have thought, however, that Campbell, explicitly leaning on the work of the Scottish theologians for whom the opposite of the worrisome 'contract' was a proper 'covenant', would have seen the potential here for an account of Paul which would be thoroughly 'apocalyptic' but in a far more recognizable historical sense. The actual second-Temple 'apocalyptists', after all, wrote what they wrote precisely because they believed that in God's covenant with Israel there lay the hidden clue to the victory of the creator God over all the principalities and powers of the world, not least the actual physical ones with which they were faced in their social and political reality. And when they spoke of 'justification', they did so within that context.[78]

Actually, they spoke of 'justification' only rarely. There are occasional mentions of 'justification' in Qumran and in the *Psalms of Solomon*, but the theme never plays the striking role it enjoys in Romans and Galatians in particular. One could, in fact, begin the enquiry at that point: what was it that caused Paul to deploy this comparatively rare Jewish theme and to give it a previously unknown prominence? Schweitzer and Wrede said, Because it was all about the quite new theme of gentile incorporation into the people of God (a theme strangely muted, if not almost absent, in Campbell). 'Justification Theory' said, Because humans are so sinful, and Jewish solutions so inadequate, that God had to provide a different way. (This makes it all the stranger that Campbell's hypothetical Jewish-Christian 'Teacher' would want to embrace such a view.) A covenantal and apocalyptic response might be, Because in the gospel events Paul saw that the divine covenant faithfulness had been revealed at last, enabling for the first time a proper 'backwards' account of the human plight, a proper vision of the victory of

[77] See *PFG*, esp. ch. 10; and see now also Wright 2014a.

[78] Campbell offers hardly any engagement with second-Temple texts. The chart (655) of thematic influences on 'Antecedent Jewish tradition', and thence to 4 Maccabees on the one hand and Paul on the other, is a small indication of a much larger world inviting exploration and offering potential resolutions for the problems which Campbell has chosen to address in other ways.

the creator God over all the powers of the world, *and, within that,* a proper understanding of how the divine condemnation of Sin in the death of the Messiah laid the foundation for the verdict 'in the right', 'forgiven', pronounced in the present time (rightly anticipating the verdict of the last day) over all who, despite having committed actual sins, believe the gospel, the Jew first and also the Greek. And it would, of course, 'nest' that whole account within a description of how this radical new and shocking event was nevertheless to be seen in retrospect as the fulfilment of the ancient divine purpose, bringing to its goal the strange, hidden but divinely guided narrative of Israel; of how the work of the spirit, and the incorporation of believers 'into the Messiah', grounded an account of redeemed humanity; and of how this redeemed humanity could resume its originally intended role, as in Genesis 1 and Psalm 8, of sharing the Messiah's redemptive and justice-bringing rule over all creation. All this, of course, sounds very much like Romans 1—8.

We must therefore agree with Campbell up to a point. Yes, it was always a mistake to isolate Romans 1—4 and make it perform a task (expounding 'justification') for which it was only partially suited. Yes, all kinds of puzzles have followed from that wrong exegetical decision, as it has been mediated through various aspects of modern culture. But thus far and no further. The puzzles and problems are not addressed, let alone solved, by cutting up Romans 1—4 into small pieces. They are addressed and solved by letting those chapters play their proper role within the larger argument of the letter as a whole, and particularly of Romans 1—8 as a whole.

Underneath all this is a puzzle about Campbell's whole project, including his earlier book, entitled *The Quest for Paul's Gospel.* Campbell (in company with 'Justification Theory') seems to take it for granted that 'the gospel' is 'how people get saved'.[79] But that already colludes with the misreading of which 'Justification Theory' is guilty. 'The gospel', in Romans at least, is not that which is defined in Romans 1.16–17. That passage expresses the *effect* of 'the gospel'. The gospel itself is defined by Paul even earlier in Romans 1, namely in 1.3–4, a passage which Campbell never really factors into his account. It is the message about Jesus himself, Jesus crucified and risen, Jesus as Israel's Messiah and the world's rightful Lord. Part of the problem of 'Justification Theory' is the Melanchthonian insistence that 'the gospel' is all about 'what it means for me'. This already turns the question towards the individual and his or her 'benefit': 'to know Christ is to know his benefits'. The truly 'apocalyptic' gospel says, by contrast, that Jesus, the Messiah, is Lord, and that the 'benefits' are found by looking away from oneself to him. By equating 'the gospel' with 'the way people get saved', Campbell has already taken a step onto his opponents' territory. A fully 'apocalyptic' account should have been bolder.

[79] e.g. 2009, 520: 'How you get saved – and that you can be – is "the good news".' Campbell is here summarizing 'Justification Theory', but he seems to be agreeing with this point.

3. Conclusion: Beyond Old and New Perspectives?

Has Campbell, then, gone beyond the new perspective, as he and some of his followers have suggested?[80] Yes and no. As with the other exponents of a would-be Pauline 'apocalyptic', he is not really on the same trajectory at all.

Why should he be? That is only one Pauline discussion among many others. Campbell shares some emphases with the various movements that sail under 'new perspective' as a flag of convenience. He reacts, for instance, against (some features of) a basically 'Lutheran' reading of Paul. He insists that insofar as Paul thought about the 'plight' of humankind this was a reaction from his vision of the 'solution', not vice versa. But his account of the supposedly Jewish-Christian 'Teacher' (the turn-or-burn preacher, offering an angry God, the flickerings of hellfire, and the salvation of individuals through a rational 'decision' called 'faith') is every bit as problematic as the caricatures to which the new perspective has objected, namely, the older Reformational projections of mediaeval Catholics dressed up as zealous Jews. The crowning irony, of course, is that if one glanced through ancient Jewish literature to see where one might find warnings about the approaching divine punishment, one might be drawn to the literature we normally call 'apocalyptic'. That is why, as we saw earlier, much liberal thought of the nineteenth and twentieth centuries rejected 'apocalyptic' as a dark, dualistic and dangerous kind of theology. We may think, and I do think, that this was a serious misunderstanding. But if we want to rehabilitate 'apocalyptic' as a key element in our understanding both of second-Temple Judaism and of Paul, as I do, we will have to do a lot more work to understand both how ancient Jewish 'apocalyptic' actually functioned, and how the fresh apocalypse of Israel's God in the gospel of Jesus the Messiah and Lord transformed this type of thought (if that is what it was) and enabled it to address the wider world.

What then shall we say about 'apocalyptic' as a category for understanding Paul? First, we must emphasize once more that the principal rhetorical effect of invoking 'apocalyptic' as a tool for interpreting the apostle is to claim a putative history-of-religions matrix. Once we cut loose from that, suggesting that the word 'apocalyptic' can now mean a variety of different things (as indeed it has come to do), any such historical claim becomes null and void. All we are left with then is a *theological* appeal to a scheme which focuses on the imminent *parousia* (Käsemann), the victory of the cross (Beker), the two 'ages' and the two 'tracks' of 'apocalyptic' (de Boer), the three cosmic 'agents' (God, humans, the powers) (Martyn), the distinction between 'sins' and 'Sin' (Gaventa), or the importance of divine sovereignty over against human initiative (Campbell). These are of course variously combined, though the differences are also important. But, to take Campbell's definition, the theologians who come to mind when we invoke divine sovereignty – Augustine, Luther, Calvin, Barth – have also insisted on the

[80] See e.g. Tilling 2014, entitled *Beyond Old and New Perspectives on Paul.*

centrality of justification, in something like its traditional sense, which Campbell rules out. If their doctrine has been corrupted, within the last four centuries of western theology, through the subtle infiltration of modern individualist, contractual or other ideas, that is a problem to be addressed in those terms, but it tells us little about Paul's original writings.

Rather, when we put Paul into his historical context within first-century Judaism itself, not least the writings loosely grouped under the label 'apocalyptic', we find all kinds of features which the modern revival of so-called 'apocalyptic' has screened out. Justification is not the only sufferer at this point (taking with it the accompanying questions of human sin, atonement, and so on). Also, and more importantly, we miss the notion of the divine covenant with Israel, and the constant sense of a long, dark story which finally reaches its goal in the shocking, fresh, but also long-promised and long-awaited new revelation. The idea of a narrative, and of a divine covenant, are not antithetical to the 'apocalyptic' idea of the divine sovereignty, or to the promise of a radical inbreaking of a new divine initiative, or to the belief that the suprahuman 'powers of the world' have usurped the divine sovereignty and are now at last to be put in their place, or to the idea of 'two ages' in which the 'age to come' will burst in upon the 'present evil age'. All those supposed elements of 'apocalyptic' are thoroughly at home within a genuine second-Temple and early Christian 'covenantal' theology. We may be grateful to Campbell, as we are to de Boer and Martyn, for raising the questions so sharply. We acknowledge the leadership of Käsemann in breaking away from Bultmann's individualistic existentialism. But, with Beker, though well beyond him too, we must insist on a fully Jewish context, and the fully Pauline integration of themes which ought not to be separated.

The conversation, of course, continues. I have mentioned the significant work of Beverly Gaventa, whose forthcoming commentary on Romans will undoubtedly move the discussion on, though in what direction remains to be seen.[81] There are various edited volumes which take Martyn's position as the starting-point and try to go forward from there – though, as I have said, I am bound to see all such attempts as inherently unstable, building on a foundation which will not sustain their weight.[82]

As I have insisted throughout, however, my opposition is not to the idea of Paul as an 'apocalyptic' theologian. My objection is to the use of that word to suggest a theological position, or rather, a bewildering range of such positions, which can then be used as Procrustean beds to stop Paul

[81] See already Gaventa 2013b.

[82] See e.g. Davis and Harink 2012; Gaventa 2013a. Martyn's concluding essay in the latter volume (Martyn 2013) opens with the claim that the volume 'will surely prove to be one of our period's most significant international events in the study of the apostle Paul' (157). Much of Martyn's own brief essay concerns the question of 'agency', that is, whether (as in hellenistic philosophy) humans can perform good works of their own accord or whether (as in Martyn's view of 'apocalyptic'), humans are enslaved to Sin until the point where, after the divine 'invasion', there are now two 'actors', God and the 'newly created' human, involved in the moral drama. This does not seem to me to add very much to the older discussions of divine sovereignty and human ability, going back at least to Luther's polemic against Erasmus in *The Bondage of the Will*, and behind that to Augustine and Pelagius. Does 'apocalyptic', after all, now simply mean 'Augustinian'?

saying several things which he, in line with many actual 'apocalypses', really does say. I too see Paul within a historically describable 'apocalyptic' framework, that of the second-Temple Jewish world, rethought in his case around the Messiah and the spirit. I too see the heart of his gospel as the message that, in Jesus, the one God has acted dramatically and decisively to overthrow the rule of the 'powers' and to liberate humans, and the world, from their grip. I, too, stress that for Paul the world's true plight is itself revealed in the gospel, and is revealed, moreover, as rendering humans, even the Jewish humans blessed by God's gift of Torah, radically incapable of initiating their own salvation and hence utterly dependent on the free gift of divine grace. I, too, stress that Paul believed that the 'age to come' had been inaugurated with the death and resurrection of Jesus, and that it would be completed in the events written about in Romans 8 and 1 Corinthians 15. I, too, insist that all this generates, for Paul, a new mode of knowing (as in passages like 2 Corinthians 5.16–17 and Galatians 4.9), a mode which with only a slight stretch can be appropriately labelled an 'apocalyptic epistemology'. But these accumulated points do not work in the way that so many have supposed. This 'apocalyptic' does not eliminate an emphasis on 'sins', on atonement, on forgiveness; it rather embraces it.[83] It does not rule out, but rather leads us to expect, an emphasis on the long, dark history of Israel, and on the divine purpose at work behind the scenes, not as an immanent process or progressive development but as part of the sovereignty of the creator God, bringing about the final great moment of judgment and mercy. And it does not rule out, but indeed it insists upon, the larger context of the *covenant*: the covenant with Abraham which God has at last fulfilled, the covenant redefined around the Messiah through whom the promises have been extended into the whole world, the covenant faithfulness of God which is both apart from Torah and yet witnessed to by Torah and prophets. As I have said, if we must choose between Bultmann and Käsemann, we must choose Käsemann. But those great thinkers claimed to stand within a tradition that appealed to history. And when we go to the actual history, we find a larger picture than either of them had imagined. Paul belongs within the first century, not within the sterile and stifling nineteenth-century European debates or their more recent successors.

It is, therefore, to history itself that we turn in the third Part of this book: the actual history of the actual communities which sprang up through Paul's work, and to which he addressed his dense and evocative letters. And by 'actual history' I mean, among other things, 'social history'.

[83] As Martyn seems now to acknowledge (2013, 163f.).

Part III

PAUL IN HIS WORLD – AND OURS?

Chapter Ten

SOCIAL HISTORY AND THE PAULINE COMMUNITIES

1. Introduction

History is stubborn. It will put up with all kinds of treatment, allow itself to be squashed out of shape, cut up into pieces, discussed, dismissed, disfigured and generally beaten up this way and that; and then, at the end of the day, it is still there, bloodied but unbowed, eyebrows raised in an ironic but insistent question. After all the tumult and shouting have died down, after the ideologies and the grand schemes have strutted their stuff, history will still be there, waiting patiently but doggedly for its turn. It won't go away.

History is important not least because it is messy. Just as individual human beings, even the ones we know best, turn out to be not exactly the way we had imagined, to have slightly but significantly different aims, hopes and fears from the ones we had supposed – and just as a real human relationship involves facing those differences and learning to accept them and work with them, rather than continuing with our previous shallow projections – so the sheer detail of what happened last week, last century, or two millennia ago continues to reassert itself. The wise historian learns to face the evidence, to accept it and work with it, rather than continuing to superimpose upon it whichever large, easy scheme had earlier been in mind. That kind of historical exercise, I submit, has always been at the heart of the study of the New Testament. At least, it should have been.

That, indeed, was what was implied in the long years when something called 'the historical-critical method' was invoked as the central task. We will do the history (it was thought), with proper Teutonic rigour, and this will demonstrate that some, perhaps much, of what ordinary western Christianity had taken for granted was in fact based on mistakes, not least on the fictions with which the early church sustained their faith. That was the agenda which ran, with twists and turns, from Hermann Samuel Reimarus in the eighteenth century through Ferdinand Christian Baur in the nineteenth, and on to Rudolf Bultmann and his successors in the twentieth. History was *subversive*, particularly when it came to ecclesial tradition. Many today, not least in North America, see themselves as engaged in the same kind of activity, and pour bitter vitriol on any whom they see as claiming to do 'history' while still retaining, and advocating, something like orthodox Christian faith. But this negative approach continues to beg the question, as, of course, do many apologists. It merely perpetuates the assumption which emerged from the social, political and religious upheavals of the second half of the eighteenth century: the assumption that the old order, whether crown or church, had had its day, and that something new was emerging. That movement appealed to 'science', and by analogy to 'scientific history', as the firm base for a brave new world. The trouble with appealing to history, of course, is that to history you must go. And history, like Caesar in Paul's famous appeal, may or may not tell you what you want to hear.

Three caveats must already be sounded. First, the word 'history' can refer, notoriously, to three things: to 'what happened', to 'what people wrote about what happened', and to 'what the historian does today', the task of trying to construct a meaningful narrative from the evidence available. History can be event, writing or task. It is a matter of 'history [event]' that Jerusalem was destroyed by the Romans in AD 70. It is a matter of 'history [writing]' that Josephus wrote about that event within his three larger narratives (the *Antiquities*, the *War*, and the *Life*). It is a matter of 'history [task]' that we today, reading those works of 'history [writing]' and many others, attempt to tell our own story of what happened ('history [event]'). The writing and the contemporary task blend into one another; in a sense, Josephus is not only a source, but also a precursor, of today's historian. But the task of research, the finished written product, and the original event are clearly not the same thing. Within this multiple ambiguity there lie many long-standing puzzles, not least the awkward difference between 'the historical Jesus' (meaning the real Jesus who lived, breathed and died) and 'the historical Jesus' (meaning the 'Jesus' whom historians, working within particular worldviews, try to reconstruct). Some, suspicious of the latter, have appeared to deny the importance of the former. Perhaps fortunately, our present concern is not with Jesus, but with Paul. A similar reaction, however, is visible here as well, as we can see when people suggest that, since the church's theologians have told us what 'justification' means, we ought not to raise awkward historical/exegetical questions about what Paul himself meant in the actual passages where he expounds and discusses it.

The second caveat is that 'facts' are complicated and hard to come by.[1] To quote a scholar whose work is central to this Part of the present book:

> Facts are not picked up like pebbles. They are won, wrested out of the maze of phenomena, invented. To find a fact, we need not only sharp eyes but also tough-minded imagination ... There is a stubbornness to facts, in which the historian, like the scientist, should rejoice.[2]

[1] See *NTPG* ch. 4, esp. 88–92.

[2] Meeks 2009, 136. In the preface to the second edition of *The First Urban Christians* Meeks explains that what kept him going in the difficult tasks leading up to that book 'was sheer stubbornness, born of curiosity, which is finally the one reliable reason for trying to be a historian': Meeks 2003 [1983], ix.

There it is again: stubbornness. Facts matter. Just because you need imagination to grasp them does not mean that they are imaginary. Far from it. Supposing they fit the theory, that doesn't necessarily mean that you made them up for that purpose. At this point the historian and the hard scientist are pretty much on the same level, the difference being that, whereas in physics you must always repeat the experiment, in history you never can. Even if Julius Caesar had crossed the Rubicon a second time, in 48 BC, that would not in itself prove that he had done the same thing a year before. Nor would a second crossing have meant the same as a first one.

The third caveat is that almost nobody comes to the raw material of history – archives, ancient manuscripts, coins, inscriptions, old photographs, letters, archaeological finds, and so on – without having at least a vague idea of a 'big picture' within which it might make sense. What counts as 'making sense' is another question: whose 'sense', what sort of 'meaning', what account of human motivation, are we assuming as the norm? But my point is that as in any study we must expect a constant dialogue between the big picture and the little details, the overall hypothesis and the data which that hypothesis will 'explain'. Those who claim to be 'neutral' ought instantly to be suspect, just as those who claim to have noticed some great pattern ought to be challenged with recalcitrant detail. To quote Wayne Meeks once more,

> the most valuable facts we discover are those which we wish were otherwise. No field of inquiry is immune from wishful thinking, but the study of religion is perhaps more at risk than most from the desire to see what ought to have been rather than what inconveniently was. That risk seems to affect more or less equally those who passionately believe and those who passionately despise.[3]

The 'big picture', of course, may be one of many quite different things. It may be a vague hunch. It may be an assumed social imperative (such as the desire for revolution, or at least radical social reform). It may be a fully worked out philosophical theory or ideology. Those who appealed to 'history' in the eighteenth century in order to construct an 'historical Jesus' very different from the normally imagined Christian portrait were often, it seems, assuming the second type (the social imperative). It was the perceived subversiveness of their project, as much as the undermining of traditional faith-claims, which caused alarm. Among the most influential figures in the study of early Christianity in the nineteenth and early twentieth centuries were some who assumed the third type (the ideology), constructing their versions of Kant and Hegel into an overarching system which would interpret everything else, all history, all human life. Within such a scheme, Paul himself, and even Jesus himself, would simply have walk-on parts, representing new movements of 'spirit', new moments in a relentless 'progress'. This is what the current proponents of 'apocalyptic' have been rejecting, following (though not always acknowledging) the similar protests of Schweitzer and Barth, and, behind them, disturbingly perhaps, Nietzsche.

[3] Meeks 2009, 136f.

The ideologies had led them, so they believed, into a disastrous blind alley. What they wanted was a radical break with the past, a totally new revelation.

The scholars whose work we will study in this Part of the book have faced the same challenges and come up with a significantly different answer. For them, the answer to ideology is not apocalyptic, but more history. Stubborn history. Not simply the history of 'great men' and their 'ideas'. Nor, particularly, the history of 'religion', though that word, cleaned up a bit, will refer to something which has a proper place within the larger historical project. Nor, especially, a 'history' which consists of the attempt to 'place' different parts of the early Christian movement within a hypothetical scheme constituted by those two great artificial constructs, 'Judaism' and 'Hellenism'. What we need, according to the investigations we shall now examine, is the history of the early Christian *communities*. And that means 'social history'.

2. Social History, Social Science and the Quest for Thick Description

(i) Introduction

'Social history' is complicated, like 'history' itself, because societies themselves are complicated. As all but the most relentless individualist will acknowledge, where two or three are gathered together something is created which is more than the sum of its parts. That is why friendship on the one hand, and family life on the other, can be simultaneously life-giving and deeply challenging, and why they provide such interesting and often elusive subjects of study. Societies matter, in history as in real life.

This is not the place to provide a proper introduction to the rise of the current movements in social history, social studies, sociology or social science, terms which both compete and overlap. Others have provided more than enough in that line.[4] My task is simply to indicate and comment on some ways in which successive tides of social study have washed up on the Pauline shore in the last generation – or, perhaps we should say, on the shores of Paul's communities, the little groups of believers that sprang up through his gospelling, to which he wrote his dense and exhilarating letters.

As with all history, part of the point of social study is to challenge the easy assumption that people in other times and places were just like us, apart from not having aeroplanes or electronic toys. In other words,

> One of the most provocative challenges for Western, European biblical scholars from social science literature . . . is the revelation that our frequently cited presumed notions of 'normal', 'natural', 'clear', or 'obvious', are nothing of the sort.[5]

[4] See e.g. Blasi, Duhaime and Turcotte 2002. The great social historian Asa Briggs, in a recent memoir, insists not only that 'we must always relate literature to history' but also that, as against G. M. Trevelyan's view that social history was 'history with the politics left out', it was in fact 'economic history with the politics put in' (Briggs 2012, 7). There is a challenge for New Testament scholars.

[5] Smith-Christopher 2013, 160.

What matters, as in all history, is the avoidance of the twin evils of anachronism and what is sometimes called 'ethnocentrism', the unquestioned assumption that one's own culture is somehow the norm for everyone else's too.[6] And since those unquestioned assumptions run deep into areas which a certain amount of history, and a good deal more exegesis and theology, have normally ignored, it is vital that we find ways of factoring them in, not just at a surface level but all the way through our investigations.[7]

This has been the aim of a lively and complex movement within the world of biblical scholarship over the last generation. Our task now is to give a brief account of this movement, not least because it forms the wider context for two of the most significant books on Paul from the last forty years. That judgment is, naturally, both subjective and subject to potentially damaging critique. But rereading the books in question, which we will study in the next chapter, has done nothing to make me think differently.

(ii) A Determined Desire for Detail

The study of the New Testament within its 'social world' has been in full swing for a generation, and many different writers have undertaken to chronicle its origins, progress and results. Though the movement has much deeper roots, there was a flurry of activity in the early 1980s, with several books and articles converging on the same theme.[8] In a discipline (biblical studies) which has usually been somewhat self-conscious about keeping to accepted patterns and pathways of study, the leading writers in this movement have been careful both to indicate the historical antecedents for their work and to explain the reasons why it has suddenly come to the fore in recent times. One of the acknowledged leaders of the movement, Gerd Theissen, speaks of the 'renewal of sociological exegesis' in the 1970s, and contextualizes the movement within such larger social contexts as the student revolts of the 1960s and the 'green' movements of the 1980s.[9] Like many others at the time, Theissen was conscious of a frustration at the way biblical studies after the Second World War had appeared to be trapped in a

[6] For this point, see e.g. Esler 1994, 22. This was a major emphasis in Malina 1981.

[7] Esler 1998, 27, 39 accuses me of perpetuating 'the idealistic fallacy' by speaking of the 'thought-forms and thought-patterns' in Paul's letters. I would suggest that, since I have emphasized the rich interplay between Paul's theology and the actual communities involved, this judgment may in fact be over-hasty.

[8] See e.g. Kee 1980 (a second edn. appeared in 1993); Malherbe 1983 [1977]; Harrington 1980; Scroggs 1980; Schütz 1982 (the 'Introduction' to Theissen 1982); Tidball 1983; Osiek 1984. A decade or so later these were joined by e.g. Holmberg 1990; Theissen 1992 (see particularly the 'Introduction', 1–32, and the challenging conclusion, 257–87); Elliott 1993; cf. too the useful chapter in Tuckett 1987, ch. 9 (136–50). More recent surveys and broad expositions include e.g. Esler 1994, esp. ch. 1 (1–18); Esler 1995, esp. Esler's own 'Introduction' (1–22); Rohrbaugh 1996; Horrell 1999, whose 'Introduction' (3–28) was then expanded in Horrell 2002. A recent important collection is Porter and Pitts 2012. Most of the above include extensive bibliographies. Among the numerous studies of particular topics one might mention two on Luke-Acts: Esler 1987; Neyrey 1991, both with interesting introductions.

[9] Theissen 1992, 15f.

world composed simply of ideas: beliefs, thoughts, and arguments, all apparently detached from the real world and real life of those who held those beliefs, who thought those thoughts, who engaged in those arguments. The 'theology of the Word' which had dominated Germany in the years of Barth and Bultmann had, whether intentionally or not, pushed the previously flourishing study of historical detail out of sight. Though the 'Chicago School' of the years between the wars had kept the rumour of social study alive in America, this was decidedly a minority interest.[10] There was a widespread assumption that the New Testament was about 'theology and ethics', with questions of social and cultural context being merely a matter of incidental backcloth, having no effect on the drama being staged.

The frustration that many felt with this approach had to do partly with a sense that the church in Europe and America needed to grapple with social and cultural issues of its own in the twentieth century, and that one way of getting at these questions might be to examine the equivalent issues in the first century. I shall return to this. But the frustration was as much historical as (in that sense) hermeneutical. It grew out of what I have called a determined desire for detail: a dissatisfaction with broad generalizations about 'the early church' which took no account of the social and economic standing of the first Christians, or of the network of assumptions, hidden social narratives and cultural symbols which shaped their everyday lives. Though it may be going too far to claim that this movement is a protest in favour of incarnation itself,[11] or that it seeks to re-unite 'body and soul',[12] it has certainly been trying to present a fuller history of early Christianity as a whole, rather than merely a history either of a few leaders, or of 'early Christian ideas',[13] or indeed of 'early Christian experience' in an existentialist sense.[14]

Such a concern, naturally, has a long 'back story', including figures such as Troeltsch, Durkheim and even Karl Marx himself, who, according to Robin Scroggs, was 'the first to have understood the basic premise of the sociology of knowledge'.[15] This, too, I think, is going too far, unless one is to work with a restricted, and indeed reductive, 'sociology of knowledge'. For Marx, the ideas people had were not just correlated with, but were actually

[10] On the 'Chicago School', and especially the work of S. J. Case, see e.g. Keck 1974, 436f.; Malherbe 1983, 5; Theissen 1992, 15; Horrell 2002, 5 (pointing out Case's adherence to a 'social gospel' theory replacing unpopular dogmas); and esp. Baird 2003, 305–30. See too the work of Kirsopp Lake in Harvard, e.g. Lake 1927, of which Stephen Neill wrote that, despite several obvious faults, 'those of us who read Lake when we were young will be inclined to think that this is one of the best books on the New Testament that has ever been written in the English language', and that, through Lake's guidance, 'we feel ourselves one with those new and struggling groups of Christians, in all the perplexities of trying to discover what it means to be a Christian in a non-Christian world. And there is the Apostle, so very much in working clothes and without a halo . . .' (Neill and Wright 1988 [1964], 178).

[11] So e.g. Malina 1981, 154.

[12] Scroggs 1980, 165f.

[13] See Keck 1974, 438: '[The Chicago School] did us the service of insisting *that* early Christianity was subject to social factors; our task is to make that insight specific and concrete without being reductionist, without deriving ideas and values from socio-economic factors in a simplistic way.'

[14] See the book of that title (Bornkamm 1969).

[15] Scroggs 1980, 177. On Troeltsch see e.g. Horrell 2002, 4, pointing out his influence on Theissen, and the lasting use within the discipline of his distinction of 'church' and 'sect' (see below).

determined by, their 'social being'.[16] Definitions of different sociological subdisciplines are themselves controversial. But most of those who pursue a sociology of knowledge in relation to the New Testament would, I think, draw back from 'determination' and settle for something like 'correlation', envisaging a complex interplay of ideas and circumstances. I suspect that the need for such correlation was understood in many pre-Enlightenment Christian circles, with the radical Reformation and Calvin's Geneva as possible examples. It was only with the Enlightenment that Gotthold Lessing's 'ugly broad ditch' between eternal and contingent truths affected the thinking of the church, and then only partially. Only after that eighteenth-century shift did it become necessary to join back together what had been split apart. However, the leftward turn in the politics of the rising western generation of the 1960s and 1970s was clearly a significant part of the context within which the new eagerness for sociological study made itself felt.

More importantly perhaps within New Testament studies, the long legacy of Rudolf Bultmann has been invoked both as a precursor to the newer movement and as part of the problem to which it offers a solution. The problem has already been noted: Bultmann's theology of the 'Word', and of the existential 'faith' which responds to it, was able to float free from the contingencies of history, and indeed to see history itself, whether the actual history of Jesus or that of his first followers, as more or less irrelevant to, or even inimical to, 'faith'. This is now seen to have vitiated what otherwise might have been a positive earlier statement of a socio-cultural reading of the New Testament, in that the celebrated form-critical reading of the gospels proposed by Bultmann was a sustained attempt to understand how Jesus-traditions had been shaped by, and perhaps generated from within, the actual life of the early Christian communities. Yet Bultmann's work stayed at a level of high generality. He never seems to have enquired as to the specific social or cultural contexts within which catechesis, controversy and other features of early Christian life actually took place.[17]

Two scholarly advances have enabled this new movement to go forward: the one routinely acknowledged and built into new systems, the other often ignored but, in my view, very necessary if the quest for full integration is to have a firm historical base. The first advance is the popularization of the social and cultural theories of Clifford Geertz on the one hand and of Peter Berger and Thomas Luckmann on the other.[18] They, along with the veteran philosopher Charles Taylor, have provided various linguistic possibilities for naming all sorts of aspects of a culture which, once seen, cannot easily be

[16] Scroggs, loc. cit., n. 45, with details.

[17] On Bultmann and his method in relation to socio-historical readings of the NT see e.g. Keck 1974, 439, 446; Kee 1980, 16; Tuckett 1987, 140, 142; Holmberg 1990, 119; Theissen 1992, 12; Horrell 2002, 6.

[18] Geertz 2000 [1973] is justly famous and still eminently readable and compelling; Berger and Luckmann 1984 [1966] introduced the notion of the 'social construction of reality' which has been a major feature of many disciplines ever since. Watson 2007 [1986], 10 describes the effect of the latter: 'This sustained reflection on the production and role of knowledge within the life-world made as profound an impression on me as any book before or since', adding in a footnote that Barth's *Church Dogmatics* might count as an exception if one were to see it as a single book.

unseen: the symbols around which humans order their lives, the narratives ('myths'?) which make up the 'script' which people understand themselves to be acting out (or which they wish they could be carrying out were they not thwarted from doing so), the praxis, including 'ritual' of whatever sort, which again is taken for granted but which shapes corporate and individual self-understanding and motivation, and the 'ethos' of a society which, again assumed rather than recognized, colours a thousand thoughts, words and actions.[19] Though both social theoreticians and practising historians will continue to modify these proposals in detail, they have released genies which cannot now be put back into the bottle. Whether we speak of a 'symbolic universe', a 'life-world', an 'ethos', a 'worldview', a 'social imaginary' or any other shorthand, we are all sociologists now, if only at second hand. (The further development of particular 'models' which put flesh on these bones is another matter, to which we shall come presently.)

The second scholarly advance which has enormously facilitated a fuller understanding of the social context and history of early Christianity is the massive work now available on the first-century Jewish world. Here there is an irony. It has been common, within the movement I am describing, to acknowledge the earlier work of Joachim Jeremias and Martin Hengel.[20] But if it is detailed social description we want, several other works cry out not only to be included in a bibliography but to be factored in to the actual, complicated and messy historical mapping: the multi-volume revision of Emil Schürer's *History of the Jewish People in the Age of Jesus Christ*, for a start, and the *Compendia Rerum Iudaicarum ad Novum Testamentum*.[21] Nor can we ignore the substantial work of by E. P. Sanders, particularly his *Judaism: Practice and Belief*.[22] If we are talking about the 'thick description' of actual societies, particularly the actual societies from which the earliest Christians came and in which many of them continued to live, then these, and many other similar works, are indispensable. By the same token the massive work now available on the complex and varied greco-roman world of the first century is a prerequisite. We are well served for detailed work on the classical world, not least through the newer archaeological accounts of many places where Paul spent considerable time.[23] By his own account, Paul stood at the crossroads between the wider Jewish world of the Diaspora and the non-Jewish world in which it was set. We have some fine studies of that complex world, and again these need to be factored in to the larger picture of the social history of Paul and his churches.[24]

[19] See Taylor 2007; Taylor's category of 'social imaginary' performs, more or less, the same role as the different categories in Geertz and in Berger and Luckmann. See the discussion on 'worldview' below. On 'ethos' in early Christianity see Keck 1974, esp. e.g. 440: he defines 'ethos' to include the 'practices and habits, problems, values and hopes of a community's style', and points out that much of this material is pre- or unconscious. Keck, as often, was ahead of the curve.

[20] See Jeremias 1969; Hengel 1974a, 1974b, 1981 [1968].

[21] Schürer 1973–87; Safrai and Stern 1974–6, and several subsequent volumes.

[22] Sanders 1992.

[23] See *PFG* 328–35; for an example of 'thick description' in one area, Mitchell 1993a and 1993b.

[24] cf. e.g. Trebilco 1991; Barclay 1996; and, more recently, collections such as Porter and Pitts 2012.

So much for the 'back story' of the sociological revolution in New Testament studies over recent decades. The movement is now well into its second generation. But before we get to that we must look in more detail at some of those who pioneered the new approaches. Social historians tend not to like doing history in terms of the stories of 'great men'. But they are rather partial to charismatic leaders, and that, in this field, is what we have had.

(iii) Leading the Way

By common consent, the launching point of the contemporary interest in the social study of early Christianity came in Edwin Judge's short book, *The Social Pattern of Christian Groups in the First Century.*[25] Judge, then in his early thirties, was on his way to becoming a highly respected historian of the Roman world of the late Republic and early empire. Still happily with us at the time of writing, he has long been Emeritus Professor at Macquarie University in Sydney, Australia.[26] Leading scholars in the field of early Christian sociology line up to heap praise on Judge's work; there are, inevitably, some dissenting voices, but these form only a background murmur against the weight of esteem he is now accorded. On the cover of the collection edited by David Scholer, Carolyn Osiek speaks of Judge's 'great contribution'; John H. Elliott says that Judge's work is 'always imaginative, always abundant in epigraphic, inscriptional, and papyrological evidence, always with a nose sensitive to social implications, always critical in the best sense'; Wayne Meeks speaks of Judge's 'quiet brilliance', and declares his work to be 'indispensable'; and Gerd Theissen, referring to Judge's book of 1960, says that it 'deserves a place of honor in the history of modern sociological exegesis.'[27]

So what makes Judge special, and what, with hindsight, did he launch? As I said, Judge's work is rooted in a lifetime of detailed study of the Roman world of late antiquity. Interpretations of the material inevitably differ, but mastering it is the first requirement, and there are few alive today who have done so more thoroughly. This gives him an ideal platform to address the problem he raised near the start of his programmatic monograph:

> It may be asserted that ideas are never satisfactorily explained merely by discovering their philosophical connections. They must be pinned down in relation to the particular circumstances in which they were expressed. The meaning is fixed at this point, and cannot be certainly ascertained until it is identified.[28]

This is a classic statement of the sociology of knowledge. Judge is not saying either that ideas are generated by, or that they can be reduced to terms of,

[25] Judge 1960.

[26] Most of Judge's work has come in technical articles, now collected in three volumes: Scholer 2008; Judge 2008; Judge 2010.

[27] Theissen 1992, 19 n. 23.

[28] Judge 1960, 8. (This small book is reprinted in Scholer 2008, 1–56.)

the social situation. But he is insisting that, without knowledge of that social situation, one cannot be sure what is meant:

> the meaning of a word is not ultimately determined by antecedent, parallel, or derived instances, but by its situation in its own context . . . While the affiliation of the ideas [in the New Testament] will generally govern their content, there will normally be a particular construction to be placed on them in relation to the particular situation. Neglect of this may result in imprecision or even error.[29]

Thus, whether we study the gospels or the epistles, it is important that we read them in the form in which they have been

> collated and formulated in Greek for the information of religious societies in hellenistic cities. If [this material] is to be understood properly, it must be understood from their point of view.[30]

This was a radical proposal in its day, arguing for something almost like a reader-response method of grappling with the texts. We may, perhaps, express surprise that Judge was able to get away with this in one of the early publications of the Tyndale Press. But his general point would now be widely accepted: if we are to understand the early Christian writings, we need to know who the groups were to whom these writings were addressed. How did they see themselves? How were they seen by others?

Judge therefore studied the different levels of institution and the different types of gathering within Roman society. The wider unit was the *politeia*, the commonwealth of the whole Republic and then of the larger Roman world under the empire. But within that the 'household' (*oikos/oikia*) was a major social unit. Judge points out that New Testament writers use both terms to express their beliefs about who they were, highlighting particularly the early Christians' sense of being 'servants of God'.[31] Within that again there was the looser, more informal notion of *koinōnia*, 'partnership' or 'fellowship', which in that social context introduces us into the world of loose 'associations', *collegiai*, professional groups and the like. Notions which have been worn smooth by constant contemporary Christian repetition thus suddenly attain the rough edges and three-dimensional shape of actual first-century reality. Judge is clear that the Christians, like their Jewish neighbours, thought of themselves as an international body, though unlike the Jews they lacked 'a recognized national seat for their cult'.[32] This is one of many points picked up later by Wayne Meeks; another, of great importance in the larger picture, is that to the outside observer one of the most striking and worrying things about this new 'association' was its novel set of theological ideas, particularly monotheism and eschatology.[33]

[29] Judge 1960, 9.
[30] Judge 1960, 10.
[31] Judge 1960, 38f.
[32] Judge 1960, 44.
[33] Judge 1960, 48.

All this prepares the reader for the central thrust of Judge's book, which is on the social constituency of Christian groups. Over against earlier views which saw almost all Christians as being among the very poor, Judge pioneered the line which has since been widely adopted, that 'their membership seems to have been drawn from a surprising variety of stations.'[34] Focusing particularly on Corinth, Judge highlights both the social diversity of the first urban Christians and the problems which this generated:

> Far from being a socially depressed group, then, if the Corinthians are at all typical, the Christians were dominated by a socially pretentious section of the population of the big cities. Beyond that they seem to have drawn on a broad constituency, probably representing the household dependents of the leading members. The interests brought together in this way probably marked the Christians off from the other unofficial associations, which were generally socially and economically as homogeneous as possible. Certainly the phenomenon led to constant differences among the Christians themselves ...[35]

This position has been contested, nuanced and developed over the last generation. Judge was right to question what had normally been seen as the consensus, and he was correct to conclude that things were more complicated than had been imagined. Further research has demonstrated that Deissmann himself, the originator of the supposed consensus, stated a somewhat more diverse picture, and that there is more to be said for seeing Paul's communities as mostly quite poor.[36] But Judge at least got the discussion going in new directions.

Since his early ground-breaking essay, Judge has added many more insights to the study of Paul and his letters. Out of many, two stand out to me at least. First, despite his earlier categorization of the Christian groups as 'religious societies', Judge has increasingly tried to distance the early church from the 'religious' world of late antiquity.[37] The first Christians did not, after all, offer animal sacrifice; they did not have a hierarchical priesthood, sacred buildings, and so on. What is more, the ancient religions did not concern themselves, by and large, either with large theological questions or with regulating the ethical behaviour of their adherents, whereas the early Christians did both. Judge has therefore proposed that the Christians were more like what he calls a 'scholastic' society, a kind of philosophical school, rather than a 'religion'.[38]

This proposal offers at best, I think, a half-truth. The early Christians did in fact do things (one thinks, obviously, of baptism and the Lord's Supper) which they saw as binding them together with one another and with the Lord whom they worshipped, and this idea of 'binding' is one possible

[34] Judge 1960, 54.

[35] Judge 1960, 60.

[36] See e.g. Meggitt 1998; Friesen 2004; Longenecker 2009, 2010, on which see below 265.

[37] See e.g. Scholer ed. 2008, 130: 'The first model to be discarded is that of "religion" itself.' Also e.g. Judge 2008, 404–9.

[38] See the important essays, 'The Early Christians as a Scholastic Community' in Judge 2008, 526–52 (orig. pub. 1960/61); and 'Did the Early Christians Compete with Cult-Groups?', ibid. 597–618 (orig. pub. 2003).

meaning of 'religion' in their world. I have discussed this in more detail elsewhere.[39] But Judge was right to stress that the early Christians were a *learning* community, and the anachronism of the word 'scholastic' (of which Judge was well aware) should not obscure the historical reality to which he was drawing attention.[40] He thus raised the right question: in their context, there is certainly not an exact fit between the first Christians and the 'religions' of their day. (Nor, indeed, does early Christianity fit with what the word 'religion' means to most people in our own day.) Gaining that kind of critical distance is what social-scientific study is all about.

Second, through his careful work of placing the first Christians within their classical environment Judge was able to demonstrate that in some respects the Christians were radical innovators, breaking the moulds of the social world they inhabited. Social-scientific study, in other words, does not mean collapsing the data into pre-existing categories; it may mean discovering that something quite new was being attempted, something which crossed over the boundaries, which attempted a new way of social and cultural living. Thus

> The followers of Jesus inherited from Judaism their sense of being a distinct community, a kind of nation of their own. The singular history of their confrontation with Graeco-Roman society is not likely to be explained simply in terms of its systems of rank and status. Their aim was not to find their place in the world as it was. They brought with them ideas and practices which undercut the classical order.[41]

This consistent theme in Judge's work was summarized in a 2003 essay in five points. The New Testament churches (1) constituted a movement of ideas, 'a kind of adult re-education'; (2) their intellectual premises differed from the philosophers' naturalistic logic, being generated instead by eschatology; (3) this resulted in a community life unconstrained by 'nationality, status, gender and numbers'; (4) this was generated by the divine gifting of each person; (5) this then 'undercuts the foundations of the public community, operating as an alternative, transnational society.'[42] These points look ahead strikingly both to the so-called new perspective on Paul and to the recent debates about the political implications of his gospel.

This conclusion, highlighting ways in which Paul's communities were significantly different from other communities in their world, will no doubt

[39] See esp. *PFG* chs. 4, 13.

[40] See Winter 2002 [1997]; in his Preface to this book (ix), G. W. Bowersock acknowledges that Winter's research on Paul and Philo has established the roots of the mid-first-century 'second sophistic' movement (see *PFG* 236f.). The more recent study of Smith 2012 has upheld Judge's substantive conclusion though preferring the term 'learning communities'. I am grateful to Professor Judge for help on these points.

[41] Judge, in Scholer 2008, 155f. (orig. pub. 1982). See too ibid. 131, 134 (from an essay orig. pub. in 1980): 'There may well be no comparable phenomenon known to history, and it could therefore prove a fundamental error to attempt to explain primitive Christianity by sociological methods which work through analogy and presuppose the repetitiveness of human behaviour … By setting powerful new ideas to work within and upon the most familiar relationships of life, Paul created in the church a social force of a unique kind.'

[42] Judge 2008, 615.

be unwelcome to those who might want to use social-scientific modelling as an a priori means of flattening out all distinctives.[43] By the same token, Judge can be faulted for the apparently uncritical way in which he uses his sources (not least Acts and the disputed Pauline letters) in his reconstruction. But his principal value for the discipline is as much because of the questions he freshly posed as because of the detailed outworking he offered. In any case, such questions must be postponed for the moment. It is time to turn from Sydney to Heidelberg.

If common consent puts Edwin Judge at the front of the line for re-introducing sociological questions into New Testament studies, a similar status belongs to Gerd Theissen. Theissen is single-handedly responsible for putting sociological and also psychological questions on the agenda of German New Testament studies from the 1970s onwards. Initially, however, his work was regarded with suspicion in his native country, being taken up with more enthusiasm in Britain and America. When the London-based SCM Press published his early work in English translation Theissen was described as 'Professor of New Testament in Bonn', which (as I recall from one of the early Oxford/Bonn theological symposia in the 1970s) came as a surprise to the then actual Bonn Professor of New Testament, Wolfgang Schrage. Theissen had been asking awkward questions from an early age, and his initial explorations, not least a string of ten or more important articles published between 1973 and 1977 on the sociological analysis of various Jesus-sayings on the one hand and of Paul on the other, had the (presumably intended) effect of rocking several boats.[44] Once you raise questions of sociology, interpretation will not be the same again. Theissen eventually obtained a professorship in Copenhagen in 1978, moving back to Germany in 1980 to occupy the chair at Heidelberg where he has remained ever since.

There is an interesting parallel, and an all-important distinction, between Gerd Theissen and Ferdinand Christian Baur. Baur, we recall, took as his famous starting-point the controversy in Corinth between the different parties. He lined them up in terms of 'Jewish Christianity' (James and Peter) and 'gentile Christianity' (Paul), and used this *religionsgeschichtlich* antithesis to find his way through not only the exegesis of 1 Corinthians but also the much larger picture of first-generation Christianity. By the 1970s, Baur had been widely criticized, the *religionsgeschichtlich* method of analysis had been challenged, but the shape of the discussion lived on, with scholars continuing to write about 'Jewish Christianity' and 'gentile Christianity' as though these were still viable categories.[45] Theissen took the bold step of

[43] An obvious example is Engberg-Pedersen 2001, 2, suggesting that 'an adequate historical analysis must leave out the category of uniqueness'. Engberg-Pedersen's strictures about the need for 'a fairly strong degree of scholarly self-consciousness about the hermeneutical categories that lie at the back of our minds' (ibid., 3) is fair enough, but of course should apply across the board; see e.g. the critique in Horrell 2005, 22–4. See Kee 1980, 104f., warning against both the 'positivists of the left', who assume there is nothing distinctive about Christianity, and the 'positivists of the right' who 'feel obligated to prove that there are no historical parallels to early Christianity.'

[44] A bibliography of Theissen's early work can be found in Theissen 1982, 25f.

[45] Even Stephen Neill does this, despite his earlier analysis of Baur: see Neill 1976.

substituting *Sozialgeschichte* for *Religionsgeschichte*: instead of 'Jews and Greeks', he focused on 'rich and poor'. The division of the 'weak and the strong' in Corinth was really, he suggested, not so much between theological positions, but between the rich, who could buy and eat anything they wanted, and the poor, who could not usually afford meat in the first place. Likewise the problem at the Lord's Supper, in 1 Corinthians 11, was a problem of rich Christians discriminating against poor ones:

> It can be assumed that the conflict over the Lord's Supper is a conflict between poor and rich Christians. The cause of this conflict was a particular habit of the rich. They took part in the congregational meal which they themselves had made possible, but they did so by themselves – possibly physically separated from the others and at their own table.[46]

The fact that this analysis of 1 Corinthians 11 would be widely accepted today is a measure of Theissen's success.

Theissen, like Judge on the one hand and Meeks on the other, has not adopted the more radical stance of those who want either to explain early Christianity purely in terms of social phenomena or to predict, from sociological models, what 'must have been' the case. His is a more central position, between (a) a phenomenological analysis of 'religious' themes without social context and (b) a reductionist analysis in which all apparently 'religious' or 'theological' themes are traced back to non-religious factors. If 'rich and poor' is the presenting problem, this is none the less, for Theissen, both a religious and a theological problem, and must be addressed in those terms. His preferred option is 'functionalism', a position which means 'taking seriously the intentionality of religious phenomena but interpreting them with reference to their contribution to the solution of basic social problems.'[47] This is obviously a broad-brush description, but it perhaps places Theissen more as a 'social historian' than a 'sociologist' as such.[48]

Theissen's overall proposal, for the interpretation of Paul in the passages under consideration, is what he calls 'love-patriarchalism':

> This love-patriarchalism takes social differences for granted but ameliorates them through an obligation of respect and love, an obligation imposed upon those who are socially stronger. From the weaker are required subordination, fidelity, and esteem.[49]

This is different from a straightforward egalitarianism, which Theissen finds in the traditions of Jesus' first followers in Galilee. Theissen borrowed the idea of 'patriarchalism' from Troeltsch, modifying it in the attempt to bring sociological and theological worlds into a Pauline combination, noting the difference between that and the more radical early Galilean movement.[50]

[46] Theissen 1982, 151.

[47] So Schütz 1982, 16.

[48] Schütz 1982, 15.

[49] Theissen 1982, 107; see the critique in Horrell 1996, ch. 4.

[50] See the summary in Schütz 1982, 14f. For Theissen's view of early Palestinian Christianity see Theissen 1978 [1977] and Theissen 1992, chs. 1–4.

If Judge in Australia, and Theissen in Germany, represent the early leaders of the modern movement for sociological approaches to the New Testament in general and Paul in particular, the Americans took up the challenge in two related ways. A group was formed within the Society of Biblical Literature to discuss 'the Social World of Early Christianity'; well-known early markers for this group include a famous essay by Wayne Meeks and a remarkable book by John Gager.[51] A different though overlapping project has been developed by other field leaders. Bruce Malina and Jerome Neyrey, individually and often in collaboration, have gone beyond sociology as such and into the related world of cultural anthropology, producing a string of books and articles which explore various 'models', mostly derived from anthropological studies of the Mediterranean world. The main initial aim, as set out in Malina's book *The New Testament World: Insights from Cultural Anthropology* (1981), has been to jolt contemporary readers, particularly students in North America, out of easy-going assumptions, and to alert them to the ways in which the culture in question was (and often still is) radically different from that which such students instinctively inhabit. As with other sociological studies, the point has been to ward off the otherwise inevitable pitfalls of anachronism and ethnocentrism.[52] Along with Malina and Neyrey we must place John H. Elliott, not least for his pioneering socio-historical study of 1 Peter;[53] and Philip F. Esler, who has tirelessly thought through a similar approach and applied it to specific New Testament books in studies which, though not commentaries in the traditional sense, none the less work through texts with fresh proposals for – in Judge's words, quoted above – the 'particular construction to be placed on them in relation to the particular situation'.[54] This is perhaps the place to mention, also, the largest English-language commentary to appear on Romans for many years, that of Robert Jewett in the *Hermeneia* series, which follows Esler in applying social-scientific analysis to the situation in Rome and hence to the interpretation of the letter.[55] Jewett argues that Paul's preaching of the shameful cross of Christ undermined greco-roman and Jewish cultural assumptions, offering the divine grace equally to every social group and so providing a radical alternative to the all-important, and dangerously divisive, implicit system of 'honour and shame'. Esler and Jewett thus follow through where Theissen had led the way with his studies of Corinth, though developing a far more rigorous system of social and anthropological modelling.[56]

Malina, Neyrey, Elliott and Esler were among the founders, and have remained core members, of 'the Context Group'. Publications from this group, too numerous to list here, have developed the thesis advanced by

[51] Meeks 1972; Gager 1975.

[52] Malina 1981; see further Malina 1986; Neyrey 1990, 1991; Neyrey and Stewart 2008.

[53] Elliott 1981.

[54] See e.g. Esler 1994, 1995, building on his earlier work on Luke-Acts (Esler 1987); and now, on Galatians (Esler 1998) and Romans (Esler 2003).

[55] Jewett 2007.

[56] One might compare, too, the much earlier proposals of Minear 1971.

Malina in the 1980s, that in 'the Mediterranean world' we can trace certain specific and powerful cultural presuppositions which can then be assumed to be true for the early Christian groups. They invite us to read the New Testament, not as initially addressed to 'people like us' dealing with 'our' concerns, but as addressing the needs and problems of people who thought and lived very differently. Thus, whereas the historian must always try to avoid anachronisms, the 'modelling' proposed by the Context Group and similar writers adopts the methods and tools of sociological analysis of a larger unit ('the Mediterranean world'), as applied in one way to the early Galilean communities, in another to the churches of Paul, then more widely again to documents like 1 Peter.[57] The 'Context Group' has been clear, and indeed forthright, in marking off its territory from 'social history' in a wider sense, being quite critical (for instance) of the eclectic and less method-driven procedure of Wayne Meeks or David Horrell.[58] But many younger scholars seem cheerfully to be crossing these boundaries, producing work in the broad stream I am describing here and drawing on many strands from Judge, Theissen and the social historians as well as Malina, Neyrey, Esler and the social scientists – insofar as that distinction can really hold.[59]

I have already said enough, under the general heading of new leadership, to introduce some of what has been going on in this area. It is now time to stand back and look at this area of study somewhat more systematically.

(iv) New Proposals from a Loose Coalition

There are, broadly speaking, four different tasks which come under the loose heading of 'social' approaches to the New Testament. They may be categorized as *description*, *explanation*, *prediction* and *application*.[60]

Taking the work of Edwin Judge as an obvious example, we are there concerned first and foremost with *description*. Judge has examined the data, particularly the classical and early Christian sources (though not so much the Jewish ones), and has proposed sharply focused and nuanced accounts of many aspects of early Christian life and writing. He has illuminated many well-known texts. A favourite example for me is 2 Corinthians 11.21–33, where Judge argues that Paul's 'boasting' is a deliberately ironic inversion of contemporary Roman practice. The passage concludes with Paul being let

[57] We might mention here also the substantial work of Stegemann and Stegemann 1999 [1995]; and, from a different angle, deSilva 1999, 2000.

[58] See e.g. Schütz 1982, 20; and cf. Horrell 2002, 11–14. Meeks has responded fairly trenchantly (Meeks 2003 [1983], ix–xii).

[59] One might instance Oakes 2001, 2009b; Barclay 2011 (the book is dedicated to Wayne Meeks) alongside Barclay 1995, which is very much in a 'Context Group' setting and mode; also e.g. John Kloppenborg.

[60] This quartet of tasks does not relate directly to the five tasks outlined by Elliott 1993, ch. 3 (investigating social *realia*; constructing an integrated social history; describing the social organization of early Christianity; studying socio-cultural constraints; use of sociological models on biblical texts). Scholer 2008, xiv is I think wrong to suggest that Judge only addresses the first three of Elliott's categories.

down over the wall and running away; this, Judge has suggested, was intended as a specific parody to the award of the much-prized *corona muralis*, awarded to the first person to scale the wall of a besieged city.[61] This kind of analysis is the province of 'history [task]' itself, the constant dialogue between original sources and contemporary reconstructions, always with the aim of a 'thick description' of 'what happened' and what it meant to people at the time.

History itself regularly includes *explanation*. But to explain something is more complex than it might seem at first sight. To explain why the can of paraffin caught fire by saying 'because it was flammable' is about as maddening, and as useless, as the famous explanation for the smashing of a valuable china ornament: 'Nobody was holding it, so it fell.' These things may be true, but what the questioner wanted was to find out why, on this occasion, the admittedly flammable paraffin burst into flames (Who dropped the cigarette end into it ... and why?), or what caused the normally secure ornament to fall to the floor (Who knocked it off the shelf ... and why?). There is a network of explanation which includes the necessary but insufficient factors (the flammability of paraffin, the weight and fragility of porcelain) but looks also for the unnecessary but sufficient element in the situation (a thoughtless smoker, a careless grandchild). The human agency in either case more or less stops the otherwise indefinite explanatory chain (unless we are to ask why the culprits were thoughtless or careless, which would push us back to speaking of mental states), but in many cases, certainly in historical description and explanation, that chain can indeed go on for a long time.[62] In the case of history, any attempt to reduce that explanation to the things which can be studied by one particular mode of enquiry is fraught with problems. Why was Julius Caesar assassinated? Why did Paul want to go to Rome? Why did Jesus tell parables? These questions, and others like them, are more complicated than is sometimes supposed. What, after all, will *count* as a good answer?

An example from another historical sphere makes the point. Many recent books have attempted to answer the question as to why the First World War broke out when it did. What on earth induced the leaders of so many countries to suppose that fighting one another in this fashion was the right way to solve current problems? One such book addresses the problem by studying the different countries and leaders involved, leading to a crucial chapter entitled, 'What Were They Thinking? Hopes, Fears, Ideas, and Unspoken Assumptions'.[63] The answer in this case explores such features as imperialism, liberalism, militarism, nationalism and, not least, Social Darwinism. Many looked forward eagerly to a war which they thought would transform

[61] See Judge in Scholer ed. 2008, ch. 2 (orig. 1968); and the Appendix in Judge 2008, 707f. (orig. pub. 1966). On the *corona muralis* see e.g. Maxfield 1981, 77f., the principal ancient sources being Aulus Gellius, *Noctes Attici* 5.6.4 and Livy 26.48.

[62] On this whole question, see the brief but helpful summary in Kirwan 1995; and the slightly fuller account in Cohen 1995.

[63] MacMillan 2013, ch. 9 (228–65).

the world; it did, but not in the way that they had hoped or imagined. But the point is that for an explanation we need to enter into the mind, the ethos, of people very different from ourselves; to see why what might look strange to us looked obvious to them. For this a full, 'thick' description is required.[64]

The problem comes, as I said, with any attempt to limit such a description to any one sphere, be it theological, social-scientific or any other. This would be tricky enough in any area of enquiry, but when it comes to early Christianity it is easy for old polarizations to resurface, with the Idealists (in this case, would-be orthodox Christians) explaining the rise of the movement in terms of divine intervention, and the Materialists, including some but certainly not all sociologists, explaining it in terms of 'social forces'.[65] This move needs to be mapped on to the larger philosophical debates in western thought, back at least as far as Hume. There is an ongoing discussion among philosophers of science as to what counts as explanation, with some pressing for such a definite chain of causality that, granted sufficient information, what can be explained could actually have been predicted (see below), and others responding that, in the case of the social sciences specifically, human behaviour cannot be so definitely determined.[66] While, therefore, the historian and the social scientist both want as much information on the table as possible, any attempt to privilege one type of analysis over another must be suspect. If quantum mechanics makes prediction difficult in the 'hard sciences', how much more should we be cautious in the social sciences.

A good example of 'explanation', one not normally noted in discussions of socio-historical study, is the difference between the beliefs of the Pharisees and the Sadducees on the matter of bodily resurrection. To a modern western mind the Pharisees, believing in resurrection, might appear to be the 'conservatives', and the disbelieving Sadducees the 'liberals' or 'radicals'. Far from it. One might have expected that the Sadducees, like aristocrats in some other cultures, would envisage a life beyond death in which they would be as well provided for as they were in the present. Indeed, knowing the Sadducees to be rich aristocrats and the Pharisees to be a party of social protest, one might have 'predicted' that the former would have a well developed view of the afterlife, at least in their own case, and the latter to be dismissing it as a way of avoiding social challenges. So why did it work the other way round? Answer: because resurrection was rightly seen as a revolutionary doctrine, proclaiming a coming divine action that would turn the world upside down. People like the Pharisees, who believed in that kind of

[64] Another modern example of a similar phenomenon is found in two disturbing books, studying certain details of American subculture : Jewett and Lawrence 2002; Jewett and Lawrence 2004.

[65] A good example of the latter might be Smith 1975, speaking (20) of 'the social forces which led to the rise of Christianity'. Hock 1980, 36 is more nuanced: Paul's trade of tentmaking is to be seen as 'at least partially responsible for his being accorded no status', and 'perhaps also as a cause of his being reviled'. Since Paul himself indicates that the gospel, scandalous to Jews and folly to gentiles, was the ultimate cause, Hock does well to moderate these suggestions.

[66] See e.g. Hempel 1965, and the discussion in Cohen 1995.

thing, might be all the more ready to engage in revolutionary actions in the present as well.[67] This essentially sociological explanation does not rule out religious or theological explanations. To hold the belief, one would need not merely a strong sense of social grievance, but also a clear and grounded belief about Israel's God as creator and judge. But the social and political factor must be allowed its full weight.

If explanation is a complex matter, not to be reduced to one level or layer of description alone, the question of *prediction* is more controversial again. As we saw, it involves such an unbreakable chain of causality that what counts as an explanation after the event could in principle count as a prediction before it. 'Prediction', used as a scientific term, then becomes possible when the observation of data leads to a hypothesis of regularity, as in the prediction of exact times for sunrise, sunset, phenomena such as eclipses, and the regular movements of the tides. Part of the point of using the word 'scientific' in relation to the observations of societies and groups is in order to claim that one can observe specific and repeated patterns of behaviour, from which, as with an eclipse, one can 'predict' not what *will* happen – we are, after all, dealing with ancient history! – but what *must have* happened, whether or not it is recorded. At one level this is unexceptional: as Ronald Hock showed in his book on Paul the tentmaker, we know enough about such occupations to be able to deduce that certain conditions, and personal challenges, 'must have been' Paul's daily lot.[68] At another, however, we may need to be wary: sometimes 'what starts as an empirical test about whether a sociological model fits the facts becomes a means whereby the model tells us what the facts must have been', at which point we may have overstepped the mark.[69] Similar things might be said, in particular, about the way 'Mediterranean culture' has been invoked as a larger category, enabling (for instance) the argument that, since most 'Mediterranean peasants' were illiterate, Jesus, being a 'Mediterranean peasant', must also have been illiterate.[70]

Of course, under certain circumstances, and with certain caveats, prediction may indeed be possible. All history employs it to some extent. Unless one is simply going to quote original sources, without adding any comment, the educated imagination must make guesses at connections. Part of the imagination's education consists of discerning potential parallels and analogies, especially within the specific culture under consideration as opposed to modern western culture, which might well provide anachronistic and/or ethnocentric pseudo-parallels. But, precisely for the reasons articulated by Edwin Judge, Wayne Meeks and many others, the systematization of such analogies into 'models' is always in danger of squeezing out the possibility

[67] See esp. Wright 2003 [*RSG*] 137–40.

[68] See Hock 1980.

[69] Tuckett 1987, 147, questioning the argument of Scroggs 1975.

[70] See esp. Crossan 1991, with the critique in e.g. *JVG* 44–65.

of radical innovation. And all the signs indicate that the first Christians were, in some respects at least, radical innovators.

In particular, we must never forget two major distinctions. First, there is an important difference between the 'hard' sciences and the 'social' sciences. The latter can never 'repeat the experiments'; human societies are not alike, and they vary with time. Second, there is considerable difference between the 'normal' social sciences, studying present-day societies and behaviour-patterns by observation, questionnaires and surveys, and studying the ancient world where surveys and questionnaires cannot be undertaken and where all we can 'observe' are limited sources. Further, though we have many sources for the ancient Mediterranean world, our sources for early Christianity are unrivalled in their vivid depiction of at least some aspects of the movement. To use social-scientific modelling to move from the supposedly known (ancient Mediterranean society in general) to the supposedly unknown (the social patterns of early Christian groups) is therefore fraught with problems, however fruitful some proposals may prove. In any case, the antithesis between the 'Mediterranean world' and the modern western world is not straightforward. In many parts of the world, including the modern western world, elements of the supposedly different ancient culture are alive and well.

The fourth and final element, never all that far away, is *application*. Scroggs points out that the 'social questions' asked by the Chicago School were directly related to the 'liberal Christianity and social gospel' which its members wanted to proclaim. Scroggs too, albeit cautiously, wants to point in the same direction. He suggests that the Marxist theologian Fernando Belo offers 'a challenge to our scholarly world' by asking

> whether New Testament exegesis has, in fact, anything to say about ecology, human oppression, economic slavery, mass malnutrition – or whether we can only be silent and leave *that* Gospel to others?[71]

Similarly Gerd Theissen suggests that sociological exegesis aims to alert interpreters to issues which they might otherwise ignore:

> Then the social consciences of theologians will no longer be roused only when they are confronted by the social problems of the present day; for those consciences will be continually schooled afresh at the very center of their theological work: in their wrestlings with the Bible.[72]

This is the point at which the strict separation of the ancient Mediterranean world and the modern western one threatens to break down. We can see this clearly in Robert Jewett's work. Having written his huge commentary on Romans to argue that Paul's main theme was the overcoming through the gospel of the honour/shame dichotomy, bringing disparate congregations together by means of the shameful message of the cross, Jewett himself

[71] Scroggs 1980, 164f., 179 (italics original); cf. Horrell 2002, 5.

[72] Theissen 1992, 29.

then engaged in a vigorous travelling campaign to persuade churches around the world to work for social and cultural reconciliation and cohesion.[73] We see the same thing in Esler's bracing challenge: 'We must expose the original meanings of the texts in a way which will facilitate their recontextualization by present-day Christian groups.'[74] It is not clear to me how this statement of intent diverges in principle from what many generations of interpreters have understood as their aim (historical study of the New Testament leading to contemporary re-application). The only difference seems to be that Esler believes that somehow 'the strangeness of the biblical world as revealed by Mediterranean anthropology' will give us access to that 'original meaning' in a way that other approaches will not.

One might already ask: if the biblical world is so strange, why should we want to recontextualize its original meanings? Might that not be sheer archaism or primitivism? How does this avoid the challenge of many interpreters of a previous generation, that we should not treat as normative today the arbitrary and contingent elements of a radically different culture?[75] How should we set about doing this recontextualization if our own world is indeed so different? I do not think these questions – the equivalents, within this newer wave of study, of other well-known challenges in biblical study and interpretation – have been properly addressed. The danger of circularity, always present in any attempt both to understand the New Testament in its own context and to 'apply' it to one's own, is just as much a problem here as anywhere else.[76] I applaud any attempt to wrestle simultaneously with historical description and contemporary application, but it seems to me that socio-historical investigation makes this more complex, not less – unless we are to settle for the kind of shallow transference which would rightly be deplored elsewhere.

There is indeed a task to be undertaken here. The best description of it I have yet found is that of Wayne Meeks, to whose work we shall shortly turn. In an article first published in an issue of the *Harvard Theological Review* honouring Krister Stendahl, he engaged critically with the work of George Lindbeck, arguing that 'the hermeneutical circle is not completed until the text finds a fitting social embodiment'.[77] Of course, as he says (an important caveat), one might indeed see what present social embodiment the text might seem to entail, and might then choose not to participate. But, against Lindbeck's approach, locating the symbolic universe of today's appropriate reader in the text itself, Meeks insists that real contemporary communities, wrestling with the flesh-and-blood issues of practical living, are required for

[73] See Jewett and Yeo 2012; and also Jewett 2013.

[74] Esler 1995, 14.

[75] cf. e.g. Nineham 1976.

[76] See the discussion in Horrell 2002, 14f.: 'one may perhaps feel that some of the radical readings present a "history" that is an idealized reflection of contemporary commitments more than of historical reality.' Horrell rightly continues with a 'nevertheless' (such approaches may challenge 'bourgeois' interpreters to consider uncomfortable possibilities), but the warning remains important.

[77] Meeks 1986a; now in Meeks, Hilton and Snyder 2002, 185–95, at 192. Here and below I refer to the latter printing.

the task of interpretation to be complete. This will need, he insists, 'a conversation between social historians of early Christianity and Christian ethicists', more even than that between exegetes and theologians, recognizing that much of Paul's work was devoted to 'moral formation and what a sociologist could only call the institutionalization of the new sect'. Thus

> A hermeneutics of social embodiment would find a place for that sometimes embarrassing worldliness and everydayness of the early Christians. It would undertake to define Christian understanding as the acquisition of competence to act appropriately in a world rendered intelligible in a peculiar way by the dialectic between texts and history.[78]

The goal, then, is clear. A socio-historical reading ought to lead neither to the old hermeneutic of discerning propositional truths, nor to a Bultmannian 'authenticity', but to a new community:

> The goal of a theological hermeneutics on the cultural-linguistic model is not belief in objectively true propositions taught by the text nor the adoption by individuals of an authentic self-understanding evoked by the text's symbols, but the formation of a community whose forms of life correspond to the symbolic universe rendered or signaled by the text.[79]

Esler paraphrases this in his own programmatic essay of 1995, but he makes more explicit the gentle caveat which Meeks had offered:

> We should acknowledge, however, that there will be occasions when we must question aspects of the way the early Christians retold the story of Jesus as their story . . . Even at the earliest stages of the Christian movement there are signs of the incorporation of ideology and imagery which seem at odds with the bedrock of our tradition – the subversive memory of Jesus. Accordingly, there will be times in assimilating their versions of the primal story when we will need to recognize and excise distortions which have crept in with the telling.[80]

All this, of course, simply pushes us back to those well-known puzzles once more. How do we know what is 'bedrock' and what is 'distortion'? How does a socio-historical approach, of whatever kind, help us in making that crucial distinction? Once we have factored in every possible aspect of the greco-roman and Jewish worlds of late antiquity, with all the social modelling we may want, we are left with the same problem, only now seen through several more lenses. What Esler is recommending is a new form of *Sachkritik*, or even simply a new version of the 'Quest for the Historical Jesus', whose 'subversive memory' he would like us to use as the yardstick

[78] Meeks, Hilton and Snyder 2002, 194.

[79] Meeks, Hilton and Snyder 2002, 193; see Meeks's fuller statement in idem, xv.

[80] Esler 1995, 18. His (unacknowledged) paraphrase of Meeks's conclusion follows: 'the goal . . . is neither the defence of propositions alleged to be ontologically true nor the unreflective iteration of biblical ideas and symbols. Rather, it is the formation of contemporary communities . . .' However, in avoiding Meeks's mention (and repudiation) of a Bultmannian solution, Esler nearly does the same thing. He continues '. . . whose identity has been informed, within their own local situations, by a critical appropriation of the "story" of the first Christians, that is, by the assimilation of the experience they had of shaping the story of Jesus, and of God's presence in the world which he represented, to the diverse exigencies of their own contexts.' That sounds like the old existentialist agenda, albeit now in new sociological dress.

for assessing other parts of the early Christian tradition.[81] Thus, when all is said and done, and agreeing fully with Meeks's main point here about understanding the 'symbolic universe' of the first Christians and then seeing what it might mean to reproduce something like that in our own world, we seem to have gone round a long circle to come back somewhere near where we began.

Or perhaps not quite. Mention of the 'symbolic universe' leads us at last to the question: what are we really looking for, in all this socio-historical investigation? How ought we to set it out, to map it, to see it whole?

(v) Mapping and Modelling the Symbolic World

Howard Clark Kee introduced his important 1980 account of sociological perspectives on Christian origins by quoting one of the great American scholars of the previous generation, Henry J. Cadbury. Cadbury was hoping, against the grain of a scholarship that had concentrated on the question of 'who wrote what and when', to probe deeper:

> More important than the immediate problems of origin, even those of exact date and authorship, are those of culture or *Weltanschauung*. To put it bluntly, I find myself much more intrigued with curiosity about how the New Testament writers got that way than with knowing who they were.[82]

I do not know what precisely Henry Cadbury meant by *Weltanschauung*, but the normal translation 'world view' or simply 'worldview' has taken its place as one label among others for the larger whole that sociologists seek to map. Kee develops the idea in his own proposals:

> From the field of ... sociology of knowledge, there is a consonant call for reconstructing the world view of a society in order to understand the specifics of its tradition and history ... What binds any society together is a vast set of common assumptions about human origin and destiny, about values, limits, responsibilities ...[83]

Kee goes on, acknowledging Berger and Luckmann as important influences, to speak of a 'life-world', a 'shared view of reality', of the historian's task as being to try to determine 'both what is meant by what is said and what is assumed by what is left unspoken', and, in that connection, of a 'network of implicit meanings', and then of the 'patterns of ritual and myth' in new movements.[84] The attempt to understand what the early Christian writers meant to say, and what their writings were heard to say, can, he says,

[81] See too Esler 1998, 28, where the biblical texts bear witness to the salvation event 'and stand to be judged for their fidelity to it'. This sweeping simplification covers a large and multi-layered set of hermeneutical assumptions and problems.

[82] Cadbury 1953, 54; quoted by Kee 1980, 11.

[83] Kee 1980, 23.

[84] Kee 1980, 23f., 28.

> be carried out effectively only when careful attention is given to the world view that is maintained by the particular group in whose service the document was produced.[85]

This is the task of 'sociology of knowledge', and the question is, how does one go about it? How do we come to terms with what Maurice Bloch graphically described as 'clumped networks of signification organized in multi-stranded, non-lineal ways'?[86] This is substantially the same question as that addressed by Jonathan Z. Smith when he calls for the investigation of the 'world of meaning which provided a plausibility structure for those who chose to inhabit it', explaining that this involves

> the empathetic reconstruction of the world of the early Christians, i.e. 'what it felt like' to live in a world described and determined by the symbols, rituals and language of early Christianity.[87]

This again is more or less what Berger and Luckmann mean by 'symbolic universe', as summarized by Esler: 'the integrated totality of the various bodies of meaning and symbolism used to legitimate a social world.'[88] In the same vein, we may cite Margaret MacDonald's important book on Paul's churches, in which she sees the letters as representing 'attempts to construct and maintain a symbolic universe which shapes and orders the beliefs and practice of the Pauline communities.'[89] Finally, we may quote from John Schütz, introducing the work of Gerd Theissen: he refers to a 'social world' as being 'the construction of a symbolic communal perception of reality'.[90]

Without wishing to labour the point further, it does appear that, despite the difference of nomenclature (worldview, symbolic world, symbolic universe, life-way, and so on), these writers are all talking about much the same sort of thing: a complex of normally hidden assumptions which may both 'legitimate' the thought and behaviour of a particular society ('that's just how we do things here'), and 'explain' it to a future historian ('that's why they thought and acted as they did'). Such a complex, it is now widely recognized, will include not only conceptual assumptions ('we all believe that X is the case'), but also 'myths' in the sense of implicit and sometimes explicit narratives about the world, 'rituals' in the sense of actions, whether overtly 'religious' or not, in which the worldview comes to some kind of symbolic expression, and actual symbols in the sense of objects or images which embody and encapsulate some key feature of the worldview. All of this, it seems to me, is both common coin in the world of social studies and common sense in thinking seriously about a 'thick description' of the past.

In modern study a good deal of this goes back, in one way or another, to the seminal and still highly readable work of Clifford Geertz, though he

[85] Kee 1980, 29.

[86] Bloch 1992, 129f., quoted in Esler 1995, 6.

[87] Smith 1975, 21.

[88] Esler 1994, 9, citing Berger and Luckmann 1984 [1966], Part II, ch. 2 (110–46).

[89] Horrell 1999, 233, summarizing the project of MacDonald 1988.

[90] Schütz 1982, 1.

reserves the term 'world view' for the 'cognitive, existential aspects' of a culture, and places alongside this what he calls 'ethos', the moral and aesthetic (and hence 'evaluative'), aspects.[91] 'Meanings', he writes,

> can only be 'stored' in symbols: a cross, a crescent, or a feathered serpent. Such religious symbols, dramatized in rituals or related in myths, are felt somehow to sum up, for those for whom they are resonant, what is known about the way the world is, the quality of the emotional life it supports, and the way one ought to behave while in it. Sacred symbols thus relate an ontology and a cosmology to an aesthetics and a morality: their peculiar power comes from their presumed ability to identify fact with value at the most fundamental level.[92]

Within this way of looking at things, the two terms 'world view' and 'ethos' belong inescapably together, not least for the practical reason that though we can separate them in thought we cannot find societies which separate them in their real life:

> The tendency to synthesize world view and ethos at some level, if not logically necessary, is at least empirically coercive; if it is not philosophically justified, it is at least pragmatically universal ... [B]etween ethos and world view, between the approved style of life and the assumed structure of reality, there is conceived to be a simple and fundamental congruence such that they complete one another and lend one another meaning.[93]

Geertz is one of those writers, like Albert Schweitzer, who demands to be quoted, for the clarity of his exposition and the illumination of his metaphors and examples. But this is enough to make the point.

Those who know my own work will not be surprised by any of this. Since 1992 I have articulated and employed a particular method of worldview-analysis which has been allied to, and which sets the context for, theological analysis. In this I have been following the sequence of thought just indicated in relation to Margaret MacDonald's work (the symbolic universe which shapes and orders the beliefs and practices) and also, as we shall see, in the work of Wayne Meeks, who offers five chapters of analysis of the social world of Paul's communities and then a sixth in which he sketches the beliefs which made sense within that social world. I set out this model in the first book in the series Christian Origins and the Question of God, applying it in detail both to the Jewish world of the first century and to the early Christian movement in general. I then applied it to Jesus; then most recently, after the intervening project on the resurrection, to Paul.[94]

In doing this I have made the mistake, if it was a mistake, of not locating this method of analysis in relation to the kind of discussion I have set out in this chapter, except for reference to Geertz on the one hand and to Berger and Luckmann on the other. Words beginning with the prefix 'socio-' have

[91] Geertz 2000 [1973], 126f., at the start of his chapter 5, 'Ethos, World View, and the Analysis of Sacred Symbols'.

[92] Geertz 127.

[93] Geertz 127, 129.

[94] cf. *NTPG* ch. 5 (121–44); *JVG* 137–44; *PFG* 22–68. The increasing length corresponds to my dawning recognition that not everyone found this as straightforward or helpful as I did myself.

not normally featured in my exposition. By the same token, I have tended to talk about 'narrative' rather than 'myth', and 'praxis' rather than 'ritual'. And I have made it clear, as many others have done, that the social description is not to be played off against a description of theological beliefs, but that we should rather see an intricate symbiosis between the two.[95] In line with the famous statement of Robin Scroggs, I have not been trying to reduce the reality of Christianity to its social dynamic, but have instead been attempting to 'guard against a reductionism from the other extreme, a limitation of the reality of Christianity to an inner-spiritual, or objective-cognitive system.'[96] All these factors, and perhaps more, may help to explain why my proposals have not received much notice from the sociologists. All the better, from one point of view: I have, quite by accident, been smuggling sociological approaches to the New Testament into discussions, and perhaps even into institutions, which might have bolted the door had they glimpsed Malina or Esler, or even Meeks, coming up the front path.

I have called the worldview-analysis in question a 'model', but of course one might properly debate whether that is the right term. The word 'model' has been applied in the discipline more to the specific proposals which might be found *within* the kind of worldview-diagram I have sketched: according to Bengt Holmberg, a 'model' in this sense is 'something less than a theory and something more than an analogy'.[97] When I called my worldview-diagrams a 'model' I meant it almost literally: something you might in principle make out of Plasticene or even Lego. But what the word has come to mean, in the recent socio-historical study of the early Christians, is the kind of specific proposal, a shorthand summary of key observations about the wider social world (perhaps, the wider 'Mediterranean world'), which could then be picked up and applied, at least in the form of a question, to specific texts and situations. This is what, at a very specific level, Ronald Hock proposed in relation to Paul as an artisan: we know quite a bit about artisans in that world, and this knowledge can help to illuminate not only what Paul's daily life was almost certainly like but also several passages in his letters where this kind of lifestyle seems to be reflected.[98]

The main 'models' which have been developed as this new wave of study has progressed are well known. One of the most obvious has been that of the 'sect'. Cross-cultural studies suggest that when a small movement breaks away from a parent body certain behaviours are likely to occur which can

[95] See, for example, Judge 1960, 48; Kee 1980, 117f.; Meeks 1983, ch. 6; Horrell 2002, 23.

[96] Scroggs 1980, 165f. This is the point at which Scroggs says that the sociology of early Christianity 'wants to put body and soul together again'. That is a shorthand, but it points towards the sort of task I have attempted. See too Holmberg 1978, 201–3, warding off 'the fallacy of idealism' to one side and 'the materialistic fallacy' on the other.

[97] Holmberg 1990, 14, quoting Carney 1975 (but without page reference). Holmberg's whole discussion at 12–17 is to the point. See too Esler 1994, 12f., stressing that a 'model' brings the interpreter's perspective into the open; that it is a heuristic tool, designed to open up the texts rather than force itself upon them; and that its object is 'to stimulate the sociological imagination'. The usefulness of a model, he states (rather obviously) is dependent upon there being 'a fair degree of comparability between the model and the data under consideration'.

[98] See Hock 1980, 18f. and *passim*.

then be invoked to explain certain features of early Christianity, though whether the early communities of Jesus' followers were the same *sort* of movement as the Pauline communities is another question.[99] The general point, however, seems to me in principle helpful, and the often-cited example of Galatians 2 is an obvious case in point.[100] Over against any assumption that what was at stake between Paul and Peter at Antioch was simply a matter of 'what one must believe in order to be saved', or indeed 'what one must believe *about* being saved' – as though the Antioch incident were simply a foretaste of the discussions of 'justification' taking place in the sixteenth or seventeenth century – the model draws attention to the fact that Paul was representing a new sort of group, in tension with the larger Jewish world, while Peter, following 'those who came from James', was to this extent going with the larger body.

One might comment at this point that it isn't clear how introducing the technical terminology of 'sect' makes this account substantially different from what one might expect within the so-called new perspective. Indeed, part of the resistance to that complex movement has come, we may suppose, from those who are wary of sociological reductionism.[101] There are, in addition, many other problems with the 'sect' model.[102] One obvious one is that the language of 'church and sect' is so clearly borrowed from later Christian history. Even when 'world' is substituted for 'church', as some have suggested, the word 'sect' has so many modern resonances that one wonders how helpful it really is as an historical tool.[103]

It draws attention, though, to two things in particular. First, it points out that when a group breaks away from a larger body there are certain things that tend to feature: strong ('charismatic'?) leadership; the need to define the boundaries of the new group and to 'legitimate' its existence; polemic against the old one; a strong sense of group identity (perhaps a 'fictive kinship'); and, quite often, an expectation of future vindication through some

[99] One of the early pioneers here was Scroggs 1975 (reprinted, with Horrell's summary of subsequent discussions, in Horrell 1999, 69–91). Esler 1987 applied this model to Luke/Acts; he expounded it briefly in his 1994, 13–17; he applied it in his 1995, ch. 4, to the Antioch conflict, and in ch. 5 to Qumran and the Johannine community. Elliott 1995, following his earlier work (e.g. Elliott 1981), offers an overview of the whole early Christian movement under the rubric 'from faction to sect', proposing a list of variables to do with the conditions for the emergence of a 'sect' and the ways in which such a group might be and behave. Watson 2007 [1986] made the notion of 'sect' a major theme.

[100] See esp. Esler 1994, 62, 68f.: Paul was proposing a sectarian position in relation to Judaism, and his opponents would have left Christianity as a 'reform movement within Judaism'.

[101] Esler 1994 ch. 4 engages in debate with Dunn; but Dunn's proposal about 'boundary markers', which Esler criticizes (1995, 4) for not being earthed in first-century reality, is no more irrelevant than the language of 'sect' itself, which as Esler admits (68) is 'modern parlance'.

[102] See, for instance, the trenchant criticisms of Scroggs and others in J. T. Sanders 1993, 114–25; the criticisms noted by Horrell 1999, 69f., 91; and the detailed critique in Harland 2003, 177–95. For Scroggs this model seems a good deal more than a tool for understanding the first century: he speaks trenchantly (71) of 'the poison of overtheologizing . . . characteristic of so much New Testament scholarship during the neo-orthodox era', and declares (89) that 'the church becomes from this perspective not a theological seminary but a group of people who have experienced the hurt of the world and the healing of communal acceptance.'

[103] As Scroggs explains (in Horrell 1999, 71f., n. 4), while Troeltsch and Weber spoke of 'church and sect', Peter Berger, following van der Leeuw, saw the sect over against 'the world'.

imminent event. Thus, to continue with the example of Galatians, if one had not noticed any of these things from reading the text, being alerted to the 'sect' model might have opened one's eyes to them; though the existence of the model scarcely 'explains' why *this* group, under Paul's leadership, believed the things it did. Here is the danger: that the 'social forces' are seen as all-powerful, with the humans who constitute the actual groups being swept up unreflectively in their path. Whatever else Paul was, he was not unreflective, and he wanted his churches to be thoughtful and intentional as well. But the point is fair. In some ways the 'sect' terminology does fit the bill.

The second point to which the model draws attention is that one can distinguish a 'sect' from a 'reform movement', with the former keen to make a clean break with the parent body and the latter eager to sustain its earlier membership and to effect, if possible, reform from within. Whether that distinction quite captures the difference between Paul's and Peter's positions at Antioch, however, is not so clear. I am not sure that Peter, or even 'those who came from James', saw themselves as reforming the Jewish world from within, granted that they, like Paul, believed in Jesus as Messiah. But again the sociological proposal, even if it needs fuller teasing out and modification, at least alerts the reader to three-dimensional possibilities, and remains as a solid protest against a 'theological reductionism'.

The proposal to understand early Christianity in terms of sectarianism contains, as I said, other elements: charismatic leadership, through which the sect comes into being; the task of 'legitimation' to create the worldview within which the sect makes itself at home, and so on.[104] Not all social 'models' function at the same level. Some nest within others.

Another element which can nest within the sectarian one is that of the 'resocialization' which follows 'conversion'. This has been widely studied, and seems fairly obvious as a general category within which to understand what was going on in Paul's churches.[105] Closely allied to this, almost as a shadow side, is the sense that members both of the new group and of the parent group – or indeed of rival 'new groups' – will quickly come to regard one another negatively, as having strayed from the true path. The technical term here is 'deviance', seen not so much as the actual behaviour of the person labelled as 'deviant' but as a social by-product of the formation of one group and the exclusion of others. As John Barclay points out in his important article on this topic, this way of looking at things 'fitted the mood of the 1960s so perfectly as to become the new orthodoxy in an amazingly short time.'[106] The sociological point seemed rather obviously to serve the protest movements of the time: what some ('the establishment'?) counted as 'deviance' was not so in fact, but was merely a way of one group defining itself

[104] This is a major element in Esler 1987.

[105] See esp. Taylor 1995; see also e.g. Kee 1980, 74–81; and now esp. Chester 2003.

[106] Barclay 1995, 115; the article is reprinted with comments and further bibliography in Horrell 1999, 289–307. The theory is applied to Luke-Acts in Malina and Neyrey 1991a.

against another.[107] 'Deviance', in other words, is a social construction, not an 'objective' truth about the behaviour or beliefs so labelled. Such analysis serves the usual purpose of constructivism, alerting people to implicit power-games behind apparently neutral statements. However, as with all such moves, the danger is that discourse then collapses into a kind of solipsism, as with the 'emotivist' ethics in which the word 'good' can *only* mean 'I like this', and the word 'bad' can *only* mean 'I don't like that'. No actual communities, and few actual individuals, can live on that basis for very long; the apparently sophisticated move of unmasking the discourse of power quickly becomes in its turn a way of asserting a different, perhaps subversive, power. However, 'deviance' theory can help to explain not only the original 'labelling', but also why events then took the turn they did. As Jack T. Sanders explains in his study of the phenomenon:

> Mainstream Judaism – constantly threatened; under severe economic, political, and military pressure; and at one point nearly destroyed – struck out at the deviant Christians in order to preserve its boundaries, its self-identity . . .; for these Christians were eroding those boundaries just at the time when gentiles were threatening to destroy them . . . Theological issues were present, but they are not sufficient alone to explain the conflict.[108]

One might comment that if, from a Jewish or early Christian point of view, one were to see the community itself as the people of God, then community identity and the pressures on it were themselves also 'theological'; but the point is taken. However, just because we can see 'labelling' going on in various directions (such as Paul labelling Peter and Barnabas as 'hypocrites' in Galatians 2.13), that does not entitle us to forget the theological questions involved (was the crucified Jesus really Israel's Messiah, and had his crucifixion radically reshaped God's people?) or to suggest that what was 'really' going on had to do simply with 'deviance' and 'conflict' (another category regularly invoked at this point).[109] Here Barclay's cautions are on target:

> Deviance theory is no magic wand with which to solve the many intricate problems which confront the historian of early Christianity. It can only be used in conjunction with minute historical analysis of the sources and cannot fill in the gaps which they leave.[110]

A rather different feature of some sectarian life was proposed by John Gager at the earlier stage of the contemporary 'social description' project. Building on the work of Festinger and others, he attempted to understand

[107] Barclay quotes the now famous definition from Becker 1963, 9: 'Deviance is not a quality of the act the person commits, but rather a consequence of the application by others of rules and sanctions to an "offender". The deviant is one to whom that label has been successfully applied; deviant behavior is behavior that people so label.'

[108] Sanders 1993, 150, summing up a long discussion (129–51).

[109] See the discussion in Schütz 1982, 18–20. He rightly (in my view) insists that a Marxist reduction of 'conflict' to economics alone is unjustified, since in reality we find 'a range of disparities exploited . . . to point up the connections between the symbols, actions and ideas of religion and the wider world of social, economic, political, and ecological realities' (19). This is more or less exactly what I try to cover in the worldview-model I have variously employed (see above, 243–7).

[110] Barclay 1995, 125.

the urgent missionary imperative of the early Christians in terms of 'cognitive dissonance': because Jesus had been crucified, and because the expected 'kingdom' had not arrived, the followers of Jesus, rather than giving up on the movement, were all the more eager to cover up for their disappointment by persuading others to join in.[111] This theory had a good run for its money, but it was never either theoretically justified or historically grounded.[112]

As to the theory, Festinger and his colleagues infiltrated a small flying-saucer cult focused on a woman who claimed to be receiving messages from outer space warning of a coming great flood, from which the group would be rescued by a flying saucer on a particular date. Her followers were secretive until the date arrived; then, when neither flood nor flying saucer materialized, they changed both their message (now, apparently, God had saved the world from the anticipated disaster) and their style, becoming zealous in propagating their belief. The problem, at the level of sociological theory, is that the group was so small that the infiltrating sociologists often formed up to a third of the members present at any one time, becoming such trusted and articulate colleagues that they were the ones delegated to talk to the press or answer the phone. This was hardly a reliable scientific experiment.

As to the history: first, what the early Christians proclaimed to the world was not at all what they had been thinking beforehand.[113] Second, we have evidence for several Jewish groups who followed this or that prophet or would-be Messiah in the second-Temple period. After the leader was killed, such groups had a choice (always assuming they had not been killed as well): give up the movement, or find a new leader. Josephus describes several such groups, and there is no sign of them suffering from 'cognitive dissonance'.[114] One hesitates to draw such a conclusion, but it looks as though the attempt to fasten a 'theory' or 'model' of this sort on to early Christianity is itself the result of the dissonance between the strongly felt desires of certain critics and the actual historical evidence about why and how Christianity began. Certainly this kind of argument ought not to gain any lasting position in the social-historical analysis of the early Christian movement.

A different kind of proposal, operating independently of ideas about the nature of sects, is that 'the Mediterranean world' took for granted certain social norms which do not obtain in today's western world. One of these, the patron/client relationship, is certainly unusual today. I still remember my astonishment, reading Juvenal's *Satires* as a schoolboy, at discovering that many ordinary Roman citizens made a pilgrimage every morning to the house of some rich 'patron' where they would be given handouts of food and perhaps money. In return (it was assumed) they would support their

[111] Gager 1975; the relevant chapter is reprinted, with Horrell's comments and suggestions for further reading, in Horrell 1999, 177–94. The key sociological texts include Festinger 1957 and Festinger, Riecken and Schachter 1956.

[112] For what follows, see my fuller comments in *RSG* 697–701, with other refs there.

[113] See *RSG* 699f.

[114] See *RSG* 557–9; and, for the wider background, *NTPG* 170–81.

patron in future political or legal contests. The patron–client system went all the way up to the emperor at the top, and all the way down to slaves and freedmen at the bottom. The status of 'benefactor' was highly prized; to be a 'mediator' or 'broker' between a patron and a client was to occupy a position of potential power; to give a gift was always a matter of careful and balanced thought.[115] The recent studies of this subject in relation to the New Testament seem to indicate that Paul, at least, both fitted in to this system and, in some respects, deliberately subverted it. This may be part of the reason why he refused to accept money from the Corinthian church, while being grateful for financial support from elsewhere, e.g. Philippi.[116] Certainly the social dynamics of a patron–client system will have been only too evident in the cities where his churches sprang up. We should not be overly hasty, however, either to draw immediate exegetical or historical conclusions from this, or indeed to suppose that the modern western world is free from similar constraints. The academic world, to look no further, is constantly reminded of the need to apply for research funding to 'benefactors' who have the power to give or to withhold. Though the idea of 'patronage' has become seriously suspect, giving off the smell of corruption, of using 'friends in high places' to secure advantages one would not obtain on one's own merits, it is also true that those in today's world who have the power to help or hinder will frequently claim that they do so on their own judgment of merit. It may well be that high-minded Romans would have made similar claims. In other words, though we today do not find queues of hungry citizens hanging around a rich man's door day by day in the way they did in ancient Rome, we are not without such systems ourselves. Here as elsewhere the apparent contrast between 'then' and 'now', much highlighted by some in the 'Context Group', seems overdrawn.

This is particularly so in relation to the most famous of their proposals, that of seeing the 'Mediterranean world' as an 'honour/shame' society.[117] A great deal has been written about this, and many attempts have been made to apply the notion to parts of the New Testament. Here the central claim is that public life in the 'world' in question was a continual contest in which 'honour' was at stake, with everyone engaged in a quest to gain 'honour' and avoid 'shame'; and that the early Christians, or some of them, may have begun to realize that there was a different kind of 'honour', and that the 'shame' which Jesus had suffered on the cross had actually turned the whole system upside down. This is undoubtedly a major dimension which ought to be factored in to our reading of many parts of the New Testament. One thinks not only of the controversies in which Jesus, challenged on this or that point, responded either with a shrewd one-liner or a subversive story,

[115] For one recent study among many, see deSilva 2000, ch. 3; applied to Luke-Acts: Moxnes 1991. A basic study of 'benefactors' is Danker 1982; see too e.g. Winter 1994; Elliott 1996.

[116] cf. 2 Cor. 11.7–11. This and similar matters are addressed in forthcoming studies by John Barclay.

[117] See Malina 1981, ch. 2; Malina and Neyrey 1991c; Esler 1994, 25–9; deSilva 2000, chs. 1 and 2. A whole issue of *Semeia* was given over to the topic (vol. 68 for 1994), including the essay by J. H. Neyrey applying the model to the Johannine passion narrative (now reprinted, with comments, in Horrell 1999, 151–76).

nor only of Paul's description of the shame of Jesus' death,[118] but also of the ways in which Paul boasts of the things which show his weakness, and claims that, despite the folly of the gospel, he is 'not ashamed' of it. But there are at least three questions which must be raised.[119]

First, it is not clear that the modern western world does not also operate quite a definite system of 'honour and shame'. It may be dressed up differently; indeed, dressing up is a case in point, as anyone who has appeared underdressed (or perhaps overdressed) at a formal dinner will know.[120] One has only to mention the relentless suburban competition for the tidiest front lawn or smartest car, or the endless media hype surrounding politicians, or the massive attention to sporting success, to see that honour and shame are alive and well in today's western culture, albeit in other forms.

It is indeed the 'other forms', this time in the ancient world, which raise the second question. Sociologists and anthropologists increasingly resist any kind of blanket application, across thousands of square miles, of any single cultural model. Just as many of us have had to learn that a phenomenon like 'the imperial cult' is not one thing but many in the first century, so similar adjustments need to be made to all large-scale generalizations.[121]

Third, as with so many sociological models, the real question is not whether we are indeed being introduced to one aspect of ancient reality, but whether other aspects can be reduced to terms of it. This is strikingly so in relation to Jerome Neyrey's attempt to read the Johannine crucifixion narrative as an ironic honour/shame contest. However important this may be, and however much traditional interpretations of the story of Jesus' death may have presented a rather one-dimensional would-be 'theological' reading, to reduce the story to this broad, supposedly 'Mediterranean' quest for honour is to concentrate on the orchestration and fail to hear the melody.

Similar things must be said about the proposal that a 'first-century personality' was 'dyadic, not individualistic'.[122] Bruce Malina, proposing this dichotomy, describes a bracing modern 'individual' who sees himself or herself as such, detached from others, living within their own 'unique social and natural environments' – contrasted with the 'dyadism' in which

> a dyadic personality is one who simply needs another continually in order to know who he or she really is ... an individual who perceives himself and forms his self-image in terms of what others perceive and feed back to him.[123]

[118] cf. e.g. Hellerman 2005.

[119] I broadly sympathize with the nuanced questions of David Horrell in Horrell 1999, 12–15, 151–3.

[120] Or for that matter to make a presentation at the Society of Biblical Literature. Academics accustomed to the informal setting of European conferences can be caught out by the American assumption that such occasions contain many coded competitions for 'honor'.

[121] On the imperial cult, see *PFG* 321–43. For a professional anthropologist's searching questions to the 'model', cf. Chance 1994, noting (143) that Malina and Neyrey, in the seminal works in question, were avoiding the theoretical issues involved, and that their work already seemed 'a bit dated'.

[122] That is the title of Malina and Neyrey 1991b; see too Malina 1981, 52–70.

[123] Malina 1981, 54f.

As a result, Malina claims, people like Jesus and Paul neither knew nor cared much about psychological states or development, or introspective analyses, and so were incapable of really understanding one another:

> first-century people did not know each other very well in the way we know people, i.e., psychologically, individually, intimately, and personally ... Jesus himself ... is a good example ... Of the twelve men he chose, we are told that one betrayed him, one denied him, and the rest quibbled a lot and eventually abandoned him in a crisis situation. Paul himself constantly has problems with the allegiance of the various groups he gathered ... All this simply indicates what poor judges of individual character, of individual psychology, people in such cultures are. This is not because they are obtuse or unobservant. Rather, it is because such abilities are culturally unimportant; there are no cultural cues of perception highlighting this feature.[124]

I find this astonishing on two counts. First, as anyone with experience of management knows, you can use all the tools and character profiling offered by our over-psychologized culture and still find yourself with a team of people who let you down, who miss the point, and who quibble among themselves. Second, as anyone but the most self-centred will recognize, people in today's western world are just as much concerned, often at a very deep level, with the opinion and valuation of their peers, their family, their colleagues, their friends, and the wider society in general. We find out, day by day, 'who we are' by interaction with these networks. Take us out of them – fly us to the other side of the world, put us in an impersonal hotel room – and one of the first things we want to do is to make contact with people, either electronically with family and friends back home, or face to face with hosts or colleagues on the spot.

Of course, there are huge variations of personality, from the introverted to the extroverted. The former may be quite happy for a while in the hotel room, curled up with a good book. The latter may seem outwardly to be more in need of overt human contact. This has nothing to do with the ancient Mediterranean world as compared with modern western culture. Granted, too, that many people who turn up for counselling or psychotherapy may begin by perceiving themselves as isolated individuals. But one of the things they will quickly learn, even the most introverted, is that life is not like that in the modern world any more than it was in the first century. Thus a married couple, seeing a therapist, will routinely be invited to talk about their wider family networks, the people who have quite literally made them who they are, and who continue (even after death) to make them that way. Sociologists are right to draw our attention to the fact that people in Paul's day understood themselves as part of a number of human networks, associations, kinships actual or fictive. If we forget this we misread the texts. But we should pause before concluding that this somehow creates a great gulf between us.

There are many other 'models' that sociologists have studied. The secondary literature is full of them. But these are I think representative. As I

[124] Malina 1981, 58f.

have said, they are not all on the same level. 'Legitimation', 'charismatic leadership', 'deviance' and 'resocialization', questions of power and authority, and probably others too, belong primarily within the larger model of the 'sect', which in turn is contrasted with the 'reform movement' as well as with the parent body, whether it be called 'church' or 'world'. 'Honour and shame', the 'dyadic personality', various models of 'conflict', and so on, belong more as wider generalizations about whole societies; insofar as they are accurate descriptions of social realities, they might be presumed to appear in different modes within different kinds of groups. Some of these will reappear in the next chapter, within a differently sketched context. And – though we have barely even mentioned this – one should also, for a complete picture, bring in the entire related fields of rhetorical criticism, the 'sociology of literature', and so forth.[125] Clearly there is a much larger map of Pauline studies, not to mention New Testament studies as a whole, than there is space to set out here. My main concern has been to display, not uncritically but still basically sympathetically, the world of discourse which has been going on over the last generation.

This world appears largely untouched by, not to say unconcerned with, the two major movements of thought in Anglophone Pauline studies in the same period. The sociologists seem innocent of the debates which have clustered around Sanders and Martyn, whom we studied in Parts I and II. Before we turn to the third member of this American trio, Wayne Meeks, we may sum up what we have found.

(vi) Sect or Reform Movement? The Social Study of Paul

By this stage some observers may have spotted a certain irony. A new group has emerged within the discipline of New Testament studies, and more specifically within Pauline studies. This group has been formed because of long-standing frustration with, and alienation from, the parent body with which it now has a decidedly contested relationship. The group has come into being not merely because of these frustrations and a desire to bring things back into a proper balance. It has emerged because of remarkable, indeed 'charismatic' leadership, whether that of Edwin Judge, Gerd Theissen, Bruce Malina, Jerome Neyrey or Philip Esler. Or, indeed, of Wayne Meeks; but to mention his name again sharpens the question. Is this group a reform movement within the study of the New Testament in its historical context, or is it actually a sect, with its own boundaries and, ultimately, its own (duly 'legitimated') symbolic universe?

A strong case can be made for seeing the 'Context Group', at least in its inception, as a sect. The group was established under the leadership of Malina and others in 1986, with clear and fresh aims, and above all with

[125] For the rhetorical criticism of the New Testament, see e.g. Kennedy 1984; Robbins 1996. A complete NT commentary using 'socio-rhetorical criticism' has been produced by Ben Witherington III; e.g. Witherington 1998.

what sometimes seems to be a top-down approach: here are the models, here is how they apply. Of course, some members of the group, such as Philip Esler, have stressed that the models are heuristic only, designed to draw out features of the historical material that might not otherwise be noticed. But the group has continued to make large claims, not simply about fresh angles of vision but about the impossibility of truly understanding the texts unless one approaches them in this way.[126] In the early days, not long before the full emergence of the 'Context Group' itself, there were regular signs of conflict between sociological approaches and the 'parent body' of mainstream New Testament studies. Scroggs accused the New Testament establishment of a poisonous over-theologizing; Watson, at least in the first edition of his famous monograph, set up a sharp either/or between sociology and theology.[127] Once the Context Group was established, its boundaries were patrolled, not least in critical reviews of the work of those who might have seemed to be doing the same sort of thing but now, apparently, were deemed not to be: like Paul rebuking Peter and Barnabas, so Malina and others sharply criticized Meeks, Judge, Horrell and others for using sociological analysis as a reform movement within the broader task of history.[128] The response which Meeks has made in various places indicates that there is indeed a boundary here, and that he is conscious of being on one side of it, with Malina and some others on the other.[129] All this begins to look like a modern, secularized version of much older battles, with dogma on one side and history on the other.

If that is anywhere near the mark, the only safe place for exegesis to stand is in the unsafe world of history. Many who have written about the social description of early Christianity have insisted that what they are doing, including the eclectic employment of this or that 'model' if it seems to be useful, is basically a thickening and thus a strengthening of the historical task.[130] In fact, when we read what was actually said by some of the early advocates of a socio-historical approach, we find them doing pretty much the same sort of thing as many other historical critics, but with extra angles

[126] See Esler 1994, 2: one cannot hope to understand either the context or the *kerygma* 'without an appropriate methodology for dealing with the social side'. This implies that nobody ever understood the Christian *kerygma* until the emergence of a methodologically sophisticated sociological method.

[127] Scroggs, in Horrell 1999, 71; Watson 1986. Neither Scroggs nor Watson, however, were members of the 'Context Group' itself.

[128] See e.g. the reviews of Meeks 1983 by J. H. Elliott (in *Religious Studies Review* 11, 1985, 329–35) and Malina (in *JBL* 104, 1985, 346–9). Note, however, Neyrey's comment about the Context Group: 'Far from abandoning the historical-critical method, they enlarged it, by calling attention to the use of the social sciences . . .' (Neyrey 1991, ix). The question is whether, though claiming to enlarge it, they in fact constrained it.

[129] See e.g. Meeks 2009, 135, speaking of 'the complaint, most forcefully advanced by Bruce Malina and some other members of the Context Group, that those of us who aim to do mere social history are not *scientific*, and therefore not worth reading', and agreeing with the response to this of Horrell's opening chapter in the same volume (Still and Horrell 2009, 6–20, esp. here at 11f.). See again Meeks's statement in 2003 [1983], xii.

[130] On the 'eclectic' use of various tools and models, see e.g. Theissen 1992, 286.

of vision factored in.[131] Kee speaks of 'the joining of historical study and social-scientific method', and sums up his project by saying that

> As we seek to discern the complexities of the process of the origins of Christianity, and to discover the variety of responses that the story of Jesus elicited in the Greco-Roman culture of the early empire, our quest is facilitated by the analytical methods developed in the social sciences.[132]

So too Stanley Stowers offers a balanced agenda:

> The models, methods and theories of the social sciences provide new and horizon-expanding opportunities for the historian. At the same time they introduce new complexities, and their use calls for a sustained critical discussion . . . about their use by historians of distant cultures.[133]

And David Horrell, commenting on the difference between social-scientific approaches and the varied liberationist readings of the last generation, gives it as his assessment that

> Social-scientific approaches to the Bible retain a much closer connection with the concerns of historical criticism than many of these other new methods, particularly some of the forms of literary criticism.[134]

As will be apparent, at this point I am sticking with the more general social-historical approach against the more dogmatic social-anthropological approach of Malina and others. However, unlike one supposed aspect of 'Mediterranean culture', this is not, or should not be, a zero-sum game. A new generation may well decide that the reinforced and protected boundary between the 'sect' and the 'reform movement' may be unnecessary and unhelpful. Things have moved on. To track that movement we need to examine the two books in this area which I regard as central and seminal.

Before we do that, three short puzzles. First, why has all this work been proceeding as though Ed Sanders, and the lines of thought which his name evokes, did not exist? If Sanders, and the varieties of new perspective which have blossomed following his work, are even half right, then the historian and the exegete are perforce committed to the study of the actual communities that came into being in the first century, and to the investigation of how they regulated their life, reinforced their boundaries, and constructed 'legitimating' frameworks of symbol, story and praxis. These movements ought to meet up, yet they seldom have. The time is ripe.

Second, many of the writers we have studied speak of the early Christians in terms of 'millenarian' movements. Some have gone so far as to liken them to the 'cargo cults' of the South Pacific.[135] This seems to me almost as basic a

[131] e.g. Kee 1980.
[132] Kee 1980, 22, 170.
[133] Stowers 1985, 168.
[134] Horrell 1999, 7; on this point, he cites Barton 1995.
[135] See the summary and discussion in Duling 1996, with helpful bibliography.

mistake as the 'cognitive dissonance' theory, for reasons discussed in the second Part of the present book. Calling the early Christians an 'apocalyptic' group, as many have done, raises questions rather than solving them, and those questions must be addressed by historical study rather than ideological projection.

Third, I do not think that any of the writers I have been studying in this chapter have really worked through the question I raised earlier on, about the 'application' of their work. Some of the early pioneers of the movement had a very clear agenda, namely the dethroning of an apparently high-and-dry 'theology' and the embracing of some kind of social ethics. Esler and Meeks both speak, as we saw, of the need to move from the full social embodiment of the gospel in the first century to an equivalent re-embodying (hedged about with critical caveats) in the present day. After all, the new socio-historical interest in the New Testament emerged during the mood of social protest in the 1960s, and it would be surprising if its results did not reflect that. But here we run into difficulty. Some of the leading lights in the movement have insisted that the sociological tools we are using are designed to enable us to think ourselves back into a society which was completely different from our own. We can't have it both ways. Either the worlds are radically different, in which case studying the ancient one will only be of help in living in the modern one if we engage in a highly complex step-by-step process of 'translation'. Or the worlds, though very different in some ways, are strangely familiar in others, so that, for instance, by alerting ourselves to the social dynamics of the first century (sometimes, indeed, with the help of cross-cultural models derived from our own day!), we might return to our communities with our eyes opened to new challenges and possibilities. Again, this would require much more careful mapping than has normally been attempted.[136]

Some, indeed, have analysed early Christianity in such a way as to make it remote, and therefore to keep it, as it were, a strange and distant movement with little or no relation to any actual or possible contemporary reality. That is the impression I gain, for instance, from the work of John Gager. But it is not the impression one gets from most of the writers studied here. Whether we like it or not, placing Paul in his world – in however multi-layered a fashion – seems almost always to raise the question: what might this mean for us today, for our own world? The social study of Paul and his communities thus points forward to, but has not usually addressed, larger questions, which are now being taken up by others. And this brings us at last to the two authors whose books form the centrepiece of the present section.

[136] A quite different critique, from its own unique angle, is offered in the classic work of John Milbank: see Milbank 1990, ch. 5.

Chapter Eleven

SOCIAL STUDY, SOCIAL ETHICS: MEEKS AND HORRELL

1. The First Urban Christians

Looking back over a long and productive scholarly career, Wayne A. Meeks summed up what he had been doing, and the puzzles with which it had left him, in the following characteristically quizzical way:

> I went to graduate school, just under half a century ago, because I wanted to learn how to do New Testament theology. The way to do that, I already vaguely understood, was by becoming a historian of early Christianity ... My fellow students and I were socialized to believe that, if we could do really good history, we would have accomplished what was required of us. In the years since, we have learned how very difficult that task was. We have also experienced some disillusionment about historiography's potential to answer the really important questions ... : what to believe, how to live, what is ultimately true. How it came about that scholars of the New Testament thought to answer such questions as those *by doing history* is itself a long and complicated and decidedly modern story. In our time that story has arrived at an unexpected peripeteia, expressed in a widespread loss of confidence ... Nevertheless, the shadow of the earlier, often misdirected, self-confidence lies over all we do. This leaves us with two large questions.
>
> First, if we could get the history exactly right, would it help us to be better at the task of being Christian – or, more important, of being human?
>
> Second, since we cannot get the history exactly right – because historiography like all science must constantly correct itself, fated to produce only probabilities, never certainty – of what use is it? Does the effort, never completed, help us in any tangible way?
>
> ... It will be obvious to most readers that my own answers to [these questions], however tentative and unformed, are affirmative ...[1]

This sums up a good deal of what we find throughout Meeks's work, even though he writes as if he only understood it all late in the day: a dogged modesty, aware that history, however well done, can only provide a twisting and often unpaved road to the great questions that face us, but convinced none the less that this is the road we must travel. Attempts by cartographers

[1] Meeks 2009, 145f., emphasis original. Webster's dictionary defines *peripeteia* as 'a sudden or unexpected reversal of circumstances or situation'.

to pretend that there really is a solid, well-paved road will lead, once more, to disillusionment. Far better to continue the patient work of a journey on difficult roads, leading towards a destination we only occasionally glimpse. The New Testament, and Paul's correspondence as one of its central features, is stranger than an easy dogmatic approach had supposed, but also much more full of possibility than an easy scepticism had wanted to believe. Meeks's work constantly reminds us of the latter as well as the former.

For that reason, and despite continuing disagreements at various points, I take *The First Urban Christians*, and the project it summed up and redirected, as one of the most hopeful signs in the English-speaking Pauline scholarship of the last generation. One or two reviewers of my *Paul and the Faithfulness of God* have expressed surprise at the significant number of times I refer to Meeks's book. There was a good reason. I envisaged Part II of my book as corresponding, in a sense, to chapters 2—5 of *The First Urban Christians*, trying to map the worldview, not least the symbols, narratives and praxis, which Paul was inculcating. I envisaged Part III as corresponding to Meeks's chapter 6, showing particularly how the 'patterns of belief' we find in Paul's letters sustained the kind of community, and the kind of worldview, we had discerned earlier on. Sharp eyes might have picked up that I began Part III with Paul's reworked monotheism, just as Meeks did in his sixth chapter. Again, there was good reason. Looking back on the last generation of Anglophone Pauline scholarship, there remain three great landmarks, Sanders, Martyn and Meeks; and the one I value most is Meeks.[2]

The First Urban Christians was the culmination of nearly two decades of publications, in all of which Meeks was addressing the same underlying question: how might we put together the social study of the actual communities of early Christians with the beliefs that their key documents were expounding? What kind of 'fit' was there between the fresh thinking of the early theologians and the fresh patterns of corporate *koinōnia*? What could we say about the kind of communities we see reflected in Paul's letters? How must they have appeared to outsiders, and what did the insiders themselves think they were doing?[3] Well-known markers along this road include Meeks's famous study of Johannine Christology through the lens of a reconstructed 'Johannine sectarianism', and the detailed study of early Christianity in Antioch.[4] Meeks, like many whom we studied in the previous chapter, was thoroughly dissatisfied with the quest for true propositions on the one hand and existentialist self-understanding on the other (rationalism

[2] For completeness' sake, I might add that Part I of *PFG* corresponds broadly to chapter 1 of *TFUC*: that is, it surveys the actual historical world, Jewish, Greek and Roman, which made up Paul's overall context. Part IV of *PFG* goes beyond Meeks's project, to ask how the worldview of Part II and the theology of Part III were seen by Paul as impacting on the world of Part I.

[3] See Meeks's own summary (2009, 134) of his seven-year approach to *TFUC*.

[4] See Meeks 1972; Meeks and Wilken 1978. For fuller bibliography see e.g. Meeks, Hilton and Snyder 2002, 276; Still and Horrell 2009, 156.

in one direction, whether conservative or radical; Bultmann in the other).[5] He saw with increasing clarity that when people had spoken of 'historical', or 'historical-critical', study of the New Testament, they had often meant the history of early Christian *ideas* as discerned on a hypothetical map of *religious* history, a map moreover which was divided into two continents, 'Judaism' and 'Hellenism', with a significant ocean between them. This was not 'history' in the sense that most historians understood it – the history, that is, of actual communities, with their characteristic ways of life, their social and cultural mores and morals, their challenges and hopes. Meeks determined to plunge into that denser world. Even though, as he now says, his early hopes for what he might find have not been fulfilled, the journey appears to have been more than worthwhile. I think he would agree.

Meeks determined early on, and has continued to insist on this point, that social history is not a matter of discovering large abstractions and imposing them on the material. He has thus, notoriously, been *persona non grata* with the 'Context Group', even though there might be some who would look from a distance, perhaps from the perspective of an ahistorical pietism, and imagine them to have much in common. Meeks describes, and responds to, the criticisms he has had from the Context Group in his Preface to the second edition of his great work:

> Several of my critics have taken me to task for my amateurishness as a social scientist – meaning that I refused to adopt a particular theoretical perspective and grind all the data through its mill. It is interesting that those who made this argument most severely were themselves amateurs in social science, for they, like myself, were biblical scholars; the sociologists and anthropologists who happened upon my work seem to have found my eclecticism quite normal.

One might comment that the sharp division here apparent bears at least an analogy to different ways of doing theology itself. If I can risk a broad generalization after long years of ecumenical debates and discussions, there are many in various traditions for whom the church's traditions have told us both what to think and what language to use in expressing those thoughts, so that the New Testament must be read as an early, and perhaps not yet fully formed, statement of things which were more completely articulated much later. This sits awkwardly, however, with the perspective of the protestant Reformers. They understood their task in terms of seeing scripture itself, in all its apparently messy and unsystematic detail, as the primary, normative witness to Jesus, requiring one to assess all later traditions, including the ones they intended to affirm, in that light. The approach of Wayne Meeks has a robust, almost Luther-like quality to it, rejecting a top-down approach in which one might find the 'single rubric', the 'one key that will make everything fall into place':

[5] See Meeks's 'Afterword' in Meeks, Hilton and Snyder 2002, 259, speaking of a 'cognitivist conception of religion' on the one hand and 'its existentialist antitype' on the other.

> There is no such key. Not the patron-client relation, not the honor-shame society, not status inconsistency, routinization of charisma, the dyadic personality, rational choice in a premarket economy, or group-grid dynamics. The constructs represented by some or even all of these metonyms and others like them may indeed help us to look from a new angle at some of the evidence at hand, or to discover evidence that we didn't know was there. They remain, nevertheless, abstractions that can never substitute for deep and long-term immersion in the scattered and enigmatic traces left by the people of the first century ... Putting the story together is finally more art than science – and the scientists I know are quick to acknowledge that there is much art in their science.[6]

As the last sentence indicates, this is more than a rejection of a certain kind of social-scientific absolutism. It is a denial of the false either/or, the great divide between 'arts' and 'science', on which a great deal of modern western life has been based. As such, Meeks's work deserves attention, not only for what it tells us about Paul, his communities, and the social and theological patterns of early Christianity, but for the marker it puts down on the map of our own larger cultural problems. Perhaps this is part of what Meeks meant when he wrote about how our understanding of the ancient world might lead to fresh communal patterns in our own.[7]

This is the perhaps surprising answer to the regular question about reductionism, usually raised by anxious traditionalists afraid of seeing their favourite theological or religious beliefs disappearing up their own sociocultural identity. Was 'justification' *really* only about the sectarian nature of Paul's communities? Might 'Christology' *only* be a reflection of the need to keep a disparate group united? Meeks has spent his career opposing all ideologies, not only the overtly theological ones in which the early Christians were treated as 'souls with ears' but also the philosophical or sociological ones which would force the historical material into inappropriate ideological patterns.[8] Like several of the scholars we studied in the previous chapter, Meeks is resolutely opposed to any 'reducing' of the New Testament's theological and religious statements either to sociology or to ideology. How this works out emerges in the final chapter of *The First Urban Christians*; what interests Meeks is not reduction but correlation.[9]

As Meeks himself has seen, *The First Urban Christians* has come to be regarded as a 'place marker' in New Testament scholarship.[10] It does not, however, stand alone. In two subsequent studies Meeks further developed

[6] Meeks 2003 [1983], xii. See the discussion of this point in Horrell 2009, 11–17.

[7] See above, 242.

[8] See e.g. Meeks 1983, 223 n. 41, anticipating Meeks's 2001 article in repudiating the long tradition of F. C. Baur which reappears in H. D. Betz and G. Lüdemann: 'I find their assumption of a single, unified, Jewish Christian, anti-Pauline movement in the first century an unnecessary inference from the sources, and not the most economical way of accounting for what little evidence we have. Moreover, German scholarship's picture of the controversies has been, I believe, too exclusively ideological. The social implications of continuing or abandoning Jewish ritual practices must have been at least as important ... as theological and christological beliefs.' Nor is this itself reductionist: 'For Paul, of course, the pragmatic factors were inseparable from theology and christology,' referring also to Dahl 1977, 95–120. See too Meeks 1983, 33: 'The conventional categories [sc. for analysing the Jewish world of the first century] suffer from vagueness, anachronism, and inappropriate definition.'

[9] Meeks 1983, 2–7, 190–2.

[10] Meeks 2003 [1983], x.

his investigation into what he called the 'moral world' of the first Christians. He distinguished this from 'ethics' as often discussed; what he was studying was not simply a list of rules in particular areas, but rather the generation and maintenance of something larger, a new worldview within which the positive things people did were the expressions and outworkings of a 'world' into which they had come and whose contours they were trying to follow.[11] There is no space here to discuss these in detail, though properly they are all part of the same project. I will content myself with a brief discussion of Meeks's main points in his major book, drawing in particular on the studies that were published in 2009 to celebrate its twenty-fifth anniversary.

Meeks begins the main argument of *The First Urban Christians* with a substantial chapter on 'The Urban Environment of Pauline Christianity'. Actually, though that is the title, the chapter ranges more broadly. It places the ancient cities of Paul's world between the smaller rural and village environment on the one hand and the Roman empire itself on the other; it traces the remarkable mobility of people within that larger world; it examines the place of women; and then, in perhaps the most interesting section, it studies 'connections', that is, the way in which people met together, congregated, and established links in that world. That leads to a careful study of the Jewish world within the Diaspora, and finally to specific accounts of the different cities where Paul spent time and established churches.

There is, of course, much more to be said. Meeks was summarizing in less than fifty pages, admittedly with substantial end-notes, a sprawling range of material on the social environment of a large, lively and culturally diverse geographical area. Every aspect of this work could be expanded a hundredfold. Mostly, however, Meeks's summaries seem fair and shrewd, though sometimes he fails to carry through his own critique of older scholarly traditions.[12] In particular, his account of the world in which Paul could arrive in a strange city and quickly find people with whom he could associate is important in helping us imagine the first evangelistic moves:

> When a stranger arrived in a city ... it is taken for granted that he knew, or could easily learn, where to find immigrants and temporary residents from his own country or *ethnos* and practitioners of his own trade ... These were the two most important factors in the formation and identification of neighborhoods.[13]

In a world where, as Meeks points out, 'privacy was rare', news would travel fast about any new, strange or fascinating arrival:

> A peddler of copper pans or magic amulets, of horoscopes or a revelation, could count on the word's getting around – once he had made his initial contacts.[14]

[11] Meeks 1986b, 1993.

[12] As e.g. his persistence with the 'north Galatian' hypothesis, despite noting its problems (42f.; though cf. the open-minded note at 49); elsewhere, as we have seen, he is critical of the ideologies which lay behind this view. (For the strong 'south Galatia' argument see e.g. Mitchell 1993b, 3f.)

[13] Meeks 1983, 29.

[14] Meeks 1983, 29.

These initial contacts would lead the newcomer into an expanding network of households, and thence into the world of 'associations' or 'clubs', a varied and disparate network of special-interest groups.

Meeks expresses regret that one cannot be more specific about the details of the cities where Paul worked. That deficiency can be made good, to some extent at least and with due caution, by exploring the one place which has been remarkably preserved for posterity: Pompeii. This is the argument of Peter Oakes, both in an essay discussing Meeks's work and in an entire book using a parallel line of thought to investigate Romans.[15] Oakes has been a member of the 'Context Group', but his work is a sign that the earlier sharp dividing line between their methods and those of Meeks and others is breaking down; his own eclectic and creative social description, as evidenced in his earlier book on Philippians, fits well within the project Meeks was undertaking.[16] His one major new point, which I am sure Meeks would be happy to take on board, is that in recent years much more has been made of the social significance of 'space' – that is, the urban space occupied by dwellings of different sizes, and the domestic space within the households. We can learn a lot from these, not least in the areas of power and honour.[17]

Having set out the broad context, Meeks addresses one of the central questions for any social analysis of Paul's churches: the question of *social level*. Following Judge and others, he confirms that the older consensus as stated by Deissmann was unsafe: Paul's churches were not after all composed almost entirely of the very poor, but 'reflected a fair cross-section of urban society'.[18] Stratification is difficult in ancient history, and one must approach it from different angles, of which the most obvious, though also one of the most potentially misleading, is the study of names. (The reason this is 'potentially misleading' is because Paul might well be naming church leaders who might not be socially representative.) Meeks follows Theissen, but takes issue with him for apparent oversimplification: social status should be understood, not as a single dimension but as 'the resultant of several different dimensions'.[19] Many members of the Corinthian church, for example, may well have been 'status-inconsistent': that is,

> They may enjoy a high rank in some dimensions, such as wealth, identification with the Latin element in the colony, support by dependents and clients, and in one or two cases perhaps also civic office, but they may be ranked lower in others, such as origin, occupation, or sex.

It will not do, then, simply to propose (as Theissen did) that the 'strong' in Corinth corresponded to the high-status, wealthy members. Things were probably more complicated.[20] Paul himself had 'status inconsistency': when

[15] See Oakes 2009a; 2009b.

[16] On Philippians see Oakes 2001.

[17] Oakes 2009a, 35.

[18] Meeks 1983, 73.

[19] Meeks 1983, 70.

[20] Meeks 1983, 70.

measured on some social scales, he was virtually part of the elite, but on others, he was near the bottom. Meeks raises the question as to whether there was something about early Christianity which was particularly attractive to people of this type, or whether conversely people of this type ('people with the sorts of drive, abilities, and opportunities that produced such mixed status') might simply stand out in the crowd, and so be noticed in written documents which survive. Both may be partly true. Meeks wisely holds back from any instant attempt at 'explanation' as opposed to description, but as his book proceeds a positive answer seems to be emerging.[21]

In the twenty-five-year review volume, the chapter on socio-economic profiling is written by Bruce Longenecker.[22] He suggests that the antithesis between Deissmann's position and the 'new consensus' may itself be inaccurate, since in fact there may have been – and Meeks allowed that there might have been – more Messiah-believers at the very poor end of the scale than appears from the written evidence. Longenecker discusses in particular the important work of Justin Meggitt, who argues that almost all Pauline Christians were among the very poor, and Steven Friesen, who has proposed more complicated stratifications through which a diverse picture, indicating a high proportion of the relatively poor, seems to emerge.[23] Paul appears to assume that his audience consists mainly of people just above subsistence level, working at basic but stable occupations.[24] Longenecker argues against the assumption that people joined the church because of their socio-economic situation, though for the poorer members of society that might none the less have been a factor. The Christian groups seem to have been at a different level from the more well-to-do members of the *collegia*, the associations of which we know in other contexts. We can rule out any suggestion that joining the church was considered a step up the scale of 'honour'. If anything it worked the other way.[25] Longenecker notes that Meeks's project does not in fact stop with *The First Urban Christians*, but continues into his further studies of the 'moral world' of the first Christians – precisely because that 'moral world' was concerned not simply with rules for personal behaviour but with the 'social practices' (such as aid for the poor and sick) by which the Christian groups were marked out from other groups with which they might otherwise be compared.[26]

So far Meeks has offered careful social analysis which, while it may affect the exegesis and understanding of Paul's letters in various ways, is perhaps not earth-shattering. With his third chapter, however, we come to a topic which has ramifications of all sorts. What sort of 'group' did the early Christians comprise? How would they have been seen in a world of many such

[21] Meeks 1983, 73; and see below, 279f.

[22] Longenecker 2009.

[23] See Meggitt 1998; Friesen 2004. Meggitt's work precipitated a discussion in the *Journal for the Study of the New Testament* 24, for 2001.

[24] Longenecker 2009, 51.

[25] Longenecker 2009, 54f.

[26] Meeks 1986b, 1993; cf. Longenecker 2009, 58f.

'groups', and how did they see themselves? Right away Meeks points out that in one respect these groups were 'peculiar' within their environment:

> the intimate, close-knit life of the local groups was seen to be simultaneously part of a much larger, indeed ultimately worldwide, movement or entity.[27]

There were not many social entities in the wider world that might have prepared people for such a phenomenon, and investigating the two-sidedness of the Christian 'groups', their local and translocal identities, may tell us quite a lot about what they thought they were.

As Judge had seen, there were various models available in the wider environment. The 'household' was basic; the 'voluntary association' was common. Both show considerable parallels with the Christian groups; both also reveal considerable divergencies, of which the translocal character of the group was again an obvious one. Likewise, the Christian groups saw themselves as 'exclusive and totalistic in a way that no club nor even any pagan cultic association was'. Pauline converts underwent an 'extraordinarily thoroughgoing resocialization', for which, according to Meeks, 'the only convincing parallel in antiquity was conversion to Judaism'.[28] If, however, the Christian groups were in one sense 'exclusive', they were in another sense 'much more inclusive in terms of social stratification and other social categories' than the clubs or associations would have been. Nobody else in Paul's world was attempting to found new communities in which social status counted for nothing. The parallel with conversion to Judaism is significant in another way: the word *ekklēsia*, though it has non-Jewish echoes as well, seems to have been used by the Christians in such a way as to evoke the Septuagint translation of *qehal* YHWH, the 'assembly of the Lord'. This points once again to the parallels with the Jewish communities, which were simultaneously closed cultic communities and members of a larger transnational entity.[29]

Meeks then discusses Judge's proposal for seeing the early Christian groups as a kind of philosophical school, and concludes that though this proposal makes important points it 'rejects far too quickly the cultic association as an analogy to the Pauline groups'. This points on to the claim, striking within a sociological work whose nature is to look for parallels and analogies in the larger social world, that the Pauline communities thought of themselves, and were seen by others, as a new kind of social reality. Granted, all social organizations that continue over time are likely to develop unique elements. But the culture of the early Christian groups we glimpse in Paul's letters was characterized, in a way that no other groups were, by three things in particular: a set of beliefs, a new moral world, and certain specific rituals. (We recall, once again, the way that 'worldview' functions: it holds together symbol, narrative, ethos, ritual and so on.) The

[27] Meeks 1983, 73.

[28] Meeks 1983, 78. Meeks allows that the Pythagoreans and Epicureans may offer partial parallels.

[29] Meeks 1983, 80.

Pauline Christians used 'the language of belonging', of fictive kinship, of the 'body of Christ', a Stoic commonplace now used 'with a concrete allusion to the human body of Jesus, crucified and raised from the dead.'[30] The metaphor could even be connected with 'a myth of cosmic restoration'.[31]

All of this makes the Pauline communities stand out in ways that the earlier 'history of religions' had not bargained for:

> A century of study by historians of religions has demonstrated that there is hardly a belief attested in the New Testament for which some parallel cannot be found somewhere in its environment or antecedents. But on balance these studies have also shown that these parallels, though often immensely illuminating, rarely explain the meaning and function of the given beliefs in their Christian contexts.

This is because, again despite older views which guessed that the development of Christian beliefs was quite a slow process,

> The first few decades after the death of Jesus were apparently a time of extraordinarily rapid emergence of new combinations of symbols and beliefs among Jesus' followers and early posthumous converts; these quickly gave to the Christian movement a character different from that of any other Jewish sect of the time.[32]

This conclusion has recently been challenged, as we shall see in due course.

Meeks then, in an important passage, describes briefly what he will spell out more fully in chapter 6: the network of belief and ethos in which that difference was expressed. This was a community in one way so very Jewish, and yet in other ways not. It was characterized by its own brand of Jewish-style monotheism, supporting a 'code of strict sexual morality' but without 'the ritual markers that protected the identity of the Jews in pagan cities'.[33] Everything was focused on the special revelation which Paul and his followers believed they had received: the secret of 'Jesus' death as God's messiah and his resurrection'. 'Those who shared this belief', writes Meeks, 'shared a religious symbol of enormous generative power.'[34] That may perhaps seem

[30] Meeks 1983, 89. Meeks suggests that the 'body' image was 'readily adapted by Jewish writers to speak of Israel', but the reference he gives (to Conzelmann 1975 [1969], 211) offers only non-Jewish parallels, and though Strack-Billerbeck (3.446–8) provide some rabbinic parallels I do not think the supposed Jewish adaptation is as clear as Meeks suggests.

[31] Meeks 1983, 90, citing Col. 1.15–20; 2.10; and Eph. 1.22 etc. Meeks regards Col. and Eph. as non-Pauline, but does not note that the theme of cosmic restoration, modelled on and enabled by the spirit's outworking of Jesus' resurrection, is the major topic of Rom. 8 as well.

[32] Meeks 1983, 91, citing Hengel's 1972 essay, 'Christology and New Testament Chronology', now printed in Hengel 1983, ch. 2.

[33] Meeks 1983, 91f. Once again we hear strong echoes of the new perspective, but without any cross-referencing. At 101 Meeks draws attention, significantly, to the fact that when Paul is discussing sexual relations between spouses he never mentions procreation.

[34] Meeks 1983, 92f. Meeks, against the run of scholarship at the time, consistently translates *Christos* as 'Messiah', seeing that from the sociological point of view it was the Messiahship of the crucified Jesus which gave the movement its distinctive shape. Meeks is however misleading to say that 'the everyday meaning of the word [*Christos*] was "ointment"' (94). In pre-Christian Greek, including the LXX, *christos* is an adjective, meaning 'anointed', or, when used in relation to medicinal oil, 'to be rubbed on', as opposed to a liquid to be poured on, which would be *pistos*. And it is hardly 'everyday', as the shortage of references in LSJ 2007 bears witness. See recently the helpful discussion in Novenson 2012, 48–53.

to be stating the obvious. Sometimes the obvious needs saying in case people overlook it.

Meeks then explores the language by which the Pauline Christians differentiated themselves from the wider world, including those Jews who did not believe in Jesus. This sense of separation was reinforced, as the identity of sects often is, by persecution and suffering.

In these ways and others, concludes Meeks, Paul and his colleagues were engaged in 'the business of creating a new social reality':

> They held and elaborated a distinctive set of beliefs, some of them expressed in dramatic claims that proved pregnant with metaphor: 'Jesus the Messiah, and him crucified.' They developed norms and patterns of moral admonition and social control that, however many commonplaces from the moral discourse of the larger culture they might contain, still in ensemble constituted a distinctive ethos. They received, practiced, and explicated distinctive ritual actions ... The resultant ... was an evolving definition of a new, visibly different subculture.[35]

It was not, however, the kind of subculture that shut itself away, maintaining its 'difference' by a strict detachment from the wider world. The 'sectarian unity' was portrayed 'with images of universal import', and the Pauline Christians thought of themselves as part not only of a local *ekklēsia* but a worldwide one, an idea which can only have come from the movement's Jewish roots.[36] Paul's travels, the letters themselves, the movements of his co-workers, and his various financial plans and arrangements, all bear witness to this.

Chapter 3 of *The First Urban Christians* thus stands at the centre of Meeks's book, arguing (in line with Edwin Judge's earlier proposals) for the substantially distinctive social nature of the Pauline churches. My only comment at this stage is to suggest that the concept of a local, tight-knit group which nevertheless saw itself as part of a larger body, perhaps a worldwide one, is indeed parallel to the synagogue communities, but it is also parallel, in a loose way at least, to two features of the Roman imperial world: the civil service and the army. In both cases local units were bound together in a common life and task, but also owing allegiance to the emperor and his worldwide rule. How much Paul or his churches were conscious of this parallel it is hard to say. Sometimes his 'imperial' language about Jesus and his followers may point in that direction, though this remains controversial. When he refers to colleagues as 'fellow-soldiers' there may perhaps be an allusion to the translocal social reality of the army.[37] Meeks is clearly right to highlight the things which made the early Christians distinctive, not least their combination of local and global identity. But, like some other 'Jewish' elements, this may simply highlight the way in which the new movement was more subversive even than its adherents realized at the time.

[35] Meeks 1983, 104f. (the word 'resultant' is here a noun with scientific overtones). This is precisely the point I was making in *PFG* ch. 1 ('A World of Difference') through an exegesis of Philemon.

[36] Meeks 1983, 108.

[37] e.g. Phil. 2.25; Phm. 2. I owe this point to Dr J. P. Davies.

This third chapter of *The First Urban Christians* is discussed by Edward Adams in the volume edited by Todd Still and David Horrell.[38] Adams draws attention to many studies that have attempted since 1983 either to resist or to strengthen the idea of a sharp difference between the Pauline churches and other contemporary social phenomena. On the one hand, writers like John Kloppenborg have drawn attention to characteristics of other social groups which may offer closer parallels than Meeks had allowed, though Adams pushes back against this, arguing that the evidence is slimmer than Kloppenborg and others have suggested.[39] On the other hand, Richard Horsley has urged that the Pauline communities saw themselves, and would have been seen by others, as in some sense an alternative society to the dominant Roman empire and its structures.[40] Adams also chronicles the ongoing debates about the social standing and relative wealth or poverty of Paul's churches, a debate which interlocks with other discussions about the possibility that some of the larger homes excavated in Corinth and other relevant cities might have been the kind of place where the church would have gathered. Further work has also been done on the question of the possible parallels, advocated by Edwin Judge, between the Pauline communities and the philosophical schools, not least a notable essay by Loveday Alexander on the evidence provided by the second-century doctor Galen.[41]

In addition to these points, Adams draws attention to the recent work in which distinctions need to be drawn, on the basis of archaeological and other evidence, between different cities such as Corinth, Thessalonica and Philippi. We cannot assume that the social profile, or self-understanding, of a Pauline community would be the same wherever such communities existed. Adams concludes by reaffirming Meeks's own summary of the ways in which these communities were both similar to, and different from, other communities in their social settings. The *ekklēsia*, writes Meeks:

> was all the old things that observers in the first century might have seen in it: a Jewish sect, a club meeting in a household, an initiatory cult, a school. Yet it was more than the sum of those things, and different from the mere synthesis of their contradictory tendencies.[42]

The fourth chapter of Meeks's classic book deals with what he calls 'governance'. Like any group that persists over time, the Pauline communities needed organization, structure and leadership, and Paul's letters offer a wide array of evidence on all this, as well as constituting in themselves a significant part of the evidence for Paul's own understanding of his regularly

[38] Adams 2009.

[39] Adams 68–71, discussing e.g. Kloppenborg and Wilson 1996; Ascough 2003. See too Harland 2009. Against Ascough's proposal that Paul's churches were not after all concerned for other similar groups elsewhere, see Still 2009, 80f.

[40] See e.g. Horsley 2004, 2005 (summarized by Adams 74–6).

[41] See Adams 73–4, discussing Alexander 1994 and others.

[42] Meeks 1986b, 120.

contested 'authority'.[43] Here a great deal of work has been done over the last generation, with Meeks once more showing the way.[44]

I find this chapter, however, the least convincing in the book, not in what it says but in what it leaves out. Meeks catalogues the 'warrants' which Paul gives for his authority: his authoritative position; the divine revelation he had received; scripture, interpreted christologically and eschatologically; Christian tradition and Pauline custom; the guiding and prompting of the spirit; and the paradigm of Jesus himself, in his crucifixion and resurrection. Meeks adds what for him are most important: the authority of the spirit in the communities on the one hand, and the model of Paul's own biography on the other hand, particularly in his giving up of rights, as in 1 Corinthians 9 or Philippians 3. Meeks highlights the fact that, when Paul indicates that certain types of behaviour are acceptable and others not, this is a matter, not of isolated rules, but (once again) of a larger worldview: 'the kinds of behavior recommended are thus joined with a set of sacred symbols and an historical ethos unique to the Christians.'[45] In all this Meeks is right to note that, though Paul can and does give specific instructions as to how Christians should conduct themselves, more often than not this is couched in very general terms.[46]

All this is fine so far as it goes. Why then do I find it less than fully convincing? Because though Meeks does indeed note the christological and eschatological interpretation of scripture, I do not think he gives sufficient weight to the theme which, as I have argued elsewhere, drills down below this. Scripture, for Paul, is not merely a miscellaneous, ahistorical source of guidance. It is the earlier, and in some ways determinative, stage of the narrative in which Paul believes that he and his communities are still living. This narrative has indeed been broken in the Messiah's crucifixion; but it continues in its new cross-shaped form, and when Paul appeals (for instance) to the exodus story in 1 Corinthians 10.1–13 he does so not simply to pick out an example from long ago but in order to stress that the erstwhile pagan converts in Corinth are part of the same, single family that was once rescued from Egypt. In a later article Meeks sees exactly this point about the single larger narrative. But I do not think he has worked through its implications for the self-understanding of the Pauline communities in general or for Paul's understanding of his own authority in particular.[47] Arguably, Paul saw himself as spearheading the scripturally rooted and messianically focused new movement of God. Through this movement, the

[43] Meeks 1983, 115: 1 Thess. shows how Paul 'fashioned the letter into an instrument for extending through time and space his instruction of converts.'

[44] Earlier important studies include Schütz 1975; Holmberg 1978.

[45] Meeks 1983, 136.

[46] Meeks 1983, 136–9.

[47] See Meeks, Hilton and Snyder 2002, 191f. [orig. 1986], speaking of 'that narrative which subsequently would form and vivify and correct the church' and asking, 'Or had the idea of that story, the plot itself, already taken shape in the rituals, preaching, moral exhortation, storytelling, prophesying, and midrash practiced by the early Christians?' Meeks is talking here about the development of the canon of scripture as a whole, but the point relates just as clearly to Paul himself.

long-awaited and paradoxical victory over all the forces of evil would have its effect in the calling of a worldwide family to join in the worship offered by the ancient people of God. All Meeks says about authority is fair enough. But it needs to be rooted in this sense of narrative, and of Paul's place within that narrative, for its full effect to be felt.[48]

This goes some way to counter the effect of the protest which, as Todd Still points out in his article discussing Meeks's fourth chapter, has now been launched from many quarters. Paul has been accused of blatant and power-hungry manipulation, of using all kinds of rhetorical tricks to fool his converts into doing what he wanted. Second Corinthians indicates that this kind of charge was levelled at him in his own day as well.[49] A much more nuanced view of the same material can be offered.[50] Meeks himself has provided a brief common-sense response to the whole question:

> One person's persuasion, of course, is another's manipulation, but I would have supposed that the principal purpose of ancient deliberative rhetoric was precisely to persuade people to feel, think, or do something toward which they were otherwise not inclined.[51]

There is no doubt more to be said, and several studies of particular churches and Paul's relationships with them have developed fresh angles of vision.[52] But at the heart of it all is a redefinition of 'power', and hence of that fuzzy modern word 'leadership'. The second letter to the Corinthians, whose very style indicates how painful it was for Paul to have to affirm his authority in the face of hostility and rivalry, says it all. If even God's own power is clothed in the weakness of the Messiah's cross, then that same pattern must be worked out in the status and authority of the apostle:

> So I'm delighted when I'm weak, insulted, in difficulties, persecuted and facing disaster, for the Messiah's sake. When I'm weak, you see, then I am strong.[53]

Meeks's fifth chapter completes his basic worldview-model. Like all communities, the groups founded by Paul engaged in certain practices which in the language of the anthropologists can properly be called 'ritual'. Here the argument is pushing on an open door, in that, behind the various theories of the sociologists, a common core of understanding coheres with a major strand within later Christian thinking. Ritual does not simply convey information, it *does something*.[54] Meeks describes the various practices reflected in Paul's letters, the meetings, singing, instruction, prayer, acclamation of Jesus, and so on, focusing eventually on the central ecclesial practices of

[48] See e.g. Rom. 10.14–21; 15.7–13.

[49] See Still 2009, 88f.: the line of critique in modern times includes Friedrich Nietzsche and George Bernard Shaw, coming up more recently to a different Shaw (1983) and others such as Castelli 1991, Moore 1994 and Marchal 2006, 2008, 2012.

[50] See e.g. Ehrensperger 2007.

[51] Meeks 2009, 143.

[52] See the sequence of books by Andrew Clarke: Clarke 1993, 2000, 2008.

[53] 2 Cor. 12.10.

[54] Meeks 1983, 141f. following a discussion of Emile Durkheim and Mary Douglas.

baptism and the Lord's Supper. Even the comparatively limited information we have about these actions in the first century speaks volumes about the fact that the communities understood themselves to be rooted in the strange fact of the crucified and risen Messiah. Jesus had inaugurated a whole new 'world'; these practices were the symbolic actions through which one entered, or was sustained within, that new reality.[55]

Here, confusingly, two things have to be said simultaneously. First, this new 'world' did indeed constitute, for Paul and his converts, a 'sacred world of unity', so that the symbolism of the Lord's Supper strengthened the 'internal coherence, unity and equality' of the Christian group, protecting its boundaries in relation to other cultic associations (in other words pagan temples). Second, this new world nevertheless confusingly overlapped with the ongoing present one, so that what might appear from one point of view as a 'sect', over against the world, could be seen from another as a reform movement challenging the wider world itself.[56] The acclamation 'Jesus is Lord' meant nothing less.[57]

In her essay on Meeks's fifth chapter, Louise Lawrence shows that Meeks's basic insight here was correct, though it can be expanded into areas quite other than those he had indicated.[58] 'Ritual', the subject of the chapter, is seen today no longer as merely reflecting a previously defined narrative, but rather as an action which is 'politically-charged, dynamic, and transformative', relating to the wider dynamics of social power.[59] Lawrence notes the points at which Meeks has been criticized here. Some have accused him of downplaying the lesser rituals. Others have proposed sharper categories, for instance a distinction between 'rituals', meaning irregular or unpredictable events involving 'status reversal or transformation', and 'ceremonies', meaning regular and predictable events which confirm existing status. Clearly baptism would exemplify the first of these, and the Lord's Supper the second.[60] Lawrence then proceeds to discuss the ways in which the study of 'ritual' (in Meeks's broader sense) has developed into new areas. First, it is a key element (as in my own work) in the 'thick description' of the biblical world, recognizing that we approach this world of action and event almost exclusively through the literary world of texts. Second, the link which Meeks already saw between ritual and the 'moral world' has been explored further, not least by David Horrell whose work I shall discuss in the second half of the present chapter.

Third, in line with the comments of Richard Horsley mentioned a moment ago, a more explicit link has been drawn between ritual and empire (or, in this case, ritual and the implicit subversion of empire). While it may

[55] Meeks 1983, 150–7 (baptism: 156, 'the integration of the baptized into another world'); 157–62 (Lord's Supper).

[56] Meeks 1983, 160.

[57] Though Meeks 1983, 152, 155 translates *kyrios Iēsous* as 'the Lord is Jesus!'.

[58] Lawrence 2009.

[59] Lawrence 99.

[60] Lawrence 104, discussing the contribution of Neyrey 1990.

indeed be stretching the point to see the ritual of baptism as a 'symbolic inversion' of the Roman imperial pride in 'water management', a case can be made, in line with several important studies, for seeing the larger world of Pauline ritual as marking out a community which gave allegiance to Jesus rather than to Caesar.[61] This is part of the emphasis of Dale Martin's ground-breaking book, which ideally should receive fuller treatment than is possible here: 'the Body of Christ ritually and symbolically constituted an alternative to the politics of Rome.' Ritual constituted a set of 'nonaggressive ripostes' through which the community declared that the emperor did not, after all, control either the human or the natural world.[62]

Finally, early Christian ritual was of supreme importance in addressing one of the great central topics of all human existence, namely life and death. 'Primary communal and formative knowledge', suggests Lawrence, 'is made known at that life/death frontier', so that by formalizing the frontier in ritual the early communities were paving a way into a new kind of knowledge, consonant with the new world of which Meeks had spoken.[63]

All this brings us at last to chapter 6 of *The First Urban Christians*, where Meeks explores the correlations between the social world of the early communities and their 'patterns of belief and patterns of life'. This kind of move has been resisted from both sides: from some sociologists, anxious lest social reality should disappear into an Idealist fog; from some theologians, similarly anxious about Materialist reductionism. Thus

> We will ask whether we can discover correlations between stated beliefs and social forms, but we will not assume that the one *causes* the other; nor shall we assume, when a given belief seems logically to imply a certain kind of behavior, that such behavior really followed, unless we have specific evidence for it.[64]

Meeks approaches this careful balance, of course, from the sociological side, resisting the temptation to write an actual outline of all Pauline theology:

> For the present we are interested in the social force of what the typical member of the Pauline churches believed.[65]

Meeks is well aware of how difficult this is to get at, but the attempt must be made, and the first move (as I have indicated earlier) is the most important. 'The affirmation that "God is one" is as basic to Pauline Christianity as it was to all Judaism.'[66] This is a specifically *Jewish* style of monotheism, significantly different from that espoused by the Stoics and (at least some of) the middle Platonists, and that is important precisely in its social effects. The monotheisms offered by the philosophers 'provided an ideology for the

[61] On 'imperial water management' see Purcell 2011 [1996], discussed by Lawrence 110.

[62] Lawrence 110, summarizing Martin 1995.

[63] Lawrence 115.

[64] Meeks 1983, 164.

[65] ibid.

[66] Meeks 1983, 163.

genial pluralism and tolerance in cultic life' which characterized the paganism of the imperial age, but the Jewish belief in 'one God', contrasted with the 'idols' of the nations, generated 'the distinctive practices that preserved their [i.e. the Jews'] communal integrity as a unique people.' And the point is this: 'Christianity took over the Jewish position completely.'[67]

This was revolutionary in the early 1980s. By making monotheism central and linking it to the social character of the early community, Meeks struck a note many have wanted to echo.[68] Before then, not many New Testament scholars gave much attention to the significance of monotheism; now, it is much more normal.[69] From his socially-aware study of monotheism, Meeks drew out several principles which, though stated only briefly, are in my view of great importance for the development of a fuller Pauline theology.

First, 'the desired social expression of faith in the one God is the exclusive unity of the worshipers'. There is an 'absolute boundary between the confession "the Lord is Jesus" and paganism.'[70] This leads Meeks directly to Ephesians and Colossians; even if pseudonymous, they reflect Paul's own social and theological dynamic. One God; one people of God. Here Paul's community was saying the same thing as the Jewish communities of his day.

Except, of course, that he was saying it about a different kind of community, one that was no longer defined by ethnicity and its markers, but by a very different set of boundary-indicators.[71] Here Meeks arrives, by a different route, at the same point as some of the post-Sanders arguments we studied in Part I. The community has been redefined around the Messiah:

> For Paul and his circle ... the unexpected, almost unthinkable claim that the Messiah had died a death cursed by the Law entailed a sharp break in terms of the way in which the people of God would henceforth be constituted and bounded.

Thus already, by the time Paul was writing his letters,

> the established pattern was ... to found in every city associations of believers in Christ, drawn from gentiles and Jews alike.[72]

And this new community, in abandoning the 'chief Jewish devices for distinguishing the covenanted people from the world of polytheism', was not doing so on the basis of an ideal of 'tolerance' or antinomianism. Their abandoning of those Jewish markers

[67] Meeks 1983, 163.

[68] See esp. *PFG* ch. 9.

[69] One of the few straws in the wind was the article of Nils Dahl, a senior colleague of Meeks's in Yale: Dahl 1977, ch. 10 (178–91).

[70] Meeks 1983, 166. Meeks sees that the same insistence on 'monotheism and unity' lies behind Gal. 3.19f., but not how to resolve the exegetical dilemma there, on which see Wright 1991 [*Climax*] ch. 8.

[71] How this works out in terms of the continuing ethnic origin of members is discussed in *PFG* ch. 15, e.g. 1426–34.

[72] Meeks 1983, 168.

> does not mean ... that they themselves did not also maintain strong boundaries to define themselves over against that world.[73]

Monotheism and election, redrawn around the Messiah: the central argument of my own recent work was sketched by Meeks thirty years earlier. It still meets enormous resistance, but it is hard to see anything wrong, historically or exegetically, with what Meeks was proposing.

This posed a problem for Paul which can be expressed in terms both of theology and of some kind of overarching narrative:

> For Paul himself, the central theological problem is not just to spell out the implications of monotheism, but to explain how the unified purpose of God through history could encompass the *novum* of a crucified Messiah.

Paul writes about all this in Romans, and the 'theological dialectic' of that letter 'cannot be separated from this social dimension of Paul's whole missionary career.'[74] The aim of this mission was not to found a small sect that would remain pure by staying well clear from the world. The church was to see itself as the spearhead of the project of new creation, the renewal of all things. Paul's missionary theology was about the creation of communities that were 'socially provisional and temporary', since the aim, remarkably enough, was universal:

> The thin network of tiny Christian cells represented itself in the audacious images of a restored, universal humanity, the creation of the only true God.[75]

All this forms part of Paul's vision of God's kingdom; though he does not often use the phrase 'the kingdom of God',

> The image of God as sovereign of the universe, enthroned in heaven, is taken for granted and extended by the depiction of Christ's exaltation to share in his reign.[76]

The six pages in which Meeks expounds all this, demonstrating at every point how it correlates with the preceding social description, are in my view the most important pages in the book, worth more as a whole and in their parts than much other recent writing about Paul.

The same cannot be said, in my view, for the section which follows, on 'Apocalyptic and the management of innovation'.[77] We do not need to repeat the detailed discussion of 'apocalyptic' from Part II of the present book. Suffice it to note that here Meeks follows the widely received opinion of the 1980s: that 'the earlier Christians really thought, as did Jewish apocalyptists, that the world was soon coming to an end.'[78] Meeks places

[73] Meeks 1983, 169.
[74] Meeks 1983, 168.
[75] Meeks 1983, 169.
[76] Meeks 1983, 170.
[77] Meeks 1983, 171–80.
[78] Meeks 1983, 171.

this within other debates, noting (for instance) that in many of the debates, particularly in Germany, there had been a stand-off between positions which called themselves 'anthropology' and 'cosmology', 'both of which the discussants use in peculiar senses.'[79] And, consonant with his whole purpose, he enquires as to how this 'apocalyptic' belief-system fits within the social dynamics of the early Christian movement. Here, like many others, he invokes the wider social phenomenon of 'millenarian movements', though as we saw most such movements have themselves been offshoots of Christianity or Judaism, and are thus not 'neutral' comparators. This points in the direction of a possible explanation for why people might join such a movement:

> people who have advanced or declined socially, who find themselves in an ambiguous relation to hierarchical structures, might be receptive to symbols of the world as itself out of joint and on the brink of radical transformation. They might be attracted to a group that undertook to model its life on that new picture of reality.[80]

This statement still holds even if, as I argued earlier, we take a different view of 'apocalyptic'. Meeks sees, in any case, that for Paul there is a sense (the strong point of Martyn's view) in which the 'apocalypse' has already occurred. Paul's thought was rooted in 'the present fulfillment of eschatological hopes', which does rather cut against the usually future-oriented view of millenarian groups.[81] Meeks also suggests that Paul's appeal to scripture in Galatians is part of an 'apocalyptic' mindset, which goes in exactly the opposite direction to Martyn: here, Meeks suggests that it is 'characteristic of apocalyptic' that one should insist that 'the radically new was already attested in scripture'.[82] As I have said elsewhere, I think there is much more going on in Galatians than has been seen by either Martyn or Meeks at this point, though it is certainly true, at the general level, that for Paul 'eschatological beliefs provided the warrants within a traditional context for sharply modified practice.'[83]

My sense throughout this section is that Meeks is being careful not to claim too much for 'apocalyptic' as a controlling or explaining category. Indeed, he warns against reading too much into it:

> when we extract from the letters the elements that we regard as apocalyptic, we are creating an abstraction. No one in the Pauline movement would have used the labels "apocalyptic" or "eschatological" to name aspects of their beliefs ... [T]he elements that we have singled out as apocalyptic in Paulinism work the way they do only because they are part of a larger, very intricate and flexible complex of beliefs. In that sense, we could as well say that all the other beliefs we are discussing in this chapter are, functionally, apocalyptic.[84]

[79] Meeks 1983, 172.
[80] Meeks 1983, 174.
[81] Meeks 1983, 176.
[82] Meeks 1983, 177.
[83] Meeks 1983, 177.
[84] Meeks 1983, 179f.

I agree with this entirely, with one exception: that for the closing word 'apocalyptic' one might as well substitute 'Jewish'. As we saw earlier, the idea of 'two ages', of the 'present age' and the 'age to come', and of the divine purposes in relation to both, is indeed part of a larger set of beliefs and also narratives: the narratives of God and creation, of God and Israel, and, in some cases, of God and a Messiah. These occur in many strands (not all) of Jewish thought. The material Meeks has studied in this section is just as comfortable, and indeed far more so, when thought of not as 'apocalyptic', in a now outdated sense, but as simply, if broadly, 'Jewish'.

The next (quite short) section on 'The Crucified Messiah' gives us the same sense of material making itself at home within a larger narrative.[85] Here Meeks rightly insists that 'the node around which Pauline beliefs crystallized was the crucifixion and resurrection of God's son, the Messiah', though I would want to add the spirit into the centre of that mix as well. For Paul, 'the belief in the crucified Messiah introduces a new and controlling paradigm of God's mode of action.'[86] That may seem obvious, but Meeks here is ruling out a view of the death of the Messiah simply as the solution to a problem. It is indeed that, for Paul, but it is much more. It is the lens through which God and God's action can be clearly seen. Meeks rightly recognizes that Paul uses the same lens to look at the church and its behaviour.

He then launches into a discussion of resurrection, showing well enough its relation to issues of power and weakness, as in chapter 4. But he does not, to my mind, really grasp the ways in which Paul's solidly Jewish account of resurrection had the remarkable social correlates which I have explored elsewhere.[87] We may agree that 'the spelling out of the meaning of even so central a belief as the resurrection of Christ was a dialectical process', which had its own social consequences. But I think this could be taken much further than Meeks did, at least in 1983.

One of the many significant features of this sixth chapter of *The First Urban Christians* is that it is only at this stage, after monotheism, 'apocalyptic', and the crucified Messiah, that Meeks turns to 'Evil and its reversal'. For many, of course, the question of how God deals with human sin, and thus rescues people for final salvation, is the centre of what they think of as 'Pauline theology', and it focuses quickly on the mechanism of what precisely Paul says about the achievement of Jesus' crucifixion. For Meeks the question presents itself differently: the task is to see how Paul refers to 'the presence or threat of evil', and to see also

> if there are any hints of the ways in which the beliefs about evil and its cure are related to social motivations, attitudes, and dispositions.[88]

[85] Meeks 1983, 180–3.

[86] Meeks 1983, 180.

[87] See *RSG* chs. 3, 4. Here as elsewhere Philo is the obvious exception to the broad rule.

[88] Meeks 1983, 184.

To address this, Meeks invokes four categories, of which the first two are the ones we so often see played off against one another. The first is 'bondage and liberation', in which, though one can make guesses at a link between human and non-human enslaving forces, this is not pursued in Paul's writings. The second sounds more traditional, though 'guilt and justification' is not quite the normal antithesis ('sin and justification'?). The third category is 'estrangement and reconciliation', highlighting the theme which Paul articulates in Romans 5.1–11 and 2 Corinthians 5.11—6.2. The fourth is 'deformity and transformation': humans are 'deformed' through weakness, sin and above all mortality, and 'salvation … is depicted as restoration of the lost image of the Creator'.[89]

On each point Meeks makes small suggestions for ways in which the antithesis in question might reflect a social situation. In the first case, one can suggest a link between 'cosmic' and human oppression or opposition, though Paul seldom says anything like this directly. In the second, Meeks notes that the language of justification is regularly linked with the coming together of Jew and gentile in the church.[90] The third follows from this, being also an expression of the reconciliation between Jew and gentile which Paul sought to achieve through his missionary career. The final category invokes images from organic life, and the dialectic of death and life is itself brought into the service of 'a point about social relations', namely that between himself and the Corinthians.[91] These are somewhat disappointing, both in their broad generalization and in their failure to do more than simply state the problem; but then Meeks was not promising a full Pauline theology anyway. At least he has pointed in a direction which many others have now followed: the linkage of what might broadly be called Paul's 'atonement' theology with actual social realia. And, to repeat a previous point, it is significant that Meeks has placed this brief summary of issues clearly awaiting further attention *within* the larger structure of (a) monotheism, (b) the redefinition of God's people around the Messiah, and (c) eschatology.

The section concludes with an even briefer discussion of 'context', suggesting that 'the scale of evil' in the Pauline correspondence is both smaller and broader than 'the political realm': personal immorality and weakness on the one hand, cosmic alienation and reconciliation on the other. One gets the decided impression that the real issues Meeks wanted to deal with in this chapter were monotheism, apocalyptic and the redefinition of both community and eschatology around the Messiah, and that questions of (what is broadly called) soteriology did not interest him so much, or perhaps did not offer so obvious a social correlation.

'Correlations', in fact, is the heading of the book's brief conclusion. Meeks summarizes his findings and then suggests ways in which people of

[89] Meeks 1983, 188.

[90] He also notes that the apparent exception, 2 Cor. 5.21, is only apparent, since the verse 'stands at the climax of Paul's apology for his missionary career'. Quite so: see *PFG* 879–85.

[91] Meeks 1983, 189.

certain social positions or in certain social contexts might have been attracted to Paul's message and communities. If the Pauline Christians were 'status-inconsistent', might that possibly be because people of that sort would be particularly attracted to 'the powerful symbols of change grounded in tradition, symbols of personal and communal transformation, symbols of an evil world encompassed by God's judgment and grace'?[92] For such people, perhaps,

> the intimacy of the Christian groups became a welcome refuge, the emotion-charged language of family and affection and the image of a caring, personal God powerful antidotes, while the master symbol of the crucified savior crystallized a believable picture of the way the world seemed really to work?[93]

Meeks grants that there are other sides to these coins, as well. Yet even with these caveats the tone of these suggestions seems to me to grate just a little with the even-handedness of the earlier analysis – and also with some fairly explicit Pauline statements, too, about the gospel being foolishness and scandalous to Greeks and Jews, and about the reason for people being drawn in to the community having to do more with a counter-intuitive belief in a well-known impossibility – the resurrection of Jesus – as a result of the power of the spirit working through the gospel announcement. Even granted that such things did not happen in a social vacuum, it still looks as though Meeks is attempting, right at the last minute, to offer some kind of sociological *explanation* for the response to Paul's message.

I suspect – and I suspect that Meeks suspects – that things were a lot more many-layered and multifaceted than this conclusion might suggest. He does say, after all, that 'the correlation between the social change of conversion and the symbolism of evil does not imply unidirectional causation', and that 'religions both respond to and create needs'.[94] Keeping this balance is hard in pastoral work in a church today. It presents huge difficulties when trying to understand a very different culture in a very different time. We can, however, agree heartily with Meeks's concluding paragraph. The radical transformation of the Mediterranean basin, and of Europe, which followed in the next few centuries began with a simple but enormous idea:

> Those odd little groups in a dozen or so cities of the Roman East were engaged, though they would not have put it quite this way, in constructing a new world.[95]

There is a sense in which, in terms of the Pauline scholarship of the late twentieth century, Wayne Meeks was doing so as well.

It fell to Dale B. Martin, one of Meeks's star pupils and now his successor at Yale, to write the twenty-five-year update on Meeks's sixth chapter.[96] He

[92] Meeks 1983, 191.
[93] Meeks 1983, 191.
[94] Meeks 1983, 184.
[95] Meeks 1983, 192.
[96] Martin 2009.

speaks appreciatively of Meeks's attempts at 'correlation', and describes the ways in which he himself has developed the idea, from his early work *Slavery as Salvation* through to more recent studies such as *Inventing Superstition*.[97] The latter work, though it covers a broader range than simply Paul's churches, argues that shifts in social structures

> *brought about* changes in the ways people viewed nature, changes in their symbolic universe, in their fundamental beliefs about themselves, the gods, demons, the body, and disease.[98]

Martin anticipated this in his earlier work *The Corinthian Body*. There he mapped the disagreements reflected in 1 Corinthians, not (as with Theissen) on to the supposed difference between 'elite' and 'popular' classes in terms of wealth and poverty, but on to the same 'elite' and 'popular' classes in terms of their notions about the body and disease:

> The higher status members ... were more likely to have been influenced by the philosophical and medical notions, whereas the lower status members ... and Paul himself assumed notions of the body and disease of the 'popular' type. These differences in social location and power correlated with differences in assumptions about the body, and those differences *caused the conflict* portrayed in the pages of 1 and 2 Corinthians.[99]

This is a bold attempt to go beyond what Meeks was doing, though it would be a bolder move yet to suggest that Martin's argument has advanced beyond the merely hypothetical.

Martin makes the point, to which I shall return, that with Meeks we have moved from 'history of religion' to something different. The 'religious' elements of what he is studying are nested within a wider social world, 'seeking "correlations" in parts of society that did not already look like "religion" to us.'[100] Meeks, he reminds us, was not tracing the genealogy of this or that practice, but searching for its setting and function in the life of the community, and for 'patterns' or 'systems' rather than isolated events or ideas.

Martin then moves on beyond his own work to consider the scholarship that has taken forward some of Meeks's proposals. I wish he had included in this the rather obvious topic of theology itself, which Meeks as we saw sketched only briefly and did not develop. Those who have seen themselves as Meeks's successors have not, it seems, been particularly interested in thinking through the implications of his theological proposals; and those who have worked on larger Pauline theological constructs have not usually troubled to do a social-scientific survey as part of the preliminary work. This is where I would submit my own recent book on Paul as crossing over the categories, though whether other members of Meeks's extended academic 'family' will recognize me as one of their own I sometimes doubt.[101]

[97] Martin 1990, 1995, 2004.

[98] Martin 2009, 121 (italics original).

[99] Martin 2009, 120, emphasis added.

[100] Martin 2009, 123.

[101] See *PFG* Parts II (social description) and III (theology).

Anyway, Martin surveys three areas which can properly be seen as following up some at least of Meeks's proposals. John Barclay suggested that, if we look at Corinth and Thessalonica side by side, it might appear that eschatology may have worked quite differently in the two different social situations.[102] David Horrell compared the situation in Corinth with that envisaged later in *1 Clement*, using Anthony Giddens's 'structuration theory' to map the changes in the mutually influential belief and 'ethos' of a community over time. He suggests that whereas in Paul's Corinthian correspondence Paul himself opposed the social hierarchies with the message of the cross, by the time of *1 Clement* things may have worked the other way round, with the social hierarchies being reinforced by the theology.[103] And Justin Meggitt, though stoutly opposing Meeks and the others in the 'new consensus' by his continued insistence that virtually all early Christians were seriously poor, follows Meeks in essaying a correlation between social status and theology, in this case between serious poverty on the one hand and the theological egalitarianism of Paul's corporate Christology on the other.[104]

Martin then offers a brief résumé of the work of the 'Context Group', pointing out that though they have been critical of Meeks they, too, have tried to sketch correlations between beliefs and practices. This leads him to a fuller discussion of 'Liberation Theology and Social Contexts', in which he focuses first on the work of Richard Horsley and his colleagues in their efforts to go beyond Meeks and discern an implicit critique of the Roman empire within Paul's theology, and then on some well-known feminist writers such as Elisabeth Schüssler Fiorenza and Antoinette Clark Wire.[105] This leads Martin to a conclusion in which he defends Meeks against the charges of reductionism and an over-optimism about the possibility of social reconstruction granted the textual base of our evidence. Nor, he points out, would it be valid to criticize Meeks or others for bringing to the texts modern categories that the actors in question would not have recognized. We all do that to a lesser or greater extent. Indeed, theologians are often worse at this than sociologists, assuming that Paul and his friends 'must have been' talking about the issues which come most readily to our minds when we hear the words they use.

I have deliberately focused on Meeks's major work, and on recent discussions both of it and of other work that has flowed from it. Those who know the field will see how sketchy this necessarily is, and how many other issues, and indeed important writers, have been left to one side. My excuse is partly personal and partly pragmatic. In personal terms, I read Meeks before I read either Geertz or Berger and Luckmann, and I ascribe my eager devouring of these writers, later on, to the way in which Meeks had raised my consciousness to the importance both of the social setting of Paul's communities and

[102] Barclay 1992, summarized by Martin 2009, 124f.

[103] Horrell 1996, discussed in Martin 2009, 125f.

[104] See Meggitt 1998, proposing a Pauline 'mutualism'; discussed in Martin 2009, 126f.

[105] Horsley 1997; 2000; Schüssler Fiorenza 1983; Wire 1990.

of the possible correlations we have been investigating. In pragmatic terms, I have preferred to sink one shaft comparatively deep into the scholarship rather than trying to provide a broader but necessarily shallower coverage. Since Meeks's work is by common consent one of the major landmarks in the Pauline scholarship of the last generation, and since (to revert to the personal) it has been a major model for my own work as well, the choice seems justified.

What then has Wayne Meeks done for Pauline interpretation? Two things in particular, I think. First, he has shifted the focus decisively from 'history of *religion*' to history, period – with a particular emphasis on social history, but on that as falling within the larger 'thick description' of the ancient Mediterranean world, and the particular cities in which Paul founded churches. The question of 'religion' is included within that, but Meeks, both in his 1983 work and in his important 2001 article, has stoutly challenged the ideological construct which had taken 'religion' as its overall subject and 'Judaism and Hellenism' as its particular binary opposition. The fact that many works continue to be written as if this revolution had not happened indicates well enough that the discipline still has much to learn from him. At the same time, he has insisted, against continuing opposition, that Paul's communities did indeed have some very distinctive features, and that some of those features have their closest analogies with features of the Diaspora Jewish communities. Once we get away from misleading *religionsgeschichtlich* assumptions of opposition between 'Judaism' and 'Hellenism', the real distinctives can stand out.

Second, Meeks has placed the study of *belief*, in this case the beliefs which Paul sought to inculcate in his communities, *within* the study of what I have called 'worldview', the large clump which includes symbol, myth, ritual and so on. He has demonstrated that, though one may indeed observe close correlations, this is not reductionist in either direction, unless of course the interpreter forces it to be so. He has repeatedly stressed Paul's urgent plea for the unity and holiness of the church, and indicated that the main correlate of this is a Jewish-style monotheism reworked around Jesus as the Messiah. Likewise, in line with Schweitzer and Wrede, and in parallel with the so-called new perspective (though without apparently noticing any of this), he has insisted that Paul's language about justification is closely correlated with the social reality of his Jew-plus-gentile communities, but he makes this point without lapsing into the sort of reductionism some have observed in Francis Watson's 1986 monograph or in the 'Context Group'. He has likewise demonstrated that some key elements of Paul's theology mean what they mean within a missionary impulse which was seeking, not to snatch people out of the world, but to generate a community which saw itself as the vanguard of an entirely new creation.

Meeks has thus insisted on studying Paul in terms of history, worldview, beliefs and mission. Since these are the four categories into which I myself have divided my major work on Paul, the reader will not be surprised (though some of Meeks's supporters may be) that I regard him as a prime antecedent for my own work.

What has Meeks *not* done for Pauline interpretation? Well, for a start, he has not developed his theological insights very far. There are many suggestive passages in his articles which indicate other lines of enquiry that might be pursued, but his energy was directed more to the moral, rather than the theological, early Christian world. He sets up four models of 'problem and solution' in Paul, but he does not try to play them off against one another, as has regularly been done in Pauline studies. Nor does he try to show how, either theologically or sociologically, they might be part of a larger coherence. I think he has missed a trick there. As I have argued elsewhere, Paul's reworking of something that can properly be called 'covenant' theology will hold the different models together, and will do so explicitly within its social and cultural world.

In addition, it is perhaps surprising (though this was usual at the time) that Meeks did not explore the possible, and some would say probable, sharp interface between Paul and his communities on the one hand and the world of Caesar and empire on the other. I agree with Dale Martin that the development of that theme by Horsley and others is a natural extension of Meeks's work, though this remains controversial.[106] A further place where more work might grow out of Meeks's studies is the hypothetical or implicit debate between Paul and the philosophers of his day. The philosophers, too, lived and reasoned within their social worlds, and quite a lot of work has been done on that correlation. Might that not be brought together with Pauline studies, so that one might envisage, not just a hypothetical debate between Paul and Seneca such as I have envisaged elsewhere, but a 'thickly described' discussion between Paul *in his social world* and some Stoics, Epicureans, Academics or indeed Cynics in *their* social contexts? That would be a large project, but I think potentially a fruitful one.[107] There is considerably more work to be done too in the area of the social level and class of Paul's communities, and of the way in which Paul's strategies for 'remembering the poor' made the sense they did at the time and were tightly integrated into everything else he believed.[108]

Meeks has been reticent about one topic which most people have in mind when reading Paul: what's in it for us? This question, asked both by people who hope to be able to agree with Paul and by people who expect to disagree with him, remains urgent across the discipline. As we saw in the previous chapter, even those who expound the sharp differences between Paul's world and our own nevertheless hint that when we do eventually find the apostle's meaning in his own world we ought to be able to make some sort of transference into our own, even if it be to say, 'Well, we now think differently.' Meeks, as we saw, hints at a 'hermeneutics of social embodiment',

[106] See the discussion in *PFG* ch. 12, and 309 below.

[107] See *PFG* ch. 14. A start in this direction is provided by Glad 1995; see too Thorsteinsson 2010.

[108] See esp. Longenecker 2010.

though recognizing that this is a difficult and complex task. It is striking that he, like the other two great American scholars of the last generation whose work I have made central to this project, does not take this very far.

When we put Meeks alongside Sanders and Martyn, some interesting parallels and contrasts emerge. Taking the 'contemporary application' first, Sanders compares Paul's 'pattern of religion' with that of 'Palestinian Judaism', leaving us with the impression that the main thing to learn is just how alike in many ways Paul and the Jewish world really are. Martyn gives few clues as to the direct application of his 'apocalyptic' reading of Paul to the preaching and life of today's church, though some of his followers have been less reticent.[109] Meeks sees that, though there is a task there to be taken up, the more immediate one is simply more detailed history. He still believes, he says,

> that people of faith need the kind of scholarship that I have tried to pursue and which will be taken in new directions by my students and successors, however diverse the motivations, goals, and methods of the scholars and however imperfect and unstable our findings – 'for we walk by faith, not by what we can see.'[110]

A strange fact, however, remains. When we reflect that Sanders, Martyn and Meeks were all at the peak of their careers between the 1970s and the turn of the century, in academic contexts of a broadly similar nature, it is noticeable that they, their students and their successors have not made common cause. They emerge from similar backgrounds; they express similar frustrations with the then normal ways of reading key biblical texts; but they go in different directions, taking their 'schools', such as they are, with them. Sanders and Meeks both give attention to 'religion', but Sanders compares Paul's religion (which turns out to be, more or less, his theology) with that of Palestinian Judaism, while Meeks places 'religion' as one element within Paul's wider social world, including but going well beyond his wider Jewish world. Sanders and Martyn both reckon that Paul's thought moved from 'solution' to 'plight', though for Sanders this is because he finds Paul's critique of Torah incoherent and seeks to explain it, while for Martyn it is because his (more or less Barthian) theology demands it. Meeks places what he calls 'apocalyptic' near the heart of Paul's belief-system, but he appears to mean by that contested term something different from what Martyn has in mind. Both constructions need adjustment in the light of further research into the Jewish world of the actual apocalypses.

None of the three, so far as I can see, gives a full or adequate account of two themes which, on anyone's readings of Paul's letters, ought to be seen as central: the question of Jesus' 'divinity', on the one hand, and the question of 'justification by faith' on the other. Meeks makes the latter one sub-theme among others; Sanders and Martyn both relativize it (not entirely unlike Schweitzer), Sanders in favour of a participationist soteriology, Martyn in

[109] e.g. Rutledge 2007.

[110] Meeks, 'Afterword', in Meeks, Hilton and Snyder 2002, 261, quoting here his own translation of the text in question, i.e. 2 Cor. 5.7.

favour of his 'apocalyptic'. These themes are so important in Paul, however, that one would have thought they would have to be dealt with. But they are naturally awkward in a comparison with Judaism (Sanders); they are not central to, and perhaps not easily factored into, the kind of 'apocalyptic' offered by Martyn; and, though Meeks does recognize that they correlate with social aspects of Paul's work, he does not pursue this in any detail.

Finally, none of the three gives, to my mind, anything like an adequate account of the underlying socio-cultural problem which Paul met in city after city (though perhaps in different ways): the relation between the Jew-plus-gentile communities who hailed Jesus as Messiah and Lord and the Jewish communities who did not. Sanders explored this to some degree, but things have moved on a long way since then, and it would be too facile to say, as some have, that he was leading the way (along with Stendahl) towards a more 'tolerant' reading of the sources. Martyn constantly implies a sharp antithesis, with the Teachers whom Paul is opposing offering a variety of Jewish 'religion' to which Paul responds with 'revelation'. Meeks realizes that we are here touching a raw nerve, but though his social studies might have led him to consider more closely the relationships between Diaspora synagogues and Paul's churches this is not a topic he pursues.

Perhaps all three, in their different ways, are offering pathways into a fuller understanding of Paul. Perhaps the brave souls who try to learn from all three will find fresh routes to an exploration of those, and other, vital themes. Or perhaps not. For myself, I regard these three as the Cephas, James and John of the American, and in a measure of the Anglophone, 'Jerusalem' of the Pauline studies of the last generation: they are *hoi dokountes styloi einai*, 'those reputed to be pillars'. That, of course, is an ambiguous role to take. Whether they will 'add anything' to those who come with other questions and ideas; whether their followers will seek to impose their will on other movements and approaches, spying out the freedom they have as exegetes; whether, in the last analysis, the blessed guild of Pauline scholars turns out to be a 'sect', a 'reform movement', or something else entirely – all that remains to be seen. For my money, the 'comparison of religions' offered by Sanders has serious weaknesses;[111] the 'apocalyptic' proposed by Martyn, even more;[112] only the relentless, undramatic, detailed, unostentatious historical work proposed by Meeks will ultimately do.

It is fascinating, and tantalizing, that as Meeks reflects on the era in which he has plied his trade he sees more clearly than ever that precisely this detailed history will end up pointing beyond itself, not just to theology, but to poetry and the imagination.[113] That hints at yet more integration than most New Testament scholars have dreamed of; at tasks, themes and even goals which will be more demanding, not less, than the most rigorous exegetical work of our forebears. As Meeks puts it, at the end of his Preface

[111] See my discussion in *PFG* 1321–5.

[112] See Part II above.

[113] Meeks, 'Reflections on an Era', in Meeks, Hilton and Snyder 2002, xxvii; and see Meeks's essay, 'Vision of God and Scripture', in the same vol., 230–53.

to the new edition of *The First Urban Christians*, only a 'deep and long-term immersion in the scattered and enigmatic traces left by the people of the first century' can take us where we need to be. Only such immersion, he writes in a passage we quoted in a different context earlier,

> can give us some sense of the diverse, complex, and dynamic webs of human relationships that constituted life in the cities where the movement that was to be 'Christianity' began to take its enduring shapes. Putting the story together is finally more art than science – and the scientists I know are quick to acknowledge that there is much art in their science.[114]

If all science includes art, then certainly the 'sciences' of history, of sociology, and of whatever we might mean by 'social history' do so as well. If the study of Paul in his world has any chance of pointing also to our own world, it will, I think, be through this kind of careful, multi-layered historical and reflective work. In that work, precisely because it is an art as well as a science, and because it exemplifies the point that ultimately the two need to be held together, we can no longer pretend to a detached, fly-on-the-wall 'objectivity'. At the very moment when we are most aware that the culture we are studying is significantly different from our own, we are also aware that we are still looking at it through our own eyes, and that the cultural spectacles we ourselves wear will have an effect on how we see the object, and how we then see differently those objects that are closer to home. It may be as well, therefore, to make all this more explicit as we move into the next phase of work. An obvious place to start, from within Pauline studies, might be the apparent use of poetry, not as a decorative embroidery around the border of beliefs expressed more clearly elsewhere, but as the clearest, if admittedly also the densest, statements of beliefs which later theologians would systematize.

One of the best recent examples of multi-layered Pauline investigation is David Horrell's *Solidarity and Difference*. To that we now turn.

2. Solidarity and Difference: History and Hermeneutics

David Horrell has featured in this narrative several times already, not least as one of the editors of the volume discussing Wayne Meeks's famous book a quarter of a century after its original publication. His own most significant work, *Solidarity and Difference: A Contemporary Reading of Paul's Ethics*, is now coming into a second edition, ten years after its original publication.[115]

The title of the book highlights, perhaps unintentionally, the dilemma I just mentioned. The ostensible subject indicated by the phrase 'solidarity and difference' is the tension between two visions of society. In the first, everyone agrees on uniform standards (the 'liberal' ideal) and attains a 'solidarity' – in which, to be sure, one of the 'standards' is at least in theory

[114] Meeks 2003, xii.

[115] Horrell 2005: page references otherwise unallocated are to this work. The 2015 edition was not available to me at the time of going to press.

the 'tolerance' of different views. In the second, the smaller identities and liberties of groups and individuals are respected without needing to be brought into conformity (the 'communitarian' ideal), thus affirming 'difference' – though also often wanting to affirm some kind of wider 'solidarity'.

I shall say more about these in a moment, but as an introductory point we note that this is precisely the dilemma of epistemology itself, not least as it applies to history in general and social history in particular. When we study human communities in the past, we are aware of all kinds of solidarities. Underneath the obvious differences between our world and theirs, we catch echoes of our own joys and sorrows, dilemmas and disagreements. That is why ancient painting, poetry and pottery (for instance) still remain so potent. But the differences matter as well. Whether we are physicists or psychologists, sociologists or archaeologists, theologians or geologists, the human art of *knowing* is found in the delicate balance between observer and observed. Horrell's book, a remarkable attempt to straddle the 'difference' between Paul's world and ours, and to allow for something we might call a 'differentiated solidarity' between the two, thus exemplifies at a second-order level the principle it expounds.

The principle itself is one which has made its way deep into popular culture at the start of the twenty-first century. As I was planning this chapter, I saw a large advertisement on a London street which said, 'Be Together, Not the Same'. It was advertising a new type of Android phone which allows you and your friends to be 'together' ('solidarity'), but with your own personal touches and style as well ('difference'). But it might have been about almost anything. Connection without conformity, solidarity without sameness: that, in theory, is what we all want.

Or is it? The clash between these two visions of society has turned ugly. On 7 January 2015 terrorists in Paris attacked the magazine *Charlie Hebdo* which had demonstrated its support for a militantly secular 'solidarity' by lampooning those who represented the 'difference' of this or that specific religion. The attackers, for their part, were standing up for their 'difference'. At the time of writing (spring 2015) the 'culture wars' in America have produced a similar tension, with a law guaranteeing the 'rights' of those who adhere to particular religions ('difference') being attacked because it might undermine certain social visions which would sign everyone up to certain new moral codes ('solidarity'). The irony there, of course, is that some of those new moral codes made their way into public consciousness by appealing to 'difference', upholding the supposed rights of minorities; but, once they had attained their object, their supporters quickly insisted on 'solidarity', resulting in what is already a cliché: 'illiberal liberalism'.[116] Such are the

[116] As Horrell (51) summarizes the point: 'Liberalism's "pretensions to neutrality" may be seen to conceal a clear preference in terms of what is and is not truly good'. He cites Mulhall and Swift 1996 [1992], 32, on liberalism's insistence that 'a good life is one which has been freely or autonomously chosen by the person living it'. This already implies, however, that the ideal 'liberal' world might well contain all kinds of 'differences', the sole uniting point being that they had all been freely chosen, which is hardly the same point. See further Horrell 201–3, which I will discuss further presently.

swirling confusions of our age. This is the complex world into which David Horrell has stepped with fresh proposals for how we should read Paul.

Horrell is a seasoned scholar, both of Paul and of other parts of the New Testament, as well as an authority on the social-scientific study of early Christianity.[117] Following the lead of Meeks, he has pursued in particular the question of the moral world of the early Christians. Even though the subtitle of his major book uses the word 'ethics', which Meeks tended to avoid, it is clear that he, like Meeks, is investigating not just isolated 'rules for behaviour' but the much larger issues of how human social life as a whole is to be lived, and what contribution Paul might make to these questions. He thus intends to contribute to the project which Meeks outlined in his article on 'Social Embodiment': what happens when we bring Paul's larger vision of a Christian 'social world' into dialogue with our own?[118]

Far more explicitly than the earlier wave of social studies of the New Testament we have so far studied in this Part of the book, Horrell is thus bringing the task of historically and sociologically aware exegesis into a creative conversation with one of the larger and more important moral debates of the western world at the start of the twenty-first century. He is treating Paul as a 'practical moral philosopher' (ix, 31) with whom it is important to enter into dialogue.[119]

The foundation of Horrell's book is an account of 'Paul's ethics as a whole' (1), seeing Paul as engaged in the 'formation and maintenance of human community' (3), exploring the kinds of values a community needs if it is to maintain both solidarity (Paul's constant appeals for unity) and 'difference' (Paul's well-known appeals for tolerance). Horrell is well aware that the charges both of naivety and of anachronism are hovering in the wings: does our contemporary formulation of the problem really reflect what Paul was doing? Do we really suppose we can so easily isolate comparable issues in our own world? The answer is in the larger project, as the two partners in the dialogue engage, seeking a fusion of horizons on the Gadamer model – although, again as Horrell well knows, the 'Paul' in the dialogue will remain *our reading of Paul.* We do not have the apostle in the room to confront us and say bluntly 'But that's not what I meant'. The danger of ventriloquism is always present, as the modern interpreter lures us into supposing that we are listening to Paul when in fact we are hearing the interpreter's own ideas about what Paul might have been saying, with the interpreter's own exegetical hand operating the 'mouth' while hidden inside a mute glove-puppet. As we have seen before, this danger afflicts equally those who want to agree with 'Paul' and those who want to disagree with him.

[117] See e.g. Horrell 1996; 2000, and other books in the bibliography to the present volume, as well as many articles. He is currently working on a major commentary on 1 Peter.

[118] Meeks, Hilton and Snyder 185–95 [orig. pub. 1986]. See Horrell 45: he is studying Paul's ethics 'not so much as rules or injunctions, separable from other aspects of his world-view, but rather as part and parcel of a community-forming discourse'; and cf. also his 95–7, defending Hays against Esler's charge that he was reducing ethics to deontology or consequentialism.

[119] My own debt to Horrell ought to be apparent from the footnotes to *PFG*, especially in chapter 6 where I took him (along with T. S. Eliot) as among my major inspirations and conversation partners.

Horrell's first main chapter reviews a wide range of current writing about Paul's ethics, introducing the themes he will later discuss. Of particular importance for his thesis is Daniel Boyarin's book on Paul, which articulates exactly the question Horrell is considering, namely

> the central moral task of engendering and maintaining human solidarity while at the same time sustaining and protecting difference and diversity.[120]

There is, to be sure, a danger of infinite regress at this point. Boyarin charges Paul with aiming at a 'sameness' which flattens out 'difference'. To the response that Paul celebrates continuing differences within that unity (so that Christian Jews are still Jews, and so on), one could reply that the word 'Christian' is still imposing on the world that idea that it matters to be a Christian, and so on.[121] At a certain point this regress must face the question: did Paul, or did he not, think that Jesus was Israel's Messiah, and did that matter? The issue is then one of *locating* the 'solidarity' and discerning its particular shape. Simply saying 'solidarity' will not get us all the way to the nuanced account we seek. For Paul, as I shall say later, and as Meeks already saw, the 'new humanity in the Messiah' was a kind of prototype for a new humanity as a whole. That results directly from the underlying creational and new-creational structure of his thought, which I believe is included in the reality described by Horrell (3) as 'the theology which constitutes the community-forming myth on which Paul draws'. (Horrell himself, however, does not include the themes of creation and new creation in this reality, which ends up dividing his reading of Paul from mine, as we shall see.) Boyarin, no doubt, would have preferred it if Paul had said that believing in Jesus was one option among many equals. But Paul would then have been able to respond that, in that case, the 'solidarity' of Boyarin's postmodern world of equal differences was now squashing the 'difference' of the specifically messianic belief about Jesus and about the new creation which had come to birth through him. Boyarin appears to be trying to do to Paul what he says Paul did to his own traditions.[122]

This already draws us into the kind of debate Horrell's book invites and encourages. His second chapter outlines the contemporary ethical dilemma as seen in two seminal thinkers: the continental philosopher Jürgen Habermas, representing the 'liberal' project of 'solidarity', and the American ethicist Stanley Hauerwas, representing the 'communitarian' project of 'difference'. For Habermas and his project of 'discourse ethics', the ideal is that people in a society should go on talking to one another until they reach agreement. For Hauerwas, they talk, if they do, in order to discern the points on which they must then agree to differ. There are many fascinating points here. Current events in the second decade of the twenty-first century

[120] Horrell 43, discussing Boyarin 1994.

[121] Horrell 2005 engages on these grounds with my review of Boyarin (now in Wright 2013b [*Perspectives*], ch. 8).

[122] See *Perspectives* 128.

make this debate even more urgent than it was twenty or thirty years ago. But for Horrell's purposes, and our own, the point is then to bring Paul into the discussion:

> How does Paul conceive of the distinctive identity of the Christian community, and how does this relate to the possibilities for the wider sharing of ethical values? Does Paul make any appeal to a universal rationality on the basis of which ethical values can be expected to be shared by all humankind, or show any indications that such a moral consensus is attainable? How, if at all, does Paul treat differences (of ethical conviction) within the community, and what kind of moral arguments does he use when faced with such diversity? ... And the over-arching question: What might the shape and structure of Pauline ethics suggest by way of critical and constructive conclusions in relation to issues raised in the liberal-communitarian debate?[123]

That is the agenda of Horrell's book: 'to sketch a contemporary debate as a context for our reading of Paul and in relation to which our reading may generate fruitful reflections' (98).

The third chapter maps out the lie of the social-historical land for Paul's communities in general and Corinth in particular. Horrell makes a virtue out of focusing attention on passages that do not normally occupy centre stage in larger construals of Paul's thought. Like so many of us, he cites Berger and Luckmann as a starting-point, bringing in Geertz as well later on, and thereby exploring the 'myth, ritual, identity and ethos' we can discern in Paul's vision of the church. He insists on the propriety of attempting a large, overall sketch, against the kind of scholarship that becomes so preoccupied with small details and differences that it can no longer 'operate in a more synthetic mode':

> To sketch an overall picture, with due attention to the variety of detail, should be neither impossible nor implausible.[124]

Horrell insists, in particular, that the 'myth', in this sense, is a larger narrative whose focus is on the events concerning Jesus but which extends much more broadly:

> This central key clearly has a 'vertical' dimension ... but it also has a horizontal dimension, a temporal extension: in the fullness of time, after the period of the law, God sent forth his son ... Thus, while Paul perceives the Christ-event as for him an 'apocalyptic' event, which has disrupted and re-oriented his very self ... and while this Christ-event requires a recasting of the stories Paul had previously held true, it is not simply a 'punctiliar' event but rather one which Paul casts within a narrative framework.[125]

[123] Horrell 82.

[124] Horrell 89.

[125] Horrell 87, citing Hays and contrasting Martyn.

He explores 'ritual' similarly: 'early Christian faith was practised and performed as well as "believed".'[126] Christian 'identity' is not so much, for Paul, the traditional paradox of 'now and not yet', a present indicative leading to a moral imperative, but is rather, he says, about 'identity-descriptors and group norms which need to be constantly affirmed' (94).

With these starting-points in place, Horrell's argument really gets going in the fourth chapter. Here he presents his case (a) that Paul's 'first and most fundamental moral value' is that of 'corporate solidarity, a form of human solidarity with egalitarian impulses' (99); (b) that by examining the symbols Paul envisages, and the language he uses, we can see '*how* that solidarity is generated' (101, emphasis original). Baptism 'symbolises the convert's transition, via "death", from one world to another' (103), though Horrell draws back from following those scholars who have argued, against the normal trend, that the 'other' world into which converts come is 'being raised with Christ'.[127] His summary of this point could hardly be bettered:

> Both rituals, baptism and Lord's supper, at least as Paul interprets them, communicate and reinforce a world-view in which the death and resurrection of Christ are the central events in a cosmic story – these events give meaning to the world, providing the fundamental hermeneutical orientation by which it is to be understood – and at the same time convey as the central theme of the Christian ethos the notion of a solidarity in Christ which transcends former divisions.[128]

This leads to an account of Paul's kinship language, which Horrell rightly sees as taken over from the Jewish context (a point which might be strengthened further), and as forming part of Paul's appeal for what Horrell calls an 'other-regarding' morality. This seems to be a way of gaining some critical distance on the otherwise overused word 'love'.[129]

This brings him to one of his central and delicate points. Paul is clearly dealing with a number of issues, on some of which he will allow for a degree of diversity. On others, however, he will 'tolerate no dissent', one of these issues being precisely 'the need for unity'. He is not working for 'a complete or blanket "sameness", an unvaried conformity', but rather for

> the kind of unanimity and shared outlook which provide the basis for solidarity, within which a circumscribed diversity may be sustained.[130]

Horrell describes 'this "intolerant" framework for tolerance' as offering 'interesting parallels between Pauline and liberal ethics'. That, indeed, is where his argument has rather obviously been tending, but I think the conclusion is over-hasty. The parallel is only on the surface. 'Tolerance' is the

[126] Horrell 91; see too 130, where the worldview-model enables Horrell to give a clear account of the way in which baptism and the Lord's Supper accomplish a 'social achievement' in their 'construction of a boundary-transcending corporate solidarity.'

[127] He cites Catchpole 2004; he might also have cited Wright 2002 [*Romans*], 533–41.

[128] Horrell 110.

[129] Horrell 115 and elsewhere.

[130] Horrell 119.

word that gives the game away: the modern liberal ideal of a 'tolerant' society is not at all the same thing as the 'love' on which Paul insists in famous passages such as Philippians 2.1–4, and I am not sure that 'other-regard' can straddle the two. Horrell argues for a subtle difference at this point between 1 Corinthians and Galatians, suggesting that in Corinth what matters is *solidarity* in Christ while in Galatia what matters is solidarity *in Christ* (121). I find this problematic for exegetical reasons; I am not convinced that Horrell has got to the bottom either of the Galatian problem or of Paul's way of addressing it. Granted that Paul does indeed issue 'angry denunciations' against those who preach 'another gospel', it misses the point to ask whether this 'vehement and inflexible stance' might 'stand in contradiction to the appeals for unity elsewhere'. The point Paul is making is precisely that his gospel insists on unity while the message of the teachers he is opposing, and indeed the actions of Cephas at Antioch, had the effect of creating two separate communities of Messiah-believers, a Jewish one and a non-Jewish one.[131] Horrell's overall point, though, is well taken, as is his insistence that the Pauline insistence on unity is not only a matter of 'equal access to salvation before God', but

> is also a social, political space, a space in which the social relationships and interactions of community members are newly conceived and restructured in the light of the world-view and ethos generated by the Christian myth.[132]

We are talking here about actual communities, not some kind of supposed 'spiritual' unity which leaves different people in different social spaces.

Does all this, then, add up to a 'liberal' reading of Paul? Horrell leans in this direction at the close of the chapter, suggesting that Paul's ideal 'bears closer comparison with the liberal democratic values of equality and fraternity'. He stresses at the same time that Paul's communities are rooted in Christology, and that this leans rather in a 'communitarian' direction – all of which might suggest that these are actually less helpful categories for understanding Paul than Horrell had been hoping. In particular, while warding off the charge of anachronism (as though Paul was two-thirds of the way to anticipating the French Revolutionary slogans, needing only 'liberty' to complete the set), Horrell does rather give the game away. It is, he says, 'implausible to deny the similarities' [between Paul and the French revolutionaries], but these may perhaps, he suggests, 'reflect, in some part, the *Wirkungsgeschichte* of these early Christian traditions' (131–2). Precisely so. This is not the time or place to examine the genealogy of eighteenth-century revolutionary slogans, but the ideals of 'freedom, equality and fraternity' do have the ring of being a secularized version of what, at its best, the church had always tried to teach and model. It is now, in fact, one of the standard critiques of the Enlightenment that it was trying to get the fruits of

[131] See Horrell 119f.

[132] Horrell 128f.

the Christian vision while denying the roots from which it had sprung.[133] That is, arguably, one of the reasons why postmodern morality has had the unhappy tendency to collapse into a competing Babel of special-interest claims ('rights'?), resulting in multiple 'differences' with precious little 'solidarity' on the horizon. But Horrell, having glanced in this direction, draws back at the close of the chapter:

> The basis for [Pauline] solidarity ... is found in Paul's Christology: as believers make the story of Christ their own, participating in his death and new life, so they leave behind the old world, and become members of one body, in Christ.[134]

The 'solidarity', in other words, is 'in Christ', and this marks a 'difference' from the wider world, even when the ideas and images for expressing the solidarity may have parallels with that world. This 'difference' is then the subject of the next chapter.

Horrell's fifth chapter is on 'the rhetoric of distinction', focusing on 'purity, boundaries and identity'. Central to this is the language and practice of 'holiness', which resonates with themes from the Jewish world, taking over the Jewish sense of separation from the pagans who worship idols and indulge in sexual immorality. I think Horrell's account could be strengthened here by a consideration of Paul's wider ecclesiology seen in terms of his reworking of the Jewish theology of election. To focus on that point would undercut the suggestion that the 'problematization' we find in Galatians might affect the analysis of purity, boundaries and identity – in other words, that Paul's opposition to ethnic boundary-lines in the Messiah's people might have implications for 'purity' boundaries as well.[135] Paul's reworking of election, by contrast, would point to the insistence, which in the present climate of scholarship is more contentious than Horrell seems to realize, that for Paul the Messiah-people formed 'a distinct group, distinguished from Jews on the one hand and Greeks on the other.'[136]

When it comes to the detail of behaviour, Horrell sees clearly that Paul is concerned as much and more with issues of 'identity' as with individual actions, though I do not think he sufficiently explores the question of why Paul saw certain actions as compromising that identity (see below). He rightly, in my view, rejects Countryman's suggestion that Paul's sexual ethics are formulated on the basis of 'property rules'; they are rather about the purity of the church as the people of God.[137] This case too, I think, might be

[133] See Habermas 2002, 162f., discussed by Horrell at 62f., 203 n. 99: 'the task of philosophy is to translate religious language into the language of public reason', since people will no longer believe the 'religious' reasons and so must seek some other basis (see too 283). The twenty-first century, one might comment, has already shown how unstable a project this kind of exercise is bound to be.

[134] Horrell 132.

[135] See Horrell 137, citing Longenecker.

[136] Horrell 139, citing 1 Cor. 1.22f.; 10.32, with Esler's comments from a sociological standpoint (Esler 1998, 141–77). For the controversy, and fuller arguments, see *PFG* 1443–9.

[137] Horrell 143; cf. Countryman 1988, 109, 197–202, 213.

strengthened by offering the wider context of Paul's view of 'new creation'. It is because the church is to model the renewal of creation itself that marriage is so important, a sign of the goodness of the original creation and of the creator's intention to restore it – a point to which we shall return.

This steers us directly towards Horrell's next question: are the ethical norms of the Pauline communities distinctive to them, or are they shared more widely in the surrounding society? What we find, he suggests, will appear to us as an 'ironic juxtaposition' of 'a sense of distinct (and morally superior) identity', on the one hand, and 'shared ethical norms' on the other (159). This irony is particularly apparent in Philippians, where 4.8 lists the good qualities in the wider world about which Paul wants Messiah-people to 'think'. Horrell does not, perhaps surprisingly, discuss the apparent balance between that verse and the next one, where Paul insists that while the congregation is to *think about* the wider world of virtue and goodness, they are to *imitate him* specifically in what they have observed of his particular way of life, with all its differences from that world (4.9; compare 2.14–16). There is indeed a considerable overlap of moral ideals, expressed up to a point in a shared vocabulary between Paul's communities and the non-Jewish world around them (though there are exceptions: philosophers have noted the absence, in ancient moralism, of humility, patience, charity and not least chastity).[138] But the main difference is that Paul claims that Christians can and should live up to the ideals which others may glimpse but not often follow (162). Many today might raise an eyebrow at the idea of Christians succeeding in such exemplary behaviour, but in the early generations it was indeed expected, and the church took steps to exercise a discipline almost forgotten in today's mainstream western churches.

The theme of 'new creation', which I mentioned a moment ago, offers an answer to the puzzles Horrell raises towards the end of the chapter. Paul's arguments, he says, 'do not actually demonstrate why certain acts should be classed as ethical or unethical'; some of his ethical convictions 'do not emerge from the theological tradition with which the ethics are motivated but are rather assumed as part of a taken-for-granted set of shared moral presumptions' (163–4). This, he says, calls into question Hauerwas's depiction of 'authentically Christian ethics as generated by the particular story which forms the community called Church' (164–5). I cannot speak for Hauerwas, but it seems to me that the particular story which Paul told and retold in one form or another always had as its widest reference point the story of creation itself and of the redemption of creation as accomplished through the Messiah and implemented through the spirit (Romans 8 and 1 Corinthians 15 are the obvious passages here). The idea of a 'new human' may be more prominent in Ephesians than in the letters normally accepted as Pauline, but, as Wayne Meeks sees, Ephesians often draws out something which is latent in the supposed 'main letters'.

[138] See Blackburn 2008 [1994], 381: 'the humility, charity, patience, and chastity of Christianity would have been unintelligible as ethical virtues to classical Greeks'. This rather striking point needs to be addressed in any account of the moral 'solidarity' between Paul's communities and their neighbours.

Horrell's sixth chapter deals with Paul's demand for 'other-regard', in relation to the two famous passages 1 Corinthians 8—10 and Romans 14—15. Do we find here an encouragement to 'tolerance' in a 'liberal' sense? If so, does this mean that Paul is, as Boyarin and others have charged, erasing cultural differences? These are clearly vital passages for Horrell's whole project. He begins with the important point that when Paul deals with food (what to eat and what not to eat) he takes a completely different line from his teaching about sexual behaviour:

> Food per se does not have the same ethical significance [as sexual behaviour] and is thus the focus for the development of different forms of ethical argument.[139]

This stands in the way of any attempt to argue from Paul's supposed 'tolerance' in the one area to a similar stance in others, but that is just the beginning. Horrell then argues that Paul's 'tolerant' stance on the question of food is based on 'a different kind of foundation and motivation for ethical decision-making, essentially a relational, other-regarding ethic with a specifically christological shape' (172). The death of Christ forms the pattern according to which the 'strong' must give up their presumed rights for the sake of the 'weak'. This ethic is 'grounded ... in Christology' (177); it is 'christologically underpinned' (181). Paul does not, then, seek to educate those he deems 'weak' in conscience. Instead, he fosters an 'other-regard' which allows differences of conviction and practice to remain (182).

This proposal has considerable merit. Certainly a christologically grounded concern for those with different views about food taboos is a central part of Paul's argument. But it seems to me surprising that Horrell rules out quite carefully what might be thought even more fundamental: Paul's emphasis on a christologically redefined *monotheism*. Here Wayne Meeks makes a strong point, as we saw earlier: monotheism, and specifically its christological form as in 1 Corinthians 8.6, is *community-defining*. The whole argument of 1 Corinthians 8, 9 and 10 is in fact held in place within this monotheistic frame, with 10.26, 31 rounding off the argument in robust (and characteristically Jewish) fashion.[140] It is because Paul's communities are to be committed to the 'one God, one Lord' version of Jewish monotheism that they know two things ahead of time: first, idols do not stand for any divine reality; second, everything God created is good, so that all foods can be enjoyed if received with thanksgiving. The whole discussion is more tightly integrated, both within itself and in relation to other matters, than Horrell allows. It is because of the nature of his monotheism that Paul can argue simultaneously for 'tolerance' on who eats what, for 'intolerance' about entering an idol-temple (because of the non-divine but still malevolent *daimonia* who haunt the premises), and for 'love' (not just 'other-regard'?) to all other Messiah-people while it is all going on. Yes: within that monotheism (that itself is significant) Paul emphasizes the crucified and

[139] Horrell 168.

[140] See *PFG* 661–70.

risen Jesus as the one because of whom 'love' is appropriate, and as the Lord with whom one would be contending if one were to eat idol-meat in an idol-temple. But this emphasis on Jesus' lordship functions within the larger category of monotheism, meaning by that not least *creational* monotheism. Paul's view of creation and new creation undergirds this argument as well as others. To this extent, though, Horrell's summary seems to me exactly right: Paul is not simply giving miscellaneous instructions, but is providing 'a different kind of moral imperative: a christologically patterned [and, I would add, monotheistically and thus creationally grounded] imperative for other-regard which should (within limits) determine ethical practice' (181 n. 53).

Can Horrell really be right, however, when he suggests that Paul is not here trying to 'educate' the 'weak'? I think not. Paul sees clearly that creational monotheism rules idol-worship 'out' and all foods 'in'; it seems strange to think that he would not want to persuade all Messiah-followers to share these convictions, even if such a process would take time. What we have here is Paul as a *pastor*: he knows that people's consciences, precisely because they are formed within larger and more complex sets of symbols, memories, narratives and so on, cannot be brought to a new position overnight. Of course, his desire for 'other-regard', or even for 'love', does not stop when people agree on things where formerly they were at odds. It goes on being the appropriate mutual stance. But the specific command for what we sometimes call 'tolerance', in this area though not in some others, applies specifically to the time, be it long or short, in which disagreement persists. The instruction to 'love' those who disagree must not be turned into an argument against allowing that 'love' to generate a new solidarity.

When it comes to Romans 14 and 15, Horrell rightly in my view resists the attempt of Mark Nanos and others to suggest that the 'weak' were non-Christian Jews. Both groups, rather, are Christian believers (183). Horrell doubts, in fact, whether the Jew/gentile dynamic is at work here in the way often proposed, though I and others have argued that the reason Paul does not make this explicit until chapter 15 is because, again for pastorally sensitive reasons, he does not want to draw attention to it, preferring to discuss differences of practice in relation to food, drink and holy days as though they are in fact what he wants them to be, points which ought not to divide Messiah-believers. But, as it turns out, Romans 14 is a classic passage for the balanced position Horrell has been looking for. It is here that Paul argues for 'a unity of mind and purpose' which is nevertheless 'not a uniformity'; a 'unified community that at the same time protects the diversity within it' (187). Paul is here seeking 'to foster the corporate solidarity of the Christian congregation in Rome while legitimating differences of ethical practice' (189). Horrell is surely correct to end this argument by stressing that in Romans 15.9–12, at the climax of Paul's argument, the point is 'to reinforce the message, central to Romans as a whole, that God's purpose was always to bring Jew and Gentile together in one worshipping community.'[141]

[141] Horrell 189.

Horrell then explores the key themes which (at least in our contemporary perception) are pushed to the fore in these discussions: conscience, freedom, tolerance and difference. The first two present few problems, but Horrell is right to stress that 'tolerance' is a modern term which carries dangerously anachronistic meanings if we try to push it back into Paul's world (193). He sees that if we suppose Paul to be advocating our kind of 'tolerance' he merely seems inconsistent, setting clear boundaries in some areas but not in others. Paul's supposed 'tolerance' makes sense within Paul's own terms. Christ alone is the basis for community solidarity, and actions which threaten union with Christ are proscribed for that reason (195).[142]

The differences between Paul's situation and ours drive Horrell at this point to some very generalized concluding summaries. If we translate the specifics of Paul's discussions into wide categories such as 'sameness' and 'difference' we will find, not surprisingly, that precision eludes us:

> Paul preserves the space for a certain kind of difference ... Paul's discourse is in some senses one which allows, indeed preserves, difference, but also in some sense requires 'sameness' ... This kind of 'sameness' – an obligatory moral framework which precisely provides the means to preserve difference – is not so different in character and structure from the kind of framework which liberal (and indeed 'postmodern') tolerance of difference presumes.[143]

The real and somewhat troubling conclusion from all this, I think, is that Horrell's thought-experiment of coming to Paul with categories from today's western world is unearthing a larger gulf than one might have hoped. It is all very well to say that for Paul 'the values of solidarity and other-regard provide precisely a basis for sustaining within a united community diversity and difference, even in terms of ethical convictions' (199). It all depends, of course, what you mean by 'ethical'. To suggest that Romans expounds 'a form of ethical relativism' may be true as far as it goes, exploiting the ambiguity of the phrase 'a form of'. I do not find it a helpful way to summarize Romans 14 and 15, even granted the caveat that Paul nevertheless places 'strict limits' on 'the degree of tolerable diversity'. We could put it this way: if Paul knew what today's world understands by the phrase 'ethical relativism', would he have agreed that he was advocating it, or even 'a form of' it?

[142] Horrell tries to avoid the implication of 'Christian superiority' by saying that Paul's tolerances and prohibitions are based simply on his own conviction (195 n. 86). He seems to downplay, here and elsewhere, Paul's *eschatological* conviction that with the Messiah's death and resurrection the new creation had already been launched. Paul was not saying 'Judaism is bad or wrong', but 'the Jewish vision of God's new world has become a reality'.

[143] Horrell 197f. The build-up of 'a certain kind ... in some senses ... in some sense ... not so different' tells its own story; and the elision of 'liberal' and 'postmodern' indicates, to me at least, that something has gone awry. 'Liberalism' in Horrell's sense is normally associated with 'modernism', while it is precisely the postmodern protest that has insisted on 'difference', so that we would have to say that postmodernism 'presupposes a super-liberalism, more pluralistic, more tolerant, more open to the right of difference and otherness' (202, quoting Benhabib 1992, 16). The question of whether such a 'super-liberalism' ('late modernity'?) tips over into an 'anti-liberalism' ('postmodernity'?) is one of the unresolved issues underneath Horrell's whole project.

Horrell seems to recognize this problem. In concluding the chapter, he notes that today's 'liberalism' tends to place 'definite and "intolerant" limits on the practice of freedom' (200), so that 'practices which contradict the fundamental ethical principles of liberalism are not tolerated' (202 n. 97). Ultimately, 'liberalism' in the classic western mode insists on certain non-negotiable values, which will then trump, when necessary, 'the values of the traditions encompassed under its umbrella of belonging' (203). Horrell suggests, daringly but with caveats, that therefore 'what Paul does to Judaism, liberalism does to Christianity' (203). A superficial parallel can indeed be seen here. Certainly, the rhetoric of the Enlightenment was relentlessly supersessionist, seeking to replace Christianity while attempting to salvage what it wanted from the wreckage. But the supersessionist model is not appropriate for Paul. The relation of his gospel to the hope of Israel is not well captured in that shorthand. The point always was that Israel's scriptures themselves looked forward to a time of fulfilment when ancient promises would come true at last. Nothing in Christianity looked forward to a secular paradise from which faith itself had been removed, to be replaced by generalized ethic. What liberalism aimed to do, and has to some extent succeeded in doing, was to cut off the branch it was sitting on. It has thereby generated the shrill assertions of postmodernity on the one hand and the communitarian (sectarian?) backlash on the other. This, I think, is a dimension of contemporary debate which has not yet been factored in to the discussions Horrell is both chronicling and advancing.

After the three central chapters 4, 5 and 6, in which he puts forward and discusses his major claims, chapters 7 and 8 of Horrell's book are comparatively straightforward. Chapter 7 argues that 'other-regard' joins 'corporate solidarity' as 'the second key metanorm of Pauline ethics' (204). This is worked out in relation to Philippians 2.5–11 in particular. First Corinthians 9 is also important: Paul gives up his 'rights', again in imitation of Christ (231). The model of the self-giving of Christ also plays a central role in Paul's appeal to the Corinthians to give generously to the 'collection' (241). This 'other-regard', then, is not something apart from Christ and his example; and the nature of this example wards off, to some extent at least, the charge that Paul is himself constructing a new discourse of power (242–3). When we express all this at a high level of generality, we can hold our breath and imagine that Paul is actually agreeing with Habermas:

> Thus, Habermas and Paul agree – though they (of course) express this thought very differently – that self-sacrifice is commendable *in situations where human relations are distorted*, and that the aim of such action is to restore or create a form of equitable solidarity within which such self-sacrifice will no longer be required.[144]

It is points like this where the larger project of the whole book comes back into focus, though now in the form of a question-mark: have we really, after all this exegesis, taken things that much further forward? The experiment

[144] Horrell 244f. (emphasis original).

has been enormously valuable, compelling us to investigate many Pauline themes and passages from new angles. Meeks's question (and that of Esler, following him) is being put to the test, though the direction of travel is not clear, at least not to me. Meeks seemed to envisage the 'hermeneutics of social embodiment' as moving from a detailed description and socio-cultural analysis of Paul towards a similarly thickly described situation in the present. But by this stage in Horrell's project it begins to feel as though he is moving in the other direction, from Habermas and Hauerwas back to Paul, and that the movement in question can only take place if, instead of thick description and attention to detail, we move towards a level of high generality. This is not to deny the value of the experiment. It is merely to raise the question as to whether, when it is all over, we have learned quite as much as we had hoped, or whether we return to our separate worlds musing once again on their radical differences and on the dangers of anachronism.

Horrell's final main chapter, chapter 8, has to do with 'ethics and outsiders'. Paul's ethical instructions are normally directed to the church; do we find in him 'any sense that all people can, should, or do have the scope to recognize common, universal ethical norms?' (247). Are Paul's ethics, in other words, distinctive, flowing from the particular story upon which the church lives, or do they 'share and presume common ethical standards' and so possess 'a more general appeal'? (247). Horrell opens with a discussion of 'natural law' and related matters in Romans 1 and 2, though without reaching any dramatic conclusions. He then focuses on Romans 13.1–7, where Paul, enjoining obligation to obey rulers, grounds this in what appear to be universal principles. Horrell even suggests that this may be deliberately non-christological in order to stress that it is universally applicable.[145] The argument is, however, still essentially Jewish and monotheistic, and indicates, against the grain of Roman claims, that the rulers are not themselves divine, but only humans with delegated authority. However, the conclusion does seem to follow: the text represents a 'universal ethics' in two senses.

> First, in the sense that all political authority is seen as ordered by God . . . A common sense of good and evil, knowable by non-Christian and Christian alike, is therefore presumed here. Secondly, in the sense that . . . the duty to submit to such authority is a universal human obligation.[146]

Horrell then examines Paul's occasional concern for the reaction of outsiders, presupposing that there might be 'a certain congruence between the norms that prevail in society at large and the ethos that distinguishes the believing community'.[147] But Paul goes further. He is concerned not merely for outward appearance but for outward *benevolence*. The church is to 'do good' to outsiders as and when opportunity affords. This includes the positive response which Messiah-followers must offer to hostility (265). This

[145] Horrell 254. His supposed parallel to this in Rom. 10.17—11.36, as argued by Stendahl 1976, 4 and others, is misleading, as I have demonstrated in *PFG* 1160f.

[146] Horrell 257.

[147] Furnish 2002, 112, quoted at Horrell 259.

outward-facing stance, Horrell suggests, moves out of the closed circle of a communitarian ethic. It is more central to Paul than is sometimes thought:

> The existence of common ground in ethics is not merely something that historical criticism can unearth, working against the flow of Paul's rhetoric . . . , but something Paul explicitly acknowledges and uses as an essential starting point for an argument about the validity of the gospel.[148]

This, Horrell suggests, is what gets lost if we read Paul simply from 'an ecclesial perspective' (272).

Here once more I sense that what is missing is the theme of creation and new creation. Paul's entire missionary strategy and motivation, and within that his understanding of the traditional philosophical topics of physics, ethics and logic, are all to be located and understood on the basis that what has begun in the resurrection of the Messiah, and in the spirit-driven life of those who belong to him, is not a *different* creation, but a *renewed* creation.[149] The contrasts between church and world, generating the radical 'difference' of holiness examined in Horrell's fifth chapter, have to do in Paul's mind with the *corruption* of the present creation, and with human collusion in that corruption. When, through the spirit's work in the gospel, humans are rescued from the corruption that has invaded them personally, they are set free to become, not something utterly different, but precisely part of 'new creation' (2 Corinthians 5.17), with a new kind of knowledge which includes the old kind even as it transcends and transforms it.

Horrell concludes his remarkable book by summarizing his findings on 'Paul among Liberals and Communitarians', a placing which, we may suppose, might be just as uncomfortable for Paul as the traditional one 'among Jews and gentiles'. His first finding is now uncontroversial: Paul's 'metanorms' are 'corporate solidarity and other-regard' (274). The second finding quickly moves into wide and qualified generalities:

> Corporate solidarity does not imply the erasure of difference: Paul is concerned to sustain diversity within the ecclesial community, including differences of ethical convictions and cultural practices, though only insofar as these fall within the limits of tolerable diversity determined in part by the obligatory metanorms.[150]

This needs further qualification to be of much use, and I do not think Horrell's exposition of it goes as far as Paul himself would want. It is one thing to say that 'the limits of tolerable diversity' are shaped by Paul's belief that 'union with Christ . . . is the crucial basis for distinguishing Christian identity' (275). But it will not do, I think, to suggest that the decision as to which actions might be 'deemed to threaten or destroy this union, notably in the realm of idolatry or sexual immorality', is derived, not from 'the Christian myth itself, but rather from Judaism and other contemporary

[148] Horrell 271.

[149] See *PFG* chs. 12, 13, 14.

[150] Horrell 274.

moral traditions' (275). Here again Horrell has nudged creational and new-creational monotheism out of the frame. Granted that this ethical strand could indeed be seen as something 'derived from Judaism', that 'derivation' was not, as is implied in Horrell's sentence, a matter of picking up a maxim or general rule from a tradition not organically related to the gospel. It was a matter of thinking through what it meant that, in the resurrection, God the creator, the covenant God of Israel, had acted to begin the project of new creation, and that by the community-forming events of gospel, baptism, Lord's Supper, and all that went with them, people were being called to be part of that new creation, worshipping the one God and living new-creational lives – which, for Paul, meant more specifically that one should avoid idolatry and sexual immorality.

The third finding is that different identities and ethical stances are relativized. This is substantially the same insight as in some types of new perspective: practices that express union with Christ are determinative for group identity and community-boundaries, 'such that other cultural/ethical practices no longer have this identity-defining significance' (276).

Horrell's fourth finding is that the community 'in Christ' is to be pure and holy, while at the same time embracing values which are shared by the wider world as well. Here again a stronger theology of creation and new creation would help. This leads to the fifth finding: that Christians are to 'do good' – namely, a 'good' that all will recognize as 'good'! – to outsiders.

The sixth and seventh findings express what I see as the strongest and the weakest points of Horrell's whole construct. First, he sees clearly that Paul's ethics are grounded in 'the myth which constitutes Paul's "theology"' (278), specifically the story of Christ and its inner meaning. Second, however, he says that Paul's theology, including Christology, 'cannot explain why Paul holds certain specific ethical convictions, for example, concerning what constitutes sexual immorality' (279). This is where, as noted above, I think Paul would respond that his views here are not simply 'derived from his wider world', especially Judaism, but grow out of his central convictions about the gospel as the news of new creation. Horrell is here, I think, trying to find a loophole which he can exploit in order to gain some critical distance from the apostle.

Paul's ethics are thus, in a sense, both communitarian and liberal. Hauerwas might like some parts of Paul but not others; Habermas, too, would applaud some elements but be uncomfortable with others. The thought-experiment of the whole project finally condenses into the question: 'How are the (liberal) values of plurality, tolerance and difference, and the social solidarity which they presume, to be fostered, motivated and exemplified, if not through some kind of traditioned story embodied in rituals and communally shared?' (285). This leads to Horrell's conclusion, in which he offers 'three possible models for the appropriation of Pauline ethics' (285). Here we find, I suggest, the heart of his proposals, the point to which all the detailed exegesis and social analysis has been leading. And here we find, too, the point of transition to the recent explosion of interest in Paul on the part of philosophers and theologians from outside the exegetical tradition altogether, at which we will glance – it will be no more than that – in the concluding chapter. Horrell thus forms, at this end of his own argument, something of a bridge to wider discussions already in progress, though whether they will lead us further away from, or back towards, an historical (indeed, a socio-historical) exegesis remains to be seen.

Horrell's three models explore what it means, respectively, to think 'with', 'beyond' and then 'against' Paul. The first points towards a more communitarian approach, the third towards the liberal viewpoint, while thinking 'beyond' Paul offers a mediating position. This is a sophisticated attempt to do what we noticed Esler and others doing earlier, wrestling with Paul's writings in their social context in order to wrestle with issues in our own.

Thinking 'with' Paul, then, leads to a churchly ethic not unlike that of Hauerwas. However, such an ethic 'need not necessarily reproduce the specific ethical conventions Paul presumes, *since these have no specifically Christian character* but are in many cases part of the overlapping moral consensus of Paul's time' (287, my emphasis). In addition, since Paul appealed to standards of good and evil widely acknowledged outside the Christian community, perhaps we too should look beyond Paul's 'rhetoric of distinction' to more 'widely shared moral norms'. Otherwise, Horrell suggests, we may end up with 'anachronistic attempts to reproduce ancient morality rather than a specifically Christian one'. Like Bultmann demythologizing ancient worldviews, he says, we may need to find ways of translating those ancient thought-forms into contemporary ones.

These are, to be sure, fine-tuned arguments. Whatever we say on any of the relevant issues needs to be carefully balanced. But as I indicated earlier I do not think the particular argument holds. What Horrell seems to have done is to have reproduced, admittedly at a highly sophisticated level, a familiar argument from earlier interpretative debates: the distinction between the bits of the New Testament which are integral to the main message and the bits which are merely 'culturally conditioned', which can therefore be set aside (as 'anachronistic') without any great loss. This founders, of course, on the impossibility of declaring any element in Paul or other early Christian writers to be free of that cultural conditioning; and, to Horrell's suggestion that certain elements are part of Paul's core narrative, we must respond that it is always possible that the interpreter has drawn that line too tightly. In the present case, we may disagree today with what Paul says about such things as idolatry and sexual behaviour. But I do not think we can say that they are simply miscellaneous maxims culled from a surrounding culture without visible links to his own 'Christian myth' – and without audible resonance with the moral culture of our own.

When it comes to thinking 'beyond' Paul, Horrell suggests that his appeal is 'for the members of the Christian community to do better than their contemporaries at meeting common ethical standards' (288). Perhaps, he suggests, the Christian story itself 'can narrate, affirm and learn from the good that is found *extra muros ecclesiae*'.[151] This brings us to the challenge of thinking 'against' Paul, which Horrell calls 'Paul's ethics for a plural society'. Paul's challenge to diversity-in-unity can perhaps, he suggests, be translated into a similar challenge to the complex and dangerous world we live in today (this is part of the challenge taken up by Alain Badiou and others, as we shall see in the next chapter). But if this is to catch on we may need to do what Plato suggested at one point, and write some new myths:

> We might therefore take from our reading of Paul's ethics the idea that human solidarity requires some shared myth, embodied in rituals, that narrates and forms that solidarity, and which may at the same time provide strong grounds for the treasuring of difference, within limits, whether through the notion of differences of faith, conscience, or whatever.[152]

Such broad generalizations invite interrogation: what sort of myths? Will any dream do? What kinds of solidarity (remembering with a shudder the secular solidarities of the twentieth century)? What differences? What limits? What strong grounds? What about those whose consciences tell them to kill people of other faiths? But at this point Horrell explicitly goes against the apostle:

> We might then conclude that to generate an ethic appropriate to our plural, indeed global, society, we need to articulate new stories, new myths, about human solidarity and difference which avoid the notion that only Christ can provide their basis, and in so doing go not only beyond but also against Paul.[153]

Once again: what sort of stories? Are there any novels, plays or movies in today's world which point the way? Some of today's stories seem positive from a Christian point of view: should we attach ourselves to them? In what way, and on what grounds should we choose? What about stories that go in a different direction? Horrell is right to point out that there are many 'myths' alive and well in the contemporary western world, and doing a good deal of damage. He instances the 'myth of the American superhero' as chronicled by Lawrence and Jewett.[154] But he seems to me both over-optimistic and curiously blind – after all his splendid exposition of Paul's subversive gospel! – in supposing that something *other than* the story of Jesus might supply 'a new story, one which encompassed, and at the same time relativized, [the Christian] identity within a wider circle of human belonging.' This is a high road towards a 'solidarity' with the prevailing culture of the day and a 'difference' from the main (and still very much alive) stream of Christian thought. Horrell appeals once more to the transition from Paul's Judaism into Paul's Christianity. He suggests that a similar transition might be appropriate today, a further 'social achievement, in which Christians too take their place among those whose differences remain,

[151] Horrell 288f.; the Latin tag means 'outside the walls of the church'.

[152] Horrell 289f.

[153] Horrell 290.

[154] See Jewett and Lawrence 2002.

but who are now united under a new basis for human solidarity' (290–1). This, perhaps, is where one needs to reaffirm the 'apocalyptic' meaning of Paul's thought, which Horrell, unlike most of the socio-historical movement, scarcely factors in to his treatment. The single moment of the Christ-event is not an 'example' (not even the finest example!) of a more general principle, in this case the idea that every so often things have to change radically. The post-Enlightenment western world has very much wanted to reduce the central event of the Pauline gospel to that status, not least to protect its own project of 'modernity', of 'humankind come of age'. History can only have one apex: modernity, claiming that for the eighteenth century, has not wanted to cede it to the first. Here there is a stark choice. To diminish the eschatological and in that sense 'apocalyptic' meaning of Jesus' death and resurrection is to give up, not some culturally conditioned appendage which we can sideline without loss, but the very centre of Paul's message. And even if it were after all appropriate to downgrade Paul's vision of the one-off messianic achievement to the status of a fine ancient example of how to navigate a tricky cultural transition, the decade since Horrell wrote those words has made the possibility of a new myth and a new social reality, which would incorporate some elements of Christianity but go beyond it into a brave new world, look even more unlikely than it was already. Horrell is offering, at this point, something very like a classic 'Enlightenment' position, reaching for a new 'saeculum' in which Christian values, or at least the ones we ourselves want to retain, may be held within a larger social reality. This has already been tried, by Thomas Jefferson among others.

I believe, however, that there are quite different options open to readers of Paul who are sensitive to the issues Horrell has raised in this remarkable book. I believe that the foundation story of the Christian myth to which Paul gave adherence, and the meaning of the rituals by which the Pauline communities were formed and shaped, had to do not only with the death and resurrection of Israel's Messiah, but with those events seen as the climactic rescue and reconstitution of creation itself. That is the theological foundation, organically related to and flowing from the very heart of Paul's belief-system (not bolted on to it from the outside as a bit of miscellaneous cultural baggage borrowed from his surroundings), for his ethic of renewed humanity, for his recognition of the goodness of the created world beyond the borders of the church, for his determination to 'do good to all', and for his vision – so clearly seen by Meeks, so apparently ignored by Horrell! – for the renewal of the whole creation under the rule of the Messiah. I believe, in other words, that the sharp antithesis of 'liberal' and 'communitarian', so sharply set out in this book and so characteristic of the modern, late-modern, or even postmodern western world, may indeed be where we have to start; but it cannot be where Paul would have us end. These two positions are the long result of the attempt (on the one hand) to turn away from a dogmatic Christianity and get its supposed benefits without its challenges, and (on the other hand) to rediscover an authentic Christian voice while downplaying or ignoring the gospel of new creation, a major Pauline theme which protects this rediscovered authenticity from collapsing into mere inward-looking sectarianism.

Granted, western theology in the last two or three centuries has oscillated to and fro on these points. It has sometimes colluded with the Enlightenment narrative, and sometimes tried to escape from it into a private world. The church in the last generation has done its best to avoid facing the challenge, which occurs within its walls as well as outside them, of how to tell the difference between the differences which make a difference (i.e. which differences threaten the true solidarity) and the differences which don't make a difference (i.e. which are to be welcomed and embraced within that flexible, multi-layered solidarity). We all know that some things are *adiaphora* (i.e. they don't make a difference), and that some things are mandatory (i.e. they do make a difference, a difference which matters). The question is, which are which, how do you tell, and who says? The notion of *adiaphora* needs then to be triangulated with the concept of 'subsidiarity' (at which level can matters be settled? The local church or some larger body?) and 'authority' (who decides, on what grounds, and with what checks and balances?). Thus, even within the household of faith, the question of 'solidarity and difference' which Horrell maps in terms of the Christian faith and the wider world makes its presence felt, and demands answers.

These are all questions which a sociological account of contemporary Christianity might help us map, so that we could all the better bring them into dialogue with the sociological account of early Christianity which David Horrell, in his many works, has helped to develop. These are questions, moreover, to which 1 Corinthians, Horrell's main text, has a lot to say – more even than we find in *Solidarity and Difference*. David Horrell's book, growing as it does out of the attempt of the last generation to do 'social history' in order to understand Paul in his own terms and his own world, and ultimately to bring that new understanding into creative dialogue with our own world, similarly understood in a multi-dimensional fashion, has opened our eyes to many facets of Paul's culture, and many questions about our own. It is one of the most creative and innovative books about Paul I have ever read. I do not think it has yet provided a blueprint for the hoped-for fusion of horizons between Paul's gospel and tomorrow's world. But it has taken a giant leap forward in helping us see what that challenge might actually look like.

Chapter Twelve

PAUL IN THE MARKETPLACE: TOWARDS A WIDER CONTEXT?

1. Back to the Areopagus

(i) Introduction

The study of Paul in his social world points to what at first glance seems to be an entirely new set of questions. These fresh questions are addressed neither by the new perspective, nor by its anxious opponents, nor by the purveyors of 'apocalyptic', nor even – and this is surprising – by those who, like Meeks, Horrell and others, have been at the forefront of the sociological study from which such questions might have emerged. In particular, however, Horrell's highlighting of 'solidarity and difference', and his probing into Paul's relevance for the larger issues which those slogans encapsulate, stands as a signpost towards these questions, though Horrell never goes down the road to see what they might look like, let alone to address them. These are the questions of what might happen if we really did put Paul in the marketplace of contemporary social, cultural and political questions, watching him debate as he did in the marketplace at Athens; or what might happen if we then took him up to the Areopagus itself and got him to explain himself more fully, and perhaps more dangerously.

Much Pauline scholarship of the last two centuries has, of course, come to the reports of Paul's activity in Athens with a suspicious mind. In part this is due to the historians' natural preference for first-hand evidence (Paul's actual letters) rather than second-hand sources (nobody really knows who wrote Acts, let alone when, let alone how reliable its sources were). There are times, however, when we may need to exercise suspicion about the suspicion. Could it, perhaps, have something to do with the desire on the part of certain historians of religion, and certain theologians, to keep Paul *away* from the marketplace, and in particular and at all costs away from the Areopagus? Many have supposed that Paul's job was to explain to people how they were to be justified by faith alone; so why would he need to trade maxims with the Stoics and the Epicureans? And if, as he said to the Corinthians about his arrival among them after only a short stay in Athens, he decided 'to know nothing in my dealings with you except Jesus the Messiah, especially his crucifixion', was he reflecting on the fact that in Athens, where he had spoken not of the cross but of the resurrection, things had not gone so well?[1] Had he not then determined to cast aside all attempts to engage with the wisdom of the world?

There is a grain of truth here, but I think only a grain. Paul's summary of the gospel he originally preached in Corinth offers a careful balance of cross and resurrection.[2] And at point after point in his letters we see him, as he says, deciding to 'take every thought prisoner and make it obey the Messiah', having torn down clever arguments and proud notions that set themselves up against the knowledge of God.[3] I have explored this elsewhere in far more detail than is possible here, and have argued that there are several ways in which we can track the implicit dialogue between Paul and the thinkers of his day.[4] Since, as I argued in the last chapter, Paul was a theologian of creation and new creation, he could not simply create a private mental or spiritual world for Messiah-followers to live in. They were citizens of the *real* world, the new creation that was springing up in the midst of the old. Just as heaven and earth overlapped in the Jewish symbols of Temple and Torah, so the Messiah-people were to live at the equally dangerous and confusing overlap of the new creation and the old. They were to speak the truth of the new creation into the world of the old, the world for which that redemptive gospel truth was designed in the first place.

But what about the implicit dialogue between Paul and the thinkers of *our* day? Suddenly the bold experiment which David Horrell has conducted, bringing Paul into dialogue with the 'liberal' philosophy of Habermas and the 'communitarian' ethic of Hauerwas, looks rather modest: what about Marx and Freud, what about Nietzsche or Walter Benjamin, what about Foucault and Derrida? What, for that matter, about Adorno and Arendt, Hegel and Heidegger, Kant and Kafka, Lacan and Levinas, and a host of others? These writers, whether Paul's current readers know them or not, have shaped the ways we think, the social, cultural and political hopes and fears that make western culture what it is. My own brief thought-experiment, bringing Paul into dialogue with Walter Benjamin (in ways quite different from how that brilliant but tragic figure is often invoked today), looks even more modest.[5] Benjamin is representative of a much wider world, a world which is, both literally and metaphorically, a closed book to most Anglophone readers of Paul.

More is the pity; and more, too, is the pity that there is no space in the present book for anything more than a glance in this new direction. One of

[1] 1 Cor. 2.2.

[2] 1 Cor. 15.3–11.

[3] 2 Cor. 10.4f.

[4] See *PFG* ch. 14.

[5] See *PFG* 1473–84.

the most recent collections of essays exploring this world runs to over six hundred pages, and it is clearly out of the question even to name all the issues involved, let alone to debate them.[6] In case there were any doubt on this point, I quote from the 'blurb' on the book's cover:

> The apostle Paul has reemerged as a force on the contemporary philosophical scene. Some of the most powerful recent affirmations of nonrepresentational, materialist, and event-oriented philosophies repeat topics and tropes of the ancient apostle. Paul is appropriated both for and against Kantian cosmopolitanism, psychoanalytic models of subjectivity and power, Schmittian political theologies, Derridean messianism, political universalism, and an ongoing refashioning of identity politics within postsecular contexts.

The book in question includes some creative engagements between Paul and his own contemporaries, but the main focus is on the fresh retrievals of Paul that are being proposed in our own day.[7]

Four comments, simply about this new project and the wider studies it represents, are already in order. First, it is fascinating to see that the cultural relativism of the 1970s appears to have dropped out of sight. It was common forty years ago, in some circles at least, to draw a thick line somewhere in the eighteenth century, and to declare that one could not translate ideas from before that time into the 'modern world', or at least not without a great deal of adjustment and distancing. There is, to be sure, a fair amount of adjustment still going on. Most of the philosophers now engaging with Paul would not share his view of the resurrection, for instance, and many would not believe in a god, whether the one of whom Paul wrote or some other. But it is taken for granted that a thinker of the distant past can in principle speak to issues that we are raising today. It seems to be assumed that there is a repository of wisdom spread across ancient thinkers. If a publisher can think it worth while to put out new studies of Epictetus and other contemporaries of Paul, more to help people navigate the modern world than to study the ancient one, we should not be surprised that those looking for meaning, for hope, for a way forward out of contemporary social, cultural and political dilemmas, might turn to the apostle himself.[8]

Second, following from that, we notice that the existentialism of Bultmann's day is largely missing. Heidegger and Sartre remain important reference points, but the focus is far more on questions of political philosophy, on the hope for a better world. Hence the 'messianism' of Derrida, following Benjamin in this respect: once the arrogant modernist dreams have been deconstructed, there must be a new possibility, a fresh hope without visible roots in the now defunct past. This is the hope that has driven a great deal of social and political thinking in the last generation or two, and it represents a turn away from the earlier preoccupation with a detached personal

[6] See Blanton and de Vries 2013. Frustratingly, the book, lacking an index, is hard to use as a guide.

[7] Among the former, see e.g. Holloway 2013; Wasserman 2013.

[8] An edition of Epictetus was published in 1995 as part of the series 'Little Books of Wisdom'; see too Epictetus and Lebell 2007; and e.g. Vernezze 2005, a book with the subtitle 'ancient wisdom for troubled times'.

authenticity, a turn signalled in New Testament studies by Käsemann's reaction against Bultmann. Bultmann was, after all, some kind of Kantian Idealist; perhaps the new Paul is some kind of 'materialist'? That, at least, is the thesis of Ward Blanton himself, one of the editors of the recent large collection, in his own trenchant re-interpretation.[9]

Third, this leads to a very different kind of political critique from that which has grown up in Pauline studies over the last generation. I have written more about the latter movement elsewhere, and I shall not repeat that discussion, except to make one or two points relevant to the present topic.[10] The sudden (mostly American) wave of fresh 'political' interpretations of Paul (and the rest of the New Testament) grew for the most part (a) from a deep dissatisfaction with the non-political readings which had become common to that point and (b) from a sense that, in the era of Ronald Reagan and later of George W. Bush, some kind of biblically based critique had to be found to counter the easy assumptions of the so-called 'religious right'. Suddenly it was no longer enough to cite Romans 13.1–7 as proof that Paul was a conservative political thinker who was happy for the ruling authorities to go on running the world in their own way. All sorts of 'subversive' themes were discerned under the surface in his writings: Jesus was Lord, therefore Caesar was not! I have elsewhere tried to bring some nuance to the earlier and somewhat monochrome statements, without I hope losing the cutting edge. But my point here is that the newer engagements on the part of contemporary (mostly European) philosophers come from an entirely different world. The 'Paul and Politics' movement associated with Richard Horsley and others was fairly thoroughly American, with its rhetoric playing out in the simplistic and increasingly divided 'culture wars' in the United States.[11] The newer movement comes mostly from the continent of Europe.

Fourth, and balancing this last comment, it is noticeable that most of the recent North American discussion of Paul and politics tries to locate Paul specifically within the Roman imperial world of his day, however hard in fact that may be. The difficulty with the project is then partly the historical one (how to be sure we are describing that world accurately, and how to evaluate those Pauline texts which may refer, or at least allude, to it) and partly the hermeneutical one (how to transfer whatever we may have learned about Paul's views of the Roman empire into the significantly different imperial worlds of our own day). With the newer continental writings, however, the movement goes the other way, reflecting perhaps a larger frustration with 'history' itself. Philosophers like Agamben, Taubes, Badiou and others start with an assumed analysis of the contemporary scene, in which the American empire has only an occasional walk-on part, playing a one-dimensional example of the supposed capitalist disaster, and then seek for

[9] Blanton 2014.

[10] See *PFG* ch. 12.

[11] See e.g. Horsley 1997, 2000; see further my remarks in *PFG* 1276f. The debate continues: see e.g. McKnight and Modica 2013; Heilig 2015.

analogies and echoes in Paul. Of course, things are never quite that simple. Some, perhaps most, of the contemporary American 'Paul and Politics' writers seem to have started from their contemporary dissatisfactions and gone back to the first century with assumed analogies in mind.[12] But there is a noticeable difference at the level of what these two schools actually write. There is an obvious analogy between the American experience and the continental European one. Both look back to glorious revolutions in the late eighteenth century (1789–94 in France, 1776 in America); both also evoke subsequent social upheavals in the middle of the nineteenth (1848 in Europe, the Civil War of the 1860s in America). But the effect of these events on the cultural, philosophical and political imagination to the west and east of the Atlantic has been significantly different, and that difference is visible in the exegetical and hermeneutical projects undertaken. The British, as usual, sit awkwardly in the middle, linked geographically to Europe but linguistically to America, suspicious of ideology and tempted by short-term pragmatism.

These remarks may serve to contextualize the newer philosophical movements, and also to explain, in a measure, why yet again the different worlds of Pauline study have not been talking to one another. As with Pauline scholarship in general, so particularly with philosophical and political angles, the Anglophone dominance has meant the screening out of other ways of lining up the questions. We may regret the lack of dialogue between the worlds represented, earlier in the present book, by Sanders, Martyn and Meeks. But that is mild compared to the lack of connection between most Anglophone Pauline scholars, including those who have written on 'Paul and politics', and the newer continental discussions. Neither side pays much heed to the other.[13] This cannot be healthy. Sooner or later somebody needs to raise the periscope and look over the high walls. Perhaps they might see another periscope, looking back. The present brief discussion is not intended to be such a periscope; merely to indicate that there is a task here awaiting attention.

Like the three main movements we have sketched in this book, the philosophical retrievals of Paul have emerged from frustration. As we saw, the new perspective was generated by a rejection of derogatory portraits of Judaism; the 'apocalyptic' movement, from Käsemann's frustration with an inward-looking (Bultmannian) existentialism; the 'social-historical' movement, from a dissatisfaction with the decontextualized twentieth-century 'theology of the Word'. The newer philosophical writings have emerged from a different, though to be sure ultimately related, frustration, already felt in the 1930s and now considerably magnified. The old European Left had been accustomed to regard the Russian Revolution as the true heir to its

[12] See e.g. Badiou 2003 [1997], 2: 'My intention, clearly, is neither historicizing nor exegetical. It is subjective through and through.'

[13] This can be confirmed by a glance at the index to the books in question (e.g. Badiou 2003 [1997]; Taubes 2004 [1993]; Agamben 2005 [2000]; Blanton 2014) – in most of which Bultmann is the only NT scholar to rate more than a passing mention.

French predecessor, but within a decade or two doubts had begun to set in, doubts which were greatly magnified when Hitler and Stalin made their brief pact in August 1939. The post-war Marxist movements suffered their apparent *coup de grâce* in 1989 with the fall of the Berlin Wall. True, history did not after all come to an end at that point, as Francis Fukuyama rashly declared.[14] The world has become, if anything, a more dangerous and confusing place, and we do not guard against these dangers, or clarify our confusions, by pretending that all questions can be subsumed under cheap left–right rhetoric ('communism lost, capitalism won'). Vital questions still remain, and we are wise to seek help.

Thus the editors of the volume on 'Paul's New Moment' introduce their work with the following trenchant scene-setting:

> At a point when the capitalist world is coming apart at the seams, we may pause and ask ourselves: what has happened to serious leftist protests against the unjust and dehumanizing logic of global capitalism? For the last few decades, any attempt to criticize the inner dark logic of capitalism has been simply dismissed as passé (or un-American). But now, as we perch precariously on the brink of total financial-capitalistic collapse [this was written, it seems, around 2008], we may wonder why and under what cultural conditions true critiques from the Left have been systematically marginalized into non-existence ... Can anyone, or any discipline, speak up?[15]

At this moment, it seems, new insights are urgently required. It is greatly to the credit of sometimes avowedly atheist philosophers that they are turning to Paul for help, just as it says a lot for the robustness of Paul's thought that he often provides them with fresh stimulus, despite their obvious disagreements at a quite basic level (on matters like the existence of God, for instance).[16] If we are to follow down the line of either Wayne Meeks's agenda of a 'hermeneutics of social embodiment', or David Horrell's proposals for addressing 'solidarity' and 'difference' – and Horrell is there doing, in a specific and focused way, more or less what these philosophers are doing, though with far more exegetical grip – then we must somehow start to engage with the newer movements.

The problem here for the mainline Pauline exegete, to be frank, is twofold. First, even to understand what the philosophers are talking about would require a crash course in European political thought over the last two hundred years. These discussions have been going on a long time, and the attempt to bring Paul into them means what it means within that longer history of discourse, most of which has not formed part of the curriculum taken by mainstream Pauline scholars, even by those of us who have studied

[14] Fukuyama 2012 [1992].

[15] 'Introduction', in Milbank, Žižek and Davis 2010, 1. Even the trenchant polemic here seems somewhat unhelpfully centred on America: 'this book's main imperative', he states, 'is to challenge the American bourgeois interpretation of Christian faith that simply hands over the world to the corporation without a fight' (4). This is plentifully illustrated in Milbank's lead article, which I shall discuss presently. This does not undermine the disjunction I mentioned a moment ago, which was between the continental philosophers (and of course their American retrievals) and the American 'Paul and politics' writers.

[16] See e.g. the trenchant statement in Badiou 2003 [1997], 1–3.

philosophy to degree level. Second, and perhaps as a result, the writing is sometimes impenetrable, at least to the uninitiated. As with all disciplines and academic traditions, and for that matter the worlds of music or sport, political philosophers use shorthand and code, which like the private argot of a sect can appear designed to prevent the outsider from finding out what is going on.

That would be a pity; because, to continue with Ward Blanton for a moment, his own project has in my view grasped one of the most important things about Paul (important, that is, in terms of how he is retrieved for our day): *that he was not a Platonist.* Blanton is reacting, in a sustained if dense argument, against the assumption of Nietzsche, Freud and others that Christianity was 'a Platonism for the masses'. Hence the title of Blanton's book: *A Materialism for the Masses*, reading Paul as passionately concerned with the material world. Thus while a line of thinkers from Nietzsche to Derrida has misread Paul, the former seeing him as the arch-purveyor of a dehumanizing glorification of 'weakness' and the latter lampooning him for his 'retrograde dualistic metaphysics', Blanton asserts that such a way of reading 'Paul'

> obscures a materialist philosophical engagement with a crucial swath of Western religious and philosophical history, thereby obscuring important resources for a new materialist philosophy of life which is a pressing need within our biopolitical or posthumanist epoch.[17]

To make Paul (effectively) a kind of Epicurean, which this position might threaten to do, would however be just as problematic in its way as to make him an Idealist. Problematic, that is, in terms once again of history and exegesis. Walter Benjamin wrote that to get at the truth of a work required 'the most precise immersion into the individual details of a given subject'.[18] It is not clear how far a project of retrieval can get if it does not pay constant attention to the one being retrieved. And that, once again, means history. Too often, I fear, the figure being invoked is a 'Paul' of cultural memory – a problem we all face, of course, but a problem to which the constant refreshing of historical study is the only answer.

What we need at this point is a map of the cultural, political and philosophical circumstances into which Agamben, Taubes, Badiou and others have written their studies on Paul, and from which Blanton and others in their work, and Davis, Milbank and Žižek in theirs, are now emerging with a further set of studies and proposals. We need the equivalent, for this large and often forbidding field, of Horrell's second chapter, where he expounds Habermas and Hauerwas as obvious representatives of the 'liberal' and 'communitarian' projects respectively. Such a project, even if boiled down to its simplest form, would require more than a chapter. The complex ideas

[17] Blanton 2014, 10f. Cf. too Milbank et al. 2010, 1: theology (and the Christian tradition) 'serves as a wellspring capable of funding a materialist politics of subjective truth.' These writers insist on the ultimate 'Event' being the incarnation, cross and resurrection of Jesus.

[18] Benjamin 1974–89, vol. 1, 208. I owe this reference to de la Durantaye 2012, 50.

and influence of Nietzsche alone would need that. All I can do here is gesture towards the area where one might begin, recognizing that neither I nor the other Pauline scholars with whom I have engaged in my own work have done more than scratch the surface somewhere near where we think the important issues may be found.

We are faced, I think, with a more dense and complex version of the hermeneutical question posed in their different ways by Käsemann and Horrell. Käsemann faced the dilemma: should Paul's gospel be seen as an individual, 'anthropological' message, as with Bultmann, or did it need to be articulated in terms of a 'cosmic' vision? That question arose sharply in the middle of the twentieth century. It was not enough, Käsemann believed, to cultivate one's own authenticity when there were forces of evil on the rampage; and since Paul used language which in its ancient setting seemed to invoke that larger battle between the righteousness of God and the powers of darkness we should try to retrieve it for our own use as well. However, as we saw in Part II above, the attempts to use such an either/or (*either* 'anthropology' *or* 'cosmology') as a template for understanding Paul founders on the actual historical exegesis of the texts, both the Jewish 'apocalyptic' texts and Paul himself. Paul resists the bifurcation, and goes on addressing his issues in his own way. With David Horrell, the dilemma has been presented in late twentieth-century terms: is Paul basically a 'liberal' or a 'communitarian' thinker? Horrell himself sees, I think, that Paul resists the antithesis, and that he finds his own way of holding together what our culture has split apart. (One could go further back in our argument, to Part I, and ask: in what ways was the question which Ed Sanders posed one which Paul himself would resist or at least rephrase?[19]) But now the question is more complicated, because it would need to go something like this: what might Paul have to say to a world which had hoped for a decisive messianic or revolutionary moment, an 'event' through which the world might be transformed for the better, and which had now suffered yet more disappointment? Deeper far than the either/or about 'Paul and empire' in some recent writing (including my own) is the question about 'Paul and western civilization'.

The question presupposes a view of the last two centuries of European history (and, in a measure, of world history, since Europe has had such a decisive influence elsewhere) in which the French Revolution forms the decisive back-marker. That is still seen by many European political thinkers as an 'event' of the first magnitude, instantiating in actual political life some at least of the ideals of the Enlightenment, declaring that it had swept away the older feudal regime, clearing the ground for … what? The answer was a highly confused nineteenth century, in which the French monarchy itself was restored, abolished again, and restored again, leading to the great revolutionary year of 1848 when revolutions broke out in several European countries, providing Karl Marx and Friedrich Engels with more than enough raw material to fuel their theories about the coming even greater

[19] See *PFG* ch. 13, esp. 1321–4.

revolution for which all these movements would eventually be seen as advance signs. The French Revolution itself had not, after all, produced a social Utopia. According to one dominant left-wing narrative, the events of 1789 had got rid of the old, creaky feudal hierarchy, thereby accidentally opening the door to the rise of the bourgeoisie, the new middle classes, who replaced the financial power of the older aristocrats with the new financial system we know (in one form or another) as capitalism. This in turn produced (at least in the view of Marx and many others) many new kinds of injustice and inequality, so that those who dreamed of a new world order found themselves caught between two times: the time of the original revolution which had raised so many hopes, and the time of the coming greater revolution in which those hopes (or at least their lineal descendants) might at last be realized.

Thinkers from Marx through Nietzsche to Walter Benjamin and others disagreed as to how this new 'event' would come. Would it be by means of active revolt and resistance? Would it be engineered by attempts at reform from within or below? Or would it arrive when the old order collapsed under its own weight? There are echoes here of biblical and theological dilemmas. Should the fleeing Israelites turn and fight the Egyptians, or should they stand still and see the salvation of the Lord? Should the would-be revolutionaries do their best to resist the new forms of tyranny, or would that be the secular equivalent of a self-help Pelagianism, when what they needed was the secular equivalent of the interruptive (apocalyptic?) divine act of rescue? Would not attempts at reform mean a compromising collusion with the forces of bourgeois capitalism, merely reinforcing them in their wicked ways? And, if there was to be a great new moment, would it come by social, cultural and economic forces operating secretly within the system, or would it come by some 'great man' emerging to point the way?

In the middle of this, it seemed that the only thing on offer from the churches was a polarization between a fundamentalism that sought to escape the world and a liberalism that sought to embrace it. That would merely restate the problem:

> But notice that these two apparently different interpretative horizons (fundamentalist and liberal) are united at a deeper, more secret level, for they each extract the struggle of Christian resistance either by giving up the world (fundamentalist) or by giving over the world (liberalism) to the powers.[20]

I do not think that the word 'liberalism' is here being used in the same sense as Horrell uses it in relation to Habermas. But the polarization noted here will be familiar to most readers.

Even at this level of generality, one can understand some at least of the tensions in European political and philosophical debate in the twentieth century. The First World War made everything much worse, of course, piling fuel on to many different fires and adding at every point new layers of

[20] Milbank et al. 2010, 4.

grief and anger. The Russian Revolution of 1917, the financial crises of the late 1920s, the collapse of the Weimar Republic, the rise of the Nazis in the 1930s – each of these, far too complex for even a brief comment here, contributed to the growing sense that only a radical new moment, perhaps a moment that might deserve the secularized but still Jewish name of 'messianic', would transform the increasingly desperate situation in the way many still hoped. All of this, cast into philosophical shorthand, stands in the background of the debates of the second half of the twentieth century and in the attempted retrievals of Paul which some have offered. Since, as I said, few if any Anglophone Pauline scholars have attempted to engage with this complex set of cultural and philosophical dilemmas, it is not surprising that the newer work has been found hard to assimilate, and is dealt with only, if at all, by philosophers rather than exegetes.[21]

After the Second World War matters did not stand still. Different varieties of revolutionary theology came and went. The old European Left held its breath for a moment in 1968 when *les événements* in Paris threatened for a moment to produce something more like what they had been hoping for. But the moment passed without lasting socio-political results, at least of the desired kind, and two decades later those still clinging to some version of the Marxist-Leninist dream suffered the ultimate disappointment with the collapse of the Soviet Union and its satellites in 1989, leaving the heavily modified Chinese version of communism, the isolated and much-mocked North Korean version, and the regimes in Venezuela and elsewhere as the tattered remnants of the biggest political experiment of modern times. This pushed the Left back against the wall, but, since that was where some of them had always thought they should be, they were prepared to wait for the crisis which would surely come, as the capitalist system tottered and fell under its own overblown weight. The financial crisis of 2007 and 2008 duly arrived – and produced, not revolution, but reaffirmation of 'the system': the western powers used taxpayers' money to bail out the banks and big businesses, rescuing the very rich from the bankruptcy which (in the view of many, not only the Marxists) they had inflicted on the very poor. The second decade of the twenty-first century, half way through at the time of writing, has itself produced increasing social and political unrest and disquiet, not only in Europe but on the global scene, as the newer militant versions of Islam wreak terror and havoc, as the running sore of Israel and Palestine seems to get worse not better, and as tensions rise once more along the old Iron Curtain. Meanwhile doubts are raised, even at a popular level, about the effectiveness of the West's much-vaunted liberal democracies – doubts which have a disturbing similarity to those which paved the way for the totalitarianisms of the previous century. These doubts then join up with the deeper theoretical disquiet expressed by many philosophical observers of the secular 'biopolitical', to which I shall return in a moment.

[21] As in the books, helpful though they are, of Milbank, Žižek and Davis 2010 and Harink 2010a. The essay by Martyn 2010 does not address Agamben and the others; those by Fowl 2010 and Elliott 2010 avoid detailed exegesis.

Many of the essayists in the recent volumes on Paul and the contemporary philosophers are engaging with this world, and the reader will now see what I meant when I said that even to offer a sketch-map of the territory would take a book much longer than the present one. The assumption which pervades much of this swathe of study is that all right-thinking observers (which means, of course, all left-thinking observers) are signed up to a kind of inaugurated eschatology, a sense of *time* in which the revolutionary events of the past have opened the possibility of further such events which would, so to speak, finish the job. It is to this cause that they are invoking Paul.

(ii) Paul, Time and Giorgio Agamben

One of the best known of these writers, dealing with the new sense of time, is the Italian philosopher Giorgio Agamben. He has written widely on issues of philosophy, politics and aesthetics, and on their intersections with Jewish and Christian thought.[22] His essay on Paul, now widely discussed, announces itself as a commentary on Romans, though in fact it uses the first few verses of the letter as a jumping-off point for much wider reflections.[23]

Agamben expounds what he understands as the Pauline stress on living in a new kind of time, 'messianic' time, a time in which everything is different, held between the event which is past and the event still to come. This is a time when, as in Bultmann's exegesis of 1 Corinthians 7, one is to live 'as if not', *hōs mē*: Agamben picks up Walter Benjamin's proposal that 'the Marxian concept of a "classless society" is a secularization of the idea of messianic time', and links this with Adorno's aphorism about the need to see everything from an ultimate, redemptive future:

> The only philosophy which can be responsibly practiced in face of despair is the attempt to contemplate all things as they would present themselves from the standpoint of redemption.[24]

For Paul, says Agamben, this begins with the radical move: not just 'as if' (living 'as if' the redemption were at hand) but 'as not', since

> The coming of the Messiah means that all things, even the subjects who contemplate it, are caught up in the *as not*, called and revoked at one and the same time.[25]

[22] See e.g. his remarkable book *The Kingdom and the Glory* (Agamben 2011 [2007]). I am grateful to my friend and colleague Professor Barbara Hallensleben of Freiburg University in Switzerland for alerting me to this work and for a fruitful discussion of Agamben.

[23] Agamben 2005 [2000], justifying the selection of these verses by suggesting that these opening verses contain the whole letter in compressed compass. This claim, while hard to justify in detail, has the merit of upstaging Rom. 1.16f., normally cited to similar effect. Subsequent references to Agamben are to this work.

[24] Adorno 1974 [1951], 247, quoted by Agamben 2005 [2000], 35.

[25] Agamben 41.

'This', says Agamben, 'is the meaning of Galatians 2.20: "It is no longer I that live . . . but the Messiah living in me."' This is the vital event that has created a new kind of time, 'a space that escaped the grasp of power and its laws'.[26] Agamben thus appears to appropriate Paul's dialectic between 'gospel and law' on behalf of the now standard political critique of 'the law' as the sign and symbol of the oppressive secular society. 'The principle of the law is thus division', he writes, and 'the Messiah is actually the instance par excellence for a conflict with the law' (47, 49). This enables him to borrow Paul's idea of a 'remnant', the term now standing for a people who embody resistance to the prevailing systems (57). All this leads to his proposal that Paul, as an apostle rather than a prophet, is speaking about 'the present time', *ho nyn kairos*, not about a time yet to come. This is a time to be characterized neither as 'the present age' nor as 'the age to come', but as

> a remnant, the time that remains between these two times, when the division of time is itself divided.[27]

Here is the central proposal of Agamben's book: Paul articulates this new kind of time, neither as mere chronological succession nor as the blank denial which belongs to end-of-the-world speculation, but as a moment to be taken hold of, to be 'bought up' or 'redeemed', indeed, to be 'seized':

> Messianic time is *the time that time takes to come to an end*, or, more precisely, the time we take to bring to an end, to achieve our representation of time. This is not the line of chronological time (which was representable but unthinkable), nor the instant of its end (which was just as unthinkable); nor is it a segment cut from chronological time; rather it is operational time pressing within the chronological time, working and transforming it from within; it is the time we need to make time end: *the time that is left us*.[28]

Agamben links this with the proposal that we should see the sabbath as a kind of messianic time, not just a different day but a different *sort* of day, creating a disjointedness within ordinary time 'through which one may – by a hairsbreadth – grasp time and accomplish it' (72). This is the moment in which 'the past (the complete) rediscovers actuality and becomes unfulfilled, and the present (the incomplete) acquires a kind of fulfillment' (75).

This leads to an explosive proposal about a Pauline notion of 'recapitulation'. Agamben rightly sees that Ephesians 1.10 offers a summary of much that is to come, not only in that letter but right across western culture:

> Having just laid out the divine project of messianic redemption, Paul writes, 'as for the economy of the *pleroma* of times, all things are recapitulated in him, things in heaven and things on earth.' This short verse is laden with meaning to the point that one could say that several fundamental texts in Western culture – such as the doctrine of apocastasis [*sic*] in Origen and Leibniz; repetition or retrieval in Kierkegaard; the eternal return in

[26] Agamben 27. This causes me to question the assertion of Griffiths 2010, 190, within an otherwise helpful article, that the 'trope' of the cross is 'noticeably absent from Agamben's reading of Paul'.

[27] Agamben 62.

[28] Agamben 67f., italics original.

> Nietzsche; and repetition in Heidegger – are the consequences of an explosion of the meaning harbored within.[29]

Though the primary emphasis of the verse might seem to concern the coming together of the two *spatial* elements (heaven and earth), Agamben picks up the notion of the 'fulfillment of time' and stresses the coming together of the *temporal*:

> Insofar as messianic time aims toward the fulfillment of time . . . it effects a recapitulation, a kind of summation of all things . . . of all that has transpired from creation to the messianic 'now', meaning of the past as a whole [*sic*]. Messianic time is a summary recapitulation of the past . . . [30]

It is therefore a mistake, though a common one, to see 'messianic time' as concerned primarily with the future. To the contrary:

> for Paul recapitulation, *anakephalaiōsis*, means that *ho nyn kairos* is a contraction of past and present, that we will have to settle our debts, at the decisive moment, first and foremost with the past.[31]

This in turn leads Agamben to a 'concrete example, a kind of small-scale model of the structure of messianic time that we have been attempting to grasp in the Pauline text' (78). This example, he says disarmingly, 'may perhaps surprise you', and it is safe to say that, for most Pauline exegetes, it will. Agamben's proposal is that western poetry, particularly the phenomenon of rhyme, exemplifies the new kind of time, generating its own time, the world which the poem creates, moving towards an end and hence 'a kind of eschatology', but possessing its own 'time' as it does so (78–9). Taking the sestina as his particular example, he suggests that

> the sestina – and, in this sense, every poem – is a soteriological device which, through the sophisticated *mēchanē* of the announcement and retrieval of rhyming end words (which correspond to typological relations between past and present), transforms chronological time into messianic time. Just as this time is not other to chronological time or eternity, but is the transformation that time undergoes when it is taken for a remnant, so too is the time of the sestina the metamorphosis that time undergoes insofar as it is the time of the end, the *time that the poem takes to come to an end.*[32]

Thus – drawing together and compressing Agamben's own larger discussion as well! – 'the movement through the six stanzas of the sestina repeats the movement of the six days of creation and together articulates their relation to Saturday . . . as a cipher of the messianic fulfillment of time' (83). This generates a potentially fruitful proposal. 'Rhyme', he says, 'issues from Christian poetry as a metrical-linguistic transcodification of messianic time

[29] Agamben 75; Agamben includes the original Greek of Eph. 1.10, as also the Danish and German technical terms in Kierkegaard and Heidegger.

[30] Agamben 75f.

[31] Agamben 78.

[32] Agamben 82f., italics original. I have corrected 'though' in the opening line of this quotation to the presumably intended 'through'.

and is structured according to the play of typological relations and recapitulations evoked by Paul' (85). But Paul's text itself then

> reveals itself as being entirely animated according to an unprecedented play of inner rhymes, of alliterations and end words . . . Paul pushes to an extreme the use of parallelism, antitheses, and homophony in classical rhetoric and Hebrew prose. But, in breaking up a period into short and abrupt *stichoi*, articulated in and stressed by rhyme, he reaches unknown heights in Greek or even Semitic prose, as though he were responding to an inner exigency and an epochal motivation.[33]

Thus, he concludes,

> rhyme, understood in the broad sense of the term as the articulation of a difference between semiotic series and semantic series, is the messianic heritage Paul leaves to modern poetry, and the history and fate of rhyme coincide in poetry with the history and fate of the messianic announcement.[34]

Whether all this will stand up to the scrutiny of specialists remains to be seen. But it makes Agamben's main point clear, as could have been done by quoting Paul, a chapter later in Ephesians: *autou gar esmen poiēma*, we are God's artwork, his 'poem'.[35]

By now the reader who has come to Agamben, or even to this brief discussion of him, expecting theology and politics may well be feeling not only surprised but also lost: this is all no doubt very interesting, but where is it going? The answer is clear. Once we understand the notion of 'the time that remains', of 'messianic time', we see that within this new kind of time *'the works of the law' are 'abolished'*. Agamben argues that Paul deliberately uses the term *katargeō* to express 'the effect of the messianic on works of the law', since the verb 'signifies the sabbatical suspension of works'.[36] Messianic time renders the works of the law inoperative: not non-existent, but powerless (97–8). This in turn reveals that several other attempts in the modern period to evade the stifling power of 'the law' are themselves to be seen as shrunken, secularized versions of an original messianic vision. 'Deconstruction is a thwarted messianism, a suspension of the messianic' (103). Nietzsche himself, despite his overt intention, is merely repeating something Paul had already glimpsed:

> *The Anti-Christ* can therefore be read as a messianic parody in which Nietzsche, in cloaking himself in the garments of the Antimessiah, is actually only reciting a script written by Paul.[37]

[33] Agamben, 85f. He offers as examples 1 Cor. 7.30f.; 15.42–4; 2 Tim. 4.7f.

[34] Agamben 87.

[35] Eph. 2.10. *Poiēma* can have the wider meaning of 'deed' or 'act', but Plato and other writers use it to refer to a poem or verse: see LSJ 1429.

[36] This is perhaps an overstatement: Agamben cites the use of *argeō* in 2 Macc. 5.25, but this is not the verb used in e.g. Gen. 2.2f. or Ex. 20.11, or indeed Heb. 4.10 (though Hebrews 3 and 4 is knocking on the door of this discussion).

[37] Agamben 112.

This leads Agamben to some concluding reflections on the different conceptions of 'faith', and to a final link back to Walter Benjamin, who had been waiting in the wings through much of the foregoing. Suggesting that the great Jewish scholar Gershom Scholem might have recognized a parallel between his friend Benjamin and the apostle Paul (I had forgotten, when proposing my own similar parallel in the final chapter of *Paul and the Faithfulness of God*, that, according to Agamben, Scholem had got there first!) he draws out the implications of such an initially unlikely match in ways which point to a transcending of the antithesis I noted earlier. The continental philosophers are trying to draw Paul into their own time, while the Americans are trying to recognize their own day in Paul's:

> These two fundamental messianic texts of our tradition [i.e. Paul and Benjamin], separated by almost two thousand years, both written in a situation of radical crisis, form a constellation whose time of legibility has finally come today ... [This idea of a time of legibility] defines a genuinely Benjaminian hermeneutic principle, the absolute opposite of the current principle [of 'normal exegesis'] according to which each work may become the object of infinite interpretation at any given moment ... Benjamin's principle instead proposes that every work, every text, contains a historical index which indicates both its belonging to a determinate epoch, as well as its only coming forth to full legibility at a determinate historical moment.[38]

Agamben is thus gesturing towards the hermeneutical gap, and is proposing a Gadamer-like fusion of horizons between Paul's ancient world and our contemporary one.[39] Just as Paul expounded *ho nyn kairos*, the 'messianic time' of the gospel, as a special sort of time in which 'the law' was to be set aside, so in the present day we may discern a kind of 'in-between time', a sabbatical moment, in which the normally all-enveloping claims of the post-revolutionary secular age can be put aside, and a genuine 'exception' made which shows up the self-serving pretensions of those who claim, in the famous Schmittian terms, the sovereign right to decide on exceptions.[40]

It should now be clear that Agamben, whom I have taken as the token representative of a wider new movement, is an astonishingly stimulating and many-sided reader of both ancient and modern texts, capable of producing bold hypotheses which I enjoy contemplating not least because they make my own look relatively modest. It is not clear, however, by what means the proposal of a new 'legibility' is to gain any foothold. It is not, in the nature of the case, something one might try to demonstrate by any

[38] Agamben 145. For my own parallel between Benjamin and Paul see *PFG* 1473–84.

[39] In the passage just quoted Agamben indicates his awareness that 'Paul and Romans are ... located firmly in the salvation-historical past, no less to be read from a temporal distance than they are by Jewett', which is what Harink 2010b, 311 says about my own work (referring also to Jewett 2007). His attempt to suggest that Jewett and I thereby refuse the proper task of commentary, which he defines as being 'to mediate the temporal gap', is falsified both by the repeated 'Reflections' in my own commentary and by Jewett's energetic propagation of his own reading of Paul as an urgent solution for contemporary problems, as in Jewett and Yeo 2012. Agamben's own careful historical and philological work, on display from time to time in the book under consideration, shows his awareness of the need for the kind of historical and linguistic study which Harink appears to regard as unnecessary and indeed unhelpful.

[40] Agamben 104–8; see further Agamben 2005 [2003]. On this, see Griffiths 2010, 181–4.

quasi-scientific method. It would have to be something discerned, perceived with some kind of prophetic insight. There may perhaps be an echo here of the famous claim by the early Barth, from which he later drew back, that, when the sixteenth-century Reformers read Paul, the wall of partition between the first and the sixteenth century melted away, so that Paul could speak directly into their new situation.[41] To this extent, what Agamben is doing is basically *preaching*: soaking himself in the text on the one hand and in critical contemporary reflection on the other hand, and allowing a fresh fusion to take place. This then invites a second-order discernment, namely that of the hearers or readers: does Agamben's proposal make good sense to us? Does it illuminate Paul from our own day, and our own day from Paul? Does it open our eyes and make us say, 'Of course! That is how things are, only we had never seen it before'? Or does it elicit only a mixed reaction? How might one adjudicate between wise and unwise hearings? Those questions need further attention – along with the similar ones which will arise from the other works, albeit very different in orientation, now regularly cited alongside Agamben.

There is one crucial respect in which the dialogue between the discussions taking place in the guild of Pauline studies and the discussions taking place among the philosophers might come into early focus. This has to do with Paul and the law. The contemporary philosophers are attempting to retrieve one of the main things that continental scholars in the nineteenth century thought they knew about Paul: that he opposed the fresh word of the gospel to 'the law', conceived as a generalized version of Israel's Torah. He thus showed the way (so it has been thought) for contemporary protests not only in favour of this or that style of antinomianism but more specifically against the whole construct of an immanent or positivistic 'law' as discussed by Carl Schmitt and others, in which the removal of any concept of 'divine right' has meant 'a secularization of theological authorizing of absolute rule'.[42] Getting rid of the divine legitimation from above ('divine right of kings') has not after all resulted in a lasting atheism, but in the implicit theism-from-below of *vox populi, vox Dei*. 'The law' has here become a way of speaking about the civil society of the western world, sustained as it were from below through the modern democratic process, in which capitalism and bourgeois values are held in place by one another under a veneer of self-congratulatory post-Enlightenment rhetoric: *we* have discovered at last how to run the world, by voting every few years and by dropping bombs on faraway people who do things differently! In other words, because *we*, the Enlightened western world, have developed by a kind of Social Darwinism into the fullest expression of a political system justified 'from below', we are in a position to justify our actions even where they constitute an apparent exception to rules that might normally apply.

[41] See above, 86.

[42] As summarized by Milbank 2010, 28; cf. 24: 'the problematic of alienation is endemic to the very notion of political representation'.

This is what has been called 'the biopolitical', discussed as such by post-Benjamin philosophers. Agamben makes the crucial distinction between this mode of existence as *bios* and a genuine human life as *zōē*. In today's late-capitalist democracies, so the theory goes, *zōē* has been collapsed into *bios*, and since the latter is defined by the paraphernalia of the modern western post-Enlightenment world people today imagine that they can safely conclude that here alone true *bios* is to be found, with disastrous consequences for the rest of the world.[43] This kind of *bios* is the form of social life in which Hobbes, Darwin and others come together and enforce, underneath what calls itself freedom, a kind of evolutionary politics which develops under its own steam and lurches between iron necessity ('that's just how things happen') and impending chaos (as witness the economic crises in the European Union and the short-term pragmatism with which they are addressed). This is the context in which hope has sprung up again for 'the event', especially 'the messianic': something new has happened, is happening, in which the 'law' of this *bios* is decisively challenged.

This is where the discussion which focused Part I of the present book becomes relevant again. It was essential to the new perspective, in its various forms, that the normal sixteenth- and nineteenth-century readings of 'the law', as a kind of ancient foretaste of the perceived moralisms of mediaeval Catholicism, did scant justice to the Jewish Torah as perceived and practised by people like Saul of Tarsus in the first century, and that neither history nor hermeneutics was well served by pretending that they were more or less the same thing. Now 'the law', as a synecdochic shorthand for the 'biopolitical', appears in the role of a secularized mediaeval moralism, playing Eck to Agamben's Luther; will it fare any better?[44] Will it, too, result (as did the 'old perspective') in renewed misrepresentations of Jews ancient and modern? Will it force us, as the Reformational readings did, into distortions of Paul himself? How might we prevent Agamben's proposed 'legibility', the arrival of a moment when certain texts spring to fresh and obvious life, from becoming, in itself, the occasion for further chaos and catastrophe?

That is only one (perhaps exemplary) problem we might face when contemplating the new philosophical proposals for reading Paul. There might be others. Would Paul not have said that the truly messianic event was the death and resurrection of Jesus of Nazareth? And does that not mean that, were he here to be interrogated, he would say that all time *since the resurrection of Jesus* is 'messianic time'? Might that not raise other disturbing questions, either about the two thousand years which have rolled along since then, or about the elevation of events in eighteenth-century Europe (and America?) to the status of a messianic moment? Might a grandiose and self-congratulatory reading of the Enlightenment not be part of the problem, part of the pride which Paul's gospel would undermine? Further, what might be the equivalent, in a post-Benjaminian vision of new time, for the

[43] See again Griffiths 2010, 181f.

[44] Johann Eck (1486–1543) was Luther's main adversary at the Leipzig Disputation of 1519, and remained a leading opponent thereafter.

Pauline emphasis on the presence and activity of the spirit? And – since some of those who cheerfully invoke Benjamin also eagerly embrace the kind of 'apocalyptic' espoused by Martyn and others – in what way do the 'apocalyptic' events of the cross and the *parousia* contextualize, and perhaps relativize, the claims of today's philosophers? This, it seems to me, might be today's version of Paul's final challenge in the Areopagus address. The debate with alternative philosophical visions is important, because the God of the gospel is the creator and re-creator God. But perhaps the resurrection of Jesus might reframe these debates in such a radical way that most will laugh, while only a few – this may perhaps be a different 'remnant' from the one which Agamben envisages – will want to hear more.

These questions are not designed to push away the challenges of Agamben and the others, as though one might then retreat to a safe ecclesial space, using a supposed historical exegesis to bolt the door and keep the intruders at bay. They are, equally, questions for all sorts of other would-be retrievals of Paul, whether by the fundamentalists who lean their weight heavily in the scales of American politics, or the radicals who seek to use Paul to oppose them, or indeed the pietists, whether catholic or protestant, who want to withdraw from the fray into the private world of prayer and liturgy. In particular, it will not do – to anticipate objections from those who never wanted to join up Pauline exegesis with the complicated and messy business of modern secular *Realpolitik* in the first place, and have no wish to start now – to complain that Paul will have nothing to say about such matters, because he writes, not about reforming society or even about a revolution, but about the gospel of Jesus. At least, any who want to register such an objection might have to reflect that they would be going back, in some senses at least, to Bultmann: they would be focusing the gospel on their own inner authenticity. That position, not least in its supposedly 'conservative' forms, is looking increasingly endangered. Of course Paul's gospel was designed to transform every aspect of human existence, inner and outer, solitary and corporate, the personal, social, cultural and political included. If therefore it is legitimate to come to Paul with the questions which dominated the three main Parts of this book – the questions of recent years to do with 'patterns of religion' ('getting in and staying in'), with apocalypse and history, and with the social formation of Messiah-followers then and now – it must also be legitimate to address the questions which concern the cultural, social, philosophical and political crises of the present day. Paul, of course, will insist on reformulating the questions, as he did before the greybeards of Athens. But he will meet them on their own terms as he does so. There is no reason a priori why we should not follow his example, appealing to him as a guide as and when responsible exegesis will permit.

It is, of course, impossible even to begin such a task here. My discussion of Agamben is a mere token of what might be done. Instead, I offer one other reflection only, on a single essay by one of the most notable writers in the recent collections, a writer who has made and is making his ongoing contribution to the transformation of the very terms in which the engagement between theology and sociology is conducted.

(iii) Paul, Biopolitics and John Milbank

John Milbank has argued in his seminal essay 'Paul against Biopolitics' that Paul provides not just *a* way, but the only viable way, of advancing beyond the destructive and enslaving 'biopolitical' and into a different kind of world. It is not obvious how Milbank thinks this theory might have any effect, since Milbank constantly wages war against those who think they are 'preaching the gospel' in a traditional fashion. (How, in other words, would his vision translate into corporate action?) But the vision is worth exploring, since in drawing on and developing the earlier work of Agamben and others Milbank is attempting to sum up a complex field and take an argument to the next stage.

Milbank first explores 'the modern biopolitical', arguing as we have already seen that the secular construct, achieved by the artificial subtraction of the transcendent from public life, results not in the supposed Utopia but in new forms of oppression and slavery. Under such a regime the churches may well carry on with their normal activities, but they will not realize that, by 'educating us into a compensating virtue and civility' they become thereby

> quasi-capitalist corporations ultimately serving the ends of immanent abstraction and local branches of the state police working toward the same end.[45]

This may seem bizarre, even extreme, but we will let the point stand for the moment – and certainly it would not be difficult to find *some* concrete examples, even if Milbank's generalizations, here as elsewhere, invite challenge or even refutation. His point, though, is that 'there can be only an authentically religious route out of the biopolitical', namely the one signalled by Paul.[46] To approach the apostle he quite rightly sees that one must look first, not at the modern 'biopolitical', but at the ancient one, at the world shaped by the theories of Aristotle and others on the one hand and by the Roman pragmatism on the other.[47] He therefore gestures, albeit briefly, in the direction of a more sophisticated analysis of Paul's Roman political world, and its philosophical underpinnings, than is normally given, though without I think getting quite to the heart of it.[48]

[45] Milbank 2010, 33.

[46] Milbank 2010, 33, 36.

[47] Milbank 2010, 33–42.

[48] In my own work I discussed Paul's philosophical and political worlds in separate compartments, knowing that this was artificial but being unwilling to make an already long book even longer by showing the ways in which they joined up. Milbank relies far too heavily, in my view, on the very debatable theories of Blumenfeld 2001 (see my summary in *PFG* 1272 and the alternative proposals which follow).

Paul, suggests Milbank, transcends both the ancient and the modern 'biopolitical' with what Milbank calls 'the politics of resurrection'. Since I shall have some critical questions to raise I want to stress that at this point I think Milbank is right on target, standing in line – *mutatis mutandis*! – with Ward Blanton's notion that Paul is offering 'a materialism for the masses'. Paul's theology is indeed all about concrete reality, the reality of a new community which by its very existence and specific nature calls into question all human communities. For Paul, 'the classical antique notion that the highest life is to be discovered only within the civic assembly is not abandoned', though for Paul the mode of entry into that life, the 'very condition for citizenship', is of a strange sort: 'a practice of detachment from the flesh bound to death, and an entering into a divinizing pneumatic sphere'.[49] Thus – and Milbank is surely conscious of the way in which he is echoing, perhaps ironically, an earlier *religionsgeschichtlich* analysis of Paul –

> the new, more fundamental political order of 'the church' that he insinuates within this regime [sc. of the existing Roman-Greek political order], like a benign parasite, is theocratic in a quite unprecedented sense. For now it is only the adherent of a mystery cult who can be a full-fledged citizen, only the person who participates in the more fundamental pneumatic life and who starts to transfigure his body in the direction of wholly purified passion who is capable of true civic virtue.[50]

Milbank speaks of 'resurrection', but I do not think he has fully grasped, let alone made use of, what Paul means by the term. He speaks of 'a prefallen life without death', and of a 'transcendental life that Paul could conceive of as eternal and as rendering possible resurrection', which would be 'a wholly counterfactual invocation of an undying reality'; of a 'corporeal resurrection' which means that 'the body also is immortal', and of a 'resurrection life' which is 'an original life before and without death, regained through an absolute endurance of death'.[51] For Paul, as we have seen, what matters is *new creation*, beginning with, and under the authority of, the resurrected Messiah. Resurrection is indeed at the heart of Paul's political theology, but much more directly than Milbank allows. The Messiah is the one 'who rises up to rule the nations' (Romans 15.12); Paul here retrieves certain key psalms, especially Psalms 2 and 110.[52] Milbank's argument here could be simplified, made more direct, and thereby strengthened.[53]

Milbank expounds Paul's resurrection-based politics in four themes, of which the first echoes the sociological analysis of the Pauline communities which we saw in the previous chapters. Paul has merged the *oikos* with the *polis*, so that the 'household' becomes the microcosm of the new political order.[54] This then grounds the second point: 'the overcoming of law and

[49] Milbank 2010, 46.
[50] Milbank 2010, 47.
[51] Milbank 2010, 42, 45, 46, 47, 48.
[52] Rom. 1.3f.; 1 Cor. 15.23–8.
[53] Milbank seems to want to leave open some sense of a gnostic interpretation of Paul: see 49f. n. 56.
[54] Milbank 2010, 48, again relying on Blumenfeld 2001.

death by trust and life'. Here Milbank offers a blend: a retrieval of an older ('old perspective'?) view of Paul as advocating 'the supercession [*sic*] of the Jewish law tout court by the gospel', on the one hand, and a particular version of the subjective reading of *pistis Christou*: 'justification occurs through a participation in Jesus' *own* exercise of trust.'[55] This leads to his 'political' proposal: that Paul envisages 'a new community of a reenvisaged Israel that is bound together by justice rather than by the law'.[56] Though one might suppose that 'trust' in this new vision might lead merely to anarchy, the law having been set aside, that is not the case. This is precisely

> a trust that God is just to an eminent and infinite extent that we cannot begin to fathom and a trust that this justice will eventually so triumph that a harmony of peaceful order will embrace not just Jews and Gentiles (who will at last discover just how their various customs may cohere) but also all God's creatures.[57]

There is, I think, a lot to be said for something like this as a reflection of Paul's hope, however strange some of Milbank's exegesis may sound:

> In trusting God we trust also that the current negative order is a violation and that 'in the end' the order of gift must be restored. It then follows that to trust others as potentially good – as potential sources of gratuitous life (which Paul's missionary and political practice endlessly attests) – is to trust their own trust in God and in eschatological finality (2 Cor. 9:6–14).

Milbank is hindered here, I think, by a failure to grasp the full biblical meaning of *dikaiosynē theou*. He is too concerned to ward off any older protestant notions of what he calls 'imputed salvation' (that phrase itself already indicates that Milbank may not be altogether familiar with the relevant discussions), and too reliant on the suggestions of Blumenfeld about Aristotelian echoes, to notice that in Israel's scriptures, notably the Psalms and Isaiah which Paul regularly echoes in the key passages, what matters is the *covenant faithfulness* of the God who is not only Israel's God but also the God of the whole creation. This means that, in Paul's key arguments, he does indeed envisage a community which is not defined by the Jewish Torah. But this bears only a loose analogy to the supposed twentieth-century *desideratum* of a civic polity which goes beyond 'the law' in the Schmittian sense ('a sovereign equity beyond the written law').[58] Paul, says Milbank, has thus 'invented the *ekklēsia* as a noncontractual economy and a nonlegal practice of human transformation'.[59]

[55] Milbank 48 n. 54, 49. At 49 he chides the RSV for concealing, through its translation of Rom. 3.25f., 'that the context here is eucharistic', a strange exegetical judgment for which Milbank offers no warrant.

[56] Milbank 2010, 52.

[57] Milbank 2010, 53.

[58] Milbank 2010, 56. Here and elsewhere Milbank enters into close readings, and sometimes refutations, of T. W. Jennings, whose book on Derrida and Paul (Jennings 2006) was followed up by an important, though in my view flawed and one-sided, reading of Romans (Jennings 2013).

[59] Milbank 2010, 57 n. 71.

This leads to Milbank's third point, which is that Paul envisages, in the redeemed community, a 'division and hierarchy of gifts'. This constitutes the church as a community in which 'the visionary anticipation of a hidden eternal present and an eschatological future ... is the architectonic foundation for the possibility of justice', because

> the world awaits a final historical event already commenced that will be also the final disclosure of the metahistorical secrets of eternal outgoings from God. Just occurrences in historical time are just only to the measure that they prefigure and make apparent this apocalyptic dimension, while the eternal metanarrative mysteriously and from all eternity includes the event of overcoming evil that has only been enacted in human time, on the cross.[60]

This brings Milbank to his fourth and final Pauline theme: 'the monarchic blended with the democratic'. Ignoring Paul's messianic language, he attempts to derive Paul's royal theme from hellenistic Pythagorean thought, and from the speculative fiction of the ancient king having 'two bodies', so that when a king died there was another hypothetical one to carry on.[61] He still seems unsure what Paul means by the resurrection: Paul announces, he says, 'the eternal rule commencing here and now on earth of a dead, executed man', meaning that 'the "fiction" (be it true or not) of his resurrection must be one that is to be forever upheld.'[62] Paul thus envisages Jesus' followers as themselves 'kings'. True enough, even though Milbank has come at this by a strange route. True also, I think, is the account of the way in which the highly important practice of 'benefaction' as a key element in ancient society is subverted by the gospel. 'An oligarchic paternalism is transformed into a process of reciprocal offering newly regarded as the primary instrument of government.'[63] Paul's vision of a new society thus goes beyond the one envisaged by Seneca, which carefully balanced the giving and receiving of gifts.[64]

Milbank thus proposes an ecclesiology which models and anticipates a form of polity which itself transcends the modern 'biopolitical' in which 'the law of exception' enables the 'sovereign' secular state to perpetuate injustice:

> If St. Paul is right, then *ekklēsia*, as founded by Christ, names the only polity, or at least possibility of a polity, that collectively lives, beyond death, as an exception even to the law of exception, because it replaces the political animal with the pneumatic body of grace-given mutual trust.[65]

[60] Milbank 2010, 59. This rather clear statement is obscured when Milbank suggests that it exhibits 'an extraordinary circular mutual dependence between an "oriental" and "gnostic" permanent apocalyptic secret and an "occidental" and "exoteric" contingent historical event' (59). This kind of history-of-religions guesswork is both undemonstrable and in any case unnecessary for a Pauline vision which is more obviously shaped by Israel's scriptures as seen in the light of the crucified and risen Messiah.

[61] Milbank 2010, 60f., following Agamben and others.

[62] Milbank 2010, 60, 62.

[63] Milbank 2010, 67. On 'benefaction' see above 251.

[64] See Barclay 2015 (forthcoming).

[65] Milbank 2010, 71.

Paul was not thereby aiming to replace the empire overnight. However,

> By insinuating a counterpolity ruled by a legally slain and divinely resurrected king, Paul uniquely opened the possibility that the unstable excesses thrown up by biopolitical processes, ancient or modern, might nonetheless gradually take on some of the character of a living excess of equity both hierarchically and unilaterally encouraged and democratically and reciprocally exchanged.[66]

One does not, perhaps, have to agree with all the sub-clauses here to see that an important point is being made. The fact, however, that Milbank continues to speak of the resurrection as 'a counterfactual' opens him up to the charge that, despite his disclaimers, there is after all something gnostic about his vision:

> human life must somehow bear within its biological spark (which itself must logically be prior to death, which is sheer negation) also a pneumatic spark that links it to undying goodness and justice and that enables it in the end entirely to root out those base passions 'of the flesh' (according to Paul) that are concerned only with survival, self-satisfaction, erotic possession of, and military triumph over, others.[67]

This can be read charitably as a detheologized statement of what Paul speaks of in terms of grace, the fruit of the spirit, and so on. Without that explicit language, it is hard to be sure. Milbank's vision of an ecclesial witness to a different way of being human remains somewhat elusive, though haunting:

> Thus it would be our ethical imperative to associate well that would of itself obscurely call forth the image of an eternal, resurrected humanity. Only the arrival of such a reality in time, however, provides the event that, for *pistis*, confirms the apocalyptic truth of such a restored ontology of undying life and thereby renders possible the project of human social justice.[68]

Whether this appeal to 'associate well' is sufficient, even supposing it were to break out in tomorrow's world, to make that noble project more than 'possible' we might question. But Milbank has here gone some way towards a more specifically Christian retrieval of the project of Taubes, Badiou, Žižek and others. Since, however, few contemporary Pauline scholars have shared the complex premise of the argument, that is, the ferocious denunciation of 'law' and its 'biopolitical' consequences, it may be doubted whether many today will want to follow him down his chosen path.

This, in my view, would be a pity. I have not taken the time to explore the other essays in the relevant volume, or the other works discussed in this new wave of studies. But the questions seem to me so important, going way beyond the rather shallow 'for-and-against-empire' discussions to which I myself have contributed in time past, that I think the journey towards a fuller Pauline political vision must include at least some travel of this kind.

[66] Milbank 2010, 72.

[67] Milbank 2010, 73.

[68] Milbank 2010, 73.

It is too bad that Milbank does not engage more directly with Paul's Jewish world. His glance towards various non-Jewish cultural references as potentially explanatory frameworks seems to me far-fetched by comparison with what was there at hand, namely, a biblically rooted vision of the divine justice constituting (or reconstituting!) the people of God as a people with the law written on their hearts – an idea which one might have thought would be more congenial to a post-Schmittian discussion than it seems to have been. This is obviously a Schweitzer-like protest (the water brought from far away, as opposed to the stream flowing close at hand), and clearly Schweitzer's point still needs to be made. In particular, the biblical theme of the divine righteousness (the *dikaiosynē theou*), as invoked in writings like *4 Ezra* roughly contemporary with Paul, envisages not only the full and final revelation of that 'righteousness' in the sense of the creator bringing true justice to the world, but also the creation thereby of a people who embody the creator's will for human community. One would therefore naturally expect that if someone like Saul of Tarsus came to believe that the creator had unveiled his *dikaiosynē* in the shocking, scandalous but also supremely powerful event of the Messiah's death and resurrection, that event would generate a community of the appropriate sort. The relationship in Paul's mind between that new messianic community and Israel's Torah is not, however, an exact anticipation of the relationship between (a) a socially just world order as envisaged in a putative post-biopolitical contemporary world and (b) the 'law' in the sense of the iron grip of a secularized or capitalistic state where nuance and critique are ruled out *ab initio*. This is the repetition, in relation to Milbank, of the point I made before in reference to Agamben. Once again, as in my comments on David Horrell's proposals in the previous chapter, one cannot see the one-off transition between (a) Israel's Torah as Saul of Tarsus had understood it and (b) the law-free (and yet law-fulfilling) gospel announced by Paul the apostle as merely a model, an example of a transition which might then be repeated variously in subsequent generations. It is part of the messianic message of Paul that what happened in and through Jesus happened uniquely, once for all. Milbank clearly wants to take that seriously. But I do not think it has yet worked its way into his articulation of the contemporary philosophical and political challenge of the gospel.

(iv) Conclusion

So what might Paul be saying in the marketplace today, or – if we dragged him to the Areopagus, as an angry postmodern mob might well do – before that supreme political and philosophical court? He would engage; there is no doubt about that. He would find the positive things that could be said about this or that aspect of culture, this or that philosophical trend, as well as the negative ones that would have to be said by way of confrontation. But it seems to me beyond question that he would do the two things which are emphasized in the Areopagus address of Acts 17. On the one hand, he would explain that idolatry is based on a mistake. The Almighty does not live in houses built with hands. I think that Paul, faced with twentieth- and twenty-first-century political constructions, might well conclude that a good deal there was idolatrous, attempting to translate *vox populi, vox Dei* into *vox populi, domus Dei*: the voice of the people turning itself into a shrine where worship and sacrifice would be offered. And I think, on the other hand, that Paul, faced with the normal tyrannical claim to supreme power by means of supreme force – in other words, the threat of violence and ultimately death – would affirm once more that the creator of all has fixed a day on which he will call the world to account, and has given assurance of this, and of the identity of the coming judge, by raising him from the dead.

This, for Paul, was no 'counterfactual', however much it was for the Athenians, who knew their Aeschylus.[69] It meant what it meant in Isaiah 11, and for the reasons specified in that prophet and in the Psalms: the root of Jesse 'rises up to rule the nations'. Ultimately, Milbank has only taken the argument half way. The resurrection of Jesus is not the foundation for a 'heavenly' or 'supernatural' faith. It is the sign of God's kingdom on earth as in heaven. That, rather than supposed new scientific evidence, explains the heavy resistance to the idea of resurrection in the post-Enlightenment world. In that world, the claim that 'religion' has been 'subtracted', leaving only the 'secular' behind, created space for the construction of a new sort of empire. Such an empire has needed to challenge the notion of resurrection for the same reason that the Sadducees did: it threatened their position of power. The resurrection does indeed challenge what Milbank and others call the 'biopolitical'. But I think it does so in ways, and by means, which the tradition of modern theopolitical thought has yet to discover.[70]

2. Paul in History, Theology and Hermeneutics

We have come a long way from Baur and Schweitzer to the newer social and political analyses of Paul and his writings. Yet the questions remain familiar, and by now we are beginning to realize that though we can indeed separate out three strands (history, theology and hermeneutics) we only ever meet them as part of a single knot. We can ask the historian's question: what can we say, with good historical warrant, about Paul himself in his own day, his own complex cultural world? We can ask the theologian's question: what can we say about the coherence or otherwise of what Paul had to say about God, Jesus, the world, human sin and salvation, and so on? And we can ask the practical question: how does this all address the world, the church, and the individual of our own day? But each of these questions at once involves the other two, and we do not get very far by pretending otherwise.

[69] *Eumen.* 647f.; see *RSG* 32.

[70] See the brief statement in *RSG* 728–31.

Properly speaking, of course, the word 'hermeneutics' refers to the combination of all three of these, with exegesis itself at the centre of it all; though in popular usage it has come to denote only the third, the question of 'application' or 'relevance'. But, as our survey has shown, however much the historian attempts to be 'neutral', however much the theologian attempts to see things through Paul's eyes rather than produce an 'etic' account based on today's way of doing things, in neither sphere is an objective or positivist position possible or even desirable. We do not have a God's-eye view, but we are in any case not supposed to; the attempt to acquire one would be Promethean. We have a human view, one among many but none the worse for that. The point of scholarship is to bring our views to the table and have them reshaped by debate. Knowledge is a corporate thing, with all persons contributing as fully as they can.

The first two questions themselves obviously join up. The task of producing a 'Pauline theology', or even a working model of such a thing, perhaps with a view to writing commentaries or preaching sermons on the letters, is itself a matter of history. It begins at one end with the history of the language, i.e. with lexicography: what did the words mean in Paul's day, was he using them in a specialized or redefined way, how did the biblical Greek of the Septuagint impinge on the Koine Greek he had spoken as a child, and so on? At the other end, it begins with the history of God-talk: how did people in Paul's world speak of God or the gods, their relation to the world, and so on? How did they speak of human beings in relation to God or the gods? How, in particular, did the Jewish people speak of these things? How, then, do we locate Paul in relation to all of the above?

In between these two starting-points, somewhere between lexicography and theology proper, we have the multiple challenges of Paul's actual arguments. What did he say about Jesus, about the spirit, about death and resurrection, about the dark powers lurking behind outward circumstances, about sin and salvation, about the *ekklēsia* and its unity, about behaviour, holiness, humility and hope? Why did *agapē* (love) mean what it meant to him? What impact did it have, what impact did he *expect* it to have, within his wider world? All these *theological* questions need *historical* answers about what Paul himself thought and wrote, and the historical question as to where Paul belongs in his wider world depends in turn on some kind of grasp, however basic or provisional, of the centre and coherence, such as it may be, of his thought. And if history and theology thus inevitably need one another, the history of research has shown that those who have tried to answer this double question have usually, and unsurprisingly, explained Paul in ways which have made sense to them in their own personal, ecclesial or cultural settings – with the exception of those, in a line including Nietzsche and others from the atheistic side, and Maccoby and others from the Jewish side, who have 'described' a supposed historical Paul upon whose head it will be easy for them to heap scorn, or even shame.[71]

[71] See Maccoby 1986.

Those, of course, are no more 'neutral' positions than are those of the preachers who are eager to mount the pulpit and tell the congregation what, in their view, Paul has in store for them this week. Mention of the preacher's task reminds us again that the question of exegesis intersects with all the others: what are the individual letters saying, and how do they say it? Exegesis, itself at the centre of anything that might be called 'hermeneutics', is the concrete location where history and theology are constantly meeting up.

The backbone of the present book, though, has been the underlying historical task. This was the task set (and controversially addressed) by Baur and Schweitzer, and continued, through many twists and turns, all the way to Sanders and his contemporaries, to Martyn and his followers, and to the social historians like Meeks and Horrell. What account can we give of the wider historical contexts within which Paul made the sense he made, and of the ways in which Paul both emerged from those contexts, fitted into them in some respects, and broke their moulds in others? (There should be little argument about his breaking of moulds. Most historical figures worth writing about have done that. Those riots in Acts, and the punishments listed in 2 Corinthians 11, cannot have been caused simply by Paul proposing minor modifications to existing worldviews.)

As we look back over the last century at those who have tried to address this question, two large shifts become visible. These might at first sight appear to pull against one another, but I suggest that in fact they belong closely together.

First, as I noted earlier in this book, we have seen the emergence of a much greater interest in, and knowledge of, the Jewish world of the first century. This has meant a much greater interest in, and grasp of, the way in which Paul can be understood from within that world, and the way in which he none the less believed and said things which many Jews then, and many since, have seen as breaking the boundaries. When we say 'Judaism' today we are thinking of a much larger, more many-sided, more historically based reality than anything which that word might have conjured up in the days of F. C. Baur.

The word 'Judaism', however, ought itself now to be questioned, and this leads to the second great shift that has taken place in the last generation or two. (Like many 'isms', the word 'Judaism' now carries specific nineteenth-century ideological baggage.[72]) In the nineteenth century it was easy for Baur and his followers to assume (a) that Christianity was a particular example of something called a 'religion', (b) that there were different types of 'religion', (c) that Judaism was the wrong type of 'religion', and (d) that Christianity was the finest example of the best type. All this was set by Baur within a protestant frame of reference which assumed that Luther had opposed the Jewish teaching about 'works of the law' (hence, that the genuine Paul could not be understood within 'Judaism'), and also within the broadly Hegelian world in which one could propose, as an *historical*

[72] See once again Meeks 2001; Martin 2001; and not least Mason 2007.

hypothesis, that great movements of thought proceeded by a process of dialectic: Jewish Christianity, gentile Christianity, and then the synthesis of 'early Catholicism'. All this wonderful edifice, however, is shaken to its foundations not only when we set Baur himself in his own cultural context, and recognize the extent to which that context extensively coloured his proposals, but also when we realize, precisely through the study of ancient history, that 'religion' in the ancient world was radically different from what that word came to mean in the eighteenth and nineteenth centuries.[73] The second great shift, then, which has been taking place in the late twentieth and early twenty-first centuries, has been a move beyond 'history of *religion*', with 'religion' imagined on the nineteenth-century model, to a larger vision. This vision looks at history as the task of social, cultural and personal description, drawing out within a much larger grid of interpretation (social construction, worldview, and so on) the many-sided nature of what people did, how they lived, and – within that and shaped by it, not as a separate category! – what they thought, how they prayed, what they believed, what they hoped for. This is where the sociologically-rooted worldview-model makes its presence felt. It serves the 'thick description' of history.

There is therefore no reductionism for those who embrace a fuller version of 'history'. Just because Baur and others treated the ancient 'religions' within a philosophically Idealist system, that is no reason to react by squashing them into a Materialist one. Equally, just because some scholars have said 'history' when they meant 'the projection of eighteenth-century post-Humean scepticism onto the past', that is no reason to declare history itself a dangerous or anti-Christian pursuit. Here of course there is no neutral ground, but it seems to me that the actual study of actual historical evidence, from the literary products of a Josephus to the material products of the latest archaeological dig, constantly speaks of an integrated world in which there was continual commerce between what people thought and believed and the symbols, stories and everyday praxis of their underlying worldview. That was true of Paul's Jewish world; it was true of the Greek world in which he grew up and whose cities he knew intimately; it was true of the Roman world which had taken over the running of the Jewish and Greek worlds, and which coloured decisively the cultures to which Paul was called to go as a missionary.

The study of Paul, then, has always involved history. But Paul's more recent interpreters have expanded the earlier 'history-of-*religions*' model, with all its ideological baggage, to the much more complicated and all-embracing one of 'history' in general. That is why, among other things, historical books on Paul have tended to get longer. 'Religion', insofar as it is a coherent category, is a vital part of all this. But we only understand what it is, and what part it might be playing, within the larger whole. The recent study of the Jewish world of late antiquity has aided this task substantially: at the formal level, by demonstrating the way in which 'religion', whether in

[73] See *PFG* chs. 4 and 13.

the ancient or the modern sense, is woven tightly in with all other aspects of life; at the material level, by providing a large amount of data which contributes to the 'thick description'.

This broadening and reconfiguring of the overall historical task is helping us get a better grip, I think, on the three major areas we have studied in this book, and the potential relationships between them. Once again we glance at Sanders, Martyn and Meeks, both for themselves and for the broad movements of thought which they may be taken to represent.

E. P. Sanders did indeed set up his project as 'a comparison of patterns of religion'. But his entire case in relation to the supposed Jewish 'pattern' was that it was broader and more complex than had been supposed, pointing to Sanders's own further detailed work on the *realia* of Jewish life and hence away from the ideological construct of 'Judaism' as a foil for a 'religion' called Paulinism (or anything else). Since Sanders saw that, for Paul, 'religion' was really a matter of 'theology', and since he was comparing it with 'Judaism' as a close cousin, it is not surprising that his historical account of Paul's theological position is quite close to that of Albert Schweitzer, who exploited the same family resemblance and stressed 'participation in Christ' as central to Paul rather than 'justification'. I regard this polarization as unwarranted, but within the discipline a vote in this direction has tended to be a vote for a more integrally Jewish reading.

Underneath the particular judgment in question, in which actual exegesis has a good deal to say, there stands the shift which, however ambiguous and itself contextual, occurred with the work of Sanders's teacher, W. D. Davies, after the Second World War.[74] What if Paul was neither a Gnostic, nor a hellenistic philosopher, but was actually a rabbi who believed that the Messiah had come? Once we sharpen this up, recognizing that the rabbis we know through Mishnah, Talmud and the rest represent a later stage in Jewish life, and that with the Scrolls, the Pseudepigrapha and Josephus we have a bigger and earlier canvas with which to work, then I think Davies's thesis, following Schweitzer's but with different source material, acts as a signpost in the right direction. To understand Paul historically we must start with his larger Jewish world and see his entire project, his own fresh thought included, as mutations from within that world.

One feature of that Jewish world, however, has been screened from view because of the residual legacy of the nineteenth-century either/or. If Paul was *either* a 'Jewish' thinker *or* a 'gentile' thinker, then presumably – so ran the implicit argument – he must, as the self-styled 'Apostle to the Gentiles', have set aside his 'Jewish' concepts in order to appeal to his non-Jewish hearers, so that he could speak to them in language they could understand. That assumption formed part not only of Baur's paradigm, but also of one of the most influential books on early Christology, Bousset's *Kyrios Christos*, which proposed that since the Jewish concept of 'Messiah' was incomprehensible to gentiles Paul must have abandoned it, treating *Christos* as merely

[74] On Davies see above 19–22.

a proper name and using the hellenistic *Kyrios* instead to refer to Jesus in the language of well-known cults.[75] My point here is not only that this is exegetically indefensible, as one of the most important modern books on early Christology has demonstrated.[76] My point is also that it misunderstands one of the central implicit claims in the Jewish world itself. Granted, the second-Temple period saw the Jewish people embattled and defensive, not often inclined to articulate a vision for the larger world. But the Psalms remained their prayer-book; and the Psalms frequently express the hope that, because Israel's God is the creator of the world, he will ultimately exert his sovereignty over, and reveal his name and his glory within, the whole creation. Quite frequently this larger hope is expressed in relation to the coming Davidic king. Often, of course, this vision is basically negative: Israel's God will condemn the wicked nations. Sometimes, however, it is positive: they will come to share in Israel's blessing.[77] Since this theme, with these biblical echoes, resonates rather obviously in Paul's writings, there was never any very good reason to suppose that a 'Jewish' history-of-religions analysis would be inappropriate for the Apostle to the Gentiles. In fact, the very idea of a gentile apostolate only made the sense it did on biblical and Jewish grounds. How many Jews of Paul's day would have resonated with his view we cannot say. But we cannot deny that the apostle consciously retrieved a wealth of well-known biblical texts to explain his vision of a Jewish message for the non-Jewish world and to locate it within its larger implicit narrative. If such a vision is hard to fit into the older history-of-religions paradigms, so much worse for the paradigms. History would tell us to acquire some better ones.

The reverse of this point is also important, and was also screened out in the older history-of-religions work. The more we study the world of the ancient Jews, the more it becomes clear that one of the strongest traditions of that world was a capacity for critique from within, rooted in the Psalms and the prophets themselves. This makes much more sense within a society as a whole than within a 'religion' per se. Once we sketch that society – complete with rival movements for royal or priestly leadership, populist pressure groups, the sudden emergence of charismatic leaders, wars of revolution, and so on – it makes sense to suppose that, the more 'Jewish' we make Paul (especially if part of that 'Jewishness' consists of his belonging to a 'messianic' movement), the more we should expect that he would have been a controversial figure *within* that Jewish world. The idea of critique from within is not, in the nature of the case, something which the older history-of-religions work was designed to discover. But history forbids us to suggest that the more we discover about Paul's basic Jewishness the less he

[75] Bousset 1970.

[76] Hurtado 2003. It would be possible to tell the story of Pauline theology in terms of the study of Christology, and in any such narrative Hurtado's book would emerge as a vital turn in the road.

[77] Obvious examples include Pss. 2; 24; 46; 48; 67; 72; 89; 93; 96; 97; 98; 99; 110 and passages such as 18.43–50; 22.25–31; 33.8–22; 47.6–9; 57.5, 11; 66.1–4; 68.28–35; 102.15f., 22; 138.4–5. This does not include the many Psalms invoking divine judgement on the nations. One might of course add passages from Isaiah, e.g. 11.1–10; 49.6f.; 52.15; and one might note Paul's use of this material.

will have any critique of his fellow (non-Messiah-believing) Jews. One sometimes gets the impression that people are interpreting the modern retrieval of Paul's Jewishness as part of a movement aimed at suggesting that Judaism and Christianity are simply two different versions of the same thing – as though there were a sort of sliding scale which moved from Krister Stendahl through Ed Sanders and onwards into a high modernist embrace of a liberal 'tolerance' all round, projected back on to the apostle himself. Whatever we say about Paul, we must be able to understand the passages in which, using biblical resources, he calls his fellow Jews to account, and why he would say things like 'through the law I died to the law'.[78] Thus, ironically perhaps – and it is a similar irony to what we see in that quotation from Galatians! – the more 'Jewish' we make Paul, within the larger world we know from detailed historical study, and the more we break out of the 'religious' straitjacket into a fuller social world in which 'religion' plays its part without dominating the landscape, the more credible it is to suppose that Paul really did occupy what he saw as a messianically defined but contested space, claiming to be at the very centre of the divine plan for Israel and the world but, by that very claim, with its radical corollaries for Torah, knowing that he was an anomaly, bound to be seen as deviant or transgressive.

These reflections serve as a signpost to a larger discussion for which there has been no room here, namely the study of Paul within contemporary Jewish writing. There is a long history of such work, by no means confined either to polemic or to attempted retrieval.[79] My point here is that Sanders, for all the limitations of his project, serves as a marker in the quest for that larger historical description of Paul within his Jewish world, a Jewish world freshly described and seen as a large and complex whole, not simply as a 'religion'. It may, indeed, be the case that some of the opposition to Sanders (from within the 'old perspective') has been sparked off by resistance on both fronts: resistance to the larger view of the Jewish world, which makes it much harder to accuse first-century Pharisees of sixteenth-century theological faults, and resistance also to the placing of 'religion' not in a safe space away from ordinary life but interwoven with politics, society, culture and an entire view of reality. It is indeed a big thing to ask people to embrace all this. They may well want to say, 'The old is better.' But once we begin to study the past in all its dimensions, we are inexorably driven this way. In my view, there is no reason to be afraid of drawing this conclusion.

Something very similar and very different needs to be said about the contribution of J. L. Martyn and his 'school'. The protest of Käsemann against Bultmann, which gave fresh energy and direction to Schweitzer's earlier project of seeing Paul within his 'apocalyptic' context (though abandoning several key aspects of Schweitzer's construction), was itself a protest against a narrow, shrivelled version of Paul's message. It expanded the horizons,

[78] Gal. 2.19.

[79] See particularly Langton 2010.

not now into the larger 'religious' world sketched by Sanders, nor yet into the larger 'social' world of Meeks and others, but into the larger 'cosmic' world of principalities and powers, of dark forces bent on determining the fate of the world, needing to be overthrown through the 'apocalyptic invasion' of God in the gospel events. This, too, was thus a protest against the boxed-in *religionsgeschichtlich* study of Paul into which Bultmann, like some others of Baur's successors, had retreated. It, too, was an attempt to restore an aspect of Paul's overall world of understanding which had been lost to view in earlier exegesis. And it, too, insofar as it represented another example of the post-war turn from a hellenistic history-of-religions explanation to a Jewish one (away from Gnosticism, towards 'apocalypticism'), can be seen as part of the same larger movement represented by W. D. Davies on the one hand and Martin Hengel on the other.

Yet, as I argued in Part II of the present book, there are serious questions about this 'apocalyptic' movement at the level of history, of theology, and of exegesis. (The questions which arise at the level of contemporary interpretation are interesting but sometimes obscure, because Martyn has left it to his followers to say more explicitly why and how this reading of Paul will give the church a fresh and welcome sense of direction.[80])

The historical question is once more basic. First, is the 'apocalyptic' theology assumed by Martyn well grounded in the relevant Jewish texts? It seems not: the proposed antitheses between 'apocalyptic' and other themes such as 'covenant', 'salvation history' and God's dealing with sin are imported into the texts, not derived from them. For Martinus de Boer, the key feature of 'apocalyptic' is the 'two ages' scheme; for Martyn, in a recent article, it seems to be 'the three-actor drama', where God is the first actor, humans the second, and the third role is taken by the 'anti-God powers' of Flesh and Sin.[81] But the two-age scheme, and the activity of anti-God powers, are not confined to 'apocalyptic' writings. Nor does either of them form part of a larger theological whole which can be played off against other elements. Second, is the 'apocalyptic' theology advocated by Martyn, principally in his Galatians commentary, an adequate way of describing the views of Paul in that document or indeed elsewhere? I have argued above, and elsewhere, that it is not. It avoids the challenge of integrating elements of Paul's thought which seem to fit together in his writings but which some modern traditions have found mutually incompatible. Granted, among those modern traditions there are varieties of would-be Pauline expression in which so much is made of an individualistic 'gospel' that all 'cosmic' or 'global' elements are left out. Granted, too, there is such a thing as a 'self-

[80] See e.g. Rutledge 2007, a work dedicated to J. L. Martyn and his wife. To applaud, as I do, the recovery of the 'cosmic' dimension in Paul's gospel is not to collude with an antithesis in which 'justification by faith' is pushed to one side. John Barclay, on the book's cover, congratulates Rutledge on providing an antidote to the '"self-help" religiosity that currently debilitates the Christian church'; but if 'self-help religiosity' is really the thing from which Martyn's reading of Galatians is designed to free the church, we are merely back to one version of the 'old perspective' (see below).

[81] Martyn 2010, 27f.; in note 24 he says that 'in the present essay I use the term "apocalyptic" to refer to the three-actor drama'.

help' religion, whether of individual moralism or corporate traditionalism. But it is not clear – to put it mildly – that Paul is opposing any of these in Galatians, just as it is not clear that there exists an ancient worldview we can usefully call 'apocalyptic' which, modified by Paul's belief in Jesus, was central to his demolition of such ideas. In fact, as we might expect granted the Käsemannic genealogy of these views, what we are faced with once more is indeed a variety of the 'old perspective', in which 'the Jews' become the type of *Homo religiosus*.[82] And with that we are back to Baur and to many problems, not only of exegesis.

One of those problems, I think, is once more the lack of integration between the scholarly worlds represented by Sanders and Martyn. At one level this is surprising. Both are trying to see Paul in relation to certain Jewish categories. Both are in some senses indebted to Schweitzer; both are reacting against the tradition of Bultmann. Both see Paul's critique of Judaism as the reflex of the gospel, with 'solution' preceding 'plight'. But at another level perhaps the lack of integration is not so surprising. Sanders takes as his theme the comparison of 'patterns of religion', but it is 'religion', in the modern sense, which Martyn rejects, seeing 'religion' as what the 'Teachers' in Galatia are offering as opposed to the 'revelation' which constitutes Paul's gospel. Sanders's comparison of patterns puts Paul up against 'Palestinian Judaism', but the world which some call 'apocalyptic' does not feature as largely there as one might have supposed. Indeed, Sanders places *4 Ezra* to one side as untypical. But considering that the scholars on both 'sides' of this divide are studying the same comparatively small body of texts, and trying to use critically aware historical methods to get at their meanings, the sense of two separate worlds, not really even in dialogue, is puzzling at least on the surface.

When, however, we put Sanders and Martyn side by side over against the world represented by Wayne Meeks, there is a different initial comparison to be made. Meeks, of course, has made his detailed study not of the Jewish world, but of the urban world of greco-roman society, the world into which Paul took his message. But this did not represent, at least for Meeks (perhaps it did for some others?), a turn back to an attempted hellenistic explanatory grid for Paul's ideas. On the contrary. Arising out of the detailed study of Paul's communities, both Meeks and Horrell recognize that Paul was insisting on certain distinctives; that Paul's communities themselves may have overlapped with, but did not conform to, existing social patterns; and that we are witnessing, not least in Paul's stress on the unity and holiness of

[82] See e.g. Martyn 2010, 22 (Paul's gospel is 'face to face with the two-ways orthodox moral drama in its Sinaitic form'), 24f. (the Teachers 'placed these Gentiles before the two ways of life and death, the two ways of Law-observance and non-Law-observance. Having placed them there, the Teachers doubtless exhorted them to use their own power of decision ... [T]he Teachers took for granted the Galatians' moral competence, their inborn ability to choose the path of Law observance'), 29 (Paul opposes the idea of 'achieving autonomous, moral progress'), 33 (Paul's God is not one 'who, after offering two ways, withdraws off stage in order to assure an autonomous decision on the part of the human agent'). I completely agree that had Paul been writing to combat such ideas he would have stressed the sovereignty of divine grace. But there is no evidence that this is the subject of Galatians; and, at the end, it is not clear that we have advanced beyond a trenchant and rather splendid reaffirmation of some form of Calvinism.

these communities, a strange, apparently anomalous but still recognizable, variety of *Jewish* socialization. The churches were not simply synagogues with an 'open' policy on wider ethnic membership. But they shared more in common with Jewish groups in the Diaspora than with any of the possible non-Jewish social models.

This is where the irony comes in. One might have supposed that with Sanders comparing 'religion', and Martyn emphasizing the divine initiative in 'apocalyptic', it would be they who would draw attention to the central features of Paul's theology. But it is not. It is left to Meeks to highlight, as a result of his rigorous sociological study, the role played by Jewish-style monotheism, not as an abstract belief which Paul's communities just happened to hold, but as the exact correlate of the kinds of communities they seem to have been, historically and sociologically speaking. And it is Meeks who sees, within this, that the Jewish monotheism in question is tightly integrated with eschatology and Christology, though his view of a Pauline 'apocalyptic' is quite different from Martyn's (and indeed from mine). And, though Sanders and Martyn both indicate that Paul moved 'from solution to plight', it is Meeks who embodies and nuances that in the structure of his exposition of Paul's main beliefs, placing monotheism, apocalyptic and Christology as the main items and treating as a subsequent question the matter of how, for Paul, this one God deals with evil, sin and death. One of the results is that, for Meeks, there is no great gulf either between 'participation' and 'justification', or between 'apocalyptic' and 'salvation history'.

It is, of course, a great oversimplification to try to boil down the current discussions into this shape. Like ancient history, the modern history of an academic discipline is bound to be full of loose ends, of research pathways leading off at a tangent, of brilliant ideas only partially worked out, and perhaps less than brilliant ideas still looking good despite being long past their sell-by date. But I hope this necessarily rapid summary of a tendentious survey will draw at least some of those loose ends together and point to further questions which might now be raised, and further suggestions as to how to raise them.

I have said less in this book than I would have liked about the task of exegesis itself. Interestingly, neither Sanders nor Meeks has written a commentary on any of Paul's letters, though others who have learned a great deal from them have done so. Martyn's famous commentary on Galatians is the heart of the American 'apocalyptic' movement, but the question can at least be raised as to whether, as with Barth on Romans, one learns more about Martyn's theological agenda than one does about what Paul himself actually wrote. That question is for another day. But it seems to me that a good way to draw this whole project to a conclusion might be to consider one of Paul's most famous paragraphs, commenting on the different angles offered by the key interpretations we have studied.

3. Antioch through Many Eyes

'When Cephas came to Antioch, I stood up to him face to face. He was in the wrong.' For Ferdinand Christian Baur, this moment of apostolic confrontation revealed the fundamental division within the early church. Cephas represented 'Jewish Christianity'; Paul was championing a 'law-free' 'gentile Christianity'. The battle would then be played out by the parties in Corinth. In the later exegesis which still looked back to Baur, the same battle could be seen in Paul's letters themselves, as the apostle, unable or unwilling to invent doctrinal formulae which said exactly what he believed, was reduced to quoting 'Jewish-Christian' sayings and altering them as he went along – such as the clearly 'covenantal' passage in Romans 3.24–6, the messianic statement of Romans 1.3–4, or, indeed, the bipartite soteriological saying in Galatians 1.4.[83] But within this scholarly tradition things had changed quite radically by the time Bultmann's successors came to debate Galatians 2. Bultmann himself read the language about justification in terms of the personal transition from 'man under sin' to 'man under grace', while others, including Käsemann, saw what was at stake in terms of the cosmos itself. Meanwhile traditional readings, within both protestant and catholic piety, continued to treat the specific questions in the passage – questions concerning the fitness of potential table companions – as mere signposts to the abstract doctrine of 'justification'. Rules for table fellowship were just examples of 'law', and one was not justified by law but by grace and through faith. It was assumed that any talk about justification and the cross was addressing the sixteenth-century question of how people got saved. Galatians 2 was read in that way, with questions of unity at the table forgotten behind the abstract issue of 'the law'.

The 'Sanders revolution' did not come about because Sanders wanted to promote a relativist agenda, though there are indeed signs of a late twentieth-century relativism in his work, and many have read him that way. Nor did it happen simply because of more detailed study of what ancient Jews actually thought and did, and in particular how they regarded their 'law-keeping', though that was clearly a central part of the argument. It came about partly because passages like Galatians 2.11–21 had a rather obvious dimension which might be called socio-cultural but was equally and emphatically theological. It was increasingly clear that these two could no longer be separated.

Let us put it bluntly. When Paul starts talking about how one is 'justified' in 2.15–16 the exegete has a choice. Either we say he has just changed the subject after the dispute described in 2.11–14. Or we conclude that his talk of 'justification', both in 2.16 and then in 2.17–21, is the continuation of the discussion of 2.11–14, which is not about 'how I get saved' or 'how I can find a gracious God', but about whether uncircumcised gentiles who believe in Jesus as Messiah should or should not eat at the same table with Jewish

[83] See above, 173–6.

believers. Paul says Yes, Cephas says No; and Paul explains his Yes – and in consequence his loud No to Cephas – *in relation to the question of how someone is declared 'righteous'*. Somehow, being declared 'righteous' and being welcomed at the table seem to be directly correlated. This, for me at least, is at the heart of the new perspective, and I continue to resist any suggestion that this reduces the gospel to a mere issue of 'table manners'.

The unity of the church is, arguably, the main theme of Galatians. The fact that one would not know this from many commentaries in the old perspective tradition is already enough to call them into question. And the unity of the church, the single family promised by God to Abraham, is here, as in Romans, the direct result of the work of the gospel and the spirit. Thus the insights emerging from the new perspective join up with the insights about the nature of the Pauline communities emerging from sociological readings, with, to be sure, Horrell's questions of 'solidarity and difference' making their presence felt as well.

Here, too, we see other major fault lines emerging. Are people 'justified' by their *faith in* Jesus the Messiah, or by *the faithfulness of* Jesus the Messiah? The old perspective, and at least one leader of the new (James Dunn), have insisted on 'faith in'. Many of us, with Richard Hays among the leaders, have argued for Jesus' own faithfulness – though there are many different and sometimes incompatible ways of construing that. Some, Hays and myself among them, have seen 'the faithfulness of Jesus' in the light of Philippians 2.8 and Romans 5.12–21, where Paul speaks of Jesus' 'obedience unto death', and have therefore seen this as a reference to the saving act of God through Jesus' death, which seems borne out by the centrality of Jesus' death in Galatians 2.19–21. Hays has stressed that this Pauline formulation is a sign that 'faith' is not 'something we do to please God'; it is not a substitute 'work', and to speak as if it is (as though 'faith' is 'the thing God really wants us to do') is to betray a fundamental misconception. I have stressed that the Messiah's 'faithfulness', here as in Romans 3.22, is his faithfulness to the divine plan for Israel, the deeply paradoxical plan which reached its *telos* on the cross. These are not incompatible. What is incompatible with my view, however, is the reading of *pistis Christou* offered by Martyn and de Boer, for whom the referent is still the death of Jesus but the meaning is the unprecedented, un-prepared-for, divine 'invasion', the 'apocalypse' without historical preparation or antecedent.

But, interrupts the old perspective once more, surely Paul is still writing about human sin and how people are saved from it? Yes, he is, though 'sin' is a rare word in Galatians (as opposed to Romans, where it is a major theme). When it is introduced here, it is in the epithet used for the gentiles in 2.15: 'gentile sinners', lesser breeds outside the law. At this point we may invoke the sociologists again: what we are talking about is the socio-cultural definition of the people of God. That is why it matters to know who is allowed to be at the same table. And the reason *that* matters is because, if the Messiah has come, he has come as the agent of the divine rescue plan. Table fellowship is not just a pleasant social occasion. It is the sign and the foretaste of Messiah-identity, and hence of benefiting from his rescuing work.

The sociological perspective then explains 2.17–18, and opens up a remarkable new insight about 'sin' and 'forgiveness' within Paul's implicit argument and wider theology. What happens if a Jew who believes in Jesus takes Paul seriously and decides to eat with 'gentile sinners', the phrase used in 2.15 to sum up how the Jews, even the Messiah-believing Jews, would naturally regard the gentiles, even Messiah-believing ones? Does such a person become a 'sinner' as well – and, if so, does that mean that the Messiah has turned out to be aiding and abetting 'sin'?[84]

One can only understand this by recognizing how ancient Jews, broadly speaking, viewed the gentile world. An important comment is necessary at this point. The idea of a Jewish 'non-mixing' practice has become controversial in some circles, because some Jewish scholars have resented what they have seen, sometimes with justification, as 'Christian' attempts to portray Judaism once more as a deficient or damaging religion. That, however, is not the point. What matters is *not a comparison of 'religion', but a claim about eschatology*. To say 'the Messiah has come' is not to say to the Jew 'your religion is the wrong sort'. It is to say 'Your religion – your calling, your whole way of life – is indeed the gift and call of the one God; and the one God has now done what he promised; although, as he also promised, what he has done is shocking and unexpected.' True, many in the Christian tradition have forgotten the eschatology and have turned this claim into a comparison not only of religion but of theology, in which Christian religion or theology is 'better' than the Jewish variety. That is a danger, even, in the 'apocalyptic' protest: we have 'revelation' while you have 'religion'! That is never Paul's point, though Sanders's 'comparison of patterns of religion' may have accidentally served to perpetuate this misunderstanding, even though he concluded that Paul did not really find anything 'wrong' with 'Judaism'. What counts is the messianic claim: Israel's God has done, in the fullness of time, the radically new thing he always promised.

Returning to Galatians 2.17–18 – and here again the new perspective and a sociological reading converge – we find the ironic choice facing those Messiah-believing Jews who follow Paul's line of thought. Either they must come with the Messiah and his people, and be, in the technical sense, 'sinners', joining uncircumcised 'gentile sinners' at the single table. Or they must 'build up once more the things which you tore down', in other words, the fence of Torah which kept Jews and gentiles separate, even in the Messiah's family. But – Paul is here using shorthand, but he explains it more fully elsewhere – if you do that, appealing to Torah to keep you safe from the contagion of 'sin', you will find that the Torah itself condemns you. It will show that you are a 'lawbreaker', a 'transgressor': not just a 'sinner', but one who breaks a known commandment.

[84] This question is cognate with the line of thought in Rom. 6.15f., though this is not often noted.

The point Paul is making, here and in Romans 3 and 4, is that in the gospel *the God of Israel has dealt with 'sin'*, both the sin that makes the gentiles 'sinners' and the sin that, expressing itself in law-breaking, makes Jews 'transgressors'. This is where the old perspective and the new perspective, and the sociological readings of Paul, all point in to a single reality. It has been customary, among those of us who defend some version of the new perspective against attacks from those who prefer the old, to point out that when Paul speaks of gentiles joining Abraham's family (the theme of Romans 4 and Galatians 3) he means that they are joining the covenant people whose purpose was to reverse and undo the sin of Adam and its effects. That itself is controversial exegetically, but my point here is subtly different. Here in Galatians 2, I suggest, Paul draws these even tighter together. *Because in the Messiah's death God has dealt with 'sin', the gentiles who come into the Messiah's people are no longer 'sinners'.* Here the word 'sin' has a meaning which goes somewhat beyond the normal two categories, actual human wrongdoing on the one hand and a cosmic power on the other. 'Sin' here is also the *sociological* category which demarcates the gentile world from the Jewish point of view. Forgiving sins is thus the way in which God welcomes gentiles – and the way, also, in which he includes Jews themselves in the messianic family.[85] This is where the opening statement of Galatians 1.4 (Jesus the Messiah 'gave himself for our sins, to rescue us from the present evil age, according to the will of God our father') joins up with the decisive climax in 2.19–20 ('the son of God ... loved me and gave himself for me').

Every word here matters in terms of the great debates that have swirled to and fro about Paul for the last two hundred years. Out of it all, and to simplify and shorten this concluding summary, there emerge three things. They draw together, I think, the strong points of all the main theories about Paul, and they do so within a context both controversial and pastoral.

First, Paul is speaking about a new identity, an identity defined not by Torah but by the Messiah. 'Through the law I died to the law, so that I might live to God'. That might seem to make no sense within the Jewish world, since God had given the Torah in the first place. Paul's point, however, is not to declare that he has moved away from the Jewish world, but that he belongs to Israel's Messiah; *and Israel's Messiah has died and been raised.* That is the centre of Paul's world, his worldview, his thinking, his praying, his gospel. Paul knows very well how shocking this is for the devout Jew. He had been there himself. But 'if "righteousness" comes through the law, then the Messiah died for nothing' (verse 21); or, to put it the other way round, a crucified Messiah means that 'righteousness' is not to be had any other way.

Here there is a further major division, near the fault line between old and new perspectives but not following it in all respects. I and others have aligned Paul's language of 'righteousness' with 'covenant membership'. This

[85] See too, interestingly, Ac. 26.17f.

has been steadfastly resisted by proponents of the old perspective, and it has been disregarded by most within the new. But the point here is Paul's new identity – and the fact that he has left behind the old one. This is directly tied to the discussion from 2.11 onwards. Paul has ceased to be defined by the law. He has ceased to be someone who must separate from uncircumcised Messiah-believers. He is now a Messiah-person, because, in coming alive after the 'death to the law', the life he now has is the Messiah's own life, lived within him.

Here is a vital element in Paul which lies at an oblique angle to the main lines charted in the present book. I have not so far featured the work of Michael Gorman, but it may be that his proposals will in retrospect be seen as pointing towards new ways of addressing old problems.[86] In a string of thoughtful and often ground-breaking studies, Gorman has drawn attention to Paul's notion of the *indwelling* of the Messiah himself as the central meaning of the transformation wrought by the gospel. 'I am, however, alive; yet it is not me, but the Messiah living in me.' For those who insist on what is called 'forensic' justification, this is seen as a second logical step, the 'sanctification' which follows the initial declaration. For those in the line from Schweitzer to Sanders, 'Christ in me' is at most the obverse of the more usual 'being in Christ'. Neither the 'apocalyptists' nor the social historians have done much, I think, to factor in this element. But Paul here and elsewhere says this kind of thing quite clearly, and since Galatians 2.19–20 is obviously the decisive climax of the argument we may assume that every element should be given due weight.

For Gorman, this is at the heart not only of Christian experience but also of 'justification' itself. He uses the word *theōsis*, 'divinization', to denote it: a previously unfashionable term, but one which Paul's language about the indwelling Messiah and spirit appears to warrant, even if its implications need to be teased out further, a task which Gorman and others have been pursuing energetically.[87] If the great paradigms of Pauline study have no room for this element, that may be a sign of their inadequacy. The question remains as to whether the notion of the believer's transformation through the indwelling of the crucified-and-risen Messiah is what Paul actually *means* by 'justification', or whether the word 'justification' and its cognates refer to something else with which this transformation is closely correlated. That requires very careful handling of the relevant texts in Romans and Philippians as well as Galatians. But I see Gorman's work, focused not least on the end of Galatians 2 as well as other key passages like Philippians 2, as a sign that in summing up the present project all I am doing is presenting a kind of interim report. There are more things in heaven and earth, and certainly in Paul, than are dreamed of in any of our schemes. Fresh lines of investigation that emerge from the very heart of dense but crucial passages in Paul show not only that all our great schemes fall short but that new

[86] See e.g. Gorman 2001, 2009, 2015.

[87] See e.g. Blackwell 2011; Litwa 2012.

pathways regularly open up. The theme of transformation might turn out to be not only a forgotten element which could point to a richer coherence but also a metaphor for what might yet happen within Pauline studies itself.

Of course, Paul is not saying 'I have been crucified with the Messiah', or that 'the Messiah lives in me', in order to suggest that he himself has had a particular 'experience' which sets him apart from others. He is referring to himself because he intends to function as a paradigm case. This is what it looks like when a Jew comes into the family of the crucified and risen Messiah. In other words (addressed by implication to Cephas, and then by resonance to the Galatian churches in relation to what the 'teachers' have been saying), the fact that the Messiah was crucified and raised, and that those who belong to him share the meaning of that event, indicates that there is indeed a new family, the messianic family, marked as such by outward membership and inward transformation. Paul's use of autobiography here, as in some other passages, is designed to avoid him saying 'you' or 'they', as though this were not his story as well. The first thing, then, is the new identity, shaped by the Messiah's death and resurrection.

The second thing is that all this has happened as a result of the plan and grace of God. Verse 21 again: 'I don't set aside God's grace'. The death of the Messiah is to be seen as the divine grace in action. This is the strong point of the 'apocalyptic' school: the dark world, ruled over by hostile powers, has been decisively invaded by God himself.[88] This again links back to 1.4, with the elements the other way round: there, the Messiah 'gave himself for our sins' in order to 'deliver us from the present evil age', while here 'the son of God loved me and gave himself for me' as the revelation in action of 'the grace of God'. Of course, Paul realizes that the death and resurrection of the Messiah, and the effect of this in terms of creating a new messianic family who can be united because sins have been forgiven, might make it look as though God has gone back on everything the ancient scriptures had said. That is why he is quick in the next chapter to expound the original terms of the Abrahamic covenant, and to show that, however surprising it seems, what has happened in the Messiah is not only the divine grace at work doing a radical new thing but the divine grace *as promised all along*. And this means that the language of 'apocalyptic invasion', though from one point of view completely justified, from another point of view can be seriously misleading. Israel's God is the creator, and the world remains his even when his rule is usurped.

This is why, as well, it is important to emphasize the last phrase of verse 19: the death to Torah has happened 'so that I might live to God'. Paul will address in the next chapter the question of an apparent disjunction between the overall divine purpose and the giving of Torah. For the moment he leaves it paradoxical. But the point he wants to stress is that in 'dying to the law' he is not abandoning Israel's God. He is living for him in a whole new way. And he wants all Jewish Messiah-believers to do the same, embodying

[88] See, e.g., Martyn 1997a, 103–5; de Boer 2011, 34; Gaventa 2012.

that whole new way by sharing fully in the Messiah's family, Abraham's family, with all who share the messianic badge of *pistis*, Messiah-faith, the badge that reminds them that, with 'sins' dealt with and forgiven, there is now no distinction between those 'in the law' and 'gentile sinners'.

Third and finally, Paul emphasizes that what matters is love: 'I live within the faithfulness of the son of God, who loved me and gave himself for me.' Paul here, as we saw, repeats the formula from 1.4: the Messiah 'gave himself for our sins'. The Messiah's death for sins is not a Jewish-Christian idea which Paul is trying to leave behind in his quest for a 'cosmic' message. The 'cosmic' message comes in too, but without forgetting the former. For Paul, it is by dealing with human sins both forensically and transformatively that the God of Israel dethrones the 'powers' that have usurped his rule. Within this frame of reference, too, one of the oldest divisions in the interpretation of Paul – as rigid in its way as the original division between Jew and gentile! – simply melts away. Is 'justification' central to Paul, or is 'participation' the centre? The line from Schweitzer to Sanders to Campbell says, Participation (perhaps in an 'apocalyptic' context). The line from Baur to Bultmann to the old perspective says, Justification. Paul says, Both, and both within a larger context; because the word 'love', in biblical usage, is itself a direct pointer to the theme which will occupy him in the next chapter, namely, the divine covenant. Within that covenant, and the family whose sociological dimensions indicate just this kind of new unity, and the transformed lives shaped from within by the Messiah's cross and resurrection, the Abrahamic promises now fulfilled through the Messiah mean that there is neither Jew nor Greek, neither apocalyptic nor salvation history, neither participation nor justification: all are one in the Messiah.

The love in question is the divine love, with the Messiah's love as the embodiment of that divine love (compare Romans 5.8; 8.37–9). The stress on love in Galatians 5 tells its own story; this theme is central at every level of Paul's thought.[89] Whether we are old perspective or new perspective, whether we study history of religion or simply history, whether we believe in apocalyptic or salvation history, whether we are social historians or social theorists, whether we read Paul as philosophers or politicians or simply as puzzled onlookers, unless this note of rescuing and transformative *agapē* sounds somewhere near the centre of our interpretation we are not reading Paul in his own terms and with his own emphases. At the heart of Paul's theology, because he believed it to be at the centre of history, was the divine act which reconfigured the world and Paul with it.[90] It was an act which would necessarily translate into further action: just as love is the ultimate mode of knowing, so love is also the ultimate hermeneutic, grounding mission as well as unity.[91] Behind all the theories and suppositions, the complexities of exegesis and the puzzles over paradigms, this stands out. 'The son of God loved me and gave himself for me.' That was the message by

[89] See 5.6, 13, 14, 22.

[90] Gal. 6.14; cf. 2 Cor. 5.13–17.

[91] See again Gorman 2015.

which, in Antioch, Paul chose to be identified, and that was how 'the truth of the gospel' identified the Messiah's followers as an apocalyptically created social, theological and missional entity. Those who study Paul, whether in the academy, the church or the wider world, could do worse than to start at this point.

BIBLIOGRAPHY

Adams, E. 2009. 'First-Century Models for Paul's Churches: Selected Scholarly Developments Since Meeks' in Still, T. D., and D. G. Horrell, eds. *After the First Urban Christians: The Social-Scientific Study of Pauline Christianity Twenty-Five Years Later*. London: T & T Clark, pp. 60–78.

Adorno, T. W. 1974 [1951]. *Minima Moralia: Reflections from Damaged Life*. London: Verso.

Agamben, G. 2005 [2003]. *State of Exception*. Chicago: Chicago University Press.

——. 2005 [2000]. *The Time That Remains: A Commentary on the Letter to the Romans*, tr. P. Dailey. Stanford, CA: Stanford University Press.

——. 2011 [2007]. *The Kingdom and the Glory: For a Theological Genealogy of Economy and Government*. Stanford, CA: Stanford University Press.

Aletti, J. N. 2010 [1992]. *God's Justice in Romans: Keys for Interpreting the Epistle to the Romans*, tr. P. M. Meyer. Rome: Gregorian and Biblical Press.

Alexander, L. C. A. 1994. 'Paul and the Hellenistic Schools: The Evidence of Galen' in Engberg-Pedersen, T., ed. *Paul in His Hellenistic Context*. Edinburgh: T & T Clark, pp. 60–83.

Allen, R. M. 2013. *Justification and the Gospel: Understanding the Contexts and Controversies*. Grand Rapids: Baker.

Allison, D. C. 1998. *Jesus of Nazareth: Millenarian Prophet*. Minneapolis: Fortress Press.

Anderson, G. A., and J. S. Kaminsky. 2013. *The Call of Abraham: Essays on the Election of Israel in Honor of Jon D. Levenson*. Notre Dame, IN: University of Notre Dame Press.

Ascough, R. S. 2003. *Paul's Macedonian Associations: The Social Context of Philippians and 1 Thessalonians*. Tübingen: Mohr.

Aulén, G. 1969. *Christus Victor: An Historical Study of the Three Main Types of the Idea of Atonement*, tr. A. G. Hebert, with a Foreword by J. Pelikan. New York: Macmillan.

Avemarie, F. 1996. *Tora und Leben: Untersuchungen zur Heilsbedeutung der Tora in der frühen rabbinischen Literatur*. Tübingen: Mohr.

Badiou, A. 2003 [1997]. *Saint Paul: The Foundation of Universalism*, tr. R. Brassier. Stanford, CA: Stanford University Press.

Baird, W. 1992. *History of New Testament Research, Volume 1: From Deism to Tübingen.* Minneapolis: Fortress Press.

——. 2003. *History of New Testament Research, Volume 2: From Jonathan Edwards to Rudolf Bultmann.* Minneapolis: Fortress Press.

——. 2013. *History of New Testament Research, Volume 3: From C. H. Dodd to Hans Dieter Betz.* Minneapolis: Fortress Press.

Barclay, J. M. G. 1992. 'Thessalonica and Corinth: Social Contrasts in Pauline Christianity.' *Journal for the Study of the New Testament* 47:49–74.

——. 1995. 'Deviance and Apostasy: Some Applications of Deviance Theory to First-Century Judaism and Christianity' in Esler, P. F., ed. *Modelling Early Christianity: Social-Scientific Studies of the New Testament in Its Context.* London: Routledge, pp. 114–27.

——. 1996. *Jews in the Mediterranean Diaspora from Alexander to Trajan (323 BCE — 117 CE).* Edinburgh: T & T Clark.

——. 2011. *Pauline Churches and Diaspora Jews.* Tübingen: Mohr.

——. 2015. *Paul and the Gift.* Grand Rapids: Eerdmans.

Barclay, J. M. G., and S. J. Gathercole, eds. 2006. *Divine and Human Agency in Paul and His Cultural Environment.* In *Early Christianity in Context,* Library of New Testament Studies 335. London/New York: T & T Clark.

Barth, K. 1936–69. *Church Dogmatics.* Edinburgh: T & T Clark. (=*CD*)

——. 1963. *Evangelical Theology: An Introduction*, tr. G. Foley. London: Weidenfeld & Nicolson.

——. 1968 [1933]. *The Epistle to the Romans*, tr. E. C. Hoskyns. Oxford: Oxford University Press.

Barton, S. C. 1995. 'Historical Criticism and Social-Scientific Perspectives in New Testament Study' in Green, J. B., ed. *Hearing the New Testament: Strategies for Interpretation.* Grand Rapids: Eerdmans, pp. 61–89.

Bauckham, R., J. R. Davila, and A. Panayotov, eds. 2013. *Old Testament Pseudepigrapha: More Noncanonical Scriptures.* Vol. 1. Grand Rapids: Eerdmans.

Baur, F. C. 2011 [1873]. *Paul the Apostle of Jesus Christ.* Grand Rapids: Baker.

Bauspiess, M., C. Landmesser, and D. Lincicum, eds. 2014. *Ferdinand Christian Baur und die Geschichte des frühen Christentums.* Tübingen: Mohr.

Becker, H. S. 1963. *Outsiders: Studies in the Sociology of Deviance.* New York: Free Press.

Beilby, J. K., and P. R. Eddy, eds. 2011. *Justification: Five Views.* Downers Grove, IL: InterVarsity Press.

Beker, J. C. 1980. *Paul the Apostle: The Triumph of God in Life and Thought.* Philadelphia: Fortress Press.

——. 1982. *Paul's Apocalyptic Gospel: The Coming Triumph of God.* Philadelphia: Fortress.

Benhabib, S. 1992. *Situating the Self: Gender, Community and Postmodernism in Contemporary Ethics.* Cambridge: Polity Press.

Benjamin, W. 1974–89. *Gesammelte Schriften*, ed. R. Tiedemann and H. Schweppenhäuser. Frankfurt: Suhrkamp.

Berger, P. L., and T. Luckmann. 1984 [1966]. *The Social Construction of Reality: A Treatise in the Sociology of Knowledge.* Garden City, NY: Doubleday, Anchor.

Bird, M. F. 2007. *The Saving Righteousness of God: Studies on Paul, Justification and the New Perspective.* Milton Keynes: Paternoster.

——, ed. and introd. 2012. *Four Views on the Apostle Paul*. Grand Rapids: Zondervan.

Blackburn, S. 2008. *The Oxford Dictionary of Philosophy*. 2nd edn. rev. Oxford: Oxford University Press.

Blackwell, B. C. 2011. *Christosis: Pauline Soteriology in Light of Deification in Irenaeus and Cyril of Alexandria*. Tubingen: Mohr.

Blanton, W. 2014. *A Materialism for the Masses: Saint Paul and the Philosophy of Undying Life*. New York: Columbia University Press.

Blanton, W., and H. de Vries, eds. 2013. *Paul and the Philosophers*. New York: Fordham University Press.

Blasi, A. J., J. Duhaime, and P.-A. Turcotte, eds. 2002. *Handbook of Early Christianity: Social Science Approaches*. Walnut Creek, CA: AltaMira Press.

Bloch, M. 1992. 'What Goes Without Saying: The Conceptualization of Zafimaniry Society' in Kuper, A., ed. *Conceptualizing Society*. London/New York: Routledge, pp. 127–46.

Blumenfeld, B. 2001. *The Political Paul: Justice, Democracy and Kingship in a Hellenistic Framework*. Sheffield: Sheffield Academic Press.

Boccaccini, G. 1991. *Middle Judaism: Jewish Thought 300 B.C.E. to 200 C.E.* Minneapolis: Fortress Press.

Bockmuehl, M. 2001. '1QS and Salvation at Qumran' in Carson, D. A., Peter T. O'Brien, and Mark A. Seifried, eds. *Justification and Variegated Nomism, Volume I: The Complexities of Second Temple Judaism*. Grand Rapids: Baker Academic, pp. 381–414.

Boer, R., ed. 2010. *Secularism and Biblical Studies*. Sheffield: Equinox.

Borg, M. J. 1984. *Conflict, Holiness and Politics in the Teachings of Jesus*. Studies in the Bible and Early Christianity 5. New York/ Toronto: Edwin Mellen Press.

——. 1986. 'A Temperate Case for a Non-Eschatological Jesus.' *Foundations and Facets Forum* 2.3:81–102.

——. 1987. 'An Orthodoxy Reconsidered: The "End-of-the-World Jesus"' in Hurst, L. D., and N. T. Wright, eds. *The Glory of Christ in the New Testament: Studies in Christology in Memory of George Bradford Caird*. Oxford: Oxford University Press, pp. 207–17.

Bornkamm, G. 1969. *Early Christian Experience*, tr. P. L. Hammer. London: SCM Press.

——. 1971 [1969]. *Paul*. London: Hodder & Stoughton.

Bousset, W. 1970. *Kyrios Christos: A History of Belief in Christ from the Beginnings of Christianity to Irenaeus*, tr. J. E. Steely. 1913. Repr. Nashville: Abingdon.

Boyarin, D. 1994. *A Radical Jew: Paul and the Politics of Identity*. Berkeley: University of California Press.

Briggs, A. 2012. *Special Relationships: People and Places*. Barnsley: Frontline Books.

Bultmann, R. 1951–5. *Theology of the New Testament*, tr. Kendrick Grobel. London/New York: SCM Press/Scribner's.

——. 1960a. *Existence and Faith*, ed. Schubert M. Ogden. Living Age Books. New York: World Publishing, Meridian.

——. 1960b. *This World and the Beyond: Marburg Sermons*. New York: Scribner's.

——. 1967. *Exegetica*. Tübingen: Mohr.

——. 2007. *Theology of the New Testament*. Introd. R. Morgan. Waco, TX: Baylor University Press.

Cadbury, H. J. 1953. 'Current Issues in New Testament Study.' *Harvard Divinity School Bulletin* 19:49–64.

Caird, G. B. 1978. 'Review of Sanders 1977.' *Journal of Theological Studies* 29:538–43.

——. 1980. *The Language and Imagery of the Bible*. London: Duckworth.

Campbell, D. A. 1992. *The Rhetoric of Righteousness in Romans 3.21–26*. Journal for the Study of the New Testament Supplement Series 65. Sheffield: JSOT Press.

——. 2005. *The Quest for Paul's Gospel: A Suggested Strategy*. London: T & T Clark.

——. 2009. *The Deliverance of God: An Apocalyptic Rereading of Justification in Paul*. Grand Rapids: Eerdmans.

——. 2012. 'Christ and the Church in Paul: A "Post-New Perspective" Account' in Bird, M. F., ed. *Four Views on the Apostle Paul*. Grand Rapids: Zondervan, pp. 113–43.

——. 2014. *Framing Paul: An Epistolary Biography*. Grand Rapids: Eerdmans.

Carney, T. F. 1975. *The Shape of the Past: Models and Antiquity*. Lawrence, KS: Coronado Press.

Carson, D. A. 2001. 'Summaries and Conclusions' in Carson, D. A., Peter T. O'Brien, and Mark A. Seifrid, eds. *Justification and Variegated Nomism, Volume I: The Complexities of Second Temple Judaism*. Tübingen: Mohr, pp. 505–48.

Carson, D. A., P. T. O'Brien, and M. A. Seifrid. 2001–4. *Justification and Variegated Nomism: Vol. 1: The Complexities of Second Temple Judaism; Vol. 2: The Paradoxes of Paul*. Tübingen/Grand Rapids: Mohr/Baker Academic.

Castelli, E. A. 1991. *Imitating Paul: A Discourse of Power*. Louisville, KY: Westminster John Knox Press.

Catchpole, D. R. 2004. 'Who and Where is the "Wretched Man" of Romans 7, and Why is "She" Wretched?' in Stanton, G. N., B. W. Longenecker, and S. C. Barton, eds. *The Holy Spirit and Christian Origins: FS James D. G. Dunn*. Grand Rapids: Eerdmans, pp. 168–80.

Chance, J. K. 1994. 'The Anthropology of Honor and Shame: Culture, Values, and Practice.' *Semeia* 68:139–49.

Charlesworth, J. H., ed. 1983. *Apocalyptic Literature and Testaments*. Vol. 1 of *The Old Testament Pseudepigrapha*. Garden City, NY: Doubleday.

——, ed. 1985. *Expansions of the 'Old Testament' and Legends, Wisdom and Philosophical Literature, Prayers, Psalms and Odes, Fragments of Lost Judaeo-Hellenistic Works*. Vol. 2 of *The Old Testament Pseudepigrapha*. Garden City, NY: Doubleday.

Chester, S. J. 2003. *Conversion at Corinth: Perspectives on Conversion in Paul's Theology and the Corinthian Church*. London: T & T Clark.

Chilton, B. D. 2004. *Rabbi Paul: An Intellectual Biography*. New York: Doubleday.

Clarke, A. D. 1993. *Secular and Christian Leadership in Corinth: A Socio-Historical and Exegetical Study of 1 Corinthians 1—6*. Leiden: Brill.

——. 2000. *Serve the Community of the Church: Christians as Leaders and Ministers*. Grand Rapids: Eerdmans.

——. 2008. *A Pauline Theology of Church Leadership*. London: T & T Clark.

Cohen, L. J. 1995. 'Explanation' in Honderich, T., ed. *The Oxford Companion to Philosophy*. Oxford: Oxford University Press, pp. 262–3.

Coleridge, S. T. 1836. *The Literary Remains of Samuel Taylor Coleridge*. Vol. 1. London: W. Pickering.

Collins, J. J. 1987. *The Apocalyptic Imagination*. New York: Crossroad.

——. 2000. 'Eschatologies of Late Antiquity' in Evans, C. A., and S. E. Porter, eds. *Dictionary of New Testament Background*. Downers Grove, IL: InterVarsity Press, pp. 330–7.

——. 2010. 'Apocalypse' in Collins, J. J., and D. C. Harlow, eds. *The Eerdmans Dictionary of Early Judaism*. Grand Rapids: Eerdmans, pp. 341–5.

Conzelmann, H. 1968. 'Current Problems in Pauline Research.' *Interpretation* 22:171–86.

——. 1975 [1969]. *1 Corinthians: A Commentary on the First Epistle to the Corinthians*, tr. J. W. Leitch. Hermeneia. Philadelphia: Fortress Press.

Countryman, L. W. 1988. *Dirt, Greed and Sex: Sexual Ethics in the New Testament and Their Implications for Today*. Philadelphia: Fortress Press.

Court, J. M. 1982. 'Paul and the Apocalyptic Pattern' in Hooker, M. D., and S. G. Wilson, eds. *Paul and Paulinism: Essays in Honour of C. K. Barrett*. London: SPCK, pp. 57–66.

Cranfield, C. E. B. 1975–9. *A Critical and Exegetical Commentary on the Epistle to the Romans*. 2 vols. International Critical Commentary. Edinburgh: T & T Clark.

Crossan, J. D. 1991. *The Historical Jesus: The Life of a Mediterranean Jewish Peasant*. Edinburgh/San Francisco: T & T Clark/Harper.

Cullmann, O. 1962 [1951]. *Christ and Time: The Primitive Christian Conception of Time and History*, tr. Floyd V. Filson. London: SCM Press.

——. 1967 [1965]. *Salvation in History*. London/New York: SCM Press/Harper and Row.

Dahl, N. A. 1977. *Studies in Paul: Theology for the Early Christian Mission*. Minneapolis: Augsburg.

Danker, F. W. 1982. *Benefactor: Epigraphic Study of a Graeco-Roman and New Testament Semantic Field*. St Louis: Clayton.

Das, A. A. 2001. *Paul, the Law, and the Covenant*. Peabody, MA: Hendrickson.

——. 2003. *Paul and the Jews*. Peabody, MA: Hendrickson.

——. 2009. 'Paul and the Law: Pressure Points in the Debate' in Given, M. D., ed. *Paul Unbound: Other Perspectives on the Apostle*. Peabody, MA: Hendrickson, pp. 99–116.

Das, A. A., and F. J. Matera, eds. 2002. *The Forgotten God: Perspectives in Biblical Theology: Essays in Honor of Paul J. Achtemeier on the Occasion of His Seventy-Fifth Birthday*. Louisville, KY: Westminster John Knox Press.

Davies, J. P. 2016. *Paul among the Apocalypses? An Evaluation of the 'Apocalyptic Paul' in the Context of Jewish and Christian Apocalyptic Literature*. Library of New Testament Studies. London: T & T Clark (forthcoming).

Davies, W. D. 1980. *Paul and Rabbinic Judaism*. 4th edn. Philadelphia: Fortress Press.

Davis, J. B., and D. Harink, eds. 2012. *Apocalyptic and the Future of Theology: With and Beyond J. Louis Martyn*. Eugene, OR: Cascade Books.

de Boer, M. C. 1988. *The Defeat of Death: Apocalyptic Eschatology in 1 Corinthians 15 and Romans 5*. Sheffield: JSOT Press.

——. 1989. 'Paul and Jewish Apocalyptic Eschatology' in Marcus, J., and M. L. Soards, eds. *Apocalyptic and the New Testament: Essays in Honor of J. Louis Martyn*. Sheffield: Sheffield Academic Press, pp. 169–90.

——. 2002. 'Paul, Theologian of God's Apocalypse.' *Interpretation* 56.1:22–33.

——. 2011. *Galatians: A Commentary*. Louisville, KY: Westminster John Knox Press.

de la Durantaye, L. 2012. 'Afterword: On Method, the Messiah, Anarchy and Theocracy' in Agamben, G., ed. *The Church and the Kingdom*. London: Seagull Books, pp. 48–62.

Deines, R. 2001. 'The Pharisees between "Judaisms" and "Common Judaism"' in Carson, D. A., Peter T. O'Brien, and Mark A. Seifrid, eds. *Justification and Variegated Nomism,*

Vol. I: The Complexities of Second Temple Judaism. Tübingen/Grand Rapids: Mohr/Baker Academic, pp. 443–504.
Deissmann, A. 1926 [1912]. *Paul: A Study in Social and Religious History*. London: Hodder & Stoughton.
deSilva, D. A. 1999. *The Hope of Glory: Honor Discourse and New Testament Interpretation*. Collegeville, MN: Liturgical Press.
——. 2000. *Honor, Patronage, Kinship and Purity: Unlocking New Testament Culture*. Downers Grove, IL: InterVarsity Press.
Dodd, C. H. 1959 [1932]. *The Epistle of Paul to the Romans*. London: Collins/Fontana.
Donaldson, Terence L. 1997. *Paul and the Gentiles: Remapping the Apostle's Convictional World*. Minneapolis: Fortress Press.
Duling, D. C. 1996. 'Millennialism' in Rohrbaugh, R. L., ed. *The Social Sciences and New Testament Interpretation*. Peabody, MA: Hendrickson, pp. 183–205.
Dunn, J. D. G. 1977. *Unity and Diversity in the New Testament: An Inquiry into the Character of Earliest Christianity*. London/Philadelphia: SCM/Westminster Press.
——. 1988. *Romans 1—8*. Word Biblical Commentary. Waco, TX: Word Books.
——. 1993. *A Commentary on the Epistle to the Galatians*. Black's New Testament Commentaries. London: A. & C. Black.
——. 1996a. *The Epistles to the Colossians and to Philemon: A Commentary on the Greek Text*. Grand Rapids: Eerdmans.
——., ed. 1996b. *Paul and the Mosaic Law*. Tübingen: Mohr.
——. 1998. *The Theology of Paul the Apostle*. Grand Rapids: Eerdmans.
——. 2008 [2005]. *The New Perspective on Paul*. Grand Rapids: Eerdmans.
——. 2009. *Beginning from Jerusalem*. Vol. 2 of *Christianity in the Making*. Grand Rapids: Eerdmans.
Duffy, E. 2005 [1992]. *The Stripping of the Altars: Traditional Religion in England 1400–1580*. New Haven: Yale University Press.
Ehrensperger, K. 2007. *Paul and the Dynamics of Power: Communication and Interaction in the Early-Christ Movement*. London: T & T Clark.
Eisenbaum, Pamela. 2009. *Paul Was Not a Christian: The Original Message of a Misunderstood Apostle*. San Francisco: HarperOne.
Eliot, T. S. 1944. *Four Quartets*. London: Faber & Faber.
Elliott, J. H. 1981. *A Home for the Homeless: A Sociological Exegesis of 1 Peter, Its Situation and Strategy*. Philadelphia: Fortress Press.
——. 1993. *What Is Social-Scientific Criticism?* Minneapolis: Fortress Press.
——. 1995. 'The Jewish Messianic Movement: From Faction to Sect' in Esler, P. F., ed. *Modelling Early Christianity: Social-Scientific Studies of the New Testament in Its Context*. London: Routledge, pp. 75–95.
——. 1996. 'Patronage and Clientage' in Rohrbauch, R. L., ed. *The Social Sciences and New Testament Interpretation*. Peabody, MA: Hendrickson, pp. 144–56.
Elliott, N. 2010. 'Ideological Closure in the Christ-Event: A Marxist Response to Alain Badiou's Paul' in Harink, D., ed. *Paul, Philosophy and the Theopolitical Vision: Critical Engagements with Agamben, Badiou, Žižek, and Others*. Eugene, OR: Cascade Books, pp. 135–54.

——. 2013. 'Creation, Cosmos, and Conflict in Romans 8–9' in Gaventa, B., ed. *Apocalyptic Paul: Cosmos and Anthropos in Romans 5–8*. Waco: Baylor University Press, pp. 131–56.

Ellis, E. E. 1961. *Paul and His Recent Interpreters*. Grand Rapids: Eerdmans.

Engberg-Pedersen, T. 2000. *Paul and the Stoics*. Edinburgh: T & T Clark.

——, ed. 2001. *Paul beyond the Judaism/Hellenism Divide*. Louisville, KY: Westminster John Knox Press.

Epictetus. 1995. *A Manual for Living*. San Francisco: HarperOne.

Epictetus, and S. Lebell. 2007. *Art of Living: The Classical Manual on Virtue, Happiness, and Effectiveness*. San Francisco: HarperOne.

Esler, P. F. 1987. *Community and Gospel in Luke-Acts: The Social and Political Motivations of Lucan Theology*. Cambridge: Cambridge University Press.

——. 1994. *The First Christians in Their Social Worlds: Social-Scientific Approaches to New Testament Interpretation*. London: Routledge.

——., ed. 1995. *Modelling Early Christianity: Social-Scientific Studies of the New Testament in Its Context*. London/New York: Routledge.

——. 1998. *Galatians*. London/New York: Routledge.

——. 2003. *Conflict and Identity in Romans*. London: Routledge.

Farrer, A. 1964. *The Revelation of St John the Divine*. Oxford: Oxford University Press.

Festinger, L. H. 1957. *A Theory of Cognitive Dissonance*. Stanford, CA: Stanford University Press.

Festinger, L., H. Riecken, and S. Schachter. 1956. *When Prophecy Fails*. Minneapolis: University of Minnesota Press.

Fortna, R., and B. R. Gaventa, eds. 1990. *The Conversation Continues: Studies in Paul and John in Honor of J. Louis Martyn*. Nashville: Abingdon.

Fowl, S. 2010. 'A Very Particular Universalism: Badiou and Paul' in Harink, D., ed. *Paul, Philosophy, and the Theopolitical Vision: Critical Engagements with Agamben, Badiou, Žižek and Others*. Eugene, OR: Cascade Books, pp. 119–34.

Fredriksen, P. 2005. 'Just Like Everyone Else, Only More So.' *Jewish Quarterly Review* 95.1:119–30.

Frey, J., and B. Schliesser, eds. 2013. *Die Theologie des Paulus in der Diskussion: Reflexionen im Anschluss an Michael Wolters Grundriss*. Neukirchen: Neukirchener Verlag.

Friesen, S. J. 2004. 'Poverty in Pauline Studies: Beyond the So-Called New Consensus.' *Journal for the Study of the New Testament* 26:323–61.

——. 2010. 'Paul and Economics: The Jerusalem Collection as an Alternative to Patronage' in Given, M. D., ed. *Paul Unbound: Other Perspectives on the Apostle*. Peabody, MA: Hendrickson, pp. 27–54.

Fukuyama, F. 2012 [1992]. *The End of History and the Last Man*. London: Penguin.

Fuller, R. H. 1963 [1962]. *The New Testament in Current Study*. London: SCM Press.

Furnish, V. P. 2002. 'Inside Looking Out: Some Pauline Views of the Unbelieving Public' in Anderson, J. C., P. Sellew, and C. Setzer, eds. *Pauline Conversations in Context: Essays in Honor of Calvin J. Roetzel*. Sheffield: Sheffield Academic Press, pp. 104–24.

Gaffin, R. B. 1978. *The Centrality of the Resurrection: A Study in Paul's Soteriology*. Grand Rapids: Baker.

Gager, J. G. 1975. *Kingdom and Community: The Social World of Early Christianity*. Englewood Cliffs, NJ: Prentice-Hall.

——. 1983. *The Origins of Anti-Semitism*. Oxford: Oxford University Press.

Garlington, D. 2004. *In Defence of the New Perspective on Paul: Essays and Reviews*. Eugene, OR: Wipf and Stock.

Gaston, L. 1987. *Paul and the Torah*. Vancouver: University of British Columbia Press.

Gathercole, S. J. 2000. 'The Critical and Dogmatic Agenda of Albert Schweitzer's *The Quest of the Historical Jesus*.' *Tyndale Bulletin* 51:261–83.

——. 2002. *Where is Boasting? Early Jewish Soteriology and Paul's Response in Romans 1-5*. Grand Rapids: Eerdmans.

——. 2006. 'The Doctrine of Justification in Paul and Beyond: Some Proposals' in McCormack, B. L., ed. *Justification in Perspective: Historical Developments and Contemporary Challenges*. Grand Rapids: Baker Academic, pp. 219–41.

——. 2013. 'Deutsche Erwiderungen auf die "Neue Perspective": eine Anglophone Sicht' in Frey, J., and B. Schliesser, eds. *Die Theologie des Paulus in der Diskussion: Reflexionen im Anschluss an Michael Wolters Grundriss*. Neukirchen: Neukirchener Verlag, pp. 115–53.

Gaventa, B. R., 2007. *Our Mother Saint Paul*. Louisville, KY: Westminster John Knox Press.

——. 2011. 'Neither Height Nor Depth: Discerning the Cosmology of Romans.' *Scottish Journal of Theology*, 64:265–78.

——. 2012. '"Neither Height Nor Depth": Cosmos and Soteriology in Paul's Letter to the Romans' in Davis, J. B., and D. Harink, eds. *Apocalyptic and the Future of Theology: With and Beyond J. Louis Martyn*. Eugene, OR: Cascade Books, pp. 183–99.

——. ed. 2013a. *Apocalyptic Paul: Cosmos and Anthropos in Romans 5—8*. Waco, TX: Baylor University Press.

——. 2013b. 'Romans' in Krans, J. et al., eds. *Paul, John and Apocalyptic Eschatology: Studies in Honour of Martinus C. de Boer*. Leiden: Brill, pp. 61–75.

——. 2013c. 'The Shape of the "I": The Psalter, the Gospel, and the Speaker in Romans 7' in Gaventa, B., ed. *Apocalyptic Paul: Cosmos and Anthropos in Romans 5—8*. Waco, TX: Baylor University Press, pp. 77–91.

Geertz, C. 2000. *The Interpretation of Cultures*. 2nd edn. New York: Basic Books.

Gerdmar, A. 2014. 'Baur and the Creation of the Judaism-Hellenism Dichotomy' in Bauspiess, M., C. Landmesser, and D. Lincicum, eds. *Ferdinand Christian Baur und die Geschichte des frühen Christentums*. Tübingen: Mohr, pp. 107–28.

Given, M. D., ed. 2010. *Paul Unbound: Other Perspectives on the Apostle*. Peabody, MA: Hendrickson.

Glad, C. E. 1995. *Paul and Philodemus: Adaptability in Epicurean and Early Christian Psychagogy*. Leiden: Brill.

Goppelt, L. 1964. 'Apokalyptik und Typologie bei Paulus.' *Theologisches Literaturzeitung* 89:321–44.

Gorman, M. J. 2001. *Cruciformity: Paul's Narrative Spirituality of the Cross*. Grand Rapids: Eerdmans.

——. 2009. *Inhabiting the Cruciform God: Kenosis, Justification, and Theosis in Paul's Narrative Soteriology*. Grand Rapids: Eerdmans.

——. 2015. *Becoming the Gospel: Paul, Participation and Mission*. Grand Rapids: Eerdmans.

Greenblatt, S. 2001. *Hamlet in Purgatory*. Princeton: Princeton University Press.

Gresham Machen, J. 1982. *God Transcendent*. Carlisle, PA: Banner of Truth.

Griffith-Jones, R. 2014. 'Beyond Reasonable Hope of Recognition? *Prosōpopoeia* in Romans 1:18—3:8' in Tilling, C., ed. *Beyond Old and New Perspectives on Paul: Reflections on the Work of Douglas Campbell*. Eugene, OR: Cascade Books, pp. 161–81.

Griffiths, P. J. 2010. 'The Cross as the Fulcrum of Politics: Expropriating Agamben on Paul' in Harink, D., ed. *Paul, Philosophy, and the Theopolitical Vision: Critical Engagements with Agamben, Badiou, Žižek and Others*. Eugene, OR: Cascade Books, pp. 179–97.

Gundry, R. H. 2005. *The Old Is Better: New Testament Essays in Support of Traditional Interpretations*. Tübingen: Mohr.

Habermas, J. 2002. *Religion and Rationality: Essays on Reason, God, and Modernity*. Cambridge: Polity Press.

Hagner, D. A. 2001. 'Paul and Judaism: Testing the New Perspective' in Stuhlmacher, P., *Revisiting Paul's Doctrine of Justification*. Downers Grove, IL: InterVarsity Press, pp. 75–105.

Hanson, A. T. 1974. *Studies in Paul's Technique and Theology*. London: SPCK.

Harink, D. 2010a. *Paul, Philosophy, and the Theopolitical Vision: Critical Engagements with Agamben, Badiou, Žižek and Others*. Eugene, OR: Cascade Books.

——. 2010b. 'Time and Politics in Four Commentaries on Romans' in Harink, ed., *Paul, Philosophy and the Theopolitical Vision*. Eugene, OR.: Cascade Books, pp. 282–312.

——. 2012. 'Partakers of the Divine Apocalypse: Hermeneutics, History and Human Agency after Martyn' in Davis, J. B. and D. Harink, eds. *Apocalyptic and the Future of Theology: With and Beyond J. Louis Martyn*. Eugene, OR: Cascade Books, pp. 73–95.

Harland, P. A. 2003. *Associations, Synagogues, and Congregations: Claiming a Place in Ancient Mediterranean Society*. Minneapolis: Fortress Press.

——. 2009. *Dynamics of Identity in the World of the Early Christians: Associations, Judeans, and Cultural Minorities*. London: T & T Clark.

Harrington, D. J. 1980. 'Social Concepts in the Early Church: A Decade of Research.' *Theological Studies* 41:181–90.

Harris, H. 1990 [1975]. *The Tübingen School: A Historical and Theological Investigation of the School of F. C. Baur*. Grand Rapids: Baker.

Hays, R. B. 1997. *First Corinthians*. Interpretation Commentaries. Louisville, KY: John Knox Press.

——. 2000. 'The Letter to the Galatians: Introduction, Commentary, and Reflections' in *New Interpreter's Bible*, Vol. 11. Nashville: Abingdon, pp. 181–348.

——. 2002 [1983]. *The Faith of Jesus Christ: The Narrative Substructure of Galatians 3:1—4:11*. 2nd edn. Grand Rapids/Cambridge: Eerdmans.

——. 2005. *The Conversion of the Imagination: Paul as Interpreter of Israel's Scriptures*. Grand Rapids: Eerdmans.

——. 2008. 'What Is "Real Participation in Christ"? A Dialogue with E. P. Sanders on Pauline Soteriology' in Udoh, F. E. et al., eds. *Redefining First-Century Jewish and Christian Identities: Essays in Honor of Ed Parish Sanders*. Notre Dame, IN: University of Notre Dame Press, pp. 336–51.

Hays, R. B., S. Alkier, and L. A. Huizenga, eds. 2009. *Reading the Bible Intertextually*. Waco, TX: Baylor University Press.

Heilig, C. 2015. *Hidden Criticism? The Methodology and Plausibility of the Search for a Counter-Imperial Subtext in Paul*. Tübingen: Mohr.

Hellerman, J. H. 2005. *Reconstructing Honor in Roman Philippi: Carmen Christi as Cursus Pudorum*. Cambridge: Cambridge University Press.

Hempel, C. G. 1965. *Aspects of Scientific Explanation and Other Essays in the Philosophy of Science*. New York: Free Press.

Hengel, M. 1974a. *Judaism and Hellenism: Studies in Their Encounter in Palestine During the Early Hellenistic Period*, tr. John Bowden. London: SCM Press.

——. 1974b. *Property and Riches in the Early Church: Aspects of a Social History of Early Christianity*, tr. John Bowden. Philadelphia: Fortress Press.

——. 1981 [1968]. *The Charismatic Leader and His Followers*, tr. James Grieg. New York: Crossroad.

——. 1983. *Between Jesus and Paul: Studies in the Earliest History of Christianity*, tr. J. Bowden. London: SCM Press.

——. 1989 [1961]. *The Zealots: Investigations into the Jewish Freedom Movement in the Period from Herod 1 until 70 A.D.*, tr. D. Smith. Edinburgh: T & T Clark.

——. 1991. *The Pre-Christian Paul*, tr. John Bowden, in collaboration with Roland Deines. London/Philadelphia: SCM Press/TPI.

Hengel, M., and A. M. Schwemer. 1997. *Paul between Damascus and Antioch: The Unknown Years*. London: SCM Press.

Hock, R. F. 1980. *The Social Context of Paul's Ministry: Tentmaking and Apostleship*. Philadelphia: Fortress Press.

Holloway, P. A. 2013. 'Paul as a Hellenistic Philosopher: The Evidence of Philippians' in Blanton, W., and H. de Vries, eds. *Paul and the Philosophers*. New York: Fordham University Press, pp. 52–68.

Holmberg, B. 1978. *Paul and Power: The Structure of Authority in the Primitive Church as Reflected in the Pauline Epistles*. Philadelphia: Fortress Press.

——. 1990. *Sociology and the New Testament: An Appraisal*. Minneapolis: Fortress Press.

Horn, F. W. 2013. *Paulus Handbuch*. Tübingen: Mohr Siebeck.

Horrell, D. G. 1996. *The Social Ethos of the Corinthian Correspondence: Interests and Ideology from 1 Corinthians to 1 Clement*. Edinburgh: T & T Clark.

——, ed. 1999. *Social-Scientific Approaches to New Testament Interpretation*. Edinburgh: T & T Clark.

——. 2000. *An Introduction to the Study of Paul*. London: Continuum.

——. 2002. 'Social Sciences Studying Formative Christian Phenomena: A Creative Movement' in Blasi, A. J., J. Duhaime, and P.-A. Turcotte, eds. *Handbook of Early Christianity: Social Science Approaches*. New York/Oxford: AltaMira Press, pp. 3–28.

——. 2005. *Solidarity and Difference: A Contemporary Reading of Paul's Ethics*. London: T & T Clark (2nd edn. forthcoming 2015).

——. 2009. 'Whither Social-Scientific Approaches to the New Testament? Reflections on Contested Methodologies and the Future' in Still, T. D., and D. G. Horrell, eds. *After the First Urban Christians: The Social-Scientific Study of Pauline Christianity Twenty-Five Years Later*. London: T & T Clark, pp. 6–20.

Horsley, R. A., ed. 1997. *Paul and Empire: Religion and Power in Roman Imperial Society*. Harrisburg, PA: Trinity Press International.

——, ed. 2000. *Paul and Politics: Ekklesia, Israel, Imperium, Interpretation*. Harrisburg, PA: Trinity Press International.

——. 2004. *Paul and the Roman Imperial Order*. London: Continuum.

——. 2005. 'Paul's Assembly in Corinth: An Alternative Society' in Schowalter, D. N., and S. J. Friesen, eds. *Urban Religion in Roman Corinth: Interdisciplinary Approaches*. Cambridge, MA: Harvard University Press, pp. 100–25.

Howard, G. 1967. 'Notes and Observations on the "Faith of Christ".' *Harvard Theological Review* 60:459–65.

——. 1969. 'Christ the End of the Law: The Meaning of Romans 10:4ff.' *Journal of Biblical Literature* 88:331–8.

——. 1970. 'Romans 3:21–31 and the Inclusion of the Gentiles.' *Harvard Theological Review* 63:223–33.

——. 1979. *Paul: Crisis in Galatia. A Study in Early Christian Theology*. Cambridge: Cambridge University Press.

Hübner, H. 1980. 'Pauli Theologiae Proprium.' *New Testament Studies* 26.4:445–73.

——. 1984 [1978]. *Law in Paul's Thought*, tr. J. C. G. Greig. Studies of the New Testament and Its World. Edinburgh: T & T Clark.

Hunter, A. M. 1951. *Interpreting the New Testament, 1900–1950*. London: SCM Press.

Hurtado, L. W. 2003. *Lord Jesus Christ: Devotion to Jesus in Earliest Christianity*. Grand Rapids: Eerdmans.

Jennings, T. W. 2006. *Reading Derrida/Thinking Paul*. Stanford, CA: Stanford University Press.

——. 2013. *Outlaw Justice: The Messianic Politics of Paul*. Stanford, CA: Stanford University Press.

Jeremias, J. 1969. *Jerusalem in the Time of Jesus: An Investigation into Economic and Social Conditions during the New Testament Period*, tr. F. H. Cave and C. H. Cave. Philadelphia: Fortress Press.

Jewett, R. 2007. *Romans*. Minneapolis: Fortress Press.

——. 2013. *Romans: A Short Commentary*. Minneapolis: Fortress Press.

Jewett, R., and J. S. Lawrence. 2002. *The Myth of the American Superhero*. Grand Rapids: Eerdmans.

——. 2004. *Captain America and the Crusade against Evil: The Dilemma of Zealous Nationalism*. Grand Rapids: Eerdmans.

Jewett, R., and K. K. Yeo. 2012. *From Rome to Bejing: Symposia on Robert Jewett's Commentary on Romans*. Lincoln, NE: Prairie Muse.

Judge, E. A. 1960. *The Social Pattern of Christian Groups in the First Century*. London: Tyndale.

——. 2008. *The First Christians in the Roman World: Augustan and New Testament Essays*, ed. J. R. Harrison. Tübingen: Mohr.

——. 2010. *Jerusalem and Athens: Cultural Transformation in Late Antiquity*. Tübingen: Mohr.

Käsemann, E., 1964 [1960]. *Essays on New Testament Themes*, tr. W. J. Montague. London: SCM Press.

——. 1969 [1965]. *New Testament Questions of Today*, tr. W. J. Montague. London: SCM Press.

——. 1971 [1969]. *Perspectives on Paul*, tr. Margaret Kohl. London: SCM Press.

——. 1980 [1973]. *Commentary on Romans*, tr. and ed. Geoffrey W. Bromiley. Grand Rapids: Eerdmans.

——. 2010 [2005]. *On Being a Disciple of the Crucified Nazarene*, eds. R. Landau and W. Kraus. Grand Rapids: Eerdmans.

Keck, L. E. 1974. 'On the Ethos of Early Christians.' *Journal of the American Academy of Religion* 42:435–52.

Kee, H. C. 1980. *Christian Origins in Sociological Perspective*. London: SCM Press.

Keesmaat, S. C. 1999. *Paul and His Story: (Re)Interpreting the Exodus Tradition*. Sheffield: Sheffield Academic Press.

Keller, T. 2014. *Prayer: Experiencing Awe and Intimacy with God*. London: Hodder and Stoughton.

Kennedy, G. A. 1984. *New Testament Interpretation through Rhetorical Criticism*. Chapel Hill, NC: University of North Carolina Press.

Kim, S. 2002. *Paul and the New Perspective: Second Thoughts on the Origin of Paul's Gospel*. Grand Rapids: Eerdmans.

——. 2008. *Christ and Caesar: The Gospel and the Roman Empire in the Writings of Paul and Luke*. Grand Rapids: Eerdmans.

Kirwan, C. A. 1995. 'Why?' in Honderich, T., ed. *The Oxford Companion to Philosophy*. Oxford: Oxford University Press.

Klein, C. 1978. *Anti-Judaism in Christian Theology*. London: SPCK.

Kloppenborg, J. S., and S. G. Wilson, eds. 1996. *Voluntary Associations in the Graeco-Roman World*. London: Routledge.

Knox, R. A. 1928. *Essays in Satire*. London: Sheed and Ward.

——. 1950. *Enthusiasm: A Chapter in the History of Religion with Special Reference to the XVII and XVIII Centuries*. Oxford: Oxford University Press.

Koch, K. 1972 [1970]. *The Rediscovery of Apocalyptic: A Polemical Work on a Neglected Area of Biblical Studies and Its Damaging Effects on Theology and Philosophy*, tr. M. Kohl. London: SCM Press.

Kümmel, W. G. 1972/3 [1970]. *The New Testament: The History of the Investigation of Its Problems*, tr. S. M. Gilmour and H. C. Kee. Nashville/London: Abingdon/SCM Press.

——. 1974 [1929]. *Römer 7 und die Bekehrung des Paulus*. Munich: Kaiser.

Lake, K. 1927. *The Earlier Epistles of St. Paul: Their Motive and Origin*. London: Rivingtons.

Lane, A. N. S. 2006. 'A Tale of Two Imperial Cities: Justification at Regensburg (1541) and Trent (1546–1547)' in McCormack, B. L., ed. *Justification in Perspective: Historical Developments and Contemporary Challenges*. Grand Rapids: Baker Academic, pp. 119–45.

Langton, D. R. 2010. *The Apostle Paul in the Jewish Imagination: A Study in Modern Jewish-Christian Relations*. Cambridge: Cambridge University Press.

Lawrence, L. J. 2009. 'Ritual and the First Urban Christians: Boundary Crossings of Life and Death' in Still, T. D., and D. G. Horrell, eds. *After the First Urban Christians: The Social-Scientific Study of Pauline Christianity Twenty-Five Years Later*. London: T & T Clark, pp. 97–115.

Levenson, J. 1984. 'The Temple and the World.' *Journal of Religion* 64.3:275–98.

Levin, B. 1982. *Speaking Up*. London: Jonathan Cape.

Litwa, M. D. 2012. *We Are Being Transformed: Deification in Paul's Soteriology*. Berlin: De Gruyter.

Loewe, R. 1981. '"Salvation" Is Not of the Jews.' *Journal of Theological Studies* 22:341–68.

Longenecker, B. W. 1991. *Eschatology and the Covenant: A Comparison of 4 Ezra and Romans 1—11*. Sheffield: Sheffield Academic Press.

——. 1998. *The Triumph of Abraham's God: The Transformation of Identity in Galatians*. Edinburgh: T & T Clark.

——. 2002. *Narrative Dynamics in Paul: A Critical Assessment*. Louisville, KY: Westminster John Knox Press.

——. 2009. 'Socio-Economic Profiling of the First Urban Christians' in Still, T. D., and D. G. Horrell, eds. *After the First Urban Christians: The Social-Scientific Study of Pauline Christianity Twenty-Five Years Later*. London: T & T Clark, pp. 36–59.

——. 2010. *Remember the Poor: Paul, Poverty, and the Greco-Roman World*. Grand Rapids: Eerdmans.

Macaskill, G. 2013. *Union with Christ in the New Testament*. Oxford: Oxford University Press.

Maccoby, H. 1986. *The Mythmaker: Paul and the Invention of Christianity*. London: Weidenfeld & Nicolson.

——. 1991. *Paul and Hellenism*. London/Philadelphia: SCM Press/Trinity Press International.

McCormack, B. L., ed. 2006. *Justification in Perspective: Historical Developments and Contemporary Challenges*. Grand Rapids: Baker Academic.

MacDonald, M. 1988. *The Pauline Churches: A Socio-Historical Study of Institutionalization in the Pauline and Deutero-Pauline Writings*. Cambridge: Cambridge University Press.

McGrath, A. E. 1986. *Iustitia Dei: A History of the Christian Doctrine of Justification*. Cambridge: Cambridge University Press.

McKnight, S., and J. B. Modica, eds. 2013. *Jesus Is Lord, Caesar Is Not: Evaluating Empire in New Testament Studies*. Downers Grove, IL: IVP Academic.

MacMillan, M. 2013. *The War That Ended Peace: How Europe Abandoned Peace for the First World War*. London: Profile Books.

Malherbe, A. J. 1983. *Social Aspects of Early Christianity*. 2nd edn. Philadelphia: Fortress Press.

Malina, B. J. 1981. *The New Testament World: Insights from Cultural Anthropology*. London: SCM Press.

——. 1986. *Christian Origins and Cultural Anthropology: Practical Models for Interpretation*. Atlanta: John Knox Press.

Malina, B. J., and J. H. Neyrey. 1991a. 'Conflict in Luke-Acts: Labelling and Deviance Theory' in Neyrey, J. H., ed. *The Social World of Luke-Acts: Models for Interpretation*. Peabody, MA: Hendrickson, pp. 97–122.

——. 1991b. 'First-Century Personality: Dyadic, Not Individualistic' in Neyrey, J. H., ed. *The Social World of Luke-Acts: Models for Interpretation*. Peabody, MA: Hendrickson, pp. 67–96.

——. 1991c. 'Honor and Shame in Luke-Acts: Pivotal Values of the Mediterranean World' in Neyrey, J. H., ed. *The Social World of Luke-Acts: Models for Interpretation*. Peabody, MA: Hendrickson, pp. 23–65.

Marchal, J. A. 2006. *Hierarchy, Unity and Imitation: A Feminist Rhetorical Analysis of Power Dynamics in Paul's Letter to the Philippians*. Atlanta: Society of Biblical Literature.

——. 2008. *The Politics of Heaven: Women, Gender, and Empire in the Study of Paul*. Minneapolis: Fortress Press.

——, ed. 2012. *Studying Paul's Letters: Contemporary Perspectives and Methods*. Minneapolis: Fortress Press.

Marshall, T. R. 2010. *The Catholic Perspective on Paul: Paul and the Origins of Catholic Christianity*. Dallas: St John Press.

Martin, D. B. 1990. *Slavery as Salvation: The Metaphor of Slavery in Pauline Christianity*. New Haven: Yale University Press.

——. 1995. *The Corinthian Body*. New Haven: Yale University Press.

——. 2001. 'Paul and the Judaism/Hellenism Dichotomy: Toward a Social History of the Question' in Engberg-Pedersen, T., ed. *Paul beyond the Judaism/Hellenism Divide*. Louisville KY: Westminster John Knox Press, pp. 29–61.

——. 2004. *Inventing Superstition from the Hippocratics to the Christians*. Cambridge, MA: Harvard University Press.

——. 2009. 'Patterns of Belief and Patterns of Life: Correlations in *The First Urban Christians* and Since' in Still, T. D., and D. G. Horrell, eds. *After the First Urban Christians: The Social-Scientific Study of Pauline Christianity Twenty-Five Years Later*. London: T & T Clark, pp. 116–33.

Martyn, J. L. 1979 [1968]. *History and Theology in the Fourth Gospel*. 2nd edn. Nashville: Abingdon.

——. 1997a. *Galatians: A New Translation with Introduction and Commentary*. Anchor Bible 33a. New York: Doubleday.

——. 1997b. *Theological Issues in the Letters of Paul*. Nashville: Abingdon.

——. 2008. 'Epilogue: An Essay in Pauline Meta-Ethics' in Barclay, J. M. G., and S. J. Gathercole, eds. *Divine and Human Agency in Paul and His Cultural Environment*. London: T & T Clark, pp. 173–83.

——. 2010. 'The Gospel Invades Philosophy' in Harink, D., ed. *Paul, Philosophy, and the Theopolitical Vision: Critical Engagements with Agamben, Badiou, Žižek and Others*. Eugene, OR: Cascade Books, pp. 13–33.

——. 2012. 'A Personal Word about Ernst Käsemann' in Davis, J. B., and D. Harink, eds. *Apocalyptic and the Future of Theology: With and Beyond J. Louis Martyn*. Eugene, OR: Cascade Books, pp. xiii–xv.

——. 2013. 'Afterword: The Human Moral Dilemma' in Gaventa, B., ed. *Apocalyptic Paul: Cosmos and Anthropos in Romans 5—8*. Waco, TX: Baylor University Press, pp. 157–66.

Mason, S. 2007. 'Jews, Judaeans, Judaizing, Judaism: Problems of Categorization in Ancient History.' *Journal for the Study of Judaism* 38:457–512.

Matlock, R. B. 1996. *Unveiling the Apocalyptic Paul: Paul's Interpreters and the Rhetoric of Criticism*. Sheffield: Sheffield Academic Press.

Maxfield, V. A. 1981. *The Military Decorations of the Roman Army*. Berkely, CA: University of California Press.

Meeks, W. A. 1972. 'The Man from Heaven in Johannine Sectarianism.' *Journal of Biblical Literature*, 91:44–72.

——. 1983. *The First Urban Christians: The Social World of the Apostle Paul*. New Haven: Yale University Press. (=*TFUC*)

——. 1986a. 'A Hermeneutics of Social Embodiment.' *Harvard Theological Review* 79:176–86.

——. 1986b. *The Moral World of the First Christians*. Philadelphia/London: Westminster/SCM Press.

——. 1993. *The Origins of Christian Morality: The First Two Centuries*. New Haven: Yale University Press.

——. 2001. 'Judaism, Hellenism and the Birth of Christianity' in Engberg-Pedersen, T., ed. *Paul beyond the Judaism/Hellenism Divide*. Louisville, KY: Westminster John Knox Press, pp. 17–27.

——. 2003 [1983]. *The First Urban Christians: The Social World of the Apostle Paul*. 2nd edn. New Haven: Yale University Press.

——. 2009. 'Taking Stock and Moving On' in Still, T. D., and D. G. Horrell, eds. *After the First Urban Christians: The Social-Scientific Study of Pauline Christianity Twenty-Five Years Later*. London: T & T Clark, pp. 134–46.

Meeks, W. A., A. R. Hilton, and H. G. Snyder. 2002. *In Search of the Early Christians*. New Haven: Yale University Press.

Meeks, W. A., and R. L. Wilken. 1978. *Jews and Christians in Antioch in the First Four Centuries of the Common Era*. Missoula: Scholars Press.

Meggitt, J. J. 1998. *Paul, Poverty and Survival*. Edinburgh: T & T Clark.

Milbank, J. 1990. *Theology and Social Theory: Beyond Secular Reason*. Signposts in Theology. Oxford: Blackwell.

——. 2010. 'Paul Against Biopolitics' in Milbank, J., S. Žižek, and C. Davis, eds. *Paul's New Moment: Continental Philosophy and the Future of Christian Theology*. Grand Rapids: Brazos Press, pp. 21–73.

Milbank, J., S. Žižek, and C. Davis, eds. 2010. *Paul's New Moment: Continental Philosophy and the Future of Christian Theology*. Grand Rapids: Brazos Press.

Minear, P. S. 1971. *The Obedience of Faith*. London: SCM Press.

Mitchell, S. 1993a. *The Celts in Anatolia and the Impact of Roman Rule*. Vol. 1 of *Anatolia: Land, Men and Gods in Asia Minor*. Oxford: Clarendon Press.

——. 1993b. *The Rise of the Church*. Vol. 2 of *Anatolia: Land, Men and Gods in Asia Minor*. Oxford: Oxford University Press.

Montefiore, C. G. 1914. *Judaism and St Paul*. London: Max Goschen.

Moo, D. J. 2013. *Galatians*. Grand Rapids: Baker Academic.

Moore, G. F. 1921. 'Christian Writers on Judaism.' *Harvard Theological Review* 14:197–254.

——. 1927–30. *Judaism in the First Centuries of the Christian Era: The Age of the Tannaim*. Cambridge, MA: Harvard University Press.

Moore, S. D. 1994. *Poststructuralism and the New Testament: Derrida and Foucault at the Foot of the Cross*. Minneapolis: Fortress Press.

——. 2006. *Empire and Apocalypse: Postcolonialism and the New Testament*. Sheffield: Sheffield Phoenix Press.

Morgan, R. 1973. *The Nature of New Testament Theology: The Contribution of William Wrede and Adolf Schlatter*. London: SCM Press.

Moule, C. F. D. 1967. 'Obligation in the Ethic of Paul' in Farmer W. R., C. F. D. Moule, and R. R. Niebuhr, eds. *Christian History and Interpretation: Studies Presented to John Knox*. Cambridge: Cambridge University Press, pp. 389–406.

——. 1977. *The Origin of Christology*. Cambridge: Cambridge University Press.

Moxnes, H. 1991. 'Patron-Client Relations and the New Community in Luke-Acts' in Neyrey, J. H., ed. *The Social World of Luke-Acts: Models for Interpretation*. Peabody, MA: Hendrickson, pp. 241–68.

Mulhall, S., and A. Swift. 1996 [1992]. *Liberals and Communitarians*. Oxford: Blackwell.

Müller, C. 1964. *Gottes Gerechtigkeit und Gottes Volk: Eine Untersuchung zu Römer 9—11*. Forschungen zum Religion und Literatur des Alten und Neuen Testaments 86. Göttingen: Vandenhoeck und Ruprecht.

Munck, J. 1959 [1954]. *Paul and the Salvation of Mankind*, tr. Frank Clarke. London/Richmond, VA: SCM Press/John Knox Press.

——. 1967 [1956]. *Christ and Israel: An Interpretation of Romans 9—11*. Philadelphia: Fortress Press.

Murphy-O'Connor, J. 1995. *Paul the Letter-Writer: His World, His Options, His Skills*. Collegeville, MN: Liturgical Press.

Murray, J. 1955. *Redemption – Accomplished and Applied*. Grand Rapids: Eerdmans.

Neill, S. C. 1976. *Jesus Through Many Eyes: Introduction to the Theology of the New Testament*. Philadelphia: Fortress Press.

Neill, S. C., and N. T. Wright. 1988 [1964]. *The Interpretation of the New Testament, 1861–1986*. 2nd edn. Oxford: Oxford University Press.

Neyrey, J. H. 1990. *Paul, in Other Words: A Cultural Reading of His Letters*. Louisville, KY: Westminster John Knox Press.

——., ed. 1991. *The Social World of Luke-Acts: Models for Interpretation*. Peabody, MA: Hendrickson.

Neyrey, J. H., and Eric C. Stewart. 2008. *The Social World of the New Testament: Insights and Models*. Peabody, MA: Hendrickson.

Nineham, D. 1976. *The Use and Abuse of the Bible: A Study of the Bible in an Age of Rapid Cultural Change*. London: Macmillan.

Novenson, M. 2012. *Christ among the Messiahs: Christ Language in Paul and Messiah Language in Ancient Judaism*. New York: Oxford University Press.

Oakes, P. 2001. *Philippians: From People to Letter*. Cambridge: Cambridge University Press.

——. 2009a. 'Contours of the Urban Environment' in Still, T. D., and D. G. Horrell, eds. *After the First Urban Christians: The Social-Scientific Study of Pauline Christianity Twenty-Five Years Later*. London: T & T Clark, pp. 21–35.

——. 2009b. *Reading Romans in Pompeii: Paul's Letter at Ground Level*. London: SPCK.

Ollenburger, B. C. 1994. 'The Story behind the Book' in Beker, J. C., ed., *Suffering and Hope: The Biblical Vision and the Human Predicament*. 2nd edn. Grand Rapids: Eerdmans, pp. 1–16.

O'Neill, J. C. 1975. *Paul's Letter to the Romans*. Harmondsworth: Penguin.

Osiek, C. 1984. *What Are They Saying About the Social Setting of the New Testament?* New York: Paulist Press.

Piper, J. 2002. *Counted Righteous in Christ: Should We Abandon the Imputation of Christ's Righteousness?* Wheaton, IL: Crossway Books.

——. 2007. *The Future of Justification: A Response to N. T. Wright*. Wheaton, IL: Crossway Books.

Porter, S. E., and A. W. Pitts, eds. 2012. *Christian Origins and Greco-Roman Culture: Social and Literary Contexts for the New Testament, Volume 1: Early Christianity in Its Hellenistic Context*. Leiden: Brill.

Portier-Young, A. 2011. *Apocalypse against Empire: Theologies of Resistance in Early Judaism*. Grand Rapids: Eerdmans.

Purcell, N. 2011 [1996]. 'Rome and the Management of Water: Environment, Culture, and Power' in Shipley, G., and J. Salmon, eds. *Human Landscapes in Classical Antiquity*. Abingdon/New York: Routledge, pp. 180–212.

Räisänen, H. 1986. *Paul and the Law*. 1983. Philadelphia: Fortress Press.

——. 2008. 'A Controversial Jew and His Conflicting Convictions' in Udoh, F. E., ed. *Redefining First-Century Jewish and Christian Identities: Essays in Honor of Ed Parish Sanders*. Notre Dame, IN: University of Notre Dame Press, pp. 319–35.

Rengstorf, K. H., ed. 1969. *Das Paulusbild in der neueren deutschen Forschung*. Wege der Forschung 24. Darmstadt: Wissenschaftliche Buchgesellschaft.

Riches, J. K. 1993. *A Century of New Testament Study*. Cambridge: Lutterworth Press.

Ridderbos, H. N. 1975 [1966]. *Paul: An Outline of His Theology*. Grand Rapids: Eerdmans.

Robbins, V. K. 1996. *Exploring the Texture of Texts: A Guide to Socio-Rhetorical Interpretation*. Valley Forge, PA: Trinity Press International.

Robinson, J. A. T. 1979. *Wrestling with Romans*. London: SCM Press.

Rohrbaugh, R., ed. 1996. *The Social Sciences and New Testament Interpretation*. Peabody, MA: Hendrickson.

Rowe, C. K. 2011. 'The Grammar of Life: The Areopagus Speech and Pagan Tradition.' *New Testament Studies* 57:31–50.

——. 2015. *One True Life: the Stoics and Early Christians as Rival Traditions*. New Haven: Yale University Press.

Rowland, C. C. 1982. *The Open Heaven: A Study of Apocalyptic in Judaism and Early Christianity*. New York: Crossroad.

——. 2010. 'Apocalypticism' in Collins, J. J., and D. C. Harlow, eds. *The Eerdmans Dictionary of Early Judaism*. Grand Rapids: Eerdmans, pp. 345–8.

Rowland, C. C., and C. R. A Morray-Jones. 2009. *The Mystery of God: Early Jewish Mysticism and the New Testament*. Leiden: Brill.

Ruether, R. R. 1974. *Faith and Fratricide: The Theological Roots of Anti-Semitism*. New York: Seabury Press.

Rutledge, F. 2007. *Not Ashamed of the Gospel: Sermons from Paul's Letter to the Romans*. Grand Rapids: Eerdmans.

Safrai, S., and M. Stern, eds. 1974–6. *The Jewish People in the First Century: Historical Geography, Political History, Social, Cultural and Religious Life and Institutions*. In Compendia Rerum Iudaicarum ad Novum Testamentum. Philadelphia/Assen/Maastricht: Fortress Press/Van Gorcum.

Sanday, W., and A. C. Headlam. 1902 [1895]. *A Critical and Exegetical Commentary on the Epistle to the Romans*. 5th edn. Edinburgh: T & T Clark.

Sanders, E. P. 1976. 'The Covenant as a Soteriological Category and the Nature of Salvation in Palestinian and Hellenistic Judaism' in Hamerton-Kelly, R., and R. Scroggs, eds. *Jews, Greeks and Christians: Essays in Honor of William David Davies*. Leiden: Brill, pp. 11–44.

——. 1977. *Paul and Palestinian Judaism: A Comparison of Patterns of Religion*. Philadelphia/London: Fortress Press/SCM Press. (=*PPJ*)

——. 1978. 'Paul's Attitude toward the Jewish People.' *Union Seminary Quarterly Review* 33:175–87.

——. 1983. *Paul, the Law, and the Jewish People*. Philadelphia/London: Fortress Press/SCM Press.
——. 1985. *Jesus and Judaism*. Philadelphia/London: Fortress Press/SCM Press.
——. 1991. *Past Masters: Paul*. Oxford: Oxford University Press.
——. 1992. *Judaism: Practice and Belief, 63 BCE — 66 CE*. London: SCM Press.
——. 2008a. 'Comparing Judaism and Christianity: An Academic Autobiography' in Udoh, F. E., et al., eds. *Redefining First-Century Jewish and Christian Identities: Essays in Honor of Ed Parish Sanders*. Notre Dame, IN: University of Notre Dame Press, pp. 11–41.
——. 2008b. 'Did Paul's Theology Develop?' in Wagner, J. R., C. K. Rowe, and A. K. Grieb, eds. *The Word Leaps the Gap: Essays on Scripture and Theology in Honor of Richard B. Hays*. Grand Rapids: Eerdmans, pp. 325–50.
——. 2009. 'Paul between Judaism and Hellenism' in Caputo J. D., and L. M. Alcoff, eds. *St Paul among the Philosophers*. Bloomington, IN: Indiana University Press, pp. 74–90.
Sanders, J. T. 1993. *Schismatics, Sectarians, Dissidents, Deviants: The First One Hundred Years of Jewish-Christian Relations*. London: SCM Press.
Sandmel, S. 1962. 'Parallelomania.' *Journal of Biblical Literature* 81:1–13.
Schiffman, L. H. 2010. 'Early Judaism and Rabbinic Judaism' in Collins, J. J., and D. C. Harlow, eds. *The Eerdmans Dictionary of Early Judaism*. Grand Rapids: Eerdmans, pp. 279–90.
Schmithals, W. 1971 [1956]. *Gnosticism in Corinth*. Nashville: Abingdon.
Schnelle, U. 2005 [2003]. *Apostle Paul: His Life and Theology*. Grand Rapids: Baker Academic.
Schoeps, H.-J. 1961 [1959]. *Paul: The Theology of the Apostle in the Light of Jewish Religious History*, tr. H. Knight. London: Lutterworth Press.
Scholder, K. 2012 [1987]. *The Churches and the Third Reich: The Year of Disillusionment, 1934: Barmen and Rome*. London: SCM Press.
Scholer, D. M., ed. 2008. *Social Distinctives of the Christians in the First Century: Pivotal Essays by E. A. Judge*. Peabody, MA: Hendrickson.
Schürer, E. 1973–87. *The History of the Jewish People in the Age of Jesus Christ (175 B.C.—A.D. 135)*. Rev. and ed. G. Vermes, F. Millar, and M Black. Edinburgh: T & T Clark.
Schüssler Fiorenza, E. 1983. *In Memory of Her: A Feminist Theological Reconstruction of Christian Origins*. London: SCM Press.
Schütz, J. H. 1975. *Paul and the Anatomy of Apostolic Authority*. Cambridge: Cambridge University Press.
——. 1982. Introduction. In Theissen, G., *The Social Setting of Pauline Christianity: Essays on Corinth*. Philadelphia: Fortress Press, pp. 1–26.
Schweitzer, A. 1912. *Paul and His Interpreters: A Critical History*, tr. W. Montgomery. London: A. & C. Black.
——. 1931 [1930]. *The Mysticism of Paul the Apostle*, tr. W. Montgomery. London: A. & C. Black.
Schweizer, E. 1982. *The Letter to the Colossians*, tr. A. Chester. 1976. London: SPCK.

Scroggs, R. 1975. 'The Earliest Christian Communities as Sectarian Movement' in Neusner, J., ed. *Christianity, Judaism and Other Greco-Roman Cults: Festschrift for Morton Smith*, vol. 2. Leiden: Brill, pp. 1–23.

——. 1980. 'The Sociological Interpretation of the New Testament: The Present State of Research.' *New Testament Studies* 26:164–79.

Seesengood, R. P. 2010. *Paul: A Brief History*. Chichester: Wiley-Blackwell.

Seifrid, M. A. 1992. *Justification by Faith: The Origin and Development of a Central Pauline Theme*. Leiden: Brill.

——. 2000a. *Christ, Our Righteousness: Paul's Theology of Justification*. Leicester: Apollos.

——. 2000b. 'In What Sense is "Justification" a Declaration?' *Churchman* 114.2:123–36.

——. 2000c. 'The "New Perspective on Paul" and Its Problems' *Themelios* 25:4–18.

——. 2004. 'Luther, Melanchthon and Paul on the Question of Imputation: Recommendations on a Current Debate' in Husbands, M., and D. J. Treier, eds. *Justification: What's at Stake in the Current Debates*. Downers Grove, IL: InterVarsity Press, pp. 137–52.

Shaw, G. 1983. *The Cost of Authority*. London: SCM Press.

Smith, B. D. 2007. *What Must I Do to Be Saved? Paul Parts Company with His Jewish Heritage*. Sheffield: Sheffield Phoenix Press.

Smith, C. S. 2012. *Pauline Communities as 'Scholastic' Communities: A Study of the Vocabulary of Teaching in 1 Corinthians, 1 and 2 Timothy and Titus*. Tübingen: Mohr.

Smith, J. Z. 1975. 'The Social Description of Early Christianity.' *Religious Studies Review* 1.1:19–25.

Smith-Christopher, D. 2013. '"And If Not Now, When?" A Sociology of Reading Micah's Notions of the Future in Micah 4:1' in Dell, K. J., and P. M. Joyce, eds. *Biblical Interpretation and Method: Essays in Honour of John Barton*. Oxford: Oxford University Press, pp. 149–62.

Spence, A. 2004. 'A Unified Theory of the Atonement.' *International Journal of Systematic Theology* 6.4:404–20.

Stanley, C. D. 1992. *Paul and the Language of Scripture: Citation Technique in the Pauline Epistles and Contemporary Literature*. Cambridge: Cambridge University Press.

——. 2004. *Arguing with Scripture: The Rhetoric of Quotations in the Letters of Paul*. New York: T & T Clark International.

Stegemann, E. W., and W. Stegemann. 1999 [1995]. *The Jesus Movement: A Social History of Its First Century*, tr. O. C. Dean. Minneapolis: Fortress Press.

Stendahl, K. 1963. 'The Apostle Paul and the Introspective Conscience of the West.' *Harvard Theological Review* 56:199–215.

——. 1976. *Paul Among Jews and Gentiles*. Philadelphia: Fortress Press.

Still, T. D. 2009. 'Organizational Structures and Relational Struggles among the Saints: The Establishment and Exercise of Authority within the Pauline Assemblies' in Still, T. D., and D. G. Horrell, eds. *After the First Urban Christians: The Social-Scientific Study of Pauline Christianity Twenty-Five Years Later*. London: T & T Clark, pp. 79–98.

Still, T. D., and David G. Horrell, eds. 2009. *After the First Urban Christians: The Social-Scientific Study of Pauline Christianity Twenty-Five Years Later*. London: T & T Clark.

Stowers, S. K. 1985. 'The Social Sciences and the Study of Early Christianity' in Green, W. S., ed. *Approaches to Ancient Judaism*. Atlanta: SBL, pp. 149–81.

——. 1994. *A Rereading of Romans: Justice, Jews, and Gentiles*. New Haven: Yale University Press.

——. 2008. 'What is "Pauline Participation in Christ"?' in Udoh, F. E., ed. *Redefining First-Century Jewish and Christian Identities: Essays in Honor of Ed Parish Sanders*. Notre Dame, IN: University of Notre Dame Press, pp. 352–71.

Strack, H. L., and P. Billerbeck. 1926–61. *Kommentar zum Neuen Testament aus Talmud und Midrasch*. Munich: C. H. Beck.

Stuckenbruck, L. T. 2014. 'Posturing "Apocalyptic" in Pauline Theology: How Much Contrast to Jewish Tradition?' in *The Myth of Rebellious Angels: Studies in Second Temple Judaism and New Testament Texts*. Tübingen: Mohr, pp. 240–56.

Stuhlmacher, P. 1966. *Gerechtigkeit Gottes bei Paulus*. Göttingen: Vandenhoeck und Ruprecht.

——. 1986 [1981]. *Reconciliation, Law and Righteousness: Essays in Biblical Theology*, tr. E. Kalin. Philadelphia: Fortress Press.

——. 2001. *Revisiting Paul's Doctrine of Justification: A Challenge to the New Perspective*. Additional essay by D. A. Hagner. Downers Grove, IL: InterVarsity Press.

Syme, R. 1939. *The Roman Revolution*. Oxford: Oxford University Press.

Taubes, J. 2004 [1993]. *The Political Theology of Paul*, tr. D. Hollander. Stanford, CA: Stanford University Press.

Taylor, C. 2007. *A Secular Age*. Cambridge, MA: The Bellknap Press of Harvard University Press.

Taylor, N. H. 1995. 'The Social Nature of Conversion in the Early Christian World' in Esler, P. F., ed. *Modelling Early Christianity: Social-Scientific Studies of the New Testament and Its Context*. London/New York: Routledge, pp. 128–36.

Theissen, G. 1978 [1977]. *Sociology of Early Palestinian Christianity*. [UK title: *The First Followers of Jesus*]. Tr. J. Bowden. Philadelphia/London: Fortress Press/SCM Press.

——. 1982. *The Social Setting of Pauline Christianity: Essays on Corinth*, ed. and tr. J. H. Schutz. Philadelphia: Fortress Press.

——. 1992. *Social Reality and the Early Christians: Theology, Ethics, and the World of the New Testament*. Minneapolis: Fortress Press.

Thielman, F. 1989. *From Plight to Solution: A Jewish Framework for Understanding Paul's View of the Law in Galatians and Romans*. Leiden: Brill.

——. 1994. *Paul and the Law: A Contextual Approach*. Downer's Grove, IL: InterVarsity Press.

——. 2005. *Theology of the New Testament: A Canonical and Synthetic Approach*. Grand Rapids: Zondervan.

Thiselton, A. C. 1980. *The Two Horizons*. Exeter: Paternoster.

Thorsteinsson, R. M. 2010. *Roman Christianity and Roman Stoicism: A Comparative Study of Ancient Morality*. Oxford: Oxford University Press.

Tidball, D. 1983. *An Introduction to the Sociology of the New Testament*. Exeter: Paternoster.

Tilling, C., ed. 2014. *Beyond Old and New Perspectives on Paul: Reflections on the Work of Douglas Campbell*. Eugene, OR: Cascade Books.

Torrance, T. F. 1957. 'One Aspect of the Biblical Conception of Faith.' *Expository Times* 68:111–14.

Trebilco, Paul R. 1991. *Jewish Communities in Asia Minor*. Cambridge: Cambridge University Press.

Tuckett, C. M. 1987. *Reading the New Testament: Methods of Interpretation*. London: SPCK.

——. 2000. 'Paul, Scripture and Ethics: Some Reflections.' *New Testament Studies* 46:403–24.

Vanhoozer, K. 2011. 'Wrighting the Wrongs of the Reformation? The State of the Union with Christ in St. Paul and Protestant Soteriology' in Perrin, N., and R. B. Hays, eds. *Jesus, Paul and the People of God: A Theological Dialogue with N. T. Wright*. Downers Grove, IL/London: InterVarsity Press/SPCK, pp. 235–59.

Vernezze, P. J. 2005. *Don't Worry, Be Stoic: Ancient Wisdom for Troubled Times*. Lanham, MD: University Press of America.

Vickers, B. 2006. *Jesus' Blood and Righteousness: Paul's Theology of Imputation*. Wheaton, IL: Crossway Books.

Vielhauer, P. 1964. Introduction [to 'Apocalypses and Related Subjects'] in Hennecke, E., and W. Schneemelcher, eds. *New Testament Apocrypha*. London: SCM, pp. 581–607.

——. 1966. 'On the "Paulinisms" of Acts' in Keck, L., and J. L. Martyn, eds. *Studies in Luke-Acts: Essays Presented in Honor of Paul Schubert*. Nashville: Abingdon, pp. 33–51.

von Rad, G. 1965. *The Theology of Israel's Prophetic Traditions*. Vol. 2 of *Old Testament Theology*. Tr. D. M. G. Stalker. New York/Edinburgh: Harper and Row/Oliver and Boyd.

Wagner, J. R. 2002. *Heralds of the Good News: Isaiah and Paul "in Concert" in the Letter to the Romans*. Leiden: Brill.

Wagner, J. R., C. K. Rowe, and A. K. Grieb, eds. 2008. *The Word Leaps the Gap: Essays on Scripture and Theology in Honor of Richard B. Hays*. Grand Rapids: Eerdmans.

Wallis, I. G. 1995. *The Faith of Jesus Christ in Early Christian Traditions*. Cambridge: Cambridge University Press.

Wasserman, E. 2013. 'Paul among the Ancient Philosophers: The Case of Romans 7' in Blanton, W., and H. de Vries, eds. *Paul and the Philosophers*. New York: Fordham University Press, pp. 69–83.

Waters, G. P. 2004. *Justification and the New Perspective on Paul: A Review and Response*. Phillipsburg, NJ: P & R Publishing.

Watson, F. B. 1997. *Text and Truth: Redefining Biblical Theology*. Grand Rapids: Eerdmans.

——. 2007 [1986]. *Paul, Judaism and the Gentiles: Beyond the New Perspective*. Rev. and expanded edn. Grand Rapids: Eerdmans.

Way, D. V. 1991. *The Lordship of Christ: Ernst Käsemann's Interpretation of Paul's Theology*. Oxford: Clarendon Press.

Westerholm, S. 2004. *Perspectives Old and New on Paul: The 'Lutheran' Paul and His Critics*. Grand Rapids: Eerdmans.

Whiteley, D. E. H. 1964. *The Theology of St. Paul*. Philadelphia: Fortress Press.

Wilckens, Ulrich. 1974. *Rechtfertigung als Freiheit: Paulusstudien*. Neukirchen-Vluyn: Neukirchener Verlag.

——. 1977. *Resurrection: Biblical Testimony to the Resurrection: An Historical Examination and Explanation*. Edinburgh: Saint Andrew Press.

——. 1978–82, 3 vols. *Die Brief an die Römer*. Cologne/Neukirchen-Vluyn: Benziger/ Neukirchener Verlag.

Williams, J. J. 2015. *Christ Died for Our Sins: Representation and Substitution in Romans and their Jewish Martyrological Background*. London: Pickwick.

Winter, B. W. 1994. *Seek the Welfare of the City: Christians as Benefactors and Citizens*. Grand Rapids: Eerdmans.

——. 2002 [1997]. *Philo and Paul among the Sophists: Alexandrian and Corinthian Responses to a Julio-Claudian Movement*. Grand Rapids: Eerdmans.

Wire, A. C. 1990. *The Corinthian Women Prophets: A Reconstruction through Paul's Rhetoric*. Minneapolis: Fortress Press.

Witherington, B. 1994. *Paul's Narrative Thought World: The Tapestry of Tragedy and Triumph*. Louisville, KY: Westminster John Knox Press.

——. 1998. *Grace in Galatia: A Commentary on St Paul's Letter to the Galatians*. Edinburgh: T & T Clark.

Wolter, M. 2011. *Paulus: Ein Grundriss seiner Theologie*. Neukirchen-Vluyn: Neukirchener Verlagsgesellschaft.

Wrede, W. 1907. *Paul*. London: Philip Green.

Wright, N. T. 1978. 'The Paul of History and the Apostle of Faith.' *Tyndale Bulletin* 29:61–88.

——. 1980. 'The Messiah and the People of God: A Study in Pauline Theology with Particular Reference to the Argument of the Epistle to the Romans.' Unpublished D.Phil thesis, Oxford University. Oxford.

——. 1989. 'Review of Watson 2006.' *Journal of Theological Studies*, n. s. 40:200–6.

——. 1991. *The Climax of the Covenant: Christ and the Law in Pauline Theology*. Edinburgh/ Minneapolis: T & T Clark/Fortress Press.

——. 1992. *The New Testament and the People of God*. London/Minneapolis: SPCK/Fortress Press. (=*NTPG*)

——. 1996a. 'Jesus' in Sweet, J. P. M., and J. M. G. Barclay, eds. *Early Christian Thought in Its Jewish Context: Essays in Honour of Professor Morna D. Hooker*. Cambridge: Cambridge University Press, pp. 43–58.

——. 1996b. *Jesus and the Victory of God*. London/Minneapolis: SPCK/Fortress Press. (=*JVG*)

——. 1997. *What St Paul Really Said*. Oxford/Grand Rapids: Lion/Eerdmans.

——. 2002. 'Romans' in *New Interpreter's Bible*, Vol. 10. Nashville: Abingdon, pp. 393–770.

——. 2003. *The Resurrection of the Son of God*. London/Minneapolis: SPCK/Fortress Press. (=*RSG*)

——. 2005. *Paul: Fresh Perspectives*. London/Minneapolis: SPCK/Fortress Press.

——. 2008. *Surprised by Hope*. London/San Francisco: SPCK/HarperOne.

——. 2009. *Justification: God's Plan and Paul's Vision*. London/Downers Grove, IL: SPCK / InterVarsity Press.

——. 2011. *How God Became King: The Forgotten Story of the Gospels*. San Francisco/ London: HarperOne/SPCK.

——. 2013a. *Paul and the Faithfulness of God*. London/Minneapolis: SPCK/Fortress Press. (=*PFG*)

——. 2013b. *Pauline Perspectives: Essays on Paul 1978–2013*. London/Minneapolis: SPCK/ Fortress Press. (=*Perspectives*)

——. 2014a. 'Justification by (Covenantal) Faith to the (Covenantal) Doers: Romans 2 Within the Argument of the Letter' in Eklund, R. A., and J. E. Phelan, eds. *Doing Theology for the Church: Essays in Honor of Klyne Snodgrass*. Eugene, OR: Wipf and Stock, pp. 95–108.

——. 2014b. 'A New Perspective on Käsemann? Apocalyptic, Covenant, and the Righteousness of God' in Harmon, M. S., and J. E. Smith, eds. *Studies in the Pauline Epistles: Essays in Honor of Douglas J. Moo*. Grand Rapids: Zondervan, pp. 243–58.

——. 2014c. *Surprised by Scripture: Engaging Contemporary Issues*. San Francisco/London: HarperOne/SPCK.

Yarbrough, R. W. 2004. *The Salvation Historical Fallacy? Reassessing the History of New Testament Theology*. Leiden: Deo Publishing.

Yinger, K. L. 1999. *Paul, Judaism and Justification According to Deeds*. Cambridge: Cambridge University Press.

Zahl, P. F. M. 1996. *Die Rechtfertigungslehre Ernst Käsemanns*. Stuttgart: Calwer Verlag.

Zetterholm, M. 2009. *Approaches to Paul: A Student's Guide to Recent Scholarship*. Minneapolis: Fortress Press.

Ziegler, P. 2011. 'The Fate of Natural Law at the Turning of the Ages: Some Reflections on a Trend in Contemporary Theological Ethics in View of the Work of J. Louis Martyn.' *Theology Today* 67:419–29.

——. 2012. '"Christ Must Reign": Ernst Käsemann and Soteriology in an Apocalyptic Key' in Davis, J. B., and D. Harink, eds. *Apocalyptic and the Future of Theology: With and Beyond J. Louis Martyn*. Eugene, OR: Cascade Books, pp. 200–18.

Ziesler, J. A. 1989. *Paul's Letter to the Romans*. London/Philadelphia: SCM Press/Trinity Press International.

INDEX OF ANCIENT SOURCES

1. Old Testament

2. Apocrypha

3. Pseudepigrapha

8. Pagan Sources

INDEX OF MODERN AUTHORS

Page numbers in **bold** type indicate key discussions of these scholars